NEW PERSPECTIVES ON
Adobe® Dreamweaver® CS6

COMPREHENSIVE

Kelly Hart
Mitch Geller

COURSE TECHNOLOGY
CENGAGE Learning·

Australia • Brazil • Japan • Korea • Mexico • Singapore • Spain • United Kingdom • United States

COURSE TECHNOLOGY
CENGAGE Learning·

New Perspectives on Adobe Dreamweaver CS6, Comprehensive

Editor-in-Chief: Marie Lee

Director of Development: Marah Bellegarde

Executive Editor: Donna Gridley

Associate Acquisitions Editor: Amanda Lyons

Senior Product Manager: Kathy Finnegan

Product Manager: Leigh Hefferon

Product Manager: Julia Leroux-Lindsey

Editorial Assistant: Melissa Stehler

Senior Brand Manager: Elinor Gregory

Market Development Manager: Gretchen Swann

Market Development Manager: Kristie Clark

Developmental Editor: Robin M. Romer

Senior Content Project Manager:
  Jennifer Goguen McGrail

Composition: GEX Publishing Services

Art Director: Marissa Falco

Text Designer: Althea Chen

Cover Designer: Roycroft Design

Cover Art: © Ingmar Wesemann/ Photodisc/
  Getty Images

Copyeditor: Karen Annett

Proofreader: Suzanne Huizenga

Indexer: Alexandra Nickerson

For product information and technology assistance, contact us at
Cengage Learning Customer & Sales Support, 1-800-354-9706
For permission to use material from this text or product, submit all requests online at **www.cengage.com/permissions**
Further permissions questions can be emailed to
permissionrequest@cengage.com

Some of the product names and company names used in this book have been used for identification purposes only and may be trademarks or registered trademarks of their respective manufacturers and sellers.

Adobe®, Dreamweaver®, Flash®, InDesign®, Illustrator®, and Photoshop® are either registered trademarks or trademarks of Adobe Systems Incorporated in the United States and/or other countries. THIS PRODUCT IS NOT ENDORSED OR SPONSORED BY ADOBE SYSTEMS INCORPORATED, PUBLISHER OF ADOBE® DREAMWEAVER®, FLASH®, INDESIGN®, ILLUSTRATOR®, AND PHOTOSHOP®.

Disclaimer: Any fictional data related to persons or companies or URLs used throughout this book is intended for instructional purposes only. At the time this book was printed, any such data was fictional and not belonging to any real persons or companies.

Library of Congress Control Number: 2012949034

ISBN-13: 978-1-133-52582-0

ISBN-10: 1-133-52582-2

Course Technology
20 Channel Center Street
Boston, MA 02210
USA

Cengage Learning is a leading provider of customized learning solutions with office locations around the globe, including Singapore, the United Kingdom, Australia, Mexico, Brazil, and Japan. Locate your local office at:
international.cengage.com/global

Cengage Learning products are represented in Canada by Nelson Education, Ltd.

To learn more about Course Technology, visit **www.cengage.com/course technology**

To learn more about Cengage Learning, visit **www.cengage.com**

Purchase any of our products at your local college store or at our preferred online store
www.cengagebrain.com

Printed in the United States of America
1 2 3 4 5 6 7 8 9 16 15 14 13 12

Preface

The New Perspectives Series' critical-thinking, problem-solving approach is the ideal way to prepare students to transcend point-and-click skills and take advantage of all that Adobe Dreamweaver CS6 has to offer.

In developing the New Perspectives Series, our goal was to create books that give students the software concepts and practical skills they need to succeed beyond the classroom. We've updated our proven case-based pedagogy with more practical content to make learning skills more meaningful to students.

With the New Perspectives Series, students understand *why* they are learning *what* they are learning, and are fully prepared to apply their skills to real-life situations.

About This Book

This book provides complete, hands-on coverage of the new Adobe Dreamweaver CS6 software:

- Presents a case-based, problem-solving approach to learning Adobe Dreamweaver CS6. Students create and publish professional-looking, accessible Web pages using CSS-based layout and styling techniques, graphics and multimedia, div tags, tables, forms, behaviors, and database connectivity.
- Covers the newest features of Dreamweaver CS6, including improvements in support of best practices in CSS-based layout, Photoshop integration, media queries, Fluid Grid Layouts, mobile sites, and mobile apps.
- Teaches students how to plan and design a successful Web site—including lessons on project management, accessibility, target audiences, end-user analysis, information architecture, and aesthetic design principles.
- Provides an understanding of the underlying HTML, CSS, and JavaScript code as students review the code for each element they add to the Web site.

New for this edition!

- Integrates HTML5/CSS3 throughout the text, highlighting new tags and best practices, including multi-screen preview and device-specific testing.
- Introduces Web fonts, the @font-face rule, and font kits, as well as adds audio, video, and animation to a site using HTML5.
- Provides in-depth coverage of media queries and the creation of adaptive/responsive, fluid grid sites.
- Includes a new tutorial in which students create a mobile site and a market-ready mobile app using the jQuery Mobile framework and PhoneGap.

"The New Perspective Dreamweaver text provides an exceptional tool in teaching the skills needed for good web design. The exercises are relevant and guide learners in developing both creative and practical real-world web design skills."

—Beth Russ
Northcentral Technical College

www.cengage.com/ct/newperspectives

The New Perspectives Approach

Context

Each tutorial begins with a problem presented in a "real-world" case that is meaningful to students. The case sets the scene to help students understand what they will do in the tutorial.

Hands-on Approach

Each tutorial is divided into manageable sessions that combine reading and hands-on, step-by-step work. Colorful screenshots help guide students through the steps. **Trouble?** tips anticipate common mistakes or problems to help students stay on track and continue with the tutorial.

VISUAL OVERVIEW

Visual Overviews

New for this edition! Each session begins with a Visual Overview, a new two-page spread that includes colorful, enlarged screenshots with numerous callouts and key term definitions, giving students a comprehensive preview of the topics covered in the session, as well as a handy study guide.

PROSKILLS

ProSkills Boxes and Exercises

New for this edition! ProSkills boxes provide guidance for how to use the software in real-world, professional situations, and related ProSkills exercises integrate the technology skills students learn with one or more of the following soft skills: decision making, problem solving, teamwork, verbal communication, and written communication.

KEY STEP

Key Steps

New for this edition! Important steps are highlighted in yellow with attached margin notes to help students pay close attention to completing the steps correctly and avoid time-consuming rework.

INSIGHT

InSight Boxes

InSight boxes offer expert advice and best practices to help students achieve a deeper understanding of the concepts behind the software features and skills.

TIP

Margin Tips

Margin Tips provide helpful hints and shortcuts for more efficient use of the software. The Tips appear in the margin at key points throughout each tutorial, giving students extra information when and where they need it.

REVIEW

APPLY

Assessment

Retention is a key component to learning. At the end of each session, a series of Quick Check questions helps students test their understanding of the material before moving on. Engaging end-of-tutorial Review Assignments and Case Problems have always been a hallmark feature of the New Perspectives Series. Colorful bars and brief descriptions accompany the exercises, making it easy to understand both the goal and level of challenge a particular assignment holds.

REFERENCE

TASK REFERENCE

GLOSSARY/INDEX

Reference

Within each tutorial, Reference boxes appear before a set of steps to provide a succinct summary and preview of how to perform a task. In addition, a complete Task Reference at the back of the book provides quick access to information on how to carry out common tasks. Finally, each book includes a combination Glossary/Index to promote easy reference of material.

www.cengage.com/ct/newperspectives

Our Complete System of Instruction

Coverage To Meet Your Needs

Whether you're looking for just a small amount of coverage or enough to fill a semester-long class, we can provide you with a textbook that meets your needs.

- Brief books typically cover the essential skills in just 2 to 4 tutorials.
- Introductory books build and expand on those skills and contain an average of 5 to 8 tutorials.
- Comprehensive books are great for a full-semester class, and contain 9 to 12+ tutorials.

So if the book you're holding does not provide the right amount of coverage for you, there's probably another offering available. Go to our Web site or contact your Course Technology sales representative to find out what else we offer.

CourseCasts – Learning on the Go. Always available...always relevant.

Want to keep up with the latest technology trends relevant to you? Visit our site to find a library of podcasts, CourseCasts, featuring a "CourseCast of the Week," and download them to your mp3 player at http://coursecasts.course.com.

Our fast-paced world is driven by technology. You know because you're an active participant—always on the go, always keeping up with technological trends, and always learning new ways to embrace technology to power your life.

Ken Baldauf, host of CourseCasts, is a faculty member of the Florida State University Computer Science Department where he is responsible for teaching technology classes to thousands of FSU students each year. Ken is an expert in the latest technology trends; he gathers and sorts through the most pertinent news and information for CourseCasts so your students can spend their time enjoying technology, rather than trying to figure it out. Open or close your lecture with a discussion based on the latest CourseCast.

Visit us at http://coursecasts.course.com to learn on the go!

Instructor Resources

We offer more than just a book. We have all the tools you need to enhance your lectures, check students' work, and generate exams in a new, easier-to-use and completely revised package. This book's Instructor's Manual, ExamView testbank, PowerPoint presentations, data files, solution files, figure files, and a sample syllabus are all available on a single CD-ROM or for downloading at http://www.cengage.com/coursetechnology.

Acknowledgments

The authors wish to thank:

Robin Romer, our favorite editor, for keeping us sane while managing the seemingly infinite complexities of this project. Thank you for all your hard work and dedication.

Charlie Lindahl (aka CyberChuck) for introducing us to an *amazing new thing* called the Web on his new Mosaic Version 0.2A browser (1993), and reminding us of why we do this through his never-ending encouragement and enthusiasm.

Richard Strittmatter of Computeam.com for his guidance, friendship and encouragement, and for knowing the answers to our most complex questions.

Mark Chapman for his unique assistance in tracking Adobe developments and changes.

The staff and management of Meshnet.com for graciously providing hosting and support.

The staff of the Sid Richardson Museum (www.sidrichardsonmuseum.org) for their support and generosity in allowing us to use images from their collection.

Exquisite Dead Guys and Matthew Skinner of Inner Mission for allowing us to use their music in the book.

Benjamin Edwards for his music instruction and insight.

Tess Haranda (www.successwithtess.com) for allowing us to use her as an inspiration for the life coach case and for her valuable coaching expertise and content.

Corey Wells and Moebius Skateboards (www.moebiusskateboards.com) for allowing us to use his story and company as the inspiration for our skateboard company case.

The Course Technology team—Leigh Hefferon, Product Manager; Christian Kunciw, Manuscript Quality Assurance Manager, and his team of testers, Susan Whalen, John Freitas, Ashlee Welz Smith, Serge Palladino, and Danielle Shaw; Jennifer Goguen McGrail, Senior Content Project Manager; and Marisa Taylor, Project Manager at GEX Publishing Services—for all their support during the creation of this edition.

Mitch would like to thank Edyie and Joe Geller, Pam, Gregg, and the rest of the family for their love and support...you guys rock! He would also like to thank John Knecht, John Orentlicher, and Don Little.

Kelly would like to thank Mary O'Brien for much needed $C_8H_{10}N_4O_2$ infusions and linguistic reality checks along with the rest of the Nu-Design.com team. She would also like to thank Matt Palmer for his love, support, and ability to bring home take-out food, and she would like to thank the dogs, Monomer, Bebe, and Bit, for enduring the trauma of "short walks."

System Requirements

This book assumes that students have a default installation of Adobe Dreamweaver CS6, a text editor, and a current Web browser (preferably Internet Explorer 9 or higher). If students are using a nonstandard browser, the browser must support HTML5 or higher. The screen shots in this book were produced on a computer running Windows 7 Ultimate with Aero turned on using Internet Explorer 9. If students use a different operating system or browser, their screens might differ from those in the book. With some Windows servers, the Dreamweaver built-in FTP client might give continuous or intermittent errors. If these errors occur, students should double-check the remote and test server configuration settings, and review the following document on the Adobe site: http://go.adobe.com/kb/ts_kb405912_en-us. In Tutorial 7, if you are using a Windows server, it must have the MIME type set for Flash Video (.flv) or it will not play back properly. Instructions can be found on the Adobe site at http://www.adobe.com/go/tn_19439 and should be completed by your hosting provider or server administrator. Tutorial 9 requires students to create or upload a database to a server. This tutorial was written for and tested on both a Linux server and a Windows server. The recommended server configurations for a Linux server are Apache 1.3.26 or higher, PHP 5.x or higher, MySQL 5.x or higher, and any current distribution of Linux. The recommended server configurations for a Windows server are Windows 2003 IIS 5.0 or higher, running .Net 1.1 framework or higher, and the IIS User must have write permission for the database directory.

BRIEF CONTENTS

TABLE OF CONTENTS

OBJECTIVES

Session 1.1
- Explore the structure and history of the Internet and the Web
- Become familiar with the roles of Web servers and Web clients
- Examine protocols, URLs, and domain names
- Review a Web page in a browser
- Review the history of Web design software

Session 1.2
- Start Dreamweaver and select a workspace layout
- Create a local site definition
- Explore the Dreamweaver tool set
- Investigate the Dreamweaver Help features
- Exit Dreamweaver

Getting Started with Adobe Dreamweaver CS6

Exploring an Existing Web Site

Case | *NextBest Fest*

NextBest Fest is a fledgling music festival devoted to tribute bands of all musical genres. The festival is held every year on the second weekend in October at the Meadowlands Racetrack in East Rutherford, New Jersey. It was started in 2008 by father-and-son tribute band aficionados Brian and Gage Lee. Brian and Gage are also the founders of Shenpa Productions. To promote the upcoming festival, Brian and Gage want to create a Web site devoted to the festival. They realize that the NextBest Fest Web site will be one of their most important marketing, promotional, and communications tools.

Gage, who is responsible for public relations and marketing, will head the Web development team. He has a background in multimedia development. Gage created a temporary NextBest Fest Web site but wants to put the new site in place as soon as possible. Gage's team will research the current market trends as well as design and create a Web site for NextBest Fest. You will work with Gage and his team to develop the site.

STARTING DATA FILES

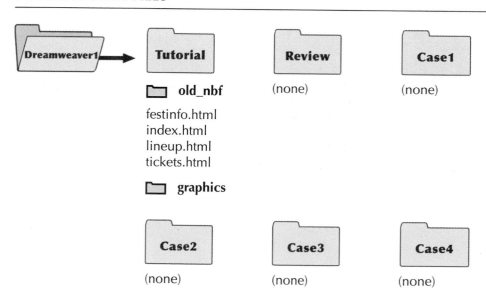

SESSION 1.1 VISUAL OVERVIEW

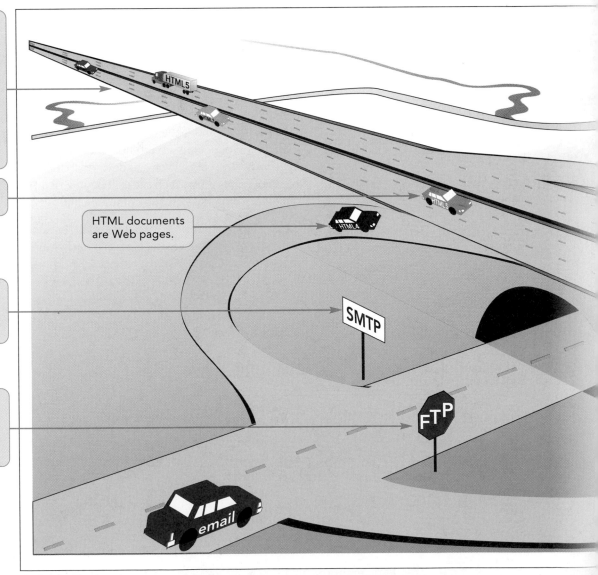

Much like a highway, the **Internet** is a global network made up of millions of smaller computer networks that are all connected and that use the TCP/IP network protocols to facilitate data transmission and exchange.

HTML5 is the current version of HTML.

HTML documents are Web pages.

A **protocol** is a set of technical specifications that defines a format for sharing information.

File Transfer Protocol (FTP) is used to copy files from one computer to another over the Internet.

THE INTERNET AND THE WEB

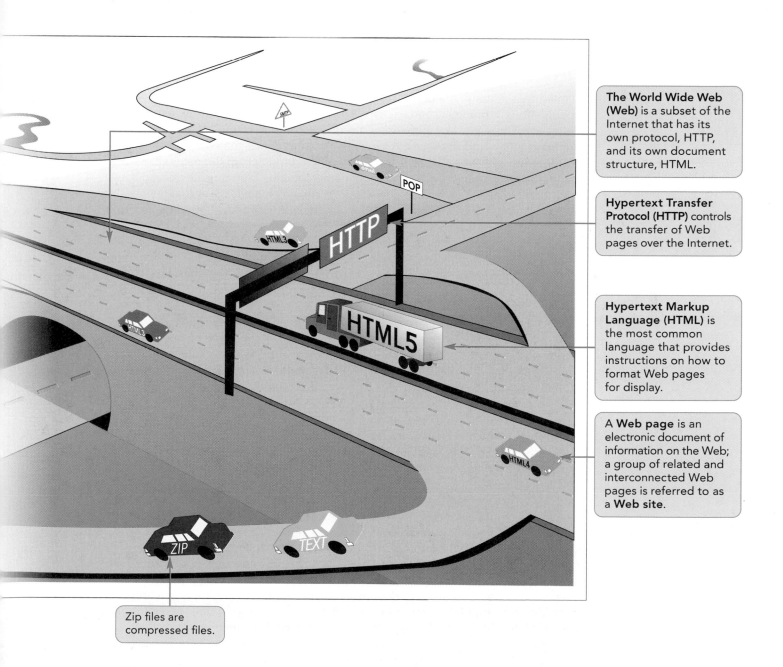

The World Wide Web (Web) is a subset of the Internet that has its own protocol, HTTP, and its own document structure, HTML.

Hypertext Transfer Protocol (HTTP) controls the transfer of Web pages over the Internet.

Hypertext Markup Language (HTML) is the most common language that provides instructions on how to format Web pages for display.

A **Web page** is an electronic document of information on the Web; a group of related and interconnected Web pages is referred to as a **Web site**.

Zip files are compressed files.

Dreamweaver and the Internet

Adobe Dreamweaver CS6 (or just **Dreamweaver**) is a Web site creation and management tool. To better understand what this means, you need to know the history of the Internet and the World Wide Web.

The concept of an Internet was introduced in the 1960s, after the USSR launched the first satellite, Sputnik. Originally, it was conceptualized as an information network that would enable the United States to communicate after a nuclear war. In the 1970s, ARPANET, an early version of the modern Internet, was used for email and the term *Internet* was coined to describe the new technology. In 1989, Timothy Berners-Lee and his team of scientists at CERN (the European Organization for Nuclear Research) invented the World Wide Web as a means for scientists to more easily locate and share data over the Internet. The Web is a subset of the Internet.

How the Internet and Web Work

The Internet is actually a series of computer networks and servers that provide a way for people to communicate and exchange information, whether they are across the street or across the globe. A **network** is a series of computers that are connected to share information and resources. A **server** is a computer designated within a network that stores and distributes information to the other computers in the network. All of the computers and servers connected to the Internet can communicate and exchange information because they all use one suite of technical specifications that defines the format they all use for sharing information. The TCP/IP network is the suite of protocols or standards that is used to facilitate data transmission and exchange over the Internet. It is sometimes called the Internet Protocol. (For additional information about TCP/IP, see *www.wikipedia.org/wiki/TCP/IP_model*. For additional information about the Internet, see *http://computer.howstuffworks.com/osi.htm*.) The illustration in the Session 1.1 Visual Overview uses a series of roadways to represent the interconnected networks that make up the Internet. As the Internet has evolved, different, higher-level protocols have been developed to allow information to be shared in different ways, but all of these new protocols rely on the TCP/IP network for data transmission and exchange. For example, **Simple Mail Transfer Protocol (SMTP)** is an agreed-upon format used by most email software. Without this standard, higher-level protocol, there would be many incompatible email formats, and you would be able to exchange email only with people who were using the same email software.

As the Session 1.1 Visual Overview illustrates, the Web is a subset of the Internet that uses higher-level HTTP (Hypertext Transfer Protocol) protocols just as email is a subset of the Internet that uses SMTP. Hypertext Transfer Protocol is a request-response protocol that uses a client-server computing model. To display a Web page, the "client" Web browser software submits an HTTP request message to a "server" that stores HTML files. The server then sends a response message that contains the requested files. Web page vehicles must follow HTTP protocols, or rules of the road to travel the Internet roadways. Because Web pages contain text and graphics, HTML (Hypertext Markup Language), a language that provides instructions on how to format Web pages for display, was created. Several versions of HTML have been adopted since Berners-Lee's team created the Web. The current version, HTML5, is much more advanced than the first version and enables modern designers to develop more complex interactions.

In addition to standards for transfer and display of information, the Web introduced the technology for hyperlinks to the Internet. A **hyperlink** (or **link**) is a node that provides a user the ability to cross-reference information within a document or a Web page and to move from one document or Web page to another.

Web Servers and Clients

The two general categories of computers involved in accessing Web pages are Web servers and Web clients. When you create a Web page or a Web site, you must post a copy of your work to a Web server to share the page with the world. A **Web server** is a specialized computer that stores and distributes information to computers and other client devices such as smartphones and tablets that are connected to the Internet. A **Web client** (or **client**) is the computer or device that an individual uses to access information, via the Internet, stored on Web servers throughout the world. A home computer with Internet access is a Web client as is a mobile phone that has Internet access. You must have access to the Internet to view a Web site. Most people connect to the Internet through an Internet service provider. An **Internet service provider (ISP)** is a company that has direct access to the Internet and sells access to other smaller entities. Some large institutions, such as universities, have direct links to the Internet and are, in essence, their own ISPs.

In addition to being connected to the Internet, to view a Web site you must have a Web browser installed on your client computer. A **Web browser** is the software that interprets and displays Web pages. The Web browser enables users to view Web pages from their Web clients, including desktop computers, laptops, tablets, and smartphones. Some of the most common Web browsers are Microsoft Internet Explorer, Mozilla Firefox, Google Chrome, and Apple Safari.

Common Web Page Elements

All Web pages have some elements. These include the Web address, hyperlinks, and content. You'll review these common elements in the next sections.

Web Address

Your residence has a unique street address that people use to locate where you live. A file on your computer has a unique path used to locate where it is stored. Likewise, every Web page has a unique address on the Internet, called a **Uniform Resource Locator (URL)**, that Web browsers use to locate where that page is stored. A URL includes the information identified in Figure 1-1.

Figure 1-1	Parts of a URL

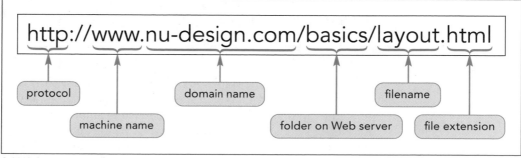

© 2013 Cengage Learning

The first portion of the URL indicates the protocol, which is usually HTTP but can be HTTPS. **HTTPS (Hypertext Transfer Protocol Secure)** means that the site is secure because it encrypts data transferred between a user's browser and the server. **Encryption** is the process of encoding and decoding data so that only the sender and/or receiver can read it, preventing others from being able to understand it. This is important when a user submits confidential or credit card information over the Web.

The protocol is immediately followed by ":/ /" which originated from UNIX (a server operating system) and essentially means "what follows should be interpreted according to the indicated protocol."

The next part of the URL is the **machine name**, which is a series of characters that the server administrator assigns to the Web server. Often, the machine name is *www*, but it can be any word, phrase, or acronym. It can often be omitted entirely. For example, the URL *online.wsj.com* for *The Wall Street Journal Online Edition* uses *online* as the machine name, and the URL *mesh.net* for Mesh Internet Solutions omits the machine name entirely. Many servers are configured to route the URL with or without a *www* to the same location. For example, *www.nu-design.com* and *nu-design.com* both go to the same place.

PROSKILLS

Written Communication: Selecting a Domain Name

A domain name is an important tool for communicating with your intended customers or target audience. The domain name you select for your Web site should provide users with useful information about the site and should be as simple, direct, and intuitive as possible. Consider the following when selecting a domain name:

1. The domain name should be short. If the company name or project title is long, brainstorm condensed versions of the name or title for the domain name that will still make sense to end users. For example, American Airlines uses *aa* for its domain name.
2. The domain name should provide information about the site, or it should communicate the brand, product, or company name to the end user. For example, the name of the Web site for the company NU Design, Inc., is nu-design.com.
3. The domain name cannot include spaces. Keep in mind that just eliminating the spaces and running words together can confuse users and sometimes produce unintended results. In the previous example, NU Design, Inc., uses a hyphen in its domain name nu-design to preserve readability and avoid the undesirable interpretation of "nude sign" as the name.
4. The top-level domain you select should be intuitive for users. For a U.S. company, .com is the most common top-level domain.

Remember, communication is key. Every communication is an opportunity to increase branding, visibility, and success for your site. Select a domain name that can inform users about your company or project or what you do. If the top-level domain/domain name combination that you want is not available, select a different domain name that still effectively represents your company or project. But keep in mind, the more complex the domain name you choose, the harder it will be for others to remember and enter the URL correctly.

The machine name is followed by the domain name. The **domain name** identifies a Web site and is chosen by the site owner. Domain names are often a word or phrase related to an organization or individual. For example, *nu-design* is the domain name for NU Design, Inc., the company owned by the authors of this book. What is commonly referred to as the domain name of a Web site is actually the domain name combined with a top-level domain. A **top-level domain** is the highest category in the Internet naming system. The top-level domain might indicate the Web site's type of entity or country of origin. Common top-level domains are commercial (.com), business (.biz), organization (.org), network (.net), U.S. educational (.edu), and U.S. government (.gov). Although .com and .org are generally available to anyone, .edu must be some type of educational entity in the United States and .gov is reserved for the U.S. government. Some top-level domains for countries are .us (United States), .ca (Canada), .uk (United Kingdom), and .jp (Japan). The domain name and top-level domain are combined to create a unique name for a Web site. No two Web sites can have the same domain name and top-level domain. For example, nu-design.com is the domain name/top-level domain for NU Design, Inc. No other Web site can use this exact combination of names. However, another site might use *nu-design.org* or *nu-design.uk*. To avoid any confusion, many companies purchase all possible domain name/top-level domain combinations and point them all to the same site. Many people commonly refer to the domain name/top-level domain combination as the domain name.

INSIGHT

Registering Domain Names

To ensure that each domain/top-level domain combination is only used once, domain names must be registered for a fee with a domain registrar and are regulated by ICANN (Internet Corporation for Assigned Names and Numbers). Domain names are purchased for one to five years, and the owner has the opportunity to renew the name before anyone else can buy it. After you own a domain name, no one else can use it. By the end of 2011, 134 million domain names had been registered worldwide (*www.domaintools.com/internet-statistics*). Before you create a Web site, be sure to verify that the name you want is available and then register the name.

The top-level domain might be followed by nested directories (also called folders) that indicate the location of the file on the Web server. The last name in the series is usually the filename, as indicated by the .html or .htm extension. Each folder and the filename are separated by a slash (/).

The different parts of a URL provide some basic information about the site you are visiting. You can also make an educated guess to determine the correct URL for a site you want to visit.

You'll open the main page of the NU Design Web site. Because you are accessing the site over the Internet from a remote server, you will enter the URL. You must be connected to the Internet to view a remote Web page in your browser.

To view the NU Design Web site in a browser:

1. Click the **Start** button on the taskbar, and then click **Internet Explorer**. The Web browser opens and displays the default page. You'll open the NU Design Web site by entering its URL.

   Trouble? If you don't see Internet Explorer on the Start menu, type Internet Explorer in the Search programs and files box, and then click Internet Explorer in the search results that appear. If you still don't see Internet Explorer, press the Esc key until the Start menu closes, and then ask your technical support person for help.

   Trouble? If you are using Mozilla Firefox, Google Chrome, or a different Web browser, use the desktop icon or Start menu to open that browser and then modify any Web browser steps in these tutorials as needed.

2. At the top of the browser window, click in the **Address** bar to select its contents.

3. Type **www.nu-design.com** to replace the contents of the Address bar, and then press the **Enter** key. The main page for the NU Design Web site opens.

   Trouble? If a message appears that Internet Explorer cannot display the Web page, you probably are not connected to the Internet. Connect to the Internet and repeat Step 3. If you do not have Internet access, you cannot view the NU Design Web site. Read but do not perform Step 4.

4. If necessary, click the **Maximize** button 🔲 on the Internet Explorer title bar to maximize the program window. See Figure 1-2.

Figure 1-2 **Internet Explorer Web browser**

URL for the current Web page

NU Design home page

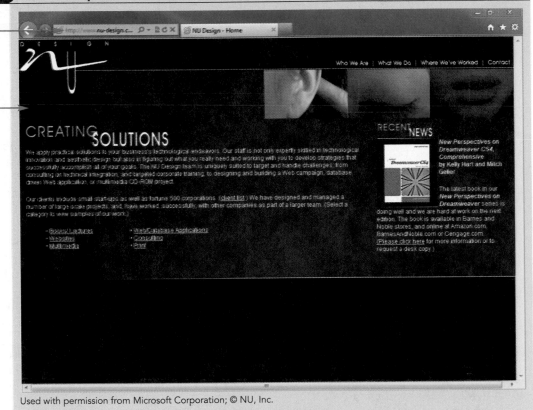

Used with permission from Microsoft Corporation; © NU, Inc.

Trouble? If the Web page you see looks different from the one shown in Figure 1-2, the content or layout of the page has changed since this book was printed. Web pages are constantly being modified and updated.

Sometimes you will want to view a Web page that is not posted to the Web. For example, a client might hand you files on a USB flash drive or a coworker might ask you to view a Web page from a local source, such as a computer hard drive or a local network server, before the Web page is posted to the Web. You can view a local copy of a Web page in your browser by typing the file path instead of the URL.

REFERENCE

Opening a Local Web Page in a Browser

- In the Address bar, type the file path, and then press the Enter key.

or

- On the menu bar, click File, and then click Open.
- Click the Browse button, and then navigate to the location where the Web page is stored.
- Click the Web page filename to select it, and then click the Open button.
- Click the OK button.

Brian wants you to view a copy of the NextBest Fest site that he created. You'll start by opening the Web site's **home page**, which is the main page of a Web site. You do not need to be connected to the Internet to view a local Web page in the browser.

To open the NextBest Fest home page in a browser:

1. Press the **Alt** key. The browser's menu bar is displayed at the top of the browser window.

2. On the menu bar, click **File**, and then click **Open**. The Open dialog box opens.

   Trouble? If the menu bar is not displayed, you can either display it or use a keyboard shortcut to access the Open dialog box. To display the menu bar, right click a blank area next to the page tab, click Menu bar on the shortcut menu, and then repeat Step 2. To use a keyboard shortcut, press the Ctrl+O keys, and then continue with Step 3.

3. Click the **Browse** button. The Windows Internet Explorer dialog box opens.

4. Navigate to the **Dreamweaver1\Tutorial\old_nbf** folder included with your Data Files, and then click **index.html** in the file list.

   Trouble? If you don't have the starting Data Files, you need to get them before you can proceed. Your instructor will either give you the Data Files or ask you to obtain them from a specified location (such as a network drive). In either case, make a backup copy of the Data Files before you start so that you have the original files available in case you need to start over. If you have any questions about the Data Files, see your instructor or technical support person for assistance.

5. Click the **Open** button. The Open dialog box reappears and includes the file path for the home page of the NextBest Fest site.

6. Click the **OK** button. The home page for the NextBest Fest site opens. See Figure 1-3.

Figure 1-3	NextBest Fest home page

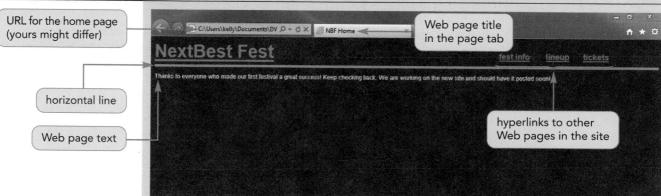

URL for the home page (yours might differ)

Web page title in the page tab

horizontal line

Web page text

hyperlinks to other Web pages in the site

Used with permission from Microsoft Corporation; © 2013 Cengage Learning

Trouble? If a dialog box opens, indicating that Internet Explorer needs to open a new window to display the Web page, click the OK button and then close all open browser windows when instructed to close the browser in these tutorials.

Trouble? If the message, "Intranet settings are now turned off by default. Intranet settings are less secure than Internet settings. Click here for options." appears, then you need to enable intranet settings. Whenever this message appears in these tutorials, click the Enable intranet settings button, and then click the Yes button in the security dialog box.

Web sites are nonlinear, which means that information branches out from the home page in many directions much like railroad tracks branch out from a train station. You can think of the home page as the hub or "train station" of a Web site. Just as people go to a train station to begin a train trip, the home page is where most people start when they want to explore a Web site. The major categories of information contained in the Web site branch out from the home page. Just as different sets of train tracks overlap, the branches of a Web site interconnect through links, and just as one train station is connected to other train stations, your Web site can be linked to other Web sites. So people can take many different routes through your Web site and end up at a variety of destinations.

Hyperlinks

Hyperlinks are how you get from one place to another in a Web page. They can be text, graphics, or buttons with active areas called hotspots that, when clicked, take you to a related section of the same Web page, another Web page in the same site, or another Web site altogether. When positioned over a link, the pointer changes to 🖑 to indicate that the area that the pointer is positioned over is a link. The NextBest Fest logo in the upper-left corner of the Web page is a link. A **logo** is usually a graphic or formatted text saved as a graphic and used by an organization for the purposes of brand identification. In this case, the logo is formatted text. A logo is often used as a link to the Web site home page. You'll use links as you review the NextBest Fest site.

Content

The main purpose of most Web sites is to provide information, which is conveyed through the site's content. **Content** is the information presented in a Web page. A Web page usually contains a combination of text, graphics, and possibly multimedia elements such as video, animation, or interactive content. The blend of these elements is determined by what most effectively conveys the intended message or information. Ignoring the content of a Web site and focusing purely on visual design is a common mistake made by inexperienced designers.

Gage created a simple design and inserted placeholder content for the temporary NextBest Fest site. The redesigned Web site will have more interesting design elements and additional content. As you review the temporary site, think about how the pages are linked and what should be added or changed when the Web site is redesigned.

To review the temporary NextBest Fest site:

▶ **1.** Read the content on the home page of the NextBest Fest site, considering what information might be appropriate to add and what design changes you would like to see.

▶ **2.** Click the **fest info** link to open the Fest Info page, and then review the page content, considering what information might be appropriate to add and what design changes would enhance the page. See Figure 1-4.

Figure 1-4   Fest Info page

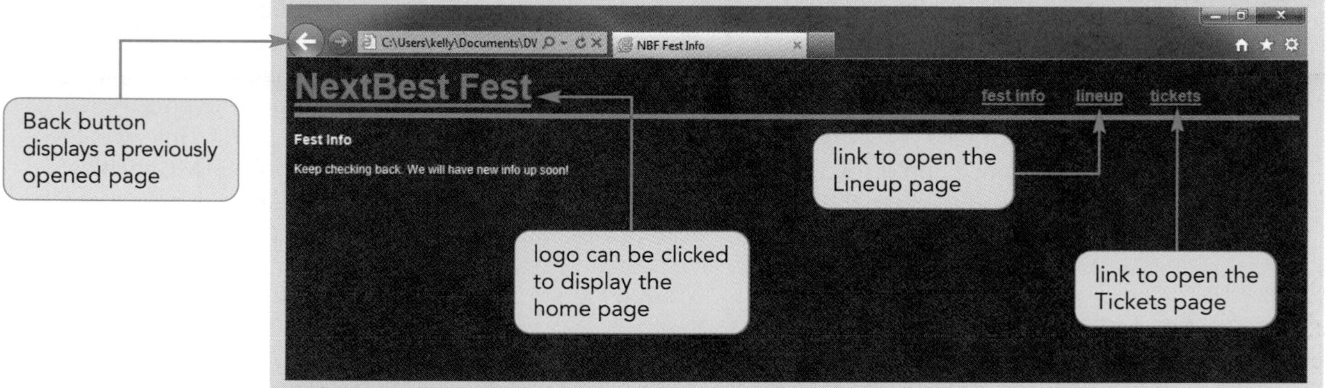

Back button displays a previously opened page

NextBest Fest

fest info   lineup   tickets

Fest Info
Keep checking back. We will have new info up soon!

logo can be clicked to display the home page

link to open the Lineup page

link to open the Tickets page

Used with permission from Microsoft Corporation; © 2013 Cengage Learning

3. Repeat Step 2 for the Lineup and Tickets pages, clicking the appropriate link to open the corresponding page.

4. Click the **NextBest Fest logo** to return to the home page.

   Now that you have reviewed the pages of the site, you will close the site and exit the browser.

TIP
You can also click File on the menu bar, and then click Exit to exit the browser.

5. On the browser title bar, click the **Close** button ⬛ x . The NextBest Fest site closes and the browser exits.

6. Repeat Step 5 to close any additional open browser windows.

From your review of the NextBest Fest site content, you might have a list of changes to suggest to Gage. For example, you might want to add a list of bands and band descriptions to the Lineup page. The page might also include links to each band's Web site.

Evolving Web Design Tools

In the early days of Web design, most Web pages contained only text and were created by typing HTML code into documents using a simple text editor such as Notepad or Simple Text. To create a Web page, you had to know how to write HTML from scratch. As the Web evolved, Web authors began to create more complex graphical interfaces. This made creating Web pages from scratch cumbersome. HTML was designed by scientists as a means of sharing information. Using HTML for graphically complex interfaces involves intricate HTML structures that are impractical for most people to type. Furthermore, artists, graphic designers, businesspeople, and nonprogrammers who wanted to create Web pages did not necessarily want to learn all the intricacies of coding in HTML. This led to the development of software packages that allowed people to design Web pages by typing, placing, and manipulating content in an environment that more closely approximated the look of the Web page they wanted to create. The software actually wrote the HTML code for them. These software packages were originally referred to as **WYSIWYG (What You See Is What You Get)** programs because the Web page is displayed in the program window as it will appear to the end user and the code is hidden from sight. Today, the acronym WYSIWYG is used infrequently because almost all software is designed to show you what you get as you work. The acronym has also been critiqued as a misnomer with Web software because what you get really depends on the specific browser and version used to view the page.

With these Web software packages, people who were not programmers could design Web pages, and designers gained even more control over the look of their sites across the various browsers. Dreamweaver grew out of this need for easy-to-use, visual tools that enable Web authors to rapidly develop reliable and well-coded Web pages. Dreamweaver has become one of the most widely used site development and management tools because of its ease of use, accurate HTML output, and powerful tool set. With Dreamweaver, you can successfully create a Web site without knowing any HTML. In Dreamweaver, you type text, insert pictures, and create hyperlinks in much the same way as you do in a word processing program. The difference is that Dreamweaver is also creating the HTML code that Web servers need to interpret the page and display it on the Internet. However, some familiarity with HTML enables you to make the site work better, fix problems that arise, and create elements that are difficult or impossible to create in Dreamweaver.

HTML5 and Apps

TIP

As of September 2011, 34 of the world's top 100 Web sites were already using HTML5.

HTML5 is the most recent version of HTML. In fact, it was still under development as of early 2012, and has not been officially recommended by W3C; the World Wide Web Consortium is an international community led by Timothy Berners-Lee and Jeffrey Jaffe that works to establish Web standards. Even though it has not yet been officially recommended, most browsers have already started supporting many of its new features in their latest releases. HTML5 streamlines the structure of HTML and introduces many new capabilities that will enable designers to use HTML to create more interactive Web pages as well as the next generation of applications, including mobile apps. An **application**, or **app**, is another name for a program or software. **Web apps** are applications that are designed to run in Web browsers and **mobile apps** are applications that are designed to run on mobile devices. Some of the new things that HTML5 has made possible include adding video and audio to a page without using additional programs to play the video or audio.

When designers say that a site has been created using HTML5, they usually mean that they have used a combination of HTML5, CSS3, and JavaScript to create the site. **Cascading Style Sheets (CSS)** is a style sheet language that you can use to specify the look, formatting, and placement of the content of a page written in a markup language like HTML. CSS3, the most current version of CSS, was developed alongside HTML5 to enable more advanced use of styles to enhance the functionality of HTML5. For example, you can create animations using only HTML5 and CSS3. **JavaScript** is a scripting language that works with HTML and is used to add advanced capabilities to Web pages. For example, HTML5, CSS3, and JavaScript are used together to enable drag-and-drop functionality on a Web page. Together these three languages form the cornerstone of modern Web pages and apps.

INSIGHT

Testing in Different Web Browsers

When creating Web sites, be aware that aspects of each Web page might display differently in the various browsers. For example, text and graphics placement and alignment might change slightly from browser to browser. These variations occur because browser manufacturers adhere only partially to some of the standards set by W3C and/or implement them differently. In addition, text might appear more or less sharp and vary in size when viewed on a Macintosh rather than a Windows PC. Images can vary in brightness as well. In addition, different versions of browsers display things slightly differently. This is partially because they support different versions of HTML. For example, some of the functionality that you can create now with HTML5 might not work in older browsers. As you learn more about coding Web pages in these tutorials, you will learn techniques for making an HTML5 site compatible with older browsers.

To ensure that all users have a good experience, test your site on every browser that your intended audience might use. Minor differences are okay. The important things to watch for are layout and functionality errors such as overlapping content, gaps, and cutoff or truncated text and graphics. Although these tutorials have you test the site you are creating only in Internet Explorer to simplify the process, you should support all of the major browsers when you design professional Web sites.

In this session, you learned about the Internet, the Web, Web servers, and clients. You explored different components of a Web page. Also, you opened the temporary NextBest Fest site in a browser, navigated between the Web pages, and reviewed the site's content. In the next session, you will view the temporary NextBest Fest site from within Dreamweaver.

REVIEW

Session 1.1 Quick Check

1. What is the Internet?
2. What is the Web?
3. Explain the difference between a Web server and a Web client.
4. What is a Web browser?
5. What is a URL?
6. In the following URL, identify the domain name and the top-level domain: *http://www.nu-design.com/index.html*.
7. Define hyperlink.
8. Explain the purpose of content in a Web site.

SESSION 1.2 VISUAL OVERVIEW

The **menu bar** is a categorized series of menus that provides access to all of the tools and features available in Dreamweaver.

The Welcome screen appears each time you start Dreamweaver and has links for creating new documents, opening existing documents, and getting help.

You can click a page worked on recently to open it.

You can use these links to take a Dreamweaver tour and complete tutorials to help you get started.

The **Property inspector** is a toolbar with buttons for examining or editing the attributes of any element that is currently selected in the active page in the Document window.

DESIGNER WORKSPACE CONFIGURATION

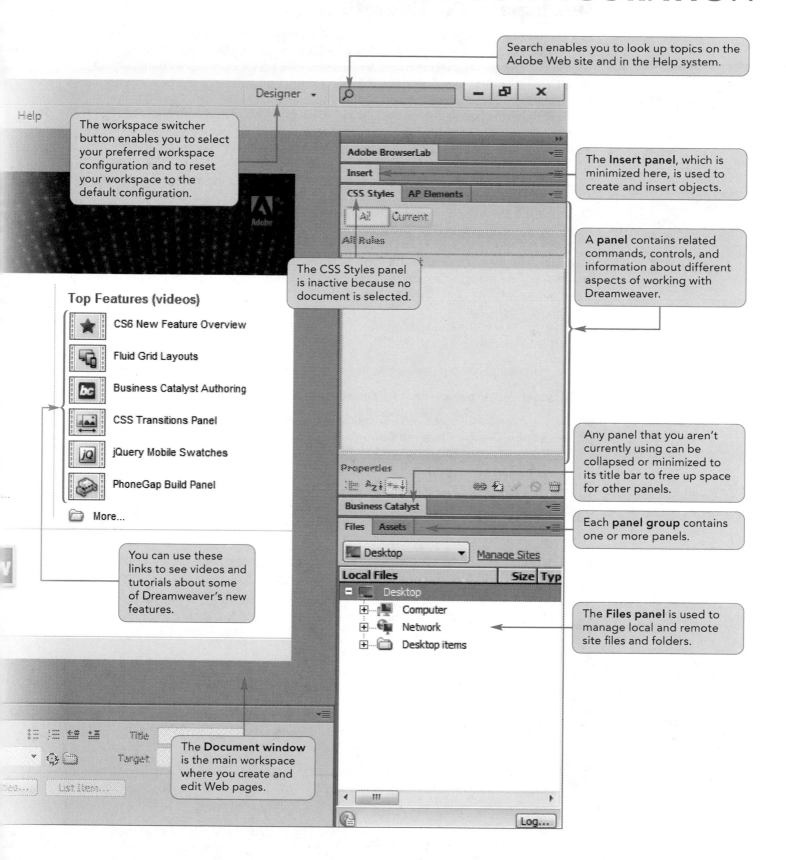

Search enables you to look up topics on the Adobe Web site and in the Help system.

The workspace switcher button enables you to select your preferred workspace configuration and to reset your workspace to the default configuration.

The **Insert panel**, which is minimized here, is used to create and insert objects.

The CSS Styles panel is inactive because no document is selected.

A **panel** contains related commands, controls, and information about different aspects of working with Dreamweaver.

You can use these links to see videos and tutorials about some of Dreamweaver's new features.

Any panel that you aren't currently using can be collapsed or minimized to its title bar to free up space for other panels.

Each **panel group** contains one or more panels.

The **Document window** is the main workspace where you create and edit Web pages.

The **Files panel** is used to manage local and remote site files and folders.

Top Features (videos)

- CS6 New Feature Overview
- Fluid Grid Layouts
- Business Catalyst Authoring
- CSS Transitions Panel
- jQuery Mobile Swatches
- PhoneGap Build Panel
- More...

Starting Dreamweaver and Selecting a Workspace Configuration

The Dreamweaver program window consists of several smaller windows, toolbars, and panels that can be configured in a variety of ways to create the workspace that best fits your needs and purposes. Dreamweaver includes nine preset workspace configurations (App Developer, App Developer Plus, Classic, Coder, Coder Plus, Designer, Designer Compact, Dual Screen, and Fluid Screen) or you can create your own. Each configuration optimizes the panels display to help you focus on working in a different way. For example, the Coder configuration optimizes the workspace for people who are mostly writing code and the App Developer configuration optimizes the workspace for people who are creating mobile and Web apps.

Dreamweaver opens in the same workspace configuration it was in when it was closed. So, depending on the working method of the person who last used the computer, Dreamweaver might open in any of the preset workspace configurations or it might open to a custom configuration if the previous user moved a panel to a new location.

In these tutorials, you will use Dreamweaver in the Designer workspace. At the beginning of each tutorial, you will reset Dreamweaver to the default Designer workspace to ensure that your screen matches the figures in these tutorials. As you become more proficient with Dreamweaver, you might find that you prefer one of the other workspace configurations.

To begin, you will start Dreamweaver, reset the Designer workspace, and then open and collapse panels.

> **TIP**
>
> To save a custom workspace, arrange the panels as desired, click the workspace switcher button, click New Workspace, type a name, and then click the OK button. The custom workspace is available from the workspace switcher button.

To start Dreamweaver and reset the Designer workspace:

▶ 1. Click the **Start** button on the taskbar, click **All Programs**, click **Adobe** or **Adobe Design Premium CS6**, and then click **Adobe Dreamweaver CS6**. Dreamweaver starts.

   Trouble? If you do not see the Adobe or Adobe Design Premium CS6 folder, type Dreamweaver in the Search programs and files box at the bottom of the Start menu, and then click Adobe Dreamweaver CS6 in the search results. If you still can't find Adobe Dreamweaver CS6, ask your instructor or technical support person for help.

   Trouble? If this is the first time Dreamweaver is started on this computer, the Default Editor dialog box opens to show the file types for which Dreamweaver will be the default editor. Click the OK button.

   Trouble? If a dialog box opens stating that the local site folder, Dreamweaver, does not exist, click the Cancel button.

▶ 2. On the menu bar, click the **workspace switcher** button to display the list of default configurations, and then click **Designer**. The workspace changes to the Designer configuration.

▶ 3. On the menu bar, click the **workspace switcher** button, and then click **Reset 'Designer'**. All the panels and windows return to their default positions in the Designer configuration.

▶ 4. On the menu bar, click the **Maximize** button ⬜, if necessary, to maximize the program window. Refer to the Session 1.2 Visual Overview to see Dreamweaver in the Designer workspace with its basic elements labeled. Note that the Business Catalyst panel on your screen will be open.

> You must reset the default Designer workspace so that your screen matches the figures.

Setting Up a New Site

Working on a Web site is a lot like working on a report. You most often keep the original report locally on your computer and distribute a copy of the report to others to review. In the case of a basic Web site, you usually work on the original site on your computer, and then use Dreamweaver to post a copy to a publicly viewable space such as a Web server. The original site stored on your computer is the *local version*, and the copy that Dreamweaver posts is the *remote version*. You make all changes and revisions to the local site, and then have Dreamweaver update the remote site. A **site definition** is the information that tells Dreamweaver where to find the local and remote files for the Web site, along with other parameters that affect how the site is set up within Dreamweaver. Dreamweaver stores a local Web site in the same format as it will be posted on the Web.

You should create the local information for the site definition (also referred to as the local site definition) before you begin working on a Web site. You can wait to create the remote information for the site definition (also referred to as the remote site definition) until you are ready to post a copy of the site to a Web server.

INSIGHT

Re-Creating a Site Definition

A site definition is stored in the Windows Registry of the computer you are using and is not kept as part of the site. If you use a different computer for a later work session, you must re-create the site definition on that computer. You can also export the existing site definition to a file and then import it to a different computer. Be sure to use the most recent version of the site when you create, re-create, or import the site definition.

Setting Up the Local Information

The **local site definition** is the information stored on the computer you are using that tells Dreamweaver where the local site folder is located. A **local site folder** (also called **local root folder**) is the location where you store all the files used by the local version of the Web site. You can use files stored anywhere on your hard drive or network to create a site; Dreamweaver prompts you to copy these files into the local site folder so that everything you need is in one convenient location. You can place the local site folder on a hard drive or on a removable disk. Working on a site stored on a removable disk can be slower than working on a site stored on a hard drive.

You add general site definition information in the Site Setup dialog box. From the Site tab, you can enter the site name and the local site folder. You could stop here and allow Dreamweaver to create the rest of the local site information based on general assumptions. Another option is to enter the rest of the local information manually on the Local Info tab in the Advanced Settings list. For these tutorials, you will enter the information manually so that you can better understand all of the components of a local site definition.

Setting Up Local Information for a New Site

- On the menu bar, click Site, and then click New Site.
- In the Site Setup dialog box, click the Site tab.
- In the Site Name box, type a name.
- In the Local Site Folder box, type a path (or click the Browse button, navigate to the Web site's folder, and then click the Select button).
- Click the Advanced Settings tab and click Local Info.
- In the Default Images folder box, type a path (or click the Browse button, navigate to the Web site's folder, double-click the folder where you want to store the images for your site, and then click the Select button).
- Click the Document option button.
- Click the Case-sensitive links checking check box to select it.
- Click the Enable Cache check box to select it.
- Click the Save button.

You'll need to enter information and select options to set up the local information for the site definition. The local site definition includes the following information:

- **Site name.** An internal name you give the Web site for your reference. This name appears on the Site menu in the Document window and in the Files panel but is not used outside of Dreamweaver. You'll use "Old NBF" as the site name for the temporary NextBest Fest site.
- **Local site folder.** The location where you store all of the files used by the local version of the Web site. You choose where to place the local site folder on your computer, network, or removable disk. The local site folder is the root folder for your local site. You can create folders within the local site folder to enable you to better organize the files in your site.
- **Default images folder.** The folder in which you store all of the graphics files used in the site. A good practice is to create a graphics folder within the local site folder as the default images folder.
- **Links relative to.** The path of hyperlinks can be relative to the current Web page (document relative links) or relative to the root directory of the site (site root relative links). Dreamweaver inserts relative paths when you create hyperlinks to pages within your site. You will use document relative links for the NextBest Fest site.
- **Web URL.** The URL of the Web site, which Dreamweaver uses to verify links. You will enter this URL in a later tutorial when you publish the NextBest Fest site.
- **Case-sensitive links.** Hyperlinks can be set to be **case sensitive** (uppercase and lowercase letters are considered different letters). Linux Web servers are case sensitive, whereas Windows Web servers are not. Linux Web servers see index.html and Index.html as different files, whereas Windows Web servers see them as the same file. Select the Case-sensitive links checking check box to avoid problems with case when you upload the site to the Web.
- **Enable cache.** A **cache** is a temporary local storage space. Dreamweaver uses a cache to speed up the processing time needed to update links when you move, rename, or delete a file. You'll usually leave the Enable Cache check box checked.

TIP

Always use lowercase letters when naming files and folders to avoid potential problems.

PROSKILLS

Decision Making: Creating a Logical Folder Structure

When creating the local site folder, use a logical folder structure and a descriptive naming system. A logical folder structure helps keep the Web site files organized. For example, it is a good idea to store each project in its own folder and to create a Web subfolder within each project folder so that the Dreamweaver files remain separate from any working files that you have not yet added to the Web site. You might, for instance, create a *nextbest_fest* project folder that contains an *nb_web* subfolder. Any text files or graphics that you have not yet added to the Web site would be stored in the *nextbest_fest* folder. The *nb_web* subfolder would be the local site folder for the new NextBest Fest site.

In addition to creating an organized file structure for each site, it is also a good idea to use consistent rules or practices when naming the site's files and pages. Remember that folder names and filenames can include any series of letters, numbers, hyphens, and underscores. They should not include spaces, symbols, or special characters, which can cause problems on some Web servers. Symbols and special characters can also have different meanings on different platforms. In these tutorials, the names of files and folders are in all lowercase letters and words are separated with an underscore, such as *nextbest_fest*.

You'll enter the local information for the site definition so you can view the NextBest Fest site in Dreamweaver on your computer.

To enter the local information for the site definition for the NextBest Fest site:

1. On the menu bar, click **Site**, and then click **New Site**. The Site Setup dialog box opens with the Site tab selected. See Figure 1-5.

Figure 1-5	Site Setup dialog box

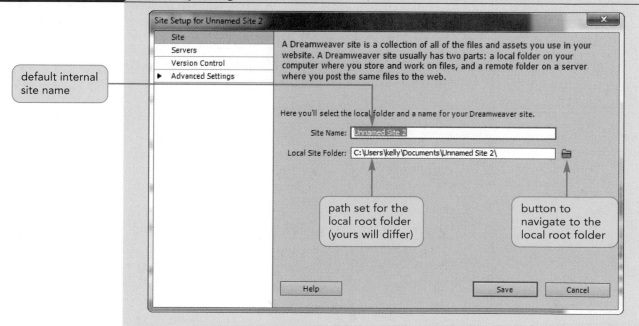

default internal site name

path set for the local root folder (yours will differ)

button to navigate to the local root folder

Trouble? If another tab is selected, you need to select the Site tab. Click the Site tab to display the site information in the main pane of the dialog box.

2. In the Site Name box, select the text, if necessary, and then type **Old NBF** as the internal name for the site. You will use Old NBF to reference the site; this name is not used outside of Dreamweaver.

3. Next to the Local Site Folder box, click the **Browse** button 📁. The Choose Root Folder dialog box opens.

4. Navigate to the **Dreamweaver1\Tutorial\old_nbf** folder included with your Data Files (the location where the NextBest Fest site is stored), and then click the **Select** button. The path to the NextBest Fest site appears in the Local Site Folder box.

5. Click the **Advanced Settings** tab, and then click **Local Info**. The local information settings appear in the main pane of the Site Setup dialog box. See Figure 1-6.

| Figure 1-6 | Local Info in the Advanced Settings tab |

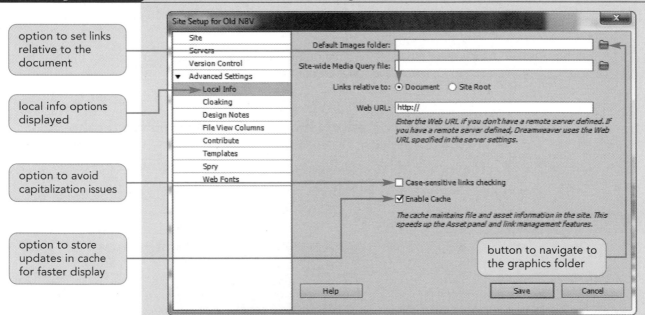

option to set links relative to the document

local info options displayed

option to avoid capitalization issues

option to store updates in cache for faster display

button to navigate to the graphics folder

6. Next to the Default Images folder box, click the **Browse** button 📁. The Choose Image Folder dialog box opens.

7. Navigate to the **Dreamweaver1\Tutorial\old_nbf** folder if necessary, click the **graphics** folder, and then click the **Select** button. Dreamweaver will store all the graphics used in the site in this folder.

8. Next to Links relative to, click the **Document** option button, if necessary. The links are set relative to the document.

9. Click the **Case-sensitive links checking** check box to select it. This avoids capitalization issues when the site is uploaded to a Web server.

> **10.** Click the **Enable Cache** check box to select it, if necessary. Dreamweaver will quickly update links whenever you move, rename, or delete a file.

> **11.** Click the **Save** button. The Site Setup dialog box closes. Dreamweaver scans the existing files and creates the files list for the site, which is visible in the Files panel.
>
> **Trouble?** If a dialog box opens with the message that the initial site cache will now be created, click the OK button.

Exploring the Dreamweaver Environment

Gage wants you to explore the temporary NextBest Fest site from within Dreamweaver. As you review the site, you will work with the Dreamweaver windows, panels, and toolbars.

TIP

Panels are docked along the edges of the program window. You can drag a panel by its tab to the center of the program window to undock it. You can drag an undocked panel to the edge of the program window to create a new docked panel group or into an existing panel group to dock it there.

Files Panel

The Files panel is located in the Files panel group. You use the Files panel to manage local and remote site files and folders. The name of the Web site that is currently selected appears in the Site button on the Files panel toolbar. After you create the local portion of the site definition on your current computer, the site name for that Web site is added to the menu—in this case, Old NBF. The local site folder for the selected site appears in the lower portion of the Files panel. When you expand the local site folder, a list of the folders and files in the local site appears. From the Files panel, you can view, move, copy, rename, delete, and open files and folders. You can also use the Files panel to transfer files to a remote site when you are ready to post the site to the Web. You will use these features of the Files panel when you begin working with the remote site and later when you add a test server to test advanced functionality.

REFERENCE

Viewing the Files List in the Files Panel

- On the Files panel toolbar, click the View button, and then click Local view.
- On the Files panel toolbar, click the Site button, and then click the Web site name.
- In the files list, click the Expand button next to the Web site folder.

The Files panel also includes an **integrated file browser** that enables you to browse files located outside of the site. After you set up your remote server information, you can select Remote view from the View button and a list of the files and folders in the remote site appears in the lower portion of the Files panel. You can expand the Files panel to fill the workspace. When the Files panel is expanded, the lower portion of the panel is divided vertically into two panes so that you can display the local and remote views of the site simultaneously.

To view the files list of the local Old NBF site in the Files panel:

▶ **1.** On the Files panel toolbar, click the **View** button, and then click **Local view**, if necessary.

▶ **2.** On the Files panel toolbar, click the **Site** button, and then click **Old NBF**, if necessary. The temporary NextBest Fest site appears in the local files list below the Files panel toolbar.

▶ **3.** Click the **Expand** button next to the Site - Old NBF folder, if necessary. The graphics folder and the Old NBF Web page files appear in the files list. See Figure 1-7.

| Figure 1-7 | Files panel with the Old NBF files list |

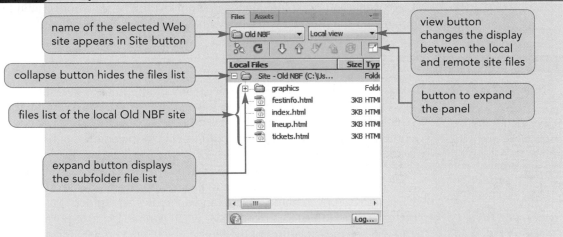

name of the selected Web site appears in Site button

view button changes the display between the local and remote site files

collapse button hides the files list

files list of the local Old NBF site

button to expand the panel

expand button displays the subfolder file list

When a Web site is selected, the folders and pages in the local site folder are displayed. Currently, the folders and pages in the local site folder of the Old NBF site are visible. A folder icon precedes the folder name; a Dreamweaver Web page icon precedes the Web page filenames. Each filename is followed by a **file extension**, which is used by Windows to determine the file type. The file extension for Web pages can be either .html or .htm. Depending on how your Web server is set up, you might be required to use one or the other for the entire site or for only the default page.

You can open any page in the Web site by double-clicking its filename in the files list. Although there are other methods for opening Web pages in Dreamweaver, this method ensures that you always open the file from the local site folder (rather than from a backup copy or another location). Each page opens in the Document window. You can open multiple pages at one time. The filenames of all the open pages appear in page tabs in the Document window title bar above the Document toolbar. The active page is displayed in the Document window, the name of the active page is displayed in the active page tab, and the file path for the active page appears on the right side of the Document window title bar.

You'll use the Files panel to open the Lineup and Fest Info pages.

To open the Lineup and Fest Info pages from the Files panel:

1. On the Files panel, double-click **lineup.html**. The Lineup page opens in the Document window.

2. Double-click **festinfo.html** in the Files panel. The Fest Info page opens in the Document window and is the active page. See Figure 1-8.

Figure 1-8   Web pages open in Dreamweaver

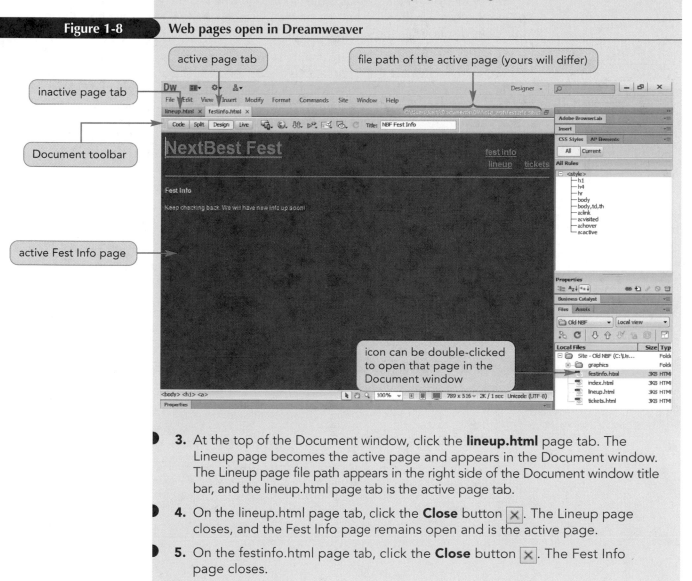

3. At the top of the Document window, click the **lineup.html** page tab. The Lineup page becomes the active page and appears in the Document window. The Lineup page file path appears in the right side of the Document window title bar, and the lineup.html page tab is the active page tab.

4. On the lineup.html page tab, click the **Close** button ☒. The Lineup page closes, and the Fest Info page remains open and is the active page.

5. On the festinfo.html page tab, click the **Close** button ☒. The Fest Info page closes.

Document Window

The Document window is the main workspace where you create and edit Web pages. You use tools from the various panels, toolbars, and inspectors to manipulate the page that is open in the Document window.

The Document toolbar, located below the page tabs, includes buttons for the most commonly used commands related to the Document window. It also includes a text box for entering the **page title**, which is the name you give a Web page that appears in the browser's title bar when the Web page is viewed in a browser window.

At the top of the Document window, the active document's file path appears at the right of the selected page tab. The file path ends with the **filename**, which is the name under which a Web page is saved. If a page has been modified, an asterisk (*) appears after the filename in the page tab until you save the page again. The page that opens by default when you visit a Web site usually has the filename index.htm, index.html, default.htm, or default.html. The Web server displays this page if the user has not requested a specific file in the URL.

Below the Document toolbar is the workspace where you create and edit Web pages. You can use the view buttons on the Document toolbar to change how the information is displayed in the workspace. The four views are as follows:

- **Design view.** Displays a nonfunctioning version of the page as it will appear in a browser. Design view is the primary view used for designing and creating a Web page. The HTML code is hidden so you can focus on how the finished product will look.
- **Code view.** Displays the underlying HTML and CSS code that Dreamweaver generates as you create and edit a page. You can also enter or edit code in this view. Code view is used primarily when you want to work directly with the HTML code.
- **Split view.** Divides the Document window into two vertical panes. The left pane shows the underlying code and the right pane shows the page as it will appear in the browser. You can move easily between the panes to either edit the code or change the design. Split view is used primarily to debug or troubleshoot a page.
- **Live view.** Displays a functioning version of the page as it will appear in a browser. Live view enables you to interact with the page just as a user will interact with the live version. You cannot edit the page in this view because the elements are functional. To make changes, you would switch to Design view or Code view, edit the page as needed, refresh the page, and then return to Live view to see the updated page.
- **Live Code view.** Displays the underlying code of a page that dynamically updates as you interact with the page. You cannot enter or edit code in this view, which is available only from Live view.

You'll look at the home page of the Old NBF site in the different views. The filename of the home page is index.html because this page displays by default when the user has not requested a specific file in the URL.

TIP

If you are having difficulty editing a page, make sure you are not in Live view.

To display the Old NBF home page in different views:

1. In the Files panel, double-click **index.html**. The Old NBF home page opens in Design view. See Figure 1-9.

Figure 1-9 Home page in Design view

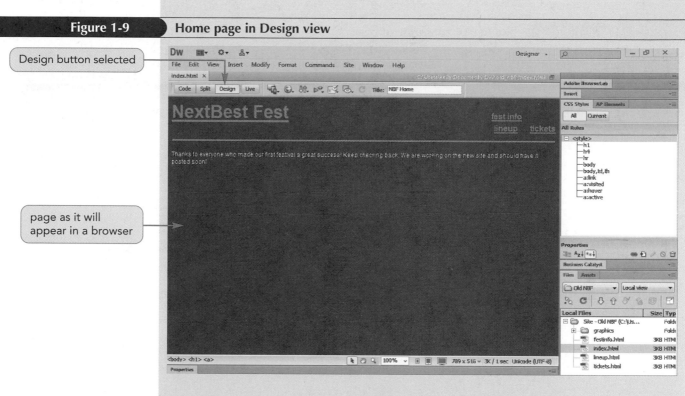

2. On the Document toolbar, click the **Split** button. The home page is displayed in Split view. See Figure 1-10.

Figure 1-10 Home page in Split view

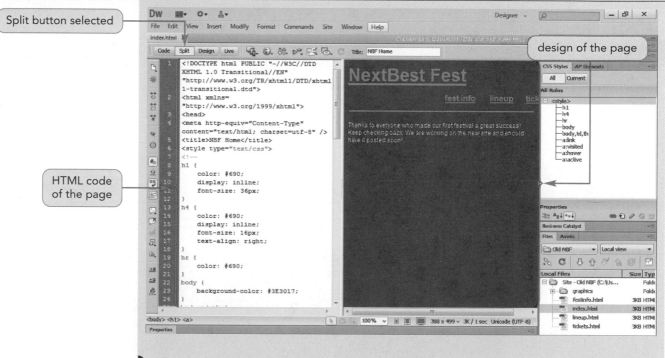

3. On the Document toolbar, click the **Code** button. The HTML and CSS code for the home page is displayed in the Document window.

4. Scroll to the bottom of the page to view the rest of the code. See Figure 1-11.

Figure 1-11 **Home page in Code view**

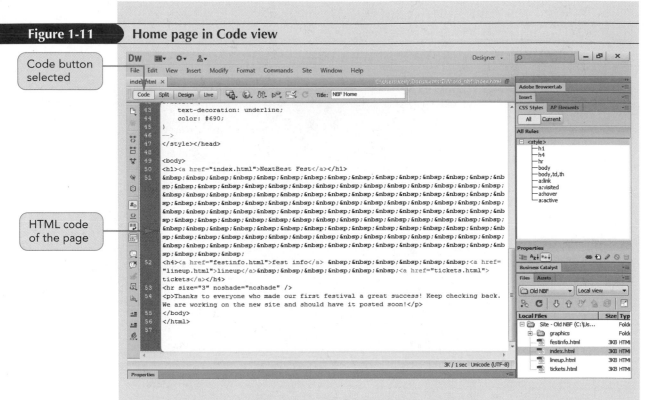

Code button selected

HTML code of the page

5. On the Document toolbar, click the **Split** button. The code and the design of the home page reappear in the Document window.

6. On the menu bar, click **View**, and then click **Split Vertically** to uncheck it. The code and design panes are rearranged to divide the Document window horizontally. See Figure 1-12.

Figure 1-12 **Split view with horizontal panes**

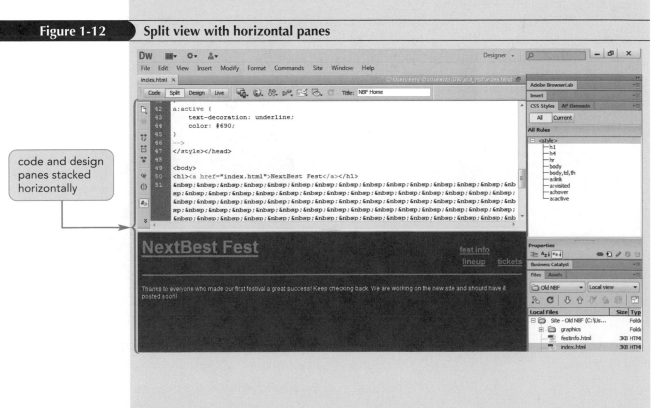

code and design panes stacked horizontally

7. On the Document toolbar, click the **Design** button. The home page returns to Design view.

8. Click the **lineup** link. Notice that the link is not functional in Design view.

9. On the Document toolbar, click the **Live** button. The home page switches to Live view.

10. Click the **lineup** link. The link is now functional and you can see that it works.

11. On the index.html page tab, click the **Close** button ⊠. The home page closes.

Status Bar

The **status bar**, located at the bottom of the Document window, displays details about the content in the Document window. The following items always appear in the status bar:

- **Tag selector.** A list of all the HTML tags used with the current selection in the page.
- **Select tool.** The pointer tool you use to select text, graphics, and so on. This is the default pointer tool.
- **Hand tool.** The pointer tool you use to drag the active page up or down in the workspace. When the Hand tool is selected, the pointer becomes 🖑.
- **Zoom tool.** The pointer tool you use to magnify the active page and zoom to a specific area. When the Zoom tool is selected, the pointer changes to 🔍. To zoom out, hold the Alt key as you click the active page.
- **Set magnification button.** A list of preset percentages you select from to zoom the page display in the workspace.
- **Mobile size, Tablet size, and Desktop size buttons.** Buttons that set the Document window dimensions for mobile, tablet, or desktop display so you can preview the site for the selected device.
- **Window Size button.** The current dimensions of the Document window in pixels. A **pixel**, which stands for picture element, is the smallest addressable unit on a display screen. The numbers change when you resize the Document window. You can set the window dimensions by manually resizing the window or by selecting one of the common monitor sizes from the menu. Before you change the window size, you must click the Maximize/Restore button to make the Document window sizable.
- **Document Size / Download Time.** The size of the current page in kilobytes (K) and the approximate time in seconds it would take to download the page over a modem transferring 56 kilobytes per second (Kbps).

You'll review status bar items as you explore and modify the Lineup page.

To use the status bar to modify the Lineup page:

1. Open the **lineup.html** page. The Lineup page opens in the Document window.

2. At the top of the page, triple-click in the **NextBest Fest logo** to select it. The tag selector in the status bar shows the HTML tags associated with the selected text. See Figure 1-13.

Figure 1-13   Status bar items

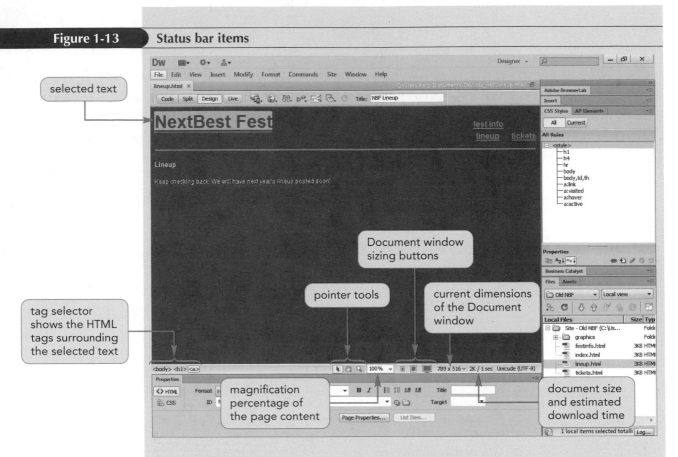

Trouble? If you don't see the <h1> tag or the <a> tag in the status bar, the tag isn't selected in the underlying code. Continue with Step 3.

3. Below the NextBest Fest logo, drag to select some of the text. Some of the following HTML tags appear in the tag selector: <body>, <h4>, <h3>, <p>, and <a>.

4. On the Document window title bar, click the **Restore** button 🗖. The Document window becomes sizable. See Figure 1-14.

Figure 1-14   **Resized Document window**

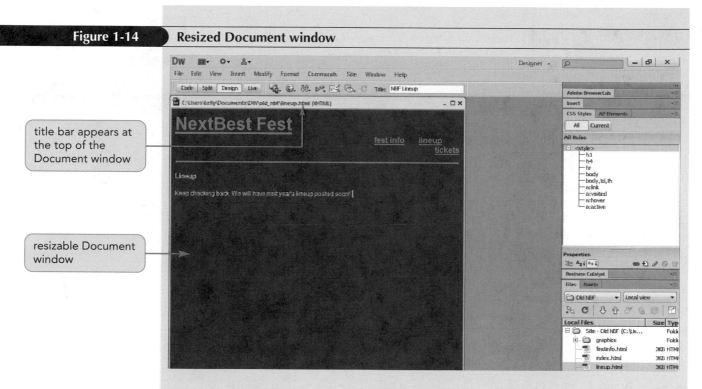

title bar appears at the top of the Document window

resizable Document window

5. On the status bar, click the **Window Size** button to open a menu of common monitor sizes, and then click **1000 × 620**. The Document window changes size.

   Trouble? If you don't see the status bar, you need to extend the Document window. Click the expand button at the bottom of the Document window. The status bar becomes visible. Click the collapse button below the Document window after you complete Step 6.

6. On the status bar, click the **Mobile size** button 📱. The Document window resizes to display the page at 480 × 800, which is the default mobile size. See Figure 1-15.

Figure 1-15 Document window resized for a mobile device

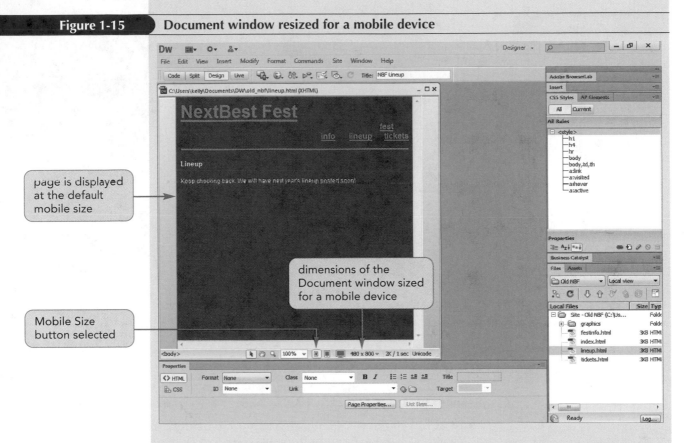

page is displayed at the default mobile size

dimensions of the Document window sized for a mobile device

Mobile Size button selected

7. On the Document window title bar, click the **Maximize** button ☐, and then click the **Desktop size** button 🖥 on the status bar. The Document window returns to its maximized state.

   Trouble? If you don't see the Maximize/Restore button, click Window on the menu bar, click Tile Horizontally to have the Document window fill the workspace, and then repeat Step 7.

8. On the status bar, click the **Set magnification** button to display the magnification options, and then click **50%**. The page content decreases to 50% magnification.

9. On the status bar, click the **Set magnification** button, and then click **100%**. The page returns to its original size.

10. On the status bar, click the **Zoom Tool** button 🔍 to change the pointer to ⊕, and then click anywhere on the Lineup page. The page content is magnified.

11. Press and hold the **Alt** key to change the pointer to ⊖, and then click anywhere on the Lineup page. The page returns to its original magnification.

12. On the status bar, click the **Select Tool** button 🔖 to change the pointer back to an arrow.

13. On the status bar, review the **Document Size/Download Time** for the page.

14. Close the page.

   Trouble? If a dialog box opens, prompting you to save changes to the page, click the No button.

Property Inspector

A frequently used tool is the Property inspector, a toolbar with buttons for examining or editing the attributes of any element that is currently selected on the active page in the Document window. A **page element** is either an object or text. You can display the attributes of any text or object that you select in the Document window. The Property inspector buttons and options change to reflect the attributes of the selected element. You can switch between viewing the HTML attributes and the CSS attributes of the selected element. Because HTML5 enables you to create interactions that happen over time, the Property inspector sometimes displays a timeline.

You'll use the Property inspector to explore the attributes of different objects in the Old NBF site.

To use the Property inspector to explore object attributes:

1. Open the **index.html** page. The home page opens in the Document window.

2. Drag to select the text in the paragraph below the horizontal rule. The Property inspector attributes reflect the HTML properties of the selected text by default. The HTML attributes associated with text are similar to those in a word processing program, such as styles (bold and italic), alignment, and indentation. See Figure 1-16.

Figure 1-16   Property inspector with HTML text attributes

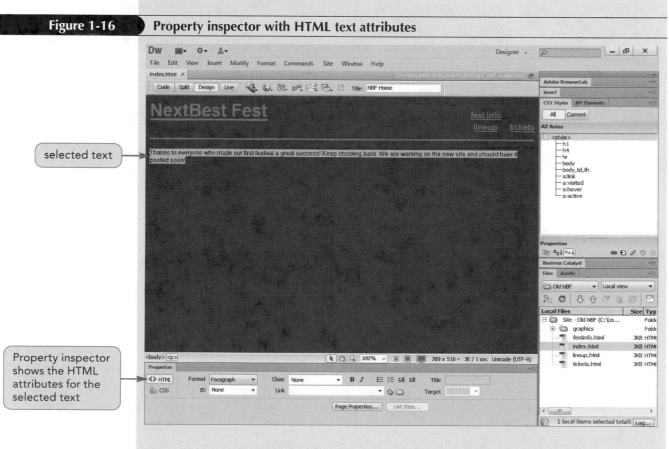

selected text

Property inspector shows the HTML attributes for the selected text

3. At the top of the page, drag to select the **tickets** link. HTML attributes in the Property inspector change to reflect the selected text link. See Figure 1-17.

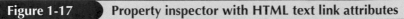

| Figure 1-17 | Property inspector with HTML text link attributes |

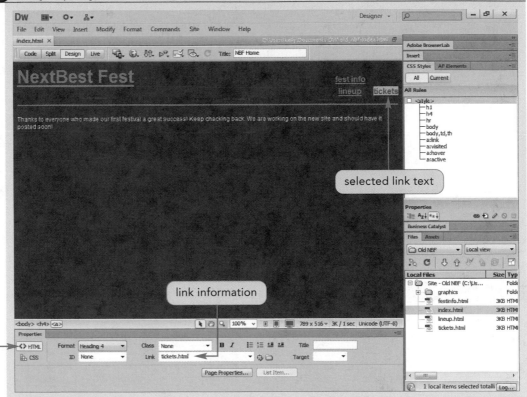

selected link text

Property inspector shows the HTML attributes for the selected text link

link information

4. In the Property inspector, click the **CSS** button. The CSS properties of the selected element appear in the Property inspector. The Property inspector displays the CSS rule that defines the style for the selected text as well as the font, alignment, size, and color of the selected text. You can also view the CSS panel or edit the CSS rule to change the appearance of the selected text. See Figure 1-18.

Figure 1-18   **Property inspector with CSS attributes**

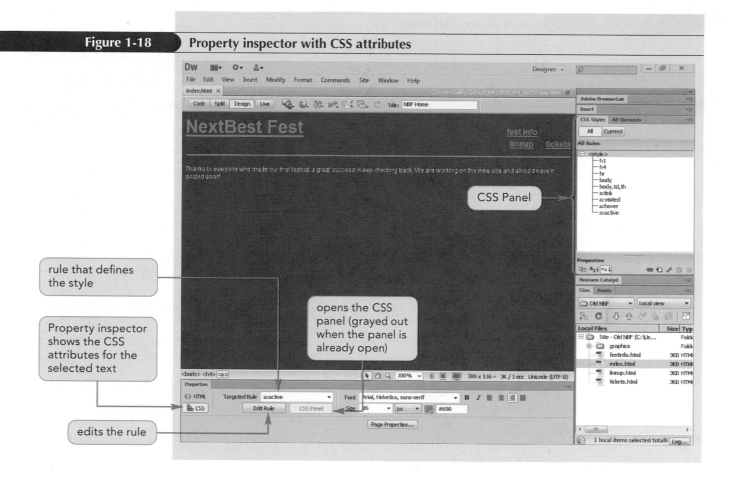

rule that defines the style

Property inspector shows the CSS attributes for the selected text

opens the CSS panel (grayed out when the panel is already open)

CSS Panel

edits the rule

Insert Panel

In Dreamweaver, anything that you create or insert into a page is called an **object**. For example, tables, images, and links are objects. Whenever you want to create a new object, you use the Insert panel. The Insert panel, located in the Insert panel group to the right of the Document window, contains buttons that are used to create and insert objects. The buttons on the Insert panel are organized into categories, which are described in Figure 1-19. Buttons with an arrow at their right contain menus of additional, related buttons with common commands. For example, when you click the Images button in the Common category, a menu of image-related buttons appears.

Figure 1-19   **Insert panel categories**

Category	Description
Common	Create and insert the most frequently used objects, such as images, hyperlinks, media elements, and tables
Layout	Draw and insert tables, div tags, Spry elements, and frames as well as switch between Standard and Expanded Tables modes
Forms	Create and insert form elements in pages that include interactive forms
Data	Insert Spry data objects and other dynamic elements, such as recordsets and repeated regions
Spry	Insert Spry elements, including widgets and Spry data objects
jQuery Mobile	Create and insert jQuery Mobile elements that you can use to create mobile applications
InContext Editing	Insert editable and repeating regions into pages so that your clients can update the content of their pages online using Adobe's InContext Editing Service
Text	Insert text and list formatting tags such as bold (b), unordered list (ul), and paragraph (p)
Favorites	Organize your most commonly used Insert panel buttons in one location

© 2013 Cengage Learning

The Insert panel displays the Common category by default. You'll explore some of the categories on the Insert panel.

To explore the Insert panel:

1. Click the **Insert** panel to open it, click the category button to display the category list, and then click **Common**, if necessary. The Insert panel is open and buttons in the Common category are displayed. See Figure 1-20.

Figure 1-20   **Common category in the Insert panel**

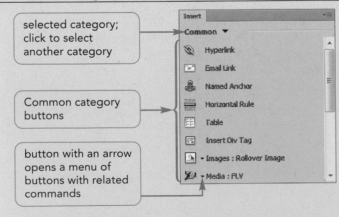

selected category; click to select another category

Common category buttons

button with an arrow opens a menu of buttons with related commands

TIP

To display the Insert panel as a toolbar, drag its panel tab below the menu bar. To switch between category tabs and a menu button, right-click a tab and click Show as Menu or click the menu button and click Show as Tabs.

2. In the Insert panel, click the **Images button arrow**. The Images menu opens. Press the **Esc** key. The Images menu closes.

3. In the Insert panel, click the category button, and then click **Layout**. The buttons for creating commonly used layout elements appear in the Insert panel.

4. In the Insert panel, click the category button, and then click **Forms**. The buttons for creating a form and inserting form elements such as buttons, menus, check boxes, and images appear in the Insert panel.

5. In the Insert panel, click the category button to display the category list, and then click **Common**. The buttons in the Common category reappear in the Insert panel.

Getting Help in Dreamweaver

As you develop a Web site, you might have a question about the purpose of a certain feature or want to review the steps for completing a specific task. The Help system provides a variety of ways to get the information you need.

The Dreamweaver Help command starts your Web browser and opens the Adobe Community Help – Dreamweaver Help / Help and tutorials window, which provides access to Dreamweaver information. There are two ways to access information about all of the Dreamweaver features: At the top of the page, to the right of the Search box, a list arranges topics by clickable subject categories, similar to the table of contents in a printed book. Search looks up information based on the keyword or phrase you enter. The selected Help topic appears in the right side of the window and can include explanations, descriptions, figures, and links to related topics as well as links to articles and information written by outside sources.

REFERENCE

Getting Help in Dreamweaver

- On the menu bar, click Help, and then click Dreamweaver Help.
- Click a topic or subtopic in the topic list to display that Help topic.
- Click in the Search box, type keywords, press the Enter key, and then click a topic in the search results.
- Click the Close button in the title bar.

or

- Click the Help button in a window or toolbar (or right-click an object and click Help on the context menu to display a context-sensitive Help topic, or click the panel menu button and then click Help).
- Click the Close button in the title bar.

You'll use Dreamweaver Help to look up information about the Document window, the Insert panel, and the Property inspector.

TIP

You can also press the F1 key to open Dreamweaver Help.

To look up information in Dreamweaver Help:

1. On the menu bar, click **Help**, and then click **Dreamweaver Help**. The Dreamweaver Help / Help and tutorials page opens in your Web browser. See Figure 1-21.

Figure 1-21 Dreamweaver Help / Help and tutorials page

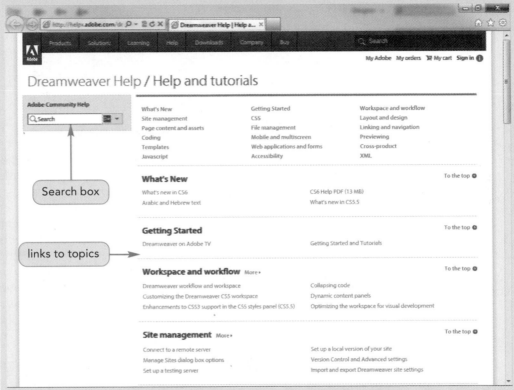

Used with permission from Microsoft Corporation

Trouble? If an Updating: Adobe Help dialog box appears, you might not have the newest version of Dreamweaver Help. Click Download now to download the latest version of Dreamweaver Help, and then click Install now to install it. Once the updated Help is installed, another dialog box will ask you to Update local help. Do this too, and then Adobe Community Help will appear in your browser.

2. In the list at the top of the page, click the **Workspace and workflow** link. The page moves down to display a list of related topics.

3. Click the **Dreamweaver workflow and workspace** link, click the **Document window overview** link, and then read the information, including the Document toolbar overview. See Figure 1-22.

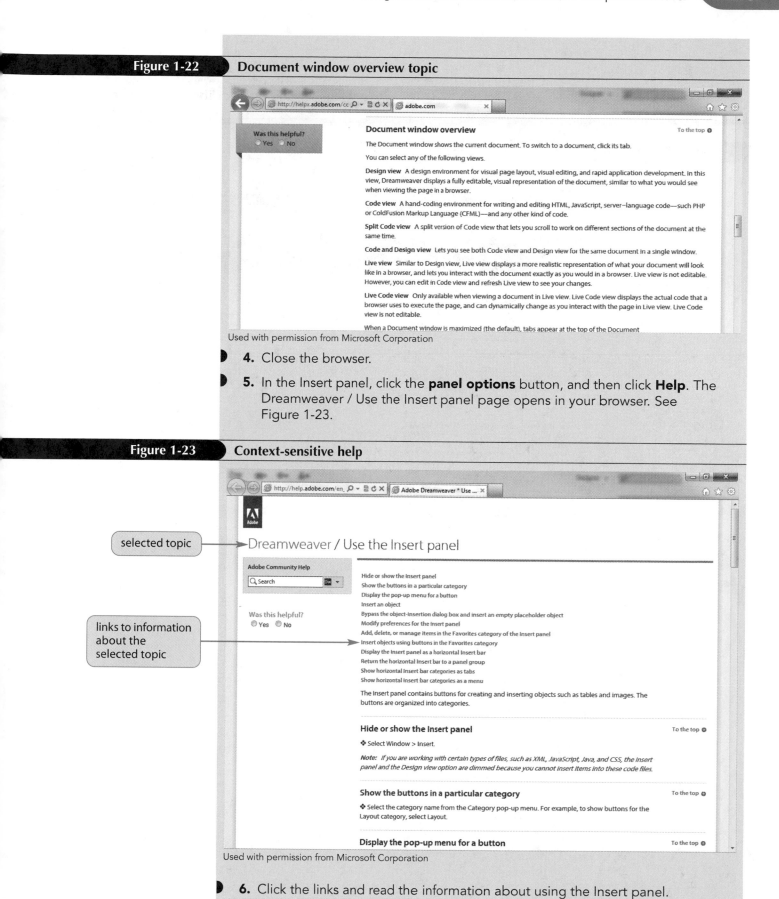

Figure 1-22   Document window overview topic

Document window overview   To the top ●

The Document window shows the current document. To switch to a document, click its tab.

You can select any of the following views.

Design view A design environment for visual page layout, visual editing, and rapid application development. In this view, Dreamweaver displays a fully editable, visual representation of the document, similar to what you would see when viewing the page in a browser.

Code view A hand-coding environment for writing and editing HTML, JavaScript, server-language code—such PHP or ColdFusion Markup Language (CFML)—and any other kind of code.

Split Code view A split version of Code view that lets you scroll to work on different sections of the document at the same time.

Code and Design view Lets you see both Code view and Design view for the same document in a single window.

Live view Similar to Design view, Live view displays a more realistic representation of what your document will look like in a browser, and lets you interact with the document exactly as you would in a browser. Live view is not editable. However, you can edit in Code view and refresh Live view to see your changes.

Live Code view Only available when viewing a document in Live view. Live Code view displays the actual code that a browser uses to execute the page, and can dynamically change as you interact with the page in Live view. Live Code view is not editable.

When a Document window is maximized (the default), tabs appear at the top of the Document

Used with permission from Microsoft Corporation

4. Close the browser.

5. In the Insert panel, click the **panel options** button, and then click **Help**. The Dreamweaver / Use the Insert panel page opens in your browser. See Figure 1-23.

Figure 1-23   Context-sensitive help

selected topic → Dreamweaver / Use the Insert panel

Adobe Community Help

links to information about the selected topic →

Hide or show the Insert panel
Show the buttons in a particular category
Display the pop-up menu for a button
Insert an object
Bypass the object-insertion dialog box and insert an empty placeholder object
Modify preferences for the Insert panel
Add, delete, or manage items in the Favorites category of the Insert panel
Insert objects using buttons in the Favorites category
Display the Insert panel as a horizontal Insert bar
Return the horizontal Insert bar to a panel group
Show horizontal Insert bar categories as tabs
Show horizontal Insert bar categories as a menu

The Insert panel contains buttons for creating and inserting objects such as tables and images. The buttons are organized into categories.

Hide or show the Insert panel   To the top ●

❖ Select Window > Insert.

Note: If you are working with certain types of files, such as XML, JavaScript, Java, and CSS, the Insert panel and the Design view option are dimmed because you cannot insert items into these code files.

Show the buttons in a particular category   To the top ●

❖ Select the category name from the Category pop-up menu. For example, to show buttons for the Layout category, select Layout.

Display the pop-up menu for a button   To the top ●

Used with permission from Microsoft Corporation

6. Click the links and read the information about using the Insert panel.

7. Scroll to the top of the page, click in the **Search** box, type **Property inspector**, and then press the **Enter** key. A list of Help topics that contain the keywords "Property inspector" and "Dreamweaver" appears in the page. See Figure 1-24.

Figure 1-24 Search Community Help

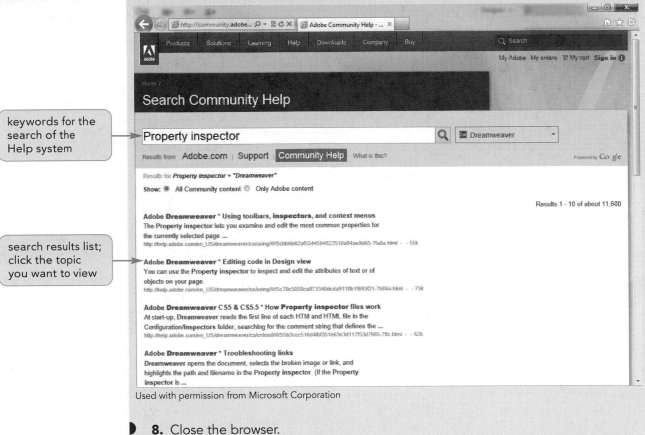

keywords for the search of the Help system

search results list; click the topic you want to view

Used with permission from Microsoft Corporation

8. Close the browser.

You can access Dreamweaver Help topics by using context-sensitive help, which opens the Help topic related to the feature you are using. You access context-sensitive help from many dialog boxes, toolbars, and panels about which you have a question. You'll use context-sensitive help to learn more about the text-formatting features of the Property inspector.

To get context-sensitive help about the Property inspector:

1. On the home page, select the block of body text below the horizontal rule.

2. In the upper-right corner of the Property inspector, click the **panel menu** button, and then click the **Help** button. Adobe Dreamweaver CS6 online help opens.

3. Read the information about editing CSS rules and setting HTML formatting in the Property inspector.

4. Close the browser.

Adobe provides additional Dreamweaver product support and Help features on its Web site (*www.adobe.com*). The Web site provides the latest information on Dreamweaver, advice from experienced users, and advanced Help topics as well as examples, tips, and updates. You can also join a discussion group to converse with other Dreamweaver users.

Exiting Dreamweaver

When you finish working, you need to close the Web site and exit the Dreamweaver program. The Exit command on the File menu exits Dreamweaver and closes all open windows. Dreamweaver prompts you to save any Web pages that you haven't yet saved. Because you haven't made any changes to the Old NBF site, you can close any open pages without saving, and then exit the site.

TIP

You can press the Ctrl+W keys to close a page, and you can press the Ctrl+Q keys to exit Dreamweaver.

To exit Dreamweaver:

▶ **1.** On the index.html page tab, click the **Close** button ⊠. The home page closes.

▶ **2.** On the menu bar, click **File**, and then click **Exit**. Dreamweaver exits.

In this tutorial, you reviewed the temporary NextBest Fest site. After setting up the local site definition, you looked at the Old NBF site and navigated its pages. In the process, you explored the Dreamweaver environment and the basic Dreamweaver tools and commands. In the next tutorial, you will begin planning the new NextBest Fest site.

REVIEW

Session 1.2 Quick Check

1. Do you need to know HTML to create a successful Web site in Dreamweaver? Why or why not?
2. True or False. If you move to another computer to work, you must re-create the site definition on that computer.
3. What is the difference between the local site and the remote site in Dreamweaver?
4. What is a site definition and where is it stored?
5. What is the local site folder?
6. Which window or panel do you use to manage local and remote site files?
7. Which view in the Document window displays only the underlying HTML code that Dreamweaver generates as you create and edit a Web page?
8. Where would you turn for information about all of the Dreamweaver features?

Practice the skills you learned in the tutorial.

PRACTICE

Review Assignments

There are no Data Files needed for the Review Assignments.

Dan and Cat Grandquist started an alternative music festival called antifest. The festival slogan—"It's what is not here that matters!"—has proven to be the festival's guiding light and the key to its local success. The festival does not have corporate sponsors or mega vendors and it does not generate much national press. However, the festival has a lot to offer. People come from all over the country to hear interesting, original, alternative music, to shop at booths full of unique items created by artisans and do-it-yourself fanatics, and to enjoy a variety of refreshments from small local restaurants and vendors. Dan believes that the festival would benefit from a Web site that would help promoters communicate the schedule, lineup, and other information to patrons.

Before he begins planning the new antifest Web site, Dan wants you to find out what other festivals do that might work for antifest without interfering with the independent image of the festival. He also wants you to review the Web sites of alternative bands that antifest patrons might visit to get some ideas about aesthetic designs that might work for the antifest site.

1. Start your Web browser.
2. Type the URL for the Web site of a favorite alternative band in the Address bar, and then press the Enter key. (*Hint*: If you don't know the URL for the alternative band Web site, try typing ***www.thenameoftheband.com*** in the Address bar, using the actual band name.) If you do not know an alternative band, start a search engine such as Google (*www.google.com*) or Yahoo! (*www.yahoo.com*) and search for **alternative bands** or **alternative music** until you find a site you like.
3. Review the home page of the Web site to see what information is included, its aesthetics, and how the information is arranged. Write a few sentences describing your findings. Be sure to include the site's URL.
4. Use hyperlinks to explore the site. Look at how information is presented and whether you can move easily between sections.
5. Click the logo, if there is one. Notice whether the logo is a hotspot, and, if it is, where it takes you.
6. Repeat Steps 2 through 5 to explore another Web site for a second band and review the information the site contains.
7. Compare the two sites that you explored. Write down your responses to the following questions:
   a. What are the similarities and the differences between the sites?
   b. Which features do you prefer? Why?
   c. Can any of the features from these sites be incorporated into the new antifest site? If so, which features?
   d. How would your suggestions help antifest's communication efforts?
8. Close the browser.
9. Start Dreamweaver, and then reset the Designer workspace.
10. Use Dreamweaver Help to learn more about working with Dreamweaver sites.
11. List four things you learned.
12. Exit Dreamweaver. Submit your answers to your instructor, either in printed or electronic form, as requested.

RESEARCH

Research existing Web sites in preparation for creating a Web site to promote a skateboard company.

Case Problem 1

There are no Data Files needed for this Case Problem.

Moebius Skateboards   Moebius Skateboards is a small, independent skateboard company located in Fort Worth, Texas. The owner, Corey Wells, is an entrepreneur and lifelong skate aficionado. In addition to designing skateboards that retail at local skate shops, Moebius sponsors a skate team that participates actively in local events. Corey organizes Feed the People, an annual skate event he founded in 2008 to raise money and food donations for the Tarrant Area Food Bank. Corey wants to develop a Web site to better market Moebius. You will work with the Moebius team to create the new site. Corey asks you to research skateboard Web sites and report back on your recommendations and findings.

1. Start your Web browser.
2. Type the URL for the Web site of your favorite skateboard company in the Address bar, and then press the Enter key. (*Hint*: If you don't know the URL for the Web site, try typing **www.thenameofthecompany.com** in the Address bar, using the actual company name.) If you do not know a skateboard company, start a search engine such as Google (*www.google.com*) or Yahoo! (*www.yahoo.com*) and search for **skateboards** or **Texas skateboard companies** until you find a site you like.
3. Review the home page of the Web site to see what information is included and how the information is arranged. Make notes about your findings, including the site's URL.
4. Use hyperlinks to explore the site. Look at how information is presented and whether you can move easily between sections.
5. Click the company's logo, if there is one. Notice whether the logo is a hotspot, and, if it is, where it takes you.
6. Repeat Steps 2 through 5 to explore the Web site for another skateboard company and review the information the site contains.
7. Compare the two sites that you explored. Write down your responses to the following questions:
   a. What are the similarities and the differences between the sites?
   b. Which features do you prefer? Why?
   c. Can any of the features from these sites be incorporated into the new Moebius site? If so, which features?
   d. How would your suggestions help Moebius's marketing efforts?
8. Close the browser.
9. Start Dreamweaver, and then reset the Designer workspace.
10. Use Dreamweaver Help to find out more about the Dreamweaver workspace.
11. Write down four things you learned about the Dreamweaver workspace.
12. Exit Dreamweaver. Submit your answers to your instructor, either in printed or electronic form, as requested.

Research existing Web sites in preparation for creating a Web site to present artwork.

RESEARCH

Case Problem 2

There are no Data Files needed for this Case Problem.

Cowboy Art Society Dr. Monomer Palmer (Moni to his friends) is a well-respected art historian who specializes in the work of western artists. He is also the founder of the Cowboy Art Society. The society has recently received a grant to create an educational Web site that presents artwork as well as historical and biographical information about western artist Charles M. Russell. Moni wants you to begin research for the new site by reviewing existing Web sites that present artwork for educational purposes and by finding current trends in art education. He also asks you to find out what image file formats are compatible with Dreamweaver.

1. Start your Web browser, type the URL for a search engine into the Address bar, and then press the Enter key to open the search engine. Two popular search engines are Google (*www.google.com*) and Bing (*www.bing.com*).

2. Search for relevant Web sites by using the keywords **western art**. (*Hint*: If too many unrelated choices appear, narrow the search by typing quotation marks around the keywords. If no matches appear, check your spelling and try again.)

3. Click the link for an appropriate page to open the Web site, and then explore the Web site, taking notes about what information is included, how the material is organized, and what images are included. Be sure to write down the site's URL.

4. Return to the search engine, and then search for Web sites about **Charles Russell**.

5. Click the link for an appropriate page to open the Web site, and then explore the Web site, taking notes about the site's content and organization. Be sure to write down the site's URL.

6. Return to the search engine, and then search for Web sites related to **art education**. Explore at least one Web site, taking notes about its content and organization. Be sure to write down the site's URL.

7. Write a memo to Moni describing your findings. List features you would like to incorporate into the new Web site. Include the URL for each site you analyzed.

8. Close the browser.

9. Start Dreamweaver, and then reset the Designer workspace.

10. Use Dreamweaver Help to find information about using images in a Web site. Use the Search feature to locate the **About images** Help topic.

11. Read the About images topic to learn about the image file formats that Dreamweaver uses.

12. Add to your memo a brief explanation of which image file formats are compatible with Dreamweaver.

13. Exit Dreamweaver. Submit the finished memo to your instructor, either in printed or electronic form, as requested.

Research competing Web sites in preparation for creating a Web site for a life coach.

RESEARCH

Case Problem 3

There are no Data Files needed for this Case Problem.

Success with Tess   Tess Haranda is a life coach who has more than 15 years of experience in the corporate world. She obtained her Core Essentials certification from the International Coach Federation. She earned a B.A. from Texas Tech University in Communication Studies and is currently employed as a public school teacher. Tess believes that a Success with Tess Web site will help take her coaching career to the next level. Tess wants you to create and maintain a Web site for Success with Tess in hopes of expanding her market through Internet exposure. Tess asks you to research the Web sites of other life coaches.

1. Start your Web browser, type the URL for a search engine into the Address bar, and then press the Enter key to open the search engine. Two popular search engines are Google (*www.google.com*) and Bing (*www.bing.com*).
2. Search for relevant Web sites by using the keywords **life coaches**. The search engine displays a list of pages that contain the words in your search.
3. Click the link for an appropriate page to open the Web site, and then explore the Web site, taking notes about the site's design, what information is included, how the material is organized, and to whom the site would appeal. Be sure to write down the site's URL.
4. Click the Back button on the browser toolbar until you return to the search engine results.
5. Repeat Steps 3 and 4 to explore at least two other Web sites for life coaches, taking notes about their content and organization and recording their URLs.
6. Write a brief report for Tess of the sites' similarities and differences, listing both content and design features that you think Tess should incorporate into her new Web site. Include the URL for each site.
7. Close the browser. Submit the finished report to your instructor, either in printed or electronic form, as requested.

Research competing Web sites and basic HTML in preparation for creating a Web site for a coffee bar.

RESEARCH

Case Problem 4

There are no Data Files needed for this Case Problem.

Coffee Lounge   The Coffee Lounge is an all-night coffee bar located in Portland, Oregon. The Coffee Lounge features live music on the weekends, an improvisational comedy open mike on Thursday nights, poetry slams on Wednesday nights, experimental film screenings on Tuesday nights, and a book club devoted to local authors on Monday nights. In addition, the Coffee Lounge encourages public art by allowing patrons and local artists to use the various pens, markers, and paints scattered throughout the club to add their mark to the walls and tables.

Coffee Lounge's owner, Tommy Caddell, believes the lounge could benefit from a Web site. He wants to use the site as a marketing tool to promote featured events, the monthly special, a different coffee blend featured each month, and sales. Tommy also wants to include a page that features a different local nonprofit organization each month. You will assist Tommy in building the site. Tommy asks you to research the Web sites of other coffee lounges and to find information about basic HTML.

1. Start your Web browser. Type the URL for a search engine into the Address bar, and then press the Enter key to open the search engine. Two popular search engines are Google (*www.google.com*) and Bing (*www.bing.com*).

2. Use a search engine to find the Web sites for coffee lounges. Search for coffee lounge Web sites by typing the appropriate keywords in the search box, and then clicking the Search button. The search engine displays a list of pages that contain the words in your search.

3. Explore at least three coffee lounge sites. For each site, write down the site's URL and any useful information about the site's content, organization, and design. (*Hint*: Use the Back button on the browser toolbar to return to the search results and link to a different Web site.)

4. Use a search engine to find the Web sites of at least three local competing coffee lounges, such as Stumptown Coffee Roasters, Backspace, Urban Coffee Lounge, and Bipartisan Cafe.

5. Write a brief memo to Tommy, describing the sites' similarities and differences and listing content and design features you would like to incorporate into the new Coffee Lounge Web site. Include the URL for each site.

6. Start Dreamweaver, and then reset the Designer workspace.

7. Search Dreamweaver Help to find topics about **Property inspector** and then read any topics about editing code.

8. Search Dreamweaver Help to find topics about **formatting text** and then read topics about text formatting using CSS and HTML.

9. Add a paragraph or two to your memo that describes what you learned about editing code and formatting text with CSS and HTML.

10. Exit Dreamweaver. Submit the finished memo to your instructor, either in printed or electronic form, as requested.

DREAMWEAVER

OBJECTIVES

Session 2.1
- Determine site goals
- Identify the target audience
- Conduct market research
- Create end-user scenarios

Session 2.2
- Design the information architecture
- Create a flowchart and site structure
- Create a site concept and metaphor
- Select colors, fonts, and a graphics style
- Develop an aesthetic concept

Session 2.3
- Create a site definition for a new site
- Add pages to a site
- Review basic HTML5 tags
- Set page properties
- Preview a Web site
- Upload a site to a remote server and preview it on the Web

Planning and Designing a Successful Web Site

Developing a Web Site Plan and Design

Case | *NextBest Fest*

A professional Web site requires a considerable amount of planning. Although planning might seem like a lot of work, it will help you avoid reworking site elements. In the end, planning will save you time and frustration. To create an effective Web site, you must have a clear idea of the site's goals; planning enables you to determine what you need from a Web site and how the site will meet those needs.

Gage, the public relations and marketing director at NextBest Fest, asks you to help plan the company's new Web site. First, you will determine site goals and identify the target audience. To do this, you will conduct market research and create end-user scenarios. Then, you will design the information architecture, create a flowchart and site structure, design the site navigation structure, and develop the aesthetic concept for the site. Finally, you will create the new site.

STARTING DATA FILES

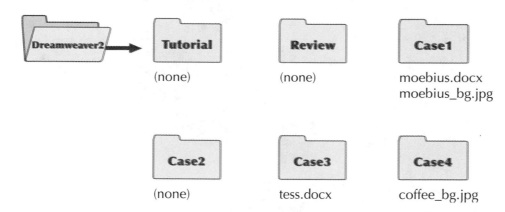

| Dreamweaver2 → | Tutorial | Review | Case1 |
| | (none) | (none) | moebius.docx
moebius_bg.jpg |

| | Case2 | Case3 | Case4 |
| | (none) | tess.docx | coffee_bg.jpg |

SESSION 2.1 VISUAL OVERVIEW

Site goals are the specific objectives you want a Web site to accomplish.

Determine the site goals and purpose.

A **site purpose** is a one-sentence, general description of your vision and aspirations for a Web site.

What is the purpose of the site?

What would the client like to accomplish?

What is the client's vision for the site?

End-user scenarios are imagined situations in which the target audience might access a Web site.

Create end-user scenarios.

Where will users view the site?

What will users use to view the site?

What type of connection will users have?

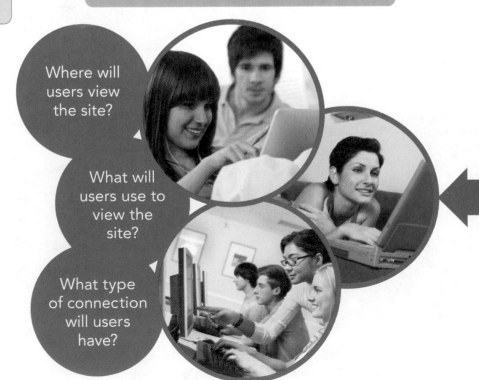

PLANNING A WEB SITE

Identify the target audience.

The **target audience** is the group of people you would most like to visit the Web site.

Who would you most like to use the site?

Considering the goals, who is most likely to use the site?

Create a detailed user profile.

A **user profile** is the demographic information you gather about the characteristics of the target audience.

Conduct market research.

Market research is the careful investigation and study of data about the target audience's preferences for a product or service.

Review sites that target your audience.

Review competing sites.

Review sites that have similar goals or vision.

Clockwise from upper left:
iStockphoto.com/Jacob Wackerhausen;
iStockphoto.com/Jacob Wackerhausen;
iStockphoto.com/Jacob Wackerhausen;
iStockphoto.com/CandyBox;
iStockphoto.com/nyul;
iStockphoto.com/mediaphotos

Managing Web Site Projects

Because Web sites are fairly large projects, it is a good idea to consider assigning a project manager to oversee the project and to coordinate the efforts of the various team members. Before the project begins, the project manager will create a project plan that outlines the project's scope, phases, tasks, due dates, and resource allocations and then present that plan to the team. Most Web site project plans are divided into the following phases: planning and analysis, designing, building, testing, and implementation or launching. Each phase includes a list of deliverables that are due during that phase of the project. For example, during the design phase of the project, the Art Department might need to deliver two completed aesthetic designs for the site. A detailed project plan that everyone can reference throughout the project helps avoid common problems like **scope creep**, which occurs when additional elements and requirements are added to a project, causing it to grow in size, complexity, cost, and so on. The project manager is responsible for making sure the team follows the project plan and delivers a quality project on time and on budget.

Gage is the project manager for the NextBest Fest project. He will coordinate the various team members and assign responsibilities and due dates during the project.

Creating a Plan for a New Web Site

Whether you are part of an in-house Web team or an independent designer hired to create a Web site, the first order of business for designing a professional Web site is to determine the goals and purpose, the target audience, and the expectations for the site. You obtain this information from the **client**, the person or persons for whom you are creating the site, and through the research you conduct during the planning phase of site design. This process usually requires a series of meetings and considerable time.

These client meetings and initial time are a crucial part of the planning process because it is impossible to design a Web site that will effectively meet the client's needs until you determine exactly what those needs are. You should come to the meetings with a list of questions to help determine the purpose of the site and the site goals that the client can answer. Questions should be tailored to the specific client and should explore things like what the client wants to accomplish with the site, how the client envisions the site fitting in with other materials and efforts, and so forth. You should explain clearly to the client what information you will need from him or her and what value his or her contribution will make to the final Web site. Throughout the project, be sure to show the Web pages to the client and other team members for feedback and evaluation.

There are many possible paths in any creative process. The Session 2.1 Visual Overview provides one possible path for creating a plan for a new Web site. As you gain experience in planning, designing, and creating Web sites, you will find that some things work better than others. You will come up with your own ideas about the new NextBest Fest site's goals, the target audience, and so on. You will then evaluate how your plan is similar to and different from the final NextBest Fest site plan approved by Gage and consider each plan's benefits and drawbacks.

Determining the Site Goals and Purpose

The first question you should ask when you begin to plan a site is: What are the primary goals and purpose for the Web site? A Web site can have one goal or multiple goals. The goals should align with the stated purpose of the site. It is a good idea to brainstorm with the client, in this case Gage, and create a list of all of the goals you can think of for the site. For example, a commercial Web site might include the following goals:

- Provide information about a product.
- Sell a product.

> **TIP**
>
> To ensure a successful project and a satisfied client, make the client aware of what to expect and communicate effectively with the client throughout the process.

- Increase brand recognition.
- Provide help or operational instructions.

This list is very general and could be expanded. The goal list for an actual site should be much more specific. For example, the first two bullets should state what the product is.

After you have a list of possible site goals, review the list and place the goals in order of importance from most important to least important. For example, the commercial Web site goals might be reordered as follows:

- Sell a product.
- Increase brand recognition.
- Provide information about a product.
- Provide help or operational instructions.

Review your list. Combine goals if possible, and then reprioritize as needed. Some of the lower-priority goals might actually be part of higher-priority goals. For example, in some cases, providing help or operational instructions might be incorporated into the general goal of providing information about the product. There is a limit to the number of goals that a Web site can effectively achieve; therefore, you will probably want to focus on the first four or five goals. Remember that site goals are most effective if they are the result of collaboration with the client. After all, just as you are an expert on Web design, the client is an expert on his or her business.

PROSKILLS

Written Communication: Developing an Effective List of Site Goals

Each part of the Web site plan needs to be documented in a well-written document. This document should outline all of the decisions that have been made during the planning process. In the case of the site goals, you need to write down all of the potential goals for the site in collaboration with the client. Then, the initial list of site goals needs to be revised for clarity, condensed for effectiveness, and ordered for priority. Keep in mind the following guidelines as you develop the list of site goals.

1. Write site goals in active voice rather than passive voice.
2. Use action verbs to help you select achievable goals rather than concepts. For example, brand recognition is a concept, not a goal; increase brand recognition is a goal. Action verbs include words such as *achieve*, *increase*, and *provide*.
3. Think about the different aspects of the site. For example, in addition to selling products, you might want to provide reliable support.
4. Make a comprehensive list of goals. Prioritize the goals in order of importance. Your final list should include no more than five goals.

As you gain experience in designing Web sites, your ability to identify and articulate goals will continue to improve.

After your list of goals is final, review the list and develop a one-sentence statement of purpose for the site. Unlike a goal, which is specific, the statement of purpose should speak to the core purpose for creating the site. Like a good mission statement, it should define your vision and aspirations for the site. For example, a good statement of purpose for an e-commerce site might be, "With this Web site, we intend to sell quality widgets, to provide exceptional, long-term customer service, and to build lifelong customer relationships."

Gage asks you to develop a list of goals and a statement of purpose for the new NextBest Fest site.

To create a list of goals and a statement of purpose for the new NextBest Fest site:

▶ **1.** Write down at least 20 possible site goals.

▶ **2.** Review the list to be sure that all statements are in active voice and use action verbs.

▶ **3.** Prioritize the goals in order of importance.

▶ **4.** Review your list, combining goals, if possible, and reprioritizing them, if necessary.

▶ **5.** Review the top five goals. Think about what you want to accomplish with the site, and make sure that your list of goals will help achieve a successful site.

▶ **6.** Write a one-sentence statement of purpose based on your final list of goals.

Gage created a list of goals for the new NextBest Fest site, and then he prioritized and combined them. From his final list of goals, he developed a statement of purpose.

▶ **7.** Compare your goals and statement of purpose with Gage's shown in Figure 2-1.

Figure 2-1	NextBest Fest site goals and purpose

Goals
1. Boost attendance and ticket sales, concentrating on three-day passes.
2. Enhance the NextBest Fest brand identity.
3. Increase the NextBest Fest brand recognition.
4. Promote the bands that play at NextBest Fest.
5. Provide press information.
6. Provide general information, including directions, lineup, and so on.
7. Link to band sites so people can hear participating bands prior to the fest.
8. Create cross-interest between bands with similar sounds.
9. Create an online audio playlist so people can hear all of the participating bands without leaving the fest site (long-term, not immediate).
10. Create other materials (such as an interactive Flash map and other Flash animations) to increase interest (long-term, not immediate).

Statement of purpose
This site will be used to promote the NextBest Fest, provide information about the festival and the participating bands to the public and the press, promote the sale of three-day passes, and increase brand recognition and festival attendance.

© 2013 Cengage Learning

You will use the site goals to make decisions about the site organization and structure. The primary goal is to increase festival attendance, compelling people to attend NextBest Fest. The secondary goal is to increase brand identity and recognition—in other words, to make people aware of the NextBest Fest and to associate it with rock 'n' roll tribute bands. The site will be organized to create a buzz about attending the fest and to emphasize the NextBest Fest name and logo. The home page will include information about the fest, including how to purchase three-day passes, and band information. The fest logo will appear at the top of every page, and the site navigation will be organized so that "fest information" and "ticket information" categories are included in the top level of the site.

The priority of the goals helps to determine the site's layout. If the first and fourth goals were switched, for example, making the primary goal to promote bands that play at the fest, the site structure might be organized differently. The band information could appear above the fest information. The band logos could appear at the top of all of the pages instead of the fest logo. The individual bands could be placed in their own categories in the top level of navigation. This is just one set of many possible changes.

When you start to examine the way that site goals and site purpose affect the structure of the final site, you can see just how important it is to carefully consider what you want to accomplish. Taking the time to establish goals and expectations from the very beginning will make the final site better organized, easily understood, and more effective.

Identifying the Target Audience

TIP

The word *user* in *user profile* refers to the target user group, not an individual user.

The target audience for a Web site is the group of people whom you would *most* like to visit the site. You identify the target audience by creating a user profile. A user profile is the information that you gather about the target audience by finding the answers to the questions shown in Figure 2-2. The user profile is a tool designed to help you determine the characteristics of the group of people you are trying to reach: the target audience.

Figure 2-2	General user profile questions

1. **What is the age range of the user?** Sites can appeal to a range of ages. The age range will depend on the site goals. Generally, the group members are linked because they share a commonality such as a habit, a characteristic, or a developmental stage.

2. **What is the gender of the user?** Sites can be targeted to males only, females only, or males and females. Not all sites are targeted to a specific gender.

3. **What is the education level of the user?** Education level will be a range. Designate education level either by the current year in school (e.g., senior in high school) or the degree earned if out of school (e.g., associate degree).

4. **What is the economic situation of the user?** Economic situation refers to the annual income level of the user as well as other extenuating economic factors, such as parental support or student loans. For example, the user may be a student who has only a part-time job. As a student, the user may have a lower income bracket, earning only $20,000 a year, but extenuating economic factors, such as parental support and student loans, may affect the user's buying power. All of this information should factor into the user's economic situation.

5. **What is the geographic location of the user?** The site can be targeted at users in a specific city, a specific region, or a specific country.

6. **What is the primary language of the user?**

7. **What is the ethnic background of the user?** Most sites are targeted at a user group with diverse cross sections of ethnic backgrounds; however, sometimes ethnicity is a factor in your target audience. For example, *Jet* magazine is targeted at African-American users.

8. **Are there other unifying characteristics that are relevant to the user?** If you know that the target group has a common characteristic that may be of use in designing the Web site, list it here. Unifying characteristics are useful if they are related to the topic of the Web site or if they could affect the goals of the site. For example, unifying characteristics might include things such as the following: target users have diabetes (for a diabetes disease-management site), target users ride dirt bikes (for a BMX motocross site), target users listen to club music (for an alternative music site), and so on.

INSIGHT

Finding More Data to Create a User Profile

You can use a variety of resources to help you create a user profile. If the client has an existing Web site, you might be able to obtain specific data about current visitors from usage logs and user registration. **Usage logs** are exact records of every visit to the site; they include information such as the time and date of the visit, the visitor's ISP, pathway through the site, browser and operating system, and so on. Some sites require visitors to register by creating a user ID and providing personal information before being allowed access. You can analyze this registration information when it is available to further define the target audience.

Gage asks you to create a user profile that identifies the target audience of the NextBest Fest site.

To identify the target audience for the new NextBest Fest site:

▶ **1.** Answer the user profile questions listed in Figure 2-2.

▶ **2.** Review your answers to ensure that the target audience you identified reinforces the final site goals and purpose listed in Figure 2-1. If it does not, reevaluate your site goals or adjust your target audience so that the two are compatible.

▶ **3.** Compare your answers to the user profile questions with those compiled by Gage, as shown in Figure 2-3.

Figure 2-3	User profile for the NextBest Fest site

1. Age: 30 to 50 (adults who listened to the music played by tribute bands in the concert lineup; concert attendance includes entire families, but adult family members drive attendance; adults are most frequently the Web site users)
2. Gender: male and female
3. Education level: high school graduates
4. Economic situation: one- and two-income households with incomes ranging from $45,000 to $90,000+
5. Geographic location: United States, but we will concentrate resources in the New Jersey area for the first three years
6. Primary language: English
7. Ethnic background: no specific ethnicity targeted
8. Other unifying characteristics: primary target user is an average adult who grew up listening to and has a nostalgic preference for the rock music played by the tribute bands appearing at the fest

© 2013 Cengage Learning

Sometimes clients and designers are hesitant to identify the target audience because they think it will limit the reach of the Web site. However, a very broad target audience can be even more restrictive than a very narrow target audience. A Web site that must appeal to many different groups of people must be more generic in some ways. For example, if the new NextBest Fest site is intended to appeal to an older audience (50 to 60 years of age) as well as to a college-aged audience (18 to 29 years of age), it can include only elements that will be attractive to and communicate effectively with both age groups. You can see how this might limit some stylistic options such as graphics, wording, and color that would be available to a Web site with a target audience that includes only a college-aged group.

Some Web sites are intended to appeal to a broad target audience. Consider the Internal Revenue Service. The IRS site, *www.irs.gov*, is designed to be an informational site available to a diverse group of people. The site contains a huge amount of information about U.S. tax laws and tax preparation. Knowing that the target audience for the IRS site is broad and that the goal of the site is to dispense information, designers chose to create a text-based site with few graphics elements so that the site will be accessible to the broadest possible group of users. The IRS site is very effective at achieving its goals. However, this primarily text-based design would not be effective if the main goal was entertainment. Although the IRS site is rich in informational content, the site is not very entertaining.

INSIGHT

Creating a Web Site That Appeals to the Target Audience

After you have identified a target audience, you can use the general information from the user profile as a basis to research and make more advanced decisions about user wants, needs, technical proficiencies, and so on. When used appropriately, the target audience information is a great tool for focusing a Web site to achieve the site goals. However, be careful with stereotypes. It is easy to draw general conclusions about the target audience without backing up those assumptions with research. This can lead to a Web site that seems targeted to the intended audience, but in practice does not actually appeal to them. For example, think about a television commercial you have seen that is supposed to appeal to your gender and/or age group. What was your reaction to a commercial that has the right look but underestimates your intelligence or misinterprets your styles and habits? Use the target audience information as a starting point for your research.

Conducting Market Research

Market research is the careful investigation and study of data about the target audience's preferences for a product or service. It also includes evaluating the products or services of competitors. The user profile provides information about the target audience. After you have created the user profile, you need to investigate the habits, interests, likes, and dislikes of that group of people as well as what competitors are doing to attract them.

Advertising and design agencies spend a substantial amount of money subscribing to services that provide in-depth market analysis of products or services and their target audiences (such as Ipsos ASI at *www.ipsos-asi.com* or The Advertising Research Foundation at *www.thearf.org*). However, independent designers usually have to rely on their own research. They look for information that will help them to build a Web site tailored to the target audience that their client wants to attract. Technical information— such as the screen size and the speeds of the computer and Internet connection that the target audience uses—identifies the technical limitations of an effective site. Information on the spending habits of the target audience identifies the potential profitability of the Web site. Information on the interests of the target audience identifies what will appeal to the target audience and what elements might be included in the site to attract visitors. Information about the culture and the customs of the target audience identifies what colors, symbols, fashions, styles, and so on will be effective in communicating with the target audience. Finally, information about competing Web sites identifies what the competition believes effectively attracts and communicates with the target audience.

The fastest way to obtain information about the habits, interests, and likes of a target audience is to use a search engine to locate Web sites with statistics and other data about the target audience's lifestyle and preferences. A **search engine** is a Web site whose primary function is to gather and report the information available on the Web

TIP

Three common search engines are Google, Yahoo!, and Bing.

related to specified keywords or phrases. Gage spent some time online and compiled the information shown in Figure 2-4 about the target audience that the NextBest Fest wants to attract.

Figure 2-4 NextBest Fest target audience information

- 76% of classic rock festival attendees are couples and families.
- Music festival patrons spend an additional $85 per day of attendance above ticket purchase.
- 82% of average U.S. households have computers with Internet access. (57% of all households have high-speed broadband connections. Of connected households, 88% have high-speed broadband connections and 12% have 56Kbps or less narrowband connectivity.)
- 72% of U.S. households can, and sometimes do, listen to audio content on their computers.
- 66% of multiday music festival attendees purchase tickets in advance, online.
- 87% of polled music festival patrons said that they had visited the festival Web site prior to attending the event to find information about bands, location, pricing, and schedule.

© 2013 Cengage Learning

You will look for additional information about the target audience for the NextBest Fest site. Make sure that you note the source of the information and the URL of each Web page you visit in case you need to refer to that source in the future.

To gather information on the NextBest Fest target audience:

1. Start your Web browser, type **www.bing.com** in the Address bar, and then press the **Enter** key. The Bing home page opens.

   Trouble? Sometimes sites "go down" and cannot be accessed. If the Bing search engine is unavailable, repeat Step 1, typing the URL for another search engine, such as *www.google.com* or *www.yahoo.com* in the Address bar.

2. Type **market research music festival** into the search box, and then click the **Search** button to start the search.

3. Review the list of Web sites, click the link for a Web site that looks promising, and then explore that site.

4. Write down all pertinent information, especially information regarding audience ages and spending habits. Make sure to include the source of the information and the URL of the Web page in case you need to refer to that source in the future. If the site contains no relevant statistics or information, continue with Step 5.

5. Click the **Back** button ◉ on the browser toolbar to return to the search results.

6. Repeat Steps 3 through 5 to gather information from other Web sites until you have documented at least five distinct facts about music festival audiences.

   Trouble? If you cannot find enough information, you can also search the keywords "market research cover bands" to find information regarding cover bands and their audiences.

The information you have collected so far gives you some understanding of the target audience's habits and likes. Now, you will switch your focus from the habits of the target audience to what you can do with the Web site to attract the target audience. You will investigate Web sites that the target audience frequents as well as Web sites of NextBest Fest competitors. You will have to make assumptions about which sites are popular with the target audience based on the information you gathered about its habits and preferences. By exploring sites that are popular with the target audience and the sites of competitors, you can familiarize yourself with graphics styles to which the target audience is accustomed as well as the colors, symbols, fashions, styles, and slang terms that have been effective in communicating with the target audience.

While you are exploring competitors' Web sites, pay close attention to their designs. What colors do the sites use? How is the information laid out? What are the navigation systems like? Is there anything unique about the sites? What aspects of the sites might appeal to the target audience? How is the space used? Can you ascertain what the sites' goals might be? Is the content presented in straightforward language or in slang specific to the target audience? Is there a lot of text on each page, or is the text broken into smaller segments? All of this information will help in designing an effective Web site for NextBest Fest.

To explore other music festival and tribute band Web sites:

1. Type **tribfest.co.uk** in the Address bar, and then press the **Enter** key. The splash screen for the Tribfest Web site opens and the home page of the Tribfest site appears in the browser window.

2. Navigate through the Web site, evaluating the colors, information layout, navigation system, use of space, content, language style (formal, conversational, slang, etc.), and so on.

3. Record your findings and make notes about anything you feel is important about the site. Note how the fact that this festival is held in the United Kingdom affects your findings. Write a brief summary of your findings and notes.

4. Visit **www.fakefestivals.co.uk**, and then repeat Steps 2 and 3 for the Fake Festivals site.

5. Search for and explore at least two other music festival sites that the target audience might frequent. For each site, write a brief summary of your findings. Were you able to locate a tribute band festival in the United States?

6. Look at the Web sites of at least two other types of festivals such as **www.aclfestival.com** (the Austin City Limits Music Festival site) or **www.coachella.com** (the Coachella music festival site). What information do they include? Does the information change when the festival is trying to target a different audience? For each site, write a brief summary of what you like and dislike about the site.

7. Search for and explore the Web sites of at least two tribute bands by typing **tribute band** into a search engine. What information do they include? Does the information change when the band is trying to target a different audience? For each site, write a brief summary of what you like and dislike about the site.

8. Close your browser.

By this point, you should have a clear idea of the target audience, including the users' habits and interests. You should also have an understanding of what you can do with the Web site to attract the target audience. You will use this information to develop end-user scenarios.

Creating End-User Scenarios

End-user scenarios are imagined situations in which the target audience might access a Web site. These scenarios help you to envision actual conditions that various end users will experience while visiting the Web site. Scenarios enable you to visualize abstract target audience members as real people. By placing characters in realistic situations, you can get a better sense of the factors that might affect the users' experiences with the Web site. You can then anticipate the end users' needs and build a Web site that incorporates these factors into the design.

Gage created two scenarios for the NextBest Fest Web site, as shown in Figure 2-5. The scenarios provide insights that go beyond statistics and facts. For example, from Scenario 1, you learn that there is a chance that the target audience will not have access to audio on the Web site; therefore, you can conclude that audio should not be a primary component for conveying necessary information.

Figure 2-5	End-user scenarios for the NextBest Fest site

Scenario 1

Hoson Wong is a construction worker from Newark, New Jersey. He lives in a three-bedroom house in the suburbs with his wife, Lola, their two daughters, and their dog, Motley. Hoson and Lola graduated from high school in 1988 and still occasionally listen to 1980s "hair band" rock. Hoson recently learned about the NextBest Fest from a foreman who heard him listening to Bon Jovi as he pulled up to a job site. After discussing the fest with the foreman, Hoson came home to get more information about the fest online. Because Hoson and Lola are saving for college for their daughters, and because the girls are still too young to need high-speed Internet access for school, Hoson and Lola get by with an older computer that has no speakers and a 56K modem connection. Hoson was disappointed with the temporary site, but he bookmarked the site and will check back frequently to find out more.

Scenario 2

Sasha and Max are roommates who have been best friends since they graduated from the Syracuse University Studio Arts Program in 1982. They are professional artists/arts educators in downtown Philadelphia. Their downtown Philly loft has recently upgraded to high-speed cable modem Internet access for all residents. Although they share a computer, Sasha and Max both find plenty of time to surf the Net.

In addition to their love for art, Sasha and Max share a love for the music of the Ramones. They recently attended a concert featuring their favorite Ramones tribute band—the Ramoones—and learned that the band is in negotiation to play at NextBest Fest. They have bookmarked the Fest Web site and are waiting for updated information.

© 2013 Cengage Learning

Gage asks you to create a third scenario for the NextBest Fest site.

To create an end-user scenario for the NextBest Fest site:

1. Review the NextBest Fest site goals and statement of purpose, user profile, and market research.

2. Create a character who might visit the NextBest Fest site. Give the character a name and attributes such as age, gender, and location.

3. Place the character in a situation where he or she is accessing the Web site. Write at least one paragraph describing the character's surroundings and the character's experience with the site.

Planning might seem time consuming and difficult, but a few hours of advanced preparation will save many hours of redesign work later. In the next session, you will work on the NextBest Fest site's informational structure and aesthetic design.

REVIEW

Session 2.1 Quick Check

1. How many goals can a Web site achieve effectively?
2. What is the difference between a site goal and its purpose statement?
3. What is the target audience for a Web site?
4. What is a user profile?
5. What happens if you draw general conclusions about the target audience without backing up those conclusions with research?
6. What is market research?
7. What are end-user scenarios?

SESSION 2.2 VISUAL OVERVIEW

Information architecture is the process of determining what you need a site to do and then constructing a framework that will allow you to accomplish those goals.

Create the information architecture.

A **flowchart** is a diagram of geometric shapes connected by lines that shows steps in sequence. In Web design, a flowchart provides a visual representation of the hierarchical structure of the pages within the site.

Create a flowchart.

Organize the available information into pages.

Determine logical categories of information.

Check the design for logic by looking at all of the elements of the site plan as though you were seeing them for the first time.

Complete the final review and get the client's approval before "going live" with the site.

Final review and sign-off.

Review the information architecture for logic.

Make sure the site is easy to use.

Check the site structure, navigation system, and content.

Make sure the site is consistent in look and feel.

Review the final design for consistency.

DESIGNING A WEB SITE

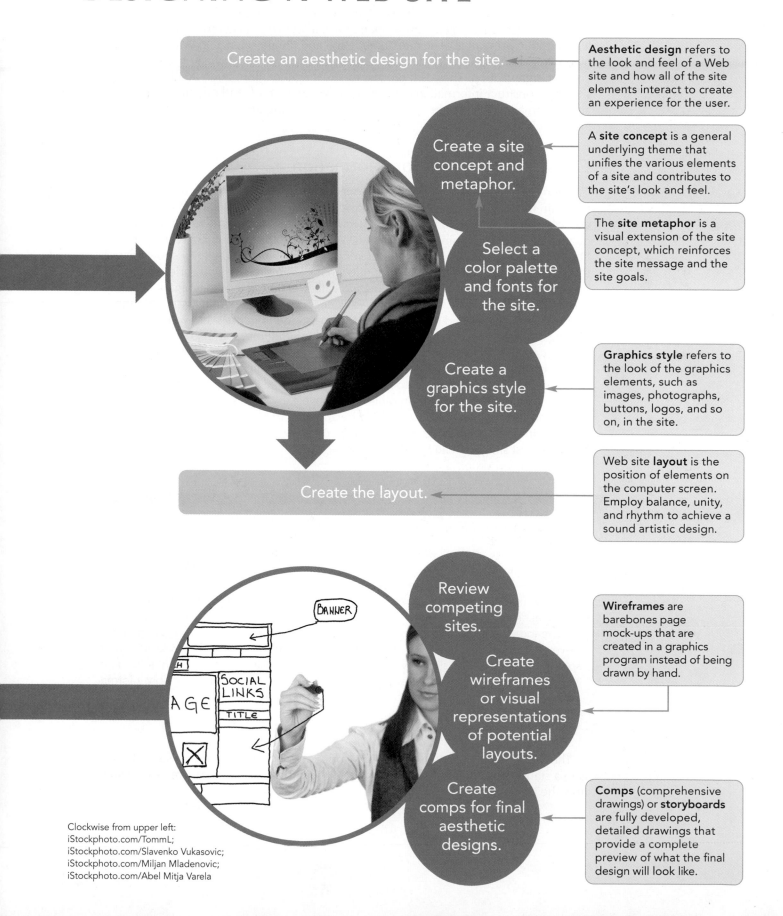

Create an aesthetic design for the site.

Aesthetic design refers to the look and feel of a Web site and how all of the site elements interact to create an experience for the user.

Create a site concept and metaphor.

A **site concept** is a general underlying theme that unifies the various elements of a site and contributes to the site's look and feel.

The **site metaphor** is a visual extension of the site concept, which reinforces the site message and the site goals.

Select a color palette and fonts for the site.

Create a graphics style for the site.

Graphics style refers to the look of the graphics elements, such as images, photographs, buttons, logos, and so on, in the site.

Create the layout.

Web site **layout** is the position of elements on the computer screen. Employ balance, unity, and rhythm to achieve a sound artistic design.

Review competing sites.

Create wireframes or visual representations of potential layouts.

Wireframes are barebones page mock-ups that are created in a graphics program instead of being drawn by hand.

Create comps for final aesthetic designs.

Comps (comprehensive drawings) or **storyboards** are fully developed, detailed drawings that provide a complete preview of what the final design will look like.

Clockwise from upper left:
iStockphoto.com/TommL;
iStockphoto.com/Slavenko Vukasovic;
iStockphoto.com/Miljan Mladenovic;
iStockphoto.com/Abel Mitja Varela

Creating Information Architecture

Creating information architecture is the process of determining what you need a site to do and then constructing a framework that will allow you to accomplish those goals. It applies the principles of architectural design and library science to Web site design by providing a blueprint for Web page arrangement, Web site navigation, and page content organization. The basic process for creating the information architecture for a site is to construct information categories, draw a flowchart, and organize the available information into pages. You will work on the information architecture for the new NextBest Fest site.

Creating Categories for Information

Categories provide structure for the information in a Web site and are used to create the main navigation system. The **main navigation system** is the interface that visitors use to move through a Web site. This interface appears in the same place on every page in the site. The main categories of a Web site are like the subject sections of a library or bookstore: fiction, poetry, reference material, and so on. They show the visitors what types of information are included in the Web site. The categories should be based on the site goals and the information gathered during the preliminary planning stages. When you create the NextBest Fest categories, think about how the information should be organized to achieve the site goals, and then use what you learned from visiting other sites to create logical groupings of information. It is also important to use category names that will be meaningful to the target audience. Avoid industry jargon and acronyms that might not make sense to the target audience.

Categories can be divided into subcategories, just like the fiction section in a library or bookstore might be divided into historical novels, mysteries, literature, science fiction, and so on. Subcategories should be arranged in hierarchical order, placing the most important subcategories first. After you know the major categories for the NextBest Fest site, you can list all the subcategories that will fall under each category in a hierarchical order.

INSIGHT

Developing an Efficient Navigation System

A Web site's navigation system should include a reasonable amount of categories and subcategories. Include no more than five main categories in a Web site so that the pages do not seem cluttered. Likewise, include no more than five subcategories for each main category because fragmenting information into too many subcategories makes the Web site more difficult to navigate. For more complex sites, you can divide individual subcategories into third-level subcategories. Before creating third-level subcategories, however, make sure that enough information exists to warrant the breakdown. Visitors dislike having to link too far into a site to find relevant information. Third-level subcategories are appropriate only when a Web site is incredibly information intensive, such as a research site, and no other means effectively conveys the information.

The best way to present the major categories and the subcategories for a Web site is in a standard outline format. Gage created the outline shown in Figure 2-6 to show how the NextBest Fest site content can be structured.

Figure 2-6   Information category outline for the NextBest Fest site

NextBest Fest Web Site Category Outline
I.   Home Page
     a.   About
          i.   Mission/Vision
          ii. Shenpa Productions
          iii. FAQs
     b.   Lineup
          i.   Band bios and links
     c.   Schedule
          i.   Three-day schedule (time, band, stage)
          ii. Fest map showing stages, exits, food booths, and facilities
     d.   Ticket Info
          i.   Ticket information and links for purchasing tickets
     e.   Contact
          i.   Company contact information for general questions, bands, press, vendors, and sponsors
          ii. Directions
          iii. Email form

© 2013 Cengage Learning

Gage asks you to create an alternate outline with another possible version of the categories and subcategories for the NextBest Fest site.

To create an information category outline for the NextBest Fest site:

1. Review the site goals and your research, and then use that information to create a list of five categories of information for the NextBest Fest site.

2. Start an outline using the categories you listed in Step 1 as section headings.

3. List all the subcategories that will be included in the first section of your outline, and then arrange them in hierarchical order.

4. Break the subcategories into their respective subcategories, where applicable, and arrange them in hierarchical order.

5. Repeat Steps 3 and 4 for each section of your outline.

6. Compare your outline with Gage's outline, as shown in Figure 2-6.

Creating a Flowchart

Next, you will work on the flowchart for the NextBest Fest site. A flowchart is a diagram of geometric shapes connected by lines that shows steps in sequence. The shapes represent steps, decision points, and dead ends. The lines represent the connection of steps. If steps must be followed in a particular order or direction, arrows are attached to the lines. In Web design, a flowchart provides a visual representation of the hierarchical structure of the pages within the site. The shapes represent different types of pages, and the lines represent connections (or relationships) between the pages.

You create a flowchart from the information category outline. The main categories become the major branches of the flowchart and the subcategories become the subbranches. Most of the time, visitors can move between pages of a Web site in any direction, so arrows are usually not included. You can use shapes to designate different types of pages in the Web site. For example, form pages can be hexagons and regular pages can be squares. A key or legend for deciphering what the shapes represent is often included in the flowchart. Figure 2-7 shows the flowchart that Gage created for the new NextBest Fest site.

TIP

There is no widely recognized standard for the shapes used to designate different Web pages.

Figure 2-7 NextBest Fest site flowchart

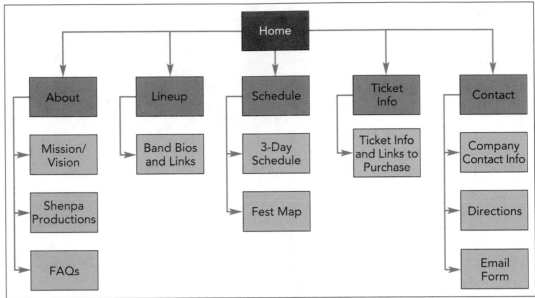

© 2013 Cengage Learning

Gage asks you to create a flowchart using the outline that you created. You can create the flowchart using flowcharting software or sketch it using pen and paper.

To create a flowchart for the NextBest Fest site:

1. Draw a rectangle at the top of the page and label it **Home**.

2. Draw rectangles in a horizontal row below the Home square for each of the main categories of your outline, and label each rectangle with one category.

3. Draw a line from each main category page to the home page to connect them.

4. Repeat Steps 2 and 3 to add the subcategory pages below the category pages. Continue until all of the information from your outline is represented in the flowchart.

5. Create a key for your flowchart by drawing and labeling the shape you used.

6. Compare your flowchart with the flowchart shown in Figure 2-7 that Gage created.

Gathering and Organizing Information

The next step in the process of creating information architecture is to gather and organize all possible sources of information. The materials that you collect will be used to create the page content for the site. It is best to err on the side of excess at this stage because the more raw materials you have to work with, the better job you can do when you actually start to create content.

Based on the site goals, the market research, the information outline, and the flowchart, you and Gage need information about the following:

- The fest and the production company
- The lineup and the bands
- The schedule
- Ticket prices and purchasing information

You will find this information in a variety of places. Much of the information you need can be found in promotional materials such as brochures, flyers, press releases, reviews, and articles. Gather all of the available graphics materials and any pertinent company documents such as the company's mission statement and employee biographies. Outside resources such as reviews, articles, and other Web sites that reference the product or service can also provide information. You will want a paper copy of all the information for ease of organization. You will also want a digital copy of anything that you can get so that later you won't have to retype the content into the pages of your site. After all the information is compiled and printed, you are ready to start organizing it.

PROSKILLS

Problem Solving: Organizing Page Content Logically

As you gather information and materials to develop and use in a Web site, the amount of data and materials can become quite large. Sorting through all of this information can sometimes feel daunting. However, the better job you do of sorting, evaluating, and organizing the information you collected, the more likely it becomes that the Web site you create will be more interesting, contain well-written content, and enable users to easily locate all of that content. Organizing the data into categories is a good first step; it lets you see exactly what you have gathered about each relevant topic. You need to sort the collected materials, piece by piece, into the categories and subcategories you established earlier. You might need to split some items, such as a brochure, into more than one category. Information that fits into more than one category should be placed in the category that will seem most appropriate to the target audience. After you have sorted the materials, review any information that is relevant but doesn't fit the planned pages. First, try to find a place in the existing structure where the information might be appropriate. If the relevant information still doesn't fit, you might consider whether that information warrants creating a separate section or a new page. Once the information is organized, it will be much easier to create the content you need from the data and materials.

Next, you will create the aesthetic design for the site. After you have designed the aesthetic structure of the pages, you will create page content out of the materials that you have assembled and organized.

Designing a Web Site

The phrase *look and feel* is used to describe the overall impact of the external characteristics of a Web site. It refers to the way that all the elements of the site design interact to create an experience for the user. The look and feel is achieved from a mixture of many smaller choices, including which colors, fonts, graphics style, and layout are selected for the design. You will make all of the choices regarding the aesthetic design elements in a site during the planning phase. As you make decisions, keep in mind how the user requirements you identified impact the design. To combine all these elements effectively, you start by creating a concept and metaphor for the site.

Best practices in Web design are to keep the aesthetic design of pages and page elements separate from the content. For example, the code that tells the page to display a specific color in the background or that tells the page to display headings at a certain size and in a certain color is stored in style sheets. You apply individual styles to the content in the pages instead of applying colors, sizes, and other attributes directly to the text in the pages. This way of working is much more efficient and enables you to change the look of all of the pages by modifying the styles applied to them.

REFERENCE

Designing a Web Site

- Create a site concept and metaphor.
- Consider accessibility issues.
- Select colors.
- Select fonts.
- Choose a graphics style and graphics.
- Sketch the layout.
- Check the design for logic.

Developing a Site Concept and Metaphor

A good concept is the basis for developing an aesthetically cohesive Web site. A site concept is a general underlying theme that unifies the various elements of a site and contributes to the site's look and feel. To develop a site concept, review some of the artwork and Web sites that appeal to the target audience and look for common underlying themes. Next, make a list of words that describes what you would like the site to convey. Try to think of words that will reinforce the site goals and words that will communicate something to the target audience. Finally, write down the concept.

After you have developed a site concept, you create a metaphor for the site. A **metaphor** is a comparison in which one object, concept, or idea is represented as another. For example, the expression "at that moment, time was molasses" and Shakespeare's famous observation that "all the world's a stage" are metaphors. The site metaphor should be a visual extension of the site concept, which reinforces the site message and the site goals. The metaphor helps to create a unified site design.

The metaphor you choose for a Web site does not have to be concretely represented in the site. For example, if the site concept is fluidity, the metaphor might be a river. The actual site does not need to be designed to look like a river, but instead could integrate elements that are commonly identified with rivers: a series of small, partially transparent, wavy lines in the page background; a flowing theme in the graphics design; and cool colors such as muted blues and silvers. The river metaphor is an instrument to focus the aesthetic choices.

For the new NextBest Fest site, Gage came up with a list of words to describe the site: *tribute*, *revival*, *logical*, *fun*, *campy*, *spectacle*, *nostalgic*, *artifacts*, and *intuitive*. Some words apply to a look that is popular with the target audience (campy, spectacle); other words apply to the flow of information (logical, intuitive). Next, Gage reviewed the art on the Facebook pages of some of the bands in the lineup at the NextBest Fest as well as the art in the sites of other bands in the same genres of music to get a feel for the artwork styles that are popular with the NextBest Fest target audience. Finally, Gage decided on the site concept—theatrical replication propelling the nostalgic past into the present moment—and the metaphor of "reclaiming." In later sections, you will see how the reclaiming metaphor helps to shape the site design by providing a foundation for color choice, font choice, graphics choice, and layout.

Gage asks you to develop another concept and metaphor for the new NextBest Fest site.

To develop another concept and metaphor for the NextBest Fest site:

▶ **1.** List at least five words that describe the site.

▶ **2.** Review your notes regarding artwork and imagery that appeals to the target audience.

▶ **3.** Choose a site concept, and then write a short description of the concept and why you selected it.

▶ **4.** Choose a site metaphor, and then write a short description of the metaphor and why you selected it.

▶ **5.** Write a paragraph that explains how you could integrate the concept and the metaphor into the site.

Considering Accessibility Issues

The Web is a public venue used by a variety of people, including people with disabilities. You will want to consider making your site accessible to them. With regard to Web design, **accessibility** refers to the quality and ease of use of a Web site by people who use assistive devices or people with disabilities. An **assistive device** is an apparatus that provides a disabled person with alternate means to experience electronic and information technologies. Some ways that you can enhance the accessibility of a Web site include providing alternate text descriptions for any graphics on the site that can be read by audio assistive devices and establishing basic text links in addition to graphical navigation structures.

Effective June 21, 2001, Section 508 of the federal Rehabilitation Act requires all United States federal government agencies, as well as public colleges and universities, to make their electronic and information technology accessible to people with disabilities. Although private companies are under no legal obligation to make their sites accessible, many try to ensure that their sites are at least partially in line with current federal guidelines. Because technologies change rapidly, the Web is the best source for current accessibility guidelines and accessibility-checking tools. You can find information about accessibility guidelines on the Section 508 Web site, *www.section508.gov*.

Adobe offers a number of tools to help you develop accessible Web sites, including templates and checking utilities. Search the Adobe site, *www.adobe.com*, using the keyword *accessibility* for information. You can also activate Accessibility dialog boxes within Dreamweaver so that every time you insert an object into a Web page, Dreamweaver prompts you for the information you need to add accessibility.

The World Wide Web Consortium (W3C) also provides information about accessibility technology, guidelines, tools, education and outreach, and research and development. It has created a Web Accessibility Initiative (WAI) whose mission is to promote usability of the Web for people with disabilities. For more information, go to the WAI page on the W3C Web site, *www.w3.org/WAI*. W3C created a checklist based on the Web content accessibility guidelines developed by WAI that designers can use to ensure a site meets the accessibility standards. The standards are split into three levels: Priority 1 must be satisfied, Priority 2 should be satisfied, and Priority 3 may be addressed. For more information, go to the Checklist of Checkpoints for Web Content Accessibility Guidelines 1.0 page, *www.w3.org/TR/WCAG10/full-checklist.html*. WAI-ARIA provides additional guidelines for making dynamic content accessible, such as a Web page that has live updates. For more information, go to the WAI-ARIA page on the W3C Web site, *www.w3.org/WAI/intro/aria*.

For now, Gage wants to adjust the new Web site design for accessibility without changing the site's look and feel. This will make the site available to as wide an

TIP

Audio assistive devices can read page elements such as page text, headers, captions, the page title, and alternative text on images, but not graphics, links, image maps, table data order, text displayed as graphics, buttons, movies, and sound.

audience as possible while maintaining a look and feel that appeals to the target audience. Gage plans to implement basic accessibility modifications into the design for the new Web site, and then create a parallel site next year that will meet all the current accessibility guidelines.

Based on a review of the current guidelines, Gage has decided to include alternate text descriptions for graphics, graphics links, and multimedia content. This alternate text can be "read" by audio assistive devices. Depending on the browser, this information will appear in place of a graphic or when the user points to an image or link. Gage wants to make the alternate text as descriptive as possible so that anyone can appreciate the site content even without seeing it.

Selecting Colors

Color is an interesting component of design because it affects the emotional response that a user has to the site. The colors you choose set the tone of the site. Before selecting colors for a Web site, you will need a basic understanding of how color applies to Web design.

The two major systems of color are subtractive and additive. The traditional **subtractive color system** uses cyan, magenta, and yellow as its primary colors; all other colors are created by mixing these primary colors. It is called the subtractive color system because new colors are created by adding pigment, such as ink and paint, and removing light. If the primary colors of the subtractive color system are combined in equal amounts, they make black—the absence of light. The **additive color system** uses red, green, and blue as its primary colors. This system is also called the **RGB system** for red, green, and blue. As with the subtractive color system, all other colors are created by combining these primary colors. It is called the additive color system because it works like a prism—new colors are created by adding varying amounts of light. If all of the primary colors of the additive system are combined in equal amounts, they create pure white light. Figure 2-8 shows how the primary colors red, green, and blue can be mixed in various combinations to create the secondary colors cyan, magenta, and yellow, and how the primary colors can be combined equally to create white.

Figure 2-8	RGB color system

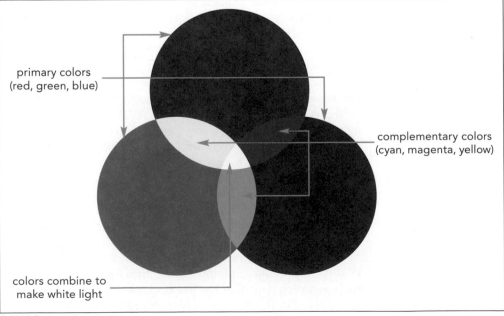

primary colors
(red, green, blue)

complementary colors
(cyan, magenta, yellow)

colors combine to
make white light

Web sites are a digital media designed to be viewed on monitors. A monitor combines hundreds of thousands of pixels (tiny dots of light that glow in different color intensities) to create images. Because monitors work with light, they use the additive RGB color system. When creating or saving graphics for the Web, you should use RGB color.

Color is a good tool for emphasizing information, such as differentiating headlines from body text, or for drawing the eye to a specific area of the page. Color can also be used to distinguish segments of the Web site. For example, you can use a different color for each major category. You can use contrasting, or complementary, colors to make one object stand out against another. You can use analogous colors to make objects blend harmoniously. Contrasting colors are opposite one another on the color wheel; analogous colors are adjacent.

Choosing a color palette can be difficult. There is no precise scientific method to ensure that you will choose the perfect colors. This is why most design teams include a graphic artist who is trained in color theory. However, even without extensive color training, you can select attractive and effective colors for a Web site. Keep in mind the following basic color concepts and strategies:

- **Keep it simple.** With color choice, more is definitely not better. Everyone has seen a Web site that looks as if it erupted from a rainbow. Too many competing colors cause the eye to race around the page, leaving the user dazed and confused.
- **Include three to six colors per site.** You will use these same colors for all of the site's elements, including the text, background, links, logo, buttons, navigation bar, and graphics. Black and white count as colors in the palette. The thousands of colors in photographic images do not count as part of the color palette.
- **Consider the mood you want to create.** Colors create a mood. Studies show that colors have certain psychological effects on people. For example, blue is calming, red is hot or intense. Think about what your target audience might associate with a color when choosing a palette for a Web site.
- **Keep the target audience in mind.** Different cultures do not always have the same psychological associations with specific colors. For example, people in the United States associate white with purity and red with danger, whereas some countries associate white with death and red with marriage. If a Web site has a global or foreign target audience, you might need to research the customs and symbols of the target culture(s).

One way to develop a color palette is to look to other works of art for inspiration. Think of what emotions and feelings you want to evoke with the Web site, and then find a painting, photograph, or other work of art that stirs those feelings in you. Evaluate the colors the artist used. Consider how the colors interact. Try to pinpoint colors that are causing the emotion. Consider how the color palette works with your metaphor. Think about how you might use that color palette in the Web site.

INSIGHT

Making Colors Accessible

Remember accessibility when selecting colors; some people cannot distinguish between colors due to varying degrees of color blindness. When designing a Web site, make sure that you use more than just color differences to convey navigation information. For example, if the only cue that a word is a link is that the text is a different color than the text around it, this will be confusing to people who cannot distinguish color variations. To ensure that everyone can easily distinguish text links from other text, you can underline, italicize, or bold the links to differentiate them stylistically.

Gage chose the colors shown in Figure 2-9 for the new NextBest Fest site. This color palette fits nicely into the reclaiming design metaphor because the varying shades of green, gray, and blue-green are reminiscent of colors popular in the early 1980s and work with the other aesthetic elements in the site to provide a slightly antiseptic feeling that provokes imagery of found objects from the past unearthed in a laboratory environment. In the site, blue-green will be used in the logo, olive will be used as an accent in the content background and as a heading color, and gray will be used in the page background and as the primary text color. Font colors are discussed more extensively in the next section.

| Figure 2-9 | **Color palette for the new NextBest Fest site** |

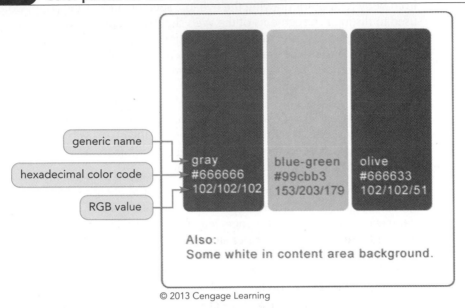

© 2013 Cengage Learning

The figure refers to the colors by their generic color names as well as their RGB values and their hexadecimal color codes. Although color names such as green, red, and yellow are easy to remember and may have more meaning to most people, they can be unreliable when trying to communicate specific color values. One person might use the word *red* to refer to the generic red family of colors, and another person might be referring to the specific color designated as red in a site's color palette. The color names used in these tutorials are the generic color names.

Many of the colors currently in use in Web sites do not have reliable color names. All colors, however, have hexadecimal color codes. Before CSS3, all well-coded HTML used hexadecimal color codes to identify specific colors. **Hexadecimal color codes** are six-digit numbers in the form of #RRGGBB where RR is replaced by the hexadecimal color value for red, GG is replaced with the green value, and BB is replaced with the blue value. The specified amounts of each of these colors are mixed together by the system to create the color you specify. **Hexadecimal** is a number system that uses the digits 0 through 9 to represent the decimal values 0 through 9, plus the letters *a* through *f* to represent the decimal values 10 through 15. Each pair of numbers in the hexadecimal color can produce 256 different values. Combining the values of the possible red, green, and blue values produces 16,777,216 unique color values. To ensure that the color you specify is understood by the browser and displayed properly, you will use hexadecimal color codes to designate colors when you create the NextBest Fest site. However, you do not need to know the hexadecimal color codes when you are selecting colors in Dreamweaver. Instead, you can click the color you want to use, and Dreamweaver will display the hexadecimal code for that color.

Finally, you should be familiar with the Web Safe Color Palette, which is still referred to frequently although it is no longer relevant. The **Web Safe Color Palette** consists of 216 colors that, when many computers could display only 256 colors at a time, provided Web designers with a reliable color palette. Because current computers can display 16+ million colors, most designers have disregarded the Web Safe Color Palette. Many of the colors currently in use in Web sites do not have reliable color names. All colors, however, have hexadecimal color codes, and all well-coded HTML uses hexadecimal color codes, RGB values, or HSL values instead of color names.

TIP

Hexadecimal color codes are not case sensitive, but it is a good idea to use capitalization consistently within a site.

RGB and HSL Color Values

CSS3 has the capability to reference colors by their RGB values or HSL (Hue, Saturation, Luminance) values in addition to their hexadecimal color codes. The advantage of using RGB or HSL values is that these systems have an additional channel, called an alpha channel, that also lets you specify the opacity of an object. An object that has an alpha channel value of 0% is fully transparent or invisible, and an object that has an alpha channel value of 100% is fully opaque. So, objects that have an alpha channel value between 0% and 100% will be partially transparent when displayed in the browser. This means you can use CSS3 styles with HTML5 to change the transparency of an object in your Web page over a period of time, creating dynamic effects. For example, you could use changing alpha channel values to make an image fade in slowly. During the planning process, you should think about opacity in addition to colors when you are designing a Web site. However, keep in mind that older browsers may not support CSS3 and, therefore, will not recognize RGB or HSL values. So consider the target audience and the site purpose and goals when deciding which color system to use in a Web site.

You need to select a color palette that will work with the site metaphor you developed. You can use a graphics program (such as Adobe Photoshop, Adobe Fireworks, or Adobe Illustrator), crayons, markers, or colored paper to create the color palette.

To choose a color palette to complement your site metaphor:

▶ **1.** Envision a set of colors that will work with your site concept and metaphor.

▶ **2.** Look at works of art for inspiration.

▶ **3.** Think about the psychological associations of the colors. Do these fit with your site goals?

▶ **4.** Draw a series of rectangles side by side (one for each color in your palette), and then fill each rectangle with one color.

▶ **5.** Write a one-paragraph explanation of your color choice and how it reinforces the site concept and metaphor. Describe where and how you intend to use the colors in the site.

Selecting Fonts

Font refers to a set of letters, numbers, and symbols in a unified typeface. Font choice is important in creating an effective Web site because a font conveys a wealth of subtle information and often creates an impression about the content before it is even read. Think about the different fonts that might be used on Web sites that present current news and events, Far East travel, and science fiction movies.

The three categories of font typefaces are serif, sans serif, and mono. These categories are also referred to as **generic font families**. **Serif typefaces** are typefaces in which a delicate, horizontal line called a serif finishes the main strokes of each character; an example is the horizontal bars at the top and bottom of an uppercase M. The most common serif typeface is Times New Roman. **Sans serif typefaces** are those in which the serifs are absent. (*Sans* means "without" in French, so *sans serif* means "without serif.") The most common sans serif typeface is **Helvetica**. A third category, mono, is sometimes used. *Mono* is short for *monospaced*. A **monospaced font** is one in which each letter has exactly the same width in the line; for example, the letter *i* (a thin letter) takes the same amount of space as the letter *m*. A common monospaced font is `Courier`. Monospaced fonts are serif fonts, but they are considered a separate generic font family in Dreamweaver. Fonts that are not monospaced are **proportional fonts** because each letter takes up a different width on the line proportional to the width of the letter. For example, the letter *i* needs less space than the letter *m*. Both the serif typeface Times New Roman and the sans serif typeface Helvetica are proportional fonts.

Before HTML5, a font had to be installed on the end user's device for the Web page to be displayed using that font. With HTML5, a designer can embed a font in the Web page code so that the end user can view the page in the specified font even if that font is not installed on his or her device. However, older browsers do not support this capability nor is it fully supported in all new browsers. As a result, using fonts installed on the end user's device is still the best practice to font selection to ensure that all users will experience the page as you have intended. According to this standard, if a font is not found on the client device, the page will be displayed in the default font the end user has chosen for his or her browser. Because of this, Dreamweaver arranges fonts into groups, which provide designers with the best chance for achieving the desired look for the page. Figure 2-10 lists the default Dreamweaver font groupings. Each group contains the most common names for the selected font; these include at least the most common PC name (for example, Verdana in the first font group in Figure 2-10), the most common Mac name when different (Geneva in the first font group in Figure 2-10), and the generic font family name (sans-serif in the first font group in Figure 2-10). When you apply a font grouping to text, Dreamweaver places a CSS style that contains all three choices around the specified text, ensuring maximum potential for aesthetic continuity across all platforms and all devices. When a browser displays a page, it checks the user's device for the first font in the group. If the device doesn't have that font, the browser checks for the second font in the list, and then, if necessary, the third font. You can also create a custom font group if you would prefer a different set of default fonts; click the Edit Font List option in the Font box in the Property inspector to add fonts to the list and create a custom list.

> **TIP**
>
> Because older browsers and most newer browsers do not support embedded fonts, it is still a good idea to use the default font groupings when you design a Web site.

| Figure 2-10 | Default font groups in Dreamweaver |

Verdana, Geneva, sans-serif

Georgia, Times New Roman, Times, serif

Courier New, Courier, monospace

Arial, Helvetica, sans-serif

Tahoma, Geneva, sans-serif

Trebuchet MS, Arial, Helvetica, sans-serif

Arial Black, Gadget, sans-serif

Times New Roman, Times, serif

Palatino Linotype, Book Antiqua, Palatino, serif

Lucida Sans Unicode, Lucida Grande, sans-serif

MS Serif, New York, serif

Lucida Console, Monaco, monospace

Comic Sans MS, cursive

INSIGHT

Deciding When to Use Embedded Fonts

If you decide to use embedded fonts, keep in mind that some users will not see the content displayed in the font you selected and the font used on their devices may cause the page content to be positioned differently in their browsers. When you learn advanced coding techniques, you can include code that lets older browsers know what font group in which to display the page. In the meantime, a good compromise is to use alternate fonts only for headings and subheadings.

Selecting a font also involves choosing a font color and size and sometimes a font style. **Font color** refers to the color that is applied to the font. The font color should be chosen from the colors you selected for the site's color palette. **Font size** refers to the size of the font. Font sizes can be relative or specific. Relative font size defines font size in respect to the default font size that the end user has set for his or her browser. Relative font sizes range from xx-small to xx-large, where xx-small, x-small, and small are smaller than the browser's default font size; medium is equal to the browser's default font size; and large, x-large, and xx-large appear bigger than the browser's default font size. Relative font sizes are often used as part of accessible design because the end user controls the default size of the base font and can change the size at which the text is displayed in the browser. Specific font sizes are fixed sizes. Using fixed font sizes enables the designer to decide exactly how a page will display in a user's browser. Pixels work well as a unit for defining a specific font size because the pixel unit is supported by major browsers. **Font style** refers to the stylistic attributes that are applied to the font. Stylistic attributes include bold, italic, and underline.

INSIGHT

Selecting Fonts When Designing a Web Site

As you select fonts for a Web site, keep in mind the following strategies:

- **Less is more.** In general, you should use no more than two fonts in a Web site to give the site a consistent look. Select one font, one font size, and one font color for the general body text (although text links in the body text will be distinguished by a different color). You can choose a second font, size, and color for headings.
- **Convert headings to images.** Sometimes headings and logos are actually text that has been converted to an image in a graphics program. By converting text into an image, you have greater control over the look of the final site because you can choose a font that is not in the Dreamweaver font list and might not be found on every computer.
- **Limit embedded fonts to page headings.** The HTML5 capability to embed a font group in page code can create dramatic headings without converting the text to an image. Limit this practice to page headings so you can maintain greater control over the page layout in older browsers that do not support HTML5. Taking advantage of this latest technique instead of creating an image enables search engines to see the heading text, which can help increase page placement.
- **Consider what you are trying to convey.** Fonts create an impression about the content of the site. Different fonts are associated with specific types of content. For example, the titles of old horror movies usually appear in a gothic font; therefore, that font is usually associated with horror movies. Choose fonts that support the concept and metaphor for your site.
- **Consider accessibility.** Visually impaired users of the Web site might have a hard time reading certain fonts or smaller sizes. Review accessibility Web sites such as *www.yourhtmlsource.com/accessibility* to find guidelines about fonts and font size.

For the font of the general body text in the NextBest Fest site, Gage decided to use gray, 14 pixels, and Arial, Helvetica, sans-serif. Gage selected the Arial, Helvetica, sans-serif group because of its simplicity, which will help give the site a minimalist look. He used gray text and the default font size because it is easy to read. The logo and headings will be graphics made from text using the CountdownD font and a combination of the Web site palette colors. Gage selected the CountdownD font, which was used prevalently on T-shirts and in advertising in the early 1980s, because it supports the site metaphor. Until the graphics are available, the font group for headings and subheadings will be Arial, Helvetica, sans-serif.

Although it is not necessary, designers often choose to format links in different colors, depending on their state. To make the site more accessible, Gage will indicate link states with colors that are different shades. This enables users who cannot differentiate between colors but can see variations in darkness and lightness to distinguish the link states. In addition, underlines will be used to indicate the link state for links in the NextBest Fest site. A **text link**, a hyperlink that has not yet been clicked, will be olive (a darker color). When the pointer is over the link, the link is in the hover state. In the hover state, the link will be underlined and blue-green (a lighter shade). An **active link**, a text hyperlink that is in the process of being clicked, will be olive. A **visited link**, a text hyperlink that has been clicked, will be displayed in olive. Using the same color for visited, active, and unvisited links is an aesthetic choice that designers make when they feel that the target audience does not want or need to track which links they have clicked. See Figure 2-11.

Figure 2-11	Font choices for the new NextBest Fest site

body text (this is the default style for all text. All exceptions to this style are specified):
Font group: Arial, Helvetica, sans-serif; color - gray #666666, size - 14 pixels

Page Headings will be:
size: heading 1; color - blue-green #99cbb3

Subheadings will be:
size: heading 2; color - olive #666633

linked text will be:
color; olive #666633

links in hover will be:
color: blue-green #99cbb3 and underlined

active links will be:
color; olive #666633

visited links will be:
color; olive #666633

© 2013 Cengage Learning

You will select a set of fonts that will go with the concept and metaphor you developed for the NextBest Fest site.

To choose fonts to complement your site concept and metaphor:

1. Start your Web browser, review accessibility Web sites for information about font choice, and then exit your browser.

2. Envision a font for the general body text that will work with the site concept and metaphor. Review the list in Figure 2-10 for a list of font grouping options.

3. Choose a font color from your site color palette for the body text.

4. Choose a color from your color palette for any text hyperlinks that will appear in the body text. Choose different colors for active links and visited links.

5. Choose a font size for the body text.

6. Choose a font, color, and size for the headings.

7. Write a brief explanation of your font choices.

Choosing a Graphics Style and Graphics

The graphics in a Web site provide the personality of the site. Recall that graphics can include images, photographs, buttons, logos, and so on. Graphics style refers to the look of the graphics elements in the site. You use elements such as texture, color, and depth or flatness to create a graphic look. Designing a consistent look for all the graphics in a Web site is one of the keys to developing a cohesive, well-made site.

INSIGHT

Choosing a Graphics Style for a Web Site

When selecting a graphics style, keep in mind the following strategies:

- **Be consistent.** If you use a cartoonish drawing for one button, use cartoonish drawings for all the buttons. If you add a photographic image to the upper-right corner of one page, consider adding photographic images to the upper-right corners of all the pages. Consistency in choosing graphics gives the site a cohesive look.

- **Design with purpose.** When you add a graphic to a page, ask yourself what the graphic adds to the page. Make sure that you have a reason for adding each graphic to the site. Also, make sure each graphic matches the other graphics in the site. For example, if you add a texture to a graphic in one page, you should probably include the same or similar texture in other pages.

- **Consider size.** Reduce all of the graphics to the smallest possible file size that you can get without sacrificing the quality of the image. The file size of each graphic contributes to the file size of the Web pages. The smaller you can keep the file size of the Web pages, the faster they will load in the user's browser. One way to ensure a small file size is to make the image resolution 72ppi, which is the resolution at which images display on a screen. You will have to use a graphics program such as Adobe Photoshop or Adobe Fireworks to do this.

- **Consider the target audience.** Review the user profile and consider the technical capabilities of the target audience. Choose graphics that will not keep users from enjoying the site because the pages load too slowly.

- **Support your concept and metaphor.** Choose graphics that reinforce the concept and metaphor of the site. Visual symbols are very powerful tools for conveying information. Consider what each graphic adds to the site, and make sure that each graphic reinforces the site metaphor.

Based on the NextBest Fest site goals, the color palette, the font choices, and the site metaphor, Gage selected a graphics style that includes flat, translucent, retro text, and found objects from the early 1980s that represent the music of the era. The objects are processed and displayed with a reduced color palette. Various graphics are layered to provide a collage of the past that is carried to the current fest. By juxtaposing design styles and images from an earlier time with modern stylistic elements and content, the site will deconstruct both the old and the new, creating a style and depth that should appeal to the target audience. Figure 2-12 shows the new NextBest Fest logo and page background as a sample of the graphics style that was chosen.

| Figure 2-12 | Sample of the graphics style for the new NextBest Fest site |

© 2013 Cengage Learning; dean bertoncelj/Shutterstock.com; Jupiterimages/Photos.com

You will choose a graphics style for the site concept that you selected for the new NextBest Fest site.

To choose a graphics style and graphics to complement your site concept:

1. Review your concept and metaphor for the site, the user profile, and the research that you gathered about sites that appeal to the target audience.

2. Make a list of the graphics that you want to include in the site such as logos, buttons, and illustrations.

3. Write a paragraph that describes the graphics style for your site. Explain how this graphics style supports your metaphor.

Determining the Layout

With the colors, fonts, and graphics style in place, you can determine the site's layout. The term *layout* comes from traditional print design. Layout is the position of elements—in this case, on the computer screen. The first decision is whether the page structure and content will be a fixed size on the screen regardless of the size of the user's browser window, or whether the page structure and content will be flexible and change to fill the user's browser window. The second decision is where in the Web pages to place the navigation system, text, logo, artwork, and so on. The layout should support the site goals and metaphor. It should be easy for a user to follow, and it should appeal to the target audience. Finally, it should also be consistent. For example, the navigation should be in the same place on all of the pages of the site to improve usability and accessibility. Most important, layout should conform to the basic tenets of sound artistic design by employing balance, unity, and rhythm. Using this approach, you should consider the space as a whole in addition to the proximity of individual elements in the page.

Balance and Space

Balance is the feeling of equilibrium when looking at the page as a whole. It is achieved by arranging objects so that their visual weight balances in the overall page composition. The two main approaches to balance are symmetrical and asymmetrical. Symmetrical balance distributes the visual weight of objects in a page evenly around the central horizontal and vertical axes of the page. Radial symmetry creates balance in a page by distributing objects equally around one center point. In juxtaposition, asymmetrical or informal, balance is created by distributing visually disproportionate objects in the page so that the visual weights of the objects achieve balance with respect to one another instead of with the page axes. Informal balance is often more visually compelling than symmetrical balance because it better incorporates the white space (or negative space) of the page into the design. **White space** is the empty space in the page and it is an important part of a well-designed Web page. If the page layout fills every inch of the screen, users can become disoriented, feel claustrophobic, and cannot move easily through the site. Leaving white space opens up the pages and enables the user to more easily navigate the pages.

> **TIP**
>
> Visually separate important elements such as navigation from page content to distinguish them and make them easier to find.

One tool for achieving open design is a frequently used design concept called the Rule of Thirds. The Rule of Thirds was created by artists in the Renaissance and states that the most interesting compositions are those in which the strongest element is off center. To implement this technique, divide the page into thirds both horizontally and vertically, and then place the objects in the page on the lines. No object should take up more than two-thirds of the page, horizontally and vertically. For example, in most Web pages, the page header takes up the top third of the page, leaving the bottom two-thirds of the page for content.

Rhythm and Unity

Rhythm is achieved in a page by repetition or alternation of objects or elements in the page. For example, a color that is repeated in different places in the page helps create a sense of rhythm or flow to the page. Unity speaks to the relationship and proximity of the individual objects in the page as they relate to the composition of the whole page. Using one graphics style throughout the site, repeating colors throughout the site, and creating balance and symmetry between the objects in the pages all help to create unity in the design.

Often, two or three effective layouts are possible. Initially, designers create rough sketches of possible layout designs. Sometimes designers create wireframes of the site layout. Wireframes are bare-bones page mock-ups that are created in a graphics program instead of being drawn by hand. Wireframes include only rough placeholder images such as boxes with text to indicate where a button will be placed. The purpose of creating wireframes is to show placement of navigation, logo, and other layout elements to the client before creating the actual artwork. Because many clients are visual and need to see some basic artwork to grasp the site's aesthetic design, often the client and design team forgo wireframes and instead choose the sketch that they like best. Then, they create comps, or storyboards, from the sketch. The comps (comprehensive drawings) or storyboards are fully developed, detailed drawings that provide a complete preview of what the final design will look like. Think of them as a pictorial overview that communicates the story of the Web site. They often include elements such as filenames, page titles, page headings, a navigation system, images, text, and link information. As you build the Web site, be sure to compare the sites with the storyboard to be sure the intended design is being implemented.

Gage developed rough sketches of two possible layouts for the new NextBest Fest site, as shown in Figure 2-13. The first sketch places the site navigation system at the top of the page, and the second sketch places the site navigation system along the left side of the page. Although both layouts are effective, Gage decided to go with Layout 1. The top navigation system makes better use of the available space and appears to flow better with the selected graphics style.

Figure 2-13 **Layout sketches for the new NextBest Fest site**

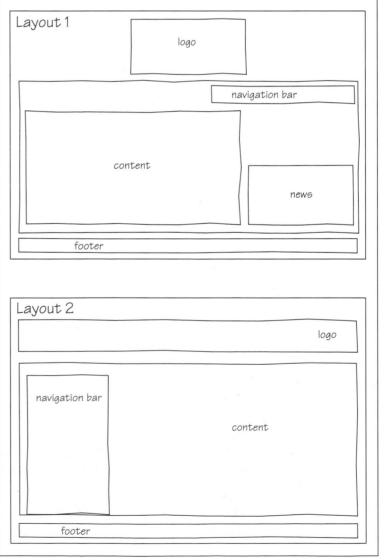

© 2013 Cengage Learning

You will draw a rough sketch of a layout that will support the site metaphor you selected.

To create a rough sketch of your site's layout:

▶ **1.** Draw a rough sketch of your site's layout.

▶ **2.** Add objects to represent items that you cannot draw, and label them. For example, draw a square the size of a photograph you plan to include, and write a brief description of the photograph inside the square.

▶ **3.** Add labels to identify the colors of each section and the lines (for example, write "white background" across the background).

▶ **4.** Write a paragraph that explains why you selected this layout. Describe how the layout reinforces the site concept and metaphor and helps to achieve the site goals.

Checking the Design for Logic

The final step of designing a site is to check the design for logic. It is important for the end user to be able to navigate through the site easily. A Web site that is attractive to view but confusing to navigate is not well designed. When you check a design for logic, look at all of the elements of the site plan as though you were seeing them for the first time and answer the following questions:

- Is the navigation system easy to follow?
- Does the graphics style support the site metaphor?
- Do the individual elements flow together to create a consistent look for the site?

If you find problems or inconsistencies in any area, you will need to work through the steps that pertain to the trouble area again, addressing the problems as you go. Gage checked the new NextBest Fest site design and is satisfied that it is logical and consistent.

With the planning and design complete, you're ready to start building the site. You will do this in the next session.

REVIEW

Session 2.2 Quick Check

1. What is information architecture?
2. What is the purpose of categories?
3. How is a flowchart used in Web design?
4. What is a site concept?
5. Why would you want to consider accessibility issues when creating a Web site?
6. Why does Dreamweaver use hexadecimal color codes rather than color names in Web sites?
7. True or False. Designing a consistent look for all the graphics in a Web site is one of the keys to developing a cohesive, well-made Web site.
8. What does the term *layout* mean?

SESSION 2.3 VISUAL OVERVIEW

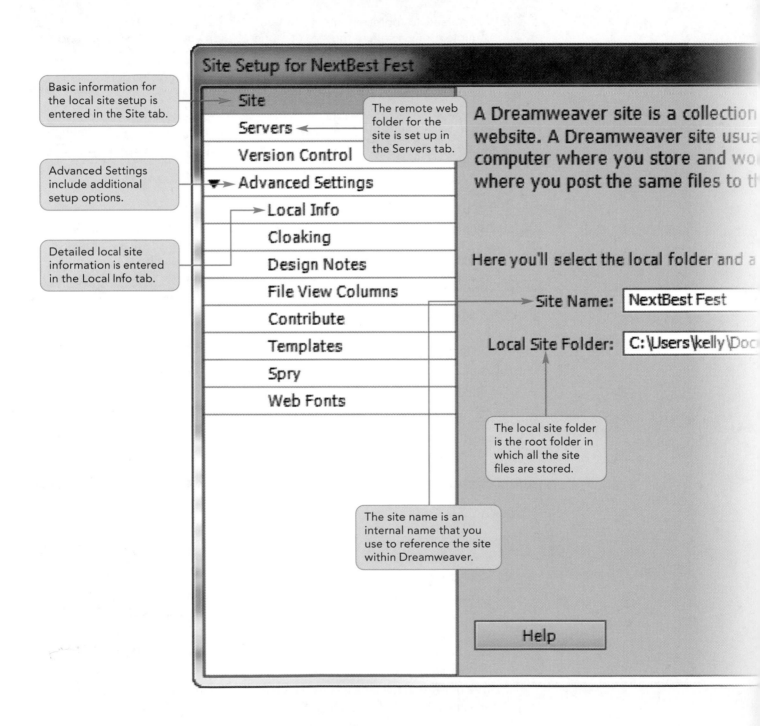

Basic information for the local site setup is entered in the Site tab.

Advanced Settings include additional setup options.

Detailed local site information is entered in the Local Info tab.

Site Setup for NextBest Fest

Site

Servers

Version Control

Advanced Settings

Local Info

Cloaking

Design Notes

File View Columns

Contribute

Templates

Spry

Web Fonts

The remote web folder for the site is set up in the Servers tab.

A Dreamweaver site is a collection website. A Dreamweaver site usu. computer where you store and wo where you post the same files to t

Here you'll select the local folder and a

Site Name: NextBest Fest

Local Site Folder: C:\Users\kelly\Doc

The local site folder is the root folder in which all the site files are stored.

The site name is an internal name that you use to reference the site within Dreamweaver.

Help

SETTING UP A SITE

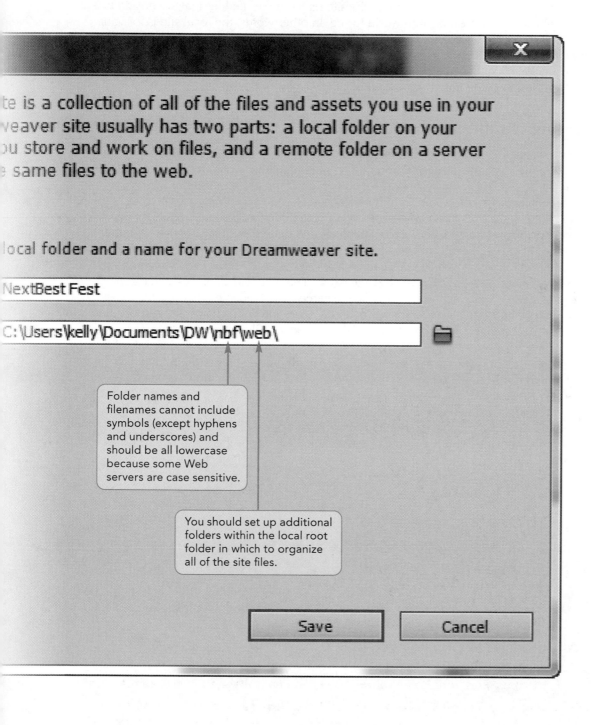

te is a collection of all of the files and assets you use in your
weaver site usually has two parts: a local folder on your
u store and work on files, and a remote folder on a server
e same files to the web.

local folder and a name for your Dreamweaver site.

NextBest Fest

C:\Users\kelly\Documents\DW\nbf\web\

Folder names and
filenames cannot include
symbols (except hyphens
and underscores) and
should be all lowercase
because some Web
servers are case sensitive.

You should set up additional
folders within the local root
folder in which to organize
all of the site files.

Save   Cancel

Creating a New Site

TIP

Do all of your work on the local site files and then post the files to the remote server only when you are ready for the world to see the finished product.

With the planning and design for the new NextBest Fest site complete, you're ready to create the Web site. You create a new Web site in Dreamweaver by setting up the site. In Dreamweaver, a Web site is all the files and assets included in the site. An **asset** is any object that you use in a Web site, such as an image, a sound, or a video. There are two copies of the site: The local copy of the site refers to the site files that are located on your computer; the remote copy of the site refers to the site files that are posted to a remote Web server for the entire world to see. In other words, the local site is for your personal, private use, and the remote site is for public use. You specify the settings for the local Web site and the remote Web site in the site definition.

You will set up the site definition with the local and remote server information for the NextBest Fest site before you begin creating pages for the site.

Setting Up the Local Information

The process for creating the local files for a new site is the same as the process for creating the files for an existing site. You need a site name and a local root folder (called a local site folder in Dreamweaver) to set up the local portion of the site.

You will use "NextBest Fest" as the site name to reference the Web site within Dreamweaver (capitalization and spaces don't matter here because this is only for internal reference). Spaces and symbols (except hyphens and underscores) are not used in folder names or filenames because they can cause problems with some operating systems. This includes the following forbidden characters: *&^%$#@!. Also, some Web servers are case sensitive, so you will use all lowercase letters when naming folders or files. You can place an underscore (_) between words to make the name more readable. Although the maximum number of characters acceptable for a URL is around 2000 characters, best practices indicate that the maximum characters you should use in a filename is 25 characters.

To keep your local root folder organized, it's a good idea to set up additional folders before you begin working on a site and then save all the site files to the folders you designated for them as you go. The local root folder for the site will be named "web," which will be stored in a project folder named "nbf" on the drive you select. Within the web folder, you will create a folder named "graphics" so that you have a designated place within the local root folder to keep the copies of the graphics that you use in the site. This folder structure, nbf\web\graphics, keeps the Dreamweaver files separate from original, uncompressed artwork and working project files stored in the nbf folder that you have not yet added to the site.

You will create the local site for the new NextBest Fest site.

To set up the local site for the NextBest Fest site:

1. Start **Dreamweaver**, reset Dreamweaver to the **Designer** workspace, minimize the Business Catalyst panel, and then close any open pages.

2. On the menu bar, click the **Site** button, and then click **New Site**. The Site Setup for Unnamed Site 2 dialog box opens.

3. Click the **Site** tab, if necessary.

4. In the Site Name box, select the text, if necessary, and then type **NextBest Fest**. NextBest Fest is the name you will use to reference the site within Dreamweaver.

TIP

You can also type the path to the folder in the Local Site Folder box.

5. Next to the Local Site Folder box, click the **Browse** button 📁 to open the Choose Root Folder dialog box, and then navigate to the location where you will store the files for the Web site.

Trouble? If you are unsure of the location in which to store the NextBest Fest site, ask your instructor or technical support person for help.

Filenames, folder names, and paths are often case sensitive. Make sure that you type the names exactly as shown in the steps.

6. Click the **Create New Folder** button 🗁, type **nbf** as the new folder name, press the **Enter** key to name the folder, select the folder, and then click the **Open** button to open the nbf folder.

7. Click the **Create New Folder** button 🗁, type **web** as the new folder name, press the **Enter** key to name the folder, select the folder, and then click the **Open** button to open the folder.

8. Click the **Select** button to set the path for the local root folder.

9. Click the **Advanced Settings** tab to display the list of options, and then click **Local Info**, if necessary. The local information settings appear in the dialog box.

10. Next to the Default Images folder box, click the **Browse** button 🖿. The Choose Image folder dialog box opens.

11. Navigate to the **nbf\web** folder (the local root folder), if necessary, and then click the **Create New Folder** button 🗁. A new folder appears in the dialog box.

12. Type **graphics** as the folder name, press the **Enter** key to name the folder, and then double-click the folder to open it.

13. Click the **Select** button to set the path for the default images folder. Dreamweaver will store all the graphics used in the site in this folder.

14. Click the **Document** option button, if necessary. The links are set relative to the document.

15. Click the **Case-sensitive links checking** check box to select it. This avoids capitalization issues when the site is uploaded to a Web server.

16. Click the **Enable Cache** check box to check it, if necessary. Dreamweaver will quickly update links whenever you move, rename, or delete a file. The information for the local site is complete. See Figure 2-14.

TIP

Sometimes Dreamweaver creates a folder in the local root folder named "_notes." This folder is necessary for Dreamweaver to display the site properly. Do not delete it.

| Figure 2-14 | Local information for the new NextBest Fest site |

links are set relative to the document

your default images folder path will differ

local information settings selected

selected to avoid capitalization issues when the site is uploaded to a Web server

selected so Dreamweaver will quickly update links whenever you move, rename, or delete a file

Setting Up the Remote Server Information

The site definition also includes remote server information (also called the remote site definition). The remote server is where the live site is posted; it is sometimes called the live server. The **remote server information** is the settings stored on the computer that you are using that tell Dreamweaver where the remote server is located and how to connect to it. Including this information in the site definition enables you to put the site on a Web server so that it can be seen on the Web. Viewing a site in a browser on the Web lets you verify that the features of the Web site work in the browser and when viewed by others over the Web. You can add more than one remote server to a Web site because designers sometimes use one server to test the site before it "goes live" for public access, and another server for the final Web server that the public will access. You set up remote servers in much the same way as you set up the local site.

REFERENCE

Setting Up Remote Servers for FTP Access

- On the menu bar, click Site, and then click Manage Sites.
- Click the site name in the list in the Manage Sites dialog box.
- Click the Edit button.
- Click the Servers tab.
- Click the Add new server button.
- Type a name in the Server Name box.
- Select FTP from the Connect using list.
- In the FTP Address box, type the FTP host address where the public version of your Web site will be hosted.
- In the Username box, type your login name.
- In the Password box, type your password, and then click the Save check box to check it if you want Dreamweaver to remember your password.
- In the Root Directory box, type the host directory name.
- Click More Options to reveal additional options.
- Click the Use Passive FTP check box to check it.
- Click the Advanced tab at the top of the dialog box.
- Click the Maintain synchronization information check box to check it.
- Verify that the Automatically upload files to server on Save check box is *not* checked.
- Verify that the Enable file check-out check box is *not* checked.
- Click the Save button in each dialog box.

Before you close the Site Setup dialog box, you will add the remote server information. First, you need to choose how you will access your Web server. Remote access is usually via FTP (File Transfer Protocol), although some larger organizations provide remote access through a local network. These tutorials use FTP to access the remote server. You will need to set the following FTP options in the remote server information:

- **Server name.** An internal name that you select to refer to the server. A server name is included so that you can easily distinguish between servers when multiple servers are available.
- **FTP address.** The full address of the FTP host, which you will use to access the Web server where the public version of the site is stored. For example, the FTP host might be *www.domain.com* or *ftp.domain.com*. Do *not* include a protocol. (A common mistake is to precede the host name with a protocol, such as ftp:// or http://.) The FTP host name is available from your hosting provider.
- **Port.** Port 21 is the default port used by FTP. Most ISPs use port 21. Unless your ISP or your instructor tells you to use another port, use port 21.
- **Username.** Your assigned login name or username.

- **Password.** Your assigned password. After you set the password, you can use the Test button to verify that you have entered the information correctly and that you can connect to the remote server.

Letting Dreamweaver Save Your Password

INSIGHT

Dreamweaver can save your password. During your work session, you should leave the Save check box checked. If you leave the Save check box unchecked, you might have to reenter your password periodically throughout your work session. If you are working on a public system, however, before ending your work session, open the Servers tab in the Site Setup dialog box and uncheck the Save check box. This ensures that the next person to use the computer cannot load your site definition and log on to your account. *If you do not uncheck the Save check box, your password remains on the computer.*

- **Root directory.** The location where your Web site files are located on the Web server. For example, the host directory might be *public_html*. You often see more folders and files if you log on to the host directory through FTP rather than with a Web browser; the Web folder is usually but not always a subfolder of your default FTP folder. The host directory is available from your hosting provider.
- **Use passive FTP.** A server parameter. This information is available from your hosting provider. If you cannot obtain this information, leave the check box checked. If you have difficulties when you preview the site on the Web, reopen the Site Setup dialog box and uncheck the Use Passive FTP check box.
- **Use IPv6 transfer mode.** Internet Protocol version 6 is a newer Internet transfer protocol that will gradually replace the existing protocol, IPv4, over the next several years. Most of today's Internet uses IPv4, which is 20 years old and beginning to have problems. IPv6 fixes a number of problems in IPv4, such as the limited number of available IPv4 addresses. You do not need to check this check box until your ISP instructs you to change to IPv6.
- **Use Proxy, as defined in Preferences.** This option is relevant only if your network includes a firewall (or other system) that requires a password for outbound connections. (This is a rare occurrence, especially in schools, because most network firewalls are not set up to restrict outbound FTP connections.) A **firewall** is a hardware or software device that restricts access between the computer network and the Internet or between a computer and other computers, protecting the computer behind the firewall.
- **Use FTP performance optimization.** This option enables Dreamweaver to increase the speed of server transfers; however, this setting does not work with all servers. Start with this setting checked; then, if you encounter problems connecting when you click the Test button, uncheck this check box and try the test again.
- **Use alternative FTP move method.** There are several methods used, within FTP, to move files. Some servers do not support all methods. Checking this check box enables Dreamweaver to try alternative methods when the most common methods do not work. Do not check this box unless you have problems connecting.
- **Maintain synchronization information.** This option enables Dreamweaver to automatically synchronize your local and remote files. Be aware that if you check this option and the remote server time or your local computer time is not accurate, Dreamweaver might overwrite new files with old files.
- **Automatically upload files to server on save.** This option automatically uploads files to the remote server when you save a page. Do *not* check this check box.
- **Enable file check-out.** This option enables multiple users to access files on the Web site. You will not use this option for these exercises.

You will set up a remote server so that you can preview the NextBest Fest site on the Web. If you do not have access to FTP, you will not be able to create and preview the remote Web site.

To set up a remote server for the NextBest Fest site:

▶ **1.** Click the **Servers** tab in the Site Setup dialog box.

Trouble? If you do not have access to an FTP host on a Web server, you cannot set up a remote server using these steps. Your instructor might provide you with directions for setting up a remote server using a local network. If you do not have access to an FTP host on a Web server, continue with Step 19 to save the site definition.

▶ **2.** Click the **Add new Server** button ➕, if necessary, click the **Connect using** arrow, and then click **FTP**. See Figure 2-15.

| **Figure 2-15** | Remote server setup for FTP access |

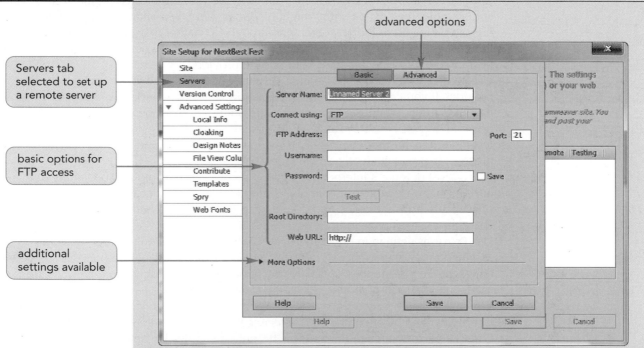

▶ **3.** Select the text in the **Server Name** box, and then type **NB Web Server**.

▶ **4.** Click in the **FTP Address** box, and then type the address to your FTP host, which enables you to connect to the server where the public version of your Web site will be hosted.

▶ **5.** Press the **Tab** key to move the insertion point to the **Port** box. If your ISP uses a different port number for FTP, type the number it provided. Most ISPs use port 21 for FTP. If you are unsure, leave 21 in this box.

▶ **6.** Press the **Tab** key to move the insertion point to the **Username** box, and then type your login or username. Remember that the username is case sensitive on many systems.

▶ **7.** Press the **Tab** key to move the insertion point to the **Password** box, and then type your password. Remember that the password is case sensitive on many systems.

8. Click the **Test** button. Dreamweaver tests the connection to ensure that you can connect to the remote server. A dialog box opens, indicating that Dreamweaver connected to your Web server successfully.

Trouble? If the connection fails, you might have entered some of the information incorrectly. Verify the information you entered in Steps 3 through 7, and then repeat Step 8.

Trouble? If you continue to have problems connecting, click More Options to display additional settings, try unchecking the Use FTP performance optimization check box and test again, then check the Use Passive FTP check box and repeat the test. If problems continue, consult your instructor or your ISP for help.

9. Click the **OK** button. The dialog box closes.

10. Press the **Tab** key to move the insertion point to the **Root Directory** box, and then type the host directory name.

11. Click the **Save** check box to check it, if you want Dreamweaver to remember your password. If you are working on a public computer, remember to uncheck the Save check box before you end your work session.

12. Review the information in the **Web URL** box; if your Web URL information differs from what Dreamweaver has inserted, type the correct information into the box.

13. Click **More Options** to display additional settings, and then click the **Use Passive FTP** check box to check it.

14. If your computer uses a firewall that restricts outbound connections, click the **Use Proxy, as defined in Preferences** check box to check it, and then enter the additional information. *Do not check the Use Proxy, as defined in Preferences check box if your computer uses a Windows or other computer-based software firewall. Most users will not check this box.*

15. Verify that the **Use FTP performance optimization** check box is checked unless this preference caused problems when you clicked the **Test** button. If it did, leave this check box unchecked.

16. Click the **Advanced** tab at the top of the dialog box.

17. Verify that the **Maintain synchronization information** check box is checked and that the **Automatically upload files to server on Save** and the **Enable file check-out** check boxes are unchecked.

18. Click the **Save** button. The Servers dialog box closes, and the NB Web Server is added to the server list in the Site Setup for NextBest Fest dialog box.

19. Click the **Save** button to save the setup information and close the dialog box. The new NextBest Fest site is set up and the nbf site folders appear in the Files panel.

Creating and Saving Pages in a Site

The new NextBest Fest is set up. Now you can work on pages for the site based on the flowchart developed during planning. Gage asks you to create, save, and set page titles for the home page.

Creating an HTML Page in a Site

- On the menu bar, click File, and then click New.
- In the category list, click Blank Page, and then in the Page Type box, click HTML.
- In the Layout box, click <none> to create a blank page or click the desired layout.
- In the DocType box, select HTML 5.
- Click the Create button.

Adding a New Page

Pages that you create for a site will be located within the local root folder specified in the local information of the site definition—in this case, the nbf\web folder. When you create a new page, you select a page category and then the type of page you want to create. You can create a page from scratch or you can use one of the prebuilt page designs that come with Dreamweaver. You can also create a page with Fluid Grid Layout, which enables you to create adaptive Web sites. Adaptive sites display differently on mobile, tablet, and desktop devices. For now, you will create a simple HTML page. In later tutorials, you will learn about the other types of pages.

You will start by creating the home page for the new NextBest Fest site.

To add the home page to the NextBest Fest site:

1. On the menu bar, click **File**, and then click **New**. The New Document dialog box opens.

2. In the category list, click **Blank Page**, if necessary.

3. In the Page Type box, click **HTML**, and then in the Layout box, click **<none>**.

4. Click the **DocType** button, and then click **HTML 5**, if necessary, to create the page in the latest version of HTML. See Figure 2-16.

Figure 2-16   New Document dialog box

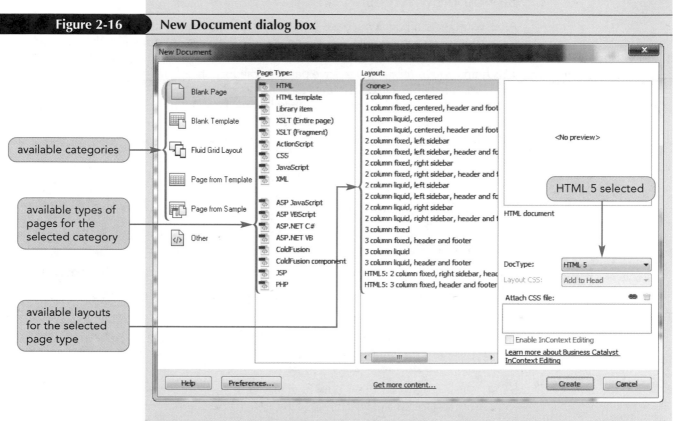

available categories

available types of
pages for the
selected category

available layouts
for the selected
page type

5. Click the **Create** button to create the page. The Untitled-1 page opens in the Document window.

6. On the Document toolbar, click the **Design** button, if necessary. The blank page switches to Design view. See Figure 2-17.

Figure 2-17   New page in Design view

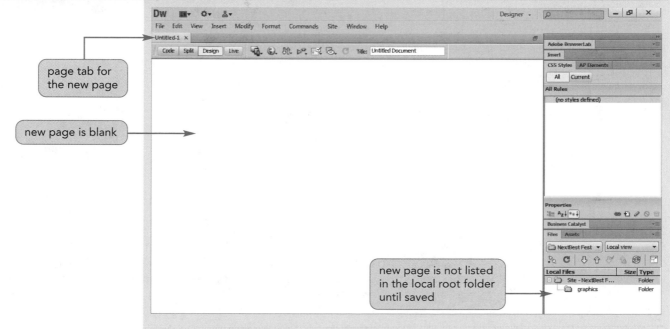

page tab for
the new page

new page is blank

new page is not listed
in the local root folder
until saved

Trouble? If your Document window is restored down, you need to maximize it. Click the Maximize button on the Document window title bar.

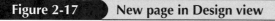

Saving New Pages

After you create a page, you need to save it. It is important to save all the pages in the local root folder for the Web site. When you use the Save As command, the Save As dialog box opens to the local root folder for the site that is selected in the Files panel. This helps you to remember to save pages in the local root folder. When you save a page, you give the page a filename.

You will save the home page with the filename of index.html (or index.htm); remember that *index* must be all lowercase letters. You will use lowercase letters for all of the page filenames. It is important to keep the case of the filenames consistent because some operating systems are case sensitive.

To save the home page:

1. On the menu bar, click **File**, and then click **Save As**. The Save As dialog box opens.

Be sure to save pages you create in the local root folder so that the site works properly on the Internet.

2. Confirm that the dialog box is open to the site's local root folder: **nbf\web**.

3. In the File name box, select the text, and then type **index.html**.

   Trouble? If your server requires .htm file extensions, type index.htm in Step 3 and use .htm as the file extension whenever .html is used in these tutorials. If you are not sure which file extension to use, ask your instructor or technical support person.

4. Click the **Save** button. The new filename appears in the page tab at the top of the Document window and in the Files panel. See Figure 2-18.

| Figure 2-18 | Saved page in the Document window |

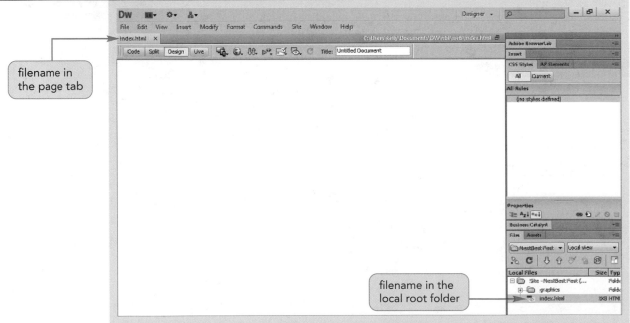

filename in the page tab

filename in the local root folder

   Trouble? If you don't see the new file in the Files panel, the Files panel is probably set to Remote view. Click the View button on the Files panel toolbar, and then click Local view.

Setting Page Titles

Before you close the page, you will set the page title for the page. Recall that the page title is the name that appears in the browser title bar. You should use the name of the Web site and a descriptive word or phrase for each page so that users can quickly determine the overall page content. For example, you will enter "NextBest Fest - Home" as the page title for the home page.

To add the page title for the home page:

1. In the Title box on the Document toolbar, select **Untitled Document**.

2. Type **NextBest Fest - Home**.

3. Press the **Enter** key. The asterisk next to the filename in the page tab indicates that changes have been made to the page since it was last saved. See Figure 2-19.

Figure 2-19   **Page title set for the home page**

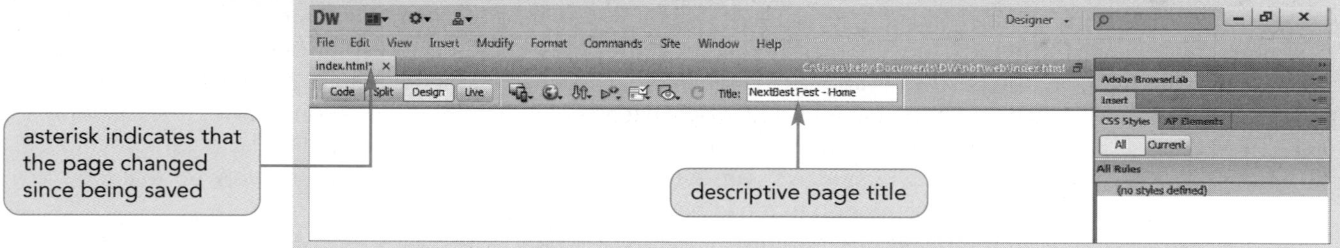

asterisk indicates that the page changed since being saved

descriptive page title

Resaving Pages

Dreamweaver has several built-in measures to help you keep your work safe. If you have not saved a page after you have edited it and you try to close the page or exit the program, Dreamweaver prompts you to save the changes you made to that page. If you use an element such as a graphic in a page and that element is not yet part of the site, Dreamweaver saves a copy of the element in the local root folder. (Dreamweaver will automatically save a copy of each graphic you use in a page if you've created a default graphics folder. Otherwise, Dreamweaver will prompt you to save a copy of the graphic or element.) By including copies of all of the files associated with a site within its local root folder, you prevent a myriad of complications from occurring.

INSIGHT

Saving Frequently

It is important to save frequently—at least every 10 minutes—and whenever you have finished modifying a page. Also, make sure that all pages in the Web site are saved before you preview the site. Anyone who has worked on a computer for any length of time can confirm that programs crash at the least opportune moment. Saving your work frequently prevents large losses.

You will resave the home page, and then you will close the page.

To resave and close the home page:

▶ **1.** On the menu bar, click **File**, and then click **Save**. The asterisk in the page tab disappears.

▶ **2.** On the page tab, click the **Close Page** button ⓧ. The home page closes.

Reviewing HTML Tags

Because many types of computers are connected to the Web and people use different operating systems and software on their computers, Web pages are not tied to any specific software package. Instead, Web pages are created in a common markup language that is viewable by a variety of software packages, including Web browsers. HTML, the most common language of the Web, uses a series of tags to tell a browser what to do with the information on a Web page and how to display it.

Even though Dreamweaver provides a graphical interface for creating a Web site in HTML, a basic understanding of HTML is important to gain a true sense of what is going on. These tutorials describe HTML version 5. Web pages are text documents that include specific markup tags that tell a Web browser how to display the elements. Tags almost always appear in sets, and each tag is included within angle brackets, < and >. The opening tag tells a browser that a certain type of information follows. The opening tag also contains any parameters or attributes that are to be applied to that information. The closing tag always starts with a forward slash, /, which tells the browser that the type of information that had been started is now finished.

Some tags are required for every Web page. These tags—HTML, head, title, and body—are described in Figure 2-20.

Figure 2-20 **Basic HTML tags**

Name	Opening Tag	Closing Tag	Description
HTML	<html>	</html>	Signify where the HTML code begins and ends; usually appear at the beginning and ending of a Web page. Everything inside the <html> and </html> tags is HTML unless specifically denoted as something else by another type of tag.
head	<head>	</head>	Contain the page title, the descriptive information for the page, which is not seen in the browser, and programming scripts.
title	<title>	</title>	Surround the page title, which appears in the title bar of the browser window when a viewer opens that page.
body	<body>	</body>	Surround all the content or visible elements on the page. Include other tags to format the content. Also contain some scripts.

© 2013 Cengage Learning

Many other tags appear within the body of a document to format the content. Other types of code, such as JavaScript and Cascading Style Sheets, are often used within HTML to add further functionality and formatting to pages. For example, you might include JavaScript that adjusts the page to optimize display for the user's browser, and you can use Cascading Styles to format the display of text, graphics, page properties, and so on. You will see these additional tags as you continue to build the pages for the new NextBest Fest site.

PROSKILLS

Teamwork: Broadening Your Understanding to Strengthen the Team

It is a good idea to gain a general knowledge and understanding of all the components involved in creating an effective Web site. No matter what your role is, understanding the project as a whole, and understanding what is required of your teammates, makes you better equipped to do your job and it makes you a more valuable member of the team. Employers look for people who can understand the big picture and can contribute to the project in ways that may move beyond the limited scope of their current position. For example, it is a good idea to gain a basic understanding of HTML, even if you are not a Web site programmer. Graphic designers benefit from this knowledge because they are better able to create useful designs when they understand the breadth and limits of the HTML code. Account managers are better able to manage client expectation and to facilitate successful projects when they understand HTML code and other aspects of programming and design. The possibilities are endless; the more you know, the more valuable you become.

You will review the HTML tags that Dreamweaver generated when you created the home page.

To review HTML tags in the NextBest Fest home page:

1. In the Files panel, double-click **index.html**. The home page opens in the Document window.

2. On the Document toolbar, click the **Code** button. The underlying HTML code for the home page is displayed. See Figure 2-21. The line numbers are only for reference; the line numbers shown in the figure might not match the ones on your screen. Also, the lines of code on your screen might wrap differently than those in the figure.

Figure 2-21	HTML code for the home page

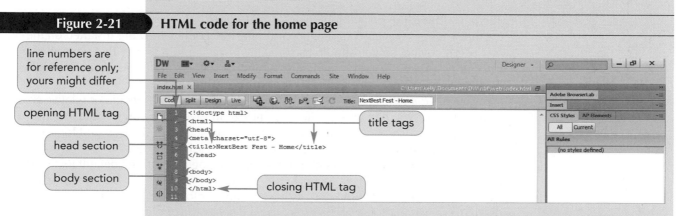

Trouble? If you cannot see all of the code, you might need to scroll. Drag the horizontal scroll box all the way to the left edge of the horizontal scroll bar.

Although you will usually work in Design view, you can create and edit your pages in Code view. You will use Code view to change the page title for the home page.

To edit the home page in Code view:

▶ **1.** In the Document window, locate the title tags.

▶ **2.** Between the title tags, select **-** (the hyphen), and then type **:** (a colon). The page title is updated to include a colon with spaces on either side as a graphics element. You will switch to Design view to review the change.

▶ **3.** On the Document toolbar, click the **Design** button. The home page is displayed in Design view. The text in the Title box on the Document toolbar shows the revised page title, which you changed directly in the code.

▶ **4.** On the menu bar, click **File**, and then click **Save**. The change you made to the home page is saved.

Setting Page Properties

After you have created the first page in the site, the next step is setting the basic page properties. **Page properties** are attributes that apply to an entire page rather than to only an element in the page. The page properties are split into six categories: Appearance (CSS), Appearance (HTML), Links (CSS), Headings (CSS), Title/Encoding, and Tracing Image. Most page properties are created with Cascading Styles, but you can change the appearance of various page elements like text color and size using HTML applied directly to each element. In most cases, it is a good idea to separate the look from the content of your pages. To follow this practice, you will use CSS to alter the appearance of page elements.

Setting the Appearance (CSS) Properties

The Appearance (CSS) category includes general page properties, or settings, for the default text, background, and margin. Text settings that you need to specify include the page font, the font size, and the text color:

- The page font is the default font that is used to display page text. Remember, browsers that are not HTML5-compliant can display fonts only if they are installed on the end user's device, so you should use the Dreamweaver font groups that were shown in Figure 2-10 to ensure the highest possibility of successful display. You will use the Arial, Helvetica, sans-serif group for the NextBest Fest site.
- Size sets the default size for text in the page. You can select a specific or relative size from the list or you can type a different font size in the box. If you select a specific size, you must also choose a unit. Pixels are the most frequently used unit for specific font size. You will use a variety of sizes in the NextBest Fest site.
- The text color sets the default color for text on the page. The initial default text color is black, which has the hexadecimal color code #000000. When you want to select a different color and do not know its hexadecimal color code, you can use the color picker to select a color swatch from a visual display and Dreamweaver will insert the corresponding hexadecimal color code. You should then enter the hexadecimal color code each time you insert the color to ensure that you use the exact same color. Figure 2-22 shows the color picker in the Page Properties dialog box.

Figure 2-22   **Page Properties dialog box with the color picker**

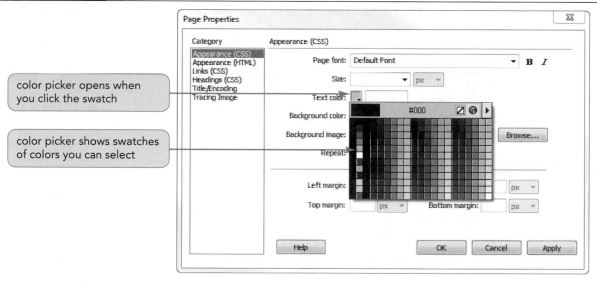

color picker opens when you click the swatch

color picker shows swatches of colors you can select

The background settings include the background color and the background image for the page. A Web page background can be an image, a color, or both. If both are used, the color will appear while the image is downloading, and then the image will cover up the color. If the image contains transparent pixels, the background color will show through. The default background is no color, and most browsers display an absence of color as white. You will use gray, which has the hexadecimal color code #666666, for the background color of the new NextBest Fest site. Later, you will add a background image to a portion of the page.

You can also set the margins for the page. **Margins** are measurements that specify where page content is placed in the page. You can specify left, right, bottom, and top page margin spaces. The new NextBest Fest site will have all margins set to 0.

You will set the Appearance (CSS) page properties for the pages you added to the new NextBest Fest site.

To set the Appearance (CSS) page properties for the home page:

1. On the menu bar, click **Modify**, and then click **Page Properties**. The Page Properties dialog box opens with the Appearance (CSS) category selected.

2. Click the **Page font** arrow, and then click **Arial, Helvetica, sans-serif**. The Dreamweaver font group is selected.

3. Click the **Size** arrow, and then click **14**. The default size for the page text is set to 14 pixels.

4. Click in the **Text color** box, type **#666666** (the hexadecimal color code for dark gray that was selected during the planning process), and then press the **Tab** key. The color box changes to dark gray to match the color code you just entered.

5. Click the **Background color** swatch to open the color picker, and then point to the **gray** swatch. The hexadecimal color code at the top of the color picker changes as you move the pointer over the color swatches.

6. Click the **gray** swatch that displays #666 in the color picker to select the lighter gray swatch as the background color. The abbreviated hexadecimal color code #666 appears in the Background color box.

7. Click in the **Left margin** box, and then type **0**.

TIP

Dreamweaver displays a three-number abbreviation of the hexadecimal color code when both characters in a pair representing red, green, or blue are the same. For example, Dreamweaver displays #345 for the hexadecimal color code #334455.

8. Press the **Tab** key twice to move the insertion point to the Right margin box, and then type **0**.

9. Press the **Tab** key twice to move the insertion point to the Top margin box, and then type **0**.

10. Press the **Tab** key twice to move the insertion point to the Bottom margin box, and then type **0**. All of the margins for the home page are set to 0. You've entered all the Appearance (CSS) properties for the home page. See Figure 2-23.

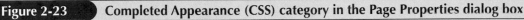

Figure 2-23   **Completed Appearance (CSS) category in the Page Properties dialog box**

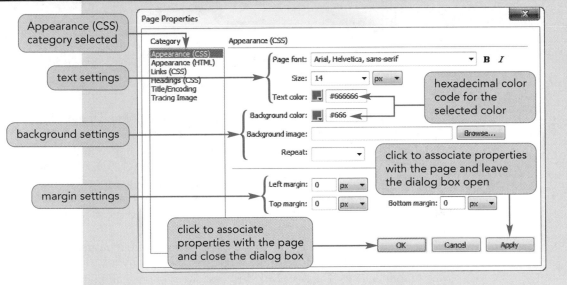

Setting the Links (CSS) Properties

The Links (CSS) category includes the page properties for hyperlinked text. You can select Same as Page Font from the Link Font list to use the page font for hyperlinked text, or you can select a different font group from the list if you want hyperlinked text to appear in another font. For the NextBest Fest site, you will use the same font for links and text, and you will not set a size.

You can set a default color for hyperlinked text in the page. If you do not specify a color for visited or active links, the browser's default colors will be used. The new NextBest Fest site will use olive for the links and the visited links and blue-green for the active links. The final attribute in the Links category is the Underline option. You can choose to always underline linked text, never underline linked text, show underline only on rollover, or hide underline on rollover. The NextBest Fest site will show underline only on rollover.

Next, you will set the page properties for the Links (CSS) category.

To set Links (CSS) page properties for the home page:

1. In the Category box, click **Links (CSS)**. The Page Properties dialog box shows the settings for the Links (CSS) category.

2. Click in the **Link color** box, and then type **#666633** (the hexadecimal color code for olive).

3. Click the **Rollover links** box, and then type **#99cbb3** (the hexadecimal color code for blue-green).

4. Click in the **Visited links** box, and then type **#666633** (the hexadecimal color code for olive).

5. Click in the **Active links** box, and then type **#99cbb3** (the hexadecimal color code for blue-green).

6. Click the **Underline style** button, and then click **Show underline only on rollover**. You've entered all the Links (CSS) properties. See Figure 2-24.

| Figure 2-24 | Completed Links (CSS) category in the Page Properties dialog box |

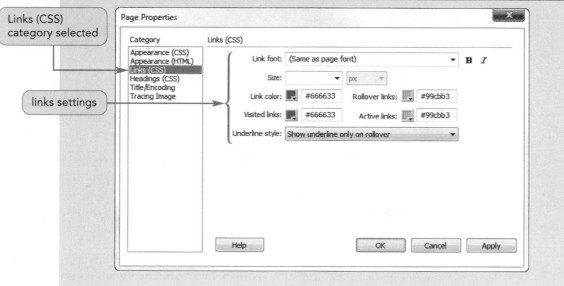

Setting the Headings (CSS) Properties

The Headings (CSS) category enables you to set font, font size, and font color attributes for the headings. There are two headings for the new NextBest Fest site. The top-level heading, Heading 1, will be 30 pixels in size and blue-green in color. The second-level heading, Heading 2, will be 20 pixels in size and olive in color.

You will set the page properties for the Heading 1 category. You will leave the default heading font setting, which is to use the same fonts that are specified for the page font in the Appearance (CSS) category.

To set Headings (CSS) page properties for the home page:

1. In the Category box, click **Headings (CSS)**. The Page Properties dialog box shows the settings for the Headings (CSS) category.

2. In the Heading 1 box, type **30**. The Heading 1 font size is set to 30 pixels.

3. Click in the Heading 1 color box, type **#99cbb3** (the hexadecimal color code for blue-green), and then press the **Tab** key. You've entered all the Headings (CSS) properties. See Figure 2-25.

| Figure 2-25 | Completed Headings (CSS) category in the Page Properties dialog box |

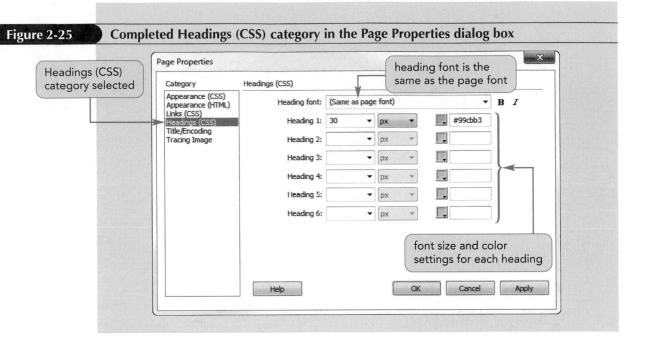

Setting the Title/Encoding and Tracing Image Properties

The Title/Encoding category enables you to set the page title and document encoding type. The page title can also be set from the Document window, as you did earlier. **Document encoding** specifies how the digital codes will display the characters in the Web page. The default Western European setting is the setting for English and other Western European languages.

The Tracing Image category enables you to select an image as a guide for re-creating a design or mock-up that was originally created in a graphics program. For example, if you created a site mock-up in Adobe Photoshop, you could import a copy of that mock-up into Dreamweaver as a tracing image. You could then use that image as a reference while re-creating the individual elements in Dreamweaver. The tracing image is visible only in Dreamweaver.

You don't need to make any changes to the Title/Encoding or Tracing Image properties for the home page. You will save and close the Page Properties dialog box, and then save and close the home page.

To save the page properties:

▶ **1.** Click the **OK** button. The Page Properties dialog box closes, and the property settings are applied to the home page. See Figure 2-26.

Figure 2-26   **Home page with the page properties set**

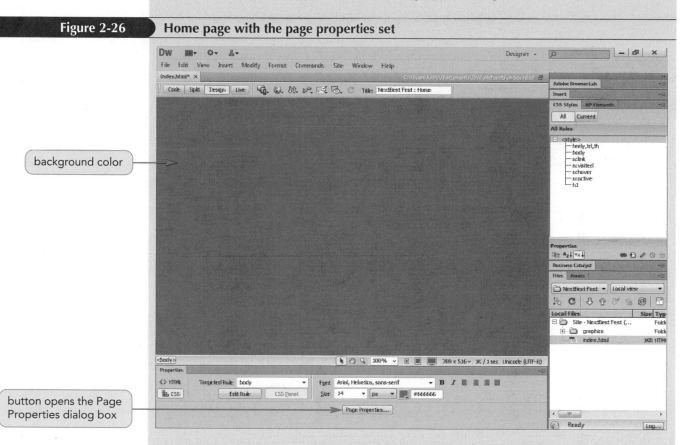

background color

button opens the Page Properties dialog box

▶ **2.** On the menu bar, click **File**, and then click **Save**. The page properties are saved with the page.

Previewing a Site in a Browser

Variations often exist in the way that different browsers display Web pages and even in the way that different versions of the same browser display Web pages. For example, elements such as fonts and colors may display differently. That is why after you have started building a Web site, you should preview it in all of the browsers that you are planning to support. NextBest Fest plans to support both Internet Explorer and Firefox, two of the most commonly used browsers.

You can preview a Web site in any browser that appears in the Dreamweaver preview list. If the browser you want to support doesn't appear in the preview list, you can add it to the list. You should designate the two browsers that you consider the target audience to use most frequently as the primary and secondary browsers. Dreamweaver defaults to the primary browser when you preview your work, and both the primary and secondary browsers have keyboard shortcuts.

To make a browser the primary browser, you check the Primary browser check box when the browser is selected in the preview list. To make a browser the secondary browser, you check the Secondary browser check box when the browser is selected. If you do not check either the Primary browser or Secondary browser check box, the browser will be added to the Preview in Browser list on the File menu, but it will not have a keyboard shortcut. These tutorials use Internet Explorer version 9 as the primary browser.

To add a primary browser to the preview list:

1. On the menu bar, click **File**, point to **Preview in Browser,** and then click **Edit Browser List**. The Preferences dialog box opens with Preview in Browser selected in the Category box. See Figure 2-27.

| Figure 2-27 | Preferences dialog box |

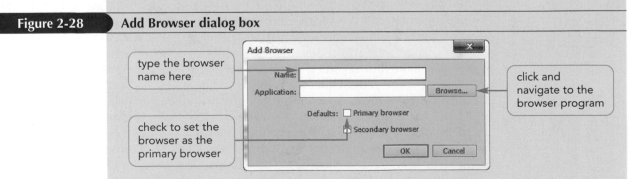

- button to add a browser to the list
- available browsers (your preview list might differ)
- selected browser is the primary browser

2. Look for the browser that you plan to use as the primary browser in the Browsers box. If the browser is listed, click the browser to select it, check the **Primary browser** check box as needed, and then skip to Step 8. If the browser is not listed, continue with Step 3.

3. If you need to add a browser to the preview list, click the Browsers **Add** button ⊞. The Add Browser dialog box opens. See Figure 2-28.

| Figure 2-28 | Add Browser dialog box |

- type the browser name here
- click and navigate to the browser program
- check to set the browser as the primary browser

4. In the Name box, type the name of the browser you are adding.

5. Click the **Browse** button to open the Select Browser dialog box, navigate to the folder containing the browser that you want to add, click the browser program icon, and then click the **Open** button. The path to the file that you selected appears in the Application box.

   Trouble? If you cannot find the browser program icon on the computer that you are using, ask your instructor or technical support person for help.

6. Click the **Primary browser** check box to insert a check mark. Dreamweaver will default to this browser when you preview your work.

7. Click the **OK** button in the Add Browser dialog box. The browser appears in the preview list.

8. Click the **OK** button in the Preferences dialog box. The primary browser is set.

You will use the primary browser to preview the home page you created for the new NextBest Fest site.

TIP

Click the Secondary browser check box to make the selected browser the secondary browser for previewing. If neither check box is checked, the selected browser will be added to the Preview in Browser list on the File menu, but it will not have a keyboard shortcut.

TIP

You can also press the F12 key to preview the page in the primary browser.

To preview the home page in the primary browser:

1. On the menu bar, click **File**, point to **Preview in Browser**, and then click **IExplore** or the name of your primary browser. (Remember to allow blocked content, if necessary, whenever you preview a page.) The browser opens and displays the home page. See Figure 2-29.

Figure 2-29   Home page previewed in Internet Explorer

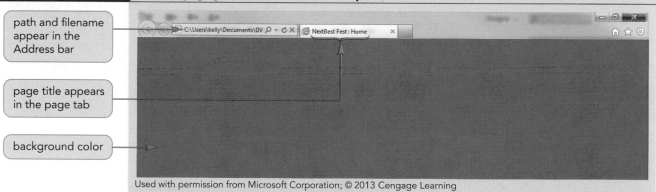

path and filename appear in the Address bar

page title appears in the page tab

background color

Used with permission from Microsoft Corporation; © 2013 Cengage Learning

2. Review the page. The background color is displayed, the page title appears in the title bar and page tab, and the filename is shown in the Address bar.

   Trouble? If a banner appears across the top of the page stating that intranet settings are now turned off by default, ask your instructor or technical support person for help.

3. Close the browser.

4. On the page tab, click the **Close Page** button ⊠. The home page closes.

Uploading a Web Site to a Remote Server

After you have created pages in a Web site, you should upload the site to your remote server: either a Web server or your network server. You upload a Web site to your remote server so that you can view the site over the Web as the end users will see it. Previewing the site from within Dreamweaver is a convenient way to check a site for problems as you work, but you should also upload the site periodically as you work on it, at least once each day, to make sure that it displays correctly. Sometimes the way a page previews within Dreamweaver is different from the way it looks when it is viewed on the Web. You set up the remote server information when you created the site definition.

REFERENCE

Uploading a Web Site to a Remote Server

- On the Files panel toolbar, click the Connect to Remote Server button.
- Select the files in the local root folder that you want to upload.
- On the Files panel toolbar, click the Put file(s) button.
- On the Files panel toolbar, click the Disconnect from Remote Server button.

All of the files that the remote version of a Web site will use must be located on the Web server. The first time you upload a site, you must include all the files and folders for the site, including the graphics located in the graphics folder. From then on, you can update the remote site by uploading only files that have changed. When you upload a Web page or group of pages, Dreamweaver prompts you to upload the dependent files. **Dependent files** are files, such as graphics files, that are used in the Web page or pages. If you have not yet uploaded these files, or if you have modified them, you need to upload these dependent files. However, if you have already uploaded them and you have not modified them, it is not necessary to upload them again. Dreamweaver transfers multiple files at the same time, reducing the time you spend waiting for files to transfer.

When you upload the pages to the remote server, be careful to use the Put file(s) button on the Files panel toolbar, not the Get file(s) button. The Get file(s) button downloads the files from the remote server to your local root folder, and you might overwrite the more current files in your local root folder. Dreamweaver also provides visual cues to indicate the file transfer direction and the files waiting to be transferred. An up arrow appears to the left of the filename when a file is being *put* to the server and a down arrow appears to the left of the filename when you *get* a file from the server. A green arrow indicates that the file is being transferred, and an orange arrow indicates that the file is in the queue to be transferred.

You will upload the new NextBest Fest site to the remote server so you can preview it on the Web.

To upload the NextBest Fest site to your remote server:

▶ **1.** On the Files panel toolbar, click the **Connect to Remote Server** button 🔌. When Dreamweaver is connected to the remote server, you see a green light on the Connect to Remote Server button.

Trouble? If you do not have access to a remote server, you cannot upload the site. Check with your instructor for alternate instructions. If there are no alternate instructions, skip to Step 9.

2. On the Files panel toolbar, click the **View** button, and then click **Local view**, if necessary.

3. Click the **graphics** folder, press and hold the **Shift** key, and then click **index.html** to select both in the local files list; these are the folder and file you want to upload to the server.

4. On the Files panel toolbar, click the **Put file(s)** button ⬆. A dialog box opens, prompting you to include dependent files. You have already selected all of the dependent files for the site—the graphics folder—in addition to the pages.

5. Click the **No** button.

6. On the Files panel toolbar, click the **View** button, and then click **Remote server**. The Files panel switches to Remote Server view, and you see the list of files you uploaded to the remote server.

7. On the Files panel toolbar, click the **Expand to show local and remote sites** button 🗗. The Files panel expands to display both the Remote Server and Local views. See Figure 2-30.

Figure 2-30   **Files panel with Remote Server view and Local view**

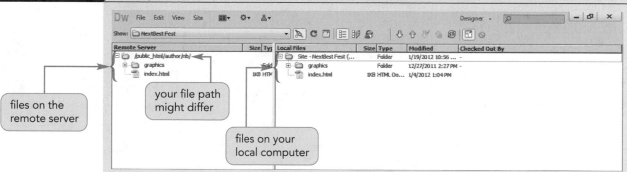

files on the remote server

your file path might differ

files on your local computer

8. On the Files panel toolbar, click the **Disconnect from Remote Server** button 🔌, click the **Collapse to show only local or remote site** button 🗗 to collapse the Files panel, click the **View** button, and then click **Local view** to return to Local view.

    If you are working on a shared computer, continue with Step 9; otherwise, read but do not perform Steps 9 and 10.

9. If you are working on a shared computer, on the menu bar, click the **Site** button, click **Manage Sites** to open the Manage Sites dialog box, make sure **NextBest Fest** is selected in the list, and then click the **Edit** button. The Site Definition for NextBest Fest dialog box opens.

10. In the Category box, click **Remote Info**, click the **Save** check box to uncheck it, click the **OK** button, and then click the **Done** button in the Manage Sites dialog box. Now, the next person who uses the computer cannot use the remote site definition to log on to your account because the password will not be saved in the remote site definition when you close Dreamweaver.

Previewing a Remote Site on the Web

When the files are uploaded to the remote site, you and others can view them in a browser. You will explore the remote site using a browser to check if the page looks the same on the Web as it does in Dreamweaver. If you find differences, such as extra spaces, write them down and discuss them with your instructor. At this point, the only difference that you should see is in the site address. When you preview over the Web, the site will have an actual Web address instead of a file path.

To view the NextBest Fest home page from your remote server:

1. Start your Web browser, type the URL of your remote site into the Address bar on the browser toolbar, and then press the **Enter** key. The index.html page of the NextBest Fest site from the remote server loads in the browser window. See Figure 2-31.

Figure 2-31 NextBest Fest home page viewed over the Web

URL to the remote site (yours will differ)

Used with permission from Microsoft Corporation; © 2013 Cengage Learning

Trouble? If the browser window displays the list of files stored on the remote site, double-click the index.html file to open the home page.

Trouble? If the browser displays a warning that the listing was denied, type the base URL of the remote site, type "/" (a forward slash), and then type "index.html" into the Address bar.

Trouble? If the page does not display correctly, the files might have been corrupted during the upload process, or you might not have uploaded all the dependent files. Repeat the previous set of steps to upload all of the files to the remote location. If you still have problems with your remote site, you might need to edit the remote site definition and click the Use Passive FTP check box to uncheck it. If you still have problems and your remote server is a Windows server, using a stand-alone FTP program to upload all the files to your remote server might solve the problem. Ask your instructor or technical support person for help.

2. Close the browser.

You have finished creating the home page for the new NextBest Fest site, setting the page properties for the home page, and previewing the page. In the next tutorial, you will create the structure of the pages.

REVIEW

Session 2.3 Quick Check

1. What is the difference between a local site and a remote site?
2. Why would you want to view a site on a remote server?
3. Where are new pages that you create for the site stored?
4. True or False. It is important to keep the case of the filenames consistent because some operating systems are case sensitive.
5. True or False. Web pages are created in a common markup language that is viewable by a variety of software packages, including Web browsers.
6. What are page properties?
7. Why should you preview a site in all of the browsers you are planning to support?
8. What are dependent files?

Practice the skills you learned in the tutorial.

PRACTICE

Review Assignments

There are no Data Files needed for the Review Assignments.

Web design teams often develop two or three Web site layouts and designs for a client, who then chooses one concept for development. The alternate design can have a different metaphor, can be based on reordered site goals, or can be geared for another target audience.

Dan and Cat are ready to get started planning the new antifest site. Dan asks you to take the lead in planning and designing the Web site. Remember that a site devoted to alternative music tends to appeal to a different audience than the NextBest Fest site. Research this target audience, and then base your decisions for the antifest site on that research.

1. Define a list of site goals for the antifest site.
2. Research and identify the target audience for the alternative music festival site.
3. Create a user profile for the site.
4. Conduct market research to gather information about indie music sites and other Web sites that cater to your target audience.
5. Develop two end-user scenarios for the site.
6. Create an information category outline arranged in hierarchical order for the site.
7. Create a flowchart for the site.
8. Develop a site concept and a metaphor for the site.
9. Choose a color palette, fonts, and a graphics style.
10. Create a rough sketch of the layout for the site.
11. In Dreamweaver, reset the workspace to the default Designer workspace.
12. Set up the local portion of the site in the Site tab and the Local Info tab (in the Advanced Settings tab). Use **antifest** as the site name. Use the Browse button to identify the local root folder as a **web** folder that you create within a folder named **anti** in the location where you are storing your Web site files. Create a folder named **graphics** in the local root folder and select that folder as the default images folder. Use case-sensitive links checking, and enable the cache.
13. Set up a remote server using FTP access for the antifest site.
14. Add the home page to the antifest site, using **index.html** as the filename and HTML 5 as the DocType. Open the **index.html** page in the Document window, and then set an appropriate page title. In the Page Properties dialog box, set the page font to Courier New, Courier, monospace; set the size to 12; set the text color to #fff; and then set the background color to #000. Set the left and top margins to 5 px and set the right and bottom margins to 0 px. Set the links, visited links, and active links colors to #f0f and the rollover link color to #fff, and then set the underline style to show underline only on rollover. Save the page.
15. Review the HTML tags for the home page in Code view.
16. Preview the page in your browser, looking for accuracy in display. The page should have a black background, and the page title that you assigned should appear in the browser title bar and the page tab. Close the browser and the open page.
17. Upload the site to your live server, selecting all the files and the folder for upload.
18. Preview the page on the Web. Again, the page should have a background and the page title you assigned should appear in the browser title bar and the page tab.
19. Submit your finished files to your instructor.

Plan and design a Web site for an independent skateboard company.

RESEARCH

Case Problem 1

Data Files needed for this Case Problem: moebius.docx, moebius_bg.jpg

Moebius Skateboards   To initiate the planning and design for the Web site you are creating for Moebius, you asked Corey to provide you with a list of site goals, ideas on a target audience, and the material that he wants to include on the site. Corey responds with a memo that outlines the decisions he has made so far. You will use the information from the memo to plan the Web site. Corey, however, did not provide all the requested information (a common occurrence when working with clients). You will use the information that was provided as a starting point. It will be necessary for you to research and make some decisions on your own.

1. In Microsoft Word or another word-processing program, open the **moebius.docx** file located in the Dreamweaver2\Case1 folder included with your Data Files, and then read the memo.
2. Review the goals that Corey listed, and then create a list of site goals for the Web site. Consider the order of importance and wording.
3. Define a target audience and a user profile for the site. (*Hint*: Search online sources to learn more about the groups of people listed in the memo.)
4. Conduct market research. Find and review at least four Web sites owned by skateboard companies or that provide information on skateboarding and the skate culture.
5. Write a paragraph documenting the findings from your market research. Include the URLs of the Web sites that you visited as well as information about categories of information, graphics style, layout, and site metaphor.
6. Create three end-user scenarios for the site.
7. Develop an information category outline. Base the categories and hierarchy on the memo and your market research.
8. Create a flowchart for the site.
9. Develop a site concept and metaphor for the site. (Even sites that have minimal design can benefit from a site metaphor.)
10. **EXPLORE** Investigate usability guidelines that deal with text. Research these guidelines at *www.w3.org/WAI*. Write down your findings and use them when making font choices.
11. Design a color palette for the site. Write a paragraph explaining your choice.
12. Choose the fonts for the site. Write a paragraph explaining your choices.
13. Plan the graphics style of the site. Write a paragraph explaining your choice.
14. Create a rough sketch of the layout of the site. Write a paragraph explaining your choice.
15. Check the design for logic by reviewing the decisions that you have made. Make sure that your design reinforces the site goals and supports the site metaphor.
16. Set up the site, using **Moebius Skateboards** as the site name and **moebius\web** as the local root folder in the folder and location where you are storing your Web site. Create a folder named **graphics** in the local root folder and select that folder as the default images folder. Use case-sensitive links checking and enable the cache.
17. Set up a live server using FTP access for the Moebius site.
18. Create an HTML page for the home page using **index.html** as the filename and HTML 5 as the DocType. Open the page in the Document window, and then enter **Moebius - Home** as the page title.

EXPLORE 19. In the Page Properties dialog box, in the Appearance (CSS) category, set the background image to the **moebius_bg.jpg** file located in the Dreamweaver2\Case1 folder included with your Data Files. Select repeat from the Repeat list, use the default font for the page font, set the text color to #66ff33, and set the text size to 12. Set the link color, rollover links, visited links, and active links to #cc00cc and set the underline style to always underline.

20. Save the page, and then preview the page in your browser. The page should have a background image, and the page title you assigned to it should appear in the page tab.

21. Review the HTML tags for the home page in Code view, and then close any open pages.

22. Upload the site to your remote server, including all the files and the folder.

23. View the pages on the Web. Again, the page should have a background image and the page title you assigned to it should appear in the browser title bar and page tab.

24. Submit your finished files to your instructor.

Plan and design a Web site for an art society.

RESEARCH

Case Problem 2

There are no Data Files needed for this Case Problem.

Cowboy Art Society Dr. Monomer (Moni) Palmer asks you to work on the plan and design of the new Web site for the Cowboy Art Society. To develop a feasible plan, you need to conduct market research on other western art sites. In addition, Moni asks you to research the current accessibility guidelines for using alternate text descriptions on graphics. You will then set up the new site, add the home page to the site, and set page properties.

1. Define the goals for the site.

2. Define a target audience and a user profile for the site.

3. Conduct market research. Find and review at least four Web sites that deal with western art. (*Hint*: Use a search engine to search for the keywords **western art**, **cowboy art**, and **Texas museums**.)

4. Write a paragraph documenting the findings from your market research. Include the URLs of the Web sites that you visited as well as information about categories of information, graphics style, layout, and site metaphor.

5. Create two end-user scenarios for the site.

6. Develop an information category outline for the site.

7. Create a flowchart for the site.

8. Develop a site concept and metaphor for the site. Write a paragraph explaining your choices.

EXPLORE 9. Investigate usability guidelines that deal with Alt text, which are messages that can be read by assistive devices. They are used with graphics buttons and so on to make the site more accessible. Research these guidelines at *www.w3.org/WAI*. Write down your findings to use when working on the site's graphics.

10. Design a color palette, choose the fonts, and select a graphics style for the site. Write a paragraph explaining your choices.

11. Create rough sketches of two layouts for the site. Write a paragraph explaining which layout you prefer and why.

12. Check the logical layout of the design you prefer by reviewing the decisions that you have made. Make sure that your design reinforces the site goals and supports the site metaphor.

13. Set up the site, using **Cowboy Charlie** as the site name and **charlie\web** as the folder and location where you are storing your Web sites as the local root folder. Create a folder named **graphics** in the local root folder, and select that folder as the default images folder. Use case-sensitive links checking and enable the cache.

14. Set up a live server using FTP access for the Cowboy Charlie site.

15. Create the home page for the site; use **index.html** as the filename and HTML 5 as the DocType. Enter **Cowboy Charlie - Home** as the page title. (*Hint*: Click HTML in the Create New category on the Welcome screen.)

16. Click the Page Properties button in the Property inspector. Set the page font to Times New Roman, Times, serif; set the size to medium because the Cowboy Art Society requested that the site conform to current accessibility standards; set the text color to #666666; and then set the background color to #7c6c53. Set the links, visited links, rollover links, and active links colors to #666666, and then set the underline style to hide underline on rollover. Set heading 1 to size xx-large and color #993300. Set heading 2 to size large and color #6a7029. Save the page.

17. Preview the page in your browser. The page should have a background color, and the page title you assigned to it should appear in the browser title bar and in the page tab.

18. Upload the site to your remote server. Remember to select all the files and the folder for upload.

19. View the pages on the Web. Again, the page should have a background color and the page title you assigned to it should appear in the browser title bar and in the page tab.

20. Submit your finished files to your instructor.

Plan and design a Web site for a life coach.

RESEARCH

Case Problem 3

Data File needed for this Case Problem: tess.docx

Success with Tess   The Web design team is in the initial planning phase of designing the Success with Tess Web site. Using your research on life coaching, you will develop a plan for the new site. You will then create the new site, add the home page, and set the page properties.

1. In Microsoft Word or another word-processing program, open the **tess.docx** file located in the Dreamweaver2\Case3 folder included with your Data Files, and then read the memo.

2. Define a list of goals for the site.

3. Define a target audience and a user profile for the site.

4. Conduct market research as needed by visiting competitors' sites.

5. Compose two end-user scenarios for the site.

6. Develop an information category outline for the site.

7. Create a flowchart for the site.

8. Develop a site concept and metaphor for the site. Write a paragraph explaining your choices.

9. Design a color palette, choose the fonts, and select a graphics style for the site. Write a paragraph explaining your choices.

10. Create a rough sketch of the layout of the site. Write a paragraph explaining your choice.

11. Check the layout of the design for logic by reviewing the decisions that you have made. Make sure that your design reinforces the site goals and supports the site metaphor.

12. Set up the site, using **Success with Tess** as the site name and **tess\web** as the local root folder in the folder and location where you are storing your Web sites. Create a folder named **graphics** in the local root folder, and select that folder as the default images folder. Use case-sensitive links checking and enable the cache.

13. Set up a live server using FTP access for the Success with Tess site.

14. Create a new HTML page for the home page using **index.html** as the filename and HTML 5 as the DocType. Use **Success with Tess - Home** as the page title.

15. Set the following page properties: Set the page font to Arial, Helvetica, sans-serif; set the font size to 12 pixels; set the text color to #333; set the background color to white #fff; and set all the margins to 0.

16. Set links, visited links, and active links colors to #ffa011, set rollover links to #ffffff, and set the underline style to hide underline on rollover. Set heading 1 to size 24 pixels and color #ffa011. Set heading 2 to 16 pixels and color #333. Save and close the page.

17. Preview the page in your browser. The page should have a background color, and the page title you assigned to it should appear in the page tab.

18. Review the HTML tags for the home page in Code view, and then close any open pages.

19. Upload the site to the remote server. Remember to select all of the files and the folder for upload.

20. View the page on the Web. Again, the page should have a background color, and the page title you assigned to it should appear in the browser title bar and in the page tab.

21. Submit your finished files to your instructor.

Plan, design, and set up a Web site for a coffee lounge.

CREATE

Case Problem 4

Data File needed for this Case Problem: coffee_bg.jpg

Coffee Lounge   Tommy Caddell asks you to develop a Web site plan and design to present to the Coffee Lounge staff at the next scheduled staff meeting. You will have to do further research to define the target audience as well as to develop content for the site, as the business has not yet generated any informational materials. Use the notes you made from your research on coffee bars and the Portland scene.

1. Construct a list of goals for the site.

2. Define a target audience and a user profile for the site.

3. Complete your market research. Review at least eight Web sites, including coffee bars; art galleries; sites geared at your target audience; sites about Portland, Oregon; and sites about the local music scene.

4. Write a paragraph documenting the findings from your market research. Include the URLs of the Web sites that you visited.

5. Compose two end-user scenarios for the site.

6. Develop an information category outline for the site.

7. Create a flowchart for the site.

8. Develop a concept and metaphor for the site. Be creative, but make sure that your metaphor will support the site goals.

9. Design a color palette, choose the fonts, and select a graphics style for the site. Write a paragraph explaining your choices.

10. Create rough sketches of two layouts of the site. Write a paragraph explaining which layout you prefer and why.

11. Check the layout of the design you prefer for logic by reviewing the decisions that you have made. Make sure that your design reinforces the site goals and supports the site metaphor.

12. Set up the site, using **Coffee Lounge** as the site name and **coffee\web** as the local root folder in the folder and location where you are storing your Web sites. Create a folder named **graphics** in the local root folder and select that folder as the default images folder. Use case-sensitive links checking and enable the cache.

13. Set up the live server definition using FTP access for the Coffee Lounge site.

14. Create the home page for the site based on your site plan. Use **index.html** as the filename and HTML 5 as the DocType. Set the appropriate page title, background, and colors in the Page Properties dialog box. You can use a background color or a background image of your choice (**coffee_bg.jpg** is provided in the Dreamweaver2\Case4 folder included with your Data Files).

15. Preview the page in your browser, verifying the page title and properties you assigned.

16. Review the HTML tags for the home page in Code view.

17. Upload the site to the remote server. Remember to select all of the files and the folder for upload.

18. View the pages on the Web, verifying the page title and properties you set.

19. Submit your finished files to your instructor.

TUTORIAL 3

OBJECTIVES

Session 3.1
- Add text to a Web page by typing, copying and pasting, or importing
- Check spelling in a Web page
- Find and replace text
- Format text using the Property inspector
- Create hyperlinks
- Examine HTML tags for hyperlinks

Session 3.2
- Explore CSS styles and style sheets
- Modify HTML tags
- Create custom style classes
- Create styles for the <a> tag pseudoclasses

Session 3.3
- Create an external style sheet
- Attach an external style sheet to a Web page
- Delete styles from a style sheet
- Create and edit CSS styles in an external style sheet
- Enable and disable CSS styles
- Examine the code for styles and style sheets
- Examine HTML tags used to format text
- Explore Web fonts and the @font-family rule

Adding and Formatting Text

Creating CSS Styles and an External Style Sheet

Case | *NextBest Fest*

Brian, president of NextBest Fest, and his son, Gage, public relations and marketing director, approved the design plan for the new NextBest Fest site. You will begin by working on the home page of the Web site. You will add text to the home page and then format the text by adding appropriate CSS styles based on the design plan. Each page of the NextBest Fest site will contain at least three text elements—the page heading, subheadings, and body text—as well as hyperlinks. Formatting provides a way to distinguish between these different types of text. When you set the page properties of the home page in the previous tutorial, Dreamweaver created CSS styles for the page heading elements, body text, and hyperlinks. In this tutorial, you will examine the code for those CSS styles and create additional CSS styles.

In this tutorial, you will also type text directly into a Web page as well as import text from files. You will use the spelling checker and Find and Replace tools to correct typing and capitalization errors in the text. You will create hyperlinks to navigate among the pages in the site. You will create and apply different types of CSS styles to the text that you added. You will create an external style sheet, which you will attach to all the Web pages in the site. The style sheet helps to ensure that the formatting remains consistent from one page to another, reduces the size of the files, and enables you to easily add other styles as needed. Finally, you will learn to add Web fonts to a page.

STARTING DATA FILES

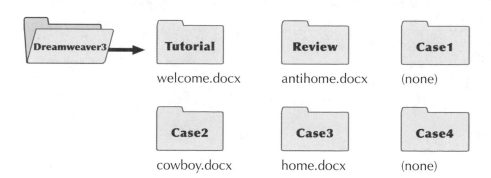

Dreamweaver3 → Tutorial
welcome.docx

Review
antihome.docx

Case1
(none)

Case2
cowboy.docx

Case3
home.docx

Case4
(none)

SESSION 3.1 VISUAL OVERVIEW

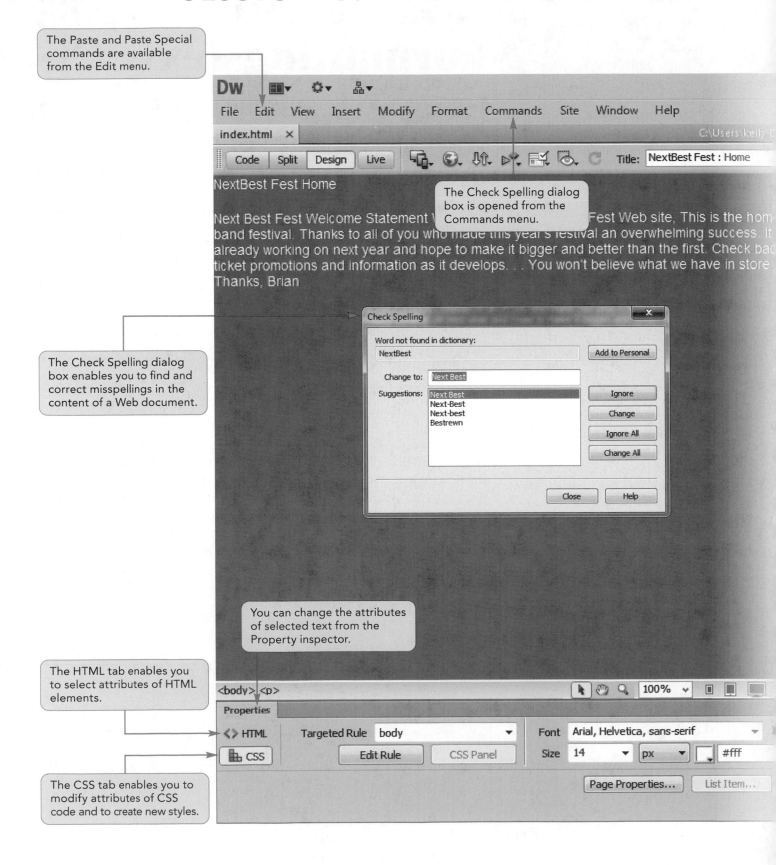

The Paste and Paste Special commands are available from the Edit menu.

The Check Spelling dialog box is opened from the Commands menu.

The Check Spelling dialog box enables you to find and correct misspellings in the content of a Web document.

You can change the attributes of selected text from the Property inspector.

The HTML tab enables you to select attributes of HTML elements.

The CSS tab enables you to modify attributes of CSS code and to create new styles.

ADDING TEXT TO A WEB PAGE

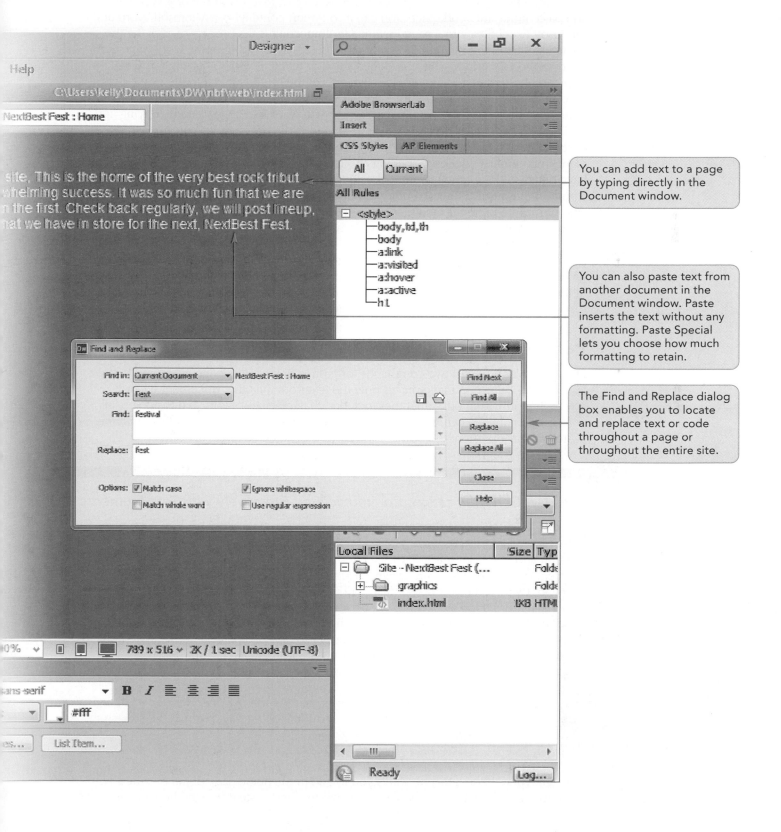

You can add text to a page by typing directly in the Document window.

You can also paste text from another document in the Document window. Paste inserts the text without any formatting. Paste Special lets you choose how much formatting to retain.

The Find and Replace dialog box enables you to locate and replace text or code throughout a page or throughout the entire site.

Adding Text to a Web Page

Text is included in almost every Web page. In Dreamweaver, you can add text to a page in several ways. You can simply type in the workspace of the Document window. You can copy existing text from another file, such as a text document or a Web page, and paste it into the workspace. You can also import content from Microsoft Word and Microsoft Excel files into a page in your site. **Importing** is the process of copying the contents of an entire file from one program into another. Typing in the workspace is a good method for adding small amounts of text or text that will be heavily formatted. Copy and pasting text lets you place segments of the original text into the exact locations in the page where you want it appear. Importing lets you insert the entire contents of the file into the location in the page where you want it to appear. Both copying and importing content are good for adding a lot of text to a site because you can avoid mistyped text. If you are copying or importing content from a word-processing document, you can first check the spelling and grammar; most word-processing programs have better spelling- and grammar-checking features than Dreamweaver and also have a built-in thesaurus. However, other errors—such as extra spaces, oddly positioned text, or misinterpreted symbols—sometimes appear in the Web page when text is copied or imported from another program. To help prevent errors, the Dreamweaver pasting options let you select how much of the original formatting to include in the pasted content. This option is not available with importing text. When you import content into a Web page, Dreamweaver simply places all of the content from the original document in the Web page. Whenever your text originates from another source, it is important to read the text and correct any errors that were introduced.

Pasting Content into a Web Page

Dreamweaver provides two commands for pasting items into a page: Paste and Paste Special. The Paste command places only the text from the other document without any of the formatting but sometimes includes characters and styles. The Paste Special command enables you to choose the level of formatting that will be retained with the pasted text. Most often, you will use the Paste Special command.

PROSKILLS

Written Communication: Communicating Effectively with Text Elements

Almost every Web page includes text elements. In fact, text is the basis of most Web sites. To ensure maximum readability, the text you add to a Web page should be clearly written and free from spelling, punctuation, and grammatical errors. Well-written Web content is concise, effectively communicates the point, and is written with the end user in mind. By the time you are ready to add the content to a Web site, you will already have the information architecture, which specifies what to include in each page. You will also have all the raw materials, including the text and the graphics, so that you are not composing on the fly. In addition, you will have set the page properties for the pages so that basic text formatting attributes are set. Logically placed headings, subheadings, lists, and indentions provide the structure that visually guides the user through the page. Font size and font color are visual indicators of information hierarchy and should be used consistently. Refer back to the comps and the site plan you developed during the planning phase as you create heading and subheading styles so that they match the look and feel of the site.

Gage typed the text that he wants you to add to the home page of the NextBest Fest site into a Word document. You will copy that text and paste it into the home page.

To add text to the home page:

1. Open the **NextBest Fest** site you modified in Tutorial 2, reset the **Designer** workspace, minimize the Business Catalyst panel, make sure the Files panel is open, and then set the Files panel to **Local view**, if necessary.

2. If you are working on a different computer than you did in Tutorial 2, re-create or import the site definition (both the local site setup and the remote server setup) on your current computer.

3. In the Files panel, double-click **index.html** to open the home page in the Document window, and then click the **Design** button on the Document toolbar, if necessary, to switch to Design view.

4. Type **NextBest Fest Home**. The text is invisible because it is the same color as the background. You will temporarily change the text color so that you can view the text in the page.

5. In the Property inspector, click the **Page Properties** button, type **#fff** in the Text color box to change the text color to white, and then click the **OK** button. The text is now visible in the Document window. See Figure 3-1.

> Remember to re-create or import the site definition each time you use a different computer to work on the site.

Figure 3-1 **Home page with new text**

> text typed in the Document window

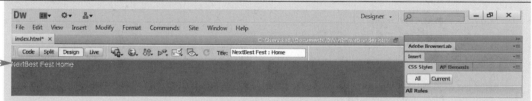

6. Use Word or another word-processing program to open the **welcome.docx** file located in the Dreamweaver3\Tutorial folder included with your Data Files. This document contains additional text you will add to the home page. The paragraph headings are bold and the text is in the Times New Roman font.

7. Press the **Ctrl+A** keys to select all of the text in the document, press the **Ctrl+C** keys to copy the text to the Windows Clipboard, and then click the **Close** button [X] on the program window title bar to close the document and exit the word-processing program.

8. Click the Document window to place the insertion point after the text you typed in the home page, if necessary, and then press the **Enter** key to move the insertion point down two lines.

9. On the menu bar, click **Edit**, and then click **Paste Special**. The Paste Special dialog box opens.

10. Click the **Text only** option button, and then click the **OK** button. The text you copied from the welcome.docx document is pasted into the page without any formatting. See Figure 3-2.

Figure 3-2	Text copied from the welcome.docx document

subheading is not bold

page name (page heading)

body text is in the Arial, Helvetica, sans-serif font group

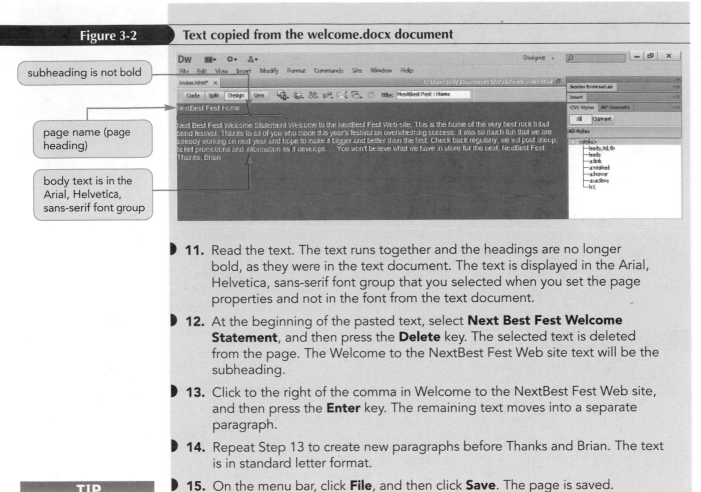

▶ **11.** Read the text. The text runs together and the headings are no longer bold, as they were in the text document. The text is displayed in the Arial, Helvetica, sans-serif font group that you selected when you set the page properties and not in the font from the text document.

▶ **12.** At the beginning of the pasted text, select **Next Best Fest Welcome Statement**, and then press the **Delete** key. The selected text is deleted from the page. The Welcome to the NextBest Fest Web site text will be the subheading.

▶ **13.** Click to the right of the comma in Welcome to the NextBest Fest Web site, and then press the **Enter** key. The remaining text moves into a separate paragraph.

▶ **14.** Repeat Step 13 to create new paragraphs before Thanks and Brian. The text is in standard letter format.

▶ **15.** On the menu bar, click **File**, and then click **Save**. The page is saved.

TIP

You can quickly save the page by pressing the Ctrl+S keys.

The home page text is entered in the Web page, ready to be corrected and formatted.

INSIGHT

Obtaining Permission to Reuse Copyrighted Content

When you are developing a Web site, you need to be aware of copyright issues related to using content created by other people. **Copyright** protects "original works of authorship," including literary, dramatic, musical, artistic, and other intellectual property, or derivative works such as unique compilations or collections of existing content as long as they are fixed in some tangible form, such as on paper or in electronic memory. Since January 1, 1978, copyright in the United States extends for the life of the author plus 70 years. So, works created before January 1, 1923, are now in the **public domain**, which means they are public property and can be reproduced without permission or charge. Works created after that date may or may not be in the public domain, and should be verified through the Copyright Office. Works created outside the United States are protected in their own countries generally for the life of the author plus 50 or 70 years, depending on the country. A copyright notice includes (1) the symbol or the word *copyright*; (2) the year of first publication; and (3) the name of the copyright owner.

To use copyrighted work, whether published or unpublished, you must obtain the copyright owner's permission unless the intended use is a **fair use**. Generally, the fair use doctrine allows you to reproduce small amounts of an original work specifically for a review, criticism, or illustration of a point. When creating commercial Web sites, you must be careful to get permission to include anything that is someone else's work. As a professional Web designer, it's a good idea to get permission to reuse anything that you didn't create yourself or that is not owned by your client.

Whenever you reuse someone else's work—including Web sites, images, sounds, video, and text from the Internet—you should indicate that the content is copyrighted and credit the original source. When you obtain permission, ask the copyright holder for the specific information they want you to include with the work. If the copyright holder doesn't specify the information or the content falls under fair use, include the name of the copyright holder, the copyright year, the work's title, and the source. For works found online, list the URL and the date accessed.

For more information, visit the U.S. Copyright Office site at *www.copyright.gov*.

Checking the Spelling in Web Pages

It is important to proofread all of the text that you add to Web pages, whether you typed it directly into the Web page or you copied it from another file. You cannot assume that text you receive from someone else has been proofread and corrected. You should also use the Dreamweaver built-in spelling checker to double-check for errors. You can choose to change or ignore one instance or all occurrences of any word that isn't found in the Dreamweaver built-in dictionary. Dreamweaver uses the spell checker engine from Linguistic Library Optimized (LILO), which supports 37 different dictionaries. The default dictionary matches the version of Dreamweaver CS6 that you install. For example, when you install the Turkish version of the software, the Turkish dictionary will be the default dictionary. You can change the default dictionary by editing the general preferences for the program.

Correcting All Spelling and Grammar Errors

Errors in spelling and grammar can detract from the overall impression of a Web site. They can make the company, product, or service seem unprofessional. So be sure to use the spelling checker and proofread the text in all Web pages. Because no spelling checker is foolproof, proofread the pages carefully looking for errors that a spelling checker won't catch, such as incorrectly used homonyms (for example, *there*, *their*, and *they're*), a correctly spelled word that is wrong in context (such as *from* versus *form*), and missing words.

You will check the spelling in the home page to be sure that the document you received from Gage was error free.

To check the home page for spelling errors:

1. At the top of the home page, click to the left of the NextBest Fest Home heading to place the insertion point at the top of the page.

2. On the menu bar, click **Commands**, and then click **Check Spelling**. The Check Spelling dialog box opens, displaying the first word that does not match any words in the built-in dictionary, in this case, the word *NextBest*. The Check Spelling dialog box suggests that NextBest be corrected to *Next Best*. See Figure 3-3.

TIP

You can also open the Check Spelling dialog box by pressing the Shift+F7 keys.

Figure 3-3	Check Spelling dialog box

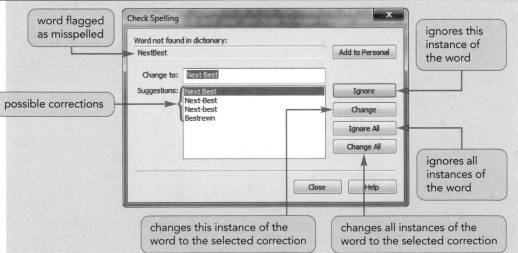

word flagged as misspelled

possible corrections

ignores this instance of the word

ignores all instances of the word

changes this instance of the word to the selected correction

changes all instances of the word to the selected correction

3. Click the **Ignore All** button to leave every instance of NextBest in the page. The Check Spelling dialog box displays *Fest*—the next word that does not match any words in the built-in dictionary. In this case, the word *Fest* is a short-ened form of *Festival* and is not misspelled. Although the spelling checker does not recognize this slang term, the target audience will recognize it.

4. Click the **Ignore All** button to leave every instance of Fest in the page and continue checking the spelling. The Check Spelling dialog box displays *tribut*. The word should be *tribute*.

5. In the Suggestion box, click **tribute**, if necessary, and then click the **Change** button to replace the highlighted word with the selected word.

6. Check the rest of the page, ignoring the remaining words that the spelling checker flags as misspelled. A dialog box opens, indicating that the spelling check is complete.

7. Click the **OK** button.

8. Proofread the page, making any necessary additional corrections, and then save the page.

Using the Find and Replace Tool

Dreamweaver has a Find and Replace tool that enables you to locate text or tags and then to replace the located elements with other text or tags. You can specify the area to search (selected text, current document, open documents, folder, selected files in site, or entire current local site) as well as the kind of search to perform. A source code search locates instances of the designated text string within the HTML source code. A text search locates instances of the designated text string within the document text. A text (advanced) search enables you to further specify the parameters of the search. For example, you can set the search to locate instances of the designated text string within only a specified tag and so on. Finally, a specific tag search locates specific tags, attributes, and attribute values so you can replace each with a new tag, attribute, or attribute value.

You will use the Find and Replace tool to locate all instances of the word *festival* in the home page and replace it with *fest* (all in lowercase). Gage selected this slang term to reinforce the festival name and to appeal to the target audience by creating a more casual tone.

TIP

You can also press the Ctrl+F keys to open the Find and Replace dialog box.

To find *festival* and replace it with *fest*:

1. At the top of the home page, click to the left of the NextBest Fest Home heading to place the insertion point at the top of the page.

2. On the menu bar, click **Edit**, and then click **Find and Replace**. The Find and Replace dialog box opens. See Figure 3-4.

Figure 3-4   **Find and Replace dialog box**

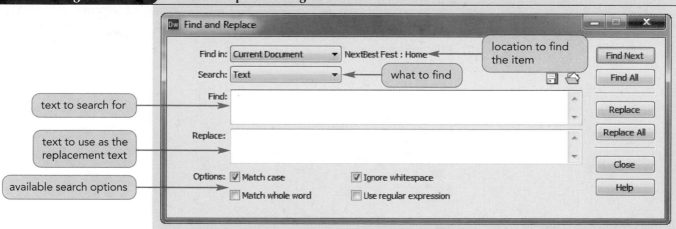

3. Click the **Find in** button and click **Current Document**, and then, if necessary, click the **Search** button and click **Text**.

4. Select any text in the **Find** box, and then type **festival**. This is the word you want to search for.

5. Click in the **Replace** box, and then type **fest**. This is the replacement word you want to use.

6. Click the **Match case** check box to insert a check mark, and uncheck all the other check boxes. Dreamweaver will look for words with the exact capitalization as in the Find box and insert words with the exact capitalization as in the Replace box.

7. Click the **Find Next** button. The first instance of the word *festival* is selected in the page. See Figure 3-5.

| Figure 3-5 | Search text found in the home page |

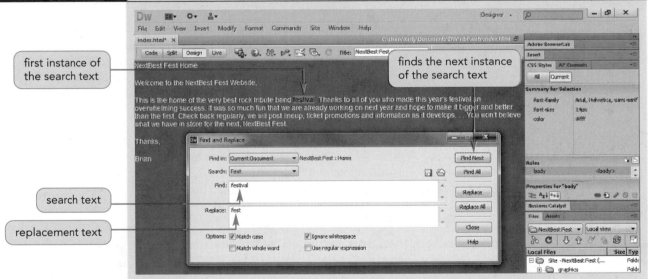

8. Click the **Replace** button. The selected instance of *festival* is replaced with *fest*, and then the next instance of *festival* is selected.

9. Click the **Replace All** button. The remaining instances of the search text in the page are replaced. The Results panel group opens to the Search panel and lists all instances where the search text was replaced in the page.

10. Review the list in the Search panel, and then right-click the panel title bar and click **Minimize** to minimize the panel group.

Formatting Text Using the Property Inspector

The simplest way to format text in Dreamweaver is to select the text in the Document window and set the attributes for the text in the Property inspector. You can set the attributes for a single letter, a word, a line of text, or an entire block of text. The attributes for text formatting are similar to those you find in a word-processing program; however, when text is formatted in Dreamweaver, CSS styles that control the look and layout of the text are added behind the scenes.

The Property inspector switches between the HTML pane and the CSS pane. From the HTML pane, you can add HTML tags to the page, apply existing CSS styles to selected text, and set text formatting attributes of bold, italic, unordered (bulleted) or ordered (numbered) lists, and indents by adding HTML tags to the selected text. From the CSS pane, you can create new CSS styles and edit existing CSS styles. Often, you use the two panes together by first creating CSS styles to customize the display of a tag in the CSS pane, and then adding the tag to selected text in the page from the HTML pane.

REFERENCE

Formatting Text Using the Property Inspector

- In the Document window, select the text that you want to format.
- In the Property inspector, click the HTML button.
- Click the Format button, and then click the HTML tag you want.
- Click the ID or Class arrow, and then click the style you want.
- Click the Bold button and/or the Italic button.
- Click the Unordered List button or Ordered List button to create a list. You can set properties for a list by using the List Item button in the Property inspector.
- Click an alignment button and/or an indent button.
- To create a text hyperlink, click the Browse for File button and navigate to the file to link to (or drag the Point to File button to the file to link to, or type the external URL in the Link box).

You will use the Property inspector to format the text in the home page based on the comps and site plan you developed during the planning phase.

To format the home page text with the Property inspector:

1. In the Document window, select **NextBest Fest Home**. You will format this text in the Heading 1 style.

2. In the Property inspector, click the **HTML** button. The HTML pane appears in the Property inspector.

3. Click the **Format** button, and then click **Heading 1**. The page heading, "NextBest Fest Home," is formatted with the Heading 1 attributes—Arial, Helvetica, sans-serif; 30 pixels; and #99cbb3 (blue-green)—you set in the page properties.

4. Click to the right of the Heading 1 text. The Heading 1 text is deselected. See Figure 3-6.

Figure 3-6   **Text formatted with Heading 1**

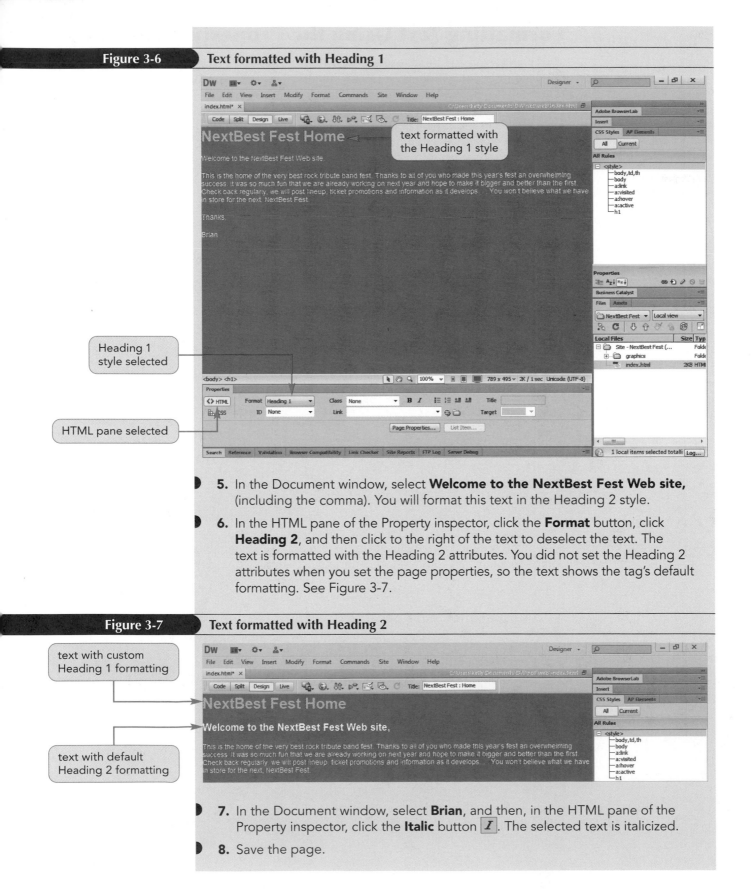

5. In the Document window, select **Welcome to the NextBest Fest Web site,** (including the comma). You will format this text in the Heading 2 style.

6. In the HTML pane of the Property inspector, click the **Format** button, click **Heading 2**, and then click to the right of the text to deselect the text. The text is formatted with the Heading 2 attributes. You did not set the Heading 2 attributes when you set the page properties, so the text shows the tag's default formatting. See Figure 3-7.

Figure 3-7   **Text formatted with Heading 2**

7. In the Document window, select **Brian**, and then, in the HTML pane of the Property inspector, click the **Italic** button *I*. The selected text is italicized.

8. Save the page.

Creating Text Hyperlinks

The NextBest Fest site plan calls for text hyperlinks at the top of each page. Hyperlinks enable users to move between pages in a Web site and to connect to pages in other Web sites. For the NextBest Fest site, you will create text hyperlinks for the main navigation system as called for in the site plan. First, you will add the link text to the home page and format it. Then, you will create the hyperlinks to the other pages you know you will create based on the site plan.

PROSKILLS

Written Communication: Creating an Effective Navigation System

Whether you are creating a Web site for personal use or for a client, moving around the site should be intuitive to end users. Creating a site that users find simple to navigate and locate content in can be challenging. When done well, users will be unaware of your efforts. It's only when a site is poorly designed and difficult to use that end users take notice. In reality, a site structure that feels effortless to navigate takes a lot of planning and effort.

To make it easier for users to move through the site, be sure to use a consistent structure in all the pages. Most important, the navigation system should be the same no matter which page is being viewed. The links in the navigation system should remain the same from page to page. The navigation system should always be located in the same place on each page of the site. It should be separated from the other content by white space. Also, the colors and font size should make the links clearly distinguishable to users so that they can easily move through the site. A well-designed navigation system ensures that users can find what they are looking for quickly and easily.

Adding and Formatting Hyperlink Text

You will insert the text for the hyperlinks—about, lineup, schedule, tickets, and contact—on a blank line above the page heading. You want to separate each word with two **nonbreaking spaces**, which are special, invisible characters used to create more than one space between text and other elements. In HTML, only one regular space appears between items no matter how many spaces you type with the Spacebar. Nonbreaking spaces enable you to separate items with multiple spaces between them. Keep in mind the difference between spaces and nonbreaking spaces when copying or importing content from a word-processing program; review the content to be sure that the text is displayed as you intended. You can use the new HTML5 <wbr> tag to insert an optional hyphen into a word that specifies where a long word can break at the end of a line. However, Internet Explorer does not support this tag.

You will format the inserted link text by setting its size and alignment. When you are working with styled text, the status bar is a valuable tool. You can use it to quickly locate the text formatting tags and move past them in the page before you paste new text so that the new text is not displayed with the wrong style. You won't set colors for the link text because you specified them when you set the page properties.

To add and format the text hyperlinks for the navigation system:

1. In the Document window, click to the left of the page heading to position the insertion point, and then press the **Enter** key. A blank line is added above the page heading and the insertion point moves down two lines.

2. Press the **Up** arrow key to move the insertion point to the blank line.

3. In the status bar, if you see the <h1> tag, press the **Left** arrow key until the <body> tag is the only tag that appears. The insertion point is now positioned before the heading 1 tag in the code so that the new text you enter will not be in the Heading 1 style.

4. Type **about**. This is the text for the first hyperlink.

5. Open the Insert panel, click the **Common** arrow, and then click **Text**. The buttons in the Text category appear in the Insert panel.

TIP

A space and a nonbreaking space look the same in Design view.

6. Scroll to the bottom of the Insert panel, click **Characters** to open the Characters menu, and then click the **Non-Breaking Space** button twice. Two nonbreaking spaces are inserted after the text.

7. Type **lineup**, and then press the **Ctrl+Shift+Spacebar** keys twice to insert two nonbreaking spaces using the keyboard shortcut.

8. Type the remaining link text, inserting two nonbreaking spaces after each of the following: **schedule**, **tickets**, and **contact**. The text for each link is followed by two nonbreaking spaces. See Figure 3-8.

Figure 3-8   **Link text typed in the home page**

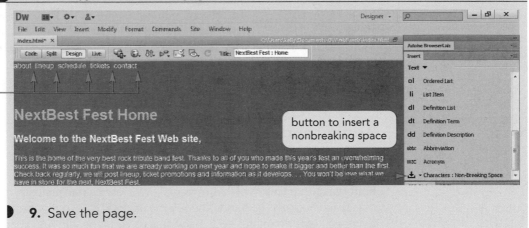

two nonbreaking spaces separate the link text

button to insert a nonbreaking space

9. Save the page.

Creating Links from Text

Text links are an accessible form of navigation because they can be read by assistive devices and provide clear information to the user. You can create text hyperlinks using the HTML pane of the Property inspector to connect the text with a specific file or Web page. The first time you link to a file, you select the link text in the Document window and type the URL in the Link box. After you create the other pages, you can use the Browse for File button or the Point to File button next to the Link box to select the appropriate file. Dreamweaver will then create the link for you. After you link to a file, it appears in the Link list so you can select new link text and then select the file from the list to create another link to that file.

Designers often create one page that includes the navigation system and structural elements, and then duplicate that page to create the other pages in the site. This saves time because the designer has to create these elements only once. If the different pages of the site were created first, the designer would have to add the navigation system and structural elements to each page in the site. Keep in mind that when the other pages of the site are created, their page names *must* match the names typed in the link path, or the link will not work. Refer to the site plan to ensure that the filenames remain consistent.

The two types of links are relative links and absolute links. **Relative links** can be relative to the document or to the site's root folder. **Document relative links** don't specify the entire URL of the Web page you are linking to; instead, they specify a path from the current page. Use document relative links to link to pages within the site; this practice allows you to move the site to a different server location or different domain, and the links will still work. **Site root relative links** specify a path from the site root folder to the linked document. Use site root relative links when you work on large sites with complex folder structures that change frequently. When you link to a page anywhere within the local root folder, Dreamweaver creates a relative link. The Web sites in these tutorials use document relative links. When you link to a page in another site, you use an absolute link. An **absolute link** contains the complete URL of the page you are linking to, which includes the filename of the page to which you are linking, such as *http://www.domainname.com/filename.html*. Use an absolute link to link to Web pages in other sites.

You will create hyperlinks from the link text you just added. Each link will connect to the corresponding Web page after you create the other pages in the site. For now, the linked text will have the styles and functionality of a link, but will not link to another page. When you set the page properties, you designated colors for four states of links (text links, rollover links, active links, and visited links). Because you have not yet added the white content background image, the linked text might blend into the background at this point. Because you are working from a site plan, you can build the site in phases, confident that the final pages will be attractive and user-friendly.

To create hyperlinks from the navigation system text:

1. In the Document window, select **about** in the home page. You will convert the selected text to a hyperlink.

2. In the HTML pane of the Property inspector, click in the **Link** box, type **about.html**, and then press the **Enter** key. The about text is coded and styled as a link. After you create the about.html page, clicking the about link will open that page. See Figure 3-9.

Figure 3-9	Text converted to a hyperlink

about text hyperlink

selected text is linked to the about.html page

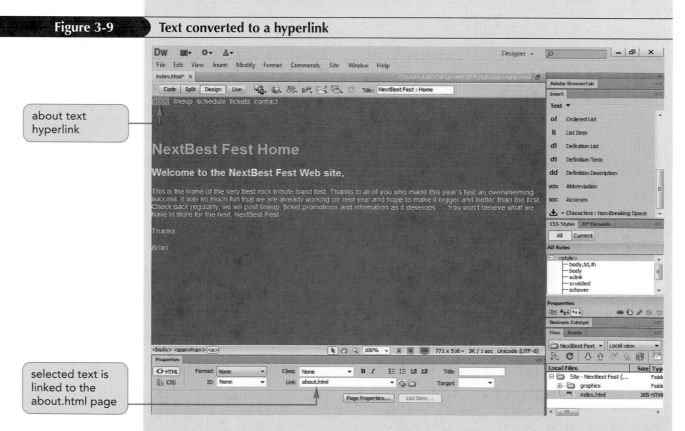

3. Click in the Document window to deselect the text. The linked text is difficult to see in the Document window. After you add the background image to the page, the linked text will be clearly visible.

4. Repeat Steps 1 and 2 to create links to the other pages you will add to the site using the following URLs: **lineup.html**, **schedule.html**, **tickets.html**, and **contact.html**.

TIP

You can quickly preview a saved page in your primary browser by pressing the F12 key

5. Save the home page.

6. In the Files panel, click **index.html** to select it, and then preview the home page in your primary browser. The links blend into the page background. See Figure 3-10.

| Figure 3-10 | Home page previewed in a browser |

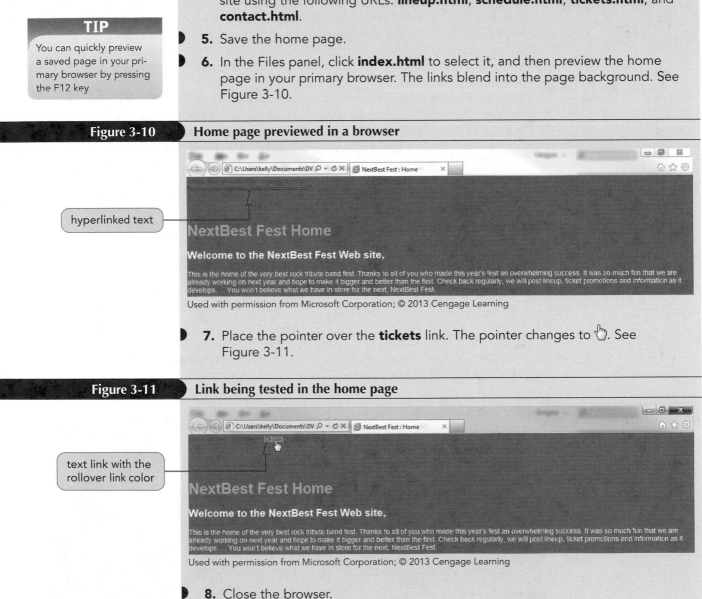

hyperlinked text

Used with permission from Microsoft Corporation; © 2013 Cengage Learning

7. Place the pointer over the **tickets** link. The pointer changes to 🖑. See Figure 3-11.

| Figure 3-11 | Link being tested in the home page |

text link with the rollover link color

Used with permission from Microsoft Corporation; © 2013 Cengage Learning

8. Close the browser.

Exploring HTML Tags for Hyperlinks

Dreamweaver inserted HTML tags when you formatted text and created hyperlinks. HTML tags, whether they apply to text, hyperlinks, or other elements, follow a specific format. As you have seen, most HTML tags come in pairs with opening and closing tags that surround the text to which the tags are applied, as in the following example:

```
<tag>Some Text</tag>
```

Opening tags are placed before the text, or other element, to which they are applied. They take the form <tag>, where *tag* is replaced by the specific HTML tag you are using. An opening tag has an opening bracket, the tag name, and a closing bracket. Closing tags are placed after the text, or other element, to which they are applied, and take the form </tag>. Again, a closing tag has opening and closing brackets, but also includes a forward slash inside the opening bracket before the tag name.

Tags can also be used together, or **nested**, which places one element inside another. With **nested tags**, one set of tags is placed around another set of tags so that both sets apply to the text they surround, such as:

TIP

Use the phrase "first on, last off" to remember that the outside opening and closing tags belong together.

```
<tag2><tag1>Some Text</tag1></tag2>
```

When working with nested tags, you must keep the opening and closing tags paired in the same order. For example, it would be incorrect to write:

```
<tag1><tag2>Some Text</tag1></tag2>
```

Some tags also contain attributes such as size, color, and alignment. These attributes are placed within the opening tag. Tag attributes are separated by a blank space, and the value of each attribute is usually placed in quotation marks, as shown in the example:

```
<tag color="x" size="x">Some Text</tag>
```

The specific tags depend on the applied formatting and the type of element. Helpful reference sites for HTML tags include *www.w3.org*, *www.htmldog.com/reference/ htmltags*, and *www.devx.com/projectcool/Article/19816*. Even though some HTML tags have attributes that enable you to specify the element's size, color, and so forth, a better practice is to keep styles separate from the content. You create styles that modify the look of page elements by creating global CSS styles that can affect multiple elements and be updated from a central location.

REFERENCE

Examining HTML Tags

- On the Document toolbar, click the Code button or the Split button.
- If the lines of code do not wrap in the Document window, click the View menu, point to Code View Options, and then click Word Wrap.
- In the Code pane, select the tag to examine.
- Right-click the selected tag, and then click Reference to display a description of the tag in the Reference panel.

Exploring HTML Tags That Apply to Hyperlinks

Hyperlinks are created in HTML with the **anchor tag**, which has the general format:

```
<a href="absolute or relative path">Link Text</a>
```

In this tag, *href* is short for hypertext reference, *"absolute or relative path"*—the URL or page for the link—is the value for href, and *Link Text* is the text on the Web page that users click to use the link. Absolute, document relative, and site root relative links have different path information in the href attribute. Figure 3-12 lists the anchor tags with the three types of links.

Figure 3-12 Anchor tags for absolute and relative links

Link	Anchor Tag	Description
Absolute	**\<a href="http://www.websitename.com"\>**Text link to a Web page outside current site**\</a\>**	Specifies the absolute or complete path to the linked page.
Document relative	**\<a href="anotherpage.htm"\>**Text link to another page within current site**\</a\>**	Specifies the location of the linked page relative to the current page; most commonly used type of linking.
Site root relative	**\<a href="/subfolder/anotherpage.htm"\>**Text link to another page within current site**\</a\>**	Specifies the location of the linked page relative to the site's root folder. Used when sites have many subfolders within the root folder and/or change frequently.

© 2013 Cengage Learning

You can set the target attribute with an anchor tag. The **target** specifies where the link opens—in the current browser window (_self), a new browser window or tab (_blank), the parent frame (_parent), or the top frame that then fills the window (_top). By default, the new page will open in the current browser window, replacing the page from which you linked. If you want the new page to replace the current page, you do not need to include a target attribute. If you want the linked page to open in a new browser window or in a new tab in the open browser window, you must specify "_blank" as the target attribute. When you specify "_blank" as the target, the code tells browsers to "open the link in a new window." However, many current browsers instead open the page in a new tab in the same browser window. To make things more complex, some browsers provide users the option to change the default for opening a link with a target of "_blank" from opening in a new window to opening in a new tab. So, you cannot always tell where the link will open. The complete anchor tag for opening a page in a new browser window or new tab in the open browser window takes the following format:

TIP

To keep a user at your site, it is a good idea to specify "_blank" as the target when you link to another site.

```
<a href="absolute or relative path" target="_blank">Link Text</a>
```

Another anchor tag attribute is the name attribute. The name attribute associates a name with a specific, named location within a Web page. With the name attribute, you can link to the named location on the current page or another page, much like a bookmark. You use the anchor tag with the name attribute in the following format:

```
<a name="anchor_name">Some Text</a>
```

In this tag, *"anchor_name"* is the name you give the anchor, and *Some Text* is the text being named as the anchor. Anchor names are case sensitive. When you create a named anchor, Dreamweaver inserts an anchor icon into the Document window beside the text. The anchor icon is not visible in a browser window.

After a location on a page has a named anchor, you can create links to it from other locations in the same page or from other pages. For example, you can create an anchor to the selected page heading text named "top," type "back to the top" at the bottom of the page, and then create a link from that text to the "top" anchor. This enables the user to jump from the bottom to the top of the Web page by clicking the "back to the top" link. The format for an anchor tag that links to a named anchor on the same page is:

```
<a href="#anchor_name">Link Text</a>
```

If you are linking to a named anchor in a different page, you need to include the path and filename to the page containing the named anchor in the following general format:

```
<a href="absolute or relative path#anchor_name">Link Text</a>
```

The # symbol always precedes the anchor name when it is used in a link.

You will look at the HTML for the hyperlinks you created in the home page.

To examine HTML tags for hyperlinks in the home page:

1. In the Document window, select the **contact** link.

2. On the Document toolbar, click the **Split** button. The page is in Split view vertically with a Code pane and a Design pane.

   Trouble? If the page is split horizontally, you need to change the page to split vertically. On the menu bar, click View, and then click Split Vertically.

3. In the Code pane, examine the anchor tag that surrounds the selected text. See Figure 3-13.

Figure 3-13   Anchor tag in the home page

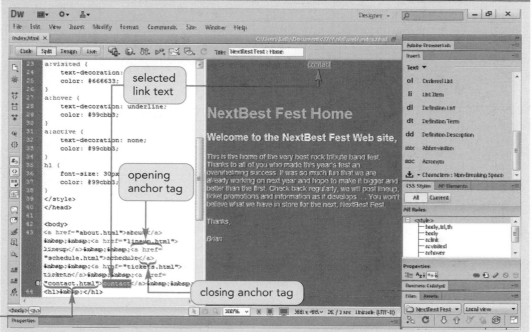

Trouble? If the lines of code do not wrap in the Document window, you need to turn on word wrap. On the Document toolbar, click the View options button, and then click Word Wrap to check it.

4. In the Code pane, select **<a href=** (the entire opening anchor tag), right-click the selected tag, and then click **Reference**. The Reference panel in the Results panel group expands, displaying the O'Reilly HTML Reference description of the anchor tag. See Figure 3-14.

Figure 3-14   Anchor tag description

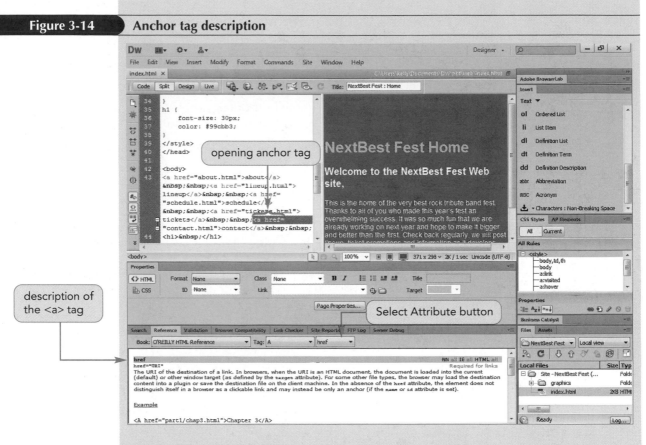

5. Read the description of the anchor tag href attribute.

6. In the Reference panel, click the **Select Attribute** button, and then click **Description**. A description of the a tag appears in the Reference panel.

   Trouble? If Description doesn't appear in the Select Attribute list, select href in the Code pane, right-click the selected attribute, and then click Reference.

7. Read the description of the a tag, and then collapse the Results panel group.

8. On the Document toolbar, click the **Design** button. The page is displayed in Design view.

So far, you have added text to a Web page, used the spelling checker, proofed the page, used the Find and Replace tool to change all instances of a word on the page, formatted the text with the Property inspector, created text hyperlinks, and reviewed the HTML tags used for the hyperlinks. In the next session, you will work with Cascading Style Sheets.

Session 3.1 Quick Check

1. What are two ways to add text to a page in Dreamweaver?
2. True or False. It is not necessary to read a page and look for errors if you use the Dreamweaver spelling checker.
3. To format text, select the text in the Document window and select formatting options in the _____.
4. _____ enable users to move between pages in a Web site and to connect to pages on other Web sites.
5. When you link to a page in the site's local root folder, what type of link is created by default?
6. What is the general format for the HTML code for the bold tag?
7. Which tag is used to create hyperlinks?

SESSION 3.2 VISUAL OVERVIEW

You can create a new style by clicking New in the CSS Styles list in the Format menu.

A **CSS style sheet** is a collection of styles that is either inserted in the head of the HTML of a Web page and used throughout that page (an internal style sheet), or is attached as an external document and used throughout the entire Web site (an external style sheet).

A **CSS style** is a rule that defines the appearance of an element in a Web page either by redefining an existing HTML tag or by creating a custom style (also called a class style or a custom class style).

A CSS style sheet stores styles that can be defined in one location and then applied to content in many other locations. This ability to separate the look of the site from the content of the site lets the designer more easily update the Web site's appearance.

When you create a Class style, you must first select the content to which the style will be applied, and then select the style from the Class list.

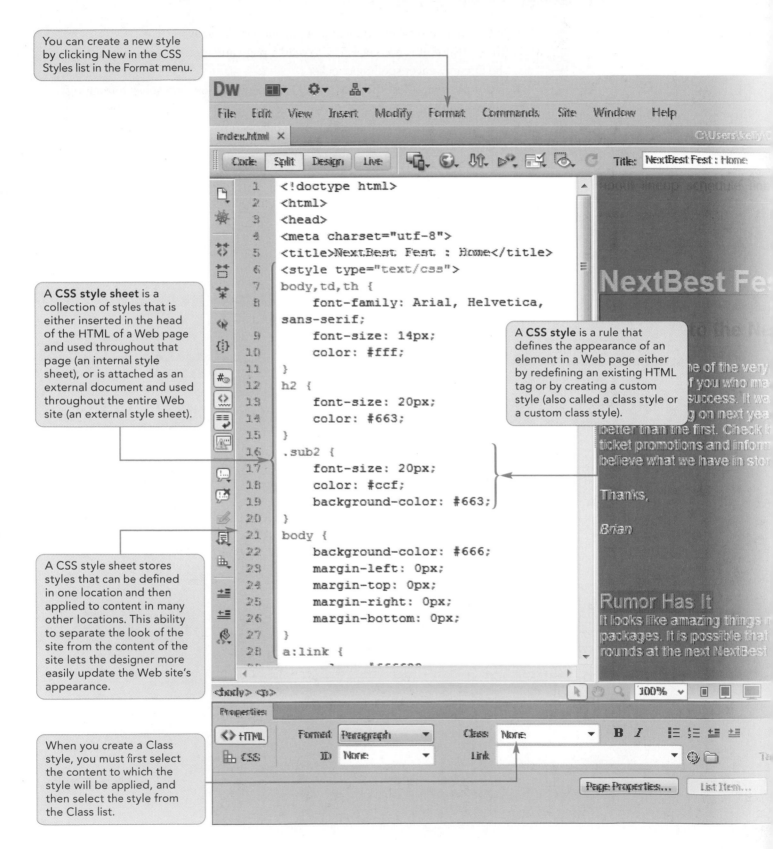

CREATING CASCADING STYLES

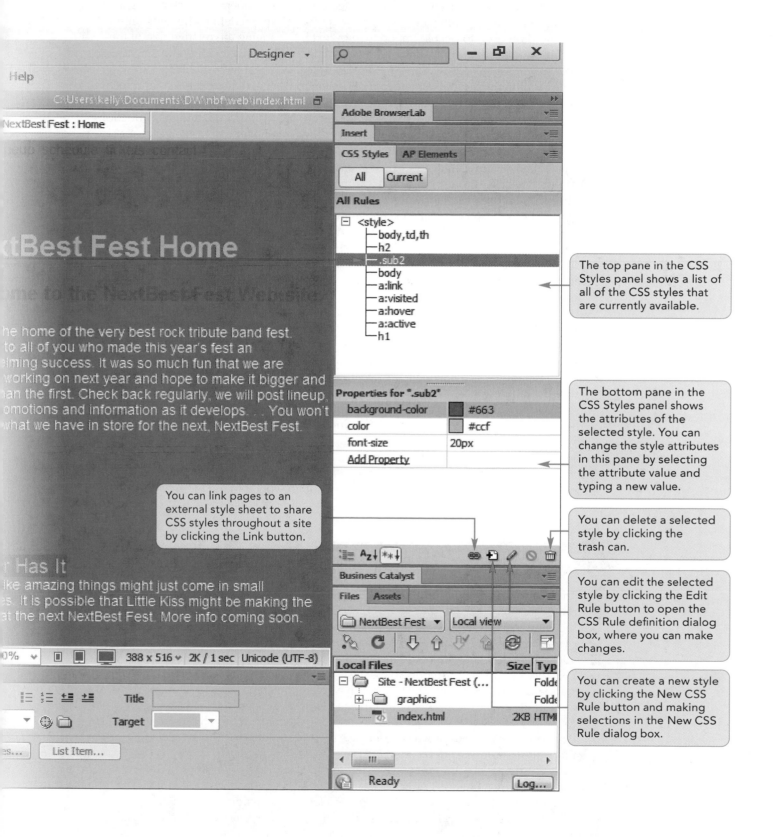

The top pane in the CSS Styles panel shows a list of all of the CSS styles that are currently available.

The bottom pane in the CSS Styles panel shows the attributes of the selected style. You can change the style attributes in this pane by selecting the attribute value and typing a new value.

You can link pages to an external style sheet to share CSS styles throughout a site by clicking the Link button.

You can delete a selected style by clicking the trash can.

You can edit the selected style by clicking the Edit Rule button to open the CSS Rule definition dialog box, where you can make changes.

You can create a new style by clicking the New CSS Rule button and making selections in the New CSS Rule dialog box.

Evolving HTML and CSS Standards

In the earliest days of the Web, designers had limited control over the way text was displayed in a browser. Text appeared in the default font and size set by the user's browser. The way it looked was also affected by the user's operating system. Designers had no font control within a Web page except for the six predefined heading tags that could be used to denote importance of text by changing the relative size of the headings. In HTML 2, bold, italic, and underline attributes were added. In HTML 3.2, another milestone in controlling the display of text was reached—the HTML font tag (or just font tag). The **font tag** allowed designers to designate in which font and relative font size the Web page should display (as long as the designated font was installed on the user's computer). Font tags were deprecated in HTML 4.01, and their functions were replaced and expanded upon by Cascading Style Sheets.

The next step in standards evolution was the introduction of **XHTML (Extensible Hypertext Markup Language)**, which is basically a combination of HTML and XML. **XML (Extensible Markup Language)** is a markup language that describes the structure of the data it contains. It provides a common and flexible method for applications and organizations to electronically exchange information. XML was created to describe or identify data, whereas HTML was designed to display data. The shift from HTML 4.01 to XHTML 1.0 continued the move toward separating style and content—XHTML structured the page content and CSS styled it for display. As an additional benefit, XHTML more strictly defines the syntax and makes it easier to format the same content for display on various devices.

In 2003, as some developers were seeing the limits of using XHTML to code pages, new interest emerged for extending HTML to create page structure rather than replacing it with XHTML. A community of people interested in evolving the Web formed the Web Hypertext Application Technology Working Group (WHATWG; *www.whatwg.org*) to work on these new standards. With this return to HTML, some developers realized that the new standards needed to be backward compatible, which means that they work with the older standards so that existing sites would continue to function without issues. The new standards also needed to include more detail than previous standards. In 2007, W3C formed a joint working group with WHATWG to work toward recommendation of these new HTML5 standards. This newest version of HTML contains all of the improvements that XHTML had and the new standards will continue to be backward compatible, enabling older Web sites to continue to work into the foreseeable future. Like XHTML, HTML5 will leave the layout and styling of content to CSS.

PROSKILLS

Written Communication: W3C Recommended HTML Standards

The World Wide Web Consortium (W3C) publishes recommendations for HTML standards. It is important to stay informed about changing standards because using old techniques to code Web pages can prevent new browsers from displaying the content of your site as you intended. This can prevent you from communicating effectively with your target audience. As new versions of HTML are developed and then accepted, the W3C assigns version numbers to these standards (a lower number equals an earlier standard). New HTML versions contain new elements, tags, and updated methods of doing things. Tags that have been replaced in new versions of HTML are kept around for compatibility with older browsers. Older tags that are in the process of becoming obsolete are called **deprecated**. Because some people use older browsers that rely on the earlier versions of HTML, deprecated tags are no longer phased out from support by user agents. A **user agent** is any device that can display Web pages, such as a computer, a smartphone, or a tablet. Specifications and standards change rapidly, so there is no easy way to predict exact adoption rates for newer standards and technologies. The W3C Web site (*www.w3c.org*) is a good reference for current trends and changes.

Exploring Cascading Style Sheets

Cascading Style Sheets were created as the answer to the limitations of HTML, and they are the current standard for layout and formatting of Web pages. A Cascading Style Sheet (CSS) is a collection of styles that is either inserted in the head of the HTML of a Web page and used throughout that page (an internal style sheet), or is attached as an external document and used throughout the entire Web site (an external style sheet). A CSS style is a rule that defines the appearance of an element in a Web page either by redefining an existing HTML tag or by creating a custom style (also called a class style or a custom class style). CSS styles define the appearance and position of text and graphics, and control most aspects of Web page layout. They allow you to specify more parameters of the design than earlier HTML specifications; for example, you can create custom list bullets.

CSS3, the latest version of CSS, has added many style properties and selectors that enable designers to do new and exciting things with pages. With CSS3, you can use multiple background images in a page, you can use an image as a border for another element, you can round the border edges, you can add shadows to box elements and text, you can create multiple columns without a table and text will flow through the columns automatically, you can change the opacity of a color, you can animate elements in your page, you can use media queries to create separate style sheets for different user devices—the list goes on and on.

Dreamweaver uses CSS styles by default to format page elements. When you defined the page properties for the NextBest Fest site, Dreamweaver added CSS styles that control the appearance of the text placed in the page. For example, the text that you pasted in the home page is displayed in the Arial, Helvetica, sans-serif font group, which you defined as the page font in the page properties. You can also create CSS styles yourself.

A CSS style sheet provides a convenient way to store styles that can be defined in one location and then applied to content in many other locations. This ability to separate the look of the site from the content of the site lets the designer more easily update the Web site's appearance. It also enables you to create pages that display appropriately on different types of media. For example, you can create a page that looks one way when viewed on a computer and a different way when viewed on a cell phone. Designers can redefine an existing CSS style, and any content to which that style has been applied is then updated to reflect the changes. This makes changing the font for all headings in a site or changing the color of body text on all the pages a simple task.

Creating CSS Styles

TIP

You can also create styles in the CSS pane of the Property inspector.

You can create styles using the CSS Styles panel located in the CSS panel group. When you create a CSS style, first you choose a selector type, then you choose the selector name, and, finally, you choose the location of the style. Selectors enable you to bind styles to specific elements in your pages, creating the boundaries or parameters of what exactly is being affected by the style. The four types of CSS selectors are class, ID, tag, and compound (based on your selection).

You create a class selector from scratch and you can apply it to any HTML element selected in the page. A class can be applied to any tag even if that tag has been redefined or has other styles applied to it. The class selector is the most versatile selector.

ID selectors are similar to class selectors with one major distinction: They can be used only once in a page. Because of this, ID selectors are frequently used to create page layouts where you define each section of a page only once.

The tag selector is an existing HTML tag that you modify. You can change and remove existing attributes or add new attributes to any HTML tag to make the tag more useful. This is probably the most common type of CSS style. When you redefine an HTML tag, the modified CSS style is used in every instance of that tag.

The compound selector is a combination of the ID, class, and tag styles and is used to redefine formatting for a group of tags only when those tags appear in the defined order. Compound selectors are especially helpful in creating a special look for text only when it displays in a certain area of the page. A dependent selector is a type of compound selector in which one element is contained in another. For example, if you define the footer area of the page using an ID style or the HTML5 footer element, you could create a compound style that tells the browser to display any text in a paragraph tag inside that area of the page in a smaller font size. This is also an example of a dependent selector.

After you decide on a type of style, you choose a name or tag to redefine. Finally, you select the location in which to define the style. You can save the style you are creating in a new external style sheet file, in an existing external style sheet file, or only within the current document. When you save the file in the current document, Dreamweaver creates an **internal style sheet** that embeds (or inserts) the styles in the head of the current Web page and applies them only throughout that document. Creating an internal style sheet is useful because it enables you to update the look of all elements on which a style is used throughout the page. For example, if you wanted to change the look of all the subheadings in a page, you could change the subheading style instead of selecting and modifying each subheading individually. An **external style sheet** is a separate file that contains all the CSS styles used in a Web site. When you define styles in an external style sheet, you can use the styles in any page in the Web site to which you connect that style sheet. Editing a style in the external style sheet will update all instances in which that style is used throughout the site. This is the most powerful way to use styles.

Every CSS style (or rule) consists of two parts: the selector and the declaration. The **selector** is the name of the style. The **declaration** defines the attributes that are included in the style. After you select the type, the name, and the location of the style, you can choose the various attributes to be included in the declaration for the style. You can combine attributes from the following nine categories to create a style:

- **Type.** Font and type settings and attributes such as font family, font size, color, decoration, and weight. More type attribute choices are available here than in the Property inspector when text is selected.
- **Background.** A color or an image, fixed or scrolling, that can be placed behind a page element such as a block of text. CSS background attributes overlay the Web page background designated with the page properties and can be added behind any page element.
- **Block.** Spacing and alignment settings for tags and attributes. Examples include the spacing between words, letters, and lines of text; the horizontal and vertical alignment of text; and the indentation applied to the text.
- **Box.** Attributes that control the placement of elements in the page. When you select a letter, a word, a group of words, a graphic, or any other element, a selection box surrounds all the selected elements. Box attributes control the characteristics of the selection box, enabling you to set margins, padding, float, and so on.
- **Border.** The dimensions, color, and line styles of the borders of the selection box that surround elements.
- **List.** The number format and its position used with ordered lists and the bullet shape or image and its position used with unordered lists.
- **Positioning.** Attributes that determine how a tag or selected content is positioned in the page.
- **Extensions.** Attributes that control page breaks during printing, the appearance of the pointer when positioned over objects in the page, and special effects added to objects. Most browsers do not support all extensions' attributes.
- **Transition.** New attributes that enable you to animate elements in your pages using nothing but HTML and CSS.

Previewing Your Site

Although CSS styles are the current standard for formatting the look and layout in Web pages, some problems still exist. HTML5 and CSS3 have not yet been adopted by WC3, but browsers have started to support the new standards to varying degrees. As a result, a Web page that works in one browser, or one version of a browser, will not necessarily work in another browser or version. To avoid problems, preview the site in every browser and version you plan to support before making the site public. This ensures that the site works and displays as you intend. In Dreamweaver, the BrowserLab extension enables you to see screen shots of a Web page as it will display in various versions of Internet Explorer, Firefox, Chrome, and Safari. It is available for free (at the time this tutorial was published) on the Adobe Web site to anyone with an Adobe User ID. In the Designer workspace, the Adobe BrowserLab panel appears above the Insert panel. You can also open the Adobe BrowserLab panel by clicking the BrowserLab extension in the extensions list on the Window menu.

Modifying HTML Tags

The simplest way to create a CSS style is to redefine an existing HTML tag. For example, the Heading 1 tag, <h1>, was introduced in an early version of HTML. It was created to give designers some control over the size at which text was displayed. The format of the Heading 1 tag changes based on how each user's browser interprets the tag, making the heading's layout and appearance inconsistent and limited. However, when you set page properties, you selected size and color attributes for the Heading 1 tag, <h1>, and Dreamweaver created a style that customized the appearance of that tag. Customizing the existing Heading 1 tag gives you a consistency that the <h1> tag would otherwise lack.

Many designers prefer to redefine HTML tags when creating CSS styles because the tags are often automatically inserted and older browsers that don't support CSS styles will apply the standard formatting of the HTML tags. For example, Dreamweaver applies the paragraph tag whenever you press the Enter key. If you modify the paragraph tag, Dreamweaver automatically applies the new formatting attributes anywhere a paragraph tag is found in the Web page. A redefined HTML tag is applied in the same way that the tag would normally be applied.

When you create a CSS style to modify an HTML tag, Dreamweaver provides an extensive list of tags from which to choose. You can change and remove existing attributes or add new attributes to any tag. When you modify the attributes associated with a tag, the changes you make will apply to every instance of that tag.

Modifying an Existing HTML Tag

- In the CSS Styles panel, click the New CSS Rule button.
- Click the Selector Type arrow.
- Click the Tag arrow, and then click the tag you want to modify.
- Click the appropriate Rule Definition option, and then click the OK button.
- Click a category, set options, and then click the OK button.

You will customize the Heading 2 tag so that the subheadings will be displayed in the approved NextBest Fest style: font—Arial, Helvetica, sans-serif; size—20 pixels; color—olive, #663. You will not specify a font because the style uses the page font defined in the page properties.

Styles **inherit** the attributes of higher-level tags when those attributes are not also specified in the current style. Because the attribute that specifies the page font was defined in the body tag, which surrounds all the other tags that format content in a Web page, the specified font family applies to the Heading 2 tag by default, unless you specify another font for this tag when you create the style. If you do specify a font in the Heading 2 tag style, it will override what was specified in the body tag; text to which the Heading 2 tag is applied will display that font instead of the one in the body tag. This happens because style sheets are **cascading**; if an attribute is defined in two styles that affect the same object, the style that is "closer" to the object in the code will override the value of the attribute in the tag that is farther away from the object in the code. The cascading effect of style sheets is very powerful because it enables you to create general styles that affect the entire page. You create additional styles only for items that are exceptions to the general style. From the CSS Styles panel, you can view the properties of a selected tag as well as the cascade of rules for a selected tag. This powerful tool enables you to see which styles are affecting the appearance of a selected tag so that you can create new styles without inadvertently affecting existing styles.

Gage wants the subheadings formatted so that they go with the style of the site. You will modify the Heading 2 tag style.

To modify the existing Heading 2 HTML tag:

1. If you took a break after the previous session, make sure that the NextBest Fest site is open, the Designer workspace is reset, the Business Catalyst panel is minimized, the Files panel is open, the index.html page is open in the Document window, and the page is in Design view.

2. Double-click the **CSS Styles** tab to expand the panel group, if necessary, click the **All** button in the top pane of the CSS Styles panel, and then drag the bottom border of the panel down to expand the Properties for portion of the panel. The CSS Styles panel lists the styles that Dreamweaver created. See Figure 3-15.

Figure 3-15 CSS Styles panel

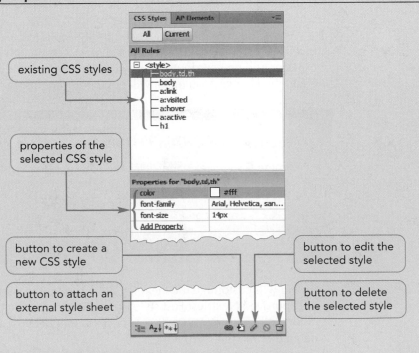

existing CSS styles

properties of the selected CSS style

button to create a new CSS style

button to attach an external style sheet

button to edit the selected style

button to delete the selected style

Trouble? If you do not see the Properties pane in the CSS Styles panel, you need more room to display the full panel. Double-click the Files panel title bar to collapse or expand the panel group as needed throughout these tutorials.

3. In the CSS Styles panel, click the **New CSS Rule** button. The New CSS Rule dialog box opens. See Figure 3-16.

Figure 3-16   New CSS Rule dialog box

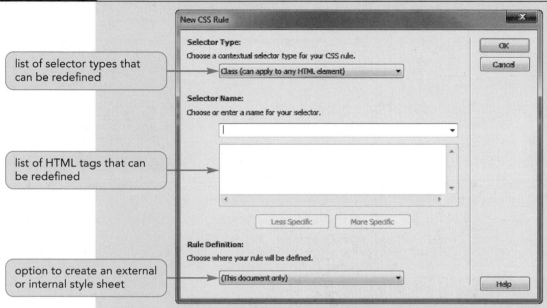

list of selector types that can be redefined

list of HTML tags that can be redefined

option to create an external or internal style sheet

4. Click the **Selector Type** button, and then click **Tag (redefines an HTML element)**. A list of tags appears in the Selector Name list.

5. Click the **Selector Name** arrow, and then click **h2**. This specifies that you will modify the <h2> tag.

6. Click the **Rule Definition** button, and then click **(This document only)**, if necessary. This creates an internal style sheet.

7. Click the **OK** button. The CSS Rule definition for h2 dialog box opens, and h2 appears in the All Rules pane of the CSS Styles panel.

8. In the Category box, click **Type**, if necessary.

9. In the Font-size box, type **20**, and then, if necessary, click the **Font-size** button, and then click **px**. The font size for the style is set to 20 pixels.

10. In the Color box, type **#663**, and then press the **Tab** key. The specified color appears in the color picker. See Figure 3-17.

Figure 3-17 | **CSS Rule definition for h2 dialog box**

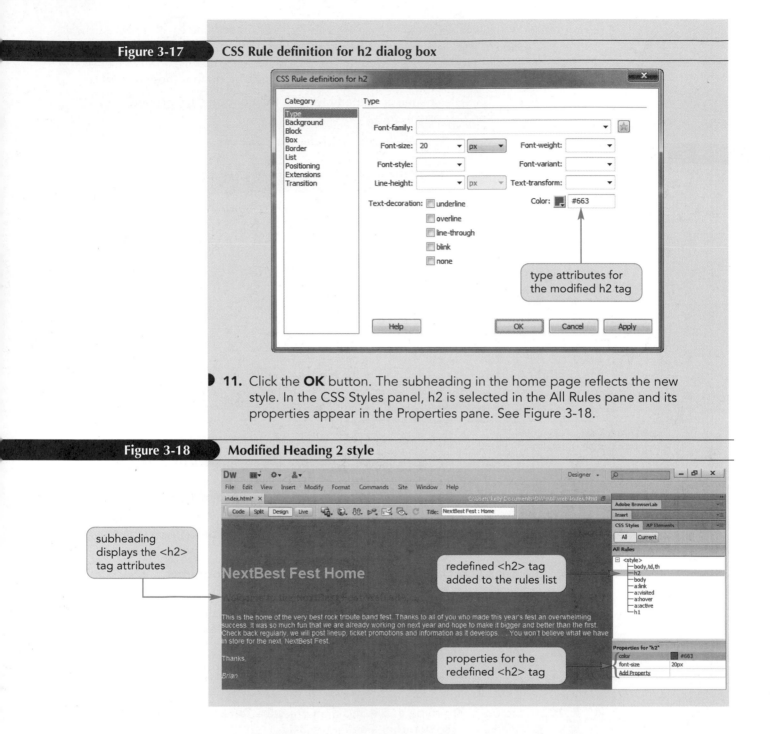

11. Click the **OK** button. The subheading in the home page reflects the new style. In the CSS Styles panel, h2 is selected in the All Rules pane and its properties appear in the Properties pane. See Figure 3-18.

Figure 3-18 | **Modified Heading 2 style**

Creating and Applying Class and ID Styles

Modifying text attributes is not limited to redefining existing HTML tags. You can also create class and ID styles, which are styles (or rules) you build from scratch and give a unique name. The process for creating a custom style is similar to redefining an HTML tag except that you name the style and specify all the attributes you want the style to include. Class styles have a period directly before the name and ID styles have # directly before the name. The name itself can include letters and numbers but no spaces. When you create these styles, Dreamweaver adds the period or # if you forget.

Some designers prefer to create class styles instead of redefining existing tags (such as the heading tags) when they create styles for elements that will be used in a limited way or as an exception to the norm. For example, when you selected the page font in the Page Properties dialog box, Dreamweaver redefined the body tag to include the selected font group. This ensures that all of the text in the Web page displays in the selected font group because the body tags are always included in the code for a Web page. If you decide to display a small section of text in a different font, a good way to do this is to create a custom style and apply the custom style only to that text. Because ID styles can be used only once in each page, designers tend to save them for structuring the page and use class styles for other formatting. You will use ID styles when you create structural elements for the pages of the NextBest Fest site.

REFERENCE

Creating a Class or ID Style

- In the CSS Styles panel, click the New CSS Rule button.
- Click the Selector Type button, and then click Class (can apply to any HTML element) or ID (applies to only one HTML element).
- In the Selector Name box, type the name of the new style.
- Click the Rule Definition button, and then click the appropriate option.
- Click the OK button to open the CSS Rule definition dialog box.
- In the Category box, click a category, and then set the options you want; repeat for each category you want to include in the style.
- Click the OK button.

Gage wants to create a Rumor Has It section on the home page to generate interest about next year's fest. You will add the new subheading to the bottom of the home page, create a class style named sub2 for the new subheading, and then apply the custom style to the new heading text. You will use the class style instead of the ID style because you might need to use this style in the home page again.

To create a class style for the new subheading:

1. In the CSS Styles panel, click the **New CSS Rule** button 🖺. The New CSS Rule dialog box opens.

2. If necessary, click the **Selector Type** button, and then click **Class (can apply to any HTML element)**.

3. In the Selector Name box, type **.sub2** (including the period before the name).

4. Click the **Rule Definition** button, and then click **(This document only)**, if necessary. This creates an internal style sheet.

5. Click the **OK** button. The CSS Rule definition for .sub2 dialog box opens, and .sub2 appears in the All Rules pane of the CSS Styles panel.

6. In the Category box, click **Type**, if necessary.

7. In the Font-size box, type **20**, and then, if necessary, click the **Font-size** button, and then click **px**. The font size for the style is set to 20 pixels.

8. In the Color box, type **#ccf**, and then press the **Tab** key. The specified color appears in the color picker.

9. In the Category box, click **Background**. The background color is located in this category.

TIP

The name of a class style always begins with a period, has no spaces, and cannot contain any special characters.

10. In the Background-color box, type **#663**. The background color is set to olive.

11. Click the **OK** button. In the CSS Styles panel, the name of the new style is selected in the All Rules pane and its properties appear in the Properties pane.

You must apply the class style to the text you want to format. When you create a new class or ID style, its name appears in the Class or ID list in the HTML pane of the Property inspector as well as in the All Rules pane in the CSS Styles panel along with any HTML tags that you have modified. You apply the style to selected text by selecting the style from the Style list in the Property inspector. To help you remember what a style looks like, when possible, each style name in the Property inspector is formatted with the style's attributes.

You will type the new heading text, and then apply the .sub2 class style to the heading.

To apply the .sub2 class style to new heading text:

1. In the Document window, position the insertion point after the paragraph text at the bottom of the home page, and then press the **Enter** key twice. The insertion point moves down four lines.

2. Type **Rumor Has It**, and then press the **Shift+Enter** keys to insert one line break.

3. Type **It looks like amazing things might just come in small packages. It is possible that Little Kiss might be making the rounds at the next NextBest Fest. More info coming soon.** to enter the text for the new section.

4. Select **Rumor Has It**. You will format this text with the new subheading style you created.

5. In the Property inspector, click the **HTML** button, click the **Class** arrow, and then click **sub2**. The new class style is applied to the selected text.

6. Click in the heading to deselect the text. See Figure 3-19.

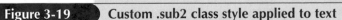

Figure 3-19   Custom .sub2 class style applied to text

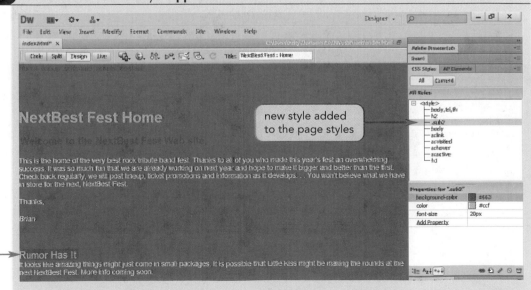

7. Save the page, preview the page in a browser, and then close the browser.

Examining Anchor Tag Pseudoclasses

When you set the page properties for the NextBest Fest site, Dreamweaver created CSS styles to customize the appearance of hyperlinks for the site. Compound selector type styles also enable you to create these styles manually. When you create a compound selector style, you redefine the formatting for a group of tags or for tags containing a specific ID attribute. In this case, you would create a CSS style (or rule) for parts, or pseudoclasses, of the <a> tag. According to style sheet standards, a **pseudoclass** is any class that is applied to entities other than HTML Specifications Standard tags. For example, the anchor tag <a> is broken into pseudoclasses that include a:link, a:hover, a:active, and a:visited. Each pseudoclass controls a portion of the hyperlink functionality of the anchor tag. The a:link portion of the tag controls the way the link text looks before the link has been visited. The a:hover portion of the tag controls the way the link text looks while the pointer is over the link text. The a:active portion of the tag controls the way the link text looks as it is being clicked. The a:visited portion of the tag controls the way the link text looks after the link has been visited. Compound selector type styles enable you to modify each part of the anchor tag in the same way that you redefine an existing HTML tag. This is just one use of the compound selector type styles.

TIP

Mobile devices often bypass the hover pseudoclass and jump straight to the active pseudoclass.

When you define parts of the anchor tag manually, you must define them in the order they appear in the CSS Selector list: a:link, a:visited, a:hover, a:active. The a:hover style must be placed after the a:link and a:visited styles so that they don't hide the color property of the a:hover style. Similarly, the a:active style must be placed after the a:hover style, or the a:active color property will display when a user both activates and hovers over the linked text. When you set the hyperlink attributes in the Page Properties dialog box, Dreamweaver creates the CSS styles for the pseudoclasses of the anchor tag that are commonly used with hyperlinks and places the styles in the correct order in the style sheet.

In this session, you created CSS styles in the home page by redefining an HTML tag and creating a class style. In the next session, you will export the styles from the home page to an external style sheet, create CSS styles in an external style sheet, and attach the external style sheet to the home page of the NextBest Fest site.

REVIEW

Session 3.2 Quick Check

1. What is a CSS style?
2. True or False. When you redefine a CSS style after it has been applied to text, the look of the content to which the style has been applied is also updated.
3. What is a CSS style that you create from scratch called?
4. True or False. You can save CSS styles in a style sheet that can be applied to all of the pages in a site.
5. How does modifying an HTML tag make it more useful?
6. When do some designers prefer to create class styles instead of redefining existing HTML tags?
7. With what letter or character do class style names start?

SESSION 3.3 VISUAL OVERVIEW

When you disable a property, Dreamweaver puts comment tags around the code, which causes the browser and Design view to ignore the property.

A **comment** is a note added to the code that does not get read or displayed by the browser.

The font-family property is disabled so it does not affect the display of the text in Design view.

The CSS tab in the Property inspector shows which rule is affected.

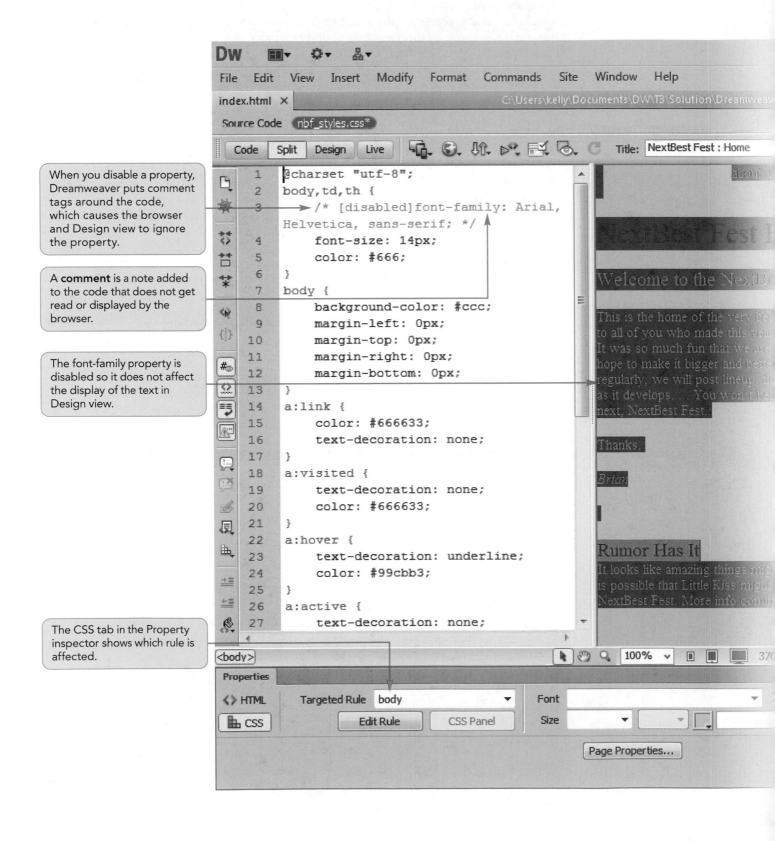

CODE FOR EXTERNAL CSS STYLES

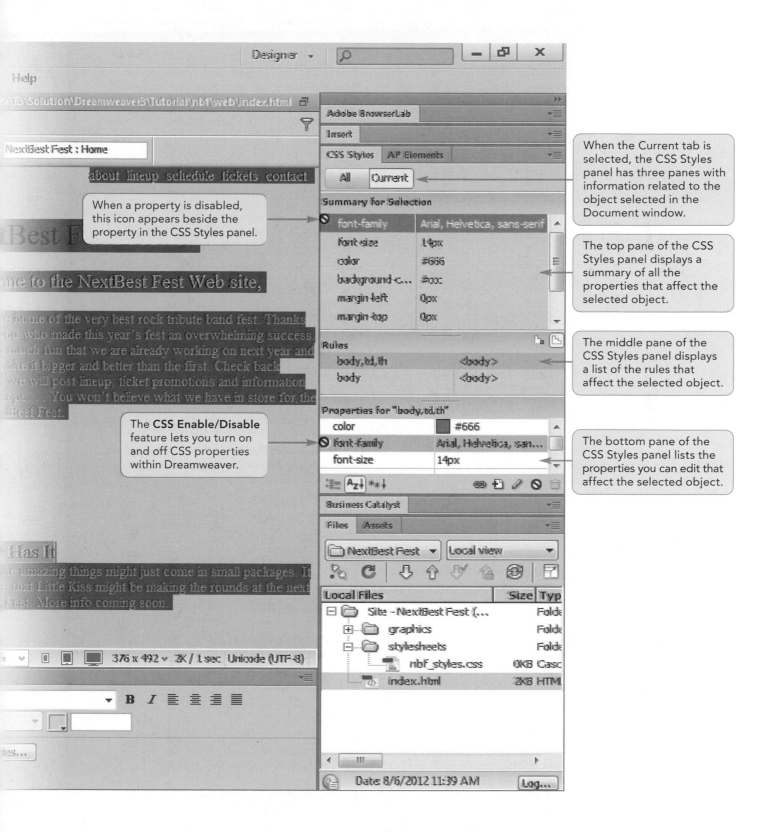

When a property is disabled, this icon appears beside the property in the CSS Styles panel.

The **CSS Enable/Disable** feature lets you turn on and off CSS properties within Dreamweaver.

When the Current tab is selected, the CSS Styles panel has three panes with information related to the object selected in the Document window.

The top pane of the CSS Styles panel displays a summary of all the properties that affect the selected object.

The middle pane of the CSS Styles panel displays a list of the rules that affect the selected object.

The bottom pane of the CSS Styles panel lists the properties you can edit that affect the selected object.

Examining Code for Internal CSS Styles

As you created and applied CSS styles to format the text in the home page, Dreamweaver added the appropriate HTML code within the head of each page. The **head** of a Web page is the portion of the HTML between the head tags. The actual code included within the head differs, based on whether you created an internal style sheet or an external style sheet.

When you create styles that apply only to the document in which you are working, the code for those styles is placed in the head of that page. If you attach an external style sheet to a Web page, a link tag to the style sheet is placed in the head of the HTML code for that page. The link tag allows the Web page to access the content of the external style sheet.

You will examine the HTML and CSS code in the head of the home page as well as the additional tags that appear throughout the page.

Viewing Code for Internal Style Sheets

When styles are defined in the current document only, the code is stored in an internal style sheet, which is also called an **embedded style sheet** because the styles are embedded (or placed) in the head of the Web page. The embedded styles can be used throughout the current Web page but not in any other page. The code usually takes the format:

```
<style type="text/css">
name {
    attribute-name: attribute value;
    attribute2-name: attribute2 value;
}
</style>
```

where *name* is the selector name, the HTML tag name, or the tag and pseudoclass name.

The style definitions (or rules) all appear inside the style tags, which are in the format:

```
<style type="text/css">style definitions</style>
```

where *type="text/css"* indicates the format of the styles that will follow. At this time, *"text/css"* is the only style type. However, the current HTML guidelines recommend that you include the style type to prevent problems if other style types are introduced in the future.

Remember, every CSS style (or rule) consists of two parts: the selector and the declaration. The selector is the style name and the declaration defines the attributes included in the style. The format for the style definition is:

```
name {
    attribute-name: attribute value;
    attribute2-name: attribute2 value;
}
```

In Dreamweaver, the selector and opening bracket are located on the first line of code for the style and are displayed in pink. You can tell by the selector whether the style is a custom class or ID style, a redefined tag, or a compound style tag. The class style name is preceded by a period (for example, .sub2). The ID style name is preceded by #. The name of a redefined tag includes the tag name at the beginning of the style (for example, h1). In the compound style, the selector is followed by the tags (preceded by a colon for pseudoclasses), or selector names, separated by commas.

The style declaration is a series of attribute/value pairs. The attribute and value are separated by a colon and a space. Each attribute/value pair is displayed in blue on a separate line that ends with a semicolon and is indented under the selector. The closing bracket appears on a separate line after the final attribute/value pair and is displayed in pink. Styles follow this same format no matter where they are located.

Dreamweaver created the internal style sheet code when you defined the page properties for the home page. You will view this embedded style sheet in Code view.

To view the code for the home page's internal style sheet:

1. If you took a break after the previous session, make sure that the NextBest Fest site is open, the Designer workspace is reset, the Business Catalyst panel group is minimized, the index.html page is open in the Document window, and the page is in Design view.

2. On the Document toolbar, click the **Code** button, and then scroll to the top of the page, if necessary. The code for the home page appears in the Document window. See Figure 3-20.

Figure 3-20   **Code for the internal style sheet in the home page**

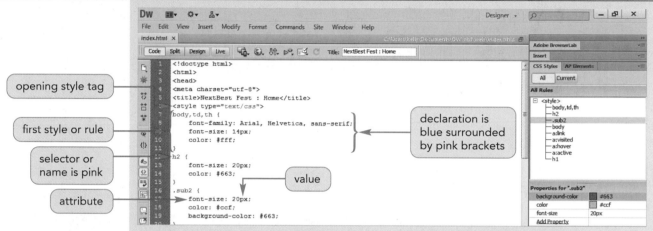

Trouble? If the code on your screen does not match the code in the figure, you do not have word wrap, line numbers, syntax coloring, and/or auto indent turned on or the new CSS styles were inserted in a different order. On the menu bar, click View, and then click Word Wrap, Line Numbers, Syntax Coloring, and/or Auto Indent to check each option as necessary. If the new styles were inserted in a different order, do not worry. It will not affect the code.

3. Examine the code associated with the styles. Locate the opening head tag, and then locate the opening style tag.

4. Locate the opening comment tag, and then locate the first rule. Each rule starts with the selector (in pink) followed by the opening bracket. The declaration (in blue) is indented beneath the selector. Each attribute/value pair is on a separate line ending with a semicolon. The attribute is separated from the value by a colon and a space. The closing bracket (in pink) is on a separate line.

5. In the All Rules pane of the Insert panel, select the **h1** rule and, if necessary, drag it to the bottom of the list, select the **h2** rule and drag it below the h1 rule at the bottom of the list, and then drag the **.sub2** rule below the h2 rule. The styles are reordered in the style sheet and the corresponding code is rearranged as well.

6. Save the page.

Using External Style Sheets

TIP

An external style sheet has the file extension .css.

Locating all of the styles for a Web site in one place is one of the greatest advantages of using CSS styles. An external style sheet enables you to separate the style of the Web site from the content of the Web site, allowing you to make stylistic changes throughout the site by updating a single file. So far, you have created and used styles within one document, or page, in the NextBest Fest site. To use these styles throughout a site, they must be located in an external style sheet, a file that contains the CSS styles defined for a Web site. A site can have as many external style sheets as you want, but it is usually simpler to incorporate all styles into one external style sheet. An exception to this guideline is when you use style sheets to create different layouts for the content of pages. For example, you might create a separate print style sheet to structure the site content so that the user can more easily print information from the site or you might have a separate style sheet for mobile devices. You can either create a style in an external style sheet or you can move the styles you created within a Web page to an external style sheet.

Moving Styles to an External Style Sheet

If you have already created styles in a specific document or page, you can move one or all of those styles to an external style sheet rather than re-create them. This lets you use those styles throughout the Web site. To keep the files in a Web site organized, you should create a folder in the local root folder of the Web site, such as a folder named *stylesheets*, and then save the external style sheet file with a descriptive name, such as *nbf_styles*, within that folder. To move CSS styles to an external style sheet, the Web page where the styles are currently located must be open.

REFERENCE

Moving Styles to a New External Style Sheet

- Open the Web page whose styles you want to move.
- In the CSS Styles panel, select the styles to move, right-click the selected styles, and then click Move CSS Rules.
- Click the A new style sheet option button, and then click the OK button.
- Navigate to the stylesheets folder in the local root folder.
- In the File name box, type a name for the style sheet.
- Click the Save button.

You want to use the styles you created for the home page in all of the other pages in the NextBest Fest site. You will move those styles to an external style sheet that you will store in a new folder named *stylesheets* in the local root folder. When you move the styles from the home page, all of the styles from the page, including the styles that Dreamweaver created when you set the page properties, are moved to the external style sheet. In this case, you will create the style sheet when you export the styles from the home page.

Be sure to move all the styles to the external style sheet to avoid conflicts that cause the page to display incorrectly.

To move the styles from the home page to an external style sheet:

1. Open the Files panel, and then select **index.html**, if necessary.

2. In the CSS Styles panel, click the **All** button, if necessary.

3. In the All Rules pane, click the first style in the list, press and hold the **Shift** key, click the last style in the list, and then release the Shift key. All of the styles are selected.

4. Right-click the selected styles, and then click **Move CSS Rules** on the context menu. The Move To External Style Sheet dialog box opens.

5. Click the **A new style sheet** option button, and then click the **OK** button. The Save Style Sheet File As dialog box opens.

6. Verify that the Save in box displays the local root folder of your NextBest Fest site. You will create a new folder in which to store the external style sheet.

7. On the dialog box toolbar, click the **Create New Folder** button 📁. A new folder is created within the local root folder of your NextBest Fest site and appears in the Save in list with the New Folder name selected.

8. Type **stylesheets**, and then press the **Enter** key. The new folder is renamed stylesheets.

9. Double-click the **stylesheets** folder to open it. You will save the external style sheet in this folder.

10. In the File name box, type **nbf_styles**. The external style sheet has a descriptive name. See Figure 3-21.

Figure 3-21   **Save Style Sheet File As dialog box**

folder where the style sheet will be saved

descriptive name for the style sheet

style sheet files have the .css extension

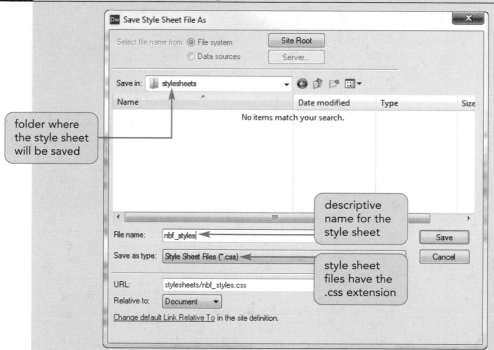

---

11. Click the **Save** button. The external style sheet file is saved within the folder you created, the styles disappear from the code for the home page, and the nbf_styles.css page appears on the Related Files toolbar located below the index.html tab at the top of the Document window. When you open a page in the Document window, the related documents associated with the open file such as style sheets or external JavaScript files appear as buttons on the Related Files toolbar so you can easily move between them and update the pages.

12. On the Files panel toolbar, click the **Refresh** button 🔃 to refresh the files list, and then in the Files panel, click the **Expand** button ⊞ next to the stylesheets folder to display the nbf_styles.css file in the files list. See Figure 3-22.

| Figure 3-22 | External style sheet created |

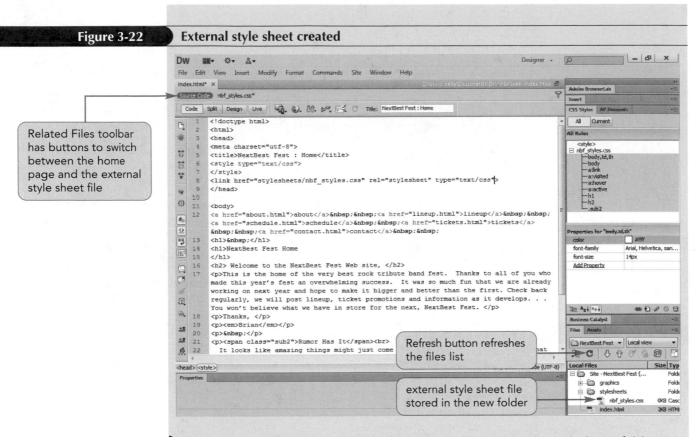

Related Files toolbar has buttons to switch between the home page and the external style sheet file

Refresh button refreshes the files list

external style sheet file stored in the new folder

▶ **13.** In the Files panel, click the **Collapse** button ⊟ next to the stylesheets folder to collapse the folder in the files list.

▶ **14.** On the Related Files toolbar, click the **nbf_styles.css** button to display the page in the Document window, and then save the file.

▶ **15.** On the Related Files toolbar, click the **Source Code** button to return to the index.html page, and then save the page.

Deleting Styles from a Style Sheet

Styles moved to a new external style sheet are automatically deleted from within the page. However, when you connect an existing external style sheet to a page, you must move all of the styles from that page to the external style sheet and then delete the styles from within the page. Otherwise, you will create multiple sets of styles with the same names, which can cause styles to conflict and lead to confusion.

Leaving some styles in the internal style sheet can negate the benefits of using style sheets because you don't have one centralized set of styles that is easily updated and used throughout the site. Also, because style sheets are cascading, the styles in an internal style sheet will override styles in an external style sheet wherever a style conflict exists.

When you delete the internal styles from a page without connecting that page to an external style sheet, the text and page properties return to their default formatting.

When you moved the styles from the home page to the external style sheet, the internal styles were automatically deleted from within that page and the page was connected to the style sheet. The page now gets its formatting from the external style sheet.

Creating a Style in an External Style Sheet

You can add new styles to an external style sheet at any time. The process of creating a style in an external style sheet is exactly the same as the process of creating a style in an internal style sheet. The only difference is that you choose the style sheet by name in the Rule Definition list when you create the new style.

Defining a Style in an External Style Sheet

- In the CSS Styles panel, click the New CSS Rule button.
- Click the Selector Type button, and then click the appropriate style selector type.
- Click in the Selector Name box, and then type a name for the new style.
- Click the Rule Definition button, and then select the style sheet name from the list.
- Click the OK button.
- In the Category box, click a category, and then set the option you want. Repeat until the style includes all the options you want.
- Click the OK button.

You need to create a style that will justify the navigation text at the right side of each page. Because this style will be used only once in each page of the NextBest Fest site, you will create a new ID style defined in the nbf_styles.css external style sheet. When you add a new style to the style sheet, the style sheet opens in the Document window. You must save the style sheet to save the new style.

To define the nav style in the external style sheet:

▶ 1. On the Document toolbar, click the **Design** button to switch to Design view, and then, in the Document window, select the navigation text.

▶ 2. In the CSS Styles panel, click the **New CSS Rule** button ⊡. The New CSS Rule dialog box opens.

   Trouble? If the buttons in the CSS Styles panel are not active, scroll to the top of the All Rules pane, click <style>, and then repeat Step 1.

▶ 3. Click the **Selector Type** button, and then click **ID**. You will create an ID style for the navigation system.

▶ 4. In the Selector Name box, type **#nav**. The new ID style will be named nav.

▶ 5. Click the **Rule Definition** button, and then click **nbf_styles.css**. The ID style will be saved in the external style sheet.

▶ 6. Click the **OK** button. The CSS Rule definition for #nav in nbf_styles.css dialog box opens.

▶ 7. In the Category box, click **Box**, and then, in the Float list, click **right**.

▶ 8. Click the **OK** button. The style is added to the style sheet.

▶ 9. If necessary, next to the style sheet name, click the **Expand** button ⊞ to view the styles. The #nav style appears in the All Rules pane of the CSS Styles panel as well as in the ID list in the HTML pane of the Property inspector. The nbf_styles.css page tab in the Document window includes an asterisk to indicate that the style sheet has been changed since it was last saved. You must save the style sheet to save the changes.

▶ 10. Click the **nbf_styles.css** page tab, save the page, and then click the **Design** button to return to the home page.

You will now add the new nav style to the navigation text.

To apply the nav style from the external style sheet:

1. At the top of the home page, select the navigation text.

2. In the HTML pane of the Property inspector, click the **ID** arrow, and then click **nav**. The nav ID style is applied to the selected text, which is right justified in the page. See Figure 3-23.

| Figure 3-23 | Navigation text with the nav style applied |

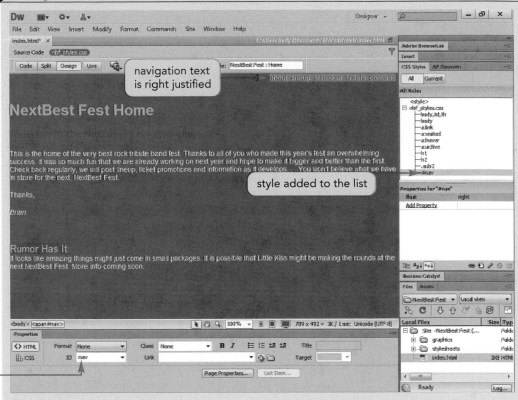

3. Save the page.

Viewing Code for External Style Sheets

When an external style sheet is attached to a page, a link tag appears within the head of the Web page and the styles are located in the style sheet, not in the head of the Web page. External style sheets are also called **linked style sheets**. Link tags do not include a closing tag or any style content information; they only convey relationship information about the linked document.

Link tags appear in the following general format:

```
<link rel="stylesheet" href="stylesheeturl.css" type="text/css"/>
```

The first part of the tag, link, identifies the type of tag. The second part of the tag, rel=, indicates the relationship between the linked document and the Web page. The relationship itself appears within quotation marks; in this case, the relationship is *"stylesheet"*—meaning that the linked document contains the CSS style for the page. Next, *href="stylesheeturl.css"* is the URL of the linked document. The URL appears within quotation marks. Finally, *type=* indicates the form of the content that will follow.

TIP

Link tags usually appear only within the head of a Web page; anchor tags are used to create hyperlinks in the body of a Web page.

MIME type is the standard for identifying content type on the Internet. The type also appears within quotation marks.

You will look at the link to the external style sheet in the home page.

To view the code in the home page:

1. On the Related Files toolbar, click the **Source Code** button.

2. On the Document toolbar, click the **Code** button. The home page appears in Code view.

3. In the Document window, scroll to the top of the home page, and then locate the link tag in the head of the page. See Figure 3-24.

Figure 3-24   **Code for the external style sheet in the home page**

opening head tag

link tag in the head of the page

closing head tag

4. Locate the closing head tag. Notice that no styles appear in the head of the page.

When styles are located in an external style sheet, you must open the style sheet to view all of the code for the styles. If you know how to enter code manually, you can edit the styles for the page by changing the code in the style sheet. Style sheets open only in Code view; Split and Design views are not available options.

You will open the nbf_styles.css style sheet in the Document window and view the styles.

To view the nbf_styles.css external style sheet:

1. On the Related Files toolbar, click the **nbf_styles.css** button.

2. In the Document window, scroll to the top of the page, if necessary. The external style sheet appears in the Document window. See Figure 3-25.

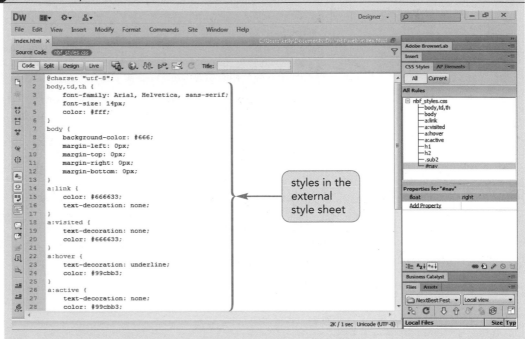

Figure 3-25   External style sheet

styles in the
external
style sheet

3. Notice that the style format is the same as in the internal style sheet.

4. On the Document toolbar, click the **Design** button to return to the home page.

Viewing Style Tags

Whether styles are located in an internal or external style sheet, using CSS styles affects the code in the body of a Web page in the same way. When you use CSS styles to modify or customize HTML tags, you do not see any additional code in the body of the Web pages. The existing tags simply reference the new definitions, which are located either in the head of the Web page or in an external style sheet.

When you select text and apply a class style, Dreamweaver adds the attributes of that class style to the text by inserting additional code within the Web page in one of three ways:

- **Adding attributes to an existing tag.** When you apply a class style to text that is already surrounded by a tag, Dreamweaver adds the additional attributes of the class style to the existing tag. For example, if you apply a class style named "class_name" to a block of text that is already surrounded by a paragraph tag, <p>, Dreamweaver adds the attributes of the custom style to that paragraph tag in the following manner:

  `<p class="class_name">Content of text block</p>`

  where class="class_name" tells the browser to format the text according to the definition in the class style named "class_name." (The class style definition will be located either in the head of the Web page or in an external style sheet.)

- **Applying a class style to a block of text or block-level element.** When you apply a class style to a block of text that is not already encompassed by a tag, Dreamweaver surrounds the entire block of text with the div tag that inserts the custom style attributes. The div tag appears in the general format:

  `<div class="class_name">Content of text block</div>`

- **Applying a class style to a text selection.** When you apply a class style to a selection smaller than a text block (such as a word, a phrase, or a portion of a text block), Dreamweaver surrounds the selection with a span tag that inserts the custom style attributes. The span tag appears in the following general format:

```
<span class="class_name">Content of text selection</span>
```

You will view the subheadings and navigation system in the home page in Split view to examine the code that Dreamweaver inserted into the page.

To examine the home page in Split view:

1. On the Document toolbar, click the **Split** button to switch to Split view.

2. On the Related Files toolbar, click the **Source Code** button. The HTML source code for the page appears in the Code pane.

3. In the Design pane, select the **Welcome to the NextBest Fest Web site,** line. The text is also selected in the Code pane.

4. In the Code pane, examine the code around the selected text. The text is surrounded by the Heading 2 tag, <h2>. No extra code appears in the page because the <h2> tag simply references the style located in the style sheet and displays the text according to the defined rule.

5. In the Property inspector, click the **CSS** button. The rule's properties appear in the CSS pane of the Property inspector.

6. In the All Rules pane of the CSS Styles panel, click the **h2** tag. The rule's properties appear in the Properties for "h2" pane of the CSS Styles panel. See Figure 3-26.

Figure 3-26   **Code for a redefined HTML tag**

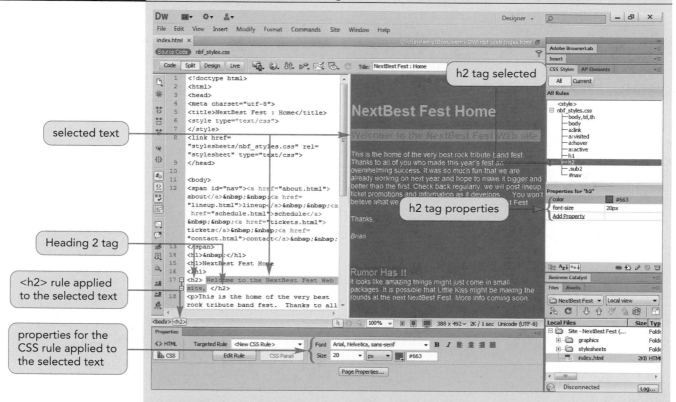

7. In the Design pane, scroll to the bottom of the page, select **Rumor Has It**, and then, in the Code pane, examine the code surrounding the selected text. The class style information is inserted into a span tag because the paragraph tag that surrounds the subheading also surrounds the following paragraph text, but the style is applied to only the heading. See Figure 3-27.

Figure 3-27 | **Class style applied with a span tag**

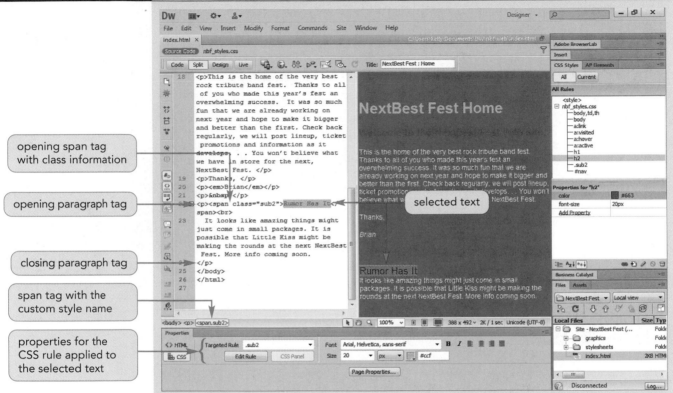

8. In the Design pane, scroll to the top of the page, select the navigation text, and then, in the Code pane, examine the code surrounding the selected text. The ID style information is again inserted into the span tag. See Figure 3-28.

Figure 3-28   Custom ID style applied with the span tag

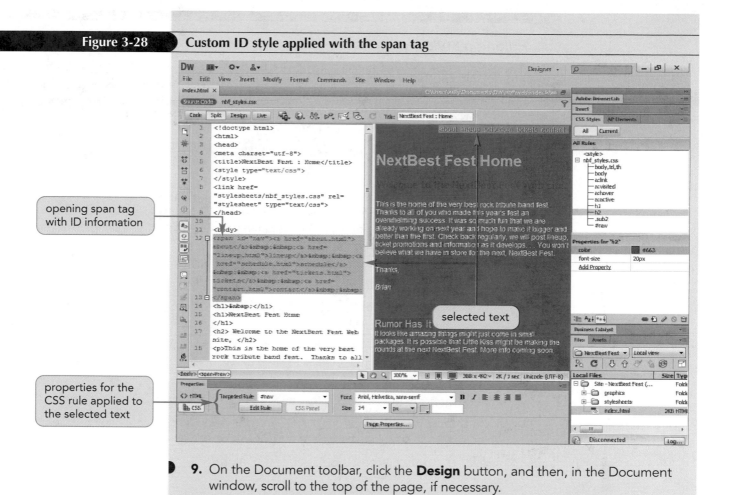

9. On the Document toolbar, click the **Design** button, and then, in the Document window, scroll to the top of the page, if necessary.

Editing CSS Styles

One of the most powerful aspects of CSS is the ability to edit styles. You edit a style by adding or removing formatting attributes from an existing style. When you edit a style, any element to which the style is applied is updated automatically to reflect the changes you made. This helps you to maintain a consistent look throughout a Web site, whether the site includes only a few pages or many. It also enables you to control the look of an entire Web site from one centralized set of specifications. Dreamweaver includes several tools to help you manage and edit your styles, including the CSS Rule definition dialog box, the Properties pane in the CSS Styles panel, and the CSS pane in the Property inspector. New features that help you to test and edit CSS styles include CSS Enable/Disable and CSS Inspect.

Editing Styles in the CSS Rule Definition Dialog Box

You can edit styles in the CSS Rule Definition dialog box. This is the same dialog box that you used to create the definitions. The changes you make override the original style attribute selections. After you have selected attributes for the style, you can view the style in the page by clicking the Apply button in the CSS Rule Definition dialog box and viewing the page in the Document window.

REFERENCE

Editing a Style

- In the All Rules pane of the CSS Styles panel, select the style to edit.
- Right-click the name of the style, and then click Edit (or in the CSS Styles panel, click the style name, and then click the Edit Rule button).
- Make the changes in the CSS Rule Definition dialog box.
- Click the OK button.

Gage wants you to make the background color of the page lighter so that you can change the text to the dark color that was approved in the Web site plan. You will select the body tag in the CSS Styles panel and edit it in the CSS Rule Definition dialog box.

To edit the background color of the page style:

1. In the All Rules pane of the CSS Styles panel, select the **body** style. This is the style you want to edit.

2. In the CSS Styles panel, click the **Edit Rule** button 🖉. The CSS Rule Definition for body in nbf_styles.css dialog box opens so you can modify the body style.

3. In the Category box, click **Background**. You will change the background color.

4. In the Background-color box, type **#ccc**. This is the hexadecimal color code for the light gray color you want to use for the background.

5. Click the **Apply** button. The background color in the home page changes to a lighter gray. See Figure 3-29.

| Figure 3-29 | Home page with the updated body style |

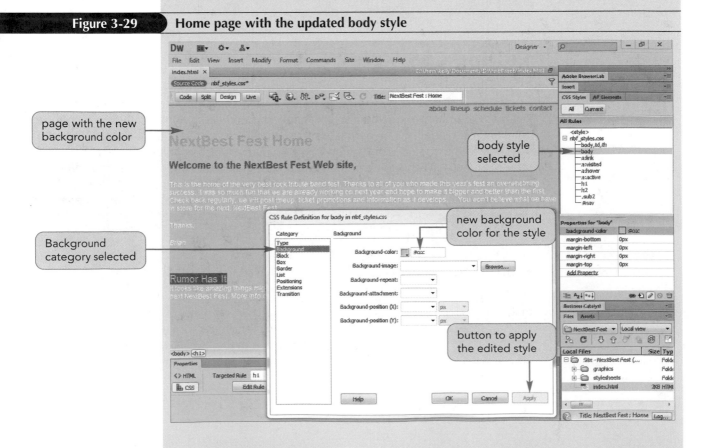

6. Click the **OK** button. The changes you made to the styles are accepted. Next, you will change the body text color.

7. In the All Rules pane of the CSS Styles panel, double-click the **body,td,th** style. The CSS Rules Definition for body,td,th in nbf_styles.css opens.

8. Select the text in the Color box, type **#666** (the hexadecimal color code for the gray color you want to use for the text), and then click the **OK** button. The body text changes to gray.

9. On the Related Files toolbar, click the **nbf_styles.css** button, and then save the style sheet. You must save the external style sheet to save the style changes you made.

10. On the Document toolbar, click the **Design** button to return to the home page, and then save the home page.

11. Preview the home page in a browser, and then close the browser.

TIP

When an edited style is in an internal style sheet, you must save the page to save the changes to the style.

Editing Styles in the Properties Pane of the CSS Styles Panel

The CSS Styles panel is another tool that you can use to examine and edit CSS styles. When you select a page element in the Document window and click the Current button in the CSS Styles panel, the panel changes from All mode to Current mode and three panes display information about styles and properties for the selected page element. Because styles are inherited and cascading, several rules might contribute to the formatting of any particular element.

The Summary for Selection pane lists the properties for all rules that affect the formatting of the selected element. Properties are listed in hierarchical order; properties that are closer to the text appear at the bottom of the list. This is useful because styles sometimes inherit properties from higher-level styles, and when a property value is set in more than one style, the value located in the style closest to the element will override the value of the higher-level style. Viewing the properties in a hierarchical list enables you to see exactly which property takes precedence.

The middle pane switches between About and Rules. The About pane specifies which rule or cascade of rules affects the property selected in the Summary for Selection pane as well as the style sheet file in which that rule is saved. The Rules pane shows the cascade or hierarchy of all the rules that affect the selected element.

The Properties pane enables you to edit CSS properties for the rule in which the property selected in the Summary for Selection pane is defined or for the rule selected in the About or Rules pane. You can show only those properties that are set; you can display the properties in alphabetical order, or you can display the properties by category (such as font, background, and so on). Properties that have values are displayed in blue at the top of the list. When a property in another rule overrides the same property in the selected rule, the property in the selected rule has a red line through it. Property names are displayed in the left column, and values are displayed in the right column. You can change or add values by typing in the value column or by selecting a value from a list. Any changes you make in the Properties pane are immediately applied to the page, so you can see how that property affects the design. You must save the page and any relevant style sheets to save the changes.

Gage wants you to remove the default bold from the h1 and h2 styles so that the styles more closely match the site plan. You will use the Properties pane in the CSS Styles panel to make the changes.

To edit the h1 and h2 styles using the Properties pane in the CSS Styles panel:

▶ 1. Collapse the **Files panel group**, and then, in the CSS Styles panel, click the **Current** button. The CSS Styles panel changes to Current Selection mode and displays the Summary for Selection pane, the About pane, and the Properties pane.

▶ 2. At the top of the home page, select **NextBest Fest Home**. The Summary for Selection pane lists the font-family from the body tag and the properties that are set for the Heading 1 text; the color property is selected by default. The About pane shows that the property selected in the Summary for Selection pane is located in the h1 rule. The Properties pane displays the properties set for the <h1> tag. You can edit a rule by changing the information in the bottom pane.

  Trouble? If you see the rules pertaining to the selected property in the middle panel, the Rules pane is displayed and you need to switch to the About pane. Click the Show information about selected property button in the middle pane title bar.

▶ 3. Click the **Show list view** button [Az↓] to display all of the available properties for the selected h1 rule, if necessary, and then drag the bottom border of each pane in the CSS Styles panel down until all of the text is visible. Dreamweaver uses the tag name as the style name for redefined HTML tags. See Figure 3-30.

Figure 3-30   **CSS Styles panel in Current Selection mode**

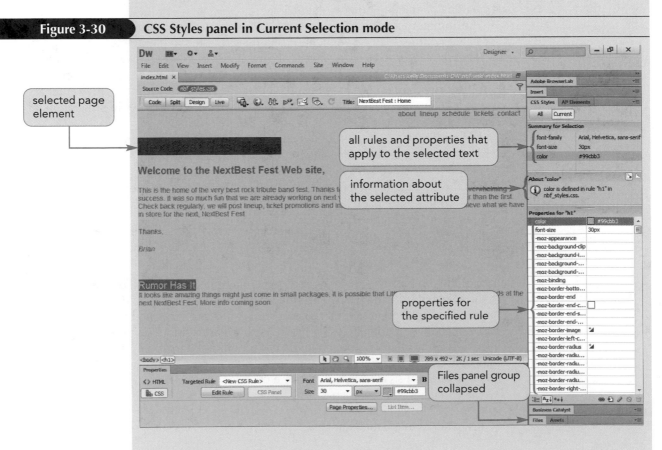

selected page element

all rules and properties that apply to the selected text

information about the selected attribute

properties for the specified rule

Files panel group collapsed

4. In the About pane title bar, click the **Show cascade of rules for selected tag** button to select it, if necessary. The cascade of rules that affects the selection is listed in the pane. You will edit the font-weight property for the h1 style in the Properties pane.

5. In the Properties pane, scroll down to font-weight, click the right **font-weight** box, and then click **normal** in the font-weight list. The font weight of the h1 tag is changed from its default bold to normal. See Figure 3-31.

Figure 3-31   **Updated h1 font-weight in the Properties pane**

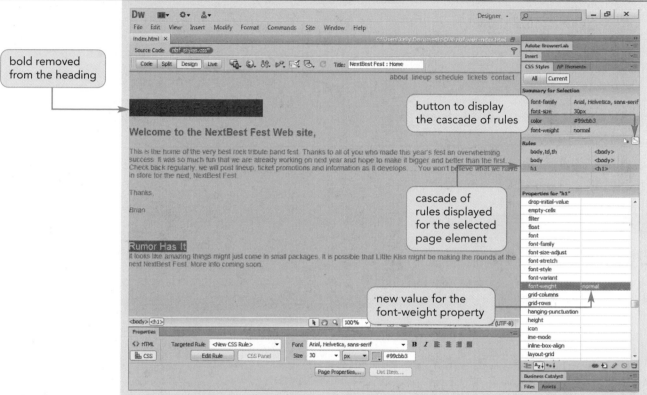

bold removed from the heading

button to display the cascade of rules

cascade of rules displayed for the selected page element

new value for the font-weight property

6. In the home page, select **Welcome...**. The relevant rules and properties for the selected text appear in the CSS Styles panel with the properties set for the h2 style listed in the Properties pane. You will edit the h2 style for the subheading in the Properties pane.

7. In the Properties pane, scroll down to font-weight, click the right **font-weight** box, and then click **normal** in the font-weight list. The subheading with the h2 style changes font weight.

8. In the Summary for Selection pane, click **font-family** to select this property, and then, in the Rules pane, click the **body,td,th** rule to see how the properties from this tag affect the current selection. The color and font-size properties have black lines through them because the color and font-size properties you set in the h2 style override the ones in this higher-level style. The font-family property has a value even though you did not select a font family in the h2 style because the body tag affects all the elements in the body of the HTML code.

9. Save the home page, switch to the **nbf_styles.css** style sheet, and then save the nbf_styles.css style sheet.

10. In the CSS Styles panel, click the **All** button.

Enabling and Disabling CSS Styles

Because styles are cascading and many styles can affect any object in a page, editing the styles for an object can become confusing. You can use the CSS Enable/Disable feature to help figure out what CSS properties are affecting an object. The CSS Enable/Disable feature enables you to turn on and off CSS properties within Dreamweaver. When you disable a CSS property, Dreamweaver places a comment around the property, which makes the property invisible until you enable the property again. When you enable a disabled property, the comment is removed and the property is again visible within Dreamweaver.

You will disable the font-family property in the body,td,th style to see how that property affects the text in the index.html page.

To disable the font-family property in the body,td,th style:

1. In the All Rules pane of the CSS Styles panel, select the **body,td,th** style. You will disable the font-family property for this style.

2. In the Properties pane, right-click the **font-family** property, and click **Disable** on the context menu. A red circle with a slash appears to the left of the property, indicating that the property has been disabled.

3. In the Document window, examine the page to see how the text has changed. See Figure 3-32.

| Figure 3-32 | Home page with the font-family property disabled |

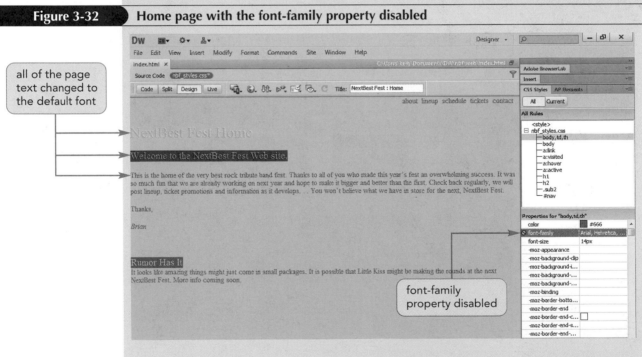

4. In the Properties pane, right-click the **font-family** property, and then click **Enable** on the context menu. The disabled font-family property is again enabled, and the page text is redisplayed in the Arial, Helvetica, sans-serif font group.

5. Minimize the CSS Styles panel.

Changing Text Appearance in the Property Inspector

You can change the appearance of selected text with the Property inspector by applying an existing style to the text or changing HTML attributes of the text in the HTML pane, or by editing the attributes of the CSS style applied to the selected element in the CSS pane. If you select an attribute in the Property inspector that is not already defined in a style, Dreamweaver opens the New CSS Rule box so that you can create a new CSS rule as usual.

PROSKILLS

Teamwork: Organizing Styles for a Site

Just as it is important to keep site files organized, it is important to keep styles organized. This is essential when you are working as part of a team. You should create a new style only when it is necessary. Also, you should limit the number of styles that are used in a site as much as possible to keep the style list manageable. If you are going to change the appearance of all the text to which an existing style is applied, you should edit the existing style. If you need a new style, you should create the style with the CSS Styles panel, and you should place the new style in the external style sheet so that you can use it throughout the site.

A good design practice is to use CSS styles for all Web page formatting, not just to define some display attributes. You should get in the habit of creating CSS styles for all formatting that you want to add to a site. Finally, you should remember to name styles with intuitive, logical names. Do not reference attributes in the style name because the red text might be blue text in the future. Maintaining these commonsense practices ensures that your team will, more easily, be able to work together efficiently.

Exploring HTML Tags Used with Text

A variety of HTML tags are used with text. You worked with text tags when you created styles by modifying the existing body tag <body> and the Heading 1 tag <h1>. Other tags also affect how text is displayed in the page. Before HTML5, tags such as italic <i> and bold <b> were used to indicate how text should be presented in the page. In HTML5, some of these presentation tags now have specific semantic meanings. For example, in HTML5, the <i> tag is used for text in an alternate voice, such as foreign words and technical terms, as well as for italicized text. Because these tags have semantic meanings as well as presentational styles, designers can change the look of the style. In other words, the <i> tag doesn't have to display tagged text in italics. Figure 3-33 describes some of the more common text tags. These tags, with the exception of the div tag, are available in the Text category on the Insert panel.

When you create Web pages in Design view, Dreamweaver places the appropriate HTML tags around the text for you. To see the HTML tags, you need to switch to either Code view or Split view.

Figure 3-33   **Common HTML tags for text**

Tag Name	Description	Sample	Browser Display
I	The <i> tag was used to add italic style to text. Now it defines a section of text in an alternate mood or voice that is offset from the surrounding text in a way that will indicate a different quality of text. It is usually displayed in italic type but you can define it with different styles using CSS. For example, you would use the i tag around stage directions in a script to separate the directions from the actors' lines. The i tag should only be used if you cannot use a more appropriate semantic element. For example, the mark tag should be used to indicate marked/highlighted text, the cite tag should be used to indicate the title of a work, and the dfn tag should be used to indicate a definition of a term.	**<i>**Some text**</i>**	*Some text*
Emphasis	Adds structural meaning to text and is to be rendered differently from other body text to designate stress emphasis. For example, if you would pronounce a word or group of words differently, you would use the emphasis tag around them. When you use the Italic button, Dreamweaver places emphasis tags around the selected text. Most browsers italicize text that is surrounded by the emphasis tag unless you redefine the tag using CSS.	****Some text ****	*Some text*
Bold	Was historically used to add bold style to text. Now the b tag defines a section of text to which you are drawing attention only for utilitarian purposes, without conveying added importance or implying an alternate mood or voice. For example, key words or product names would be surrounded by the b tag. Now you should use a style to make text surrounded by the b tag look different from surrounding text; it is not necessary to make the text in the b tag bold.	****Some text****	**Some text**
Strong	Adds structural and semantic meaning to text and is to be rendered differently from other body text to designate a strong emphasis. When you use the Bold button, Dreamweaver places strong tags around the selected text. Browsers bold text that is surrounded by the strong tag, unless you have used CSS to change the style of the tag.	****Some text ****	**Some text**

Unordered list	Creates a list of bulleted items.	**<ul>**
		    <li>Item1**</li>**
		    <li>Item2**</li>**
		 </ul>
			• Item1
			 • Item2

Figure 3-33   **Common HTML tags for text (continued)**

Tag Name	Description	Sample	Browser Display

Ordered list	Creates a list of numbered items.	**<ol>**
		  <li>Item1**</li>**
		  <li>Item2**</li>**
		</ol>
			1. Item1
			2. Item2

Paragraph	Designates a block of text that starts and ends with a break (a skipped line) and by default is left aligned with a ragged right edge. Dreamweaver places paragraph tags around blocks of text when you press the Enter key.	**<p>**Some text in a paragraph.**</p>** **<p>**Another paragraph.**</p>**	Some text in a paragraph. Another paragraph.
Blockquote	Specifies a section of text that has been quoted. Usually indents text from both the left and right margins, and can be nested for deeper indents. Added in Dreamweaver with the Text Indent button; the Outdent button removes a blockquote tag.	<p>Introductory text</p>**<blockquote>** <p>Some text</p> **</blockquote>** <p>Closing text</p>	Introductory text Some text Closing text
Div	Divides a page into a series of blocks. Divs are powerful because you can wrap them around text, graphics, and other objects and create CSS styles that affect everything in the tag. You can insert a div from the Layout tab of the Insert panel.	**<div>**Some text, a paragraph, or other element**</div>**	Some text, a paragraph, or other element

Pre	Preserves the exact formatting of a block of text when it is displayed in a Web page by rendering text in a fixed pitch font and by preserving the associated spacing with white space characters. For example, a poem surrounded by pre tags would maintain indents, multiple spaces between words, and new lines that would otherwise be discarded when it was rendered in a browser.	**<pre>**Some
		preformatted text
		might
		  look like
		this.**</pre>**
			Some
			preformatted text
			might
			  look like
			this.

Break	Forces a line break on a page. Used singly without a closing tag because it does not surround text and add attributes. Add by pressing the Shift+Enter keys or clicking the Line Break button in the Characters list in the Text category of the Insert panel.	Some** **text	Some text
Nonbreaking space	Inserts a space that will be displayed by the browser. (Browsers will display only one regular space between items in a Web page, regardless of how many regular spaces are entered.) Use nonbreaking spaces to add more than one visible space between items or to ensure that a line does not break between items. The nonbreaking space is a special character (not a tag) that is often used like a tag to format text. Insert by pressing the Ctrl+Shift+Spacebar keys or by clicking the Non-Breaking Space button in the Characters list in the Text category of the Insert panel.	Some text	Some text

You will examine the code for HTML tags that apply to text in the home page. You will also use the Reference panel to gather additional information about some of the tags.

To examine the code for HTML text tags in the home page:

1. On the Document toolbar, click the **Code** button, and then on the Related Files toolbar, click the **Source Code** button. The home page appears in Code view.

2. Scroll to the top of the page, locate the **body** tag, and then locate the first paragraph tag **<p>** below the body tag.

3. Right-click the paragraph tag **<p>**, and then click **Reference** on the context menu. The Reference panel opens, displaying information about the paragraph tag. See Figure 3-34.

| Figure 3-34 | Reference panel for the selected HTML paragraph tag |

description of the selected tag

4. Read the information in the Reference panel, and then look at the code in the Code pane. There are five sets of paragraph tags.

5. Select the entire fifth paragraph tag, including the text within the opening and closing tags, and then click the **Split** button on the Document toolbar. The linked text is selected in the Design pane of the Document window.

6. In the Design pane, select the **NextBest Fest Home** text. The text is also selected in the Code pane.

7. In the Code pane, click in the opening **<h1>** tag before the selected text, right-click the selected tag, and then click **Reference** on the context menu. A description of the <h1> to <h6> tags appears in the Reference panel. Read the description.

8. In the Code pane, select the line break tag **
, right-click the selected tag, and then click **Reference on the context menu. Read the description of the <br> tag.

9. Examine the code for the rest of the page, using the Reference panel to learn about any tags that you do not recognize.

10. Collapse the **Results panel group**, click the **Design** button on the Document toolbar, and then save the nbf_styles.css style sheet and close the home page.

Exploring Web Fonts

TIP

Before Web fonts, designers had to place a graphic image in the page of text that used a font not installed on the end user's computer.

In Dreamweaver CS6, Web pages can now include fonts that are not installed on the end user's computer. This is accomplished by using Web fonts and the @font-face rule. A **Web font** is a font that is hosted on a Web server and that can be embedded in Web pages. A font library hosts many collections of Web fonts that you can use if you do not want to host your own Web fonts. Two popular Web font libraries are *https://typekit.com* and *http://www.google.com/webfonts#HomePlace:home*. The **@font-face rule** is a new CSS rule used to embed fonts in a site.

REFERENCE

Adding a Web Font

- Select the font you want to use.
- Secure an End User License Agreement (EULA) that allows you to use the font as a Web font.
- Find or create a font kit.
- In Dreamweaver, add the Web font. The Web font appears on the fonts list so you can select it when you create or modify a style.
- Create a style that uses the Web font. Dreamweaver adds a webfonts folder to the site that contains all of the variations of the font as well as a style sheet that has the @font-face rule.
- Apply the style to use the font in your site.
- View the page in Live view to see the font in Dreamweaver or preview the page in a browser.

Using Web fonts is a multistep process. The first three steps happen outside of Dreamweaver.

First, you must decide what font you want to use. You want to select a font that matches the look and feel of the site that you outlined in your site plan. The font should reinforce the site metaphor. The font should be easy to read and appeal to your target audience.

Second, you must secure an End-User License Agreement (EULA) to use the font as a Web font. Like original artwork, most fonts are protected by copyright and you must purchase a license to use them. Many older EULAs do not include Web font permissions, so be sure to double-check the terms of your agreements before you use fonts as Web fonts. Some free Web fonts are available, but the agreements often limit you to using the fonts only for personal, noncommercial projects. It is the designer's responsibility to secure the proper permissions, so be sure to check the appropriate license agreements and permissions before you embed a font in a site.

Third, you must find, gather, or create a set of files that includes a definition of the font in each font format for each browser and user agent that you plan to support. This is important because different browsers and user agents recognize different font formats for Web fonts. The following list explains which font formats work in different browsers and user agents:

- TrueType Fonts (TTF) work in most browsers and user agents except Internet Explorer, Safari, and Apple devices such as the iPhone and iPad.
- Embedded OpenType (EOT) fonts work only in Internet Explorer.
- Scalable Vector Graphics (SVG) fonts work in Apple devices such as the iPhone and iPad.
- Web Open Font Format (WOFF) is an emerging font that is in the process of being standardized as a W3C recommendation. Currently, Firefox 3.6, Google Chrome 5, Opera, Internet Explorer 9, Safari, and other browsers support the format. W3C expects WOFF to become the only interoperable font format supported by all browsers.

When you use Web fonts in a site, you actually include a **font kit**, which includes fonts, font variations, and descriptive information. If you do not know how to create a font kit, you can obtain one from a Web site that provides font kits. For example, the Font Squirrel site (*www.fontsquirrel.com*) makes available hundreds of font kits that they claim are 100% free for commercial use. However, the fine print on the @font-face Kits page states that "there is no guarantee that our interpretation of each license is correct in allowing @font-face usage." This means that you use these fonts at your own risk. To find other sites that provide font kits, search the Web for "Web fonts" or "font kits."

At this point, you can start Dreamweaver and use the Web fonts in your site. The first time you use a Web font, you must add it to the list of potential fonts you can use in your site. You can do this from the Web Fonts Manager dialog box, which you open by clicking Web fonts on the Modify menu. After you add the font, the font appears in the font list on the CSS tab of the Property inspector. After you create a style that uses the font, Dreamweaver creates a webfonts folder in your local root folder that contains all of the definitions for the font as well as a style sheet that uses the @font-face rule.

The following code shows the @font-face rule that is created in the style sheet in the webfonts folder whenever you use a Web font in a page:

```
@font-face {
    font-family: 'name of font';
    src: url('name of font_Pro-webfont.eot');
    src: url('name of font_Pro-webfont.eot?#iefix')
format('embedded-opentype'),
        url('name of font_Pro-webfont.woff') format('woff'),
        url('name of font_Pro-webfont.ttf') format('truetype'),
        url('name of font_Pro-webfont.svg') format('svg');
}
```

In this code, font-family specifies the name of the font, where *'name of font'* is the actual name of the Web font being used in that @font-face rule. The next lines of the code list the URLs where the browser can locate the specific format it needs to display that Web font in the page. The second line of code lists the location where the browser can find the EOT format of the Web font, which Internet Explorer uses to display the Web font.

INSIGHT

Advantages and Disadvantages of Web Fonts

Before Web fonts, designers had to place a graphic image in the page of text that used a font not installed on the end user's computer. Web fonts have several advantages over using a graphic image to include unique fonts, including the following:

- Web fonts are fully searchable.
- Web fonts are accessible to assistive devices.
- Web fonts can be translated by in-browser translation apps and services.
- You can use CSS to modify text formatted with a Web font as you can other fonts by setting line height, letter spacing, text alignment, and so forth.

Even with these advantages, you should use Web fonts sparingly because slight variations exist in the way different user agents display the Web fonts. For example, the current versions of Firefox and Opera briefly display the wrong font when the page is loading and the Web font has not yet been downloaded. Also, user agents that do not understand the @font-face rule will pass over the rule when displaying the text; because CSS is cascading, text will be displayed based on the closest rule. For example, the text may be displayed in the default font specified for the site in the page properties. Finally, keep in mind that fonts are protected by copyright and many EULAs do not include Web font use in the agreement.

You use the Web font the same way you use any of the other fonts in the list. For example, you can create styles that use the font, like you did when you modified the body tag. A Web font displays in a page the same way that any other font would display. Figure 3-35 shows the home page of the NextBest Fest site with the NextBest Fest logo displayed using a Web font. Just from looking at the logo, you cannot tell whether the logo uses a Web font or a font installed on your computer.

Figure 3-35   Home page with Web fonts

logo text formatted
with a Web font

other text formatted
with fonts installed
on the end user's
computer

Used with permission from Microsoft Corporation; © 2013 Cengage Learning; dean bertoncelj/Shutterstock.com;
Jupiterimages/Photos.com

Because of the problems with licensing, you will not add Web fonts to the NextBest
Fest site.

Updating a Web Site on a Remote Server

As a final review of your work, you will post the updated files for the NextBest Fest site
to your remote server. Because you have already uploaded the entire site, you need to
upload only the files that you have changed to update the remote site—the home page
and the external style sheet.

REFERENCE

Uploading a Site to the Remote Server

- On the Files panel toolbar, click the Connect to Remote Server button.
- On the Files panel toolbar, click the View button, and then click Local view.
- Press and hold the Ctrl key, and then click all of the files and folders on the local site
  that have been modified or added.
- On the Files panel toolbar, click the Put file(s) to "Remote Server" button.
- In the dialog box that opens and prompts you to include dependent files, click the
  No button.
- On the Files panel toolbar, click the View button, and then click Remote server.
- On the Files panel toolbar, click the Disconnect from Remote Server button.

You will upload the modified page and new dependent file in the NextBest Fest site
to the remote server. Then, you will preview the site on the Web.

To upload modified pages of the NextBest Fest site to your remote server:

▶ **1.** Expand the **Files panel group**, and then, on the Files panel toolbar, click the **Connect to Remote Server** button ☒. Dreamweaver connects to the remote host.

▶ **2.** On the Files panel toolbar, click the **View** button, and then click **Local view**.

▶ **3.** In the Files panel, click the **stylesheets** folder, press and hold the **Ctrl** key, click **index.html**, and then release the Ctrl key.

▶ **4.** On the Files panel toolbar, click the **Put file(s) to "Remote Server"** button ⬆. A dialog box opens, prompting you to include dependent files.

▶ **5.** Click the **No** button. You already selected the new dependent file for the site when you selected the stylesheets folder.

▶ **6.** On the Files panel toolbar, click the **View** button, and then click **Remote server**. A copy of the stylesheets folder and the updated files appear in the remote files list in the Files panel.

▶ **7.** On the Files panel toolbar, click the **Disconnect from Remote Server** button ☒.

▶ **8.** On the Files panel toolbar, click the **View** button, and then click **Local view**.

Next, you will preview the updated site in a browser. The site will include all of the new styles and text that you added to the local version.

To preview the updated site in a browser:

▶ **1.** Start your Web browser, type the URL of your remote site into the Address bar on the browser toolbar, and then press the **Enter** key. The home page opens in the browser window.

▶ **2.** Read the text on the home page and examine the text to ensure that the formatting is displayed correctly.

▶ **3.** Close the browser.

In this session, you exported the styles from the home page to an external style sheet, created CSS styles in an external style sheet, and examined the code that creates CSS styles. Finally, you uploaded the updated home page and the new external style sheet to your remote server, and then previewed the remote site. In the next tutorial, you will use CSS to create the page structure for the pages in the NextBest Fest site.

Session 3.3 Quick Check

1. What is the file extension for an external style sheet?
2. True or False. You can apply CSS styles that you create in one Web page to text in another Web page in the same site.
3. Why is it a good idea to delete unneeded styles from a style sheet?
4. Why do you need to remove the current formatting from text in a Web page before attaching an external style sheet?
5. What happens when you edit a CSS style?
6. Why is an internal style sheet also called an embedded style sheet?
7. True or False. A link tag has a closing tag.
8. What is the rule that is used to embed Web fonts in pages?

Practice the skills you learned in the tutorial.

Review Assignments

Data File needed for the Review Assignments: antihome.docx

Cat wants you to create an external style sheet with styles for headings and sub-headings for the antifest site. She has a document with content for the home page that she wants you to add to the site to begin generating interest in and promoting next year's fest.

1. Open the **antifest** site you created in Tutorial 2, open the **index.html** page in the Document window, and then switch to Design view.

2. In the CSS Styles panel, switch to the All pane, and then expand the <style> list, if necessary.

3. Click the first style in the list, press and hold the Shift key, click the last style in the list, and then release the Shift key to select all the styles in the list.

4. Right-click the selected styles, and then click Move CSS Rules on the context menu to open the Move To External Style Sheet dialog box.

5. Click the A new style sheet option button, and then click the OK button to open the Save Style Sheet File As dialog box.

6. Create a new folder named **stylesheets** in the local root folder, name the external style sheet **antistyles.css**, and then save the style sheet in the new folder to move all the styles from the home page to the external style sheet.

7. In the Files panel, open the stylesheets folder to view the new style sheet.

8. In a word-processing program, open the **antihome.docx** document located in the Dreamweaver3\Review folder included with your Data Files, select and copy all the content in the document, and then close the document.

9. In the Document window, use Paste Special to paste the content into the home page, selecting Text with structure (paragraphs, lists, tables, etc.) and unchecking the Clean up Word paragraph spacing check box. The content is pasted into the page with its formatting intact but is displayed in the font you selected for the page properties.

10. Save the page, and then use the spelling checker to correct any spelling errors. Do not change the spelling of antifest, which is an intentional combination of "anti" and "fest" that forms the festival name.

11. Proofread the page content, being sure to pay careful attention for contextual errors. In the heading text of the home page, the word *worlds* should be *world's*.

12. Format the page heading, "antifest, home of the world's freest festival," as Heading 1, and then create a new CSS rule with the tag selector type in the antistyles.css style sheet that modifies the h1 tag, as follows: text-transform: lowercase; color: #0f0.

13. Format the subheading, "site expansion project," as Heading 2, and then create a new CSS rule with the tag selector type in the antistyles.css style sheet that modifies the h2 tag, as follows: text-transform: lowercase; color: #ff3.

14. Save the home page and the antistyles.css style sheet, and then preview the home page in a browser.

15. Upload the index.html page and the stylesheets folder to your remote server, and then preview the page over the Internet.

16. Submit your finished files to your instructor.

Add and format text links and page content for a Web site to market a skateboard company.

APPLY

Case Problem 1

There are no Data Files needed for this Case Problem.

Moebius Skateboards   The Moebius Skateboards team is competing at a local event this weekend, so Corey wants a basic site ready before the competition. You will create a simple text navigation system and add content to the home page of the Moebius Skateboards site. You will also create and apply styles to the new content, and then export the styles to an external style sheet for the site. Because you have not yet created the structural elements that will provide a cleaner page background for the site, the home page content is not readable. To make the site content legible in time for the coming event, you will modify the text formatting, temporarily making the text larger and black. Because you are using CSS styles, this is simple to do.

1. Open the **Moebius Skateboards** site you created in Tutorial 2, Case 1, and then open the **index.html** page in Design view.
2. In the All pane of the CSS Styles panel, select all of the existing styles, and then move the CSS rules to a new external style sheet.
3. Save the new external style sheet as **moebius.css** in a new folder named **stylesheets** that you create in the local root folder of your Moebius Skateboards site. The styles move from the home page to the new style sheet. Save the home page and the style sheet.
4. At the top of the home page, type the following navigation text using two nonbreaking spaces before and after each slash: **about / boards / team / events / contact**. Press the Enter key to move the insertion point down two lines.
5. Select the navigation text, and then in the CSS Styles panel, click the New CSS Rule button.
6. In the New CSS Rule dialog box, create a new rule using ID as the selector type, **#nav** as the selector name, and moebius.css style sheet as the rule definition location.
7. In the CSS Rule definition for #nav in moebius.css dialog box, in the Type category, change the font size to 16 px. In the Background category, change the background color to #999. In the Box category, change the float to right. In the Border category, make sure the three Same for all check boxes are checked, change the top style to double, change the top width to thin, and change the top color to #6f3. If necessary, apply the #nav style to the navigation text.
8. In the home page, if no space appears between the border of the box that surrounds the text and the beginning of the first word, or between the end of the last word and the border, add a nonbreaking space.
9. Create the following links from the navigation text to the pages that you will create: about – **about.html**, boards – **boards.html**, team – **team.html**, events – **events.html**, contact – **contact.html**.
10. Press the Right arrow key until the <p#nav> tag no longer appears in the status bar (indicating that the insertion point is past the tag in the code), and then press the Enter key to move the insertion point down two lines. (*Hint*: There should be two paragraph tags between the navigation and the text that you will type in Step 11.)
11. Type the following text exactly as shown (including the intentional spelling error), pressing the Enter key after each line:
    Moebius Skateboards
    skateboarding is not a style, it is a lifestyle.
    Check Out Team Moebius
    Members of Team Moebius will be at the Mansfield Public Skatepark exhibition event Wed. Nov. 12th at 5pm. Come join us for a good show and some suprises. . .
    Check the spelling of and proofread the text you just typed.

12. Apply Heading 1 to "Moebius Skateboards," using the Format list in the HTML pane of the Property inspector to apply the h1 tag.

13. Apply Heading 2 to "Check Out Team Moebius," using the Format list in the HTML pane of the Property inspector to apply the h2 tag.

14. In the CSS Styles panel, select the body,td,th style, and then in the Properties pane, use the color picker to change the color attribute to Orange,#f30, and change the font-size attribute to 16. All of the text in the home page changes to a larger, orange-red font.

15. Save the home page and the moebius.css style sheet, and then preview the home page in a browser.

16. Upload the index.html page and the stylesheets folder to your remote server, and then preview the page over the Internet.

17. Submit your finished files to your instructor.

Add and format text links, create an external style sheet, and apply styles to text you add to a Web site for an art society.

CHALLENGE

Case Problem 2

Data File needed for this Case Problem: cowboy.docx

Cowboy Art Society   Moni wants you to add content to the Web site you are creating for the Cowboy Art Society. He has provided the content for the home page in a Microsoft Word document, which you will import. You will create a navigation system that will appear on all of the pages and add a horizontal rule to each page. You will move the current styles to an external style sheet, and then you will use these styles to format the text. Finally, you will upload the site to a remote location and preview it. The society believes it is important that the site be accessible to everyone who wants to learn about the artist Charles Russell. Moni asks you to follow accessibility guidelines while creating the site. After you import the content into the home page, you will see that the text does not meet accessibility guidelines because it is not easily distinguished from the background by someone with impaired vision. The site plan specifies that you will add a background behind the content, which will make the text clearly visible. You will do this in a later tutorial.

1. Open the **Cowboy Charlie** site you created in Tutorial 2, Case 2, and then open the **index.html** page in Design view.

2. Move the styles from the home page to an external style sheet named **cowboy.css** stored in a new folder named **stylesheets** that you create in the local root folder for the site, and then save the page and the style sheet.

3. In the Document window, click to place the insertion point in the home page. You will import content from a Word document into the page.

⊕ EXPLORE

4. On the menu bar, click File, point to Import, and then click Word Document to open the Import Word Document dialog box. Browse to the Dreamweaver3\Case2 folder included with your Data Files, click **cowboy.docx**, and then click the Open button. The content is imported into the page.

5. In the Document window, place the pointer after "Cowboy Charlie," press the Enter key to insert two lines, and then press the Delete key to move the next line of text two lines below this line. Repeat this step after the word *Poetry*, after the Welcome to the World of Cowboy Charlie heading, and after the end of the first paragraph.

6. Select the Cowboy Charlie text, create a class style named **.logo** that is saved in the cowboy.css style sheet, and then, in the Type category, select xx-large for the font size.

7. Apply the logo style to the logo. (*Hint*: Use the Class list in the HTML pane of the Property inspector to apply the style to the logo.)

8. In the home page, create the links to the navigation text, as follows: Charles M. Russell – **russell.html**, Artwork – **artwork.html**, Poetry – **poetry.html**.

9. Apply the h1 tag to the page heading text.

10. Create an ID style named **#nav** that is saved in the cowboy.css style sheet, and then, in the Box category, change float to right.

11. Apply the nav style to the navigation text. (*Hint*: Select nav from the ID list in the HTML pane of the Property inspector.)

⊕ **EXPLORE**   12. In the home page, select the logo. In the Insert panel, in the Common category, click Horizontal Rule. A horizontal rule (line) appears below the logo.

⊕ **EXPLORE**   13. In the Property inspector, uncheck the Shading check box. The rule is not shaded.

14. Save the home page and the cowboy.css style sheet, and then preview the home page in a browser.

15. Upload the index.html page and the stylesheets folder to your remote server, and then preview the page over the Internet.

16. Submit your finished files to your instructor.

Create an external style sheet, and then create, edit, and apply new CSS styles to text you add to a Web site for a life coach.

CHALLENGE

Case Problem 3

Data File needed for this Case Problem: home.docx

Success with Tess   With a plan and design in place for the Success with Tess Web site, you are ready to add and format the text for the site. Tess has already written the home page text. You need to move the existing styles to an external style sheet. You will also edit the existing CSS styles and create new styles as needed. Finally, you will add and format the text on the home page.

1. Open the **Success with Tess** site you created in Tutorial 2, Case 3, and then open the **index.html** page in Design view.

2. Move the styles from the home page to an external style sheet named **tess.css** stored in a new folder named **stylesheets** in the local site folder of the site. Save the home page and the style sheet.

3. In a word-processing program, open the **home.docx** document located in the Dreamweaver3\Case3 folder included with your Data Files, select and copy all the content in the document, and then close the document.

4. In the Document window, use Paste Special to paste the content into the home page, selecting Text with structure (paragraph, lists, tables, etc.) and unchecking the Clean up Word paragraph spacing check box. The content is pasted into the page with its formatting intact but is displayed in the font you selected for the page properties.

5. Check the spelling of and proofread the text you just pasted.

6. In the Document window, select all of the text in the first line of the home page and use the HTML pane in the Property inspector to apply the Heading 1 tag.

7. Create links in the navigation text, as follows: About Tess – **about_tess.html**, Coaching – **coaching.html**, Specials – **specials.html**, Contact – **contact.html**.

8. Use the HTML pane in the Property inspector to apply the Heading 2 tag to the following heading text: What, Where, and Who do you really want to be in life? and TESS-timonials.

9. Italicize the following text below the TESS-timonials heading, using the Italic button in the HTML pane of the Property inspector: From A.K., Flower Mound, TX and From J.R., Denton, TX.

10. Save the home page and the tess.css style sheet, and then preview the home page in a browser.

11. Upload the index.html page and the stylesheets folder to your remote server, and then preview the page over the Internet.

12. Submit your finished files to your instructor.

Create a navigation system, and then create and apply CSS styles to text in a Web site for a coffee bar.

CREATE

Case Problem 4

There are no Data Files needed for this Case Problem.

Coffee Lounge   Tommy wants you to start working on the navigation system and the styles for the Coffee Lounge site. He asks you to create CSS styles, add appropriate text to the Web site, and then format the text you added. You will view the code, upload the modified pages to the remote site, and then preview the remote site.

1. Open the **Coffee Lounge** site you created in Tutorial 2, Case 4, and then open the **index.html** page.

2. Move the styles from the home page to an external style sheet, using an appropriate style sheet name and location.

3. Add content to the home page of the site. Include logo text, navigation text, headings, and content that you develop based on the site plan created for the Web site.

4. Create at least two new CSS styles for the page, and then apply appropriate styles to the logo text and the headings.

5. Create links from the navigation text to the pages you will create for the site. Follow your site plan so that the links will work once you create the new pages.

6. Read the content that you have added to the page to ensure that it supports the site goals.

7. Use the spelling checker and then proofread the content to ensure that there are no misspellings or typing errors.

8. Save the home page and the style sheet, and then preview the home page in a browser.

9. Upload the index.html page and the stylesheets folder to your remote server, and then preview the page over the Internet.

10. Submit your finished files to your instructor.

DREAMWEAVER

Using CSS for Page Layout

Working with Floating and AP Divs

OBJECTIVES

Session 4.1
- Explore CSS layout
- Compare types of floating layouts
- Examine code for CSS layouts
- View prebuilt CSS layout pages
- Insert floating divs and nest divs
- Add rounded corners to a div with CSS
- Duplicate pages

Session 4.2
- Draw AP divs
- Select, resize, and move AP divs
- Add content to AP divs
- Adjust AP div attributes
- Examine code for AP div tags
- Modify AP div stacking order
- Nest AP divs
- Inspect code with CSS Inspect

Case | *NextBest Fest*

The existing NextBest Fest site provides basic information for users while you create the full interesting and dynamic site. Now Gage wants you to work on the page structure for the pages of the new NextBest Fest site. First, you will review the CSS templates that Dreamweaver provides to become familiar with their code techniques. Then, you will create the structure for the site's pages.

Gage wants the site to use a floating, fixed-width design so that it maintains a consistent look, regardless of the user's browser window size. You will create the site with a fixed-width layout at 955px, which is optimized for a 1024 × 768 display. The team's research determined this is appropriate for the target audience. After you create the home page layout, you will move the existing content into the new structure. Then, you will create the other pages you need for the site. You will also create a page that promotes the location of next year's Fest.

STARTING DATA FILES

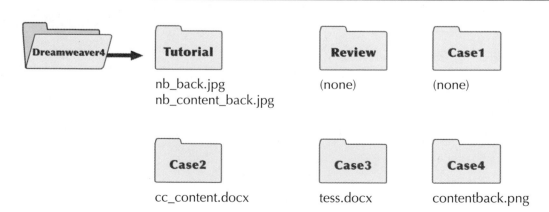

Dreamweaver4 → Tutorial
nb_back.jpg
nb_content_back.jpg

Review
(none)

Case1
(none)

Case2
cc_content.docx

Case3
tess.docx

Case4
contentback.png

SESSION 4.1 VISUAL OVERVIEW

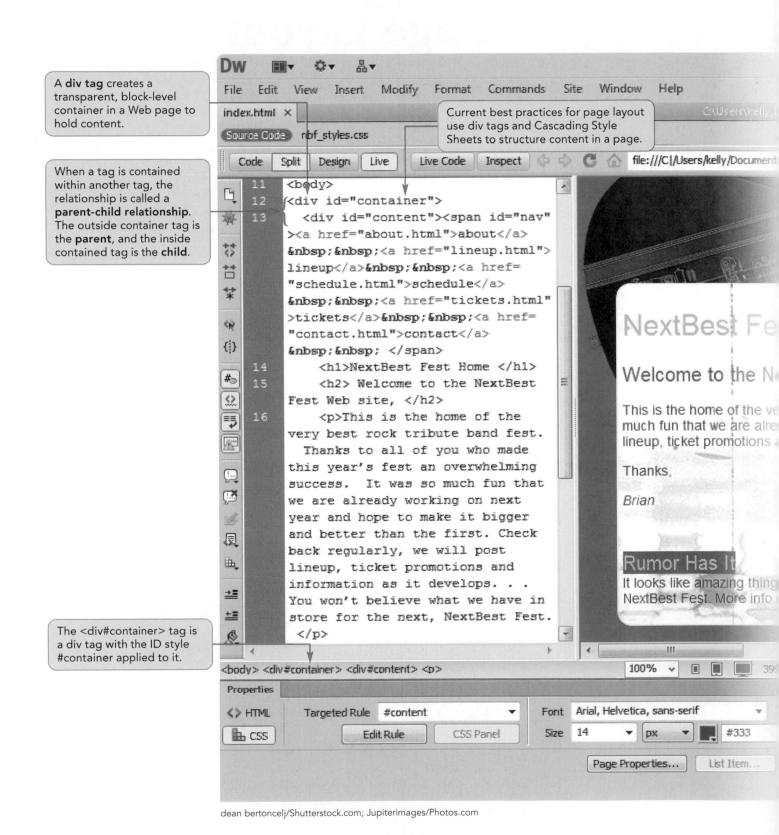

A **div tag** creates a transparent, block-level container in a Web page to hold content.

Current best practices for page layout use div tags and Cascading Style Sheets to structure content in a page.

When a tag is contained within another tag, the relationship is called a **parent-child relationship**. The outside container tag is the **parent**, and the inside contained tag is the **child**.

The <div#container> tag is a div tag with the ID style #container applied to it.

```
11  <body>
12  <div id="container">
13    <div id="content"><span id="nav"
    ><a href="about.html">about</a>
      <a href="lineup.html">
    lineup</a>  <a href=
    "schedule.html">schedule</a>
      <a href="tickets.html"
    >tickets</a>  <a href=
    "contact.html">contact</a>
       </span>
14      <h1>NextBest Fest Home </h1>
15      <h2> Welcome to the NextBest
    Fest Web site, </h2>
16      <p>This is the home of the
    very best rock tribute band fest.
    Thanks to all of you who made
    this year's fest an overwhelming
    success.  It was so much fun that
    we are already working on next
    year and hope to make it bigger
    and better than the first. Check
    back regularly, we will post
    lineup, ticket promotions and
    information as it develops. . .
    You won't believe what we have in
    store for the next, NextBest Fest.
    </p>
```

dean bertoncelj/Shutterstock.com; Jupiterimages/Photos.com

USING DIV TAGS FOR PAGE LAYOUT

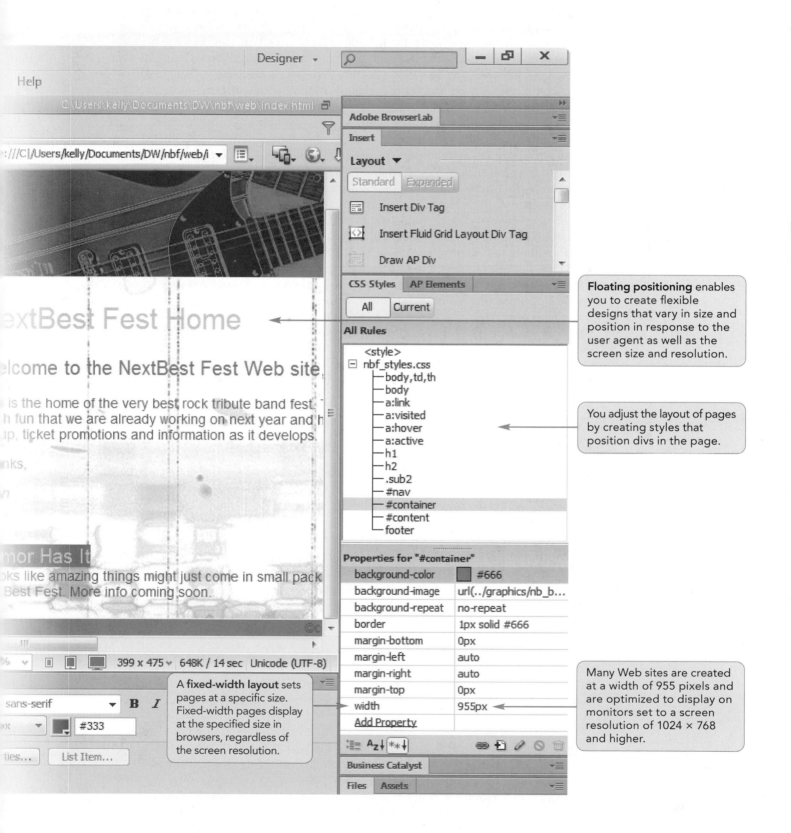

Floating positioning enables you to create flexible designs that vary in size and position in response to the user agent as well as the screen size and resolution.

You adjust the layout of pages by creating styles that position divs in the page.

A **fixed-width layout** sets pages at a specific size. Fixed-width pages display at the specified size in browsers, regardless of the screen resolution.

Many Web sites are created at a width of 955 pixels and are optimized to display on monitors set to a screen resolution of 1024 × 768 and higher.

The Evolution of Layout Techniques

In the earliest days of the Web, text and images were aligned to the left of the page. Designers soon discovered that they could use tables to provide a vertical and horizontal structure for the content of a Web page. This grid structure provided some flexibility in arranging the content and elements in the Web page. Although this method was used effectively for many years, the resulting HTML code was cumbersome because tables were designed to display tabular data, not to provide hidden structure for the pages. Tables are no longer used to structure Web pages. Because you might still encounter pages that used tables to structure content, you will learn more about this method when you add tables and tabular content to the site in another tutorial.

The second early method for structuring pages was frames. Frames divided a Web page into multiple HTML documents. Each frame contained a single HTML document with its own content and, if necessary, its own scroll bars. A Web page with frames was held together by a frameset, which is a separate HTML document that defines the structure and properties of a Web page with frames. This method is also outdated and rarely used.

CSS page layout is the current standard for laying out professional Web pages. This method of page layout uses div tags and Cascading Style Sheets (CSS) to structure content in a page. In CSS page layout, the div tag is commonly placed around text, images, and page elements to structure and position the chunks (or divisions) of content in the page. The div tag creates a transparent, block-level container in a Web page to hold content. You can place almost any other tag in a div tag.

As with other tags, you can add CSS styles to a div tag. You adjust the layout of pages by creating styles that position the divs in the pages. Although this sounds simple enough, it can be a bit challenging because browsers react slightly differently to the styles you create and because users view Web pages on various user agents, including smartphones and tablets, as well as on different sized screens and at varying screen resolutions.

Positioning Div Tags in Web Pages

TIP

Floating positioning relies heavily on the float attribute to position the divs in a page.

The two general methods for positioning div tags in Web pages are absolute and floating. **Absolute positioning (AP)** enables you to specify the exact pixel in the browser window in which the upper-left corner of the div tag will be placed. Floating positioning enables you to create flexible designs that vary in size and position in response to the user agent as well as the screen size and screen resolution. Although absolute positioning seems like a great idea, it is difficult to use effectively for page layout because of the variety of user agents, screen sizes, and screen resolutions on which the page could be viewed. However, designers sometimes use absolute positioning in very specific cases to achieve certain effects. Floating positioning is used most frequently for page layout.

Comparing Floating Layouts

The three general types of page layout that use floating divs are fixed width, liquid, and elastic. Fixed-width layouts let you set a specific size for the pages. Fixed-width pages display at the specified size in the user's browser, regardless of the screen resolution. In some cases, the page is justified to the left of the browser window when the user's screen is larger than the specified page size. In other cases, the page is positioned in the center of the user's browser window. The display size you set for the page depends on the target audience. Research indicates that users almost always have at least a 1024 × 768 screen resolution when viewing a page on a monitor, but not necessarily when viewing the page on a tablet or mobile device. Pages created for a 1024 × 768 resolution should have a width of 955 pixels to provide room for the **browser chrome** (the borders of the Web browser window, including the frames, menus, toolbars, and scroll bar).

Liquid layouts adjust to fit the user's browser width. When the user resizes the browser window, the page adjusts to fit the new size. Liquid layouts are sometimes called fluid layouts because content seems to flow to fill the size of the user's browser window. This type of layout maximizes the use of the available space (sometimes referred to as browser real estate), but without a lot of planning and a good understanding of advanced techniques, designers have less control over the look of the pages. Liquid layouts lead to a myriad of potential problems. For example, when the browser window is particularly wide, such as on a 24-inch wide-screen monitor, content can look sparse and be difficult to read. Unless you understand the problems you might encounter, this type of design can limit your control over design elements such as symmetry and white space, and the design suffers as a result. However, when used well, fluid layouts can be used to create sites that display appropriately on various devices and at different resolutions. This means that a site can detect the screen size being used and adjust to display appropriately whether the user is viewing the site from a mobile device, a tablet, or a monitor. You will use these advanced techniques when you learn about the Dreamweaver Fluid Grid Layout in Tutorial 8.

Elastic layouts are fixed-width designs that use ems instead of pixels as the unit for div and text styles. An **em** is a unit of measurement that is relative to the size of the font. This enables the text and the page layout to change size when the font size of the user's browser display changes. It does not change when the browser window is resized. When users can change the text and layout display size in their browser, the site becomes more accessible for users with assistive devices and impaired vision.

INSIGHT

Using Prebuilt CSS Layout Pages

The prebuilt CSS layout pages in Dreamweaver provide files for building commonly used CSS page layouts. These pages are not templates; they are more like the basic architecture from which you can create your own designs. There are many discrepancies in the way that browsers interpret and display CSS layout. These pages are helpful tools because they contain the fixes that enable the content to display similarly across the most common browsers. Without cross-browser fixes in place, creating CSS layouts can be a frustrating process.

The prebuilt CSS layout pages that use fixed-width, fluid, and elastic layouts contain div tags, a list of CSS styles, and placeholder content. By selecting and replacing placeholder content, and by editing the existing CSS styles and creating new styles, you can create your own Web pages using the prebuilt pages as a starting point. You can also move the styles to an external style sheet and use them in all of the pages in your site.

Exploring CSS Layout Code

Prebuilt pages are a good place to start learning about the underlying code used for CSS layout. Dreamweaver adds comments, which are notes added to the code of HTML pages that do not get read or displayed by browsers. Comments are often used in the code of the prebuilt pages to help designers understand what the code is used for and how it works. It is a good idea to add comments to your code to explain what you have done. This is not only helpful when other designers must look at your code, but comments also help you recall what you did when you need to edit the pages in the future.

The two types of comments you can add to the code of pages are HTML comments and c style comments. In Code view, all comments are displayed in gray. HTML comments are used within the HTML code in the page and are coded as

```
<!--comment-->
```

where *comment* is the content of the comment. C style comments are used within the CSS or JavaScript code in a page, or in the external style sheet, and are coded as

```
/* comment */
```

where *comment* is the content of the comment.

In the prebuilt pages, Dreamweaver adds a comment before each of the closing div tags. This is helpful because all closing div tags look alike in the code as

```
</div>
```

and because the order of the closing tags makes a difference in the way the code works. Remember that tags are paired sets (opening and closing) and that the rule is first on last off. The comments help distinguish one closing div tag from another and ensure that the tags are in the right order in the page.

The prebuilt pages also use good coding practices to make the code easier to understand. Programmers usually insert each new tag at the beginning of a line, when possible. When a tag is contained within another tag, the relationship is called a parent-child relationship. The outside container tag is the parent, and the inside contained tag is the child. Programmers usually indent the child tag to indicate that the child tag is contained inside a parent tag. The convention of using indents to indicate hierarchy is considered good practice because it makes the code easier to follow and to understand.

You will examine a prebuilt page with a fluid or liquid layout. Flexible layouts enable you to maximize the design to fill the user's browser window.

> **TIP**
>
> When you create CSS layouts with multiple divs in the page, Dreamweaver does not add comments to the code, so you should do this yourself.

To view prebuilt CSS fluid layout pages:

1. Reset Dreamweaver to the **Designer** workspace, minimize the **Business Catalyst** panel, open the Files panel, and then open the **NextBest Fest** site you created in Tutorial 3.

2. On the menu bar, click **File**, and then click **New**. The New Document dialog box opens.

3. Click **Blank Page**, and then click **HTML** in the Page Type box.

4. In the Layout box, click **2 column liquid, left sidebar**. A preview of the selected page layout appears at the right of the dialog box.

5. Below the preview, click the **Layout CSS** button, and then click **Add to Head**, if necessary. See Figure 4-1.

> **TIP**
>
> You can also click More in the Create New section of the Welcome screen to open the New Document dialog box.

Figure 4-1   New Document dialog box

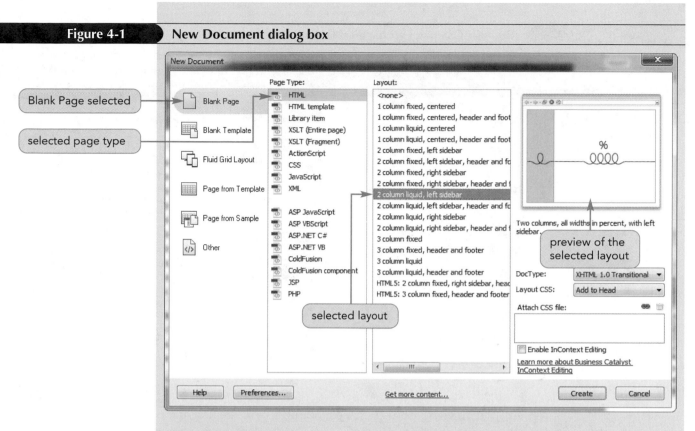

6. Click the **Create** button. A page with the selected layout opens in the Document window.

7. Switch to **Split** view so you can see both the code and the page design.

8. In the CSS Styles panel, click the **Current** button. See Figure 4-2. In this prebuilt layout, divs are used with CSS styles to create a page that has two columns that are fluid, increasing or decreasing with the size of the user's browser window.

Figure 4-2   Prebuilt CSS page with a fluid layout

comments for the page are gray

placeholder content

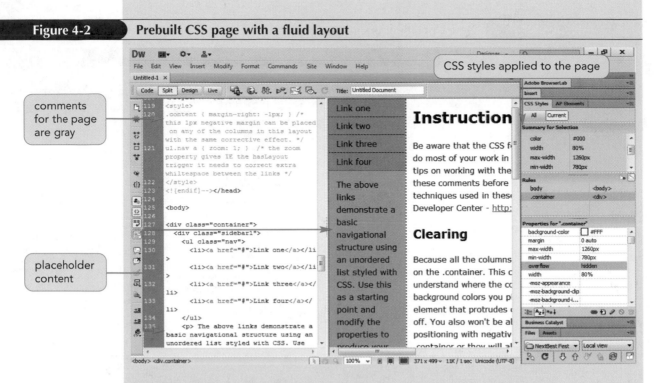

CSS styles applied to the page

9. Scroll to the top of the Code pane, look at the styles, and read the comment containing notes that were added to explain how the prebuilt page works.

10. Save the page as **fluid.html** in the local root folder of your NextBest Fest site, and then preview the page in a browser. See Figure 4-3.

Figure 4-3   Preview of the prebuilt CSS page with a fluid layout

page layout adjusts to reflect the display area

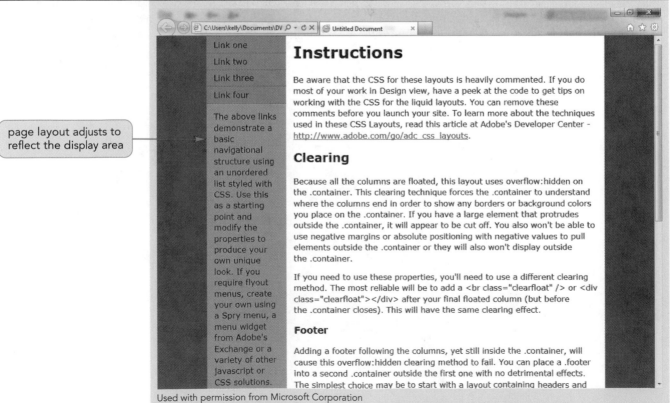

Used with permission from Microsoft Corporation

11. Resize the browser window. The text remains the same size but the column widths change.

12. Close the browser, and then close the page.

As you can see, pages with a fluid layout change to fit the available display area. This type of flexible layout enables you to maximize a design to fill the screen. Next, you will examine a fixed-width layout.

To view a prebuilt CSS fixed-width layout page:

1. On the menu bar, click **File**, and then click **New**. The New Document dialog box opens with Blank Page and HTML page type selected.

2. In the Layout box, click **1 column fixed, centered, header and footer**, and then click the **Create** button. A page with the selected layout opens in the Document window.

3. Click in the **Design** pane, and then, in the status bar, click the **<div .container>** tag, scrolling down if needed to see the selected div. See Figure 4-4.

Figure 4-4   **Prebuilt CSS page with a fixed-width layout**

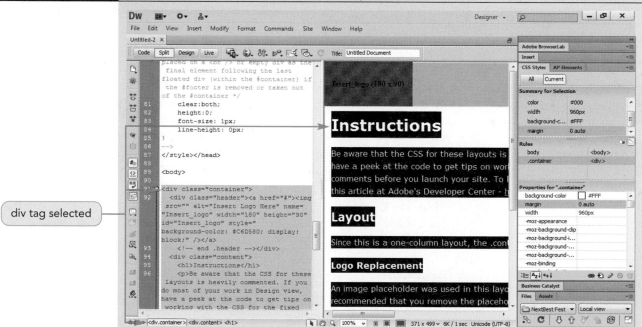

div tag selected

The <div .container> tag is a div tag with the class style .container applied to it. You can tell it is a class tag because the name is preceded by . (a period). The opening and closing tags, as well as everything between them, are selected in both the Code pane and the Design pane. In the Design pane, a yellow border surrounds everything in the page because the div tag is acting as the outside container that holds all of the other page elements and code.

4. Switch to **Code** view, collapse the Property inspector, if necessary, and then scroll until you can see the top and bottom of the selected tag in the Document window. See Figure 4-5.

Figure 4-5   **Selected div tag in Code view**

opening div tag
has the class
style .container

closing div tag
with the class
style .container

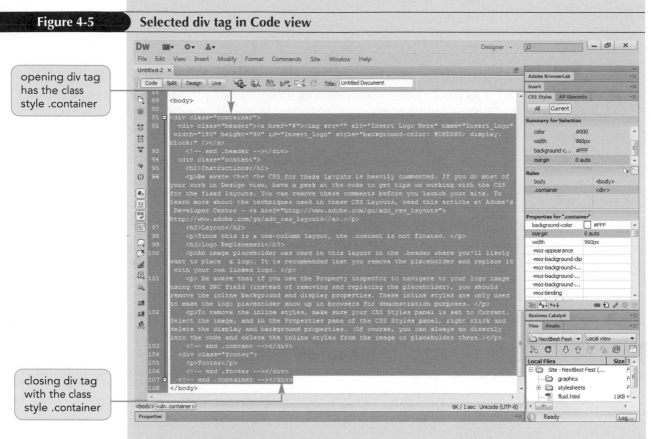

TIP

Printing can be helpful
when reviewing code.
You can print the code
for a page by pressing the
Ctrl+P keys.

In Code view, it is clear that the class style .container is applied to the opening div tag because class="container" is added to the div tag, resulting in the code <div class="container">. The opening and closing div tags surround all the other elements in the body of the page. All of the other tags are indented to make the code easier to follow and understand. Dreamweaver also adds a comment (in gray) before the closing div tags to help you distinguish one closing div tag from another.

5. Switch to **Design** view, expand the Property inspector, and then click in the Document window to deselect the div and its content. See Figure 4-6.

Figure 4-6   Fixed-width page in Design view

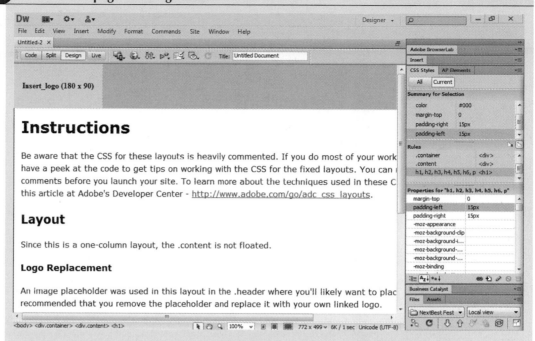

6. In the CSS Styles panel, click the **All** button, expand the style list, click **container**, and then review the style properties in the Properties pane, adjusting the panel size as needed to view the bottom pane. The width is set to 960px, which means that the page will remain at a fixed width of 960 pixels even if the size of the text or browser window changes.

7. Save the page as **fixedWidth.html** in the local root folder of your NextBest Fest site, and then preview the page in a browser. See Figure 4-7.

Figure 4-7   **Preview of the fixed-width page**

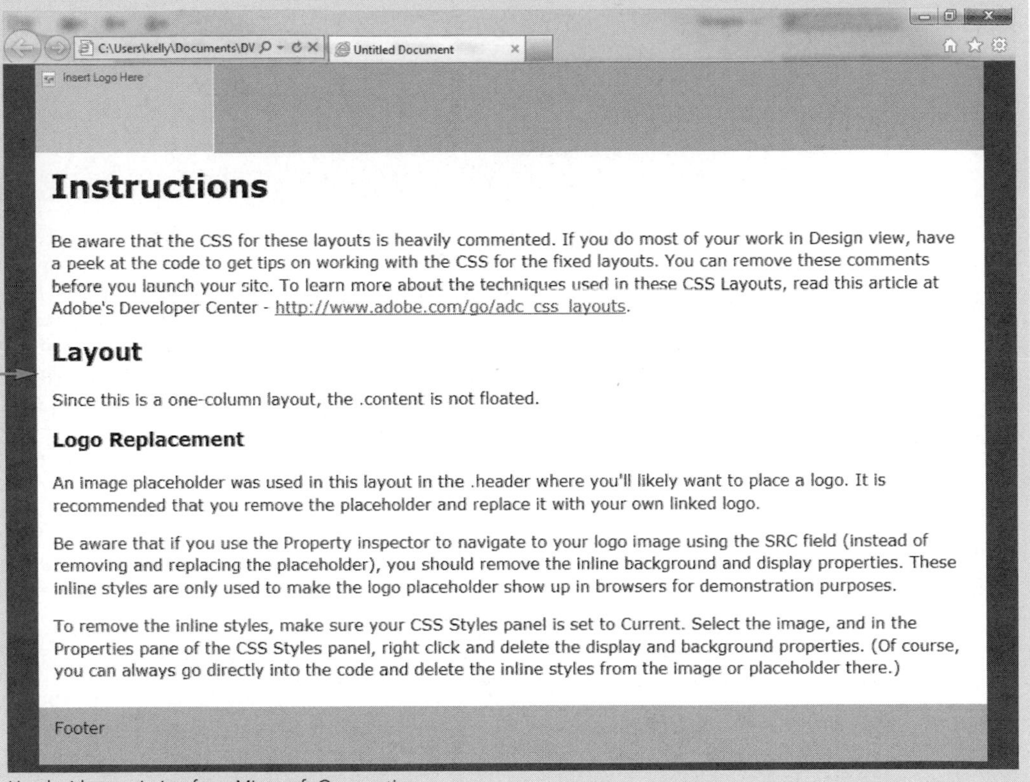

page width doesn't change even when the browser window changes size

Used with permission from Microsoft Corporation

8. Resize the browser window. The page width doesn't change even when the browser window changes size. You will use this fixed-width layout style for the NextBest Fest site.

9. Close the browser, and then close the page.

You do not need any of the prebuilt pages you reviewed for the NextBest Fest site. You will delete these pages from the local root folder so that the site contains only the files for the pages you want.

To delete the prebuilt CSS layout pages:

1. In the Files panel, click **fluid.html** to select it in the files list, and then press the **Delete** key. A dialog box opens, confirming that you really want to delete the selected file.

2. Click the **Yes** button. The page is deleted from the local root folder of your NextBest Fest site.

3. Repeat Steps 1 and 2 to delete the **fixedWidth.html** page from the local root folder.

Planning a CSS Layout

You can create custom CSS layouts. Before you begin creating a CSS layout, you should determine which CSS elements the pages require. For example, most pages need a heading area, a content area, and a footer area in each page of the site. This information was decided during the planning phase and is outlined in the site plan. Because each page will have only one heading, a content area, and a footer area, you will use ID type styles.

Gage created the diagram shown in Figure 4-8 to specify how div tags will be used to create the page structure for the NextBest Fest site. You will use this to create the layout of the home page.

| Figure 4-8 | Div placement for the layout of the NextBest Fest site |

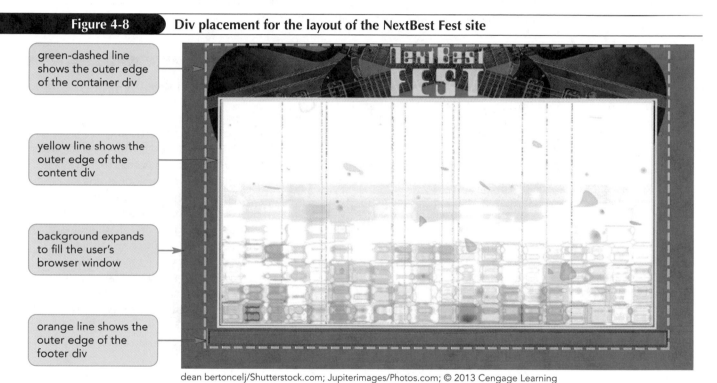

green-dashed line shows the outer edge of the container div

yellow line shows the outer edge of the content div

background expands to fill the user's browser window

orange line shows the outer edge of the footer div

dean bertoncelj/Shutterstock.com; Jupiterimages/Photos.com; © 2013 Cengage Learning

Determining the Display Order of Div Tags

Div tags appear in the page in the order in which they appear in the code. For example, if you want the heading div to appear above the content div in the page, you must place the heading div above the content div in the page. You accomplish this by placing the pointer in the desired location in the Document window before inserting the new div tag. As you add each new div to the page, create a comment in the code before the closing tag to help you identify it more easily.

Using Container or Wrapper Div Tags

A **container div tag** or **wrapper div tag** is a regular div tag that you place around the other divs and elements in a page. Designers often create a CSS style that specifies the width, padding, alignment, and sometimes background color of the container div tag to set a boundary and the page dimensions. Container divs are frequently used to create fixed-width pages. The opening container div tag is usually the first tag below the body tag in the page code and the closing container div tag is usually the last tag before the closing body tag.

Creating Common CSS Style Attributes for Layout

If you want a div to have any specific attributes or characteristics, you must create CSS styles and apply them to the div. The style attributes that are most useful for layout are found in the Box category and include width, height, float, clear, padding, and margin. For example, you can create styles that specify a certain height, width, and padding for the div that control the display of the div content in the browser window. You can also use other categories of style to control the attributes of content contained in the div. For example, you can create styles to specify an alternate font size or color for text in the div. To include columns in the layout, you create styles that use the float attribute and apply them to the divs that will be columns to enable them to float beside each other in the browser window. You can also use the float attribute to specify how other elements flow around each other in the page.

PROSKILLS

Written Communication: Developing a Meaningful Style Naming System

Best practices suggest that when you create styles, you should use names that refer to the way each style is used rather than its aesthetic characteristics. As Web sites evolve, the characteristics of each style might change. For example, if you name a subheading style *blue_medium* to reflect the text color and later change the look of the site so that subheading text is red and large, the style name no longer makes sense. But if you name the style *b_headings*, it will always be clear that this style should be used to format text that is designated as a second-level subheading (often called a B head) according to the hierarchy of heading text in your site plan. In addition, you cannot use special characters or spaces when you name styles. When you need to separate words, a good idea is to use an underscore (_) instead of a space. If you do not name styles logically, as the site evolves and the styles change, you can end up with a site that is difficult for designers to work with because the style names no longer describe the style characteristics.

After you know what divs you must create and what CSS styles you need for a site, and you have developed a flexible naming schema for the styles, you can add the divs to the page and create the styles in an external style sheet.

Inserting Div Tags

When you insert a new div into a page, you choose where, in the code, the div tag is placed. Your choices include at insertion point, before tag, after start of tag, before end of tag, and after tag. In these cases, the tag being referenced is the tag selected in the status bar. In addition, you can apply an existing class or ID style to the div when you create it, or you can create a new CSS rule, which will automatically be applied to the div.

You will create the div tag that will act as a container for the home page layout, and then you will create an ID style called container and apply it to the new div.

To insert a div tag into the home page:

TIP

You can also insert a div tag from the Common category of the Insert panel.

1. Open the **index.html** page, verify that it is displayed in **Design** view, and then, in the status bar, click the **\<body\>** tag.

2. Open the **Insert** panel, and then, in the **Layout** category, click the **Insert Div Tag** button. The Insert Div Tag dialog box opens. See Figure 4-9.

Figure 4-9   Insert Div Tag dialog box

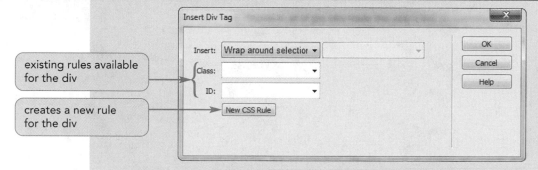

existing rules available for the div

creates a new rule for the div

3. Click the **Insert** button, and then click **Wrap around selection**, if necessary.

4. Click the **New CSS Rule** button. The New CSS Rule dialog box opens.

5. Create a new CSS rule using **ID** as the selector type, **#container** as the selector name, and **nbf_styles.css** for the rule definition, and then click the **OK** button. The CSS Rule Definition for #container in nbf_styles.css dialog box opens.

6. In the **Background** category, type **#666** in the Background-color box, click the **Browse** button to open the Select Image Source dialog box, navigate to the **Dreamweaver4\Tutorial** folder included with your Data Files, double-click **nb_back.jpg** to set the image path and name in the Background-image box, and then select **no-repeat** from the Background-repeat list.

7. In the **Box** category, type **955 px** in the Width box, uncheck the **Same for all** check box in the Margin section, type **0** in the Top and Bottom margin boxes, and select **auto** in the Right and Left margin boxes.

8. In the **Border** category, check the **Same for all** check boxes, if necessary. In the Top box, select **solid** from the Style list, type **1** in the Width box, type **#666** in the Color box, and then click the **OK** button. The container ID style appears in the ID list in the Insert Div Tag dialog box. The div tag border will not be noticeable because it is the same color as the background. You must create the border because the div tag needs something in the foreground so it displays properly in the page.

9. Click the **OK** button. The container ID style is added to the div, the div is inserted into the home page, and the new style is added to the style sheet.

10. Press the **Right** arrow key to deselect the page content. See Figure 4-10.

Figure 4-10   Div tag in the home page

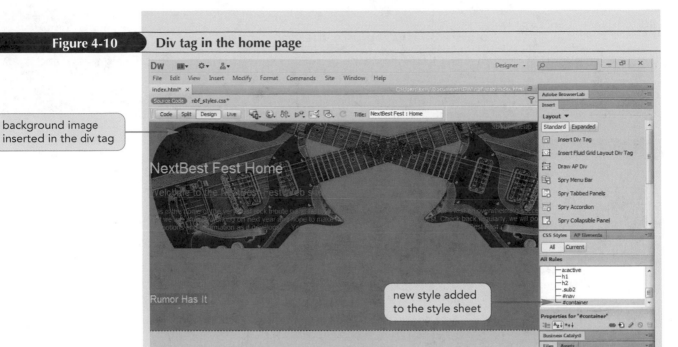

background image inserted in the div tag

new style added to the style sheet

dean bertoncelj/Shutterstock.com

▶ **11.** Save the page and the style sheet, and then preview the page in a browser. See Figure 4-11.

Figure 4-11   Preview of the home page with the div tag

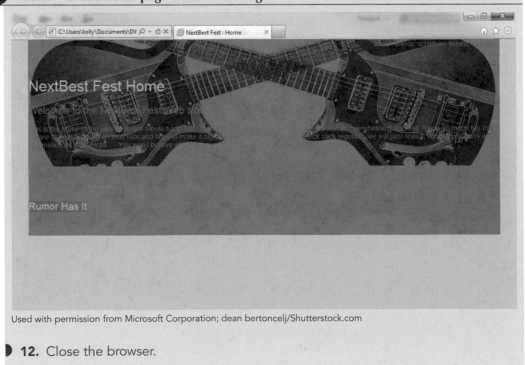

Used with permission from Microsoft Corporation; dean bertoncelj/Shutterstock.com

▶ **12.** Close the browser.

The container div is visible in the page because the color of the page background is lighter than the color of the container div background. Next, you will add a comment before the closing div tag to help you identify it in the future.

Adding Comments to the Code in HTML Pages

Dreamweaver does most of the coding work for you behind the scenes. You can also work with the code yourself. When you are creating complex code that you might need to edit later or when you are working in a team environment, it is a good idea to add comments to the code to help you and others understand the code in the future. This use of comments is similar to the comments that Dreamweaver added to the prebuilt CSS pages to help you to better understand what is going on with the code in those pages.

Because you will add another div tag to this page, and because all closing div tags look the same, Gage wants you to add a comment in the code before the closing tag of the container div to help the team identify the closing div tag.

To add a comment about the div tag to the home page:

1. Click in the **Document** window, and then, in the status bar, click the **<div#container>** tag.

2. Switch to **Code** view, and then click the **Source Code** button, if necessary. The opening and closing div tags, as well as everything between them, are selected. See Figure 4-12.

Figure 4-12 **Code view with the selected div**

content in the div tag selected

closing div tag

selected div tag

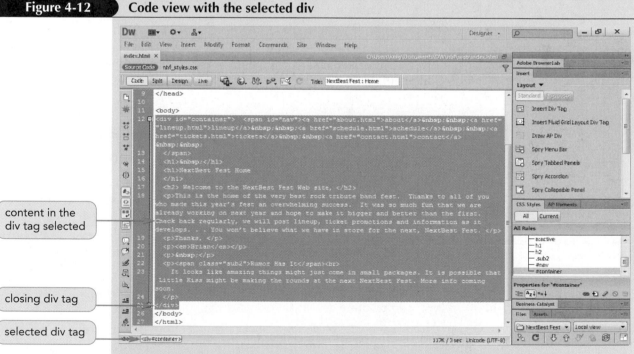

3. Place the insertion point before the closing div tag. You will insert the comment here.

4. On the Coding toolbar, click the **Apply Comment** button, and then click **Apply HTML Comment**. Opening and closing comment tags are inserted in the code with the insertion point positioned between them ready for you to type the comment text. See Figure 4-13.

Figure 4-13   **Comment code added to the home page**

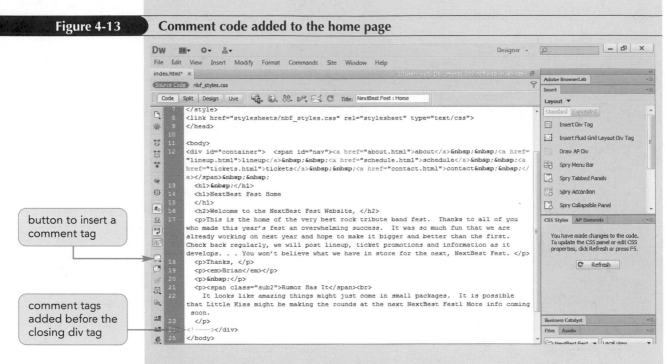

button to insert a comment tag

comment tags added before the closing div tag

5. Type **closing container tag** as the comment text. The comment text is inserted within the opening and closing comment tags in the code for the page.

6. Switch to **Design** view.

You will continue to add div tags to create the structure of the home page. For each tag, you will include a comment tag to help the team distinguish each div. Next, you will add the content div tag within the container div.

To add the content div tag inside the container div:

1. In the status bar, click the **<div#container>** tag. The container div is selected.

2. In the **Common** category of the Insert panel, click the **Insert Div Tag** button. The Insert Div Tag dialog box opens.

Make sure the div tag is inserted exactly where specified so the page will display correctly.

3. Click the **Insert** button, click **After start of tag**, click the right **Insert button**, and then click **<div id="container">**. The new div will be inserted within the container div.

4. Click the **New CSS Rule** button. The New CSS Rule dialog box opens, so you can create a new style for the div.

5. Create a new CSS rule using **ID** as the selector type, **#content** as the selector name, and **nbf_styles.css** for the rule definition, and then click the **OK** button. The CSS Rule Definition for #content in nbf_styles.css dialog box opens.

6. In the **Background** category, click the **Browse** button, navigate the Select Image Source dialog box to the **Dreamweaver4\Tutorial** folder included with your Data Files, double-click **nb_content_back.jpg** to set the image path and name in the Background-image box, and then select **repeat-y** from the Background-repeat list.

7. In the **Box** category, in the Padding section, type **5** in the Top box, uncheck the **Same for all** check box in the Margin section, type **130** in the Top margin box, type **37** in the Right and Left margin boxes, and then type **10** in the Bottom margin box.

8. In the **Border** category, make sure the three **Same for all** check boxes are checked, select **solid** from the Top list in the Style section, select **thin** from the Top list in the Width section, and then type **#cff** in the Top box of the Color section.

9. Click the **OK** button in the CSS Rule Definition for #content in nbf_styles.css dialog box, and then click the **OK** button in the Insert Div Tag dialog box. The content div is inserted into the page.

10. Click in the Document window to deselect the content div. See Figure 4-14.

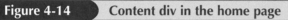

Figure 4-14	Content div in the home page

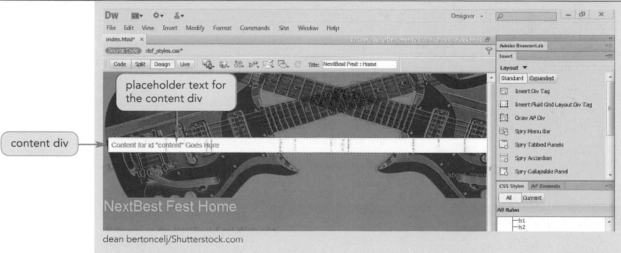

dean bertoncelj/Shutterstock.com

You want the content div to surround the page content. To do this, you need to move the closing content div tag to the bottom of the body of the page.

To move the closing content div tag:

1. In the status bar, click the **<div#content>** tag to select the content div, and then switch to **Code** view. The opening and closing content div tags are selected so that you can see where they appear in the code.

2. Click in the line above the closing container div tag and the comment, but after any code in that line, and then press the **Enter** key. A blank line is added to the code.

3. Select the closing content div tag, and then drag it to the blank line.

4. Place the insertion point before the closing content div tag, and then press the **Spacebar** twice to indent the tag, if necessary.

5. On the Coding toolbar, click the **Apply Comment** button 💬, click **Apply HTML Comment** to insert a comment, and then type **closing content tag** in the comment to identify the tag. See Figure 4-15.

Figure 4-15   **Comment added to the closing content div tag**

opening content
div tag

comment to
identify the
closing content
div tag

closing div tags are
indistinguishable without
the comments

6. Save the page, save the style sheet, and then switch to **Design** view.

7. Select the **Content for id "content" Goes Here** placeholder text, and then press the **Delete** key to delete the placeholder from the home page.

8. Save the page, and then preview the page in a browser. The container div background color is different from the page background image. See Figure 4-16.

Figure 4-16   **Preview of the home page with divs**

Used with permission from Microsoft Corporation; dean bertoncelj/Shutterstock.com; Jupiterimages/Photos.com

9. Close the browser, collapse the Insert panel, in the All Rules pane of the CSS Styles panel, select the **body** style, and then, in the Properties pane, change the background color to **#666**. The background color blends with the background image.

10. In the All Rules pane, select the **body,td,th** style and then, in the Properties pane, change the color to **#333**.

11. In the Document window, click in the blank line after the navigation text, and then press the **Delete** key to move the heading text up in the page.

12. Save the style sheet and the page, and then preview the page in a browser. The container div background blends into the page background.

13. Close the browser.

HTML5 includes new tags that you can style using CSS and use as containers like you do the div tag. Some of the new tags are header, footer, nav, aside, section, article, and figure. As you can see, each tag name indicates its purpose. The header tag includes an identifier for a section of a page, such as heading, label, logo, or banner. The footer tag includes a footer for the closest element above it, such as a figure, and usually contains information about who created the element as well as copyright data. The nav tag includes large-scale navigation information, such as site navigation. The aside tag includes tangentially related content, such as a tip or a pull quote. The section tag includes related content. The article tag includes the text of a newspaper, magazine, or other article. The figure tag includes a graphic or image that is positioned within the content. Best practices specify that, when applicable, you should use one of these tags instead of a div tag because these tags have meaning to machines and assistive devices. Search engines, assistive devices, and other programs that search the Web for specific types of content know what kinds of information these tags contain, and they can use the tags when searching or interacting with the pages of a site.

The final basic layout element you will create for the home page is the footer, which will include the site's copyright notice. As with the other layout elements, the footer needs to appear on all the pages in the site. The footer tag does not appear on the Insert panel so you will insert a div, create a style for the footer tag, and then change the code in the page. You will place the footer inside the content div.

TIP

You can find more information about proper use of the new tags at www.w3.org/community/ webed/wiki/HTML/ Elements#Sections.

To add a footer to the home page:

1. In the status bar, select the **<div#content>** tag to select the content div. You will nest the footer div within the content div.

2. In the **Common** category of the Insert panel, click the **Insert Div Tag** button. The Insert Div Tag dialog box opens.

3. Click the **Insert** button, click **After tag**, click the right **Insert** button, and then click **<div id="content">**. The new div will be inserted within the content div.

4. In the Insert Div Tag dialog box, click the **New CSS Rule** button. The New CSS Rule dialog box opens, so you can create a new style for the div.

5. Create a new CSS rule using **Tag** as the selector type, **footer** as the tag, and **nbf_styles.css** for the rule definition, and then click the **OK** button. The CSS Rule Definition for footer in nbf_styles.css dialog box opens.

6. In the **Block** category, select **center** from the Text-align list.

7. In the **Box** category, select **both** from the Clear list, uncheck the **Same for all** check box in the Margin section, type **0** in the Top and Bottom boxes, and then type **37** in the Right and Left boxes.

8. Click the **OK** button in the CSS Rule Definition for #footer in nbf_styles.css dialog box, and then click the **OK** button in the Insert Div Tag dialog box. The div is added inside of the container div, below the content div.

9. In Design view, select the placeholder text in the div. You will enter the copyright notice in the div.

10. In the **Text** category of the Insert panel, click the **Characters button arrow**, and then click the **Copyright** button. The copyright symbol © is entered in the div.

11. Type **copyright NextBest Fest 2015**. The copyright notice is entered in the div.

12. Switch to **Code** view, scroll down to the new div, select **div** in the opening div tag, and then type **footer**.

13. Select **div** in the closing div tag, type **footer**, and then return to **Design** view. See Figure 4-17.

Figure 4-17	Footer added to the home page

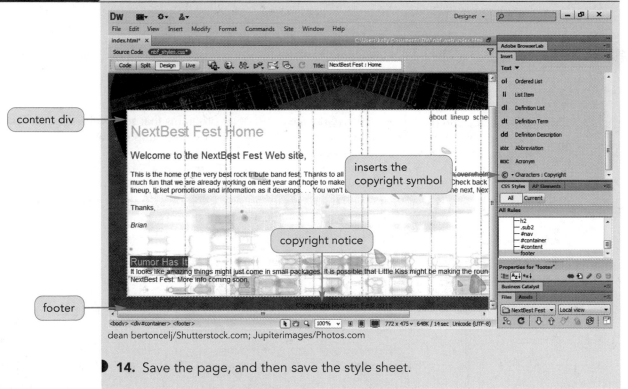

dean bertoncelj/Shutterstock.com; Jupiterimages/Photos.com

14. Save the page, and then save the style sheet.

Duplicating Pages

You have created the basic layout for the pages of the NextBest Fest site. Now that the basic page structure is in place in the home page, you can duplicate the home page to create the other pages of the site. Duplicating pages is a smart way to work because not only do you save time, but you also are assured that the basic page structure is the same for all the pages in the site.

You will duplicate the home page to create the other pages planned for the NextBest Fest site.

TIP

You can also press the Ctrl+D keys to duplicate the selected page in the Files panel.

To duplicate the home page:

▶ 1. Collapse the CSS Styles panel, and then close the **index.html** page.

▶ 2. In the Files panel, right-click **index.html** to open the context menu, point to **Edit**, and then click **Duplicate**. A duplicate of the home page, named index – Copy.html, is created and appears in the files list.

   Trouble? If you do not see index – Copy.html in the files list, you probably need to refresh the Files panel. On the Files panel toolbar, click the Refresh button.

▶ 3. In the Files panel, click **index – Copy.html** to select the page name, click **index – Copy.html** again to open the page name for editing, type **about.html**, and then press the **Enter** key. The duplicated page is renamed.

▶ 4. Open the **about.html** page in Design view.

▶ 5. On the Document toolbar, in the Title box, change the page title to **NextBest Fest : About**.

▶ 6. In the Document window, select the page heading, type **About**, and then delete the remaining content from the page, leaving the navigation text and the footer text.

▶ 7. Save the page, and then close it.

▶ 8. Repeat Steps 2 through 7 to create the following pages: **lineup.html**, **schedule.html**, **tickets.html**, and **contact.html**, using the appropriate file-name and the corresponding page title and page heading.

You have created all of the pages needed for the NextBest Fest site. You will preview the pages in a browser, and confirm that the navigation system works by linking between the pages.

To preview the site pages and test the navigation system:

▶ 1. Open the **index.html** page, and then preview the page in a browser.

▶ 2. In the browser window, click the **about** navigation link to open the about.html page.

▶ 3. Click each of the following links to move between the pages you created and test that all of the links work: **lineup**, **schedule**, **tickets**, and **contact**.

▶ 4. Close the browser.

Editing the Style Sheet from the CSS Styles Panel

The most powerful thing about having an external style sheet connected to each page in a site is that any change made in one place will affect all of the pages in the site. You can edit a style from within the CSS Styles panel.

Gage thinks that the footer text appears too far below the content div in the pages. This is caused by the 10px bottom margin of the content div. He wants you to change the bottom margin to 0px. Rather than changing the bottom margin in each page, you will make the change just one time in the external style sheet.

To change the #content div in the nbf_stylesheet.css:

1. Collapse the Insert panel, expand the CSS Styles panel, click the **All** button, if necessary, and then, in the All Rules pane, click **#content**. The attributes of the #content style appear in the Properties pane.

2. In the margin-bottom box of the Properties pane, select **10px**, type **0**, and then press the **Enter** key. The footer text moves closer to the content div, reflecting the new bottom margin value.

3. Scroll down the home page as needed to view the footer. See Figure 4-18.

Figure 4-18 | **Footer div with new bottom margin**

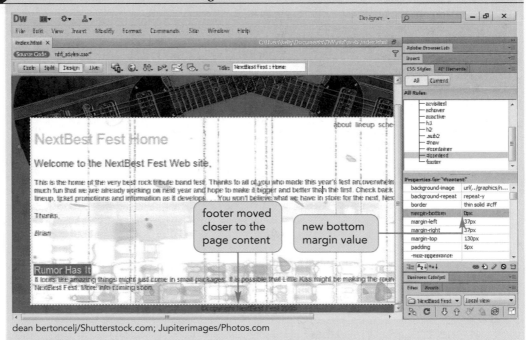

dean bertoncelj/Shutterstock.com; Jupiterimages/Photos.com

4. Save the style sheet, and then preview the page in a browser.

5. Use the navigation system to open the other pages of the site, and confirm that the footer changed position in those pages.

6. Close the browser.

Gage has seen sites that display divs with rounded corners. He likes this new style and thinks that it will appeal to the target audience. Because the new NextBest Fest site uses CSS3, you can change the content div to display with rounded corners. You will accomplish this by adding a value of 15px to the border-radius attribute of the # content rule.

To change the #content div to display rounded edges:

1. In the CSS Styles panel, in the All Rules pane, click the **#content** rule, if necessary.

2. At the bottom of the CSS Styles panel, click the **Show only set properties** button ⁺⁺↓.

3. Scroll to the bottom of the Properties pane, click the **Add Property** link, and then scroll down as needed to select the **border-radius** property.

4. Click in the right **border-radius** box, type **15px**, and then press the **Enter** key. The value is entered, but the appearance of the div does not change in the Document window. You need to switch to Live view to see the effect of the border-radius property.

5. On the Document toolbar, click the **Live** button to switch to Live view. The rounded corners of the div are now visible.

6. Save the style sheet, and then preview the page in a browser. See Figure 4-19.

| Figure 4-19 | **Preview of the home page with updated #content style** |

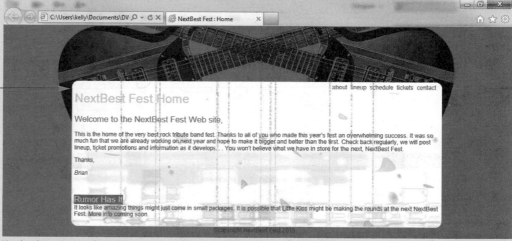

div with rounded corners

Used with permission from Microsoft Corporation; dean bertoncelj/Shutterstock.com; Jupiterimages/Photos.com

7. Close the browser, and then, on the Document toolbar, click the **Live** button to return to Design view, and then close the page.

In this session, you learned about CSS-based layout techniques. You examined Dreamweaver's prebuilt CSS layout pages, including elastic, fluid, and fixed-width layouts. You used div tags and CSS styles to create a fixed-width layout for the NextBest Fest site. In the next session, you will work with AP div tags.

REVIEW

Session 4.1 Quick Check

1. What is a div?
2. What are the three types of fluid layouts?
3. What are comments?
4. Why would you want to add comments before the closing div tags?
5. Do div tags work with CSS styles?
6. How do you select a div?
7. Why is it a good idea to create the page structure for one page, and then duplicate that page to create the other pages of the site?

SESSION 4.2 VISUAL OVERVIEW

Absolute positioning is used when an object will always remain in the same place, regardless of the size of the browser window.

An **AP (absolutely positioned) div** is a div tag that is located a specific number of pixels from the top and left corner of the browser window.

A selected AP div is outlined in yellow or blue.

A **guide** is a vertical or horizontal line you drag from a ruler into the Document window to help you place and align objects in a page. It is visible only in Dreamweaver.

AP div tags are positioned relative to the left (L) and top (T) margins of the page. The top of this selected AP div is 23 pixels from the top margin of the page.

DW

File   Edit   View   Insert   Modify   Format   Commands   Site   Window   Help

index.html ×   C:\Users\kelly\Documents\DW\T4\Solutions\Dreamwea

Source Code   nbf_styles.css

Code | Split | Design | Live   Title: NextBest Fest : Home

TICKETS
AVAILABLE

st Home

Welcome to the NextBest Fest Web site,

This is the home of the very best rock tribute band fest. Thanks to all of you who m much fun that we are already working on next year and hope to make it bigger and lineup, ticket promotions and information as it develops. . . You won't believe what

Thanks,

Brian

You can change the width (W) and height (H) of the selected AP div here or with the sizing handles on the selected AP div.

Rumor Has It
It looks like amazing things m   ackages. It is possible that I i

`<body>` `<div#TICKETS.featured>` `<h1>`   100%   739 x

Properties

CSS-P Element   L 20px   W 160px   Z-Index 2   Bg image

TICKETS ▼   T 20px   H 160px   Vis default ▼   Bg color   #fff

Overflow visible ▼   Clip: L   R

T   B

USING ABSOLUTELY POSITIONED DIV TAGS

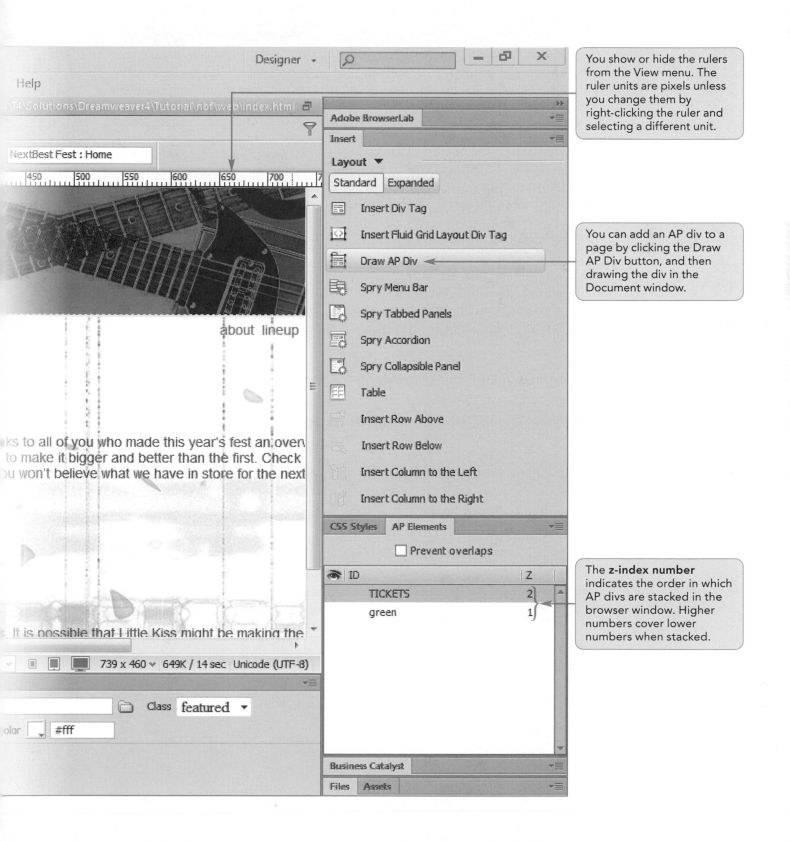

You show or hide the rulers from the View menu. The ruler units are pixels unless you change them by right-clicking the ruler and selecting a different unit.

You can add an AP div to a page by clicking the Draw AP Div button, and then drawing the div in the Document window.

The **z-index number** indicates the order in which AP divs are stacked in the browser window. Higher numbers cover lower numbers when stacked.

Using Absolutely Positioned Div Tags

With absolute positioning, div tags can be positioned anywhere on the screen with accuracy and reliability, and they remain in place relative to the top and left margins of the page (or top and left margins of the object in which they are placed) regardless of how a user resizes the browser window. AP (absolutely positioned) divs can be stacked on top of one another so that their content overlaps. They can be animated, made visible or invisible, and have their stacking order (the order in which they overlap) changed. You can also use CSS styles to customize the display attributes of an AP div just like with a regular div tag. Although AP divs are useful for positioning content in an exact location in a Web page, relatively positioned divs are a better choice when creating an entire Web site because they provide more flexibility and enable you to create designs that display differently on different user agents.

Gage wants you to add some promotional text outside of the content area in the home page. You will use AP divs to place the text in the upper-left corner of the browser window so that the content maintains a consistent position. This text is designed to promote ticket sales and will link to the tickets page.

Drawing AP Divs

You draw an AP div in a page in Design view. The borders of each AP div you draw are visible within Dreamweaver to make them easier to work with. The borders do not appear in the browser window.

You will draw an AP div in the home page. The AP div will contain a link to the tickets page.

To draw an AP div in the home page:

1. If you took a break after the previous session, make sure the NextBest Fest site is open in Dreamweaver, the Designer workspace is reset, the Business Catalyst panel is minimized, the Files panel is open, and the index.html page is open in Design view.

2. On the menu bar, click **View**, point to **Rulers**, and then click **Show**. The rulers appear along the top and left sides of the Document window.

3. If the units on the ruler are not pixels, right-click a ruler, and then click **Pixels**.

4. In the **Layout** category of the Insert panel, click the **Draw AP Div** button. The pointer changes to ┼.

5. Position the pointer approximately **10 pixels** below the top of the page and approximately **10 pixels** from the left border of the page, and then drag to draw an AP div approximately **100px** wide and **50px** high. The rectangular AP div appears in yellow in the upper-left corner of the page when you release the mouse button. See Figure 4-20.

TIP

You can also press the Ctrl+Alt+R keys to show or hide the rulers.

Figure 4-20	AP div drawn in the home page

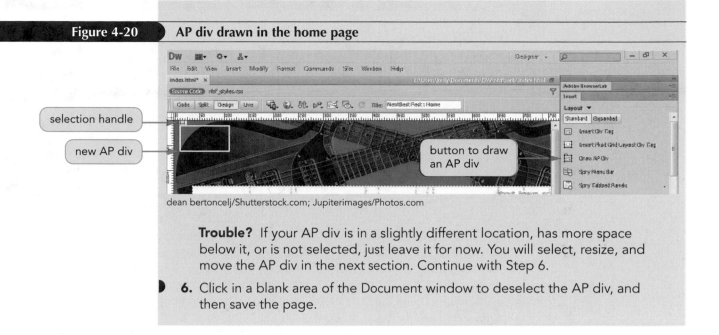

selection handle

new AP div

button to draw an AP div

dean bertoncelj/Shutterstock.com; Jupiterimages/Photos.com

Trouble? If your AP div is in a slightly different location, has more space below it, or is not selected, just leave it for now. You will select, resize, and move the AP div in the next section. Continue with Step 6.

6. Click in a blank area of the Document window to deselect the AP div, and then save the page.

Selecting, Resizing, and Moving an AP Div

Divs are container objects. As a container object, an AP div can be active or selected. When an AP div is active, its border is visible and a selection handle appears in its upper-left corner. You can change the Visual Aids settings to also display layout backgrounds and the box model to help identify CSS issues. You must select the div before you can reposition or resize it. When an AP div is selected, resize handles surround it and a selection handle appears in its upper-left corner. You can use the resize handles to change the dimensions of the AP div to fit the content you enter. If the page contains multiple AP divs on top of one another, the selected AP div temporarily becomes the top item so that you can work with its contents.

You might also want to reorder or move AP divs. Each AP div is positioned in a page using x-, y-, and z-coordinates, much like graphs. The x- and y-coordinates correspond to the AP div's Left and Top positions, respectively. Left and Top refer to the distance from the left and the top of the page unless the AP div is nested inside another AP div or regular div, in which case, Left and Top refer to the distance from the left and the top of the parent AP div or regular div. When viewed in a browser window, the AP div remains in the exact same place, even when the browser window is resized. The z-coordinate—called the z-index number—determines the stacking order (the order in which the AP div is stacked in the user's browser window when more than one AP div is used in a page). When AP divs overlap, the higher-numbered AP divs are at the front of the stack and are seen in front of those that have lower numbers. If a top AP div has transparent areas, AP divs stacked below it are visible in those areas. The areas of the top AP div that contain text, background color, or images obscure any AP divs stacked below it.

REFERENCE

Working with AP Divs

- To make an AP div active, click in the AP div.
- To select an AP div, click the edge of the AP div in the Document window when its border is visible (or click the selection handle of the active AP div, or click the name of the AP div in the AP Elements panel).
- To resize an AP div, drag any resize handle until the AP div is the desired size (or enter exact height and width values in the Property inspector).
- To move an AP div, drag the AP div by its selection handle to the desired location (or press the arrow keys to shift the selected AP div one pixel at a time to the desired location, or enter Left, Top, and z-index numbers in the Property inspector).

The rulers and guides enable you to more easily place elements in a specific position in the page. Rulers, which you have already used, provide markings in pixels, inches, or centimeters to help you to position elements in the page. Guides are lines that you drag from the horizontal and vertical rulers into the Document window to help you place and align objects, such as AP divs, in a page. You can drag multiple guides into the page, move visible guides to new positions in the page, or drag unneeded guides from the Document window back to the ruler to remove the guide from sight. Guides are visible only within the Dreamweaver environment.

You want to reposition the AP div from below the navigation bar to the right. You will use guides to help you position the AP div.

To select, resize, and move the AP div in the home page using guides:

1. Click in the Document window anywhere outside of the AP div, and then place the pointer over the border of the AP div. The border becomes red. See Figure 4-21.

Figure 4-21   AP div in the home page

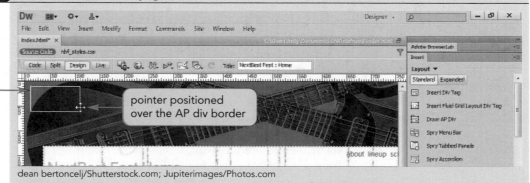

dean bertoncelj/Shutterstock.com; Jupiterimages/Photos.com

2. Click the red border of the AP div. The AP div is selected. Resize handles surround the selected AP div, its border is yellow, and its selection handle appears. The AP div's width and height values appear in the Property inspector in the W and H boxes.

3. Place the pointer over the yellow border of the selected AP div. An indicator that opens the code navigator appears. See Figure 4-22.

| Figure 4-22 | AP div selected in the home page |

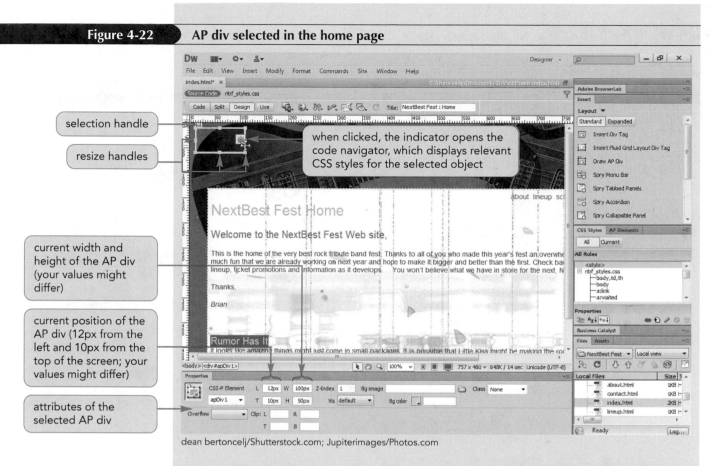

selection handle

resize handles

when clicked, the indicator opens the code navigator, which displays relevant CSS styles for the selected object

current width and height of the AP div (your values might differ)

current position of the AP div (12px from the left and 10px from the top of the screen; your values might differ)

attributes of the selected AP div

dean bertoncelj/Shutterstock.com; Jupiterimages/Photos.com

4. Drag from the vertical ruler to the **20-pixel** mark on the horizontal ruler (the tooltip shows 20.00 px), and then release the mouse button. (If you cannot get the exact location, just drag to the closest mark possible.) A vertical guide appears in the page over the AP div and other elements.

5. Drag the middle-left resize handle of the AP div to the guide, as shown in Figure 4-23. In the Property inspector, the W value changes as you drag the AP div border.

Figure 4-23   **AP div being resized**

resize handle being
dragged to reposition
the outer border; the
yellow border will not
move until the mouse
button is released

width value changes
as the AP div resizes

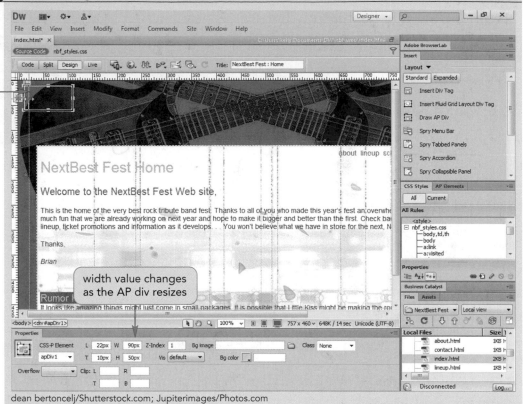

dean bertoncelj/Shutterstock.com; Jupiterimages/Photos.com

6. Release the mouse button. The left border of the AP div is adjusted.

7. Position the pointer over the AP div selection handle. The pointer changes to ✛. You will drag the AP div to a new position.

8. Drag the AP div selection handle down in the page until the top of the div is at **20px**. You know the AP div is in the exact location because 20px appears in the T box in the Property inspector, as shown in Figure 4-24.

Figure 4-24 | Repositioned AP div

drag the selection handle to move the AP div

repositioned AP div snaps to the guide

left value remains unchanged as you drag the AP div

top value changes as you drag the AP div

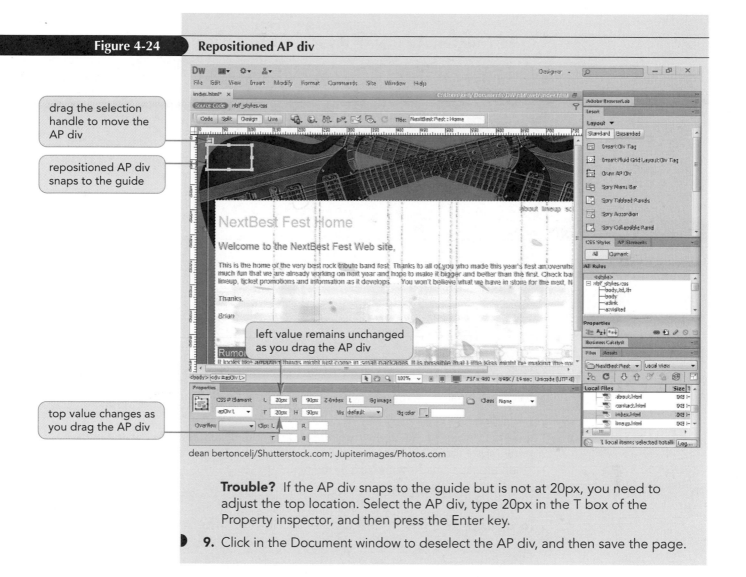

dean bertoncelj/Shutterstock.com; Jupiterimages/Photos.com

Trouble? If the AP div snaps to the guide but is not at 20px, you need to adjust the top location. Select the AP div, type 20px in the T box of the Property inspector, and then press the Enter key.

▶ **9.** Click in the Document window to deselect the AP div, and then save the page.

Adding Content to an AP Div

Like other divs, an AP div can contain almost any type of content, including text, graphics, forms, multimedia content, and other divs. You add content to an AP div using the same methods you use to insert content directly into a Web page. You can also move existing content from the page to an AP div by dragging it. AP divs must be active to accept content. To enter text into an AP div, for example, you first click in the AP div to make it active.

Gage wants you to type TICKETS into the new AP div. This new content will help promote ticket sales, which is one of the goals for the site. He also wants a user to be able to click anywhere in the AP div to open the tickets page. You will add content to the AP div you created in the home page, and then create a hyperlink to the tickets page.

To add content to the AP div in the home page:

1. In the Document window, click in the AP div to make it active, and then type **TICKETS**. The text content is added to the AP div.

2. Select the text, and then, in the HTML pane of the Property inspector, format the text with **Heading 1**. The AP div expands to fit the enlarged text.

3. Click outside of the AP div to deselect it. A dotted yellow line indicates the actual dimensions of the AP div. Although the div appears to have expanded to accommodate the formatted text, the original size of the div has not changed. See Figure 4-25.

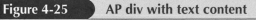

Figure 4-25 | **AP div with text content**

dotted line shows the actual dimensions

text entered into the AP div

dean bertoncelj/Shutterstock.com; Jupiterimages/Photos.com

The right border of the AP div expanded automatically, but the width value in the Property inspector still reflects the original width. You will update the AP div width, and then create a link from the text to the tickets page.

To update the width and create a link from the AP div:

1. Click the border of the AP div, and then click a right resize handle to extend the width. The width is updated in the CSS pane of the Property inspector and the dotted yellow line disappears. A second solid yellow line still runs horizontally across the div, below the text. See Figure 4-26.

Figure 4-26   **AP div width updated in the Property inspector**

resized AP div

updated width value

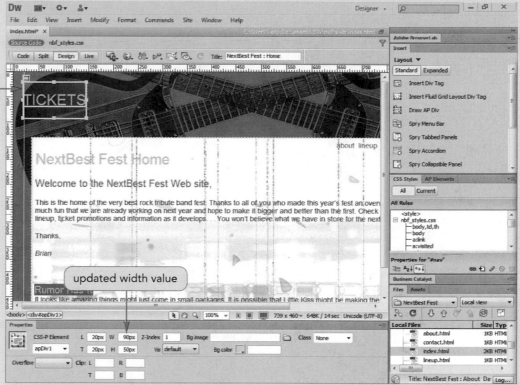

dean bertoncelj/Shutterstock.com; Jupiterimages/Photos.com

Trouble? If the AP div width does not update, you need to adjust the width. Select the AP div, type 90px in the W box of the Property inspector, and then press the Enter key.

2. In the Property inspector, type **160px** in the H box, and then type **160px** in the W box, if necessary, to change the height and width of the AP div. The AP div is now a larger square and the horizontal yellow line disappears.

3. Collapse the CSS Styles panel. The Files panel expands to fill the extra space and all the pages in the root folder are visible.

4. In the AP div, select the **TICKETS** text. You will link the selected text to the tickets page.

5. In the HTML pane of the Property inspector, click and drag the **Point to File** button 🎯 to the **tickets.html** page in the Files panel. See Figure 4-27.

Figure 4-27 **AP div text linked to the tickets.html page**

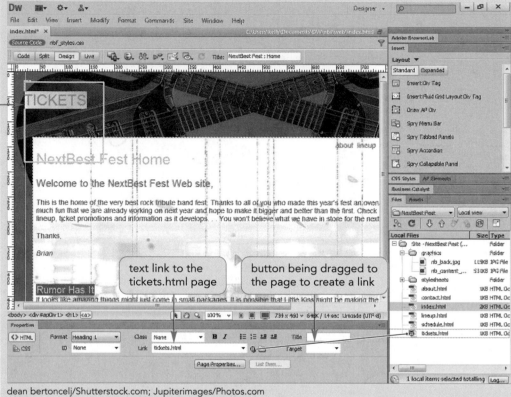

formatted text link

text link to the tickets.html page

button being dragged to the page to create a link

dean bertoncelj/Shutterstock.com; Jupiterimages/Photos.com

6. Release the mouse button. In the HTML pane of the Property inspector, tickets.html appears in the Link box, indicating that the selected text is linked to the tickets page of the Web site.

The AP div position is absolute. It remains fixed in the same location at the exact pixels you specified regardless of the size of the browser window. The positions of the other divs are relative. They reposition to remain in the center of the page as the browser window resizes. The content in the AP div is complete. You will preview the page in a browser to test the link and see how it remains in position no matter how the browser window is sized.

To preview the home page with the AP div:

1. Save the page, and then preview the home page in a browser.
2. On the browser window title bar, click the **Maximize** button 🔲 , if necessary, to maximize the browser window. See Figure 4-28.

| Figure 4-28 | Home page previewed in maximized browser window |

AP div position is absolute

container and content divs reposition based on the size of the browser window

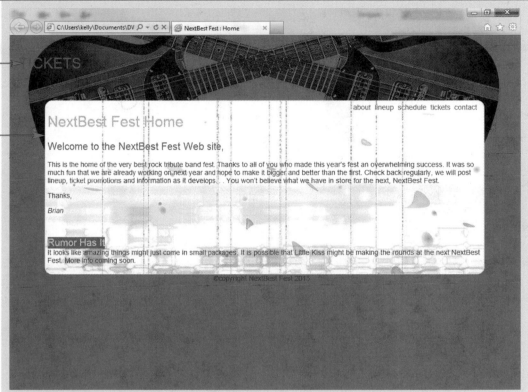

Used with permission from Microsoft Corporation; dean bertoncelj/Shutterstock.com; Jupiterimages/Photos.com

3. On the browser window title bar, click the **Restore Down** button ▣. The window decreases in size. The AP div remains in the same location even though the window changed size, but the other divs shift position to remain in the same relative position in the window. See Figure 4-29.

Figure 4-29	Home page previewed in restored down browser window

AP div's absolute position remains in the same location regardless of the browser window size

container and content divs' relative positions change as the browser window resizes

Used with permission from Microsoft Corporation; dean bertoncelj/Shutterstock.com; Jupiterimages/Photos.com

Trouble? If the browser window did not change size, drag the lower-right corner of the browser window up and left to decrease its size.

4. Click the **TICKETS** link. The tickets page opens.

5. Close the browser.

Adjusting AP Div Attributes

You can change the attributes for a selected AP div in the Property inspector, or you can create a CSS style with the desired attribute values and attach that style to any AP divs that you want to have the same attributes. To adjust the attributes in the Property inspector, the AP div must be selected. When the AP div is selected, the Property inspector includes the following attributes:

- **CSS-P Element.** A unique name for the AP div. The name cannot contain spaces or symbols because it will be used in HTML code to refer to the AP div. If you don't specify a name, Dreamweaver assigns the name apDiv1 to the first AP div you draw, apDiv2 to the second, and so on.
- **L and T.** The horizontal (L) and vertical (T) positions of the AP div measured in pixels from the left margin and the top margin. If the AP div is nested within another AP div, the values reference the distance from the left and top edge of the parent AP div instead of the page margin. These numbers adjust automatically to reflect the AP div's position in the page when you drag the AP div.
- **W and H.** The horizontal (W) and vertical (H) dimensions of the AP div. If you delete the width, the AP div will scale with the browser window.
- **Z-Index.** A number that indicates the AP div's stacking order. AP divs with higher numbers are stacked in front of AP divs with lower numbers.

- **Vis.** The visibility options that specify whether the AP div is visible when the Web page is loaded. If the AP div is hidden when the page is loaded, different actions by the user can make it visible. Default uses the browser's default visibility, which is usually visible. Inherit, the default for most browsers, sets the same visibility property as the parent AP div of a nested AP div. Visible displays the AP div content when the page is loaded. Hidden hides the AP div content when the page is loaded.
- **Bg image.** The path to the background image file for the AP div. If no image is specified, the Web page background is seen through the AP div.
- **Bg color.** The hexadecimal color code for the background color of the AP div. If no color is specified, the AP div is transparent and the Web page background is seen through the AP div.
- **Class.** A list of the styles you created. You can select a style to apply to the AP div.
- **Overflow.** The options for how the AP div appears in a browser window if its content exceeds its specified size. Visible expands the AP div to display the overflow content. Hidden maintains the AP div's size and prevents the overflow text from being displayed in the browser. Scroll adds scroll bars to the AP div (whether or not they are needed) in Internet Explorer, and in Firefox it behaves like the auto option. Auto displays scroll bars for the AP div in the browser only if the content overflows. Overflow options are not supported in all browsers.
- **Clip.** The portion of the AP div that is visible in a browser. Clip does not work correctly in all browsers.

You need to name the AP div that you created in the home page. Because the content of the AP div you created might overflow the AP div's boundaries, you also need to adjust the Overflow attribute.

To adjust the AP div's attributes in the Property inspector:

1. In the Document window, click the AP div border to select the AP div.

2. In the Property inspector, double-click the **CSS-P Element** box to select the name that Dreamweaver assigned to the AP div, and then type **TICKETS**. The AP div is renamed.

3. In the Property inspector, click the **Overflow** button, and then click **visible**. The tickets AP div will expand to display any overflow content.

4. Save the page.

You will create a CSS style to add a colored background and a colored medium-width double line around the TICKETS AP div. You will also adjust the border radius to change the visible shape of the background to a circle. Because these attributes will be saved in a style, you can quickly apply them to other elements you create in the NextBest Fest site.

To create the new CSS style and edit the existing div style:

1. Expand the CSS Styles panel and collapse the Insert panel.

2. In the CSS Styles panel, click the **New CSS Rule** button , create a **Class** selector named **.featured** that is defined in the **nbf_styles.css** style sheet, and then click the **OK** button.

3. In the Background category, click in the **Background-color** box, and then type **#fff**.

4. Click **Border** in the Category box, click **double** from the Top list in the Style section, click **medium** from the Top list in the Width section, and then type **#99cbb3** in the Top box in the Color section.

5. Make sure that the **Same for all** check boxes are checked in the Style, Width, and Color sections, and then click the **OK** button.

6. In the Document window, select the **TICKETS** AP div, and then, in the Property inspector, click the **Class** arrow, and then click **featured**. The featured style is applied to the TICKETS AP div.

7. In the CSS Styles panel, click the **All** button, if necessary, and then click **#TICKETS** in the style list. The #TICKETS rule that defines the TICKETS AP div is selected. You will edit the properties for the TICKETS AP div in the CSS Styles panel.

8. In the Properties pane, click the **Add Property** link, select **border-radius**, and then type **90px** in the corner radius box in the right column. The AP div now has completely rounded corners so it will display as a circle in the browser window.

9. Click in the Document window to deselect the TICKETS AP div, and then click the **Live** button. In Live view, you can see the circular display area of the TICKETS AP div. See Figure 4-30.

Figure 4-30   **The TICKETS AP div with the featured CSS style applied**

double line border surrounds the AP div with rounded edges that create a circle

border-radius property added

TICKETS rule selected

dean bertoncelj/Shutterstock.com; Jupiterimages/Photos.com

10. Click the **Live** button to return to Design view, save the page, and then save the style sheet.

11. Preview the page in a browser. The double lines around the AP div are visible.

12. Close the browser.

Examining the Code for AP Div Tags

Remember that a div tag is a generic, block-level HTML tag that can be used for many things; you have examined the div tag in the tutorial. When you create an AP div, Dreamweaver places an ID style in the head of the page that defines the type of positioning, the AP div's left and top coordinates, the width and height, the overflow value, and the z-index number. The style is placed in the head of the page instead of in the external style sheet because absolute positioning is usually so specific that you generally apply it to only one element in a site. If you plan to use an AP div in multiple pages of a site, you can move the style to the external style sheet. Because the tickets AP div will appear in only the home page and because you do not want to clutter an external style sheet with a lot of styles that will be used only one time and in one page, it is okay to leave the style in the head of the page. Dreamweaver uses the CSS-P Element name entered in the Property inspector as the ID style name.

When you view the code for the TICKETS AP div in the home page, you see its ID style name in the internal style sheet in the head of the page. The following code shows the TICKETS AP div code (the exact measurements of your AP div might be slightly different):

```
<style type="text/css">
#TICKETS {
    position:absolute;
    left:20px;
    top:20px;
    width:160px;
    height:160px;
    z-index:1;
    overflow: visible;
    border-radius:  90px;
}
</style>
```

The following code for the AP div tag is placed in the body of the page:

```
<div class="featured" id="TICKETS">
    <h1><a href="tickets.html">TICKETS</a></h1>
</div>
```

The CSS-P Element name (or the ID style) that you assigned in the Property inspector is placed in the opening div tag, as shown in the first line of the code. In the code, id is the attribute name, and everything to the right of the equal sign in the quotation marks is the value. The div tag also references the external featured style that you created. The AP div content appears between the opening and closing div tags. When you drag an AP div tag to a new position or when you change its attributes in the Property inspector, Dreamweaver updates the ID style.

INSIGHT

Creating AP Div Positioning Styles

It is sometimes useful to create external styles to define the AP div positioning, for instance, if you plan to use the same positioning for multiple AP divs (similar to the way you used regular divs when you created multiple pages). If you create a site that enables users to choose from a variety of looks for the display of the pages (depending on which style sheet is attached to the page), creating external styles for the AP divs enables you to change the location of the AP divs in each style sheet to accommodate the corresponding look. You can also use this technique to create pages that display differently in different types of devices such as phones.

There are many other reasons to create external styles to define the AP div positioning. When you drag an AP div whose positioning is defined externally to a new position in the page, the style is updated with the new positioning coordinates in the same way that an ID style would be. This can cause problems if you have attached more than one AP div to the style and want to reposition only one AP div. As you can see, both methods of AP div positioning have drawbacks and benefits. However, because Dreamweaver automatically places AP div positioning styles in the head of the page, this tutorial uses that method.

You will examine the HTML code for the tickets AP div in the home page.

To examine the HTML code for the tickets AP div:

1. In the home page, select the **TICKETS** AP div, switch to **Split** view, and then click the **Source Code** button on the Related Files toolbar. The home page appears in Split view with the AP div tag code found in the body of the page selected.

2. Scroll the Code pane until all of the AP div code is visible, and then locate the ID style. See Figure 4-31.

| Figure 4-31 | **TICKETS AP div in Split view** |

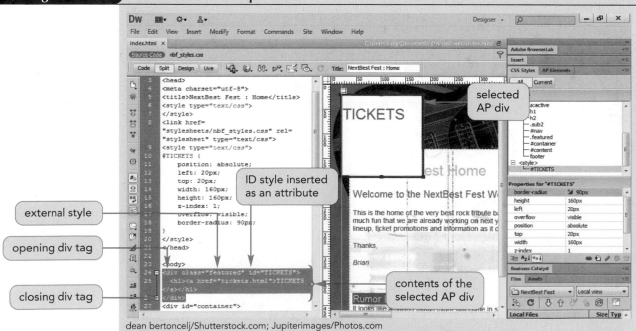

dean bertoncelj/Shutterstock.com; Jupiterimages/Photos.com

▶ **3.** In the Code pane, locate the content of the **TICKETS** AP div.

▶ **4.** Locate the anchor **<a>** tag that links the text to the tickets.html page.

▶ **5.** Scroll the Code pane to the head of the page, if necessary, to view the internal style sheet, and then review the ID style for the tickets AP div. See Figure 4-32.

Figure 4-32   **Code for the TICKETS AP div's ID style**

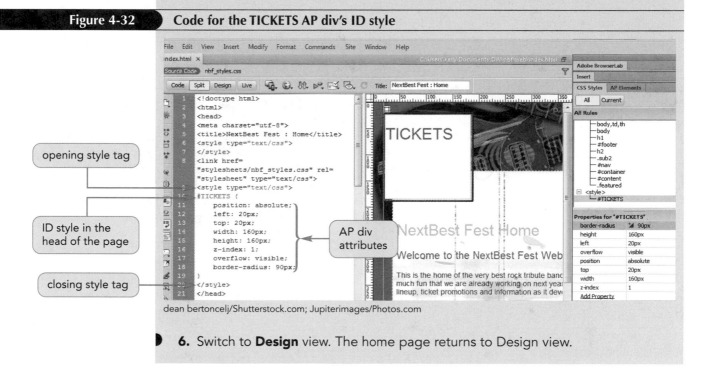

dean bertoncelj/Shutterstock.com; Jupiterimages/Photos.com

▶ **6.** Switch to **Design** view. The home page returns to Design view.

Modifying AP Divs

AP divs give you precise control over the placement of the content in pages. After you have added an AP div to a page, you will most likely need to modify it. You can change the stacking order of AP divs and you can nest one AP div inside another.

Adjusting Stacking Order

One benefit of using AP divs in a Web page is that they can be stacked or overlapped. Think of each AP div as a clear acetate sheet such as those used for overhead projectors. You can stack one on top of another and still see the bottom AP div through any transparent portions of the top AP div. If the top AP div does not have any transparent portions, the bottom AP div is hidden from view. Stacking enables you to create more sophisticated and interesting layout designs. Also, because AP divs can be animated, stacking enables you to create interesting user interactions. For example, you could stack two AP divs that contained text so that the back AP div is hidden by the front AP div and then animate the AP divs to switch their stacking order when the user clicks a button. This brings the back AP div to the front so that its text is visible.

Each new AP div you create is assigned the next consecutive z-index number—the first AP div you create is 1, the second is 2, and so on. On the screen, AP divs with higher z-index numbers appear in front of those with lower z-index numbers. You can change the stacking order by changing the z-index numbers. For example, an AP div with the z-index number of 2 appears behind an AP div with a z-index number of 3. If you change the first AP div to a z-index number of 4, then it will appear in front of the second AP div with an index number of 2 when they are stacked. You can set more than one AP div with the same z-index number to make them appear at the same level.

PROSKILLS

Problem Solving: Keeping Up with CSS Developments

Web designers are constantly pushing the limits of what can be done with CSS and how it can be used to lay out Web pages. New techniques for using CSS are being developed all the time. However, using the latest trendy techniques is not always a good idea because cutting-edge techniques are often buggy and can produce unreliable results. In addition, incorporating the latest trends while still following best practices for creating a site can be challenging. As the designer, you must do your research to ensure that new innovations you use will not cause problems in a site. It is your job to ensure that the client's best interest and the functionality of the site are always at the forefront of the decisions you make.

Designers must keep up with the latest techniques and know when they should rely on older techniques. At Web sites such as *www.csszengarden.com*, designers contribute CSS page layouts they have created that demonstrate new and innovative ways to use CSS. Online magazines such as *webdesignermag.co.uk* discuss best practices as well as innovative techniques for using CSS. Visiting sites like this regularly can help you to keep up to date with the latest innovations and current industry standards for best practices. This knowledge can make you a stronger Web designer and a more valuable employee.

Gage wants you to add the word AVAILABLE below TICKETS, center the text in the circle, and create a more dramatic border around the existing TICKETS AP div. You will add the background and border in a second AP div that you will place behind the TICKETS AP div in the home page.

To add text to the TICKETS AP div and create a new AP div:

1. In the TICKETS AP div, click before the TICKETS text, and then press the **Shift+Enter** keys to move the text to a second line.

2. Click after the TICKETS text, select the **<a>** tag in the status bar, and then press the **Right** arrow key to move past that tag.

3. Press the **Enter** key to create a new line, type **AVAILABLE** on the new line, select the **AVAILABLE** text, and then, in the HTML pane of the Property inspector, click the **Formatting arrow** and click **Heading 2** to format the text.

4. Select all of the text in the TICKETS AP div, and then, in the CSS pane of the Property inspector, click the **Align Center** button 🖹 to center the text in the AP div.

   Trouble? If the text doesn't center in the AP div, you need to edit the TICKETS style. In the CSS Styles panel, select the TICKETS style, and then click the Edit Rule button. In the Block category, select Center in the Text-align list, and then click the OK button.

5. Switch to **Live** view to see the text in the modified TICKETS AP div, and then return to **Design** view.

6. In the **Layout** category of the Insert panel, click the **Draw AP Div** button. You will create a second AP div in the home page.

7. In the home page, draw a new AP div the approximate width and height of the TICKETS AP div directly below the TICKETS AP div but not overlapping it. See Figure 4-33.

TIP

To align selected AP divs to the last selected AP div, click Modify on the menu bar, point to Arrange, and then click the appropriate command.

Figure 4-33	Second AP div drawn in the home page

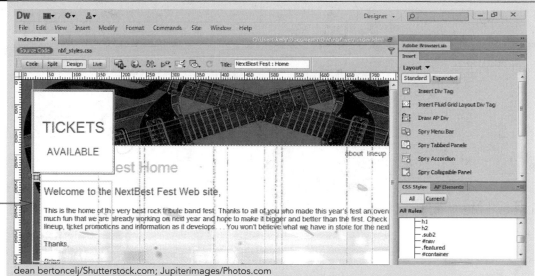

new AP div below the TICKETS AP div

dean bertoncelj/Shutterstock.com; Jupiterimages/Photos.com

Trouble? If the AP div is not positioned or sized correctly, you need to move or resize it. Click the AP div's selection handle to select the AP div, and then drag the AP div to the correct position or drag a resize handle to resize it.

8. Select the new AP div, and then, in the Properties pane of the CSS Styles panel, change the width and height to **190px**. The new AP div is resized.

9. Collapse the Insert panel, and then select **apDiv1** in the All Rules pane of the CSS Styles panel.

10. Using the **Add Property** link in the Properties pane, add a background-color of **#663**, a border-radius of **120px**, and a border of **medium double #99cbb3** to the new AP div. The new AP div now has a background color and border.

11. Drag the new AP div by its selection handle to left-align the AP div with the guide and position it below the TICKET text.

12. Click outside of the AP div to deselect it, and then switch to **Live** view to preview AP divs in the home page. See Figure 4-34.

Figure 4-34   **Second AP div formatted**

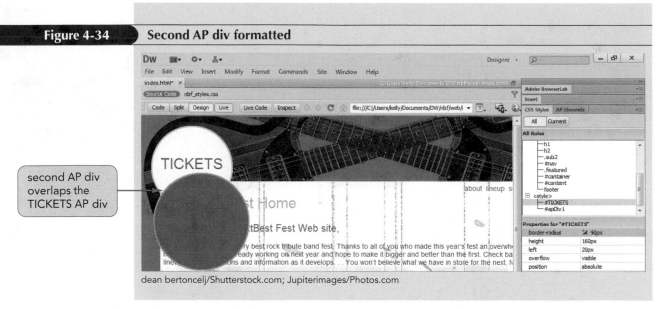

second AP div overlaps the TICKETS AP div

dean bertoncelj/Shutterstock.com; Jupiterimages/Photos.com

You will expand the AP Elements panel, name the new AP div in the Property inspector, and then look at the stacking order in the AP Elements panel. Dreamweaver gives a generic name to each new AP div—the first unnamed AP div is apDiv1, the second is apDiv2, and so on. After you rename the first AP div you create, the next AP div you create is named apDiv1.

To rename the new AP div in the home page:

1. In the CSS panel group, click the **AP Elements** tab. The AP Elements panel expands. See Figure 4-35.

Figure 4-35   **AP Elements panel**

drag to resize the ID and Z columns

default ID of the new AP div

new AP div has a higher z-index number and appears in front of the TICKETS AP div

z-index numbers

dean bertoncelj/Shutterstock.com; Jupiterimages/Photos.com

2. On the Document toolbar, click the **Live** button to return to Design view.

3. Click the border of the new AP div to select it.

   Trouble? If the TICKETS AP div becomes selected and moves to the top of the stack, obscuring the available AP div, click in a blank space to deselect the TICKETS AP div, and then select the available AP div.

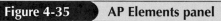

4. In the Property inspector, double-click **apDiv1** in the CSS-P Element box to select the text, type **green**, and then press the **Enter** key. The ID name changes in the AP Elements panel.

In the AP Elements panel, AP divs appear in their current stacking order. The green AP div has a z-index of 2, which means that it is in front of the TICKETS AP div, which has a z-index of 1. This is evident in the Document window.

To adjust the stacking order of the AP divs in the home page:

1. In the Z column of the AP Elements panel, select the number **2** to the right of the green AP div, and then type **1** to change its z-index number.

2. In the Z column, select the number **1** to the right of the TICKETS AP div, type **2** to change its z-index number, and then press the **Enter** key. The TICKETS AP div became selected when you changed its z-index number.

3. In the Document window, click the **green** AP div to select it, and then, in the Property inspector, type **5px** in the L box and type **5px** in the T box. The green AP div is repositioned in the page.

4. Click in the Document window outside of the AP divs to deselect them. The center of the green AP div is obscured by the TICKETS AP div. See Figure 4-36.

| Figure 4-36 | AP divs stacking order changed in the AP Elements panel |

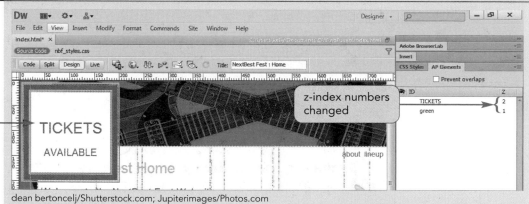

TICKETS AP div obscures the center of the green AP div

z-index numbers changed

dean bertoncelj/Shutterstock.com; Jupiterimages/Photos.com

5. Select the **green** AP div. The border of the green AP div becomes yellow. Although the stacking order has changed, its content is visible because the green AP div is selected.

6. Save the page, and then preview it in a browser. See Figure 4-37.

Figure 4-37   Home page with AP divs previewed in Internet Explorer

TICKETS AP div
appears in front of
the green AP div

Used with permission from Microsoft Corporation; dean bertoncelj/Shutterstock.com; Jupiterimages/Photos.com

▶ **7.** Close the browser.

Creating Nested AP Divs

You might want two or more AP divs to move together, which you can do by nesting AP divs. A **nested AP div** is an AP div contained within an outer (parent) AP div. With AP divs, nesting does not refer to the AP divs' physical positions but instead to the underlying code. This means that the nested AP div does not have to touch its on-screen parent to be nested. The nested AP div is indented under the parent in the AP Elements panel.

Nesting is used to group AP divs. When AP divs are nested, if you move the parent, the nested AP div will move with it. This is because the position of the nested AP div is relative to the left and top borders of the parent rather than to the left and top borders of the page. A nested AP div also shares other attributes with its parent. It might be necessary to change your preferences for AP Elements to enable Dreamweaver to nest AP divs. You will check your preferences.

To change the AP Elements preferences:

▶ **1.** On the menu bar, click **Edit**, and then click **Preferences**. The Preferences dialog box opens.

▶ **2.** Click the **AP Elements** category to display the AP Elements preferences.

▶ **3.** Click the **Nesting: Nest when created within an AP div** check box, if necessary, to check it.

▶ **4.** Click the **OK** button.

Nesting is now enabled. Next, you will draw a new AP div in the TICKETS AP div. Then you will move the AP divs together.

To create a nested AP div:

▶ **1.** Click inside the **TICKETS** AP div.

▶ **2.** In the Layout category of the Insert panel, click **Draw AP Div**, and then draw an AP div that fills the blank area inside of the TICKETS AP div above the TICKETS text.

3. Type **test** in the new AP div. See Figure 4-38.

Figure 4-38   Nested AP div

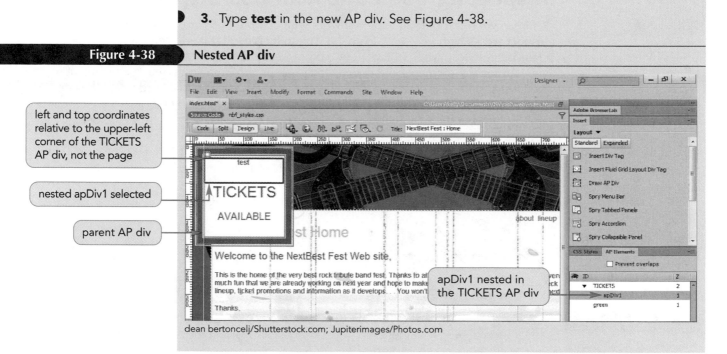

left and top coordinates relative to the upper-left corner of the TICKETS AP div, not the page

nested apDiv1 selected

parent AP div

apDiv1 nested in the TICKETS AP div

dean bertoncelj/Shutterstock.com; Jupiterimages/Photos.com

In the AP Elements panel, the new AP div, named apDiv1, is indented under the TICKETS AP div and the TICKETS AP div has a down arrow to the left of its name. These cues indicate that the new AP div is nested in the TICKETS AP div. You will move the AP divs so you can see how the nested AP div is affected by the parent AP div.

To move the nested AP div:

1. Click the **selection handle** of the TICKETS AP div and drag it horizontally across the page so that the right side of the TICKETS AP div is close to the right edge of the screen. The TICKETS AP div and the apDiv1 are repositioned at the right of the screen, but the green AP div remains in its original position because the apDiv1 is nested in the TICKETS AP div and is positioned relative to the TICKETS AP div.

2. Click the **selection handle** of the apDiv1 AP div, and then drag it below the TICKETS AP div. Only the apDiv1 AP div moves.

3. Move the **TICKETS** AP div back to its original position. Because the apDiv1 AP div is still nested in the TICKETS AP div, it moves back to the left side of the screen.

4. Close the page without saving. You do not want to save the nested AP div.

5. Collapse the CSS Styles panel group.

Inspecting CSS Code with CSS Inspect

A Dreamweaver tool that helps you work with complex CSS code is CSS Inspect. **CSS Inspect** works with Live view to enable you to identify HTML elements and their associated CSS styles. When in Live view, CSS Inspect changes the display to Split view so you can see the elements and code at the same time. When you point to an element in the Design pane, that element is highlighted in blue with a yellow border and the corresponding code in the Code pane is selected. The styles affecting the selected element are displayed in the CSS Styles panel. This way, you can see how the rules are being applied to the selected element so that you can determine why that element might not be displaying as you expected. This process of determining what is not working in code is called **debugging**. CSS Inspect works similarly to frequently used developer tools like Firebug and Web Inspector.

You will turn CSS Inspect on and examine the home page.

To examine the code in the home page with CSS Inspect:

1. Open the **index.html** page, minimize the Insert panel and the Files panel, and then switch to **Live** view.

2. On the Document toolbar, click the **Inspect** button. A bar appears at the top of the Document window saying that "Inspect mode is most useful with certain workspace settings."

3. Click the **Switch now** link to switch Dreamweaver to its most useful workspace settings.

4. In the Document window, move the pointer over the **NextBest Fest Home** page heading. The heading is selected in Design view, the h1 tag is selected in the Code pane, and the CSS rules affecting the selected text are displayed in the CSS Styles panel. See Figure 4-39.

> **TIP**
>
> Inspect view is most useful with the CSS Styles panel open; Current view, Live view, and Live Code enabled; and the Document window in Split view.

Figure 4-39 **Home page with CSS Inspect enabled**

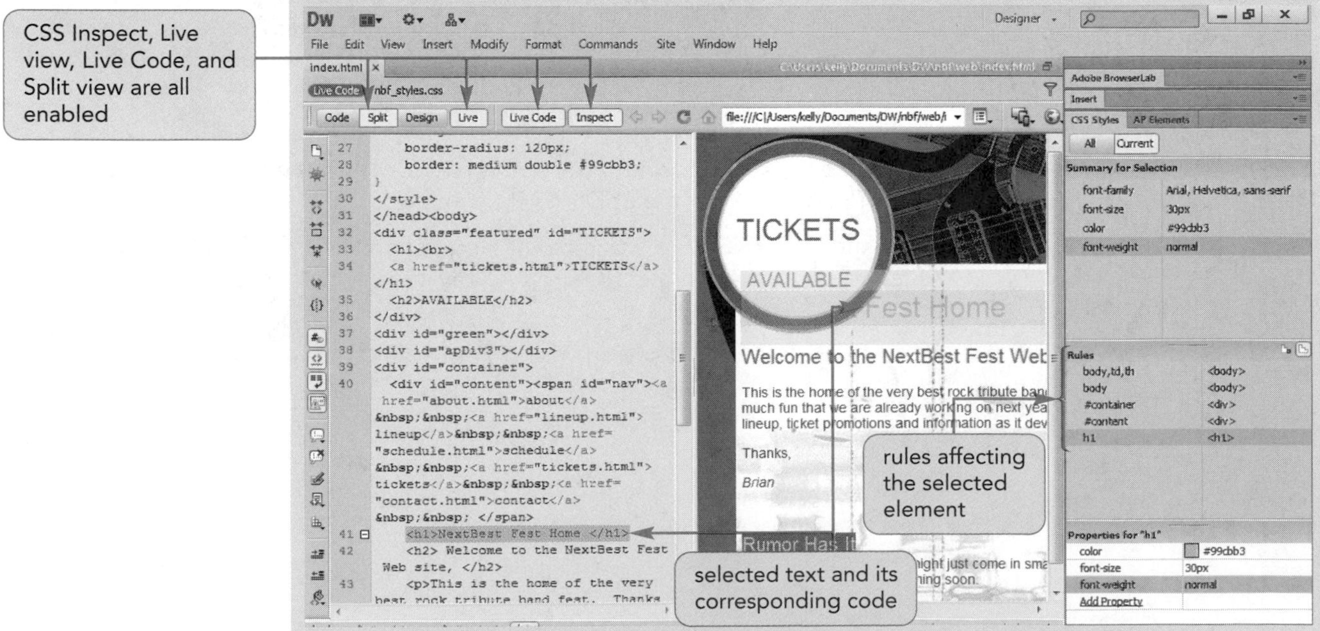

dean bertoncelj/Shutterstock.com; Jupiterimages/Photos.com

Trouble? If you cannot see most of the information in the CSS Styles panel, drag the top or bottom of each pane to resize them as needed.

> **5.** Move the pointer over various page elements to view the code and CSS styles for each element.

> **6.** On the Document toolbar, click the **Inspect** and **Live** buttons to turn them off, and then click the **Design** button to return to Design view.

Updating the Web Site on the Remote Server

As a final review of the changes you made to the NextBest Fest site, you will update the files on your remote server and preview the pages over the Web. You need to upload every page of the site. When you upload the pages, you will also need to include the dependent files so that the new graphics and CSS styles are uploaded to the remote server. Then you will preview the site on the Web.

To upload and preview the updated remote NextBest Fest site:

> **1.** Connect to your remote host.

> **2.** Use the **Put file(s) to "Remote Server"** button ⬆ on the Files panel toolbar to upload the updated pages and new dependent files to your remote site.

> **3.** Disconnect from your remote site.

> **4.** In your browser, open the home page of your remote NextBest Fest site.

> **5.** Preview each of the pages, reviewing the content and testing the links. The site includes all the content and styles that you added to the local version.

> **6.** Close the browser.

In this session, you worked with absolutely positioned divs. You drew AP divs, inserted content in the AP divs, adjusted AP div attributes, and examined AP div code. You also adjusted the stacking order of the AP divs and nested AP divs. Finally, you used CSS Inspect to examine the code in the home page. In the next tutorial, you will work with graphics and tables.

REVIEW

Session 4.2 Quick Check

1. What is the z-index number?
2. Describe the Vis attribute of AP divs.
3. True or False. AP divs cannot be overlapped.
4. Do AP divs with higher z-index numbers appear in front of, or behind, AP divs with lower z-index numbers?
5. Which property do you change to create an AP div that displays rounded corners?
6. Does a nested AP div need to be positioned inside of its parent?
7. What is CSS Inspect?

Review Assignments

There are no Data Files needed for the Review Assignments.

Cat wants you to create an alternate home page, using a prebuilt CSS page to create a 2 column liquid, left sidebar, header and footer layout. You will use this layout for the other pages of the antifest site. You will create the page, edit the existing styles in the internal style sheet, and then move the styles from the internal style sheet to the external style sheet. You will attach the style sheet to the page, and then add new content, including the navigation system and an AP div that contains the logo text. After the page structure is in place, you will duplicate the home page to create the other pages of the site.

1. Open the **antifest** site you created in Tutorial 3, and then, in the Files panel, delete the index.html page.

2. Use the New Document dialog box to create a blank page with the HTML page type; the 2 column liquid, left sidebar, header and footer layout; and the HTML 5 Doc Type.

3. Save the page as **index.html** in the local root folder of the antifest site.

4. Use the CSS Styles panel to attach the antistyles.css external style sheet located in the stylesheets folder in the local root folder of the antifest site. (*Hint*: Use the Attach Style Sheet button.) The styles from the style sheet appear in the page; you cannot see the main text because you set its style to white.

5. Switch to Code view, locate the internal style sheet at the top of the page, select the body style and its content, and then press the Delete key to remove the style from the internal style sheet. Delete the h1, h2, h3, h4, h5, h6, and p styles. Delete the a:link, a:visited, a:hover, a:active, and a:focus styles. You deleted these styles from within the new index.html page because you have already defined these in the style sheet and it is poor practice to have two sets of styles for one tag.

6. Delete the following styles because you will not need them with your layout (and it is a good idea to delete unused styles): ul,ol,dl .content ul, .content ol, ul.nav, ul.nav li, ul.nav a, ul.nav a:visited, ul.nav a:hover, ul.nav a:active, and ul.nav a:focus.

7. In the All Rules pane of the CSS Styles panel, expand the style list, select the .container style, and then click the Edit Rule button. Change the background color to #000. Change the border to a solid style, a thin width, and the #f0f color. Click the OK button. Switch to Design view. The container background area changes to black, and a pink border surrounds the page area.

8. In the All Rules pane of the CSS Styles panel, select the .header style, and then, in the Properties pane, change the background color to #000 and add a new margin property with a value of 10px. The content area changes to black and the div moves 10 pixels in from the container div.

9. In the All Rules pane of the CSS Styles panel, select the .sidebar1 style, and then click the Edit Rule button to open the CSS Rule definition for .sidebar1 dialog box.

10. In the Background category, change the background color to #400040. In the Box category, check the Same for all check box for Padding, then change the top margin to 10 and check the Same for all check box. In the Border category, change the top style to dotted, change the top width to thin, change the top color to #0f0, check all the Same for all check boxes, if necessary, and then click the OK button. The new style attributes are applied to the sidebar1 column. (*Hint*: These changes cause the .content div to move below the .sidebar1 div in the page; you will fix that in the next step.)

11. In the All Rules pane of the CSS Styles panel, select the .content style, and then click the Edit Rule button. In the Box category, change the padding to 0, click the Same for all check box, and then change the width to 74%. Click the OK button. The placeholder text in the content div moves back up in the page.

12. In the All Rules pane of the CSS Styles panel, select the .footer style, and then, in the Properties pane, change the background color to #000. The footer area changes to black and the placeholder footer text is visible.

13. Save the page, preview the page in a browser, and then close the browser.

14. In the All Rules pane of the CSS Styles panel, select all the internal styles in the list under styles, right-click the selected styles, and then click Move CSS Rules.

15. In the Move to External Style Sheet dialog box, select antistyles.css from the style sheet list, if necessary, and then click the OK button. The styles are removed from the page's internal style sheet and added to the external style sheet.

16. Save the page, and then save the style sheet.

17. In the Document window, select the Insert logo image, delete it, insert a nonbreaking space, type **antifest**, and then select the text and apply the h1 tag.

18. Select all of the text in the sidebar 1 div (make sure that the ul.nav tag is selected in the status bar), press the Delete key (if you have problems, locate the tags in the code and delete them), and then type the following navigation text, pressing the Shift+Enter keys after each word except the last: **home**, **lineup**, **schedule**, **tickets**, and **directions**.

19. Create the following links from the navigation text to the pages that you will create: home – **index.html**, lineup – **lineup.html**, schedule – **schedule.html**, tickets – **tickets.html**, and directions – **directions.html**.

20. Select the footer placeholder text, read the text, and then type © **copyright 2015, antifest, inc.**, inserting the copyright symbol from the Characters list in the Text category of the Insert panel, and then center the text.

21. Save the page, save the style sheet, create four duplicates of the page, and then rename the duplicated pages as **lineup.html**, **schedule.html**, **tickets.html**, and **directions.html**.

22. Preview the pages in the browser, test the navigation links, and then close the browser.

23. In the Title box on the Document toolbar, enter **antifest – home**, read the placeholder text in the main content area, select the heading in the main content placeholder text, and then type **antifest, home of the world's freest festival**.

24. Select the top paragraph of placeholder text, and then type **antifest is an independent music festival that has been created to provide you with an opportunity to hear some of the best, independent music in the world. This is a grassroots festival. We do not accept any corporate sponsorship so that we can continue to keep the music pure.** (including the period).

25. Select the h2 level heading placeholder text, and then type **news**.

26. Select the remaining paragraphs of placeholder text, and then type **Next year's festival lineup is already taking shape. We already have confirmation from a few of your favorite bands, including sloth child and black lab. . . stay tuned for more.** (including the period). Save and close the page.

27. For each of the remaining pages you created for the site, open the page, change the page title to correspond to the filename (for example, lineup.html has the page title **antifest – lineup**), replace the main content heading placeholder text with the name of the page (for example, lineup.html has the name **lineup**), replace the rest of the content with **coming soon.**, and then save and close the page.

28. Preview the pages in the browser, testing the links, and then close the browser.

29. Upload the pages and the stylesheets folder to your remote server, and then preview the site over the Internet.

30. Submit the finished files to your instructor.

Create the page structure and the remaining pages for a Web site for a skateboard company.

APPLY

Case Problem 1

There are no Data Files needed for this Case Problem.

Moebius Skateboards   You will create the structure for the pages of the Moebius Skateboards site by adding divs to the home page and moving the existing content into these new divs. You will also create styles for the divs you add. Then you will create the rest of the pages for the site.

1. Open the **Moebius Skateboards** site you created in Tutorial 3, Case 1, and then open the **index.html** page in Design view.

2. Click in the Document window, and then select the <body> tag in the status bar.

3. Insert a div tag that wraps around the selection, and then create a new CSS rule using ID as the selector type, **#container** as the selector name, and defined in the moebius.css style sheet.

4. In the Background category, change the background color to #333. In the Box category, change the top width to 80%, uncheck the Same for all check box in the Margin section, and then change the top margin to 10px and the right and left margins to auto.

EXPLORE

5. In the Border category, change the top style to solid, change the top width to medium, and then, in the Color section, click the color picker to change the pointer to an eye dropper and click one of the lighter yellow-greenish stars in the background image to change the swatch color to match the yellow-green (#d9f666 or something close should appear in the color column). Click the OK button in each dialog box to add the new div around the content in the page.

6. Select the <div#container> tag in the status bar, and then, in Code view, before the closing div tag, add a comment with the text **closing container tag**.

7. In Design view, click inside the container div, select the tag in the status bar, insert a div tag after the start of the <div id="container"> div, create a new CSS rule using ID as the selector type, **#content** as the selector name, and defined in the moebius.css style sheet, and then, in the Box category, set the margins to 5px.

8. In the Document window, select the content div, and then, in Code view, drag the closing div tag to the line above the container div. (*Hint*: Press the Enter key to create a blank line, if necessary.)

9. Indent the new tag two spaces, if necessary, insert a comment that identifies the tag in the code, and then save the page and the style sheet. The content div tag surrounds the content in the home page.

10. In Design view, select the **skateboarding is not a style, it is a lifestyle.** text, drag it beside the placeholder text at the top of the content div, delete the placeholder text, add quotes around the remaining text, and then select the content div tag in the status bar.

11. Insert a div tag after the content div tag, create a new CSS rule using ID as the selector type, **#logo** as the selector name, and defined in the moebius.css style sheet, and then set the background color to #919f3d and change the text alignment to center.

12. Move the Moebius Skateboards logo text into the logo div and delete the placeholder text from the div. If the logo text loses its formatting, reformat the logo text as Heading 1.

13. In the CSS Styles panel, edit the #nav style, changing the color to #919f3d in the Border category.

14. Edit the a:link, a:visited, a:hover, and a:active colors to #872970 to better match the colors of the site.

15. Create a new style for the h2 tag that changes the color of the tag to #872970.

16. In the Document window, remove the extra blank lines that were below the logo text, remove the h1 tag if it is still in the page, remove any extra lines after the last line of text in the content div, and then save the page and the style sheet.

17. Duplicate the home page five times to create the other pages of the site, and then rename the duplicated pages as **about.html**, **boards.html**, **contact.html**, **events.html**, and **team.html**.

18. Open each page, update the page title to replace Home with the corresponding page name, change the page heading to include the corresponding page name, and then replace the remaining text below the page heading and above the logo text with **check back soon, more is on the way. . ..**

19. Save and close the pages, preview the pages in a browser, test the links and review the pages, and then close the browser.

20. Upload the pages and the stylesheets folder to your remote server, and then preview the pages over the Internet.

21. Submit the finished files to your instructor.

Create an accessible elastic site structure for a Web site to present artwork of Charles M. Russell.

CHALLENGE

Case Problem 2

Data File needed for this Case Problem: cc_content.docx

Cowboy Art Society   The next step in the site you are working on for Moni and the Cowboy Art Society is to design the page layout and then create the other pages in the site. You will create a new home page that is an HTML page with a 2 column elastic, left sidebar, header and footer layout so that the page is accessible to people with vision impairments. (You will use the prebuilt 2 column fixed, left sidebar, header and footer layout, and you will change the width of the div tags from px to em to create the elastic layout that will vary with the users' text size.) After you copy the existing content and navigation from the home page to the new page, you will delete the old home page. You will attach the page to the existing style sheet, and then move the styles from the new home page to the style sheet. Finally, you will create the rest of the pages for the site.

1. Open the **Cowboy Charlie** site you created in Tutorial 3, Case 2, and then open the **index.html** page in Design view.

⊕ EXPLORE

2. Create a new HTML document with the 2 column fixed, left sidebar, header and footer layout and the HTML 5 DocType.

3. Delete all of the styles that you will not need from the head of the page, including: body; a:link; a:visited; a:hover, a:active, a:focus; ul.nav li; ul.nav a, ul.nav a:visited; ul.nav a:hover, ul.nav a:active, ul.nav a:focus.

4. Select the Header placeholder image and delete it, then type **Cowboy Charlie** and press the Enter key. Apply the h1 tag to the text.

5. Copy the navigation text (including the span tag that surrounds the text) from the home page, paste it into the header area of the new page, move past the closing span tag, and then press the Enter key to add a line. (*Hint*: Make sure that you are outside of the closing h1 tag when you paste.)

6. Copy the page heading and content from the home page and paste the text into the main content area of the new page, replacing the placeholder text.

7. Delete the placeholder text in the sidebar1 div, press the Backspace key, if necessary, to remove the bullet point from the page, type **did you know:**, press the Enter key, and then, for the rest of the content in the sidebar1 div, type:

    In 1886, Charlie Russell sent his first important oil painting, Breaking Camp, to the St. Louis Exposition and Music Hall Association art show and the following events also occurred:

    - The Statue of Liberty, a gift from the French, was dedicated in New York Harbor.

    - Geronimo's Apaches surrendered to the U.S.

8. Select the *did you know:* text, and then bold the selected text.

9. Replace the Footer placeholder text with © **copyright Cowboy Art Society, 2015**.

10. Delete the index.html page, save the new page as **index.html** in the local root folder, and then connect the new page to the cowboy.css style sheet.

11. In the style list, change the container style width to 46 em, and then add a solid, thin, border with the color #666. (Don't worry if the navigation text appears to move from the heading div; it will be appropriately placed when you view the page in a browser.)

12. In the style list, change the #header style background color to #cabb8e.

13. Edit the #sidebar1 style so that the color in the Type category is #cabb8e, the background color in the Background category is #6a7029, the margins in the Box category are 5 px for all borders, the padding is 10px for the Top and Bottom borders, and the width is 10 em.

14. Edit the #content style to have a width of 35 em.

15. In the style list, change the #footer style background to #cabb8e.

16. Move the internal styles to the external style sheet, and then save the page and the style sheet.

17. Edit the #nav style to include 10px of padding on the right side only.

18. Save the page and the style sheet, preview the page in a browser, and then resize the browser window to confirm that the size of the Web page does not change with the size of the browser window.

⊕ **EXPLORE**   19. Change the text size in the browser window to Larger to confirm that the Web page expands to accommodate the larger text, and then return the text size to its original setting. The ability of the Web page to expand to display larger text is what makes elastic pages accessible to people with vision impairments. (*Hint*: You can change the text size in Internet Explorer 9 by right-clicking in a blank area in the top tab, clicking Command bar, selecting Text size from the Page list, and then changing the text size.)

⊕ **EXPLORE**   20. Duplicate the index.html page as needed to create the remaining pages in the site, naming the pages to correspond to the filenames you used when you created the navigation links. (*Hint*: You can quickly duplicate a selected page by pressing the Ctrl+D keys and you can quickly rename a selected page by pressing the F2 key and typing the new filename. To see the filenames used in the links, click the navigation text to display the link in the HTML pane of the Property inspector.)

21. In the home page, change the page title to **Cowboy Charlie – Home**, and then save the page.

22. Using Word or another word-processing program, open the **cc_content.docx** document located in the Dreamweaver4\Case2 folder included with your Data Files, and then enter the appropriate content in each of the pages you created for the site, including the page title, the page heading, the main content area, and the sidebar1 div content (replacing the current did you know facts). Save and close the pages.

23. Preview the site in a browser, click each link and read the text on each page, and then close the browser.

24. Upload the pages and the stylesheets folder to your remote server, and then preview the pages over the Internet.

25. Submit the finished files to your instructor.

Case Problem 3

Data File needed for this Case Problem: tess.docx

Success with Tess   With the plan and design for the Success with Tess site approved, you are ready to create the pages of the site. Tess has already written the text for the pages, although you can edit and enhance that content to achieve the site goals. For now, Tess's only contact information is a telephone number, which will be the sole avenue to drive business to Tess until she obtains her new email address. You need to move the existing styles to an external style sheet, and then edit the existing CSS styles and create new styles. You will create the other pages for the site, and then add and format the text on those pages.

1. Open the **Success with Tess** site you created in Tutorial 3, Case 3, and then open the **index.html** page in Design view.
2. Select the body tag in the status bar, and then insert a div tag that wraps around the body tag.
3. Create a new CSS rule for the div using ID as the selector type, **#container** as the selector name, and defined in the tess.css style sheet. In the Background category, set the background color to #fff. In the Box category, set the width to 750px, set the top margin to 0, and then set the right and left margins to auto. In the Border category, create a border that has a solid style, a thin width, and a line color of #ffa011.
4. Inside the container div, create a **header** div with a height of 150px, place the logo text inside the header, and then delete the placeholder text. (*Hint*: When you select the text, select the h1 tag in the status bar to ensure that the h1 tags surrounding the logo text move with the text.)
5. Create a **content** div after the div #header that has 5px margins to separate the text from the outside border of the container div, move the content into the content div, and then delete the placeholder text.
6. In Design view, select the content div, and then switch to Code view to see that everything in the div tag is highlighted in blue, including the opening and closing div tags. This is one method for locating a closing div tag if you have not added comments to distinguish one closing div tag from another.
7. In Design view, create a **logo** div inside the header div that has a white background color and solid, thin, color #06c borders. Float the logo div right; set the left, right, and bottom margins to 15px; set the top margin to 5px; set the padding to 5px; and then center-align text in the div.
8. Move the logo text into the logo div, and then move the insertion point before Call and press the Enter key to move the text to another line, and then delete the placeholder text.
9. Create a **footer** div outside of the container div, set the text color to #fff, set text-align to center, set the width to 750, set the top margin to 0, and then set the right and left margins to auto.
10. Select the existing body style and change the background color to #06c, and then select the a:hover and change the color to #06c333.
11. Select the existing h2 style, change the color to #06c333, and then delete the placeholder text in the footer div. Enter the following content into the footer div: © **Tess, 2015**.
12. Save the page and the style sheet, preview the page in a browser, and then close the browser.
13. Duplicate the home page to create the other pages of the site, and then rename the duplicated pages with the filenames you used when you created the links for the navigation text.

⊕ EXPLORE

14. Open each new page, enter an appropriate page title, and then add content to the pages of the site using the information in the **tess.docx** document located in the Dreamweaver4\Case3 folder included with your Data Files. You can shorten and edit the content Tess provided to maximize the user's experience and better achieve the site goals. Create additional styles as needed to format the content.

15. Save the pages and the style sheet, and then preview the pages in a browser.

16. Upload the pages and the stylesheets folder to your remote server, and then preview the pages over the Internet.

17. Submit the finished files to your instructor.

Create a navigation system, and create and apply CSS styles to text in a Web site for a coffee bar.

CREATE

Case Problem 4

Data File needed for this Case Problem: contentback.png

Coffee Lounge   Tommy wants you to create structure for the pages of the Coffee Lounge site, to create styles, as necessary, to create the other pages of the site, and to add text to the site. He will provide the events calendar and list when the schedule is confirmed.

1. Open the **Coffee Lounge** site you created in Tutorial 3, Case 4, and then open the **index.html** page in Design view.

2. Design a page structure that follows your site plan and reinforces the site goals. Keep the target audience in mind when you decide on the page width, the way you will structure information, and what type of layout (fixed-width, liquid, elastic) you will use. Create a sketch that shows the divs and where you will use them in the page structure.

3. Create the divs you need for the page structure or use one of the prebuilt CSS layouts.

4. Create and modify existing styles for the site as needed. You can use the **contentback.png** image located in the Dreamweaver4\Case4 folder included with your Data Files to create a translucent white background for the container div.

5. Duplicate the index.html page to create the other pages of the site, and then rename the duplicated pages with filenames that match the links you created for the navigation system.

6. Open each new page, change the page title, and then add appropriate headings and content to the page. Use your research to create a simple food and drink menu and to create the other page content.

7. Draw an AP div in the home page, name the AP div **feature**, create an appropriate style for the AP div, and then add text that advertises this week's featured coffee drink.

8. Save the pages and the style sheet, and then preview the pages in a browser, testing the links and reading the content.

9. Upload the pages and the stylesheets folder to your remote server, and then preview the pages over the Internet.

10. Submit the finished files to your instructor.

Working with Graphics and Tables

Creating Smart Objects, Rollovers, Image Maps, and Tables

OBJECTIVES

Session 5.1
- Review graphic formats and compression
- Add, format, edit, and replace graphics
- Use Multiclass Selection to apply several classes at the same time

Session 5.2
- Create graphic hyperlinks and an image map
- Create a rollover
- Create and update a Smart Object
- Insert part of a Photoshop file

Session 5.3
- Create tables and import tabular data
- Work with tables, table elements, and CSS styles
- Explore the HTML code of tables
- Understand how tables were used to structure pages

Case | *NextBest Fest*

Gage commissioned an artist to design a new graphic logo for the NextBest Fest. He wants this logo added to each page of the NextBest Fest site and linked to the site's home page. To match the style of the new logo, the artist created graphics to replace the existing text links in the navigation system. Gage also wants you to add tables containing the latest festival schedule to the schedule.html page. He will update the table as new acts sign on. In addition, Gage wants you to add a page to the Web site to promote individual bands.

STARTING DATA FILES

Tutorial

bon_journo.jpg
brian.jpg
fest_map.png
hot.png
nb_logo.gif
nb_logo.png
nb_logo.psd
nb_logo_2.png
nb_logo_2.psd
satellite_schedule.xlsx
sitedesign.psd
tickets.png
tickets_over.png

Review

anti_logo.jpg
anti_logo.psd
anti_logo_over.jpg
anti_logo_over.psd
bands.docx
bl_cd.jpg
sc_cd.jpg

Case1

asher.png
corey.png
dustin.png
m_logo.jpg
m_logo.psd
m_logo_over.jpg
m_logo_over.psd
paris.png

Case2

art.docx
bucker.jpg
cc_head.jpg
cc_head.psd
cowpunching.jpg
grubpile.jpg
utica.jpg

Case3

tess_head.psd
tess_logo.png
tess_logo_over.png

Case4

coffee_menu.xlsx
lounge_logo.png
lounge_logo.psd
lounge_logo_over.png
lounge_logo_over.psd

SESSION 5.1 VISUAL OVERVIEW

The Select Image Source dialog box lets you navigate to the image you want to insert in a page.

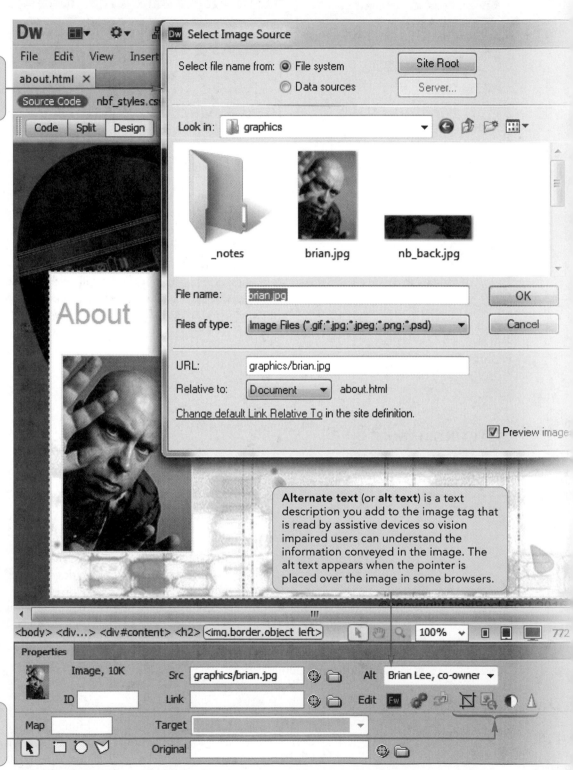

Alternate text (or **alt text**) is a text description you add to the image tag that is read by assistive devices so vision impaired users can understand the information conveyed in the image. The alt text appears when the pointer is placed over the image in some browsers.

You can crop, resample, change the brightness and contrast of, and sharpen images in the site.

dean bertoncelj/Shutterstock.com; Jupiterimages/Photos.com; iStockphoto.com/upsidedowndog

ADDING IMAGES TO PAGES

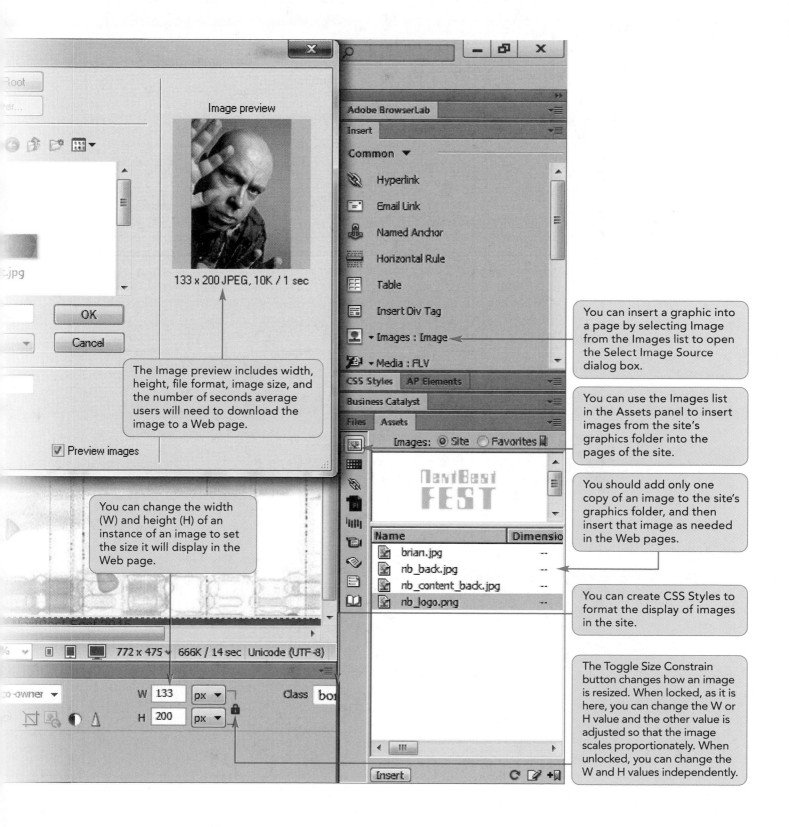

Image preview

133 x 200 JPEG, 10K / 1 sec

The Image preview includes width, height, file format, image size, and the number of seconds average users will need to download the image to a Web page.

✓ Preview images

You can change the width (W) and height (H) of an instance of an image to set the size it will display in the Web page.

You can insert a graphic into a page by selecting Image from the Images list to open the Select Image Source dialog box.

You can use the Images list in the Assets panel to insert images from the site's graphics folder into the pages of the site.

You should add only one copy of an image to the site's graphics folder, and then insert that image as needed in the Web pages.

You can create CSS Styles to format the display of images in the site.

The Toggle Size Constrain button changes how an image is resized. When locked, as it is here, you can change the W or H value and the other value is adjusted so that the image scales proportionately. When unlocked, you can change the W and H values independently.

Understanding Graphics and Compression

TIP

The smaller the graphic's file size, the faster the graphic will load in a browser.

The NextBest Fest site plan calls for a graphic logo to be included in each page. The logo will increase the brand recognition for NextBest Fest, which is a major goal of the site. Because the logo was designed with the site metaphor in mind, it will enhance the intended look and feel of the site. Other graphics will be added as needed to carry the look and feel of the site throughout the pages.

Because graphic files are usually large, the graphics you add to a Web site are stored in compressed file formats. **Compression** shrinks file size by using different types of encoding to remove redundant or less important information.

PROSKILLS

Decision Making: Using Graphics Effectively

We live in a visually oriented world, and there are millions of images available to use in a Web site. Because of the variety available, choosing which graphics to use in a site can be challenging. You should use graphics to make a Web site more interesting and provide valuable information. For example, maps and graphs can summarize information more succinctly and intuitively than words. As a society, we are accustomed to distilling information from images. The graphics you add to a Web site should enhance the feel you are trying to create and provide users with visual clues about the page content and/or the site's intended message. Most important, the graphics you add to a Web site should reinforce the site goals.

When choosing graphics for a Web site, consider what each graphic will add to the page. Consider the following questions before including an image. If the graphic does not add anything to the page, it should not be used.
• Will the graphic supply information or reinforce the page content?
• Will the graphic aid the user in navigating through the site?
• Will the graphic help the page to maintain the look of the site?

In addition, graphics you add to a site should be an appropriate file size. Consider the total file size of all the graphics in the Web page and the connection speed the target audience will have. If you are going to include only one graphic in a page, its file size can be larger. If you are going to include several graphics in a page, the size of each graphic will contribute to the amount of time it takes a user's browser to download the page. In this case, you might want to make the file size of each graphic smaller. If the target audience is using a mobile device over a slower 3G network, graphic-intensive pages might take longer to download, so keep the graphics to a minimum or choose graphics with small file sizes. Remember to evaluate each graphic's importance to the page. A user is more willing to wait for a page to download if that page is interesting and provides content the user is looking for. So, be sure to carefully consider the size and purpose of each image before choosing to place it in a site. The decisions you make affect the effectiveness of the site and the user's experience.

Figure 5-1 lists the approximate times it takes to completely download files of various sizes over a standard 56 kbps (kilobits per second) dial-up connection, a DSL connection, cable modem connection, and 3G and 4G wireless connections. As you can see, how many images and other types of content you will want to include in a site is very dependent on anticipated connection speeds of the target audience.

Figure 5-1	Approximate download times for different file sizes

Connection Type	Average Speed	MSNBC Home Page (200 kB)	NY Times Home Page (600 kB)	3 Minutes MP3 (4 MB)	3 Minutes Web Video (10 MB)
Dial up	56 kbps	30 seconds	1 minute 30 seconds	9 minutes 31 seconds	23 minutes 50 seconds
3G	800 kbps	2 seconds	6 seconds	~41 seconds	~102 seconds
4G	1.5 mbps	1.5 seconds	~3 seconds	~22 seconds	~56 seconds
DSL	3 mbps or higher	< 1 second	~1.5 seconds	~11 seconds	~28 seconds
Cable	10 mbps or higher	< 1 second	< 1 second	~3 seconds	~8 seconds

© 2013 Cengage Learning

All browsers can display graphics in the GIF and JPEG file formats, and all newer browsers can display the PNG file format as well. The GIF, JPEG, and PNG formats all compress graphic files but in different ways. If you want to use graphic images that are in another format, you need to use a graphics-processing program such as Adobe Photoshop, Adobe Photoshop Lightroom, or Adobe Fireworks to convert them to GIF, JPEG, or PNG.

Using GIF

GIF (Graphics Interchange Format) was invented by the CompuServe Company to provide its customers with a means to exchange graphic files online. Unisys, which now owns the patent on the type of compression used in GIFs, requires that software producing GIFs license the GIF patent. However, graphics compressed as GIFs can be used free of charge. Files saved as GIF images have the file extension .gif.

The GIF format is usually used on images that have large areas of flat, or nongradient, color. **Nongradient** refers to color that is one shade and does not vary with subtle darkening or lightening. Many line-drawn graphics and nonphotographic images use GIF. GIF supports a palette of up to 256 colors, one of which can be used for single-color transparency. GIF transparency is usually used to create a clear background for graphics. For example, if you want an image to appear in a Web site without its background, you can make the background transparent so that the color of the Web page or the background image behind it is visible. In GIF format, greater compression (and, therefore, smaller file size) is achieved by further limiting the graphic's color palette. In other words, the fewer colors used in a GIF image, the smaller its file size. You need to find a balance between how colorful an image you want to use and how fast the target audience can load the image.

The new NextBest Fest logo that will appear in each page of the Web site is shown in Figure 5-2. You could compress the new logo using GIF because it is composed of flat colors and has a transparent background. The transparent background enables the logo to be laid over the background of the Web pages seamlessly. The logo file size is 7 K.

| Figure 5-2 | NextBest Fest logo as a GIF image |

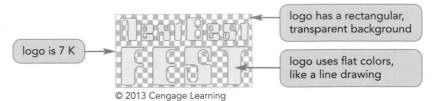

logo has a rectangular, transparent background

logo is 7 K

logo uses flat colors, like a line drawing

© 2013 Cengage Learning

Using JPEG

A committee from the Joint Photographic Experts Group created the **JPEG** format to digitize photographic images. Files saved as JPEG images have the file extension .jpg. The JPEG format is usually used on photographic images and graphics that have many gradient colors. The JPEG format can support millions of colors but not transparency.

JPEG is a **lossy** compression format, which means that it discards (or loses) information to compress an image. Because it was designed for photographic images, JPEG discards the information that is less perceptible to the human eye, such as the fine details in the background of a photograph. As an image is further compressed, additional information is discarded, the blurry spots increase in size, and the image becomes less and less sharp. So, as with a GIF image, you must make a trade-off between the image quality and the file size (or download time).

Both the container div background image and the content div background image are JPEG images because each contains a variety of gradient colors, which will be compressed more effectively in this format. Figure 5-3 shows the two JPEG images.

| Figure 5-3 | Backgrounds as JPEG images |

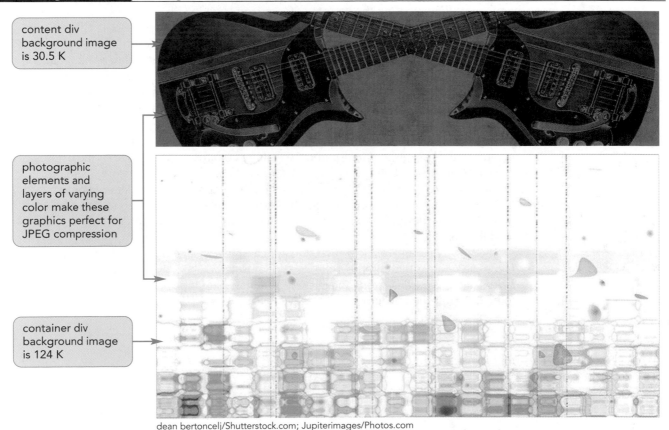

content div background image is 30.5 K

photographic elements and layers of varying color make these graphics perfect for JPEG compression

container div background image is 124 K

dean bertoncelj/Shutterstock.com; Jupiterimages/Photos.com

Using PNG

PNG (Portable Network Graphics), a graphic compression format, was created by a group of designers who were frustrated by the limitations of existing compression formats. PNG files use the file extension .png. PNG supports up to 48-bit true color or 16-bit gray scale. It uses **lossless** compression, so no information is discarded when the file is compressed. It also supports **variable transparency**, the ability to make the background of the image transparent at different amounts; for example, a background can fade (using gradient shades of color) from a dark color to transparent. Generally, PNG compresses files 5 percent to 25 percent better than GIF. For transmission of photographic style images, JPEG is still a better choice because the file size of a photographic style image compressed with JPEG is usually smaller than the file size of a photographic style image compressed with PNG. The only drawback of the PNG format is that variable transparency usually does not display correctly in Internet Explorer 6 and earlier versions. Internet Explorer 7 and 8 have strong but not full support of variable transparency of PNGs. Because the current release of Internet Explorer is version 9, and version 10 is on the way, it is probably fine to use PNGs in a Web site. However, it is always a good idea to test the page in the browser to be sure that it displays correctly.

> **TIP**
>
> It is considered good practice to ensure that a site works on the latest two versions of any browsers that you are supporting.

Figure 5-4 shows the graphic that advertises that tickets are now on sale saved in the PNG format. Because the graphic has gradient colors fading to transparency, the image is a perfect example of variable transparency.

Figure 5-4	Tickets graphic as a PNG image

gray background shows through the transparent area

tickets image is 38 K

transparent background

© 2013 Cengage Learning

Adding Graphics to Web Pages

The first time you place a graphic in a Web site, you use the Insert panel to place the graphic in the page. When you add the graphic to the Web site, it is stored in the graphics folder within the site's local root folder, which you specified during the site setup, so that Dreamweaver always knows where to locate the image file. You need to include only one copy of each graphic in the graphics folder, even when you plan to use the same image multiple times in a site. After a graphic is stored in the local root folder, it appears in the Assets panel. Then, you can use either the Files panel or the Assets panel to insert that graphic into the pages.

When you place a graphic in a page, you are actually placing an image tag, <img>, in the page. The image tag tells the page to display the graphic stored in the graphics folder at that spot in the Web page. When the same graphic appears multiple times in a site, Dreamweaver retrieves the graphic from the graphics folder and displays it in the various locations. If you decide to change a graphic in the site, you can simply replace the old graphic in the graphics folder with a new one that has the same filename, and each page that contains an image tag for the old graphic then displays the new one.

Adding a Graphic to a Web Page

- In the Common category of the Insert panel, click the Images button arrow, and then click the Image button.
- Select the file to insert in the Select Image Source dialog box.
- Click the OK button.

or

- In the Files panel group, click the Assets tab.
- On the Assets panel toolbar, click the Images button.
- Click the file you want to insert, and then click the Insert button in the Assets panel.

or

- Drag the image from the Files panel or the Assets panel to its position in the page.

After you insert a graphic, you can select it. A selected graphic is surrounded by a black box with squares in the corners. The squares are **resize handles**. If you drag a resize handle, it enlarges or shrinks the selected object.

Sizing and Compressing Graphics

Graphics are an integral part of Web pages. Before you add graphics to a site, make sure that each graphic is saved at the proper size for insertion into the pages. Do not resize a graphic after it has been added to a Web page unless you resample the graphic or you use an external editor because the graphic is included in the page at its original size and then resized on the user's computer. This can make the Web page load much more slowly. Also, compress each graphic to the smallest possible file size you can achieve without losing image quality. Be sure to retain the original uncompressed graphics in addition to the compressed Web versions because you might need to return to the original version to create another variation of the graphic in the future. A compressed graphic cannot be returned to its original resolution. Also, be sure to use descriptive and meaningful names for the graphic files. Logical naming structures save you time later in identifying the files.

Making Graphics Accessible

When you add graphics to a page, Dreamweaver prompts you to add an alternate text description. The alt text is placed in the alt attribute in the image tag. It is read by assistive devices, enabling vision impaired users to understand the information conveyed in the image. The alt text appears in place of an image in browsers that only display text, in regular browsers when a download of an image is interrupted or slow, and when a user mouses over an image in some browsers. Current accessibility guidelines state that you should provide text alternatives for any nontext content in Web pages. Special instructions include the following:

- **Controls or inputs.** If nontext content is used as a control, such as a button, use alt text to explain its purpose. For example, alt text for the NextBest Fest logo graphic could be "NextBest Fest logo and link to the home page."
- **Decoration and formatting.** If nontext content is purely decorative, use it in a way that enables assistive devices to ignore it. For example, the background images in the container and content divs do not have alternate text and can be ignored by assistive devices because they are used as background images.

- **Conveys information.** If nontext content conveys information, also provide that information in an accessible way—a short alt text description, and, if necessary, an in-depth description. For example, designers often include a paragraph above or below an image that conveys the image's information. When Dreamweaver prompts you to provide the short alt text description, it also enables you to create a link to an in-depth description that you can use to provide detailed information, if necessary.
- **Images of text.** To conform to the strictest level of accessibility guidelines, images of text (or text that is actually a graphic such as a button that contains text) should be used only for pure decoration.

Using the Insert Panel to Add Graphics

Gage has provided the redesigned NextBest Fest logo as a GIF graphic. You will add the logo at the top of every page in the site, starting with the home page.

To add the logo to the home page using the Insert panel:

1. Reset Dreamweaver to the **Designer** workspace, collapse the Business Catalyst panel, open the Files panel, open the **NextBest Fest** site you modified in Tutorial 4, and then open the **index.html** page in Design view. The home page opens with the insertion point in the upper-left corner of the content div.

   Trouble? If the insertion point is not in the upper-left corner of the content div, you need to place it there. Click in the upper-left corner of the content div.

2. In the status bar, select the **<div#content>** tag, and then press the **Left** arrow key. Although the pointer still appears in the content area of the page and it might seem like it is in the TICKETS div, the insertion point moved before the content div in the code.

   > Be sure to move the insertion point before the content div in the code so that the logo is inserted in the main container div.

3. Switch to **Code** view, confirm that the insertion point is positioned directly before the content div in the code, and then return to **Design** view.

4. In the **Common** category of the Insert panel, click the **Images button arrow**, and then click the **Image** button. The Select Image Source dialog box opens.

5. Navigate to the **Dreamweaver5\Tutorial** folder included with your Data Files, and then click the **nb_logo.gif** graphic file. The Image preview box shows the graphic and lists its specifications.

6. Click the **OK** button, and then click the **Yes** button in the dialog box that opens to save a copy of the image in the graphics folder, if necessary. The Image Tag Accessibility Attributes dialog box opens.

7. Type **Logo for the NextBest Fest and link to the home page of the site.** in the Alternate text box. See Figure 5-5.

Figure 5-5 **Image Tag Accessibility Attributes dialog box**

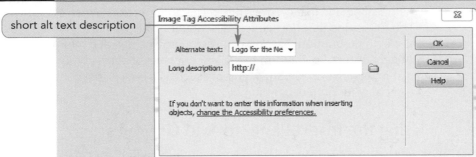

short alt text description

8. Click the **OK** button. A copy of the NextBest Fest logo is saved in the graphics folder in the site's local root folder. The image appears at the top of the page behind the TICKETS div and is selected. The content div moves lower in the page because you set a 150px top margin for the div in its CSS style.

9. Collapse the CSS Styles panel, and then, in the Files panel, next to the graphics folder, click the **Expand** button to view the folder's contents. See Figure 5-6.

Figure 5-6 **NextBest Fest logo in the home page**

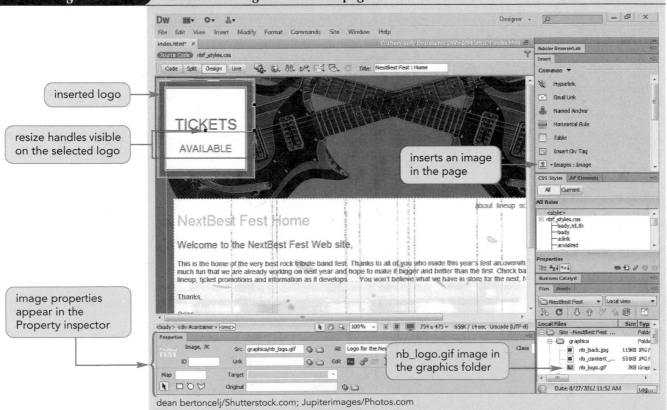

inserted logo

resize handles visible on the selected logo

inserts an image in the page

image properties appear in the Property inspector

nb_logo.gif image in the graphics folder

dean bertoncelj/Shutterstock.com; Jupiterimages/Photos.com

Trouble? If you don't see the nb_logo.gif file in the graphics folder, you need to refresh the files list. On the Files panel toolbar, click the Refresh button.

10. Click a blank area of the Document window to deselect the logo, and then save the page.

Formatting Graphics Using CSS Styles and the Property Inspector

You can change some attributes of inserted graphics by formatting them. You format graphics either by creating a CSS style and applying it to the graphic, or by selecting the graphic and setting its attributes in the Property inspector. In general, you should use CSS to format images rather than HTML attributes that are inserted directly into the image tag. This keeps all the styles in one place and allows you to make global changes to all instances of the style. This is especially important if you plan to add the same attributes to multiple graphics in the Web site.

The process for creating and applying CSS styles to graphics is the same as the process for creating and applying CSS styles to text. All of the same attribute categories are available. CSS styles are commonly used to add borders to graphics; define the border style, width, and color; add margins or padding to graphics; and align or position graphics. You can also insert an image in a div tag and apply CSS styles to the div. Finally, you can redefine the image tag, <img>, if you have style elements that you want to apply to all of the images in a site.

TIP

If you define an attribute in the style that is not applicable to a graphic element, such as a font group, the display of the graphic element is not affected.

INSIGHT

Naming Class and ID Styles

When creating class or ID styles, use naming strategies that enable you to identify the styles by the ways they will be used rather than by their attributes. For example, you do not want a style that makes subheadings orange and bold to be named *blueskinny* because the original style made the subheading text blue and narrow. A better name for the style would be *subheadings*. Remember, the beauty of CSS is that you can quickly and easily change the look of styles over time. Use meaningful names that will not become outdated.

You will create a CSS style for the NextBest Fest logo.

To create and apply a CSS style to the logo:

1. Expand the **CSS Styles** panel and collapse the Insert panel.

2. In the CSS Styles panel, click the **New CSS Rule** button ⊞, and then create a **Class** selector named **.logostyle** and defined in the **nbf_styles.css** style sheet.

3. In the **Box** category, change float to **right**, uncheck the **Same for all** check box in the Margin section, set the top margin to **0**, and then set the right margin to **40%**. This will center the logo in the container div.

4. In the Border category, verify that the **Same for all** check box in the Width section is checked, and set the Top width to **0**. This setting ensures that the logo does not have a border.

5. Click the **OK** button. The .logostyle rule is added to the site's style sheet and is ready to be applied to the logo.

6. In the home page, click the **NextBest Fest logo** to select it.

   Trouble? If you cannot click the logo, switch to Code view, select the image tag, and then return to Design view.

7. In the Property inspector, click the **Class arrow**, and then click **logostyle**. The style is applied to the logo, which moves to the top center of the container div when you preview it in Live view.

8. Turn on **Live** view. The logo is visible in the home page as it will appear in a browser. See Figure 5-7.

| Figure 5-7 | Formatted NextBest Fest logo in the home page in Live view |

logo moved to the top center of the container div

dean bertoncelj/Shutterstock.com; Jupiterimages/Photos.com

9. Save the page, and then save the style sheet.

If you are formatting only one graphic, you can create a CSS style and apply that style to the graphic. Or, you can use the Property inspector to set HTML attributes that are included in the image tag that surrounds the selected graphic. When a graphic is selected in the Document window, the Property inspector displays a small picture of the graphic and the following graphic attributes:

- **ID.** A descriptive name of the graphic. The ID is used in some advanced forms of programming to instruct Dreamweaver or the browser what to do with the graphic. The ID can differ from the filename, but it should identify the graphic. The ID must begin with a letter or an underscore; the rest of the name can contain letters and numbers, but no spaces or symbols.
- **W and H.** The horizontal and vertical dimensions of the graphic in pixels. If you resize a graphic in Dreamweaver, the page will load more slowly because Dreamweaver must transmit the original graphic to the end user's computer and then resize it on the client computer. Also, resizing a graphic larger than its original size will degrade the image quality. Instead, use an external image-processing program to resize a graphic, or resample the graphic after you adjust its width or height. Resampling is discussed in the next section.
- **Reset Size.** The button that appears between the W and H boxes after you change a graphic's width or height to restore the selected graphic to its original dimensions.
- **Src.** The path to the graphic's source file (which includes the filename). The path is either relative or absolute, depending on what you selected when you inserted the graphic. A relative path is used most commonly because the path still works even if the site's URL changes or its root directory moves.
- **Alt.** An alternate text description of the graphic that appears in place of the graphic when the page opens in a browser that displays only text or is set to download images manually. In some browsers, the alt text also appears in a tooltip when the pointer hovers over the graphic. You should add alt text to all graphics except background images that are used only for decoration. Alt text allows you to convey the graphic's content or purpose to individuals with visual disabilities who rely on audio assistive devices to communicate the graphic information.

- **Class.** A list of the CSS Class styles you created that you can apply to a selected graphic. Text attributes defined in the style do not affect the graphic's display.
- **Original.** A link to the original image file.

Next, you will add a descriptive name for the logo graphic.

To enter an ID for the NextBest Fest logo graphic:

▶ 1. Switch to **Code** view, and then select the **NextBest Fest logo** img tag, if necessary. The logo is selected and the img tag appears in the status bar.

▶ 2. In the Property inspector, click in the **ID** box, type **nb_logo**, and then press the **Tab** key. The ID is entered for the logo, which remains selected. The image tag for the selected image is highlighted in blue.

▶ 3. Locate the id attribute, and then locate the ID you just entered in the tag.

▶ 4. Return to **Design** view, turn off **Live** view, save the page, and then preview the page in a browser. See Figure 5-8.

| Figure 5-8 | Logo previewed in a browser |

logo has some jagged edges

Used with permission from Microsoft Corporation; dean bertoncelj/Shutterstock.com; Jupiterimages/Photos.com

▶ 5. Examine the logo text. Notice that jagged edges appear around some of the letters.

▶ 6. Close the browser.

What makes text look smooth to the eye is that the edges of the letters have a slight gradient, which is called **anti-aliasing**. The GIF compression format only allows one color to be transparent. Any other colors in the gradient become solid, which shatters the illusion of smooth text. As a result, you sometimes see blocky sections, called **artifacts**, around the letters. Because artifacts appear around the new logo, you will replace the GIF with a PNG that allows for gradient transparency.

Replacing a Graphic

Web sites are dynamic and updatable media. Because of this, it is frequently necessary to replace an existing image with a new image or an updated version of the same image. When you replace an image, the CSS styles applied to the original image are automatically applied to the replacement image.

When you replace an image that does not appear anywhere else in the site and that you do not plan to use again, you should delete its file from the graphics folder. This helps keep the graphics folder organized and current. It also minimizes the files being stored. One extra compressed image stored in a folder might not seem like much, but over time as you continue to update the site, keeping unused files can make the contents of the graphics folder confusing, outdated, and unnecessarily big.

You will replace the nb_logo.gif image with the new nb_logo.png image, and then delete the old image from the graphics folder.

To replace the logo in the home page:

▶ **1.** In Design view, double-click the **nb_logo.gif** image in the home page. The Select Image Source dialog box opens.

Trouble? If you cannot see the nb_logo.gif image or you cannot click the image in the home page, switch to Code view, and then click the folder button to the right of the Src box in the Property inspector to open the Select Image Source dialog box.

▶ **2.** Navigate to the **Dreamweaver5\Tutorial** folder included with your Data Files, double-click **nb_logo.png**, and then click the **Yes** button in the dialog box that opens to save a copy of the image in the graphics folder, if necessary. The logo graphic in the home page is replaced with the PNG logo graphic and is selected.

▶ **3.** Turn on **Live** view to see the new logo. See Figure 5-9.

Figure 5-9	PNG logo in the home page

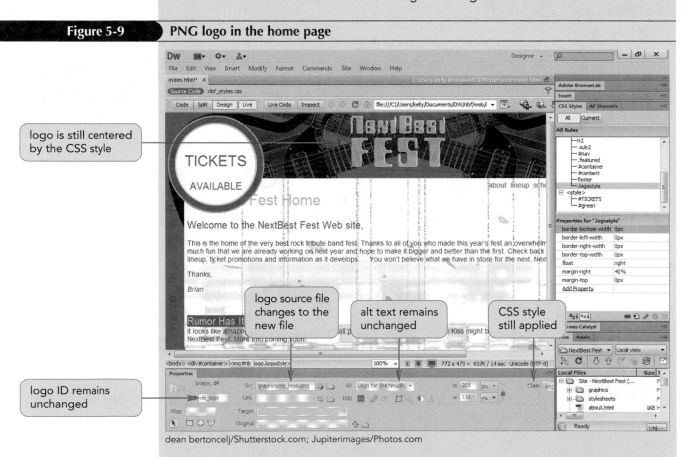

logo is still centered by the CSS style

logo source file changes to the new file

alt text remains unchanged

CSS style still applied

logo ID remains unchanged

dean bertoncelj/Shutterstock.com; Jupiterimages/Photos.com

▶ **4.** Save the page, and then preview the page in a browser. See Figure 5-10.

Figure 5-10 PNG logo previewed in a browser

Used with permission from Microsoft Corporation; dean bertoncelj/Shutterstock.com; Jupiterimages/Photos.com

5. Close the browser.

Because you will no longer use the nb_logo.gif image in the NextBest Fest site, you can delete it from the graphics folder to minimize the size of the site files.

To delete the nb_logo.gif file from the site:

1. In the Files panel, expand the **graphics** folder, if necessary.

2. Select the **nb_logo.gif** file, and then press the **Delete** key. A dialog box opens to confirm the deletion.

3. Click the **Yes** button. The file for the unneeded logo is removed from the graphics folder.

Next, you will add the logo to the about.html page of the NextBest Fest site. The nb_logo.png file is stored in the graphics folder within the local root folder. You will insert the copy of the file in the graphics folder into the page rather than saving a second copy of the file in the graphics folder.

To add the logo to the about.html page:

1. Open the **about.html** page in Design view, and then click in the **content** div.

2. In the status bar, click the **<div#content>** tag to select the content div, and then press the **Left** arrow key to move the insertion point before the content div.

3. In the **Common** category of the Insert panel, click the **Image** button in the Images list. The Select Image Source dialog box opens.

4. Navigate to the **nbf\web\graphics** folder in the local root folder, and then double-click **nb_logo.png**. The Image Tag Accessibility Attributes dialog box opens.

5. In the Alternate text box, type **NextBest Fest logo linked to the home page.** (including the period), and then click the **OK** button. The NextBest Fest logo appears in the upper-right corner of the about.html page and the content div moves down.

6. With the logo selected, in the Property inspector, click the **Class arrow**, and then click **logostyle**. The style is applied to the logo, which moves to the center of the page.

7. Save and close the about.html page.

Using the Assets Panel to Insert Graphics

Another way to add graphics to Web pages is to use the Assets panel. In Dreamweaver, assets are the images, colors, URLs, Flash, Shockwave, movies, scripts, templates, and library items that you use throughout a site. The **Assets panel** is used to manage these assets. The Assets panel helps you keep track of the assets in the site by listing them all in one place.

The Site list displays all the assets used in the site, which can become quite lengthy in large sites. To make the list easier to work with, you can add assets you use frequently to the Favorites list. Assets in the Favorites list are simply references to the assets in the Site list. To help organize either list, you can create folders to store items in. You can place an asset in the site or edit an asset from either list.

After a graphic is stored in the site's local root folder, you can use the Assets panel to place the graphic in other pages. When you display images in the Assets panel, the graphic image appears in the upper pane and the graphic's filename, type, size, and location appear in the lower pane.

TIP

To add an asset to the Favorites list, right-click the asset in the Site list or the Files panel, and then click Add to Favorites. To remove the asset from the Favorites list, click the asset, and then click the Remove from Favorites button.

To open the Assets panel:

1. In the Files panel group, click the **Assets** tab. The Assets panel opens.

2. Collapse the **CSS Styles** panel group to provide more room for the Assets panel.

3. On the Assets panel toolbar, click the **Images** button ⬛, if necessary, and then at the top of the Assets panel, click the **Site** option button, if necessary. The images in the NextBest Fest site are listed in the Assets panel.

4. In the Images list of the Assets panel, click **nb_logo.png**. The selected image appears in the top pane of the Assets panel. See Figure 5-11.

Figure 5-11 **Images in the Assets panel**

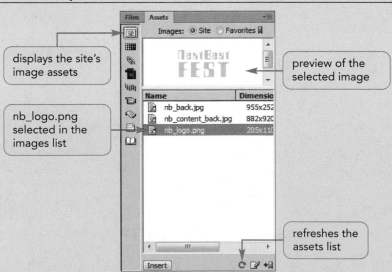

displays the site's image assets

preview of the selected image

nb_logo.png selected in the images list

refreshes the assets list

Trouble? If you don't see the nb_logo.png file in the Assets panel, click the Refresh button at the bottom of the Assets panel. If you see additional files in the list, right-click any of the files, and then click Recreate site list on the context menu.

The NextBest Fest logo needs to be placed in the contact.html page of the NextBest Fest site. You will use the Assets panel to place the logo in the page.

To insert the NextBest Fest logo using the Assets panel:

1. In the Files panel group, click the **Files** tab to expand the Files panel.

2. Open the **contact.html** page in Design view. The insertion point is positioned in the upper-left corner of the content div.

3. In the status bar, click the **<div#content>** tag to select it, and then press the **Left** arrow key to move the insertion point before the content div.

4. In the Files panel group, click the **Assets** tab. The Assets panel opens.

5. In the Assets panel, click **nb_logo.png** in the Images list, and then click the **Insert** button. The Image Tag Accessibility Attributes dialog box opens.

6. In the Alternate text box, type **NextBest Fest logo and link to the home page.** (including the period), and then click the **OK** button. The logo is inserted in the contact.html page and the content div moves down.

7. In the Document window, select the **logo**, if necessary.

8. In the Property inspector, click the **Class arrow**, and then click **logostyle**. The style is applied to the logo, which moves to the right side of the page.

9. Save and close the contact.html page, and then, in the Files panel group, click the **Files** tab to open the Files panel.

Editing Graphics from Dreamweaver

You can change the appearance of a graphic by editing it. Unlike formatting, which changes the way the graphic is displayed by defining values for attributes such as borders, alignment, and spacing, editing a graphic is the process of changing and manipulating the actual image. Because you must often adjust graphics while you work on a Web page, Dreamweaver includes the following basic graphics-editing components that you can use even if a graphics-editing program is not installed on your computer:

- **Edit.** The button to set Adobe Photoshop or Adobe Fireworks as the external image editor for each image file type (.jpg, .gif, .png). You can then open a selected image in the external image editor, edit and save the image, and then view the edited image in Dreamweaver in the Document window.
- **Edit Image Settings.** The button to open the Image Preview dialog box, in which you can compress or convert for best display all or part of an image file inserted in a page and scale all or part of the image file.
- **Crop.** An image-editing process that **crops** or reduces the area of a graphic by deleting unwanted outer areas. For example, you might want to crop the surrounding area and other people from a photograph of your family at an amusement park to emphasize your family.
- **Resample.** An image-editing process that **resamples** or adds or subtracts pixels from a resized graphic. Resizing a graphic does not change its file size. Resampling a graphic changes its file size and improves its image quality at the new size and shape. Only bitmap graphics (JPEGs, GIFs, and PNGs) can be resampled.
- **Brightness and Contrast.** An image-editing process that adjusts the brightness and contrast of the pixels in a graphic so you can lighten a graphic that is too dark or darken a graphic that is too light.
- **Sharpen.** An image-editing process that increases contrast of a graphic's edges to improve definition. You can adjust the sharpness of a blurry image to make it clearer.

INSIGHT

Keeping a Copy of Unedited Graphics

When you edit a graphic, usually the actual graphic is altered and the edits cannot be undone. It is a good idea to keep a copy of the original graphic outside the local root folder so that you can reinsert the original graphic in the page if you dislike the edited version. All of the original graphics used in the NextBest Fest site are included with your Data Files.

Gage wants you to insert and edit images of him and of Brian in the about.html page. You will start with the image of Brian.

To insert and resize the brian.jpg image:

1. Open the **about.html** page in Design view, and then click in the line below the page heading.

2. In the **Common** category of the Insert panel, click the **Image** button in the Images list. The Select Image Source dialog box opens.

3. Navigate to the **Dreamweaver5\Tutorial** folder included with your Data Files, double-click **brian.jpg**, type **Brian Lee, co-owner of Shenpa Productions.** in the Alternate text box, click the **OK** button, and then click the **Yes** button in the dialog box that opens to save a copy of the image in the graphics folder, if necessary. The graphic appears in the page below the heading. The graphic's file size and image appear in the Property inspector.

4. In the Document window, drag the brian.jpg graphic's right resize handle until **250** appears in the W box in the Property inspector. The graphic is resized but its file size remains unchanged. The Reset to Original Size button appears so you can return the graphic to its original settings. See Figure 5-12.

Figure 5-12	Resized graphic

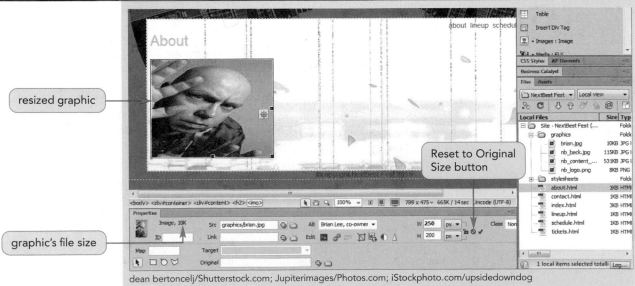

resized graphic

Reset to Original Size button

graphic's file size

dean bertoncelj/Shutterstock.com; Jupiterimages/Photos.com; iStockphoto.com/upsidedowndog

5. In the Property inspector, click the **Reset to Original Size** button ⊘. The brian.jpg graphic returns to its original size.

6. In the Document window, double-click the **brian.jpg** graphic. The Select Image Source dialog box opens and the graphic's width, height, and file size appear below the graphic in the Image preview box.

   Trouble? If the graphic does not appear in the Image preview box, click brian.jpg in the list of filenames to select it.

7. Click the **Cancel** button. The Select Image Source dialog box closes.

8. In the Property inspector, type **300** in the W and H boxes, and then, in the Document window, double-click the **brian.jpg** graphic. The graphic's original width, height, and file size still appear below the Image preview box because visually resizing an image does not change its dimensions or file size in the graphics folder. (Remember, if you include a visually resized graphic in a page, the original graphic is loaded in the user's browser and then resized on the client computer, slowing down the Web page.)

9. Click the **Cancel** button. The Select Image Source dialog box closes.

Next, you will resample the brian.jpg graphic to change its file size and improve its image quality at the new size and shape. Because resampling changes the file size of the actual graphic, it can create some problems. For example, if the same graphic is used in more than one location in a site, every instance of the graphic will have the new file size. Instances of the graphic that were not resized will probably display poorly.

To resample the brian.jpg image:

1. In the Property inspector, click the **Resample** button 🖼️. A dialog box opens, warning that the resampling action will permanently alter the selected graphic.

2. Click the **OK** button. The dialog box closes, and the graphic's new file size appears in the Property inspector.

3. Double-click the **brian.jpg** graphic. The Select Image Source dialog box opens, and the graphic's new width, height, and file size appear below the Image preview box. Resampling the graphic changes the file size of the actual graphic in the graphics folder. See Figure 5-13.

Figure 5-13   **Resampled graphic**

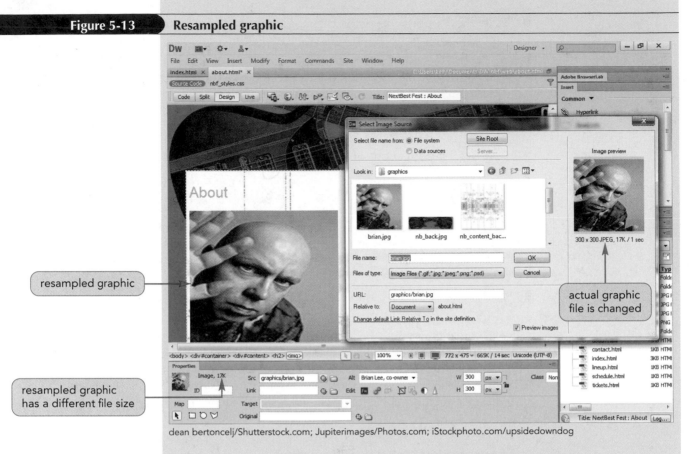

resampled graphic

resampled graphic has a different file size

dean bertoncelj/Shutterstock.com; Jupiterimages/Photos.com; iStockphoto.com/upsidedowndog

4. Click the **Cancel** button. The Select Image Source dialog box closes.

You will crop the brian.jpg image by removing excess space around Brian so that he fills the entire image. When you click the Crop button, a dark filter with a clear center appears over the graphic. You select the area of the graphic to keep in the page by dragging the resize handles of the inner clear area. You can crop only rectangular areas. Clicking the Crop button a second time removes any areas of the graphic that are covered by the dark filter.

To crop the brian.jpg image:

1. In the Property inspector, click the **Crop** button. A dialog box opens, warning that the cropping action will permanently alter the selected graphic.

2. Click the **OK** button. The dialog box closes. In the Document window, a filter appears around the edges of the brian.jpg graphic and resize handles appear around the clear inner square.

3. Drag the resize handles so that they are flush against the top, left, and bottom sides of the image, and then drag the right resize handle to the left until the right border is almost touching Brian's head. See Figure 5-14.

| Figure 5-14 | Crop area set for the graphic |

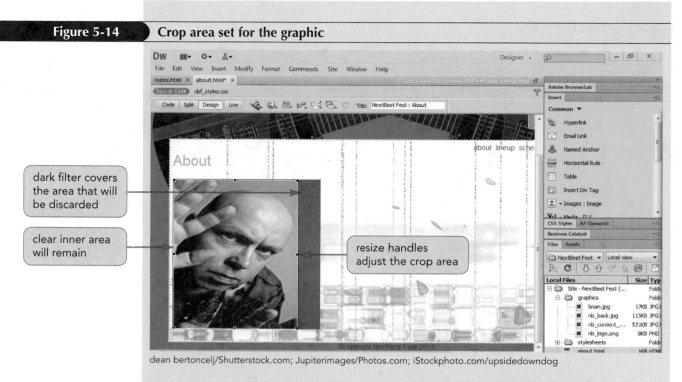

dark filter covers
the area that will
be discarded

clear inner area
will remain

resize handles
adjust the crop area

dean bertoncelj/Shutterstock.com; Jupiterimages/Photos.com; iStockphoto.com/upsidedowndog

4. Press the **Enter** key. The brian.jpg graphic is cropped, and its new width, height, and file size appear in the Property inspector.

The last edits you will make to the brian.jpg image are to adjust its brightness, contrast, and sharpness. In addition to using the brightness and contrast controls to correct an image, you can also use these controls to create stylized looks for the images.

To adjust the brightness, contrast, and sharpness of the brian.jpg image:

1. In the Property inspector, click the **Brightness and Contrast** button ◑. A dialog box opens, warning that the action will permanently alter the selected graphic.

2. Click the **OK** button. The Brightness/Contrast dialog box opens.

3. Drag the **Brightness** slider to the right until **50** appears in the box. The graphic is lighter.

4. Drag the **Contrast** slider to the right until **25** appears in the box. The contrast between the graphic's colors is increased, creating an effect that makes Brian appear a bit crazed. See Figure 5-15.

Figure 5-15

Brightness/Contrast dialog box

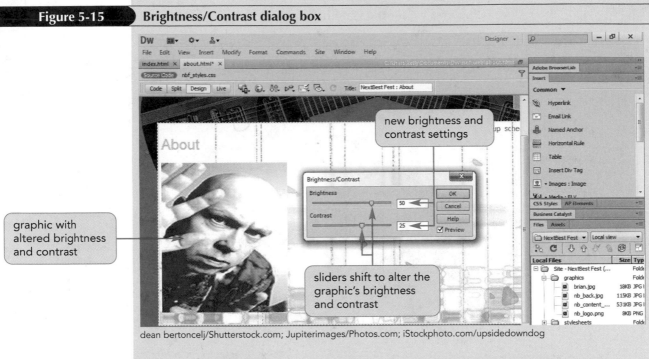

graphic with altered brightness and contrast

new brightness and contrast settings

sliders shift to alter the graphic's brightness and contrast

dean bertoncelj/Shutterstock.com; Jupiterimages/Photos.com; iStockphoto.com/upsidedowndog

5. Click the **OK** button. The Brightness/Contrast dialog box closes, and the changes are applied.

6. In the Property inspector, click the **Sharpen** button △. A dialog box opens, warning that the action will permanently alter the selected graphic.

7. Click the **OK** button. The Sharpen dialog box opens.

8. Drag the **Sharpen** slider to the right until **10** appears in the box. See Figure 5-16.

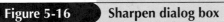

Figure 5-16 **Sharpen dialog box**

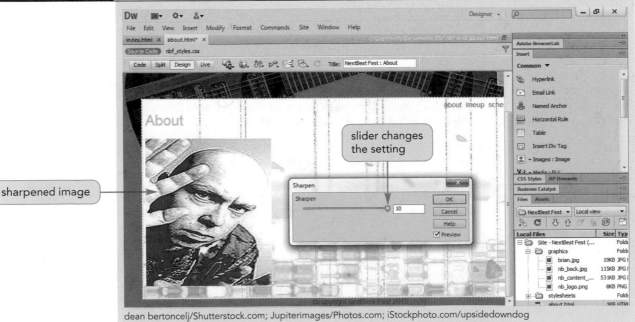

sharpened image

slider changes the setting

dean bertoncelj/Shutterstock.com; Jupiterimages/Photos.com; iStockphoto.com/upsidedowndog

9. Click the **OK** button. The dialog box closes, and the settings are saved.

You don't want to use the edited brian.jpg graphic. First, you will delete the edited version of the image from the page and from the graphics folder. Then, you will reinsert the original, unedited image.

To delete the edited brian.jpg image and reinsert the original file:

▶ 1. In the Document window, select the **brian.jpg** graphic, and then press the **Delete** key. The graphic is removed from the page.

▶ 2. In the Files panel, expand the **graphics** folder, if necessary, select the **brian.jpg** file, and then press the **Delete** key. The file is removed from the graphics folder.

   Trouble? If a dialog box opens warning that the file you are deleting is linked to other files, click the Yes button to delete anyway.

▶ 3. In the Document window, click in the line below the page heading, if necessary, to place the insertion point.

▶ 4. On the **Common** tab of the Insert panel, click the **Image** button in the Images list. The Select Image Source dialog box opens.

▶ 5. Navigate to the **Dreamweaver5\Tutorial** folder included with your Data Files, double-click **brian.jpg**, type **Brian Lee, co-owner of Shenpa Productions.** in the Alternate text box, click the **OK** button, and then click the **Yes** button in the dialog box that opens to save a copy of the image in the graphics folder, if necessary. The graphic appears in the page below the heading.

With the brian.jpg image reinserted in the about.html page, you are ready to format the image. You will create two styles. One style will left-align an object and add a margin around it. The second style will add colored borders around the object. You will create two styles because Brian wants to left-align several elements, but he does not want colored borders displayed around all of the elements. In this case, he wants both styles applied to the brian.jpg image, but only the first style applied to the video or sound files you will add to the site later. Creating two styles streamlines your work flow because you will be able to use the styles together or separately, which makes them much more useful. The Multiclass Selection dialog box enables you to apply multiple class styles at the same time. You will create the new styles, and then apply both styles to the brian.jpg image.

To create and apply styles to the brian.jpg image:

▶ 1. Expand the **CSS Styles** panel, collapse the Insert panel, and then create a **Class** selector named **.object_left** and defined in the **nbf_styles.css** style sheet.

▶ 2. In the **Box** category, set the float to **left**, and set all of the margins to **5 px**.

▶ 3. Click the **OK** button. The style is saved.

▶ 4. Create a second class style named **.border** that is defined in the **nbf_styles.css** style sheet.

▶ 5. In the **Border** category, make sure the **Same for all** check box is selected, set the top style to **solid**, set the top width to **thin**, and then set the top color to **#cff**.

6. Click the **OK** button. The style is saved and both styles are ready to apply to the brian.jpg image.

7. In the Document window, select the **brian.jpg** image, if necessary.

8. In the Property inspector, click the **Class arrow**, and then click **Apply Multiple Classes**. The Multiclass Selection dialog box opens.

9. Click the **border** and **object_left** check boxes to select them, and then click the **OK** button. The two styles you selected are applied to the image.

10. Press the **Right** arrow key to deselect the image and position the insertion point to the right of the image. See Figure 5-17.

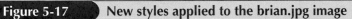

Figure 5-17 New styles applied to the brian.jpg image

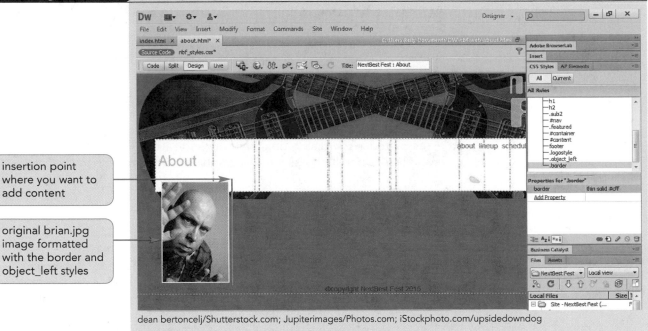

insertion point where you want to add content

original brian.jpg image formatted with the border and object_left styles

dean bertoncelj/Shutterstock.com; Jupiterimages/Photos.com; iStockphoto.com/upsidedowndog

With the brian.jpg image placed and formatted, you will add information about Brian's role in the company next to his image in the about.html page.

To add content to the about.html page:

1. Type **Brian Lee** to enter Brian's name next to his picture.

2. If the text you typed is formatted with a style, select the text, click the **Format** button in the Property inspector, and then click **none**.

3. Press the **Enter** key, and then type **Brian is the co-owner of Shenpa Productions, the company that produces the NextBest Fest. Brian is a lifelong music aficionado. He created the NextBest Fest so that he could spend his time concentrating on his two greatest loves: tribute bands and his son/business partner, Gage.** (including the period).

4. Press the **Enter** key four times to move the insertion point below Brian's image.

5. Check the spelling and proofread the content you just entered.

6. Select **Brian Lee**, and then format the text as **Heading 2**. The h2 tag is added to the text.

7. Turn on **Live** view, and then review the image and other content you added to the about.html page. See Figure 5-18.

Figure 5-18 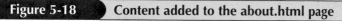 Content added to the about.html page

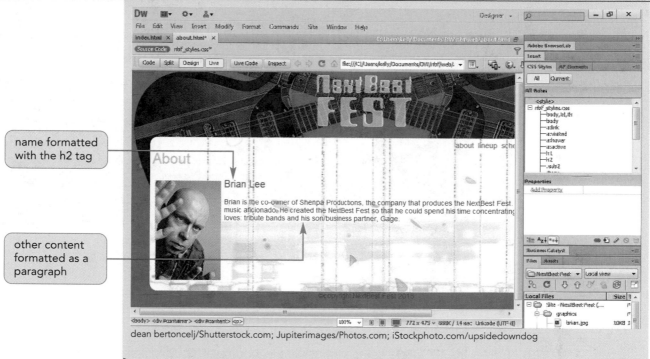

name formatted with the h2 tag

other content formatted as a paragraph

dean bertoncelj/Shutterstock.com; Jupiterimages/Photos.com; iStockphoto.com/upsidedowndog

8. Turn off **Live** view to return to Design view.

9. Save the about.html page and the nbf_styles.css style sheet.

In this session, you reviewed the different graphic formats that browsers can display, and then you added graphics to pages in the Web site. In the process, you entered alt text and applied multiple class styles to the graphic at the same time. You also replaced a graphic file. Finally, you explored different ways to edit a graphic in Dreamweaver. In the next session, you will create graphic hyperlinks and then you will insert and edit a graphic using Photoshop.

Session 5.1 Quick Check

1. What does compression do to a graphic file?
2. What are the three graphic formats that browsers can display?
3. What is the best graphic file format to use for photographs?
4. Why would you add alt text to an image?
5. What are assets in Dreamweaver?
6. Why would you use the Assets panel?
7. _____ reduces the area of a graphic by deleting unwanted outer areas.
8. True or False. When you delete an image from a Web page, it is also deleted from the local root folder.

SESSION 5.2 VISUAL OVERVIEW

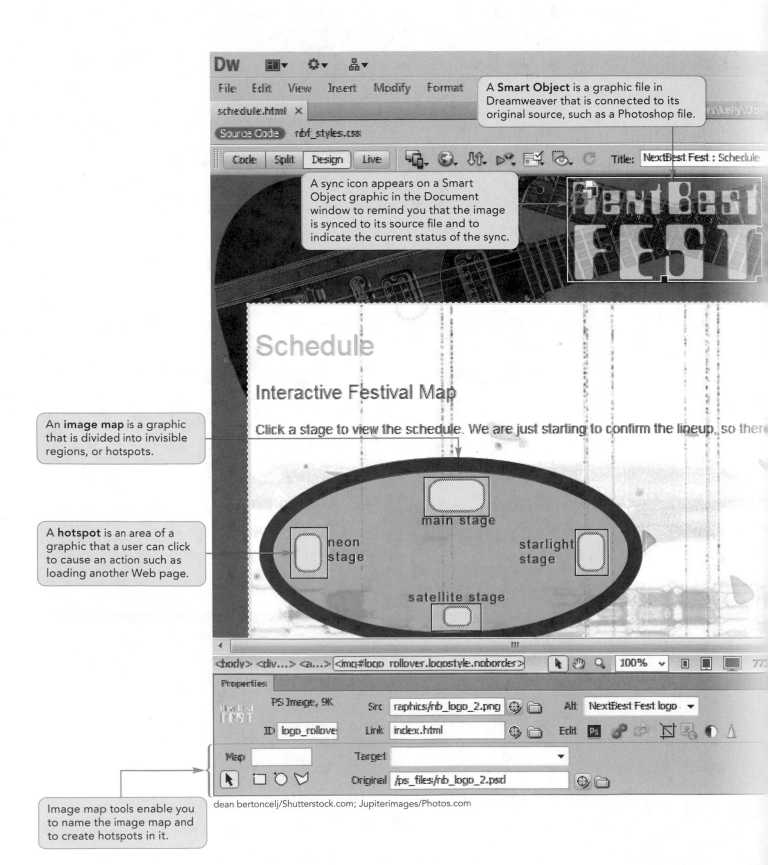

A **Smart Object** is a graphic file in Dreamweaver that is connected to its original source, such as a Photoshop file.

A sync icon appears on a Smart Object graphic in the Document window to remind you that the image is synced to its source file and to indicate the current status of the sync.

An **image map** is a graphic that is divided into invisible regions, or hotspots.

A **hotspot** is an area of a graphic that a user can click to cause an action such as loading another Web page.

Image map tools enable you to name the image map and to create hotspots in it.

dean bertoncelj/Shutterstock.com; Jupiterimages/Photos.com

LINKS, HOTSPOTS, AND ROLLOVERS

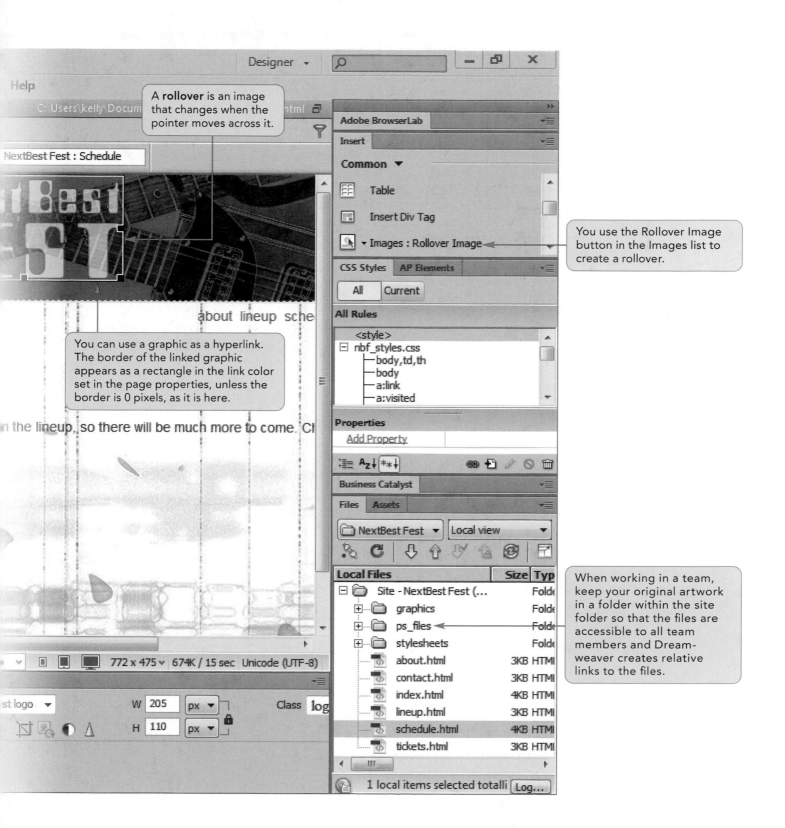

A **rollover** is an image that changes when the pointer moves across it.

You use the Rollover Image button in the Images list to create a rollover.

You can use a graphic as a hyperlink. The border of the linked graphic appears as a rectangle in the link color set in the page properties, unless the border is 0 pixels, as it is here.

When working in a team, keep your original artwork in a folder within the site folder so that the files are accessible to all team members and Dreamweaver creates relative links to the files.

Creating Graphic Hyperlinks

Another common use of graphics is as hyperlinks. You can create a link for an entire image, or you can divide the image into smaller sections and create a link for each of those sections.

Linking an Image

The process for creating a graphic hyperlink is similar to the process for creating a text hyperlink. After you have created a link to a page, you can select it as the link for a selected graphic using the Link box in the Property inspector. When a graphic is linked, the border appears as a rectangle around the graphic in the color you set for links in the page properties, unless the border is 0 pixels.

You will create a graphic link from the NextBest Fest logo to the home page. You will not see a rectangle around the graphic because you set the border of the NextBest Fest logo to 0px in the .logostyle style. Using a logo as a link to the home page of a site is a common convention that the NextBest Fest target audience should be familiar with. You will start by creating the link in the about page. Because creating the link does not affect the appearance of the logo graphic, you won't create a link from the logo on the home page to itself.

To create a graphic link from the logo to the home page:

▶ **1.** If you took a break after the previous session, make sure that the NextBest Fest site is open, the Designer workspace is reset, the Business Catalyst panel is collapsed, the Files panel is open, and the index.html and about. html pages are open in Design view.

▶ **2.** In the about.html page, switch to **Code** view, and then select the **NextBest Fest logo** code to select the logo.

▶ **3.** In the Property inspector, next to the Link box, click the **Browse for File** button ▢, and then double-click **index.html** in the Select File dialog box. The link information appears in the Link box, the code is added to the page, and an <a> tag appears around the code for the image.

▶ **4.** Save the page, and then preview the page in a browser. You will test the logo.

▶ **5.** Point to the **logo**. The pointer changes to 🖑, indicating that the logo is a link.

▶ **6.** Click the **logo**. The home page appears in the browser window.

▶ **7.** Close the browser.

TIP

You can also use the Point to File button in the Property inspector to link the selected graphic to a page.

Creating an Image Map

In addition to creating a link from an entire image, you can create multiple links from different areas of an image. An image map is a graphic that is divided into invisible regions, or hotspots. A hotspot is an area of a graphic that a user can click to cause an action such as loading another Web page. Image maps are useful when you want to link parts of a graphic to different pieces of information. You frequently use image maps and hotspots when you view maps on the Web such as Google Maps and MapQuest. In a music festival site, each stage of the concert venue that appears in an image could be a hotspot so that when a user clicks a particular stage, the corresponding lineup and schedule information appears on the screen.

Creating an Image Map

- In the Document window, select the graphic.
- In the Property inspector, type a name in the Map box.
- For each hotspot, click the rectangular, oval, or polygonal hotspot tool in the Property inspector, and then drag over the image in the Document window to create a rectangle or circle hotspot, or click at various points to create a polygon hotspot.
- For each hotspot, type alternate text in the Alt box in the Property inspector.

You can create three types of hotspots: rectangle, circle, and polygon. After the hotspots are created in the image, you create separate links for each hotspot. When a hotspot is selected, the Property inspector displays the hotspot and pointer tools and the following hotspot attributes:

- **Link.** The Web page or file that opens when the hotspot is clicked.
- **Target.** The frame or window in which the linked Web page will open. This option is available only after you specify a link for the hotspot.
- **Alt.** The alternate text description for each link.
- **Map.** The unique descriptive name of the image map. You do not have to name image maps; however, some advanced coding requires objects to be named so they can be referenced. If you do not name the image map after you create the first hotspot, Dreamweaver assigns the name *Map* to the first image map, *Map2* to the second image map, and so on. Map names must begin with a letter or an underscore, and they can contain letters and numbers but not spaces or symbols.

Gage wants you to add a map graphic to the schedule.html page, and then use the graphic to create an image map.

To insert the map graphic in the schedule.html page:

1. Open the **schedule.html** page in Design view.

2. In the Document window, move the insertion point after the page heading text by pressing the **Right** arrow key until no heading tags appear in the status bar.

3. Press the **Enter** key to move the insertion point to a new line, type **Interactive Festival Map**, press the **Enter** key, and then type **Click a stage to view the schedule. We are just starting to confirm the lineup, so there will be much more to come. Check back frequently!** (including the exclamation point).

4. Check the spelling and proofread the text you just typed.

5. In the Document window, select the **Interactive Festival Map** text, and then format the text with **Heading 2**.

6. If more than two empty lines appear above the heading 2 text, delete the extra empty lines.

7. Click at the end of the text you just entered, and then press the **Enter** key. You will insert the map graphic on this line.

8. In the **Common** category of the Insert panel, click the **Image** button in the Images list. The Select Image Source dialog box opens.

9. Navigate to the **Dreamweaver5\Tutorial** folder included with your Data Files, double-click **fest_map.png** to insert the graphic, and then click the **Yes** button in the dialog box that opens to save a copy of the image in the graphics folder, if necessary.

10. Type **Map of the festival stages with links to stage schedules located below.** (including the period) in the Alternate text box, and then click the **OK** button. A copy of the festival map graphic is saved in the graphics folder and the graphic appears in the page.

11. Deselect the graphic, if necessary. See Figure 5-19.

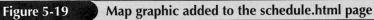

| Figure 5-19 | Map graphic added to the schedule.html page |

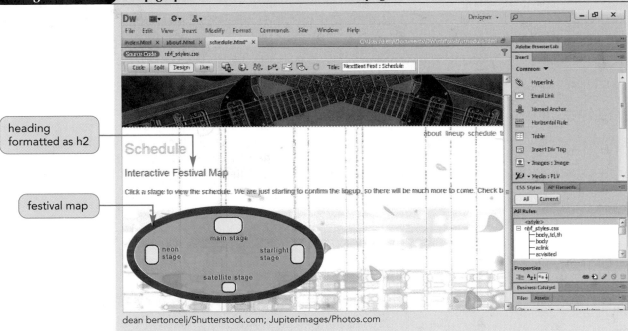

dean bertoncelj/Shutterstock.com; Jupiterimages/Photos.com

Next, you will add hotspots to the map, which turns the graphic into an image map. You want to create a hotspot for each stage on the map. You will use a rectangle hotspot because the stages are fairly rectangular in shape. You should draw the hotspot slightly larger than the object you want users to click to be sure that the area is completely covered by the hotspot. You will add alt text to each hotspot so that assistive devices can convey the purpose of the hotspots.

To create the image map from the festival map:

1. In the Document window, select the **fest_map** graphic.

2. In the Property inspector, click in the **ID** box, and then type **fest_map_im**.

3. In the Property inspector, click the **Rectangle Hotspot Tool** button ☐. In the Document window, the pointer changes to ┼.

4. In the Document window, click just outside the upper-left corner of the main stage and drag to just beyond the lower-right corner to draw a hotspot that covers the stage. A dialog box opens, prompting you to add alt text for the hotspot.

5. Click the **OK** button, and then, in the Alt box in the Property inspector, type **Main stage with hotspot linking to the schedule below**. See Figure 5-20.

| Figure 5-20 | Hotspot added for the main stage |

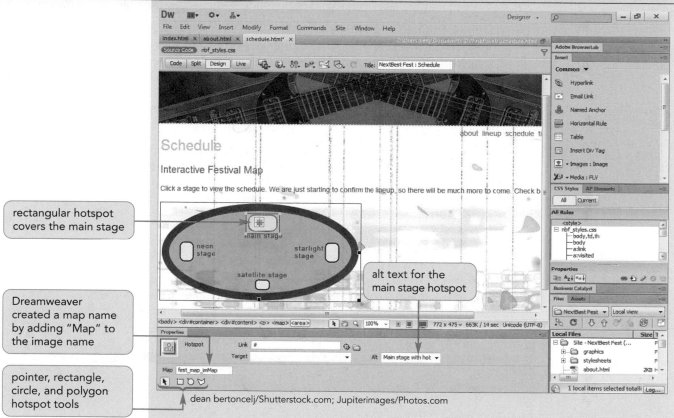

rectangular hotspot covers the main stage

alt text for the main stage hotspot

Dreamweaver created a map name by adding "Map" to the image name

pointer, rectangle, circle, and polygon hotspot tools

dean bertoncelj/Shutterstock.com; Jupiterimages/Photos.com

6. Repeat Steps 4 and 5 to create hotspots for the other three stages, replacing the stage name in the alt text for each hotspot.

7. Save and close the page. When all of the schedule information is available, Gage will link the hotspots to the appropriate location in the page.

Creating Rollovers

A rollover is an image that changes when the pointer moves across it. In actuality, a rollover enables two seemingly stacked graphics—the original graphic and the rollover graphic—to swap places during a specified browser action, such as a mouseover, and then to swap back during another specified browser action, such as when the pointer is moved off the images. The two graphics must be the same size.

Inserting Rollovers

You can insert rollover buttons that change when the user points to them and that link the user to another page when the button is clicked. When you use the Rollover Image button to create rollovers, Dreamweaver does more than just create code to make the images swap. After you fill in the requested information in the Insert Rollover Image dialog box, Dreamweaver creates all of the code to make four separate things happen:

- The graphics preload when the Web page is loaded so that they are in place when a browser action such as a mouseover occurs.
- The graphics swap occurs when the pointer is placed over the graphic.
- The graphics swap occurs again when the pointer is moved off the graphic.
- If a URL is specified in the When clicked, Go to URL box of the Insert Rollover Image dialog box, the user is hyperlinked to the new page when the graphic is clicked.

Technically, a rollover is a JavaScript behavior. A JavaScript behavior is a set of JavaScript instructions that tell the browser to do specified things. After you enter the image name, the original image source file, the rollover image source file, and a URL, if appropriate, Dreamweaver adds the JavaScript for you.

The image name is the name that appears in the Property inspector when one of the rollover graphics is highlighted. The image name does not replace the filename of either graphic you designate. The image name must begin with a letter or an underscore and cannot have any spaces or special characters. Use a descriptive name that includes the word *roll* or *rollover* to remind you that a graphic has rollover behaviors attached to it. Unless the word *roll* or *rollover* appears in the image name, you cannot tell that a graphic has rollover behaviors attached to it without looking at the code or previewing the page in a browser.

REFERENCE

Inserting a Rollover

- In the Common category of the Insert panel, click the Rollover Image button in the Images list.
- In the Image name box, type a name for the rollover image.
- Click the Original image Browse button, navigate to the file you want to insert as the original image, and then double-click the image.
- Click the Rollover image Browse button, navigate to the file you want to insert as the rollover image, and then double-click the image.
- Click the Preload rollover image check box to check it.
- In the Alt box, type alternate text for the image.
- Click the When clicked, Go to URL Browse button, navigate to the page to which you want to link, and then double-click the filename.
- Click the OK button.

As a site grows in depth and sophistication, it is common to update elements to make them better. You will update the TICKETS div in the home page to include a rollover image that draws more attention to the tickets promotion.

To insert a rollover image in the featured div in the home page:

1. In the **index.html** page, select the **TICKETS AVAILABLE** text in the featured div, and then press the **Delete** key. The text is deleted from the div.

2. In the **Common** category of the Insert panel, click the **Images button arrow**, and then click the **Rollover Image** button. The Insert Rollover Image dialog box opens.

3. In the Image name box, type **featured_roll**. Remember, the image name cannot include spaces. Whenever you see the name in the Property inspector, you will be reminded that the image has rollover behaviors.

> Be sure to type the image name without spaces; otherwise, the rollover behavior will not work.

4. Next to the Original image box, click the **Browse** button, navigate to the **Dreamweaver5\Tutorial** folder included with your Data Files, double-click **tickets.png**, and then click the **Yes** button in the dialog box that opens to save a copy of the image in the graphics folder, if necessary. A copy of the tickets.png graphic is added to the graphics folder, as you can see from the path in the Original image box.

5. Next to the Rollover image box, click the **Browse** button, navigate to the **Dreamweaver5\Tutorial** folder included with your Data Files, double-click **tickets_over.png**, and then click the **Yes** button in the dialog box that opens to save a copy of the image in the graphics folder, if necessary. A copy of the tickets_over.png graphic is saved in the graphics folder, as you can see from the path in the Rollover image box.

6. Click the **Preload rollover image** check box to insert a check mark, if necessary. Both graphics will load with the Web page.

7. Click in the Alternate text box, and then type **Image advertising that tickets are available and a link to the tickets page.** (including the period).

8. Next to the When clicked, Go to URL box, click the **Browse** button, and then double-click **tickets.html** in the local root folder of your NextBest Fest site. The tickets.html page is added to the When clicked, Go to URL box.

9. Click the **OK** button. The Insert Rollover Image dialog box closes, and the rollover image is added to the home page.

10. Press the **Right** arrow key to position the insertion point to the right of the rollover images, and then click the **tickets.png** graphic to select the logo rollover. The only information that identifies this graphic as a rollover is its name, which appears in the ID box in the Property inspector. See Figure 5-21.

Figure 5-21 Rollover in the home page

rollover inserted in the page

h1 tag surrounds the image, creating extra space above and below the image

button to insert a rollover image

name indicates that the graphic has rollover behaviors

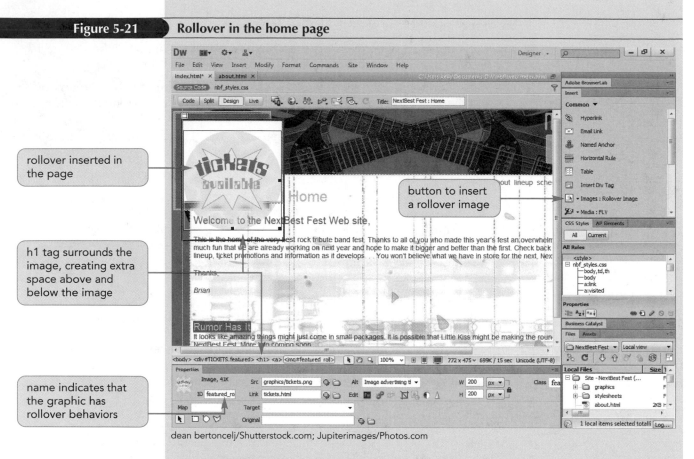

dean bertoncelj/Shutterstock.com; Jupiterimages/Photos.com

11. Turn on **Live** view, and then point to the new rollover image. The text changes color when the pointer is positioned over the image.

12. Turn off **Live** view to return to Design view.

With the rollover image in place, you need to adjust the div styles to accommodate the new graphics. You will do that next.

To edit the TICKETS div in the home page:

1. In the Document window, select the **green** div, and then press the **Delete** key. The div and its content are removed from the home page.

2. In the Document window, select the **TICKETS** div, and then, in the Property inspector, change its width and height to **200px**, if necessary.

3. Collapse the Insert panel, select the **featured** style in the All pane of the CSS Styles panel, and then, in the Properties pane, delete the background color from the style.

4. In the CSS Styles panel, select the **green** style, and then delete it.

5. In the CSS Styles panel, select the **TICKETS** style, and then, in the Properties pane, change border-radius to **100px**.

6. In the Document window, select the **TICKETS** div, if necessary, and then, in the Property inspector, type **15px** in the L box and type **0px** in the T box. The TICKETS div is repositioned in the page.

7. In the Document window, click in the **TICKETS** div, and then, in the Property inspector, click the **Format arrow** and click **None** to remove the h1 tag and move the image to the top of the div.

8. Create a new class style named **.noborder** in the style sheet, set the border width to **0**, and then select the **Same for all** check box, if necessary.

9. In the Document window, select the new **tickets** graphic, if necessary, and then apply the **noborder** style. The style you just created is applied to the rollover.

10. Save the page, and then save the style sheet.

11. Open the **tickets.html** page in Design view, place the insertion point below the page heading, type **You can take advantage of our lower advanced ticket prices by calling our offices to purchase tickets NOW. To purchase tickets, please call 732.555.1234 and one of our representatives will take your order.** (including the period), and then press the **Enter** key.

12. Check the spelling and proofread the text you just typed, and then save the tickets.html page.

13. Preview the index.html page in a browser, and then point to the **tickets** image. The rollover image appears in the browser. See Figure 5-22.

| Figure 5-22 | Rollover previewed in a browser |

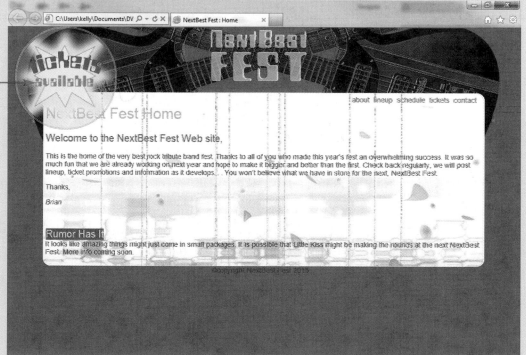

rollover image

Used with permission from Microsoft Corporation; dean bertoncelj/Shutterstock.com; Jupiterimages/Photos.com

Trouble? If an extra space appears above the graphic, close the browser, delete the extra space from the div, and then repeat Step 13.

Trouble? If a security warning bar appears in the browser, click Allow Blocked Content, and then click the Yes button to view the page in the browser. Do this whenever content you have created is blocked.

▶ **14.** Click the rollover image to open the tickets.html page, and then close the browser.

▶ **15.** Close the tickets.html page and the index.html page.

Editing a Rollover

You can modify a rollover by changing the original graphic, changing the rollover graphic, or editing the code of the rollover. For example, you might need to replace a graphic with an updated design, or you might decide to open the linked page in a new browser window. You can edit a rollover graphic in three ways:

- Delete the original graphic and insert a new rollover using the Rollover Image button. This deletes all the code, as well as the graphic, so you can create a new rollover from scratch.
- Replace the original graphic or the rollover graphic with a new one, leaving the attached code unchanged. To replace the original graphic, select the graphic and then select a new source file in the Property inspector. To replace the rollover graphic, select the graphic, click the Behaviors button in the Tag Inspector panel, double-click onMouseOver in the behaviors list, and then select a new source file for the rollover graphic.
- Edit the code for the rollover graphic in Code view if you know JavaScript, or edit the behaviors in the Behaviors panel.

For now, you will leave the original and rollover graphics.

Integrating Photoshop and Dreamweaver

You can set the Dreamweaver preferences to select Adobe Photoshop or Adobe Fireworks as an external image editor for each image file type (.jpg, .gif, .png). After you select an external editor for a file type, you can open a selected image in the external image editor, edit and save the image, and then view the changes in the Dreamweaver Document window. This tutorial uses Adobe Photoshop to edit images in Web pages.

Adobe Photoshop CS6 is the industry-standard software for creating, editing, and working with bitmap graphic images. Its integration with Dreamweaver enables you to move seamlessly between the two programs, streamlining your work flow and increasing your productivity. You can insert Photoshop files into Web pages in Dreamweaver or you can copy parts of Photoshop images and paste them into pages. When you do this, you create the optimized GIF, JPEG, or PNG images that will be displayed in the site's pages. This is extremely helpful because Web site content can change frequently and in today's busy world, every saved second counts.

Teamwork: Improving Productivity and Efficiency

Companies often rely on marketing campaigns to highlight a corporate message, image, or goal to customers and investors. To create an effective campaign, designers and writers work together to develop the various pieces in the marketing campaign. Using the different programs such as Illustrator, Photoshop, Fireworks, Flash, Dreamweaver, and InDesign that are part of one suite like Adobe Creative Suite makes it much easier for different members of a team to share resources as various elements of the project are completed. Team members can simultaneously work on different elements that are used in a variety of pieces in the campaign. This helps to streamline the work flow because as each element is developed, it can be reused by the rest of the team in other elements. This means elements from one document can be used in multiple layouts while preserving the links to the original artwork. For example, the same logo might be used in a brochure created in InDesign as well as in a Web site created in Dreamweaver. Later, any creative changes made to the original artwork seamlessly flow through to the various layouts in which that element is used. Improvements, like this integration feature, enable you to increase productivity and efficiency, but they also require that you keep up with current developments and remain flexible in your approach to development and design.

You should move any Photoshop file that you are going to insert into a page to the site's local root folder. If you insert a Photoshop file located outside of the site's root folder into a Web page, Dreamweaver creates an absolute local file path to the Photoshop file. The absolute path might not work from another computer, which can cause problems if you share the file with a team or if you change computers. When you store the Photoshop file in the site's local root folder, Dreamweaver creates a relative path to the file and anyone who has access to the site files can access the Photoshop file.

If you do not have Photoshop: You can read the rest of this session, but do not perform the steps. Instead, use the nb_logo.png and the nb_logo_2.png images to create a rollover that links to the home page from all of the pages in the site. Your site will not differ from the figures shown in the tutorials. The only differences will be that instead of the Photoshop documents inserted into the pages, you will have GIF, PNG, or JPEG images inserted in the pages.

You will move the nb_logo.psd file to the root folder of your NextBest Fest site. You can do this directly from the Files panel.

To move the nb_logo.psd file to the local root folder:

1. In the Files panel, click the **Site** button, and then click the folder where you store your Data Files.

2. In the files list, navigate to the **Dreamweaver5\Tutorial** folder included with your Data Files.

3. Right-click **nb_logo.psd**, point to **Edit** on the context menu, and then click **Copy**. The file is copied to the Windows Clipboard.

4. In the Files panel, click the **Site** button, and then click **NextBest Fest**. The site's files are displayed in the files list.

5. In the files list, navigate to the root folder of your NextBest Fest site.

6. Right-click the **root** folder, and then click **New Folder** on the context menu. A new folder is inserted within the web folder.

▸ **7.** Type **ps_files** as the name of the new folder, and then press the **Enter** key.

▸ **8.** Right-click the **ps_files** folder, point to **Edit** on the context menu, and then click **Paste**. The nb_logo.psd file is pasted into the ps_files folder in the local root folder.

Creating a Photoshop Smart Object

When you select a Photoshop file to insert into a Web page in Dreamweaver, the Photoshop file is not inserted directly into the Web page because .psd files are uncompressed files that cannot be displayed in Web browsers. Instead, the Image Preview dialog box opens and you are prompted to select optimization settings that enable Dreamweaver to create a compressed .gif, .jpg, or .png file that is inserted into the page. The graphic is inserted as a Smart Object, which is a graphic file in Dreamweaver that is connected to its original source file—in this case, a Photoshop file. A sync icon appears at the upper-left corner of the Smart Object graphic in the Document window to remind you that the image is synced to its source file and to indicate the current status of the sync.

REFERENCE

Inserting a Photoshop File into a Dreamweaver Web Page

- In the Document window, click where you want to insert the image.
- In the Common category of the Insert panel, click the Images button arrow, click Image, and then double-click the image to insert (or copy the image in the Photoshop window, and then in Dreamweaver paste the image in the Web page).
- In the Image Preview dialog box, select optimization settings, and then click the OK button.
- In the Save Web Image dialog box, enter a filename and storage location, and then click the OK button.

When you insert a Photoshop file in a Web page, Dreamweaver opens the Image Preview dialog box so you can optimize the image for Web display. There are two goals of optimizing an image for Web display. The first goal is to create an image that can display over the Web because the Photoshop .psd file cannot display in a browser. The second is to create the smallest possible file size so that the image loads quickly while maintaining good image quality so that the image displays in the Web page in the user's browser as you intended.

Figure 5-23 describes the basic optimization settings available for each format. The Image Preview dialog box also enables you to resize a graphic, but it is better to do that in Photoshop.

Figure 5-23	Basic image optimization settings

Format	Setting	Description
JPEG	Quality	Adjusts the quality of the image. A setting of 80 provides very good quality with a fairly low file size, but you can adjust to find the optimal setting for the image.
GIF/PNG 8	Palette	Sets the colors used in the image's compression. Because GIF/PNG 8 images can include a maximum of 256 colors, Adaptive provides the best results for color images because it enables Dreamweaver to select the best 256 colors for the image's compression while gray scale provides the best results for noncolor images.
	Loss	Removes spots of color, decreasing the image's file size. This usually looks more like an image effect and should be avoided unless you want a stylized look.
	Colors	Adjusts the image's quality/file size because GIF and PNG 8 formats compress images by adjusting the number of colors in the image. The maximum number of colors is 256, but you can decrease the number of colors in the color palette.
	Transparency	Enables you to set index, alpha, or no transparency for the image. The gray/white checked pattern in the background of the image denotes the transparent area.
	Matte	Enables you to select a colored matte as the image background. Selecting the white swatch with the diagonal red line indicates that the graphic will have a transparent background.
PNG 24	No real settings for this format.	
PNG 32	Transparency	Enables you to set index, alpha, or no transparency for the image. The gray/white checked pattern in the background of the image denotes the transparent area.
	Matte	Enables you to select a colored matte as the image background. Selecting the white swatch with the diagonal red line indicates that the graphic will have a transparent background.

© 2013 Cengage Learning

Image optimization can be a trial-and-error process. For each image, you want to find the smallest file size that still looks good when displayed on the user's screen. To do this, you select an image format (GIF, JPEG, or PNG), and then you adjust the settings. If you are unsure which format will be best for an image, you might need to repeat the process several times to end up with an image that looks good and has a small file size. Keep in mind that the smaller the file size, the faster the image downloads when users load the page in their browsers.

You will delete the logo from the home page of the NextBest Fest site, and then insert a PNG image that you create from the original Photoshop image. As with any other image you insert in a Web page, you can use CSS styles to format the graphic.

To insert a Photoshop image file in the home page:

1. Switch the about.html page to **Code** view, select the **nb_logo.png** code, and then delete it from the page. The original logo is no longer in the page.

2. In the **Common** category of the Insert panel, click the **Image** button in the Images list.

3. Navigate to the **ps_files** folder in the local root folder of your site, and then double-click **nb_logo.psd**. The Image Optimization dialog box opens, enabling you to select a preset option to create a compressed image that will be created from the Photoshop file for display in the Web site.

4. Click the **Preset arrow**, and then click **PNG 32 for Background Images (Gradients)**.

5. Click the **Transparency** check box to select it, if necessary. See Figure 5-24.

| Figure 5-24 | Image Optimization dialog box |

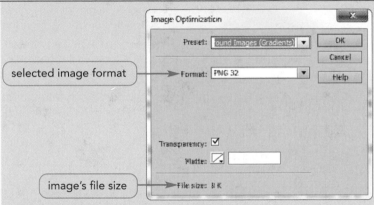

6. Click the **OK** button, and then click the **Save** button in the dialog box that opens to save a copy of the image in the graphics folder, if necessary. The Image Tag Accessibility Attributes dialog box opens.

7. In the Alternate text box, type **NextBest Fest Logo and link to the home page.** to enter the alt text for the image, and then click the **OK** button. The Smart Object is inserted in the upper-left corner of the home page.

8. Switch to **Design** view, and then scroll to the right to see the new image, if necessary.

9. With the image selected, in the Property inspector, click the **Class arrow**, and then click **logostyle**. The logostyle style is applied to the <a> tag that surrounds the graphic, and the content div moves up in the page. See Figure 5-25. The graphic will appear in the center of the page when the page is viewed in a browser.

Figure 5-25 Logo inserted in the about.html page

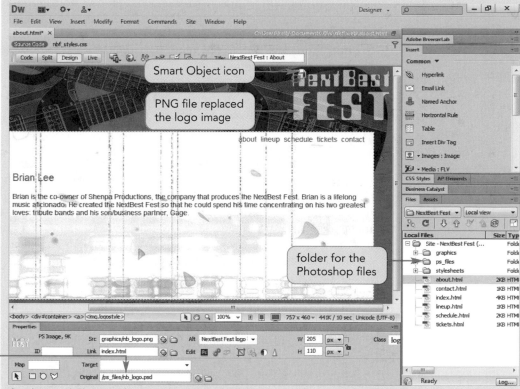

dean bertoncelj/Shutterstock.com; Jupiterimages/Photos.com

10. In the status bar, select the **<img.logstyle>** tag. The logo image is selected.

11. In the Property inspector, click the **Class arrow**, click **Apply Multiple Classes**, make sure the **logostyle** check box is checked, click the **noborder** check box to check it, and then click the **OK** button. The noborder style and the logostyle are applied to the image tag.

12. Save the page.

Because you saved the Smart Object over the original nb_logo.png file that was in the graphics folder, all of the pages in which the image had been placed have the Smart Object in them. You will check that the home page was updated with the Smart Object.

To confirm that the Smart Object is updated in the home page:

1. Open the **index.html** page in Design view.

2. Turn on **Live** view, examine the logo image, confirming that the updated image appears in the page.

3. Turn off **Live** view to return to Design view, and then close the index.html page.

Editing a Photoshop Source File for a Smart Object

One benefit of Web pages is that you can quickly and regularly update their content and styles. Although Web pages change frequently, you should not modify and then resave the compressed Web graphics that are displayed in the pages. Each time you resave a compressed image file, the file compresses further. Each compression degrades the image quality because the types of compression that are used for the Web are often lossy forms of compression. Instead, you should modify the original, uncompressed Photoshop file, and then recompress the updated image. This preserves the quality of the artwork in the Web pages. This process is fairly simple because Dreamweaver preserves the link between the Smart Object inserted in a Web page and the original Photoshop file.

Because Photoshop is an image-processing program, you can change just about anything in the image. For example, you can change the image size or color, you can rotate and bend an image, you can add text and textures to an image, and you can combine multiple images. The editing capabilities increase exponentially when an image is created with layers. In Photoshop, **layers** enable you to separate the elements that make up the image. Layers stack the elements of an image one on top of another to create the complete image. You can think of layers as pieces of acetate that are stacked to form a cell of a cartoon animation. Areas of a layer that do not contain image elements are transparent, so you can see the elements that appear on the layers below that one. You can also move or change elements in one layer without changing or moving elements in other layers.

Gage wants the NextBest Fest logo to use a different color. You will open the original Photoshop file for the NextBest Fest logo, modify the logo color, and then update the Smart Object.

> ### To open and edit the original logo image file in Photoshop:
>
> ▶ 1. In the Document window, select the **nb_logo.png** Smart Object, and then, in the Property inspector, click the **Edit** button. The original nb_logo.psd file opens in Photoshop.
>
>   **Trouble?** If you cannot select the image in Design view, switch to Code view, select the nb_logo.png Smart Object, return to Design view, and then click the Edit button in the Property inspector.
>
> ▶ 2. Click the **Layers** tab, if necessary, to display the Layers panel. See Figure 5-26.

Figure 5-26	Original logo image in Photoshop

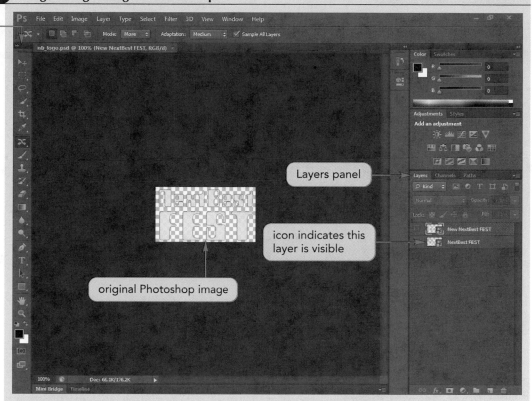

Tools panel

Layers panel

icon indicates this layer is visible

original Photoshop image

Trouble? If a dialog box opens, warning that some text layers contain fonts that are missing, the font used in the logo image is not installed on your computer. Click the OK button, and be careful not to double-click any layers that contain fonts.

Trouble? If the Photoshop program window on your screen looks different from the one shown in the figure, Photoshop is not set to its default configuration on your computer. To reset Photoshop to the default Essentials workspace, click Window on the menu bar, point to Workspace, and then click Reset Essentials.

3. In the Layers panel, to the left of the New NextBest FEST layer, click the **visibility** box. The Indicates layer visibility icon 👁 appears and the layer becomes visible.

4. In the Layers panel, to the left of the NextBest FEST layer, click the **Indicates layer visibility** icon 👁. The icon disappears from the box and the layer becomes invisible. See Figure 5-27.

Figure 5-27 Modified logo image in Photoshop

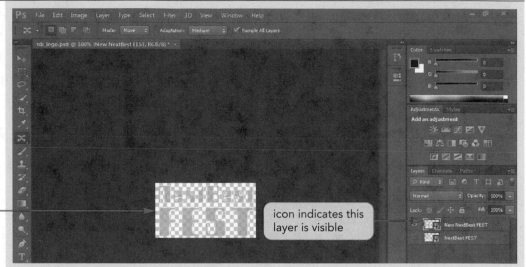

new NextBest Fest layer is visible

icon indicates this layer is visible

5. On the menu bar, click **File**, and then click **Save**. The changes you made to the image are saved.

6. On the taskbar, click the **Adobe Dreamweaver CS6** button to return to the Dreamweaver program window. See Figure 5-28.

Figure 5-28 Modified logo image not updated in the home page

Smart Object icon indicates the logo is not yet updated

dean bertoncelj/Shutterstock.com; Jupiterimages/Photos.com

Updating a Smart Object in Dreamweaver

After you have modified and saved the original Photoshop file and you return to the Dreamweaver program window, the bottom arrow on the sync icon for the Smart Object that is connected to the updated Photoshop file is red to indicate that the file has changed and that you need to update the Smart Object from the original file. When you update the Smart Object, Dreamweaver uses the setting you selected when you created the Smart Object to create a new, compressed image from the Photoshop file. When you sync a Smart Object in one page, Dreamweaver updates all the instances of that Smart Object.

To update the Smart Object:

▶ **1.** In the Document window, switch to **Code** view, select the **logo** code, and then return to **Design** view.

▶ **2.** In the Property inspector, click the **Update from Original** button ⬚. Dreamweaver creates a new image using the same settings that you used to compress the original image. The updated Smart Object still has all the same CSS styles applied to it as well as its alt text.

▶ **3.** Click a blank area of the Document window to deselect the logo. See Figure 5-29.

Figure 5-29   **Modified logo image updated in the home page**

dean bertoncelj/Shutterstock.com; Jupiterimages/Photos.com

▶ **4.** Save the about.html page. The updated Smart Object also appears in the other pages of the site.

▶ **5.** Open the **contact.html** page in Design view, confirm that the updated logo appears in the page, and then close the page.

Pasting Part of a Photoshop File in Dreamweaver

You can copy a piece of an image in Photoshop and then paste it into a Web page. This is helpful when you design the layout of an entire Web page in one Photoshop file, such as when you create a comp, but you create the working page in Dreamweaver. With this method, you copy only the images you need from the Photoshop document and then in Dreamweaver re-create the other elements such as the page layout, background color, and text with CSS or HTML. When you paste the portion of the Photoshop document into a Web page in Dreamweaver, the Image Optimization dialog box opens so you can create an optimized image. The portion of the Photoshop file is added as a Smart Object in Dreamweaver, and there is a link to the original file just like when you opened a Photoshop file in Dreamweaver.

You will open the sitedesign.psd file in Photoshop and copy only the logo into the content section of the page to see how this is done.

To copy part of a Photoshop file into the home page:

1. On the taskbar, click the **Adobe Photoshop CS6** button to return to the Photoshop program window.

2. On the menu bar, click **File**, and then click **Open**. The Open dialog box opens.

3. Navigate to the **Dreamweaver5\Tutorial** folder included with your Data Files, and then double-click **sitedesign.psd**. The file opens in Photoshop.

   Trouble? If a dialog box opens, warning that you do not have the font in which the logo was made installed on your computer, you can open the document but not edit the text. Click the OK button, and then read but do not perform the rest of the steps.

4. Click the **Layers** tab to open the Layers panel, if necessary.

5. On the menu bar, click **View**, point to **Show**, and then click **Guides** to display the guides if they are hidden.

6. On the menu bar, click **View**, and then click **Fit on Screen** to resize the image to fit in the workspace. See Figure 5-30.

Figure 5-30	Site design displayed in Photoshop

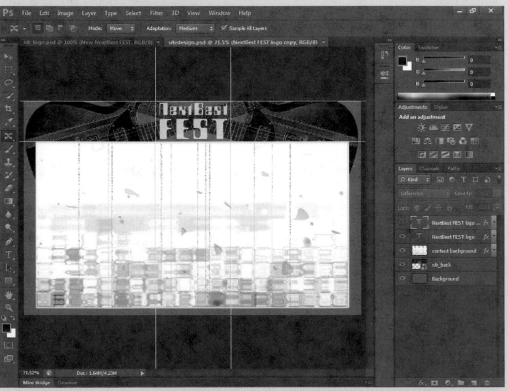

dean bertoncelj/Shutterstock.com; Jupiterimages/Photos.com

7. In the Tools panel, click the **Rectangular Marquee Tool** button to select it.

8. In the Document window, click the upper-left corner where the top and left guides intersect, drag to the lower-right corner where the right and bottom guides intersect, and then release the mouse button to create a rectangular selection as indicated by the guides. See Figure 5-31.

Figure 5-31   **Logo selected in the site design**

Rectangular Marquee tool selected

rectangle drawn to select the part of the logo within the guides

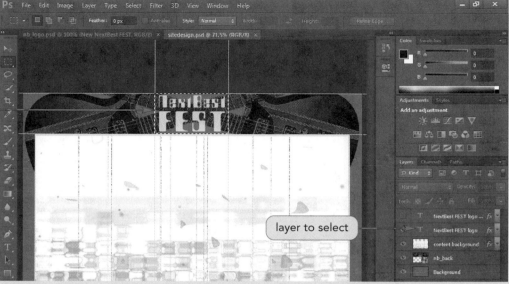

layer to select

dean bertoncelj/Shutterstock.com; Jupiterimages/Photos.com

9. In the Layers panel, select the **NextBest FEST logo** layer.

10. On the menu bar, click **Edit**, and then click **Copy**. The selections are copied to the Windows Clipboard.

11. In the taskbar, click the **Adobe Dreamweaver CS6** button. The Dreamweaver program window becomes active.

12. In the about.html page, click in the line below the last line of content. This is where you want to paste the logo.

13. On the menu bar, click **Edit**, and then click **Paste**. The Image Optimization dialog box opens and the logo appears in the page.

14. Select **JPEG** from the Format list, if necessary, select **80** from the Quality list, and then click the **OK** button.

15. Save a copy of the graphic in the **graphics** folder for the site using the default filename but do not add alt text. The logo is inserted below the text in the content div in the about.html page.

16. Scroll the page down, if necessary, to view the logo. See Figure 5-32.

Figure 5-32   **Logo pasted in the content div**

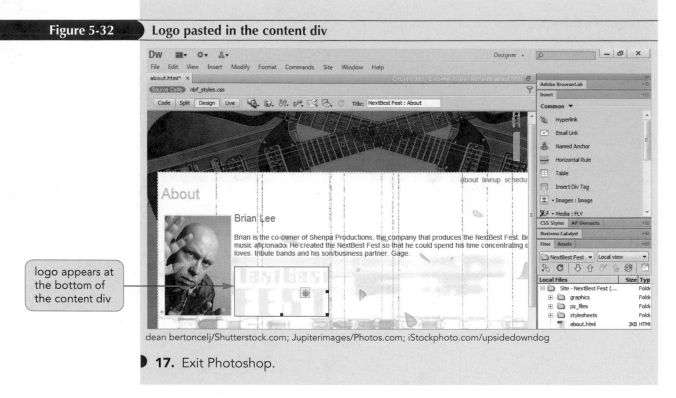

dean bertoncelj/Shutterstock.com; Jupiterimages/Photos.com; iStockphoto.com/upsidedowndog

▶ **17.** Exit Photoshop.

Because the image you pasted into the page is a Smart Object, you could modify the original Photoshop file, and then copy and paste the updated image into the page, just as you did with the previous Smart Object you included in the site.

Creating a Rollover Using a Smart Object

You can use Smart Objects in all the same ways you can use a regular image: as a page background, as a div background, as a rollover, and so on. You will add the nb_logo_2.psd file to the ps_files folder, and then you will create a rollover for the NextBest Fest logo. Before you do that, you will delete the logo from the body of the about.html page because Brian feels that the page is too cluttered. You will also delete the unneeded file from the graphics folder to keep the file size of the site as small as possible and to keep the files uncluttered.

To create the NextBest Fest logo rollover Smart Object in the about.html page:

▶ **1.** In the about.html page, select the **sitedesign.jpg**, and then press the **Delete** key. The logo is removed from the page.

▶ **2.** In the Files panel, delete the **sitedesign.jpg** from the graphics folder, and then click the **Yes** button to confirm the deletion. The unneeded file is removed from the site.

▶ **3.** In the about.html page, delete the **nb_logo.png** Smart Object from the page.

▶ **4.** Using the Files panel, copy the **nb_logo_2.psd** file located in the **Dreamweaver5\Tutorial** folder included with your Data Files, and then paste the file in the **ps_files** folder in the local root folder of your site.

5. In the **Common** category of the Insert panel, click the **Rollover Image** button in the Images list. The Insert Rollover Image dialog box opens.

6. In the Image name box, type **logo_rollover** to name the image.

7. Next to the Original image box, click the **Browse** button, navigate to the **ps_files** folder in the local root folder of your site, and then double-click **nb_logo_2.psd**. The Image Optimization dialog box opens so you can create the optimized Smart Object.

8. Select **PNG 32** from the Format list, check the **Transparency** check box, if necessary, and then click the **OK** button. The Save Web Image dialog box opens.

9. Save the **nb_logo_2.png** image in the **graphics** folder in the site's root folder.

10. Next to the Rollover image box, click the **Browse** button, navigate to the **graphics** folder in the root folder of your site, and then double-click the **nb_logo.png** Smart Object. Dreamweaver will remember that the image is a Smart Object every time you place an instance of the image into a page in the site.

11. Check the **Preload rollover image** check box, if necessary, type **NextBest Fest Logo and link to the home page.** in the Alternate text box, type **index.html** in the When clicked, Go to URL box, and then click the **OK** button. The logo rollover is inserted into the page and remains selected.

12. In the Property inspector, click the **Class arrow**, click **Apply Multiple Classes**, check the **noborder** and **logostyle** check boxes, and then click the **OK** button. The style is applied to the logo rollover.

13. In the Document window, deselect the logo rollover.

14. Open the CSS Styles panel, select **logostyle** in the All Rules pane, and then change the margin-right property to **33%** in the Properties pane. The new logo rollover moves back to the center of the screen. See Figure 5-33.

| Figure 5-33 | Final logo rollover in the about.html page |

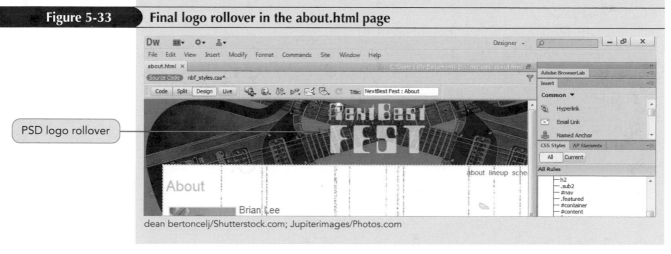

dean bertoncelj/Shutterstock.com; Jupiterimages/Photos.com

The logo rollover is complete and ready to add to every page of the site. You will copy the new rollover, and then paste it in each page.

To add the logo rollover to the other pages in the site:

▶ **1.** In the Document window, select the **logo**, and then, on the status bar, select the **<a.logostyle>** tag. The <a.logostyle> tag surrounds all the code for the logo and the rollover.

▶ **2.** On the menu bar, click **Edit**, and then click **Copy**. The code is copied to the Windows Clipboard.

▶ **3.** Open the **index.html** page in Design view, and then select the **logo**. You will replace this older logo.

▶ **4.** On the menu bar, click **Edit**, and then click **Paste**. The logo is pasted in the page.

▶ **5.** Select the **logo**. The logo ID logo_rollover appears in the Property inspector, confirming that the original logo image was replaced with the rollover logo.

▶ **6.** Save the page, and then close the page.

▶ **7.** Repeat Steps 3 through 6 to paste the logo rollover into the rest of the pages of the site: **contact.html**, **lineup.html**, **schedule.html**, and **tickets.html**.

▶ **8.** Save the style sheet.

▶ **9.** Open the **index.html** page, and then preview the page in a browser. See Figure 5-34.

| Figure 5-34 | Final logo in the home page previewed in a browser |

PSD logo rollover

Used with permission from Microsoft Corporation; dean bertoncelj/Shutterstock.com; Jupiterimages/Photos.com

▶ **10.** Go to each page of the site, testing that all of the pages display correctly and that the rollover appears in each page.

▶ **11.** Close the browser, and then close the home page.

In this session, you created graphic hyperlinks, an image map, and rollovers. You learned how to integrate Photoshop and Dreamweaver. You inserted a Photoshop image into a Web page, modified the original Photoshop image, and then updated the Web page image. You also inserted part of a Photoshop image into a Web page. In the next session, you will work with tables.

REVIEW

Session 5.2 Quick Check

1. What is an image map?
2. What is a hotspot?
3. What is a rollover?
4. What type of software is Photoshop?
5. What are the two ways to insert a Photoshop file into a Web page in Dreamweaver?
6. Why would you optimize an image for Web display?
7. What is a layer used for in Photoshop?
8. True or False. When you sync a Smart Object in one page, Dreamweaver updates all the instances of that Smart Object.

SESSION 5.3 VISUAL OVERVIEW

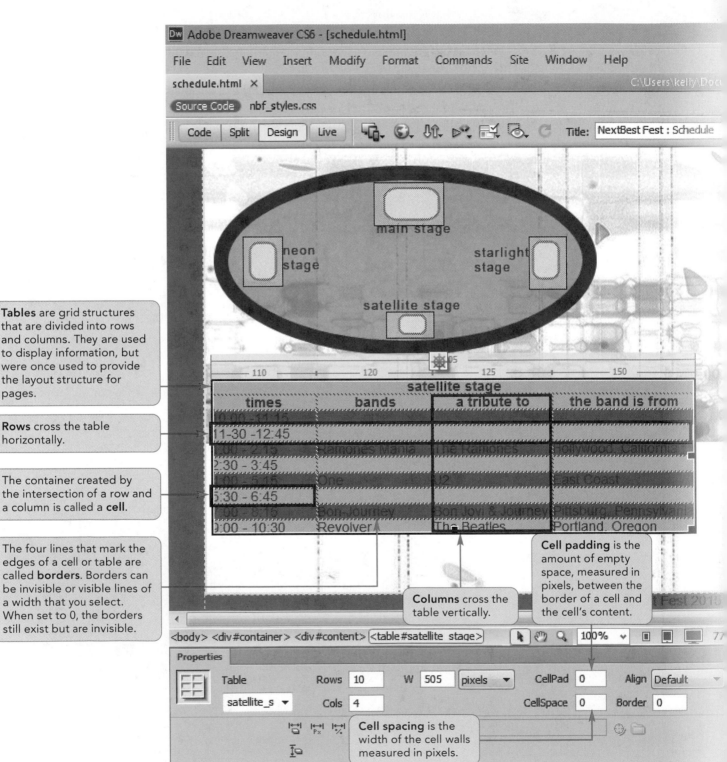

Tables are grid structures that are divided into rows and columns. They are used to display information, but were once used to provide the layout structure for pages.

Rows cross the table horizontally.

The container created by the intersection of a row and a column is called a **cell**.

The four lines that mark the edges of a cell or table are called **borders**. Borders can be invisible or visible lines of a width that you select. When set to 0, the borders still exist but are invisible.

Columns cross the table vertically.

Cell padding is the amount of empty space, measured in pixels, between the border of a cell and the cell's content.

Cell spacing is the width of the cell walls measured in pixels.

Jupiterimages/Photos.com

CREATING AND FORMATTING TABLES

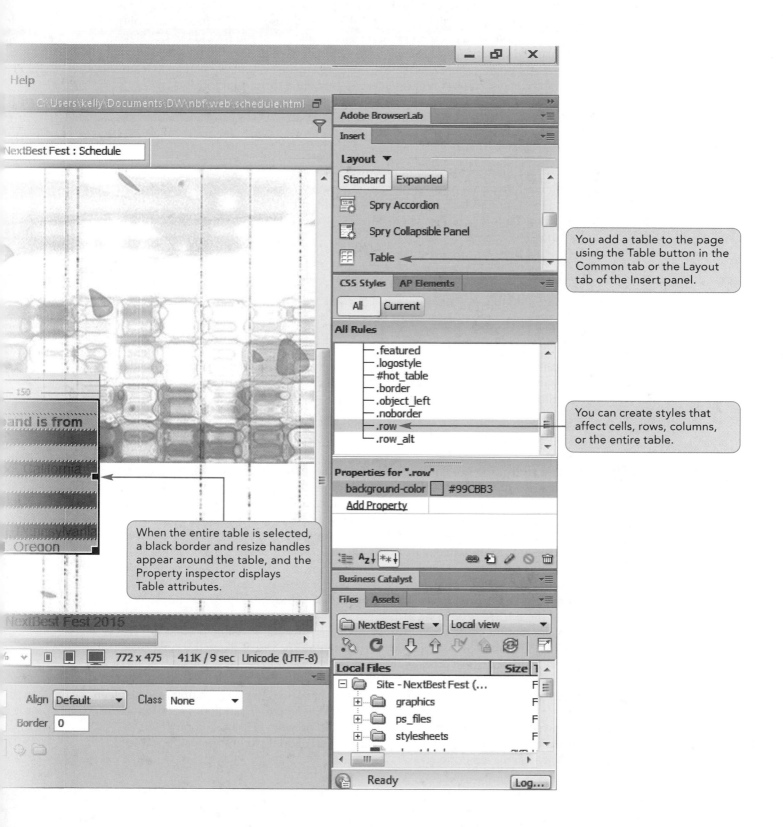

You add a table to the page using the Table button in the Common tab or the Layout tab of the Insert panel.

You can create styles that affect cells, rows, columns, or the entire table.

When the entire table is selected, a black border and resize handles appear around the table, and the Property inspector displays Table attributes.

Creating Tables

In the earliest days of the Web, text and images were aligned to the left of the page. Designers soon discovered that they could use tables to provide a vertical and horizontal structure for the content of a Web page. This provided more flexibility in arranging the content and elements in the Web page. Tables are still used in Web pages to simplify the presentation of data. Current best practices specify that you should use CSS styles to create all of the page layouts, although tables are sometimes used to increase layout options. Although it is not advisable to use tables in this way, it is important to learn about how tables might be used because you will encounter them occasionally.

REFERENCE

Inserting a Table

- In the Common category of the Insert panel, click the Table button.
- In the Rows box, type the number of rows.
- In the Columns box, type the number of columns.
- In the Table width box, type a percentage value, click the Table width arrow, and then click percent.
- In the Border thickness box, type a border width (type 0 if you do not want the table structure to appear on the Web page).
- Click the OK button.

Inserting a Table

You can quickly insert a table in a Web page by selecting where to insert the table and its parameters. Dreamweaver then inserts the HTML code for the table. You can specify the following table parameters:

- **Rows.** The number of rows for the table. You can also add rows to the table later.
- **Columns.** The number of columns for the table. You can also add columns to the table later.
- **Table width.** The horizontal dimension of the table specified in pixels or as a percentage of the width of the browser window. Using pixels creates a table that has a somewhat fixed width—the table will still expand as needed to fit the content, but it will not change size when the browser window is resized. Using a percentage creates a table that adjusts in size as the Web page is resized in the browser window. All the cells start with equal widths, but you can adjust the height and width of cells, rows, and columns.
- **Border thickness.** The size of the table border in pixels. A border of 0 creates an invisible table structure. If you don't specify a value, most browsers display the table as if the thickness were set to 1. It is a good idea to specify a border thickness to ensure that the table is displayed correctly. By default, invisible borders are visible within Dreamweaver so you can see the table structure, making the table easier to work with. You must preview the page in a browser to see how the table content will look without borders.
- **Cell padding.** The amount of empty space, measured in pixels, maintained between the border of a cell and the cell's content. When no cell padding is specified, most browsers display the table as if the cell padding were set to 1. Although this is usually fine, it is a good idea to specify a cell padding to ensure that the table is always displayed correctly.

TIP

Changing one cell's width changes the width of all cells in the column; changing one cell's height changes the height of all cells in the row.

- **Cell spacing.** The width of the cell walls measured in pixels. If you set the border to 0, the table still will be invisible no matter what you set the cell spacing to. When no cell spacing is specified, most browsers display the table as if the cell spacing were set to 2. Although this is usually fine, you should specify a cell spacing to ensure that the table is always displayed correctly.
- **Header.** The table cells that contain heading information (also called header cells). None specifies no header cells, Left makes the first column of cells header cells, Top makes the first row of cells header cells, and Both makes both the first row and the first column header cells. Designating header cells enables users who rely on assistive devices to more easily understand the table information.
- **Caption.** A table title that is displayed outside of the table. The optional caption can aid users who rely on assistive devices.
- **Align caption.** The alignment of the caption in relation to the table.
- **Summary.** A description of the table. Assistive devices read the summary, but the text is not displayed in the page.

You will create a table to hold the satellite stage schedule in the schedule.html page.

To insert a table for the satellite stage schedule:

1. If you took a break after the previous session, make sure that the NextBest Fest site is open, the Designer workspace is reset, the Business Catalyst panel is collapsed, and the Files panel is open.

2. Open the **schedule.html** page in Design view, click to the right of the map, and then press the **Enter** key to move the insertion point below the map.

3. In the **Common** category of the Insert panel, click the **Table** button. The Table dialog box opens. You will set the table parameters.

4. In the Rows box, type **10**, press the **Tab** key, and then, in the Columns box, type **4**. The table will have 10 rows and 4 columns.

5. Press the **Tab** key, type **600** in the Table width box, click the **Table width** button, and then click **pixels**. The table width will be 600 pixels.

6. Press the **Tab** key, and then, in the Border thickness box, type **0**. The table borders will be invisible.

7. Press the **Tab** key, and then, in the Cell padding box, type **1**. One pixel of space will be maintained between the cell border and its content.

8. Press the **Tab** key, and then, in the Cell spacing box, type **2**. The cell walls will be 2 pixels.

9. In the Header area, click **Top**. The first row of the table will be header cells.

10. Click in the **Summary** box, and then type **Schedule for the satellite stage.** (including the period). Assistive devices will be able to read the summary text, but it will not appear in the browser window. See Figure 5-35.

TIP

The Table button is also available in the Layout category of the Insert panel.

Figure 5-35 Completed Table dialog box

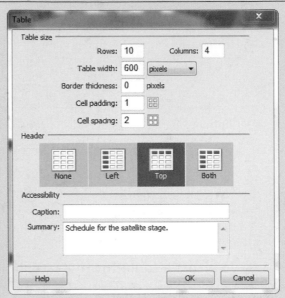

11. Click the **OK** button. The table appears in the Document window and is selected. You might need to scroll down to see the entire table. See Figure 5-36.

Figure 5-36 Table inserted in the schedule.html page

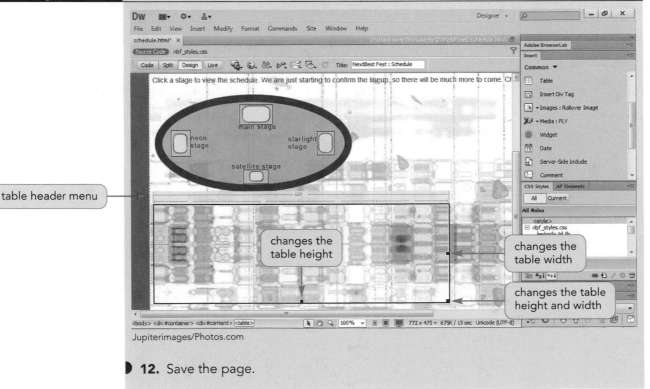

table header menu

changes the table height

changes the table width

changes the table height and width

Jupiterimages/Photos.com

12. Save the page.

When you create a table, Dreamweaver inserts a nonbreaking space in each cell. Some browsers collapse cells that are empty, destroying the table structure. The nonbreaking space is invisible, but it keeps the cells from collapsing. To view a nonbreaking space, you must be in Code view or Split view.

You will view the nonbreaking space in the first cell of the table.

To view the nonbreaking space in the schedule table:

▶ **1.** Click in the upper-left cell of the table. The insertion point moves into the first cell.

▶ **2.** Switch to **Split** view. In the Code pane, a nonbreaking space ( ) appears to the right of the insertion point.

▶ **3.** Return to **Design** view.

Adding Content to Cells and Importing Tabular Data

To add text to a cell, you simply click in the cell and type. If you have difficulty locating the rows, columns, and cells of the table, move your mouse over the table; as you move over various elements, the borders of those elements will have a red highlight enabling you to select the desired element. After you click in a cell, pressing the Enter key adds another paragraph within the cell. You can also copy data between cells using the Copy and Paste commands. When you type or paste text into a cell, the text wraps within the cell to fit the width you defined. If you check the No wrap check box in the Property inspector, the cell will expand to fit the text when the page is viewed in a browser, but remain wrapped when viewed in Dreamweaver. In addition, you can import data stored in a spreadsheet into a table.

Keyboard commands help you move through the table. To move the insertion point to the next adjacent cell, press the Tab key. Pressing the Tab key in the last cell of the table adds a new row to the table. Press the Shift+Tab keys to move the insertion point to the previous cell. You also can use the arrow keys to move the insertion point to an adjacent cell.

In addition to text, you can insert graphics into table cells. You do this the same way you insert graphics into a page. When a graphic is inserted into a cell, the cell's column width and row height expand as needed to accommodate the graphic.

PROSKILLS

Written Communication: Reusing Content to Reinforce Marketing

Companies hire professional copy writers and trained marketing people to craft the content that will be used in all their public communication. This is done intentionally to present a specific image to their customers and investors. As the different elements are drafted, they can be reused in different formats. In the world of marketing and communications, it is a good practice to reinforce a message by presenting the same content in different ways. The same content is often used in many contexts, including printed brochures, promotional letters, and advertisements, as well as the Web site, to reinforce the message being conveyed. Reusing material helps to create a specific branding and identity for the business or product. When creating content for a Web site, don't overlook content that has already been developed. Make sure that you use existing materials to reinforce the overall message that the client is trying to convey. To create a good Web site, consider how that Web site will fit into the client's overall marketing plan, and make sure that the site you design and build has the greatest possible effect.

When you use existing material, rather than retyping content that is already available in another file (and possibly introducing errors into the text), you can copy that text from its original source and paste it into the Web pages. When you want to place data stored in a spreadsheet or a table into a table in a Web page, you can save the data in a delimited format (such as comma, tab, semicolon, colon, or other delimited format) and then import the data into the table. Comma-delimited format inserts commas between pieces of data to indicate how data should be divided into table cells. Most spreadsheet programs and programs that create tables will let you save the tabular data in comma-delimited (.csv) format, but, if you have Microsoft Excel, this is not necessary. You can import the contents of an Excel worksheet directly into a table in Dreamweaver.

The NextBest Fest schedules are stored in Excel worksheets. Gage wants you to import the satellite_schedule.xlsx file into the table you created on the schedule.html page.

To enter and import text into the schedule table:

1. Click in the upper-left cell in the table, type **satellite stage schedule**, and then press the **Tab** key. The text you typed is entered in the first cell in the table, and the active cell is the second cell in the first row. You could continue to type all of the tour dates information, but it is faster to import the data from the Excel file.

2. Click in the upper-left cell in the table, press and hold the **Shift** key as you click in the lower-right cell, and then release the Shift key. All of the cells in the table are selected. Selecting all the cells in a table is different from selecting the table itself. You need to select the table in which you want to import data.

3. Point to the upper-left border of the table until the pointer changes to ↖⊞, and then click the table border. The table is selected. You will import the tabular data into the selected cells.

4. On the menu bar, click **File**, point to **Import**, and then click **Excel Document**. The Import Excel Document dialog box opens.

5. Navigate to the **Dreamweaver5\Tutorial** folder included with your Data Files, and then double-click the **satellite_schedule.xlsx** file. The data in the Excel worksheet is imported into the table, the table width changes to accommodate the content, and the table loses its cell padding and cell spacing. See Figure 5-37.

TIP

To import tabular data, you can also click the Import Tabular Data button in the Data category of the Insert panel, or click Insert on the menu bar, point to Table Objects, and click Import Tabular Data.

Figure 5-37   **Tabular data imported into the table**

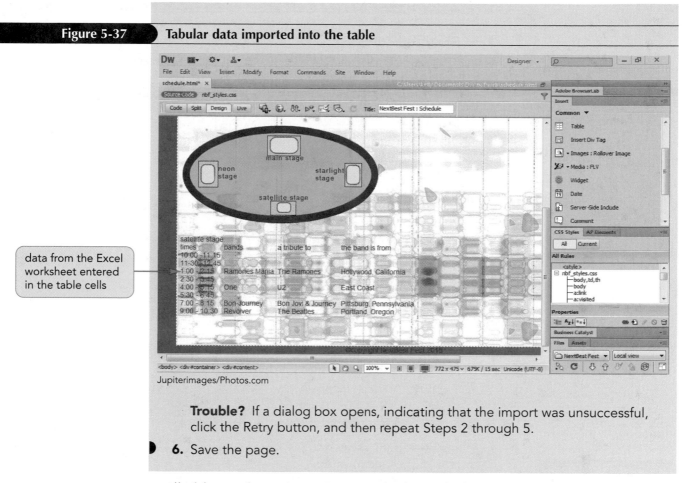

data from the Excel worksheet entered in the table cells

Jupiterimages/Photos.com

Trouble? If a dialog box opens, indicating that the import was unsuccessful, click the Retry button, and then repeat Steps 2 through 5.

6. Save the page.

All of the text formatting options can also be applied to text in a table. Text formatting attributes are available in the Property inspector when you select a cell, a row, or a column. You can also create CSS styles for table text.

Selecting Tables and Table Elements

You often need to modify a table and its elements to fit a particular Web page layout or specific content. To work with a table or table element, you must select it. You can select a table cell, a row, a column, or the table itself. When you move the pointer over an element, it is highlighted to enable you to more clearly see what you are selecting. Any time the table or a table element is selected, the table header menu appears at the top of the table. You can switch from Standard Table mode to Expanded Table mode, which increases the width of the cell walls, to more easily select various table elements.

Using Expanded Tables Mode

If you are having difficulty selecting a table element, you can use Expanded Tables mode. **Expanded Tables mode** temporarily adds cell padding and spacing to all of the tables in the page so that you can more easily select table elements and more precisely position the pointer inside cells. You select tables and table elements in Expanded Tables mode in the same way you do in Standard mode. Tables in Expanded Tables mode might not be positioned precisely in the page because of the additional cell padding and spacing. Be sure to return to Standard mode before you check the final page layout.

To switch to Expanded Tables mode, click the Expanded button on the Layout tab of the Insert panel. To return to Standard mode, click the Standard button on the Layout tab of the Insert panel.

Selecting a Table

When you want to change attributes that affect the entire table, the whole table must be selected. When the entire table is selected, a solid black line surrounds the table, and resize handles appear on the left side, in the lower-right corner, and at the bottom of the table. The attributes in the Property inspector also change to reflect the entire table.

You will select the table in the schedule.html page.

To select the table in the schedule.html page:

1. In the Insert panel, switch to the **Layout** category. The table is currently displayed in Standard mode.

2. In the Document window, click outside the table to deselect the table.

3. Right-click the table, point to **Table** on the context menu, and then click **Select Table**. The table is selected, the table tag is selected in the status bar, and the table attributes appear in the Property inspector. See Figure 5-38.

TIP

You can also select a table by clicking the menu button above the table, and then clicking Select Table.

| Figure 5-38 | Table selected in the schedule.html page |

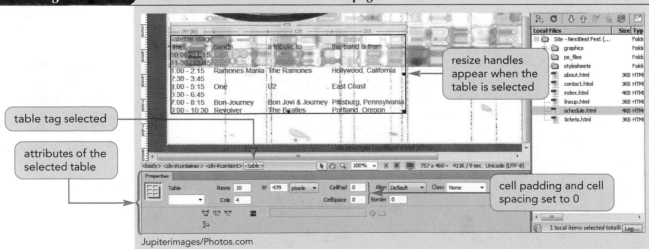

Jupiterimages/Photos.com

4. Click anywhere in the Document window outside the table to deselect it.

5. Position the pointer over the upper-left corner of the table to change the pointer to ⊞, and then click. The entire table is selected.

Selecting a Table Cell

You must select a cell to adjust its attributes. The borders of a selected cell are solid black. Any content in the cell is selected as well. Clicking in a cell displays the cell properties in the Property inspector but does not select the cell. You can also select multiple cells. The borders of all the selected cells are solid black, and any content within the selected cells is also selected.

You will select a single cell and a group of cells in the table in the schedule.html page.

To select cells in the table:

▶ **1.** Press and hold the **Ctrl** key, click the cell at the upper-left corner of the table, and then release the Ctrl key. The cell is selected. See Figure 5-39.

Figure 5-39   **Cell selected in the table**

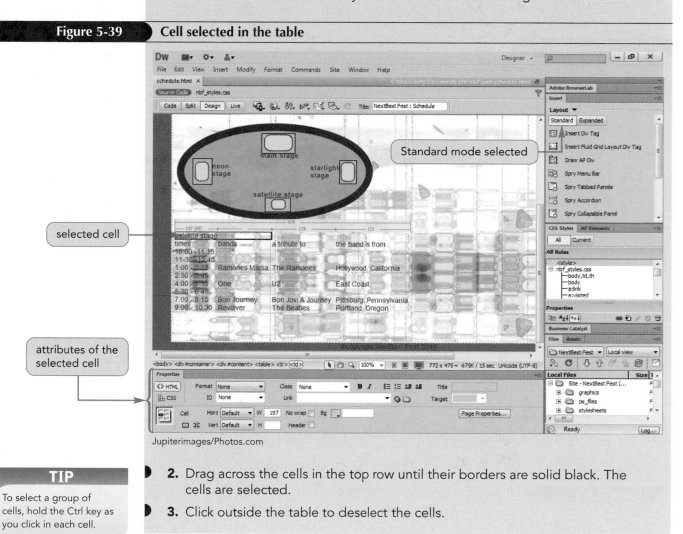

Jupiterimages/Photos.com

▶ **2.** Drag across the cells in the top row until their borders are solid black. The cells are selected.

▶ **3.** Click outside the table to deselect the cells.

TIP

To select a group of cells, hold the Ctrl key as you click in each cell.

Selecting Columns and Rows

You can use the pointer to select one or more columns or rows. The borders of all the cells in the selected column or row are solid black. You can also tell that a column or row is selected because the word *Column* or *Row* appears in the Property inspector alongside an icon showing a highlighted column or row in a table. Selecting all the cells in a row or column is the same as selecting the row or column.

You will select a column in the schedule table, and then you will select a row of cells.

To select a row and a column in the table:

1. Click in the table, move the pointer above the top border of the fourth column of the table, click the column width value to display the menu, and then click **Select Column**. The fourth column of the table is selected. See Figure 5-40.

Figure 5-40	Column selected in the table

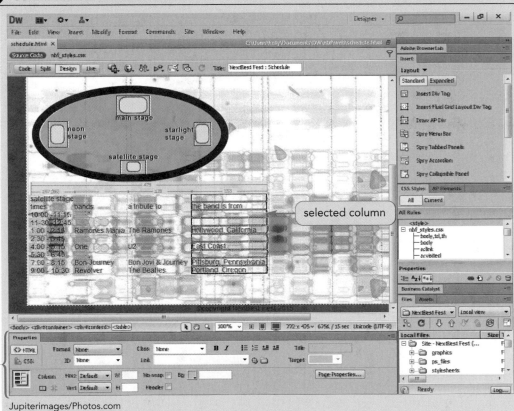

attributes of the selected column

Jupiterimages/Photos.com

2. Point outside the left border of the second row of the table. The pointer changes to ➡.

3. Click the left mouse button. The second row of the table is selected.

4. Click outside the table to deselect the row.

Working with an Entire Table

After a table is selected, you can change the attributes of the table, resize the table, move the table, or delete the table.

Previewing Tables in Different Browsers

Differences occur in the way that browsers handle tables, such as the differences in the way browsers display table border color. Some versions of Firefox do not display the table border color correctly. Because of differences like this, it is very important to preview Web pages that use tables in all of the different browsers that you intend to support. If you find problems in the way a browser displays the tables you have created, you can look at sites from browser manufacturers such as *microsoft.com* and *firefox.com* to research issues and fixes for specific browsers and browser versions.

Modifying Table Attributes

You can change the attributes of an existing table in the Property inspector, you can create a CSS style with the table attributes you want to use, or you can create a CSS style to modify the <table> tag to change the attributes of all the tables in the site. When the entire table is selected, the Property inspector includes the attributes of the HTML tag for the selected table, including the attributes from the Table dialog box: rows, columns, width, border, cell padding, and cell spacing. It also includes the following additional formatting attributes:

- **Table ID.** A unique descriptive name for the table. The table ID helps you to distinguish between multiple tables in a Web page. Also, some programming languages use the ID to refer to the table. The table ID must begin with a letter or an underscore, and can contain letters and numbers but not spaces or symbols.
- **Align.** The position of the table within the Web page, using the HTML attribute. Table alignment can be the browser's default alignment, left, right, or center. Remember, you can also create CSS styles to align the table.
- **Clear row heights and Clear column widths.** Buttons that remove all row height and column width settings from the table.
- **Convert table widths to percent and Convert table widths to pixels.** Buttons that change the current table width from pixels to a percentage of the browser window or from a percentage of the browser window to pixels.

You will name the table in the schedule.html page, and then modify some of its attributes.

To change the table attributes:

1. In the Document window, select the table.

2. In the Property inspector, in the Table box, type **satellite_stage**.

3. In the Property inspector, double-click in the **CellPad** box, and then type **0**, if necessary. This eliminates any space between the cell border and the cell content.

4. In the Property inspector, double-click in the **CellSpace** box, type **0**, if necessary, and then press the **Enter** key. This eliminates the space between cells in the table.

5. Save the page.

Resizing and Moving a Table

You can resize a table in the same way that you can resize an image. When a table is selected, you can adjust its height and/or width by dragging resize handles. The new width value appears in the Property inspector in the unit (percentage or pixels) specified for the attribute. The height attribute does not appear in the Property inspector because most of the time, it is not necessary to define a height for a table. If you adjust the table's height value, the height attribute is added to the code for the table. You can move a table on the page by cutting and pasting the table or by dragging the table to the new location.

You will adjust the width of the satellite_stage table.

To resize the satellite_stage table:

1. If the rulers are not visible, on the menu bar, click **View**, point to **Rulers**, and then click **Show**.

2. If the rulers' units are not set to pixels, on the menu bar, click **View**, point to **Rulers**, and then click **Pixels**.

3. Click the middle-right resize handle on the table to make the Document window active and keep the table selected. The pointer changes to ⟺.

4. Press and hold the left mouse button, and then drag to the right about **150 pixels** until the pointer is at 600 pixels on the ruler, but do not release the mouse button. A dotted border shows the new dimensions of the table. See Figure 5-41.

Figure 5-41	Table being resized

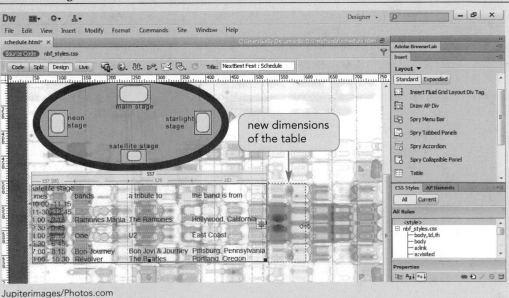

Jupiterimages/Photos.com

Trouble? If the exact numbers on your screen differ from those in Figure 5-41 (in other words, if the table is in a different position relative to the measurements on the rulers), then your screen size is different from the one shown in the figure. Continue with Step 5.

5. Release the mouse button. The Width value in the Property inspector changes, reflecting the larger table size. The table does not need to be this large, so you will try a smaller size.

▶ **6.** Drag the middle-right resize handle on the table to the left about **300 pixels** to reduce the table size. The Width value in the Property inspector reflects the smaller table size. The text is difficult to read in the smaller table, so you will return to the original table size.

▶ **7.** In the Property inspector, double-click in the **W** box, type **450**, press the **Enter** key, and then make sure **pixels** is still selected. The table returns to its original size.

▶ **8.** On the menu bar, click **View**, point to **Rulers**, and then click **Show**. The rulers are hidden.

▶ **9.** Position the pointer in the upper-left corner of the selected table. The pointer changes to ▦.

Trouble? If you have difficulty getting the pointer to change to the correct shape, switch to Expanded Tables mode, repeat Steps 9 through 11, and then return to Standard mode.

▶ **10.** Press and hold the left mouse button, and then drag the table above the map. The table moves to the new location. The original position is more appropriate, so you will move the table back to that location.

Trouble? If there is no blank line between the page heading and the map, release the mouse button when the indicator line is to the left of the map.

▶ **11.** Press the **Ctrl+Z** keys to undo the move, and then save the page.

Deleting a Table

Sometimes you will need to remove a table from a Web page. To delete a table, simply select the table, and then press the Delete key. The table, as well as any content in the table, is removed from the page.

Working with Table Cells

You can customize tables by modifying individual cells or groups of cells. When a cell or a group of cells is selected, you can change its attributes in the Property inspector, including modifying the formatting attributes of the cell content and changing the cell properties.

Modifying Cell Formatting and Layout

Cells have a different set of attributes than tables. You can change the attributes of a selected cell, and the attributes of any content within the cell, in the Property inspector. Cell attributes include text formatting because within a table, content can be contained only in cells.

You can format the content of an entire table by selecting all the cells in the table and then changing the text formatting attributes. Text formatting attributes are not available when you select the table itself because the HTML code for text formatting is in the tags for the individual cells and rows, not in the code for the table itself. This setup allows for formatting variations within cells and makes tables more flexible.

In addition to the familiar text formatting attributes, you can use the following options in the Property inspector to change the cell's layout attributes:

- **Merges selected cells using spans.** The button to join all selected cells into one cell. This button is active only if more than one cell is selected.
- **Splits cell into rows or columns.** The button to divide a single cell into multiple rows or columns. This button is active only when a single cell is selected.
- **Horz.** The horizontal alignment options for the cell's content. Content can be aligned to the browser's default setting, left, right, or center.
- **Vert.** The vertical alignment options for the cell's content. Content can be aligned to the browser's default setting, top, middle, bottom, or baseline.
- **No wrap.** The option to enable or disable word wrapping. Word wrapping enables a cell to expand horizontally and vertically to accommodate added content. If the No wrap check box is checked, the cell will expand only horizontally to accommodate the added content.
- **Header.** The option to format the selected cell or row as a table header. By default, the table header content is bold and centered; however, you can redefine the header cell tag with CSS styles to create a custom look.
- **Bg.** The background color for the selected cells. If no color is specified, the Web page background is seen through the cell. The background color for a cell takes precedence over the background image or color for the table.

When a single cell is selected, the word *Cell* and an icon of a table with a selected cell appear in the lower-left corner of the Property inspector. You can then verify that you have selected the correct element before you begin to adjust the attributes.

You will merge the cells in the top row of the table to use the table header.

To merge the top row and make the new cell the table header:

▶ **1.** Select the cells in the top row of the satellite_stage table.

▶ **2.** In the Property inspector, click the **Merges selected cells using spans** button 🔲. The cells are combined into one.

▶ **3.** In the Property inspector, click the **Header** check box to insert a check mark. The text moves to the center of the table and becomes bold because this is a header cell. See Figure 5-42.

| Figure 5-42 | **Four cells merged into one header cell** |

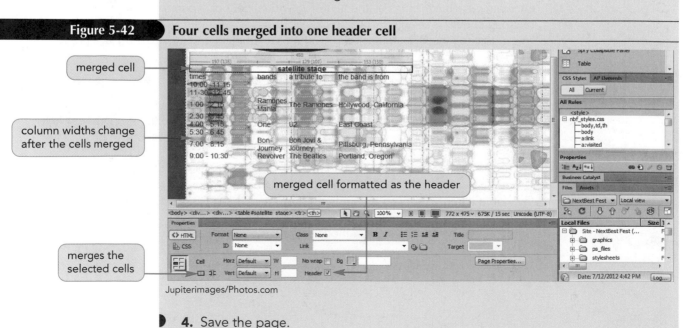

Jupiterimages/Photos.com

▶ **4.** Save the page.

Adjusting Row Span and Column Span of Cells

You can adjust the height and width of individual cells of a table. **Row span** is the height of the cell measured in rows. **Column span** is the width of the cell measured in columns. You can change the row and column spans by increments of one. For example, increasing a cell's row span makes the selected cell span the height of two rows of the table. If you increase the row span of a cell twice, the cell becomes three rows high. Decreasing the row span removes one increment. If a cell is only one row high, decreasing the row span does not work. Adjusting column span works the same way. Increasing the column span of a cell makes the selected cell span the width of two columns of the table. If you increase the column span of a cell twice, it becomes three columns wide. Decreasing the column span removes one increment. If a cell is only one column wide, decreasing the column span does not work.

Working with Rows and Columns

Table rows and columns provide the vertical and horizontal structure for the content of the table as well as for the content of some Web pages. When a row or column is selected, you can change its attributes and resize, add, or delete the entire row or column. Selecting all of the cells in a row or column is the same as selecting the row or column.

Modifying Rows and Columns

The attribute options available for rows and columns are the same as those for cells. When you modify attributes while a row or column is selected, the changes apply to all of the cells in the selected row or column. Before you change attributes, you should verify that the correct element is selected by looking in the Property inspector.

You want to change the second row of the table to a header row.

To change row attributes in the satellite_stage table:

1. In the Document window, select the second row of the satellite_stage table.

2. In the Property inspector, click the **Header** check box to insert a check mark. The content of each cell in the row is centered and in boldface.

3. Save the page.

Resizing Columns and Rows

When a table is created, columns are all of equal width and rows are all the default height. You can adjust the width of a selected column by typing a new value in the W box or by dragging a column's left or right border to the desired position. When you adjust a column width manually, Dreamweaver calculates the width you selected. You can adjust the height of a selected row by typing a new height value into the H box or by dragging the row's top or bottom border to the desired position. When you adjust a row height manually, Dreamweaver calculates the height you selected.

You will resize the columns in the table to better fit the content.

To resize columns in the satellite_stage table:

1. Position the pointer on the right border of the first column. The pointer changes to ◀║▶.

TIP

You can press the Shift key as you drag a row or column border to retain the other row or column sizes.

2. Drag the border to the left so that the first column is approximately **110 pixels**. When you decrease the first column's width, the second column width increases.

   Trouble? If you have difficulty determining the column width, look in the Width box in the Properties inspector. The width changes as you drag the border.

3. Repeat Steps 1 and 2 for each column, dragging the right border so that the second column is **120 pixels**, the third column is **125 pixels**, and the fourth column is **150 pixels** (this will expand the width of your table). See Figure 5-43.

Figure 5-43 | **Resized table columns**

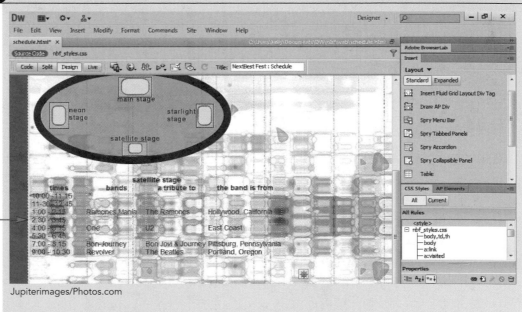

columns better fit the table content

Jupiterimages/Photos.com

4. Save the page.

Adding and Deleting Columns and Rows

As you work, you might find you need more or fewer columns and rows in a table. To insert a column, you select a cell or a column and use the Insert Column command. A new column of the same width as the selected cell or column is inserted to the left of the selection. To insert a row, you select a cell or a row and use the Insert Row command. The new row is added above the selected cell or row. You can also add a new row at the end of the table by clicking in the last cell of the table and pressing the Tab key. You can add multiple columns or rows by using the Insert Rows or Columns command; when you click this command, a dialog box opens and you set the number of columns or rows you want to insert and where you want to insert them relative to the selection.

If you need to remove extra columns or rows, you can select the column or row and then use the Delete Column or Delete Row command. Be aware that all of the content in that column or row is also deleted. You can also press the Delete key to remove a selected column or row and all of its content.

Using CSS to Format a Table

The correct way to format tables is with CSS styles. Although some formatting options are available in the Property inspector when table elements are selected, these table formatting options are deprecated in the current version of HTML. The proper way to format tables is by creating a series of CSS styles and applying those styles to the table elements. You can apply styles to the entire table, rows, columns, cells, and even the table content.

Gage asks you to create two row styles for the table. You will apply these styles to alternating rows of the table.

To format the satellite_stage table with CSS styles:

▶ 1. Create a new CSS rule using **Class** as the selector type, **.row** as the selector name, and defined in the **nbf_styles.css** style sheet.

▶ 2. In the **Background** category, type **#99cbb3** in the Background-color box, and then click the **OK** button. The background color of the table is added to the style. You will apply the new .row style to the satellite_stage table.

▶ 3. Select the first two rows of the table, press and hold the **Ctrl** key as you select every other row in the table, and then release the **Ctrl** key. The first two rows and then alternating rows of the table are selected.

▶ 4. In the Property inspector, click the **Class arrow**, and then click **row**. The .row style is applied to the selected rows. See Figure 5-44.

| Figure 5-44 | Table with the .row style applied to alternating rows |

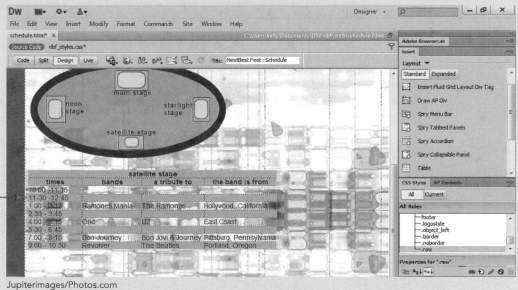

alternating rows with the .row style applied

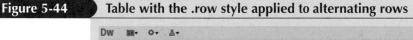

Jupiterimages/Photos.com

▶ 5. Create a new CSS rule using the **Class** selector type, **.row_alt** as the selector name, and defined in the **nbf_styles.css** style sheet.

6. In the **Background** category, type **#663** in the Background-color box, and then click the **OK** button. The second table style is created.

7. Select the third row of the satellite_stage table, press the **Ctrl** key as you select every other row, and then release the **Ctrl** key. You will format the selected rows with the .row_alt style.

8. In the Property inspector, click the **Class arrow**, and then click **.row_alt**. Alternating rows of the table are formatted with the new style.

9. Press the **Right** arrow key to deselect the rows, and then switch to **Live** view. See Figure 5-45.

Figure 5-45   **Table with the new format attributes applied**

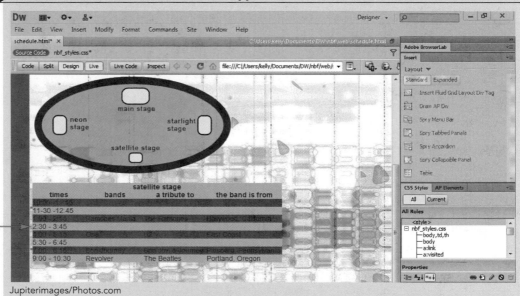

alternating colors added to the table rows

Jupiterimages/Photos.com

10. Turn off **Live** view to return to Design view, save the page and the style sheet, and then preview the schedule.html page in a browser.

11. Close the browser, and then close the schedule.html page.

Exploring the HTML Code of Tables

Four types of tags are associated with tables: table tags, table row tags, cell tags, and header cell tags. Although you can select columns of cells, no HTML tags exist to define columns. All of the tags associated with tables are **bracketing tags**, which consist of an opening tag and a closing tag that bracket the content to which they are applied. The following explains the parameters of these tags:

- **Table tags.** A set of table tags surrounds every table. Table tags take the form:

```
<table attribute1="value" attribute2="value">tags defining table
rows and cells</table>
```

  If you apply attributes to the entire table (when the table is selected), the parameters for those attributes appear in the opening table tag.

- **Table row tags.** A set of row tags surrounds every row. An opening table row tag always appears after the opening table tag because every table must have at least one row. Table row tags take the form:

```
<tr>all the tags for the cells in the row</tr>
```

  If you apply attributes to a row of cells, the parameters for those attributes usually appear in the tags for the cells, not in the tag for the row.

- **Cell tags.** A set of cell tags surrounds every cell (except those cells you designate as header cells). Cell tags are nested inside the row tags. Every table must have at least one cell. Cell tags take the form:

```
<td attribute1="value" attribute2="value">text in the cell</td>
```

  Every cell in the table has its own set of cell tags (unless it is a header cell), and any attributes applied to the cell are contained in the opening cell tag. Attributes that you apply to columns appear in the cell tags for each cell in the column.

- **Header cell tags.** A set of header cell tags surrounds every cell that you designate as a header cell by checking the Header check box in the Property inspector while the cell is selected. Like regular cell tags, header cell tags are nested between the row tags. Header cell tags take the form:

```
<th attribute1="value" attribute2="value">text in the cell</th>
```

- Every header cell in the table has its own set of header cell tags, and any attributes applied to the cell are contained in the opening tag.

  A table might seem complex; however, all table code can be broken down into the four types of tags just described. Figure 5-46 shows the table in the schedule.html page in Code view.

Figure 5-46 Table tags in Code view

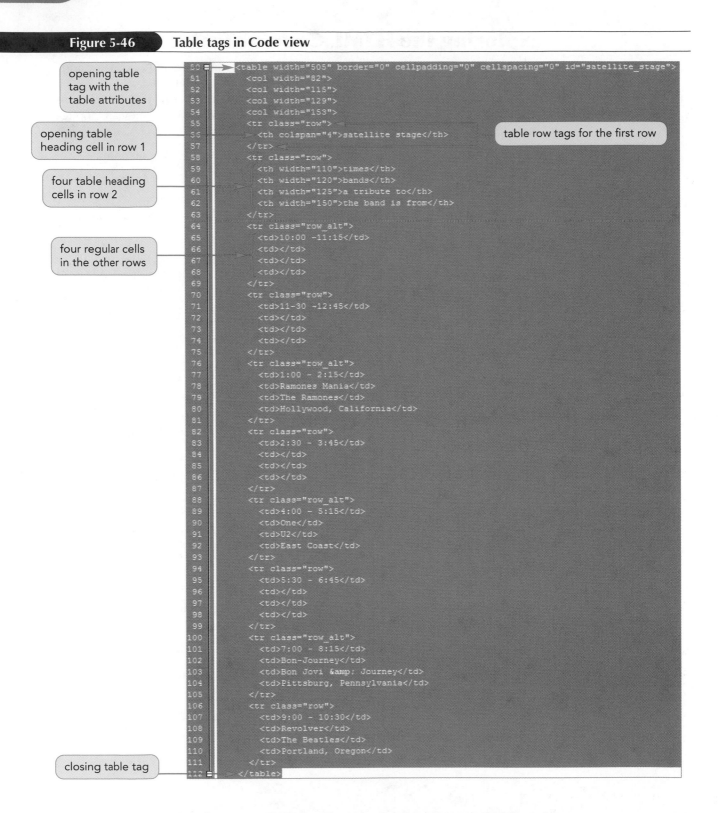

opening table tag with the table attributes	`<table width="505" border="0" cellpadding="0" cellspacing="0" id="satellite_stage">`
	`<col width="82">`
	`<col width="115">`
	`<col width="129">`
	`<col width="153">`
opening table heading cell in row 1	`<tr class="row">`
	`<th colspan="4">satellite stage</th>` — table row tags for the first row
	`</tr>`
four table heading cells in row 2	`<tr class="row">`
	`<th width="110">times</th>`
	`<th width="120">bands</th>`
	`<th width="125">a tribute to</th>`
	`<th width="150">the band is from</th>`
	`</tr>`
four regular cells in the other rows	`<tr class="row_alt">`
	`<td>10:00 -11:15</td>`
	`<td></td>`
	`<td></td>`
	`<td></td>`
	`</tr>`

```
50   <table width="505" border="0" cellpadding="0" cellspacing="0" id="satellite_stage">
51     <col width="82">
52     <col width="115">
53     <col width="129">
54     <col width="153">
55     <tr class="row">
56       <th colspan="4">satellite stage</th>
57     </tr>
58     <tr class="row">
59       <th width="110">times</th>
60       <th width="120">bands</th>
61       <th width="125">a tribute to</th>
62       <th width="150">the band is from</th>
63     </tr>
64     <tr class="row_alt">
65       <td>10:00 -11:15</td>
66       <td></td>
67       <td></td>
68       <td></td>
69     </tr>
70     <tr class="row">
71       <td>11-30 -12:45</td>
72       <td></td>
73       <td></td>
74       <td></td>
75     </tr>
76     <tr class="row_alt">
77       <td>1:00 - 2:15</td>
78       <td>Ramones Mania</td>
79       <td>The Ramones</td>
80       <td>Hollywood, California</td>
81     </tr>
82     <tr class="row">
83       <td>2:30 - 3:45</td>
84       <td></td>
85       <td></td>
86       <td></td>
87     </tr>
88     <tr class="row_alt">
89       <td>4:00 - 5:15</td>
90       <td>One</td>
91       <td>U2</td>
92       <td>East Coast</td>
93     </tr>
94     <tr class="row">
95       <td>5:30 - 6:45</td>
96       <td></td>
97       <td></td>
98       <td></td>
99     </tr>
100    <tr class="row_alt">
101      <td>7:00 - 8:15</td>
102      <td>Bon-Journey</td>
103      <td>Bon Jovi &amp; Journey</td>
104      <td>Pittsburg, Pennsylvania</td>
105    </tr>
106    <tr class="row">
107      <td>9:00 - 10:30</td>
108      <td>Revolver</td>
109      <td>The Beatles</td>
110      <td>Portland, Oregon</td>
111    </tr>
112  </table>
```

closing table tag → (line 112 `</table>`)

Using a Table to Create Page Structure

Designers most often use CSS to provide structure for the layout of Web pages, and use tables only to display tabular data. However, before CSS was fully supported, designers primarily used HTML to create style and structure for pages, which means that tables were frequently used to structure the page layout. You still need to know how to edit tables that are used for layout because some existing Web sites are structured with tables and you might encounter them at some point.

Io become familiar with tables used for layout, you will create a temporary promotional page for a band that will be playing at NextBest Fest. A link from the home page of the site, when clicked, will load the new page in a new browser window. The new page will use tables for structure. It will not have a navigation system because it is a pop-up promotion instead of a regular page in the site. Before you begin, it is a good idea to sketch what you want the page content to look like, just as you did before you added div tags to a page. Planning the page layout enables you to determine where to place the cells and tables on the page so that the information can be conveyed effectively. Figure 5-47 shows a sketch of the layout for the new page.

Figure 5-47	Sketch of the layout for the new page

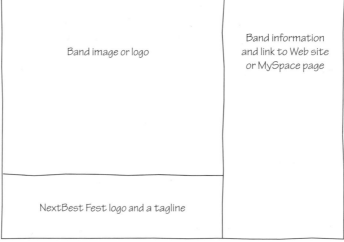

© 2013 Cengage Learning

You will start by creating the hot.html page, adding a page heading, and attaching the external style sheet to the page.

To create the hot.html page and attach the nbf_styles.css style sheet:

1. On the menu bar, click **File**, and then click **New** to open the New Document dialog box.

2. Click **Blank Page** in the left column, click **HTML** in the Page Type column, click **<none>** in the Layout column, select **HTML 5** in the DocType list in the right column, and then click the **Create** button. A new page opens in the Document window.

3. In the Title box on the Document toolbar, type **NextBest Fest - What's Hot**, and then press the **Enter** key. The page title is entered.

4. Save the page as **hot.html** in the local root folder of your NextBest Fest site. The hot.html page appears in the Files panel.

5. In the CSS Styles panel, click the **Attach Style Sheet** button ⊞. The Attach External Style Sheet dialog box opens.

6. If necessary, click the **Browse** button, navigate to the **stylesheets** folder in the local root folder of your NextBest Fest site, and then double-click **nbf_styles.css**. The external style sheet is attached to the hot.html page.

7. Click the **OK** button, and then save the page.

Inserting a Table for Page Structure

Now that you have created a page, you will create the structure for the page content with a table in the same way that you structured page content using divs. You will create a table, add content to the table, and create CSS styles for the table.

To create the table in the hot.html page:

▶ 1. In the **Common** category of the Insert panel, click the **Table** button. The Table dialog box opens.

▶ 2. Create a table that has **2** rows, **2** columns, **90%** table width, **0** border thickness, **5** cell padding, **0** cell spacing, and no header cells, and then click the **OK** button. The table is inserted into the page. See Figure 5-48.

Figure 5-48   **Table for the hot.html page structure**

table information appears below the table when the table is at the top of the page

▶ 3. Select the right column, and then, in the Property inspector, click the **Merges selected cells using spans** button ⊡. The cells are merged.

▶ 4. Click in the merged cell, and then, in the Property inspector, select **Left** from the Horz list, select **Top** from the Vert list, and type **100%** in the W box. The right column expands to fill most of the table.

▶ 5. Click in the upper-left cell, and then, in the Property inspector, select **Center** from the Horz list, select **Bottom** from the Vert list, type **410** in the W box, and type **310** in the H box.

▶ 6. Click in the lower-left cell, and then, in the Property inspector, select **Center** from the Horz list and select **Top** from the Vert list.

▶ 7. Save the page. See Figure 5-49.

| Figure 5-49 | Table with formatted cells |

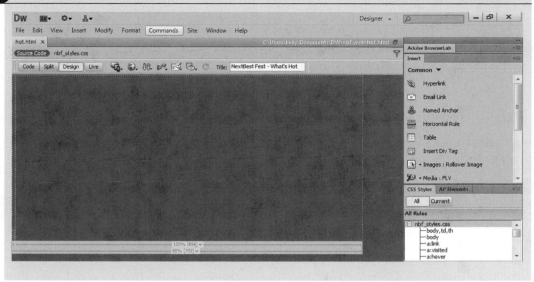

Next, you will create a style with a light green background and a blue border. You will apply the style to the table, and then you will center the table in the hot.html page.

To create a style to format the table in the hot.html page:

1. Create a new CSS rule using **ID** as the selector type, **#hot_table** as the selector name, and defined in the **nbf_styles.css** style sheet.

2. In the **Background** category, type **#000** in the Background-color box.

3. In the **Box** category, in the Margin section, click the **Same for all** check box to remove the check mark, type **0** in the Top box, and then type **auto** in the Right and Left boxes.

4. In the **Border** category, in the Style section, select **solid** from the Top list, in the Width section, select **thin** from the Top list, in the Color section, type **#99cbb3** in the Top box, and then click the **OK** button.

5. In the Document window, select the table, and then, in the Property inspector, click the **ID** arrow and click **hot_table**. The style is applied to the table.

6. In the Document window, click in a blank area to deselect the table. See Figure 5-50.

Figure 5-50 **Table with the #hot_table style applied**

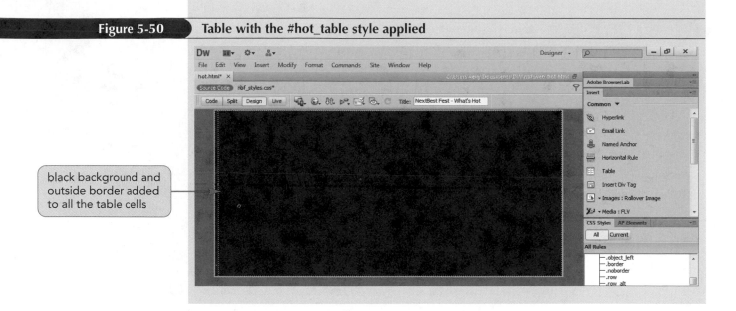

black background and outside border added to all the table cells

Adding Content to a Table for Page Structure

With the table structure in place, you are ready to add content to the table. The content will include both graphics and text. After you insert the first graphic, you will adjust the column to fit snugly against the graphic.

To add content to the table in the hot.html page:

1. Click in the upper-left cell, insert the **bon_journo.jpg** image located in the **Dreamweaver5\Tutorial** folder included with your Data Files, and save a copy of the image in the graphics folder, if necessary.

2. Enter **The logo for Bon-Journo, the featured band.** as the alt text for the graphic.

3. Place the pointer over the dotted line that represents the right border of the first column and drag it as needed until the border is against the image.

4. Click in the right column, type **Bon-Journo is one of the nation's greatest dual tribute bands. The band is dedicated to the music of Bon Jovi and Journey.** (including the period), and then press the **Enter** key.

5. Type **The band is thrilled to be playing at this year's NextBest Fest. Check back soon for a link to the new Bon-Journo Web site and additional tour dates.** (including the period).

6. Select the text you just typed, and then format the selected text as **Heading 2**.

7. Click in the lower-left cell, insert the **nb_logo_2.png** logo located in the graphics folder, and then enter **Logo for the NextBest Fest** as the alt text. The logo Smart Object is inserted into the cell.

8. Place the insertion point after the logo, press the **Shift+Enter** keys to create a new line, type **Look Who's Coming to Play**, and then format the text as **Heading 1**. See Figure 5-51.

Figure 5-51   Content added to the table

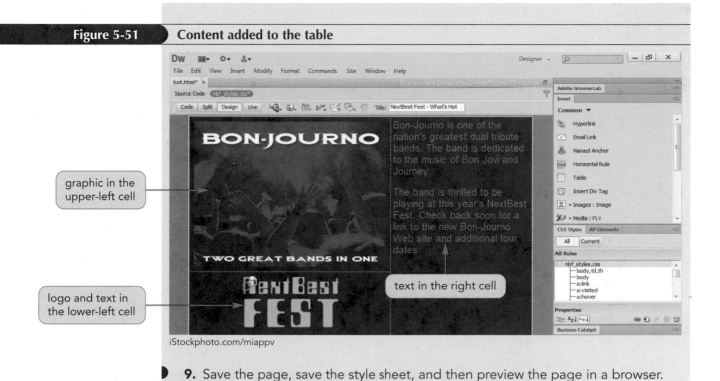

graphic in the upper-left cell

logo and text in the lower-left cell

text in the right cell

iStockphoto.com/miappv

9. Save the page, save the style sheet, and then preview the page in a browser. See Figure 5-52.

Figure 5-52   hot.html page previewed in browser

fixed-width column

adjustable-width column

Used with permission from Microsoft Corporation; iStockphoto.com/miappv

10. Drag the lower-right corner of the browser window to reduce the window size. The table changes size with the browser window.

11. Close the browser, and then close the page.

Next, you will add a link from the lineup.html page to the hot.html page. You will target the hot.html page to open in a new browser window.

To link the lineup.html page to the hot.html page:

1. Open the **lineup.html** page in Design view.

2. Click in the line below the heading text, insert the **hot.png** image located in the **Dreamweaver5\Tutorial** folder included with your Data Files, save a copy of the image in the graphics folder, if necessary, and then enter **Link to the What's Hot page.** as the alt text.

3. Select the **hot.png** graphic, link the graphic to the **hot.html** page, and then select **_blank** in the Target list. The What's Hot page will open in a new browser window.

4. In the Property inspector, click the **Class arrow**, and then click **noborder**. The graphic will not have a border.

5. Save the page, and then preview the page in a browser. See Figure 5-53.

Figure 5-53   Targeted link in the lineup.html page

click to open the hot.html page in a new window

Used with permission from Microsoft Corporation; dean bertoncelj/Shutterstock.com; Jupiterimages/Photos.com

6. Click the **what's hot** link. The hot.html page opens in a new browser tab.

7. Close the browser, and then close any open pages.

Updating the Web Site on the Remote Server

As a final review of the changes you made to the NextBest Fest site, you will update the files on the remote server and review the pages over the Web. You need to upload every page of the site because you have made changes to every page. When you upload the pages, you will also need to include the dependent files so that the new graphics and new CSS styles are uploaded to the remote server. Then you will preview the site on the Web.

To upload and preview the updated remote NextBest Fest site:

▶ 1. Connect to your remote host.

▶ 2. Use the **Put file(s)** button ⬆ to upload the updated pages and new dependent files to your remote site.

▶ 3. Disconnect from your remote site.

▶ 4. In your browser, open the home page of your remote NextBest Fest site.

▶ 5. Preview each of the pages, reviewing the new content and testing the links. The site includes all the new styles and content that you added to the local version.

▶ 6. Close the browser.

In this session, you created a table, added content, and formatted the table in both Standard mode and Extended Tables mode. Gage is pleased with the new pages.

REVIEW

Session 5.3 Quick Check

1. What is a table cell?
2. True or False. Table borders can be invisible.
3. Explain the difference between cell padding and cell spacing.
4. Explain what pressing the Tab key does when you are entering data into a table.
5. Describe what happens when you merge two cells.
6. What is the opening HTML tag for a table row?
7. What is the opening HTML tag for a table cell?
8. True or False. Designers most often use tables only to display tabular data, although they are sometimes still used to structure the page layout.

*Practice the skills
you learned in
the tutorial.*

PRACTICE

Review Assignments

Data Files needed for the Review Assignments: anti_logo.psd, anti_logo_over.psd, anti_logo.jpg, anti_logo_over.jpg, bl_cd.jpg, sc_cd.jpg, bands.docx

Cat wants you to replace the logo text on the home page with a rollover image, and then add that image to every page of the site. If you have Photoshop, you will add a Smart Object; otherwise, you will use JPEG images. You will insert a div that wraps around the new rollover and apply a new style to the div. Cat also wants you to add album images, band names, and band descriptions to the lineup.html page as new bands sign on to play at the fest. You will organize this page content in a table.

1. Open the **antifest** site you modified in Tutorial 4, and then open the **index.html** page in Design view.

2. In the Document window, select the antifest header text and additional blank lines, delete them, and then, in the Common category of the Insert panel, click the Rollover Image button in the Images list.

3. In the Image name box, type **anti_roll**.

4. *If you are using Photoshop:* Create a ps_files folder in the root folder for the site and save a copy of the **anti_logo.psd** and the **anti_logo_over.psd** files located in the Dreamweaver5\Review folder included with your Data Files. Click the Original image Browse button, double-click anti_logo.psd located in the ps_files, set the format as JPEG and the quality to 80, click the OK button, save the JPEG in the graphics folder when prompted, and repeat this process to insert anti_logo_over.psd as the rollover image.

   If you are not using Photoshop: Click the Original image Browse button, double-click **anti_logo.jpg** located in the Dreamweaver5\Review folder included with your Data Files, click the Rollover image Browse button, and then double-click **anti_logo_over.jpg**.

5. In the Alternate text box, type **antifest logo and link to the home page.**

6. In the When clicked, Go to URL box, type **index.html**, and then click the OK button to insert the logo rollover in the page.

7. Create a new Class style named **.center** and defined in the antistyles.css style sheet. In the Block category, select center from the Text-align list, and then click the OK button. (If a dialog box opens, indicating that center is a standard HTML tag, click the Yes button to use the name anyway. This class style won't conflict with the tag.)

8. In the status bar, select the <a> tag (not just the anti_logo image), and then, in the Layout category of the Insert panel, click the Insert Div Tag button.

9. In the Insert Div Tag dialog box, select Wrap around selection, select center from the Class list, and then click the OK button to insert the div around the rollover code. (*Hint:* If the image is not centered, select the <a> tag in the status bar, switch to Code view, remove any extra spaces and so on outside the <a> tags and inside of the div.) Save the page and save the style sheet.

10. In the status bar, select the <div.center> tag to select the div surrounding the roll-over, and then copy the div.

11. Open the **directions.html** page in Design view, select the antifest logo text and any additional spaces, paste the div to replace the text with the logo rollover, and then save and close the page. Repeat this process to replace the logo text with the logo rollover in all the other pages of the site.

12. Open the lineup.html page, select the "coming soon." text, type **As we start to verify our lineup, we will post information about new bands here, so check back frequently.**, and then press the Enter key.

13. In the Common category of the Insert panel, click the Table button. In the Table dialog box, create a table with 3 rows, 3 columns, 100% table width, 0 border thickness, 5 cell padding, 0 cell spacing, no header cells, **Table contains band album artwork, band names, and band descriptions for bands performing at antifest.** as the summary, and then click the OK button to insert the table into the page.

14. Click in the upper-left cell, insert the **bl_cd.jpg** image located in the Dreamweaver5\Review folder, type **black lab cd cover** as the alt text, and then, in the Property inspector, set Horz to Left and set Vert to Top.

15. Click in the first cell of the second row, insert the **sc_cd.jpg** image located in the Dreamweaver5\Review folder, type **sloth child cd cover** as the alt text, and then, in the Property inspector, set Horz to Left and set Vert to Top.

16. Drag the right border of the first column to the left so that it is snug against the album cover art.

17. Click in the second cell of the top row, type **black lab**, apply the h2 tag, set Horz to Left, and then set Vert to Top.

18. Repeat Step 17 to enter and format **sloth child** in the second cell of the second row, and then drag the right border of the second column to the left so that it is snug against the text. (If the footer is over the second row of the table, click in the container div, below the sidebar 1 div, and press Enter if necessary. This should send the footer below the table.)

19. Using Word or another word-processing program, open the **bands.docx** document located in the Dreamweaver5\Review folder, copy the black lab text, paste the text into the table in the first cell of the third column, and then delete the words "Black Lab" at the beginning of the text.

20. Repeat Step 19 to enter the sloth child text in the second cell of the third column.

21. Select the third column of the table, and then set Horz to Left and Vert to Top.

22. Save the page, preview the page in a browser, notice that the table displays the data and information in a logical way, and then close the browser.

23. Upload all the pages and dependent files to your remote server, and then preview the site over the Internet.

24. Submit the finished files to your instructor.

Add a logo rollover and create tables to insert page content for a Web site about a skateboard company.

APPLY

Case Problem 1

Data Files needed for this Case Problem: m_logo.psd, m_logo_over.psd, m_logo.jpg, m_logo_over.jpg, asher.png, corey.png, dustin.png, paris.png

Moebius Skateboards   As you continue working on the Moebius Skateboards site, you will add a rollover containing new logo art to the pages of the site. You will also create a table in the team.html page to organize content, which includes each team member's picture and name.

1. Open the **Moebius Skateboards** site you modified in Tutorial 4, and then open the **index.html** page in Design view.

2. Delete the logo text from the page. In its place, insert a rollover named **moebius_roll**, using the **m_logo.psd** and **m_logo_over.psd** images located in the Dreamweaver5\Case1 folder included with your Data Files, compressed as JPEGs and inserted as Smart Objects, with a link to the index.html page and **Moebius Skateboards logo linked to the home page.** as the alt text. (If you do not have Photoshop, create the rollover using the **m_logo.jpg** and **m_logo_over.jpg** images.) The logo is inserted at the bottom of the page and is centered in the page.

3. Create a new class style named **.noborder** in the moebius.css style sheet, specify 0 width for all in Borders, select the new logo image in the Document window, select the <img#mobius_roll> tag in the status bar, and then apply the noborder style.

4. Select the rollover by clicking the <a> tag in the status bar to select all the code for the rollover, copy the code, and then, in each of the other pages, replace the logo text with the new logo rollover.

5. Save the pages, preview the pages in a browser, testing the rollover link to the home page, and then close the browser and the pages.

6. Open the **team.html** page, and then delete the "check back soon, more is on the way. . ." text.

7. Insert a table that contains 2 rows, 4 columns, 100% table width, 0 border thickness, 5 cell padding, 0 cell spacing, no header, and no accessibility text.

8. In the top row of the table, one in each cell, insert the following four team member images located in the Dreamweaver5\Case1 folder, with alt text *Member Name* **Moebius team member** (replacing *Member Name* with the name from the corresponding image): **asher.png**, **corey.png**, **dustin.png**, and **paris.png**. After inserting an image, drag the right border of the cell to the left until it is snug against the image.

9. In the bottom row of the table, below each image, type the appropriate team member name, and then format the names with the h3 tag.

10. Select the top row of the table, and then set the horizontal alignment to Left and the vertical alignment to Top.

11. Select the bottom row of the table, and then set the horizontal alignment to Center and the vertical alignment to Top.

12. Create a Tag style for the h3 tag that is defined in the moebius.css style sheet, and then, in the Type category, change the color to #919f3d.

13. Save the page, preview the page in a browser, and then close the browser and the page.

14. Upload the site to your remote server, and then preview the pages over the Internet, checking the links and new content.

15. Submit the finished files to your instructor.

Add a logo image
with a hotspot
and a table with
the artwork
of Charles M.
Russell.

APPLY

Case Problem 2

Data Files needed for this Case Problem: cc_head.psd, cc_head.jpg, cowpunching.jpg, grubpile.jpg, utica.jpg, bucker.jpg, art.docx

Cowboy Art Society   Moni wants you to add heading graphics that contain the site logo at the top of the pages in the Cowboy Charlie site. You will create a hotspot over the logo that links to the home page. You will also create a table in the artwork.html page in which you will add images of Charlie's artwork along with painting information and descriptions.

1. Open the **Cowboy Charlie** site you modified in Tutorial 4, and then open the **index.html** page in Design view.
2. In the CSS Styles panel, edit the .header style. In the Box category, set the right and left padding to 0, and in the Positioning category, set overflow to hidden.
3. Delete the logo text in the Document window, create a new **ps_files** folder in the local root folder, and then save a copy of the **cc_head.psd** image located in the Dreamweaver5\Case2 folder included with your Data Files. Insert the cc_head.psd image as a Smart Object, save the compressed image in the JPEG format at 70 quality, and then save a copy in the graphics folder. (If you do not have Photoshop, insert the **cc_head.jpg** image into the page.) Do not add Alternate text; you will add it to the hotspot.
   The logo is inserted at the top of the page and the navigation text shifts down. The image is larger than the page area, but because the div style is set to hide anything that flows over the area of the div, it will not display this way in the browser window. (If the image is not flush against the left border of the div, you need to select the h1 tag and change the formatting to none. This will remove the extra space.)
4. Turn on Live view to ensure that the image will not be visible outside of the div area, and then turn off Live view to return to Design view.
5. Select the image, and then draw a rectangular hotspot that covers the portion of the image inside the div area.
6. Select the hotspot, if necessary, link the hotspot to the index.html page, and then enter **Charles Russell image and link to the home page.** as the alt text.
7. Save the page and the style sheet, select the <div .header> tag in the status bar, and then copy the selected code.
8. Open the **poetry.html** page in Design view, select the <div.header> in the status bar, paste the code, and then save and close the page. You do not need to type alt text for the image because it is covered by the image map.
9. Repeat Step 8 for the remaining pages of the site.
10. Open the **artwork.html** page, delete the text below the Charlie's Art heading text, and then insert a table that has 4 rows, 3 columns, 100% table width, 0 border thickness, 5 cell padding, 0 cell spacing, no header, and **Charles Russell paintings, painting information, and description** as the summary.
11. In the first cell of the first row, insert the **cowpunching.jpg** image located in the Dreamweaver5\Case2 folder, and then enter **Cowpunching Sometimes Spells Trouble** as the alt text. In the first cell of the second row, insert the **utica.jpg** image, and then enter **Utica** as the alt text. In the first cell of the third row, insert the **grubpile.jpg** image, and then enter **Grubpile** as the alt text. In the first cell of the fourth row, insert the **bucker.jpg** image, and then enter **Bucker** as the alt text.
12. Select the first column, and then set the horizontal alignment to Left, set the vertical alignment to Top, and set the width to 150.
13. In Word or another word-processing program, open the **art.docx** document; copy the artist name, painting name, medium, and dimensions for each image; and then paste the content in the corresponding cell in the second column of the table.

14. Select the second column, and then set the horizontal alignment to Center, set the vertical alignment to Top, and set the width to 135.

15. In the art.docx document, copy the text description for each image, and then paste it into the corresponding cell in the third column of the table.

16. Select the third column, and then set the horizontal alignment to Left and set the vertical alignment to Top.

17. Save the page, preview the page in a browser, and then close the browser and any open pages.

18. Upload the site to your remote server, and then preview the pages over the Internet, checking the links and new page content.

19. Submit the finished files to your instructor.

Use Photoshop to insert and modify Smart Objects in the Web pages of a site for a life coach.

CHALLENGE

Case Problem 3

Data Files needed for this Case Problem: tess_head.psd, tess_logo.png, tess_logo_over.png

Success with Tess Tess wants you to insert a heading image in the top of each page of the site. Tess also has a new logo rollover that you will insert into a div and link to the home page of the site. You will use Photoshop to modify the image and then insert the rollover.

1. Open the **Success with Tess** site you modified in Tutorial 4, and then open the **index.html** page in Design view.

2. In Photoshop, open the **tess_head.psd** image located in the Dreamweaver5\Case3 folder included with your Data Files.

⊕ **EXPLORE** 3. In the Tools panel, click the Rectangular Marquee Tool button, select Fixed Size from the Style list at the top of the document window, enter **750px** in the Width box, and then enter **200px** in the Height box.

⊕ **EXPLORE** 4. In the Layers panel, select the head5 layer, make the layer visible by clicking the eye icon at the left of the layer to display the open eye icon, place the pointer at the upper-left corner of the image, and then click the left mouse button. The rectangular marquee surrounds the entire image.

5. Copy the image in Photoshop, and then, in Dreamweaver, paste the image inside the header div at the upper-left corner of the home page.

6. Select JPEG as the format and enter 80 as the quality, and then save a copy of the image to the graphics folder with the name **tess_head5.jpg** in the local root folder. Do not add alt text because the image is purely decorative.

7. Delete the logo div from the page, and then save and close the page.

8. Repeat Steps 3 through 7 to insert the head4 layer into the about_tess.html page, saving the image as **tess_head4.jpg**; to insert the head3 layer into the coaching.html page, saving the image as **tess_head3.jpg**; to insert the head2 layer into the contact.html page, saving the image as **tess_head2.jpg**; and to insert the head1 layer into the specials.html page, saving the image as **tess_head1.jpg** in the graphics folder. (*Hint*: In the Layers panel, click the layer to select it.)

⊕ EXPLORE

9. In the index.html page, draw a new AP div at the upper-right corner of the page.

10. Select the AP div, switch to Code view, drag the new div directly after the opening <div id="header"> tag so that it is embedded in the header div, and then return to Design view.

11. Click in the new AP div, insert a rollover named **logo_roll**, use **tess_logo.png** located in the Dreamweaver5\Case3 folder included with your Data Files as the original image, use **tess_logo_over.png** located in the Dreamweaver5\Case3 folder included with your Data Files as the rollover image, enter **Success with Tess logo and link to the home page.** as the alt text, and then link to the URL index.html. Create a new class style named **.noborder** in the style sheet, set the Borders to 0, and then select the <a> tag surrounding the rollover and apply the new style.

12. Select the AP div, set the left to 650px, set the top to 2px, set the width to 210px, and set the height to 125px. (The logo may appear to move too far to the right; it will display correctly in the browser because the page is centered in the screen.)

13. Select the <div#apDiv1> tag in the status bar, copy the code, open the **about_tess.html** page, click inside the header div (if the image is selected, press the Left arrow key to move the insertion point before the image), paste the apDiv1 div, and then save and close the page. Repeat this process to paste the new div into the rest of the pages in the site.

14. In the CSS Styles panel, select the #header style, change the height to 200px, and then save the style sheet.

15. Save the page, and then preview the site in a browser. (If the logo is displayed outside of the page, it is because your screen is not optimized to display at 1024 × 768. It is important to remember that one of the problems with using AP divs is that they are located in a fixed position and the location is not liquid.)

16. Upload the site to your remote server, and then preview the pages over the Internet.

17. Submit the finished files to your instructor.

Add a rollover graphic and import an Excel worksheet into a table in a Web site for a coffee lounge.

CREATE

Case Problem 4

Data Files needed for this Case Problem: lounge_logo.psd, lounge_logo.png, lounge_logo_over.psd, lounge_logo_over.png, coffee_menu.xlsx

Coffee Lounge   Tommy asks you to add graphics and tables to the Coffee Lounge site. You will add the new Coffee Lounge logo with a rollover linked to the home page to every page of the site. Then, you will import an Excel worksheet containing the new coffee drink menu to the menu page.

1. Open the **Coffee Lounge** site you modified in Tutorial 4, and then open the **index.html** page in Design view.

2. Replace the current logo, if there is one, with a graphic logo with a rollover that links to the home page and includes alternate text. You can use the logo graphics provided by the design team in the Dreamweaver5\Case4 folder included with your Data Files or create your own. The design team has provided the logo and rollover as Photoshop files as well as PNG files (**lounge_logo.psd** or **lounge_logo.png** as the original image and **lounge_logo_over.psd** or **lounge_logo_over.png** as the rollover image). If you have Photoshop, you can modify the provided Photoshop file to match your design.

3. Adjust the CSS style of the head div to accommodate the size and placement of the new rollover image.

4. Copy the logo and its functionality to all the other pages of the site.

 EXPLORE

5. Open the coffee & food page, and then import the **coffee_menu.xlsx** Excel workbook located in the Dreamweaver5\Case4 folder. When you import the workbook, Dreamweaver creates a table to match the structure of the worksheet content.

6. Format the new content, adding new styles as necessary.

7. Save the pages, preview the site in a browser, and then close the browser.

8. Upload the site to your remote server, and then test the pages over the Internet, checking all the links and the added page.

9. Submit the finished files to your instructor.

Creating Reusable Assets and Forms

Creating Meta Tags, Library Items, Templates, and Forms

OBJECTIVES

Session 6.1
- Explore the head content of a page
- Add keywords to a page
- Add a meta description to a page
- Explore libraries and create a library item
- Add a library item to Web pages

Session 6.2
- Create a template
- Create Web pages from a template
- Edit a template
- Create a nested template

Session 6.3
- Add a form to a Web page
- Set form attributes
- Add form objects to a form

Case | *NextBest Fest*

Gage has some additions and changes for the NextBest Fest site. He wants you to add keywords and a meta description to each page, which will be useful when he lists the pages with search engines. He also wants you to convert commonly used site elements, such as the footer, into library items. In addition, he wants you to create templates for the site. Templates will make it simpler to add new pages and update the look and feel of all the existing pages. Finally, he wants to gather some additional information about the users of the NextBest Fest site, and asks you to add a form to the contact.html page that users can fill out and submit.

STARTING DATA FILES

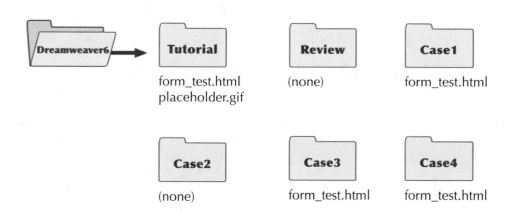

Dreamweaver6 →	Tutorial	Review	Case1
	form_test.html placeholder.gif	(none)	form_test.html

Case2	Case3	Case4
(none)	form_test.html	form_test.html

SESSION 6.1 VISUAL OVERVIEW

Search engines look for information about a page in meta tags included in the head content. A **meta tag** contains information about the page, gives information to the Web server, or adds functionality to the page. The exact purpose of each meta tag is defined by its attributes.

A **keyword** is a descriptive word or phrase that is placed in the meta tag with the attribute name="keywords". You add one keywords meta tag to the head of each page and then list all the keywords for the site in that tag. When someone searches for a word or phrase in a search engine, these keywords may be used to identify pages to display in the search results.

A **meta description** is a short summary of the Web page that is placed in the meta tag with the attribute name="description". Some search engines display the page description pulled from the description meta tag in their search results.

All Web pages contain head content (anything placed within the <head> tags). Head content typically adds functionality to a page when viewed in a browser or provides information about the page for search engines. Head content is not usually visible in a browser.

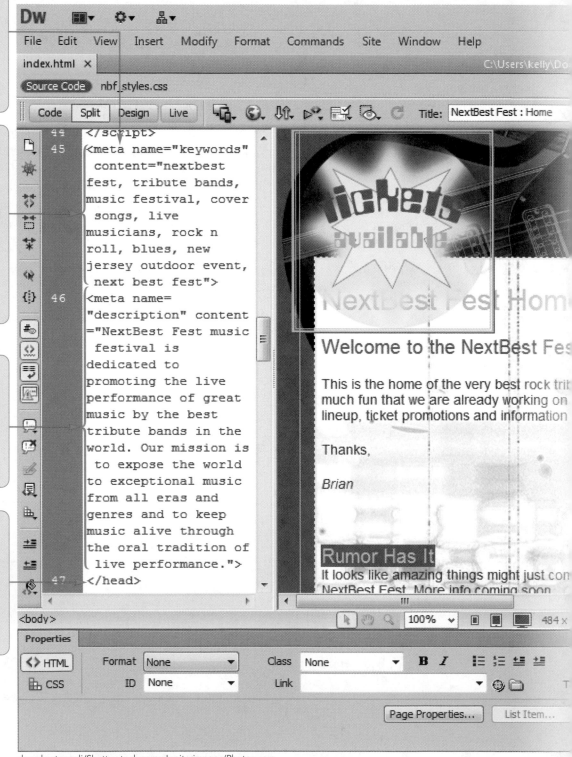

dean bertoncelj/Shutterstock.com; Jupiterimages/Photos.com

META INFORMATION & LIBRARY ITEMS

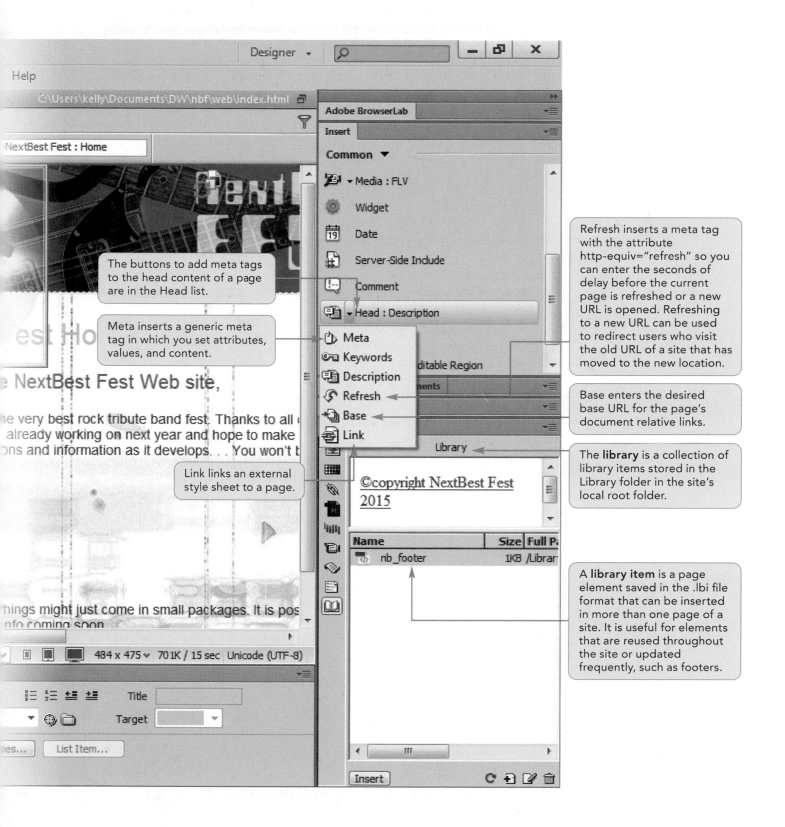

The buttons to add meta tags to the head content of a page are in the Head list.

Meta inserts a generic meta tag in which you set attributes, values, and content.

Link links an external style sheet to a page.

Refresh inserts a meta tag with the attribute http-equiv="refresh" so you can enter the seconds of delay before the current page is refreshed or a new URL is opened. Refreshing to a new URL can be used to redirect users who visit the old URL of a site that has moved to the new location.

Base enters the desired base URL for the page's document relative links.

The **library** is a collection of library items stored in the Library folder in the site's local root folder.

A **library item** is a page element saved in the .lbi file format that can be inserted in more than one page of a site. It is useful for elements that are reused throughout the site or updated frequently, such as footers.

Optimizing Web Pages for Search Engine Placement

Optimizing the pages in a Web site for search engine placement is an important part of designing a Web site because search engines enable people to find the site. Optimizing a page means doing everything you can to the page to ensure that it is ranked highly in targeted search engines. Each search engine has a different set of formulas that determine page placement. These placement formulas change frequently and are a closely guarded secret to prevent designers from using this information to manipulate page placement. Optimizing Web pages does not automatically get them placed in search engines, but the practice will help a site receive higher listings when it is listed. Not having a Web site listed appropriately with search engines is like having a business located in an unmarked building with no published address: There is no way for people to know about the amazing things inside.

Of the many things you can do to optimize Web pages for search engine placement, the two most basic things you should do to every Web page are to add keywords and a meta description to the head content, which is anything placed within the <head> tags. Head content typically adds functionality to a page when viewed in a browser or provides information about the page for search engines. Head content is not usually visible in a browser.

PROSKILLS

Decision Making: Listing a Web Site with Search Engines

Often a Web designer's job includes publicity, search engine placement, and site marketing. You must think strategically to obtain a favorable search engine placement, which includes being placed in listings by the top search engines and obtaining a listing within the first page of results.

You should concentrate on getting a site placed in the top search engines to get the most listings for the site. Although there are hundreds of search engines, three engines direct more than 90 percent of traffic. Some longer-standing top search engines are Google, Bing, and Yahoo!, which as of March 2012 had market shares in the United States of 66.3 percent, 18 percent, and 15.7 percent, respectively (*http://blog.compete.com/2012/04/11/march-2012-us-search-market-share-report*, accessed April 24, 2012). The major search engines also feed information to many smaller engines. Unfortunately, the major search engines sometimes change the way they rank sites, making it more difficult to maintain high rankings. So, as part of your decision-making process, research which search engines have the highest market share and evaluate which search engines your target audience uses most frequently.

To list a site with search engines, go to the Web site for each search engine and follow the listing guidelines provided. You can also pay a service to list the site for you. In addition, some search engines send out **robots** (also called bots and spiders), software that searches the Web and sends information back to the engine, to compile the information used to list pages in the search engines. Because robots might not find your site on their own, it is important to submit a site listing to each search engine you want a site to be listed with. The site listing tells the search engine to dispatch a robot to index your site content. To maintain a favorable listing position, you must list the pages yourself or pay a service to list them for you. Finally, be sure to relist the pages in the site with each engine to maintain a favorable position. Some engines allow you to relist pages monthly, whereas others prefer that you relist only a few times a year. Guidelines for relisting pages can be found with the listing information on the Web site for each major search engine.

Choosing the right search engines, following the listing guidelines, and continuing to evaluate and relist sites helps your site maintain a favorable listing position.

Adding and Editing Keywords

Keywords are one of the elements some search engines use to index Web pages, although their importance has diminished. A keyword is a descriptive word or phrase that is placed in the meta tag with the attribute name="keywords". You add one keywords meta tag to the head of each page, and then list all the keywords for the site in that tag. When people search for a word or phrase in a search engine, the keywords in the meta tag are used to track and identify the pages to display in the search results.

The keywords you choose should be the words you think most people will type into search engines to look for that site or the words you want people to find the site under. Be sure to include all of the words and phrases the target audience would use to do a general search for the product or service the site promotes even if they do not know the company exists. Remember to include the name of the company and products or services in the list. It can also be helpful to include common misspellings of the company or product name. For example, good keywords for the NextBest Fest site are "NextBest Fest," "tribute festival," and the names of the participating bands.

Keywords can be individual words or short phrases that are fewer than six words. (Some search engines might penalize you for adding longer phrases by decreasing your ranking order or by dropping your site from the index.) When you use phrases, generally each word is indexed separately and together. For example, if you use the phrase *tribute music* for the site, the word *tribute* and the word *music* will both be indexed as well as the phrase *tribute music*. Also, the root of the word is indexed as well; for example, if you include the word *jazzy*, the word *jazz* is also indexed.

You can use as many keywords as you would like; however, many search engines use only the first 10 words in the keywords list to index a site. So make sure that the first 10 words listed are the most important keywords for the site. Additionally, search engines often give higher placement to sites that use the keywords within the page content, page titles, navigation system, text links, and image names, so make sure that the Web site contains the keywords many times. For example, because the NextBest Fest site uses the words *tribute* and *music* many times within the text of the pages, its pages may be ranked higher in value under these keywords than the pages of a site that use these same keywords but page content does not actually include these words. A more extreme example is if you used the word *hippopotamus* in the keywords list for the pages in the NextBest Fest. The pages might receive a lower ranking under that keyword because the word *hippopotamus* never appears in the page content. Conversely, using the keywords excessively in the page content of a site can lead to penalties, including decreased ranking of the site or complete removal of the site from the index because many search engines see this as an attempt at spamming or attempting to artificially inflate the site's listing position.

INSIGHT

Researching Search Engine Optimization

Search engine optimization (SEO) standards are constantly changing. It is a good idea to review current trends before choosing the keywords for a site. You can find current information by using your favorite search engine to search on the following keywords: "current search engine optimization trends" or "seo trends" or "optimization guidelines." The search results will also include placement companies that have used these keywords to attract new clients.

Some placement techniques are considered unethical (referred to as *black hat*) and usually work only until the search engines discover them. The search engines then disallow these techniques and decrease the ranking of pages that use them. Ethical placement techniques are often referred to as *white hat* techniques.

In recent years, meta keywords have become less important to search engine ranking than page content. You should still include meta keywords in a site because they might be important to some search engines and won't hurt the site's ranking.

Adding Keywords and Exploring the HTML Code

Although you can type the meta keywords tag directly in Code view, it is simpler to use a dialog box to list the keywords for a page and let Dreamweaver create the code. When entering keywords, you should use all lowercase letters because in most search engines, lowercase letters represent both uppercase and lowercase letters, whereas uppercase letters make an item case specific. You should also separate each word or phrase with a comma. When you add keywords to a page, the following code is inserted into the head of the page:

```
<meta name="keywords" content="keyword1, keyword2, keyword3">
```

Meta tags are unpaired tags, which means that each tag stands alone and not as part of a set of opening and closing tags. Like all tags, the meta tag starts with an opening bracket followed by the name of the tag, *meta*. The tag name is followed by a series of tag attributes and values. The first attribute in the keywords meta tag is *name* and its value is the type of meta tag, *"keywords"*. The second attribute is *content* and its value is the content of the tag, or the list of keywords. The tag ends with a forward slash and a closing bracket.

You will insert the list of keywords into the NextBest Fest home page.

To add keywords to the NextBest Fest home page:

▶ 1. Reset the Dreamweaver workspace to the **Designer** configuration, collapse the Business Catalyst panel, expand the Files panel, open the **NextBest Fest** site you modified in Tutorial 5, and then open the **index.html** page in Design view.

▶ 2. In the **Common** category of the Insert panel, click the **Head button arrow**, and then click the **Keywords** button. The Keywords dialog box opens so you can type the words you want. Remember to use all lowercase letters and to separate each word or phrase with a comma.

▶ 3. In the Keywords box, type **nextbest fest, tribute bands, music festival, cover songs, live musicians, rock n roll, blues, new jersey outdoor event,** (including the final comma). See Figure 6-1.

Figure 6-1 **Keywords dialog box**

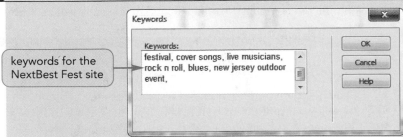

keywords for the NextBest Fest site

▶ 4. Click the **OK** button, and then save the home page. The meta keywords tag is added to the head of the page. Its exact location within the head content depends on where the insertion point was located in the page when you clicked the Keywords button.

TIP

You can also enter or edit the keywords list directly in Code view.

5. Switch to **Code** view, and then scroll, if necessary, to view the meta keywords tag in the Document window. The tag is located in the head section at the top of the page.

6. In the Document window, click in the meta keywords tag, and then, in the status bar, click the **<meta>** tag. The <meta> tag is selected in the status bar and the Document window, and the list of keywords appears in the Property inspector. See Figure 6-2.

Figure 6-2   **Meta keywords tag in Code view**

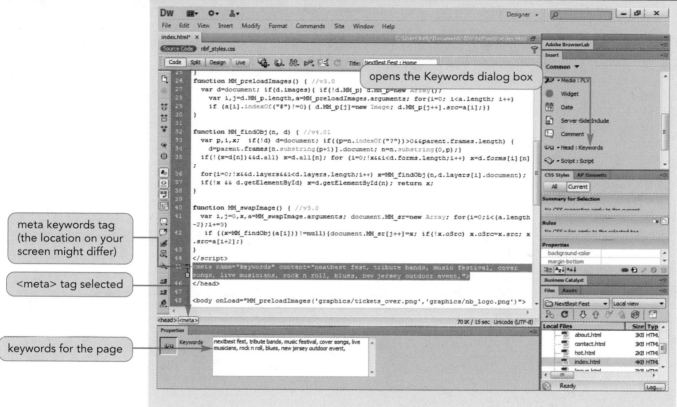

meta keywords tag (the location on your screen might differ)

<meta> tag selected

keywords for the page

Editing Keywords

Sometimes, you will want to add another keyword to the list, delete a keyword from the list, or correct the spelling of a keyword in the list. You can do any of these by editing the list of keywords that has already been added to a page.

Gage's research shows that NextBest Fest is frequently mistyped as "next best fest." You will add this misspelling to the list of keywords in the home page.

To edit the list of keywords:

1. In the Property inspector, click after the last comma in the Keywords box, press the **Spacebar**, and then type **next best fest**. The new keyword is added in the Property inspector, but is not yet added to the code.

2. In the Document window, click outside the meta keywords tag, and then click in the meta keywords tag again. The updated keywords list appears in the code and the Property inspector.

3. On the status bar, click the **<meta>** tag. The meta keywords tag is selected in the Document window. See Figure 6-3.

| Figure 6-3 | **Edited keywords list** |

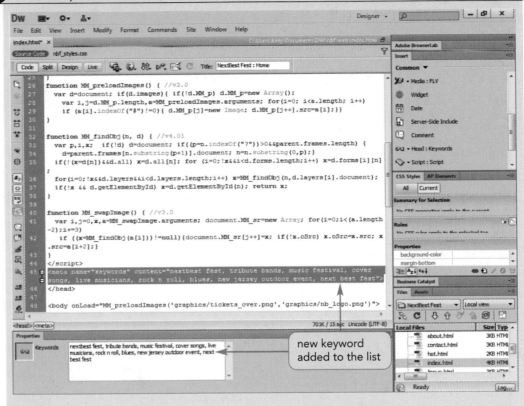

4. Save the home page.

Adding and Editing a Meta Description

Many search engines also use the meta description to index Web pages. A meta description is a short summary of the Web page or site that is placed in the meta tag with the attribute *name="description"*. The description should contain a concise summary of the page or site's content and goals. For example, the NextBest Fest site description will be "NextBest Fest music festival is dedicated to promoting the live performance of great music by the best tribute bands in the world. Our mission is to expose the world to exceptional music from all eras and genres and to keep music alive through the oral tradition of live performance." Some search engines also display the first part of the description in the search results page when a user looks up a word or phrase. Therefore, it is a good idea to use the first line or two of the description as a short caption for the site. Think of it as a newspaper headline, summarizing the highlights of the page content. Some engines also penalize a page with very long descriptions, so you should make your description fairly short—no more than six average lines of text.

Adding a Meta Description and Exploring the HTML Code

When you add the meta description, be sure to use standard capitalization, spelling, grammar, and punctuation for ease of reading. Users quickly scan search results looking for a particular topic or site and might skip difficult-to-read descriptions. The meta description tag is similar to the meta keywords tag:

```
<meta name="description"  content="The description text goes here.">
```

The tag begins with an opening bracket followed by the name of the tag, *meta*. The *name* attribute has the value of *"description"* to specify that this tag provides a summary of the Web site. The value of the *content* attribute is the description text. The tag ends with a forward slash and a closing bracket.

You will add a meta description for the NextBest Fest site to the home page.

To add a meta description to the home page:

▶ 1. In the Document window, click at the end of the meta keywords tag (to the right of ...*next best fest*">), and then press the **Enter** key. The insertion point is positioned below the keywords, which is where you will add the meta description.

▶ 2. In the **Common** category of the Insert panel, click the **Head button arrow**, and then click the **Description** button. The Description dialog box opens.

▶ 3. In the Description box, type **NextBest Fest music festival is dedicated to promoting the live performance of great music by the best tribute bands in the world. Our mission is to expose the world to exceptional music from all eras and genres and to keep music alive through the oral tradition of live performance.** (including the period). See Figure 6-4.

Figure 6-4 **Description dialog box**

meta description for the NextBest Fest site

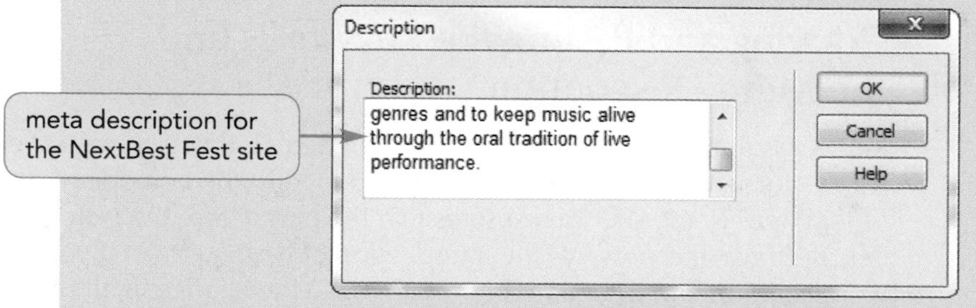

▶ 4. Click the **OK** button. The description appears below the keywords in the Document window.

▶ 5. In the Property inspector, click the **Refresh** button, if necessary.

▶ 6. In the Document window, click in the meta description tag, and then, in the status bar, click the **<meta>** tag. The description appears in the Property inspector, and the meta tag is selected in the Document window. See Figure 6-5.

TIP

To edit a meta description, click in the description in the Document window in Code view, and then change the description in the Property inspector or the Document window.

Figure 6-5 **Meta description tag in Code view**

meta description tag

description in the Property inspector

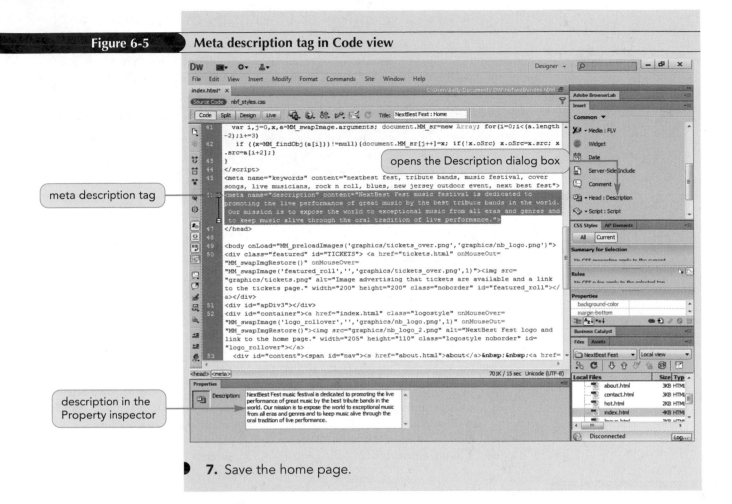

7. Save the home page.

Copying and Pasting the Keywords and the Meta Description

Keywords and descriptions should be added to all the pages of a Web site. Rather than retype the same text, you can copy the code from the home page and paste it into the other pages in the site. This ensures that the pages have the exact same keywords and descriptions, and prevents the introduction of typing errors. If you later update the keywords and meta description, be sure to make the change in all of the pages.

You will add the keywords and description to the other pages of the NextBest Fest site.

To copy and paste the keywords and the description into the other pages:

1. In Code view, select the meta keywords and description tags, right-click the selected tags, and then click **Copy** on the context menu.

2. Open the **about.html** page in Code view, place the insertion point after the meta charset tag at the top of the page, and then press the **Enter** key. You will add the keywords and description on the new, blank line.

3. Right-click the blank line you just inserted, and then click **Paste** on the context menu. The meta keywords and description tags are added in the blank line.

4. In the Property inspector, click the **Refresh** button. The code is updated. See Figure 6-6.

Figure 6-6 | **Meta tags added to the about.html page**

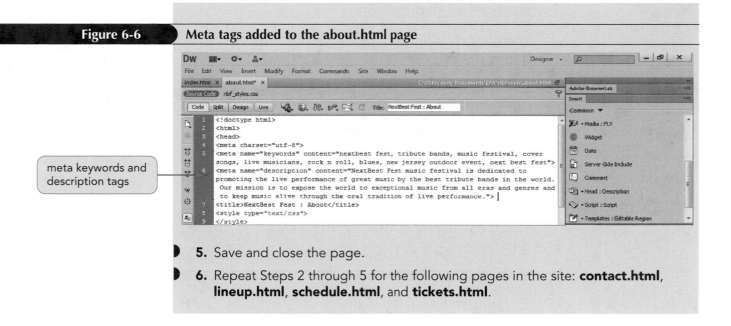

meta keywords and description tags

5. Save and close the page.

6. Repeat Steps 2 through 5 for the following pages in the site: **contact.html**, **lineup.html**, **schedule.html**, and **tickets.html**.

Using Library Items

Sometimes you need to add the same element to many pages of a site. To save time and ensure consistency, you can save the element as a library item. A library item is a page element saved in the .lbi file format that can be inserted in more than one page of a site. A library item can include most elements in the body of a Web page, including bits of code, text, images, tables, forms, and formatting. You cannot create a library item for head content. So, a library item cannot contain the meta description or the meta keywords. Library items are stored in the library, which is a folder that Dreamweaver adds to the local root folder when you create the first library item for the site.

The library and library items are Dreamweaver authoring tools. This means that unlike other items that you have added to pages (CSS styles, for example), libraries and library items do not exist outside Dreamweaver. When you upload the site to a remote server, you do not need to upload the Library folder because each page that includes a library item contains the corresponding library item code.

INSIGHT

Creating Library Items for Page Elements

Library items help you automate site design and decrease redundant work. You should create library items for any element that you intend to reuse in several pages of a site or update frequently such as footers or a list of upcoming events. Using library items not only saves you time, but it also ensures consistency of those elements throughout the site. Repeated elements are often placed in the same location on all pages. It is a good idea to delete unused library items from the library to keep your site uncluttered and well organized.

Creating a Library Item

You can create as many library items as you need for a site. To create a library item, you simply create the element in a page; select all the text, the formatting elements, and anything else you want to include in the library item; drag the selected element to the library; and then name the library item. Choose a descriptive name that will help you identify the content of the library item. As with other filenames, use only alphanumeric characters, do not use spaces or special characters, and do not start the name with a number. Every library item is saved in the .lbi file format.

When you create the page element for a library item, you can format the element with CSS styles. The library item will display the CSS styles only if the style sheet with those rule definitions is attached to the page in which the library item is inserted. If you use one style sheet for a site, as you do with the NextBest Fest site, the library item will look the same in all the pages. If you use two or more style sheets that define a style in different ways, the library item can have various looks, depending on which style sheet is attached to a page.

REFERENCE

Creating a Library Item

- Create the page element to use for the library item.
- Drag the selected page element to the library in the Assets panel.
- Type a name for the new library item, and then press the Enter key.

or

- On the Assets panel toolbar, click the Library button.
- In the Assets panel, click the New Library Item button.
- Type a name for the new library item, and then press the Enter key.
- In the Assets panel, click the Edit button.
- Create the page element you want as the new library item.
- Save and close the library item.

You will create a library item for the footer in the NextBest Fest pages that includes the footer text, formatting, and a link.

To create a library item for the NextBest Fest footer:

1. Switch to **Design** view, scroll to the bottom of the home page, and then select the footer text.

2. Collapse any open panels except the Files panel group, and then click the **Assets** tab in the Files panel group. The Assets panel appears.

3. On the Assets panel toolbar, click the **Library** button 📖. The library appears in the Assets panel.

4. Drag the selected footer to the library and then click the **OK** button if a dialog box opens warning that the selection may not look the same when placed in other documents. An untitled library item is added to the library. See Figure 6-7.

Figure 6-7   Library displayed in the Assets panel

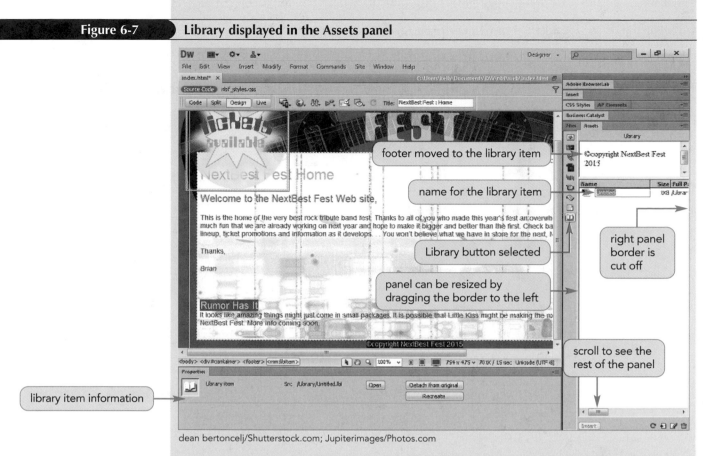

dean bertoncelj/Shutterstock.com; Jupiterimages/Photos.com

5. Type **nb_footer**, and then press the **Enter** key to name the library item.

6. Click in the Document window, and then press the **Right** arrow key to deselect the footer, if necessary. The footer is highlighted in yellow, indicating that it is a library item. See Figure 6-8.

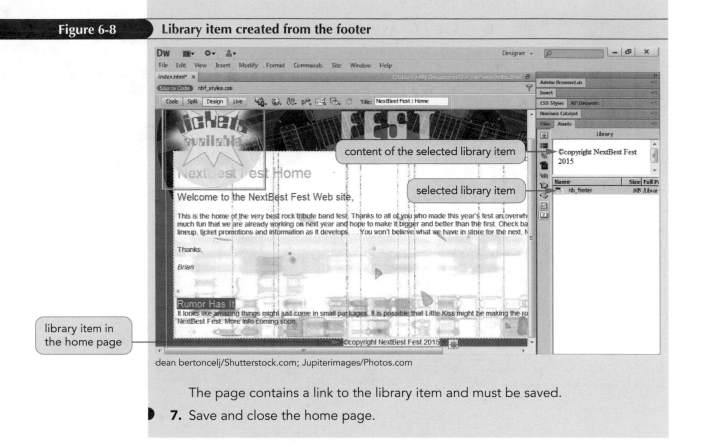

Figure 6-8 | Library item created from the footer

dean bertoncelj/Shutterstock.com; Jupiterimages/Photos.com

The page contains a link to the library item and must be saved.

7. Save and close the home page.

Adding a Library Item to Web Pages

You can add a library item to any page in the Web site. You can add the same library item to a page as many times as you want, and you can add as many different library items to a page as you need.

You will add the nb_footer library item to the other pages of the NextBest Fest site.

To add the footer library item to the rest of the NextBest Fest pages:

1. Display the Files panel, and then open the **about.html** page in Design view.

2. Display the library in the Assets panel.

3. Drag the **nb_footer** library item from the Assets panel to the right of the footer text at the bottom of the about.html page. The nb_footer library item is inserted in the page.

4. Select the original footer text, and then press the **Delete** key. The original footer is removed from the page.

5. Save the page, and then close it.

6. Repeat Steps 1 through 5 to add the nb_footer library item to each of the following pages: **contact.html**, **lineup.html**, **schedule.html**, and **tickets.html**.

Exploring the Code for a Library Item

When you include a library item in a Web page, the HTML code for the element is inserted into the page along with a hidden link to the library item. The nb_footer library item has the following code:

```
<!-- #BeginLibraryItem "/Library/nb_footer.lbi" -->&copy;
copyright NextBest Fest 2015 <!-- #EndLibraryItem -->
```

The library item starts with a comment tag. Comment tags are unpaired tags that are used to add notes to the code. Comment tags are used to denote library items because they do not appear in the page, affect the way the HTML is rendered, or cause problems even if the page is edited in another program. Every library item begins with a comment tag that tells Dreamweaver that a library item has started, <!--#BeginLibraryItem, includes a path to that library item, "/Library/nb_footer.lbi", followed by two dashes and the closing bracket of the comment tag. All code for the page element in the library item follows the comment tag. Each library item ends with a second comment tag that tells Dreamweaver the library item is ending, <!--#EndLibraryItem-->.

You will view the code for the nb_footer library item in the about.html page.

To view the nb_footer library item code in the about.html page:

▶ **1.** Open the **about.html** page in Design view.

▶ **2.** In the Document window, select the footer, and then switch to **Code** view. The code for the nb_footer library item is selected in the Code pane. See Figure 6-9.

| Figure 6-9 | Code for the nb_footer library item |

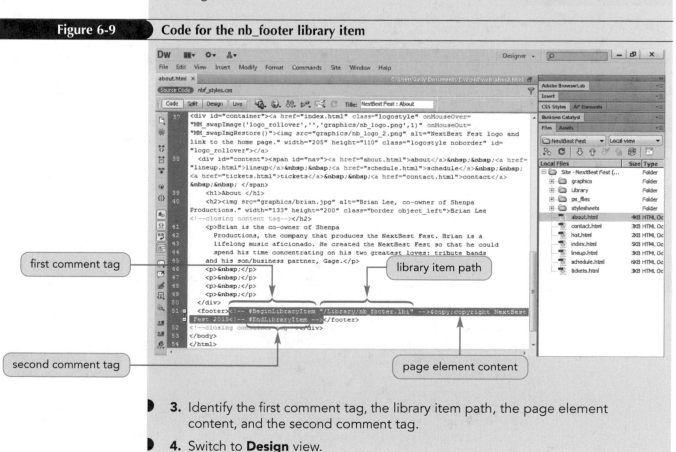

▶ **3.** Identify the first comment tag, the library item path, the page element content, and the second comment tag.

▶ **4.** Switch to **Design** view.

Editing a Library Item

When you edit a library item, every instance of the library item in the site is updated at one time. This is faster and more accurate than editing the same element in many pages. For example, to change the footer content to include an email link, you make the change only once in the library item and Dreamweaver changes the footer in every page that includes the footer library item. An **email link** is a link in a browser window that a user can click to start his or her default email program and open a blank message window with the email address from the link entered in the To field; it is also referred to as a mailto link. To create a unique version of the library item, such as changing the footer content on only one page, you must replace the library item with the unique version.

Gage wants the footer to include an email link so users can quickly contact the company. This way, users can easily provide feedback about the site or request information.

To edit the nb_footer library item:

> **1.** With the nb_footer library item selected in the Document window, click the **Open** button in the Property inspector. The nb_footer library item opens in the Document window. The text is not styled because the style sheet is not attached to the library item. When you view the library item in the pages, it will again display the appropriate style. See Figure 6-10.

Figure 6-10   **Document window with the nb_footer library item**

nb_footer library item

footer text without the style sheet attached

> **2.** In the Document window, select the footer text. You will change the text to an email link.

> **3.** In the Property inspector, type **mailto:info@nextbestfest.com** in the Link box, press the **Enter** key, and then, in the Document window, deselect the text. See Figure 6-11.

Figure 6-11   **nb_footer library item with linked text**

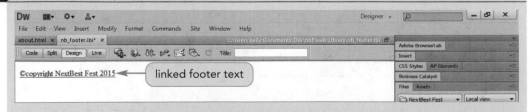

linked footer text

> **4.** Save the nb_footer library item. The Update Library Items dialog box opens, listing all the pages that contain the library item. See Figure 6-12.

Figure 6-12   Update Library Items dialog box

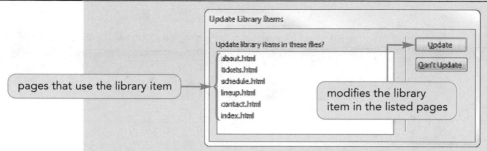

pages that use the library item

modifies the library item in the listed pages

5. Click the **Update** button to update the library item in the listed pages. Dreamweaver updates all the pages that contain the library item and the Update Pages dialog box opens.

6. Click the **Show log** check box to insert a check mark, if necessary. The log of updates appears in the dialog box. See Figure 6-13.

Figure 6-13   Update Pages dialog box

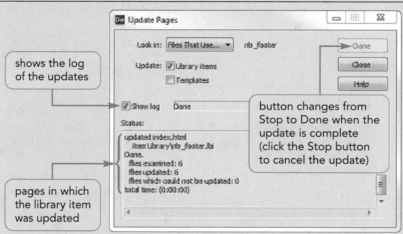

shows the log of the updates

pages in which the library item was updated

button changes from Stop to Done when the update is complete (click the Stop button to cancel the update)

7. Click the **Close** button to close the dialog box, and then close the nb_footer library item.

8. Scroll to the bottom of the about.html page, if necessary. The footer is a link and is displayed with the appropriate CSS styles.

9. Save the page, and then preview the page in a browser. The link is difficult to see against the gray background. You will create a compound style to fix this after you test the link. See Figure 6-14.

Figure 6-14   **Preview of the about.html page with the email link footer**

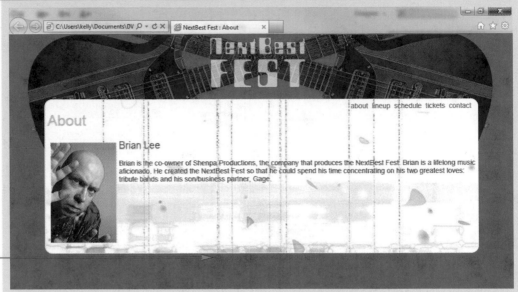

email link in the footer is difficult to see against the gray background

Used with permission from Microsoft Corporation; dean bertoncelj/Shutterstock.com; Jupiterimages/Photos.com; iStockphoto.com/upsidedowndog

10. Click the **footer** link to test the email link (a message window opens with the email addressed to info@nextbestfest.com), close the message window, and then close the browser.

    Trouble? If a message window does not open, an email program might not be installed or configured on your computer. Close any dialog boxes and windows that open, and then continue with Step 11, but do not test the footer in the other pages.

11. Using the CSS Styles panel, create a new CSS rule with a **Compound** selector type named **footer a:link, footer a:visited** and defined in the **nbf_styles.css** style sheet, and then click the **OK** button.

12. In the **Type** category, change the color to **#cff**, and then click the **OK** button. The compound style enables you to specify that the linked and visited state of a tag changes color only when it is located in the footer div. The text in the library item is now accessible to visually impaired people.

13. Save the style sheet.

14. Preview the about.html page in a browser, test the footer, and then close the message window.

15. In the browser window, go to the home page, test the footer, and then close the message window. Because the footer is a library item, it will look and function the same in all the pages.

16. Close the browser, and then close the page.

Deleting a Library Item

You can delete a library item from Web pages or from the library. If a library item is no longer needed in a specific page, you can delete it from the page by selecting the library item in the page and then pressing the Delete key. That instance of the library item is deleted, but the library item remains available in the library. If a library item is no longer needed anywhere in a site, you can delete it from the library by selecting the library item in the library and clicking the Delete button in the Assets panel. If you delete a library item from the site that is still being used in some pages, the content of the library item remains in those pages, but is no longer a library item.

In this session, you added the keywords and description meta tags to the head content of pages and you added a library item to the NextBest Fest site. In the next session, you will create templates for the site.

REVIEW

Session 6.1 Quick Check

1. What does optimizing a Web page mean?
2. What is a meta tag?
3. True or False. Head content is usually visible in a browser.
4. What are keywords?
5. What is a meta description?
6. What are library items?
7. What type of tag begins and ends the code for a library item?
8. Why are library items useful?

SESSION 6.2 VISUAL OVERVIEW

A **template** is a special page that separates the look and layout of a page from its content by "locking" the page layout. You designate what is locked in a page by creating editable regions and noneditable regions.

Editable regions are areas that can be changed in pages created from a template. They have a turquoise tab and border in Dreamweaver.

A **repeating region** is a region that can be duplicated within pages made from the template, so that the region can expand without altering the page design.

Noneditable regions are areas that can be changed in the template, but not in the pages created from a template. Any area that is not specifically designated as editable is a noneditable region.

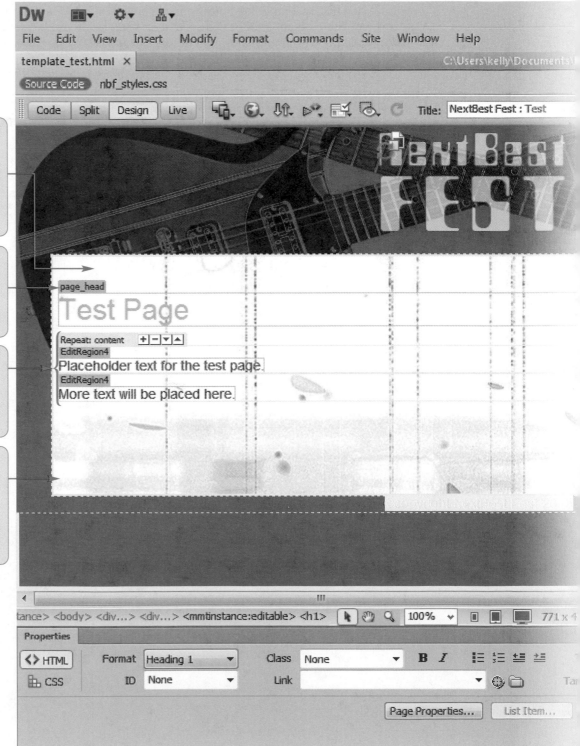

dean bertoncelj/Shutterstock.com; Jupiterimages/Photos.com

CREATING AND USING TEMPLATES

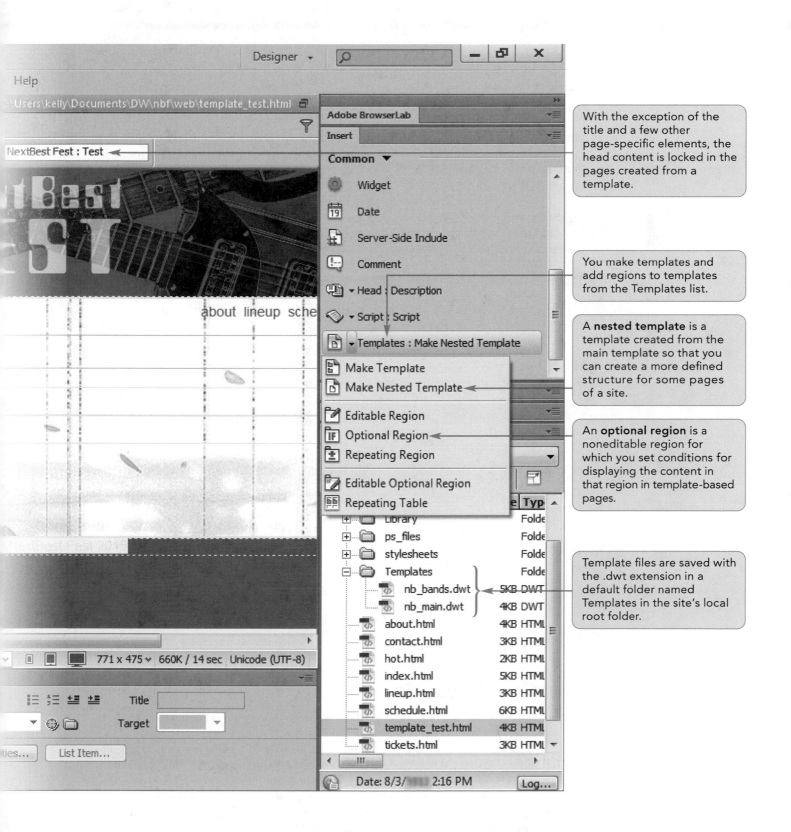

With the exception of the title and a few other page-specific elements, the head content is locked in the pages created from a template.

You make templates and add regions to templates from the Templates list.

A **nested template** is a template created from the main template so that you can create a more defined structure for some pages of a site.

An **optional region** is a noneditable region for which you set conditions for displaying the content in that region in template-based pages.

Template files are saved with the .dwt extension in a default folder named Templates in the site's local root folder.

Understanding Templates

Professional designers sometimes plan and design Web sites based on templates. A template is a special page that separates the look and layout of a page from its content by "locking" the page layout. A template is used to create multiple Web pages that share the same layout, use the same attached style sheet, and contain the same content. Elements that appear in every page of the site, such as the page background, the logo, the navigation bar, and the footer, are placed in the noneditable regions of the template. Elements that vary from page to page, such as the page heading and unique content, are included in editable regions. The style sheet that is attached to the template will be attached to all of the pages created from the template. Because the pages in the NextBest Fest site have a consistent layout and design, you will create a template for the site.

Templates, like style sheets, reduce much of the redundant work that goes into creating and maintaining a Web site. You set up the page layout only once in the template. Then, anyone can use that template to quickly create new pages with that layout. The content added to the pages does not affect the layout or design. If you later decide to modify the page layout, you need to make the changes only in the template. All of the template-based pages that are connected to the template are updated to reflect the changes. This saves you time and ensures consistency across the pages.

INSIGHT

Creating Multiple Templates for a Site

A site usually has only one main template, but you can use more than one main template if some pages have distinctly different styles. For example, if Gage wants the NextBest Fest site to highlight each band playing at the fest on a separate Web page with a different look and feel than the other pages, you could create a second main template. Using more than two main templates in one site is generally not a good idea because the site can get cumbersome and confusing. In addition, it is easy to forget to make changes that affect the whole site to every template. So, carefully consider whether you really need to use a second template in a site.

Also, you should create a new template for each site. Copying a template from one site to another causes all of the relative links in the template (including links to graphics and other materials used in the template) to become absolute links. To use the template in the new site, you must change the links to relative links and copy the materials used in the template to the new site's local root directory. Likewise, choosing a template from another site when you create a new Web page causes the same problems, and does not move a copy of the template to the new site. It also places the links in a locked area of the template so you cannot change them (unless you remember to uncheck the Update page when template changes check box), so you will not be able to view the template content when you post the new page to the Web. Because of these problems, you should create a new template for each site.

Creating a Template

Templates can be created from a new blank page or an existing page in a site. When you create a template from a blank page, you must add all the elements you want to include in pages made from the template. In the NextBest Fest site, for example, you must attach the CSS style sheet to the template, create any new CSS styles you plan to use, insert the logo at the top of the template page, and add the keywords and meta description. When you create a template from an existing page, all of these shared elements are already in the page. The page from which you created the template is unaffected and is not attached to the template.

Decision Making: Planning a Template

Creating a template requires more planning and forethought than creating individual pages. You must thoroughly plan the page layout before creating the site to ensure that you set up the appropriate editable regions—the only regions that can contain unique page content. For example, the template for the NextBest Fest site needs an editable region for the page heading, which is unique content that appears in the same location on every page. You also need an editable region for the unique page content that appears below the page heading.

You need to include editable regions for each general area of the page, but try to avoid creating too many editable regions, which limit the flexibility of the pages. For example, if subheadings are not used on every page of the site, do not create a separate editable region for subheadings. Instead, include subheadings in the editable region for the main page content as needed.

Keep in mind that templates can limit your flexibility to vary the page content. For example, to a large extent, head content is locked in pages created from templates, so you cannot add many common elements to template-based pages that add code to the head content. Also, you cannot add content outside the established editable regions. So, be sure to carefully consider the page content and layout for all the pages of the site when deciding how to structure a template.

When you create a new template, you need to save it with a unique name. As with other filenames, use only alphanumeric characters, do not use spaces or special characters, and do not start the name with a number. If you create more than one main template in a site, choose a name that clearly identifies the template. The template file is saved with the .dwt extension in a default folder named Templates in the site's local root folder. If the Templates folder does not already exist, Dreamweaver creates one. You can view all the templates for a site in the Assets panel when the Templates button is selected.

Creating a Template

- Open an existing page, and then, in the Common category of the Insert panel, click the Make Template button in the Templates list (or in the Assets panel, click the Templates button, and then click the New Template button or click File on the menu bar, click New, click Blank Template, click HTML template in the Template Type box, click a layout in the Layout box, and then click the Create button).
- Type a name for the template, and then save the template.
- If you created a new template from the Assets panel, select the template in the Assets panel, and then click the Edit Template button.
- Add editable regions to the template using the buttons in the Templates list in the Common category of the Insert panel.
- Save the template.

Gage is developing a series of new pages with information about classic music and the tribute band scene in the United States. You will create a template for these pages based on the tickets.html page, which has the most basic layout of all the existing pages and is the easiest to modify.

To create a template from the tickets.html page:

1. If you took a break after the previous session, make sure that the NextBest Fest site is open and the Designer workspace is reset, the Business Catalyst panel is collapsed, and the Files panel is expanded.

2. Open the **tickets.html** page in Design view. You will modify this page to create the template layout.

3. In the **Common** category of the Insert panel, click the **Templates button arrow**, and then click the **Make Template** button. The Save As Template dialog box opens. See Figure 6-15.

Figure 6-15   Save As Template dialog box

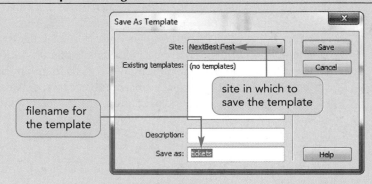

4. If necessary, click the **Site** button, and then click **NextBest Fest**. This is the site in which you will save the template.

5. In the Save as box, select any existing text and type **nb_main**, and then click the **Save** button. A dialog box opens, prompting you to update links.

6. Click the **Yes** button. Dreamweaver creates a copy of the page with the name nb_main.dwt, creates a Templates folder in the site's local root folder, and then saves the template in that folder.

7. Collapse the CSS Styles panel, and then, in the Files panel, click the **Expand** button ⊞ next to the Templates folder to expand the folder, if necessary. See Figure 6-16.

Figure 6-16   **New template page**

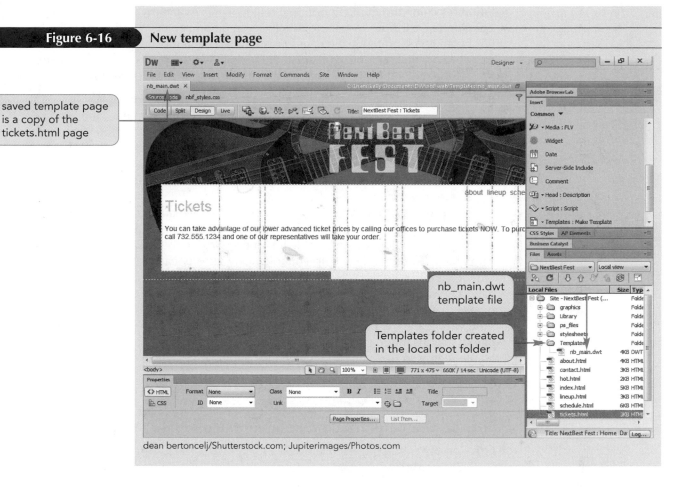

saved template page is a copy of the tickets.html page

nb_main.dwt template file

Templates folder created in the local root folder

dean bertoncelj/Shutterstock.com; Jupiterimages/Photos.com

Adding Regions to a Template

When you create a template, the entire document is locked. In other words, the page is one big noneditable region and only the template itself can be edited. You must add at least one editable region to the template to be able to change page content and other elements in the pages created from the template. Anything outside an editable region can be altered only within the template.

You can add the following types of regions to a template:

- **Editable region.** An area in a template-based page that can be edited. Any area can be defined as an editable region. You can designate either an entire table or a single table cell as editable; you cannot designate multiple cells as one editable region. Also, AP divs and their content are separate elements. Designating an AP div as editable enables you to move it. Designating the area inside the AP div as editable enables you to change its content.
- **Optional region.** A noneditable region for which you set conditions for displaying the content in that region in template-based pages. You set parameters for displaying the optional region content when you create the template. The regions are displayed in the pages created from the template only if those conditions or parameters are met.
- **Repeating region.** A region that can be duplicated within the pages made from the template, enabling the region to expand without altering the page design. For example, you can designate a table row as a repeating region, and then you can repeat the table row in the template-based pages to create expanding lists.

- **Editable optional region.** An optional region that is editable.
- **Editable tag attribute.** A tag attribute that you unlock in a template so that the attribute can be edited in the pages created from the template. For example, you can "lock" which graphic appears in the template-based pages, and then create an editable tag attribute that enables the person editing these pages to set the graphic's alignment.

With the exception of the title and a few other page-specific elements, the head content is locked in the pages created from a template. This means that you cannot add navigation bars and many other common elements that place code into the head of the page to template-based pages. Elements that add code to the head of a page must be added either directly in the template or, sometimes, in a library item that is placed in an editable region.

Regions added to templates are invisible elements. When you show invisible elements, a border appears around the regions in both the template and the template-based pages, and a tab appears at the top of each region in the Document window. Although the border and tab help you to quickly identify each region, they also interfere slightly with the way the layout appears in the Document window. To see a page as it will appear in browsers, you must hide the invisible elements or preview the page in a browser or in Live view.

You will delete the page-specific content from the nb_main template as you create editable regions in the template. You will begin by making the page heading an editable region so that you can change the heading for each new page created from the template.

To add the page heading as an editable region to the template:

1. On the menu bar, click **View**, point to **Visual Aids**, and then click **Invisible Elements**, if necessary, to check it. You will be able to see any invisible elements you add in the page.

2. In the Document window, select the **Tickets** page heading, and then, in the status bar, click the **<h1>** tag to ensure that the opening and closing h1 tags are selected.

3. In the **Common** category of the Insert panel, click the **Templates button arrow**, and then click the **Editable Region** button. The New Editable Region dialog box opens.

4. In the Name box, type **page_head**, and then click the **OK** button. The new editable region is added to the template and a tab appears over the text.

5. Press the **Right** arrow key to deselect the text. A blue border surrounds the editable region with the page heading. See Figure 6-17.

Figure 6-17   **Editable region added to the template page**

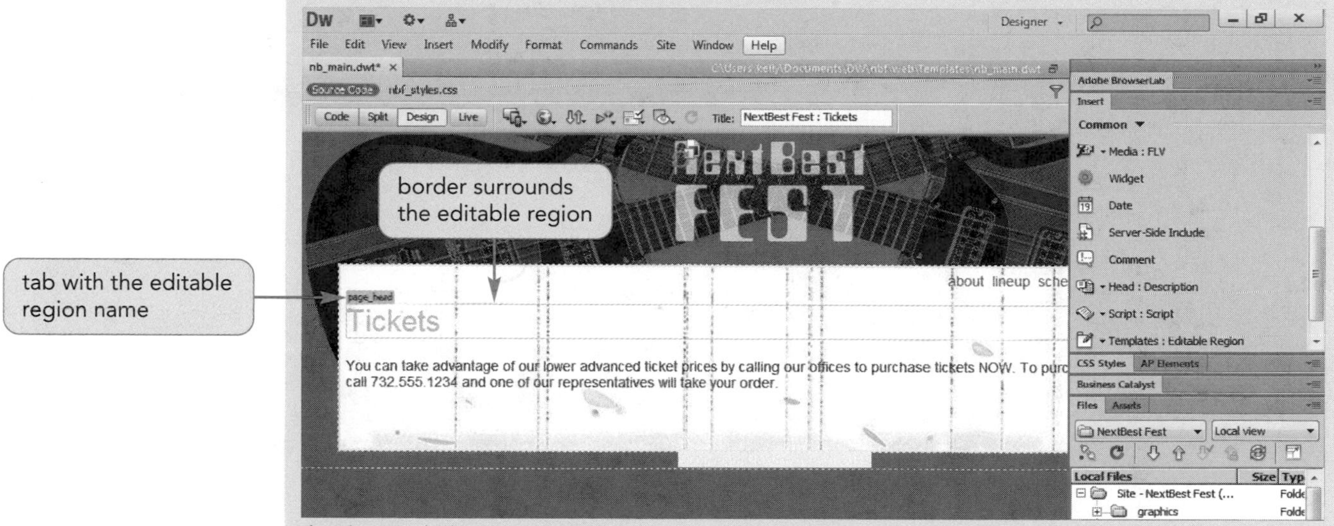

border surrounds
the editable region

tab with the editable
region name

dean bertoncelj/Shutterstock.com; Jupiterimages/Photos.com

> **Trouble?** If the tab is not visible in the Document window, invisible elements are hidden. On the menu bar, click View, point to Visual Aids, and then click Invisible Elements.

▶ **6.** Select the **Tickets** heading text, and then type **Heading**. This text replaces the page-specific content with a generic placeholder for the page heading.

Next, you will create a repeating region with a table. The Repeating Table button adds the table to the repeating region and adds an editable area in the table so you can enter content to the table in pages created from the template.

To create a repeating table in the template:

▶ **1.** In the Document window, delete all of the text below the page heading and above the footer.

▶ **2.** In the **Common** category of the Insert panel, click the **Templates button arrow**, and then click the **Repeating Table** button. The Insert Repeating Table dialog box opens.

▶ **3.** Type **1** in the Rows box, type **1** in the Columns box, type **0** in the Cell padding box, type **0** in the Cell spacing box, type **100** in the Width box, select **Percent** from the button, if necessary, and then type **0** in the Border box. This creates a borderless one-cell table the full width of the page. See Figure 6-18.

Figure 6-18 **Insert Repeating Table dialog box**

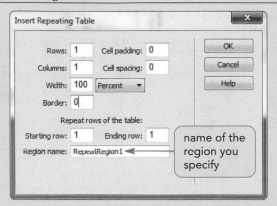

name of the region you specify

4. In the Region name box, type **content**, and then click the **OK** button. A repeating table named *content* with an unnamed editable region is placed in the page below the page heading.

5. Click in a blank area of the page to deselect the table. See Figure 6-19.

Figure 6-19 **Repeating table with an editable region**

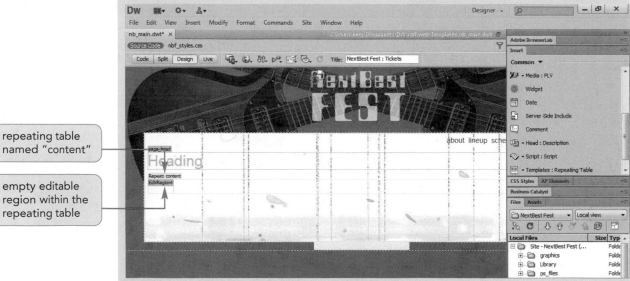

repeating table named "content"

empty editable region within the repeating table

dean bertoncelj/Shutterstock.com; Jupiterimages/Photos.com

6. In the repeating table, click in the editable region, and then type **Add content here.** (including the period). This placeholder text will act as a reminder to enter appropriate content in the template-based pages.

7. In the Document toolbar, select **Tickets** in the Title box, and then type **New**.

8. Save and close the page.

9. In the Files panel, click the **Collapse** button ⊟ next to the Templates folder.

Creating Web Pages from a Template

After you create a template, you should test it by creating a page from the template. You can create a Web page from a template in two ways. You can create a new page based on the template and then add the appropriate content to the editable regions. Or, you can apply the template to an existing page that already contains content.

Creating a New Template-Based Page

Creating a new page from a template is similar to creating a new, blank page. The only difference is that when you create the page, you select the template you want to base the page on. After the page is created, you add content to the editable regions, and then save the page as usual.

REFERENCE

Creating a Template-Based Page

- On the menu bar, click File, and then click New.
- Click Page from Template in the New Document dialog box.
- Select the current site, and then select the template from which you want to create the page.
- Click the Create button.
- Enter the appropriate content into the editable regions of the page, and then save the page.

Gage wants to see a sample page from the new template. You will create a new page from the nb_main.dwt template, and then add a new page heading and some content to the test page.

TIP

You can also press the Ctrl+N keys to open the New Document dialog box.

To create a new Web page from the nb_main.dwt template:

1. On the menu bar, click **File**, and then click **New**. The New Document dialog box opens.

2. Click **Page from Template**. The Page from Template options appear in the dialog box.

3. In the Site box, click **NextBest Fest**, if necessary, and then, in the Template for Site "NextBest Fest" box, click **nb_main**. A preview of the selected template page appears in the dialog box. See Figure 6-20.

Figure 6-20 **Page from Template options in the New Document dialog box**

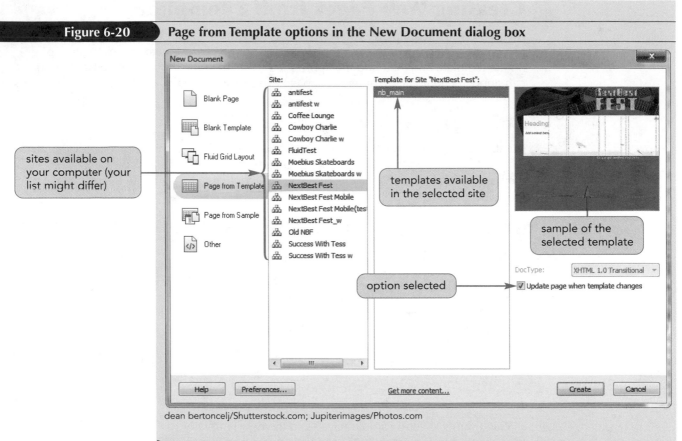

sites available on your computer (your list might differ)

templates available in the selected site

sample of the selected template

option selected

dean bertoncelj/Shutterstock.com; Jupiterimages/Photos.com

▶ **4.** Verify that the **Update page when template changes** check box is checked. This keeps the template-based page attached to the template.

▶ **5.** Click the **Create** button. A new page based on the nb_main template opens in the Document window. See Figure 6-21.

Figure 6-21 **Page created from the nb_main template**

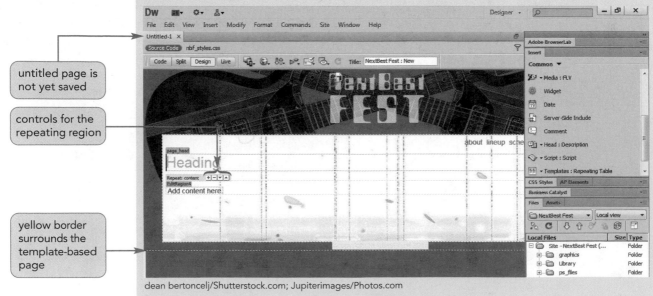

untitled page is not yet saved

controls for the repeating region

yellow border surrounds the template-based page

dean bertoncelj/Shutterstock.com; Jupiterimages/Photos.com

▶ **6.** Save the page as **template_test.html** in the local root folder.

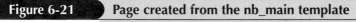

As a further test, you will add content to the editable regions in the new template-based page. You will add a page heading, add multiple rows of content to the repeating table, and update the page title.

To add content to the editable regions in the template_test.html page:

1. In the Title box on the Document toolbar, select **New**, type **Test**, and then press the **Enter** key. The page title changes to reflect the content of the new page.

2. In the page_head editable region, select the **Heading** placeholder text, and then type **Test Page**.

3. In the editable region in the repeating table content, select **Add content here.** (including the period), and then type **Placeholder text for the test page.** (including the period).

   You will test the repeating table by adding a second row to the table.

4. In the Repeat: content tab, click the **Add** button ⊞. A second editable region appears in the page.

5. Select the text in the new editable region, if necessary, and then type **More text will be placed here.** (including the period). See Figure 6-22.

TIP

To create a new line in the editable region of a repeating table, press the Enter key in the region.

Figure 6-22   New content in the template_test.html page

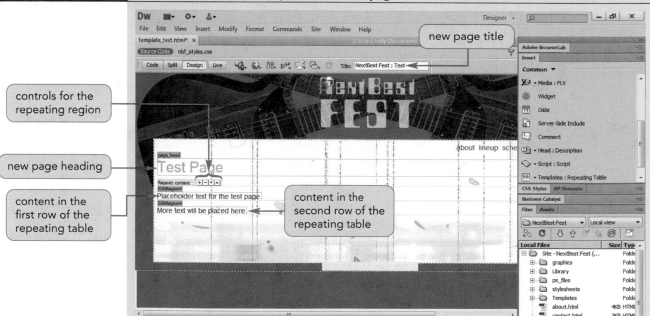

controls for the repeating region

new page heading

content in the first row of the repeating table

content in the second row of the repeating table

new page title

dean bertoncelj/Shutterstock.com; Jupiterimages/Photos.com

6. Save the page, and then preview the page in a browser. See Figure 6-23.

Figure 6-23   Preview of the template_test.html page in a browser

Used with permission from Microsoft Corporation; dean bertoncelj/Shutterstock.com; Jupiterimages/Photos.com

7. Close the browser, and then close the page.

Applying a Template to an Existing Web Page

If you already have a page with content, you can apply a template to it. To apply a template to an existing Web page, open the page in the Document window, select the template in the Assets panel, and then click the Apply button. When you apply a template to an existing page, the page uses the layout of the template page and a dialog box opens so you can designate into which regions the existing content will be placed. This can get a bit confusing, especially with complex pages that contain a lot of content. It is usually easier to create a new template-based page and move the content from the existing page into the new page.

Shared Site Formatting Options

Templates are one avenue for creating shared site formatting. However, you can gain many of the same benefits through efficient use of CSS positioning and styling. Because of this, templates are not used as frequently as they once were. The main benefit of using templates is that they prevent anyone who is allowed to update the site's content from accidentally changing the site's code.

For large Web sites, another option is to store the site content in a database and then add code to the pages that enables the pages to dynamically display the content from the database in a format appropriate for the site design. This approach also lets you create a content management system that enables clients to edit the page content from within a Web browser. If you cannot create a database in which to store the site content, you can purchase or subscribe to one of the many commercial systems available and then customize it as needed.

Adobe provides **Business Catalyst**, which is an online hosted service that enables you to create hosted, database-driven Web sites and integrated online stores. It also has a content management system that allows in-context editing so your clients can make simple changes to page content from within a browser. Like other commercial options, Business Catalyst is a fee-based service that requires a monthly or annual subscription.

Editing a Template

One of the most powerful aspects of using templates is that you can adjust all of the template-based pages in a site at once by editing the template. As with CSS styles and library items, this saves you time and ensures that all of the pages maintain a consistent design. Adjusting elements in the editable regions of a template affects only new pages created from that template. Existing template-based pages are not affected because these adjustments might overwrite content you added to those pages. However, repositioning editable regions, adding new editable regions, or adjusting anything in a noneditable region affects all new and existing template-based pages.

You can also delete regions from the template. When you delete an editable region from the template, you choose what happens to the content in that region in the existing template-based pages. You can move any content from the deleted region to another editable region or you can delete that content from the page. You can add, edit, or delete content from the noneditable regions. Any changes made to the noneditable regions in the template affect all pages created from the template—whether new or existing.

Gage wants every page in the new, template-based portion of the site to have a subheading below the page heading. You will add an editable region for the subheading to the template.

To edit the nb_main.dwt template:

▶ 1. Open the **nb_main.dwt** template in Design view, click the blank area to the left of the Repeat: content region, press the **Enter** key, and then press the **Up** arrow key, if necessary, so that there is a blank line above and below the insertion point. Two new lines are created below the page_head region.

▶ 2. In the **Common** category of the Insert panel, click the **Templates button arrow**, and then click the **Editable Region** button. The New Editable Region dialog box opens.

▶ 3. In the Name box, type **sub_head**, and then click the **OK** button. The new editable region appears in the site.

   Trouble? If the sub_head text is not visible, it is blocked by the tab of the content repeating table and you need to hide the invisible elements. On the menu bar, click View, point to Visual Aids, and then click Invisible Elements to hide the tab and view the text, complete Step 4, and then show the invisible elements.

▶ 4. Click in the **sub_head** placeholder text in the sub_head region, and then, in the Property inspector, click the **Format** button and click **Heading 2**. The sub_head text is formatted.

▶ 5. Click next to the sub_head text to deselect the text. See Figure 6-24.

Figure 6-24 | **Edited template page**

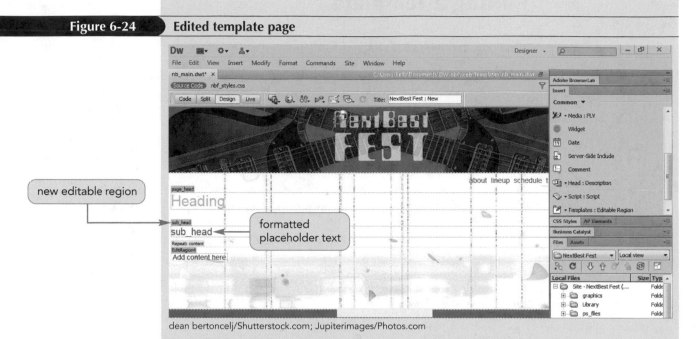

new editable region

formatted placeholder text

dean bertoncelj/Shutterstock.com; Jupiterimages/Photos.com

6. Save the template. The Update Template Files dialog box opens, asking whether to update the pages created from the template to reflect the changes in the template. You want this change to appear in the existing template-based pages—in this case, the template_test.html page.

   Trouble? If a dialog box opens, stating that the page_head region is in a block tag, click the OK button. This dialog box might open whenever you save the page; if it does, click the OK button each time.

7. Click the **Update** button to update the page, review the changes in the Update Pages dialog box when the update is complete, and then click the **Close** button.

8. Close the nb_main.dwt template, and then open the **template_test.html** page in Design view. The subheading has been added to this page, which you created from the template.

9. Select the placeholder text in the sub_head region, and then type **template test subheading**. The text appears, as specified, in the h2 style.

10. Save the template_test.html page, and then switch to **Live** view to preview the page. See Figure 6-25.

Figure 6-25   **Edited template_test.html page previewed in Live view**

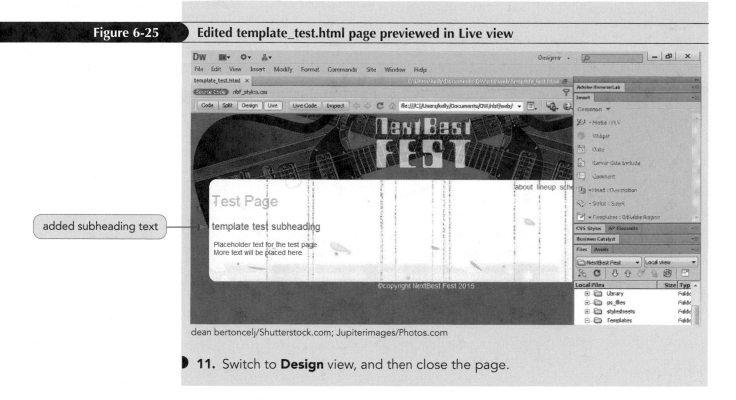

dean bertoncelj/Shutterstock.com; Jupiterimages/Photos.com

▶ **11.** Switch to **Design** view, and then close the page.

Deleting a Template

If a template is no longer relevant for a site, you can delete it. You delete a template from a site by selecting the template in the Assets panel and clicking the Delete button. When you delete a template, the pages that were created from that template still contain the template markup code. You must also detach the pages from the attached template to make them regular Web pages. To detach a page from a template, open the template-based page, click Modify on the menu bar, point to Templates, and then click Detach from Template.

Creating Nested Templates

A nested template is a template created from the main template so that you can create a more defined structure for some pages of a site. A nested template inherits all of the features of the main template. In other words, each nested template contains the same editable and noneditable regions as the main template and is linked to the main template. You can add additional editable regions to the nested template, but only within the editable regions in the main template. Any change you make to the main template affects all the nested templates as well as any pages created from the main template and the nested templates. Any change you make to a nested template affects only the pages created from that nested template.

With nested templates, you maintain even greater control over the look of the pages in a site because you further limit the choices people have when they enter content into those pages. For example, if many pages in the NextBest Fest site had subheadings below the page heading followed by a paragraph of text and another subheading, you could create a nested template with an editable region for a subheading followed by an editable region for text within the editable region that is designated for content in the main template.

You create pages from a nested template in the same way that you create pages from the main template. Any changes you make to the main template flow through to nested templates.

INSIGHT

Using Nested Templates

Nested templates are also useful when a Web site includes more than one major style of page, such as a site with both informational pages and product pages. If the informational and product pages have different styles but the same basic page properties (CSS styles, navigation bar, and so on), you can create a main template for the site and a nested template for each type of page. Another example is a site that has the same basic layout for all pages, but uses a different background color for each major section of the site. You might create a nested template for each section and change only the background color. You save time and eliminate work because the basic layout for each type of page is already designed and all your pages are still connected to the same main template.

At some point, Gage plans to add a new page to the site to promote each band that plays at the NextBest Fest. All the band pages will have the same layout. You will create a nested template based on the main template with the special layout for these pages.

To create a nested template for the nb_main template:

1. Open the **template_test.html** page in Design view.

2. In the **Common** category of the Insert panel, click the **Templates button arrow**, and then click the **Make Nested Template** button. The Save As Template dialog box opens.

3. Type **nb_bands** in the Save as box, and then click the **Save** button to save the nested template. The Update Links dialog box opens.

4. Click the **Yes** button to update the linked pages. The nb_bands.dwt page opens.

5. Delete all the text in the EditRegion within the Repeat: content region and delete the second EditRegion. You will create a table in this editable region.

6. Create a table with **2** rows, **2** columns, **100%** width, **0** border thickness, **0** cell padding, **0** cell spacing, and a **Top** header. The new table appears in the nested template.

7. Merge the bottom cells, top-align both cells in the top row, and then left-align the upper-right cell.

8. In the upper-left cell, type **Add content here.** (including the period).

9. In the upper-right cell, insert the **placeholder.gif** graphic located in the **Dreamweaver6\Tutorial** folder included with your Data Files. You do not need to add alt text to this placeholder graphic because it will be replaced with a graphic before the site goes live.

10. In the bottom cell, type **Add additional content here.** (including the period). See Figure 6-26.

Figure 6-26   Nested template page

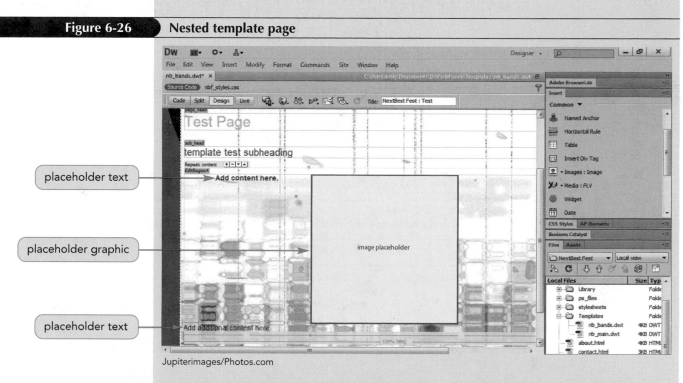

placeholder text

placeholder graphic

placeholder text

Jupiterimages/Photos.com

▶ **11.** Save the nested template. The nested template appears in the Templates folder in the Files panel.

   Trouble? If you do not see nb_bands.dwt in the Templates folder, you might need to refresh the Files panel. On the Files panel toolbar, click the Refresh button to display the new template in the Templates folder.

▶ **12.** Switch to **Live** view to preview the nested template. You can see what pages created from the new template will look like in a browser.

▶ **13.** Return to **Design** view, and then close the nb_bands.dwt template.

   In this session, you created a template, added editable regions to the page, and then created a new page based on the template. You also created a nested template and edited the main template. In the next session, you will add a form to the contact.html page.

Session 6.2 Quick Check

REVIEW

   1. What is a template?
   2. Why would you use a template?
   3. Explain the difference between editable regions and noneditable regions.
   4. What are the two ways to create templates?
   5. How does editing a template affect pages that were already created from that template?
   6. What happens when you delete an editable region from the main template?
   7. What is a nested template?
   8. True or False. The main template inherits all of the characteristics of nested templates.

SESSION 6.3 VISUAL OVERVIEW

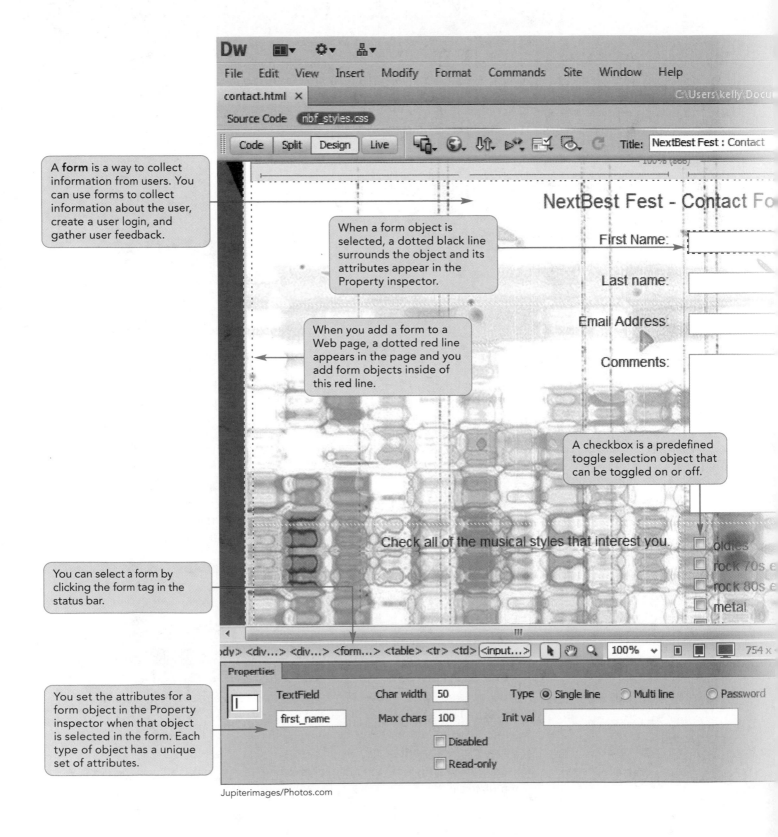

A **form** is a way to collect information from users. You can use forms to collect information about the user, create a user login, and gather user feedback.

When a form object is selected, a dotted black line surrounds the object and its attributes appear in the Property inspector.

When you add a form to a Web page, a dotted red line appears in the page and you add form objects inside of this red line.

A checkbox is a predefined toggle selection object that can be toggled on or off.

You can select a form by clicking the form tag in the status bar.

You set the attributes for a form object in the Property inspector when that object is selected in the form. Each type of object has a unique set of attributes.

Jupiterimages/Photos.com

CREATING FORMS

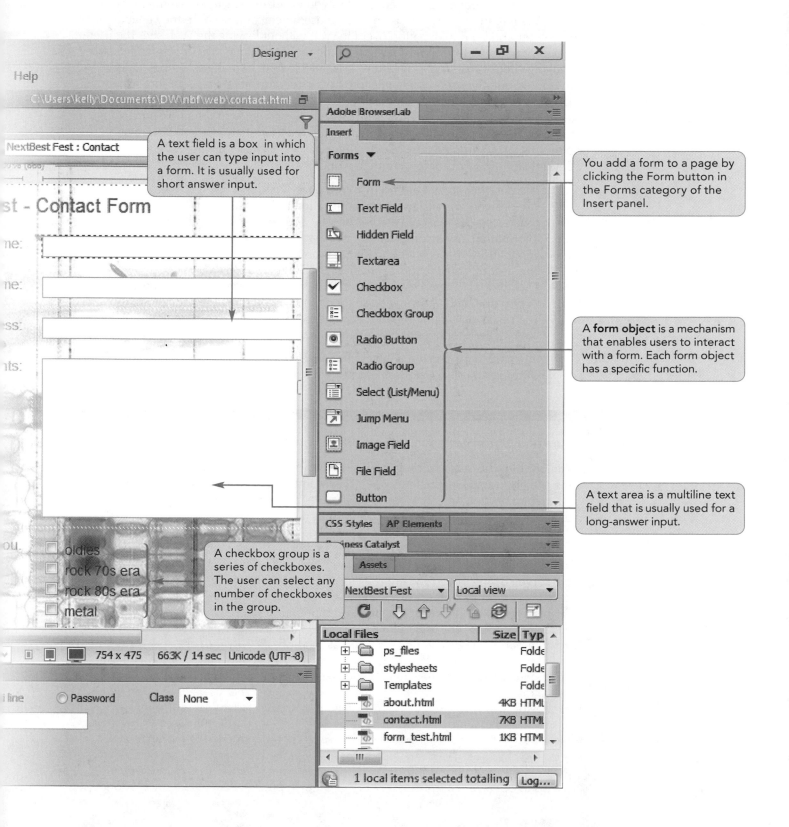

Understanding Forms

Forms are an important element in Web design because they provide a way to interact with users. You can use forms to collect information about the user, create a user login, and gather user feedback. User feedback lets you evaluate the site to determine if it is meeting the intended goals. Forms encourage user interaction because they enable the user to enter and send information over the Web without leaving the Web site. The user inputs information into the Web page by typing requested data into designated fields or clicking check boxes, option buttons, lists, and so forth to make selections. After the form is filled out, the user submits the form, which sends the information somewhere, usually to the server, for processing. Forms do not process the information that was entered. After the form information is processed, the server (or information-processing destination) sends requested information back to the user, such as search information, or performs tasks based on the collected information, such as logging in a user.

Several steps must occur for a form to work:

1. The designer creates a form in a Web page.
2. The designer installs a script or application in the designated information-processing destination, which is usually a server, to process the form information. (Most forms cannot work without server-side scripts or applications that process the information.)
3. The user fills out the form and clicks the Submit button.
4. The information-processing destination, such as a server, receives the information and a server-side script or application processes the information.
5. The server or information-processing destination sends requested information back to the user or performs an action based on the form's information.

You will create a form in the contact.html page so site visitors can communicate with NextBest Fest and so NextBest Fest can gather information about the site visitors.

PROSKILLS

Written Communication: Gathering Feedback

The people who visit and use a Web site can provide valuable feedback about the site, including what other content they want to see in the site; how well the navigation, layout, and other technical aspects of the site function; how to enhance their experience; and if the site accomplishes its intended goals.

There are many ways to interact with and gather information from users. You can ask them to fill out online forms with questions about preferences, desires, or interests. You can ask users to participate in a survey. You can use a form to create the survey online or you can email users and ask them to respond. You can also call customers directly if you have their contact information and interview them, which enables you to ask follow-up questions and probe for deeper information. Finally, you can gather several users into a focus group and lead a discussion to obtain their input in person. Focus groups are often used to obtain live feedback about a site's usability. In some cases, the focus group is observed as they move through the site and questioned about the site's functionality, navigation, and so forth.

No matter how you obtain user feedback, remember that users have taken time to provide you with their opinions. Be sure to follow up to let them know that you appreciate and value their input. It is a good idea to let participants know how their responses will impact your future plans and to ask them to provide more feedback after the changes have been implemented. By gathering user input, acting on that input, and keeping users informed of how their input affects change, you keep a dialogue open with users that makes them feel appreciated and valued. An added benefit is that users become more invested in the site as well as your brand, goals, and products.

Creating a Form

You can create a form in any Web page. Before you create a form, you should plan what information you want to collect, how the form should be designed to best collect that information, and in which page to create the form. For example, Gage wants to collect information from users to determine which of the bands playing at NextBest Fest they are listening to and what types of music they like. He also wants to collect their contact information and enable them to submit questions to the NextBest Fest staff. The form will be in the contact.html page.

The general process for creating a form is to add a form to a Web page, set form attributes, and then add form objects.

REFERENCE

Creating a Form

- Add the script that will process the form data to the server or information-processing destination.
- Click in the page where you want the form to appear, and then in the Forms category of the Insert panel, click the Form button.
- Set the form attributes, including Form ID, Action, Method, Enctype, and Target.
- Add form objects and explanations for each form object to the form, and then set the attributes for each form object, including a name.
- Add a Submit button to the form.
- Test the form in a browser.

Adding a Form to a Web Page

The first step in creating a form is to add the form to a page. This places a container in the page for the form content that you will add. Try to insert the form in the page location where you want the form to appear, although you can reposition the form if needed. When you add a form to a Web page, Dreamweaver inserts <form> </form> tags in the code for the page, and a red dotted line appears in the Document window in Design view. The red dotted line designates the form area in Dreamweaver and is invisible in the browser window.

You will add a form at the bottom of the contact.html page.

To add a form to the contact.html page:

1. If you took a break after the previous session, make sure that the NextBest Fest site is open and the Designer workspace is reset, the Business Catalyst panel is collapsed, and the Files panel is expanded.

2. Open the **contact.html** page in Design view.

3. Click in the blank line below the page heading. You will insert the form on this new line.

4. Collapse the CSS Styles panel.

5. In the **Forms** category of the Insert panel, click the **Form** button. A red dotted line that designates the form area appears in the contact.html page below the content. See Figure 6-27.

Figure 6-27 **Form added to the contact.html page**

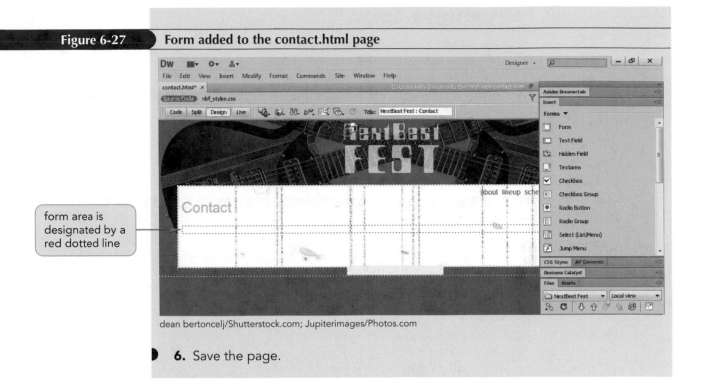

form area is designated by a red dotted line

dean bertoncelj/Shutterstock.com; Jupiterimages/Photos.com

6. Save the page.

Setting Form Attributes

After you add a form to a page, you can adjust the form attributes in the Property inspector when the form is selected. You must set all of the form attributes except the Target attribute, which is optional. Form attributes include the following:

- **Form ID.** A unique name for the form. The form ID enables the form to be referenced or controlled with a scripting language. If you do not name the form, Dreamweaver generates a name. A form ID can include alphanumeric characters, spaces, underscores, and dashes, but cannot begin with a number.
- **Action.** The path to the location of the script you will use to process the form data. You must install the script or create the page in the desired location prior to setting the Action. You can also type "mailto:" followed by an email address in the Action box to send the form information to a specified email address (the mailto: link works only if the user is on a computer configured to send email), or you can type the name of a JavaScript function in the Action box if you are using JavaScript to process the form.
- **Method.** The way form data will be sent to the location specified in the Action box. POST embeds form data in an HTTP request. When you use the POST method, the form data is not visible. POST is the preferred method for most forms. GET appends the form data to the end of the path specified in the Action box. When you use the GET method, form data is limited to 8192 characters of information and is visible because it is added to the end of the URL. GET is frequently used for search engine requests. Default uses the browser default of the user's browser to send form data. The script or application you use to process form data might affect the method that you will need to use to send the form data.

- **Target.** The target destination for any response from the form. For example, if the script attached to the form sends a response to the user such as "We have received your information." that response appears in the target destination. Target options are the usual _blank, _parent, _self, and _top.
- **Enctype (encoding type).** The Multipurpose Internet Mail Extensions encoding type (MIME type) for the form data. The MIME type is a file identification based on the MIME encoding system, which is the standard for identifying content on the Internet. Most forms use the application/x-www-form-urlencoded MIME type. The multipart/form-data MIME type is used for uploading files, such as when you use a file-upload field in a form.

You will set each of these attributes for the form in the contact.html page.

To set up the form in the contact.html page:

1. Copy the **form_test.html** file located in the **Dreamweaver6\Tutorial** folder included with your Data Files, and then paste it into the site's local root folder. This Web page contains a script that will let you test the form by displaying the data the form will send to the server when the Submit button is clicked.

2. In the contact.html page, click the red dotted line to select the form. The form attributes appear in the Property inspector.

3. In the Form ID box, type **contact**. This is the unique name for the form.

4. In the Action box, type **form_test.html**. The action will eventually point to a script placed on the server to process the form data. While the programming team is writing the script, the action points to the test script Web page you copied into the local root folder.

5. Click the **Method arrow**, and then click **GET**. The form data will be appended to the end of the path specified in the Action box.

6. Click the **Enctype arrow**, and then click **application/x-www-form-urlencoded**. This specifies the encoding type.

7. Click the **Target arrow**, and then click **_blank**. The form response will appear in a new page. See Figure 6-28.

Figure 6-28 Form attributes added to the form

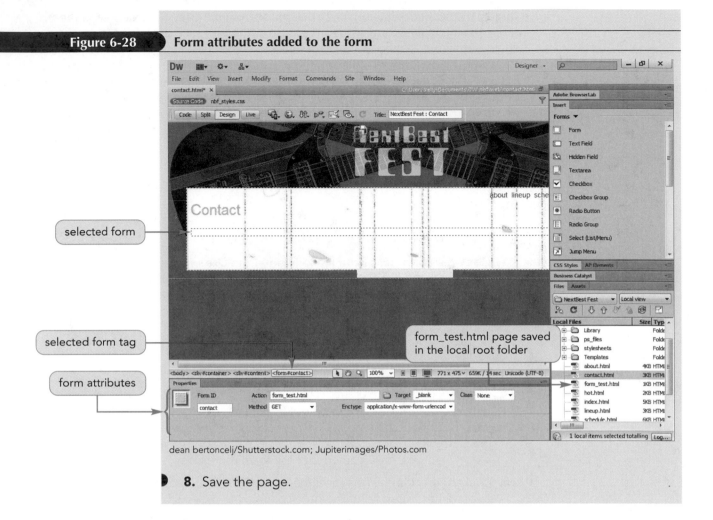

dean bertoncelj/Shutterstock.com; Jupiterimages/Photos.com

8. Save the page.

Adding Form Objects

You must add form objects to a form to make it useful. A form object is generally a mechanism that enables users to interact with a form. Each form object has a specific function:

- **Text fields and text areas.** A box into which a user can type input in a form. Text fields are usually used for short-answer input. Text areas are usually used for long-answer input. Text fields are displayed as a single-line box; text areas are displayed as a multiline box. Both can accept either single or multiple lines of input. The input can be displayed as typed or as a series of dots or asterisks to protect private information. For example, a password typed into a browser window is usually displayed as a series of asterisks.
- **Hidden fields.** Fields used to include information in a form that will be sent along with the form data to the server or designated processing location and which the user cannot see. For example, you can use a hidden field to send the name of the form with the collected form data.
- **Checkbox and checkbox group.** A predefined toggle selection object in a form. Each checkbox can be toggled "on (checked)" or "off (unchecked)," enabling the user to check any number of items in a series of checkboxes. For example, you might use a checkbox group to allow a user to select all the types of music he or she listens to.

- **Radio button and radio group.** A group of selection objects that work together in a form. The user can select only one radio button from a radio group. Unlike a checkbox, which can be toggled on and off independently, a selected radio button can be deselected only when the user selects another radio button within the radio group.
- **Select (List/Menu).** A list of preset input choices in a form. List presents a list of possible input choices in a designated area, providing a scroll bar, if necessary, that enables users to navigate through the list. The user can select multiple items in a list. Menu presents the user with the input choices in a drop-down menu. The user can select only one item from a menu.
- **Jump menu.** A special menu that contains a list of active links to other pages, graphics, or any type of file that can be opened in a browser. When a user selects an item from the jump menu, the new page or document opens. Unlike other form objects, the jump menu can be used within or outside a form because it includes form tags and a Submit button.
- **Image field.** A graphic used as a Submit or Reset button in a form. You can also use graphics as buttons that perform other tasks by adding behaviors.
- **File field.** A file upload field in the form that enables the user to upload a file from the client computer to the server. The file field contains a Browse button and a text box. The user can select the file using the Browse button or, in some browsers, the user can type the file path into the text box. You must use the POST method to send files from the browser to the server, and your Web server must be set up to handle this type of file upload.
- **Button.** A button in the form that performs the behavior you specify. The button can be designated as a Submit button or a Reset button, or it can have no designation. A Submit button sends the form data to the location you designated for processing. A Reset button clears any content that the user added to or modified in the form so that the user can start over. You can also add behaviors to the button, enabling it to perform other functions.

You will use text fields, checkboxes, radio buttons, a list, a Submit button, and a Reset button in the contact form.

You set the attributes for a form object in the Property inspector when that object is selected in the form. Each type of object has a unique set of attributes. However, every object has a name attribute. It is important to name every form object because the scripting language uses this name to identify the form object. If you do not name an object, Dreamweaver names it for you, using the object type and a number as its name. It is better to use a descriptive name for form objects because the name will be paired with its corresponding data when sent to the processing destination. When you view the data collected from forms, the name identifies the information beside it. For example, you will name the text field where users input their last name "LastName" so that when you view the data, you see LastName beside the data captured in the last name field. Without this descriptive name, you might have trouble distinguishing the user's first name from the user's last name.

Creating the Form Structure

The main purpose of a form is to interact with a user in some way. To do this effectively, you must create a form that is simple and intuitive for the user to use. The requested information should be organized logically within the form. For example, all similar or related information should be placed together so users can enter that data, such as all their personal information, at the same time. You should also include a label with brief instructions or a description of the information being requested for each form object so users know what to do.

Once you know how you want to organize the requested information, you have to decide the best way to lay out the form objects in the form. Although you can use line breaks, paragraph breaks, and tables within forms to lay out the form objects, a table is usually the simplest way to structure forms. For example, you could insert a two-column table in a form that includes a separate row for each form object. Then, you can right-justify the form labels in the left column and left-justify the corresponding form objects in the right column. This creates a form that is well organized and easy to follow. It also creates a form that is fairly stable across browsers. Different versions of browsers sometimes display form objects in slightly different ways. Putting form objects in a table helps to keep them in the same place in a page regardless of how a user's browser displays the form. However, the form layout might still vary slightly in different browsers.

You will use a two-column table without a border to organize the contact form.

To add a table to the contact form:

1. Click in the form area, and then insert a table with **9** rows, **2** columns, **100%** width, **0** border thickness, **10** cell padding, **0** cell spacing, **Top** header, and **This table contains a form for gathering information about user preferences and for communicating with the fest staff.** as the summary.

2. Align the left column to the **Right** and **Top**.

3. Align the right column to the **Left** and **Top**.

4. Merge the cells in the top row. You will add the form heading to this merged row.

5. Type **NextBest Fest – Contact Form** in the top row, center the form heading text, format the heading text in the **Heading 2** style, and then deselect the text. See Figure 6-29.

Figure 6-29 | **Contact form with the inserted table**

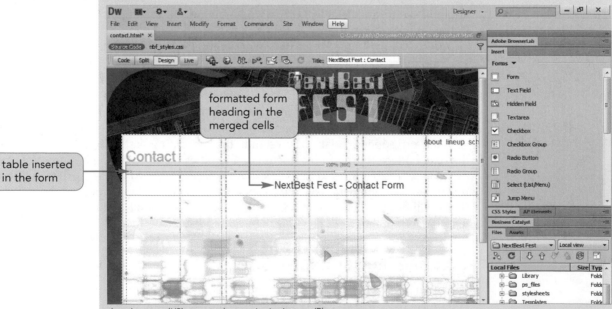

dean bertoncelj/Shutterstock.com; Jupiterimages/Photos.com

The rows and columns may be hard to see against the page background. To make the table easier to work with, you will create a style that formats the table as light gray. You will delete the style when you are finished working on the table.

> **6.** Using the CSS Styles pane, create a new CSS rule with a **Tag** selector type named **table** and defined in the **nbf_styles.css** style sheet.

> **7.** In the Background category, type **#ccc** in the Background-color box, and click the **OK** button. The background of the table turns light gray and the cells are easier to see.

Inserting Text Fields and Text Areas into a Form

Text fields and text areas are used to gather information that a user types. Most commonly, they are used for collecting name, address, and email address information. You can set a number of attributes to control how each text field or area appears and functions in the form. In addition to name, the attributes include the following:

- **Char width.** The maximum number of characters that can be displayed. When the character width value is smaller than the maximum characters value, the text field or area will not display all the input without scrolling.
- **Max chars/Num lines.** The maximum number of characters the user can input into a single-line text field or the number of lines in a multiline text area. You can use Max chars to limit a user's response. For example, you can limit a text field used to input the zip code to five characters.
- **Type.** The designated appearance. Single line creates a text field that is one line in height. Multi line creates a text area that is more than one line in height and has scroll bars. Password displays the data as dots or asterisks to protect the data.
- **Init val.** The initial value or text that is displayed until the user types new input.

You will add single-line text fields for collecting the user's first name, last name, and email address. Then you will add a multiline text area for collecting user comments.

To add text fields to the contact form:

> **1.** Click in the upper-left cell of the table below the form heading, type **First Name:** to enter the label for the first text field, and then press the **Tab** key to move the insertion point to the next cell.

> **2.** In the **Forms** category of the Insert panel, click the **Text Field** button. The Input Tag Accessibility Attributes dialog box opens. Because you provided a detailed summary in the table tag and because this form is an optional feature, you will not add accessibility attributes to the form objects.

> **3.** Click the **OK** button to close the dialog box. A text field is inserted in the cell. You will set its attributes in the Property inspector.

> **4.** Select the text field, and then, in the Property inspector, type **first_name** in the TextField box, type **50** in the Char width box, type **100** in the Max chars box, and then click the **Single line** option button, if necessary. The first_name text field will display 50 characters, accept up to 100 characters of input, and be one line in height. See Figure 6-30.

Figure 6-30   **Text field added to the form**

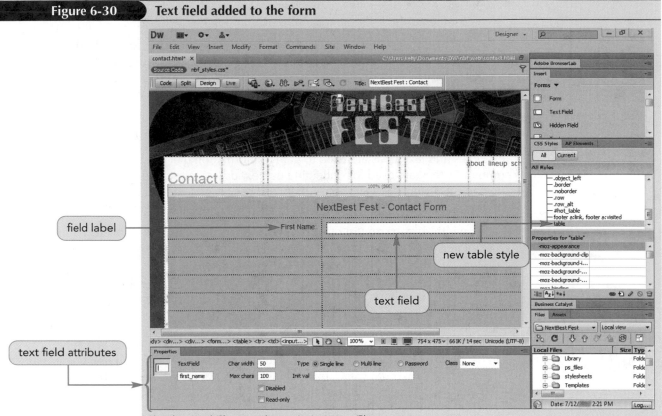

field label

new table style

text field

text field attributes

dean bertoncelj/Shutterstock.com; Jupiterimages/Photos.com

Next, you will add the last_name label and text field to the third row of
the table.

5. Click in the left column of the third row of the table, type **Last Name:** to
enter the label, and then press the **Tab** key to move the insertion point to
the next cell.

6. In the **Forms** category of the Insert panel, click the **Text Field** button, and
then click the **OK** button to close the Input Tag Accessibility Attributes
dialog box. The second text field is inserted in the table.

7. Select the text field, and then, in the Property inspector, type **last_name** in
the TextField box, type **50** in the Char width box, type **100** in the Max chars
box, and click the **Single line** option button, if necessary.

You will add the Email Address label and text field to the fourth row
of the table.

8. Click in the left column of the fourth row, type **Email Address:** to enter the
label, and then press the **Tab** key to move the insertion point to the next cell.

9. Repeat Steps 6 and 7 to insert a third text field, typing **email_address** in the
TextField box, **50** in the Char width box, and **100** in the Max chars box, and
clicking the **Single line** option button, if necessary.

You will add the comments label and text area to the fifth row of the table.

10. Click in the left column of the fifth row, type **Comments:** to enter the label,
and then press the **Tab** key to move the insertion point to the next cell.

▶ **11.** In the **Forms** category of the Insert panel, click the **Textarea** button, and then click the **OK** button in the Input Tag Accessibility Attributes dialog box. A multiline text area is added to the cell.

▶ **12.** Select the text area, and then, in the Property inspector, type **comments** in the TextField box, type **44** in the Char width box, type **10** in the Num lines box, and click the **Multi line** option button, if necessary. See Figure 6-31.

Figure 6-31  Form with text fields

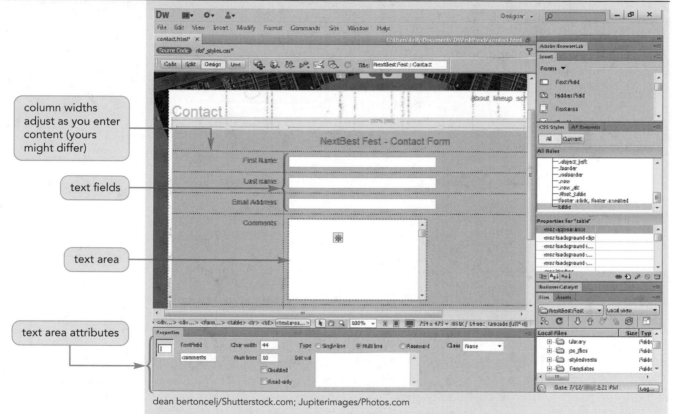

dean bertoncelj/Shutterstock.com; Jupiterimages/Photos.com

▶ **13.** Save the page, preview the page in a browser (the form has three text fields and one text area), and then close the browser.

Previewing a Form with Live Code View and Inspect Mode

Live view and Live Code view provide a quick way to preview and test the form. You can also toggle on to Inspect mode to identify the HTML elements and associated CSS styles that affect specific elements of the form. In the Live Code pane, the border, margin, padding, and content of the elements are highlighted in different colors. As you point to an element in the Live View pane, the corresponding code is highlighted in the Live Code pane. You can also see all of the styles that are affecting that element in the CSS Styles panel. Any properties of the CSS rules that are not affecting the selected element have a line through them so that you can track down why that element is not displaying as you intended. In addition, you can test the form in Live view by filling out the form and submitting it. These features make it easier to preview and debug interactive pages from within Dreamweaver. However, you should still preview the pages in all of the browsers your target audience will use so you can catch browser display variations that do not appear in Live view.

You will view the contact.html page in Live view, and then test the form you just created.

To preview and test the form in the contact.html page:

▶ **1.** Switch to **Live** view.

▶ **2.** Scroll down the contact.html page to view all the text fields and the text area. The table and form elements display the same way they do in a browser, not as they do in Design view. See Figure 6-32.

Figure 6-32	Form in Live view

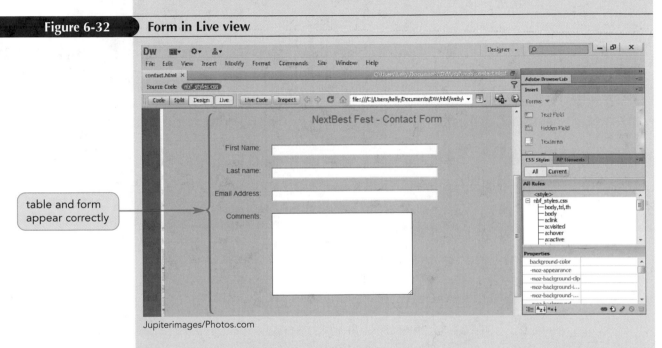

table and form appear correctly

Jupiterimages/Photos.com

▶ **3.** Click in the **First Name** text field. The field is active and will accept input.

▶ **4.** Type your first name, click to the left of the text box, and then click the **Live Code** button. The Document window switches to Split view. The source code for the page is displayed in the left pane and the code for the active text field is highlighted in blue. Live view is displayed in the right pane.

▶ **5.** Scroll as needed to view the text field. See Figure 6-33.

Figure 6-33   Form in Split view

Figure 6-33   Form in Split view

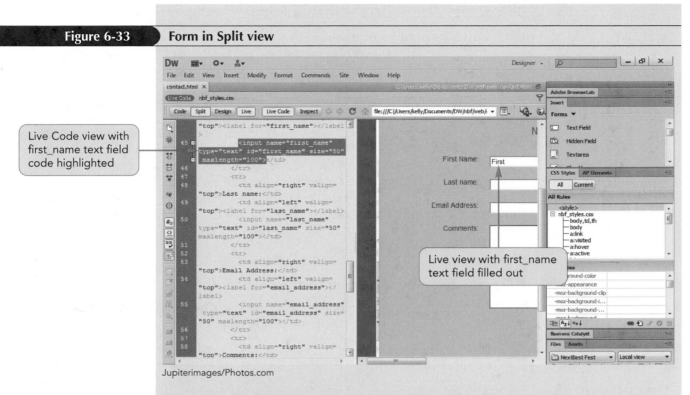

Live Code view with first_name text field code highlighted

Live view with first_name text field filled out

Jupiterimages/Photos.com

6. Click the **Inspect** button to switch to Inspect mode and arrange the panels in the optimal way to debug the HTML and the CSS.

7. In the Live View pane, point to various elements in the page. The elements you point to are highlighted and the Code pane adjusts to display and highlight the corresponding code. See Figure 6-34.

Figure 6-34   Form in Inspect mode

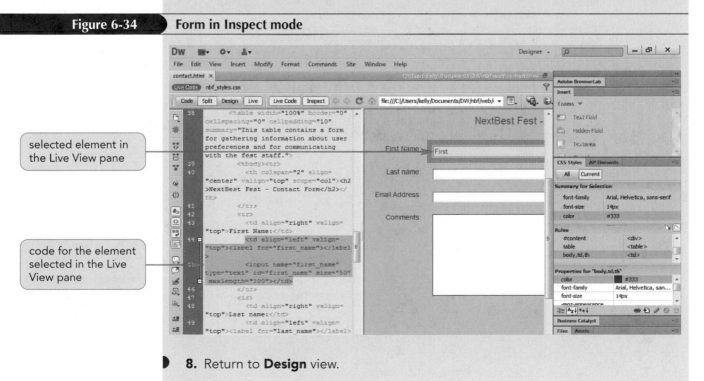

selected element in the Live View pane

code for the element selected in the Live View pane

8. Return to **Design** view.

Inserting Checkboxes into a Form

Checkboxes have only two attributes in addition to name. Because some forms use many checkboxes, it is often convenient to use a code, instead of a name, in the script to process them. When you include a series of related checkboxes, it is a good idea to use a checkbox group. Adding checkboxes as a group enables you to include a group name in addition to the names or codes of the individual checkboxes. The other checkbox attributes are Checked value and Initial state. Checked value is where you can assign a value or a numeric code for a checkbox. The Checked value is sent to the processing location along with the name when the checkbox is checked. Nothing is sent to the processing location if the checkbox is unchecked. Initial state sets whether the checkbox starts out checked or unchecked when a user first views the form.

Gage wants to find out what styles of music users enjoy to determine a lineup of tribute bands that will most appeal to them. You will use a checkbox group to collect this information.

To add a checkbox group to the contact form:

▶ 1. Click in the left column of the sixth row, type **Check all of the musical styles that interest you.** (including the period), and then press the **Tab** key to move the insertion point to the next cell.

▶ 2. In the **Forms** category of the Insert panel, click the **Checkbox Group** button. The Checkbox Group dialog box opens. See Figure 6-35.

| Figure 6-35 | Checkbox Group dialog box |

button to add more checkboxes to the group

two checkboxes already in the group

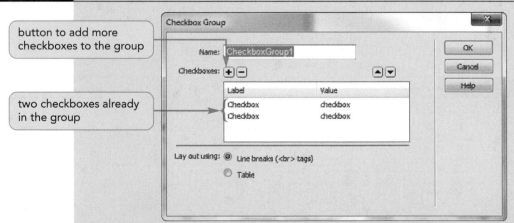

TIP

If you use POST as the method for the form, you must add brackets [] at the end of the Checkbox Group name for this method to work.

▶ 3. In the Name box, select the text, if necessary, and then type **music_style_preferences**. This clearly identifies the purpose of the checkbox group.

▶ 4. Click in the first row of the Label column, and then type **rock 70s era** to add the label that will appear beside the first checkbox in the browser window.

▶ 5. Press the **Tab** key to move to the first row of the Value column, and then type **r70**. This text will identify the checkbox when you receive the form.

▶ 6. Press the **Tab** key to move to the second row of the Label column, type **rock 80s era**, press the **Tab** key to move to the Value column, and then type **r80**. The second checkbox is entered.

▶ 7. Click the **Add Item** button ⊞ to add another checkbox, and then create a checkbox with the label **metal** and the value **m**.

8. Repeat Step 7 to create checkboxes with the following labels and values:

   blues   **b**
   funk   **f**
   oldies **o**
   pop   **p**

9. In the Checkboxes box, select **oldies**, and then click the **Move Item Up** button ▲ until the oldies checkbox moves to the top of the list. The oldies checkbox will appear first in the group.

10. In the Lay out using section, click the **Line breaks** option button, if necessary.

11. Click the **OK** button. The checkbox group is inserted into the page.

12. Click a blank section of the page to deselect the group. See Figure 6-36.

Figure 6-36	Form with checkboxes

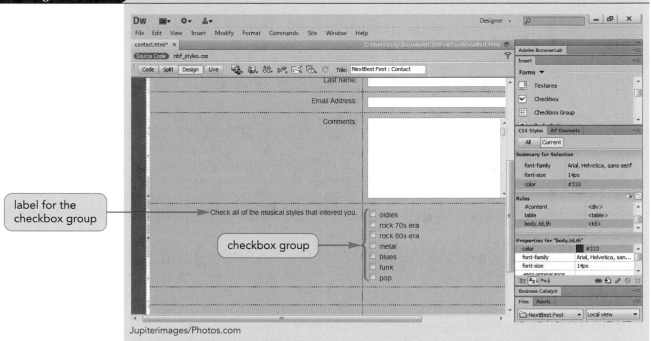

label for the checkbox group

checkbox group

Jupiterimages/Photos.com

Now that you have added the group, you can select each checkbox individually and examine or adjust additional attributes.

13. In the Document window, click the **oldies** checkbox (not its label). The checkbox attributes are displayed in the Property inspector. If you were adding individual checkboxes, this is where you would enter the checkbox name and value. See Figure 6-37.

Figure 6-37 **Selected checkbox**

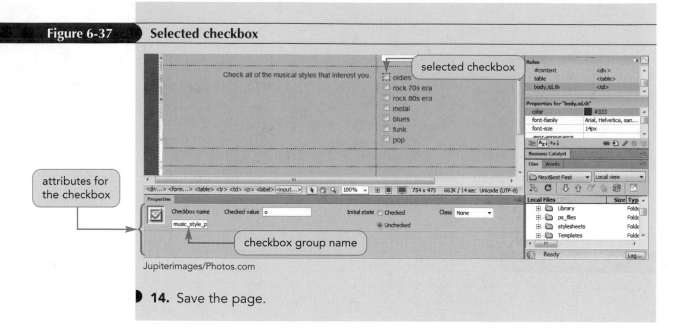

Jupiterimages/Photos.com

▶ **14.** Save the page.

Adding Radio Buttons to a Form

Radio buttons are a group of selection objects that work together in a form. Users can select only one radio button from a radio button group. You can insert a group of radio buttons into a form using the Radio Group button in the same way that you insert a checkbox group. When you click the Radio Group button, a dialog box opens so you can name the radio group, label each radio button with the text you want to appear beside it in the form, and enter a value for the Checked value of each button. You will not use radio buttons or a radio group in the contact form.

Adding Lists to a Form

Lists are another way to enable users to choose several items from a group. There are a few attribute choices associated with lists. Height enables you to set how many rows are visible in the list box. You can add as many items to the list as you want. If the list includes more items than are visible in the list box, scroll bars enable the users to view all of the selections. The Selections check box enables you to set whether users can select only one item in the list (unchecked) or more than one item in the list (checked). The List Values button opens the dialog box in which you type the items that will appear in a list or edit existing items in a list. You can also associate a value with each item, which can be used by a script to identify the list item. The Initially selected list enables you to select one or more items from the list to appear selected in the list. This option is often used to create a default selection, such as selecting New Jersey from a list of states because NextBest Fest is based there and more users will likely be from that area. If you prefer the list to appear as a menu, click the Menu option button in the Type section.

Gage wants to know which bands in next year's lineup users listen to. You will add a list field to the form that includes bands that are scheduled to perform at next year's fest.

To add a list to the contact form:

▶ **1.** Click in the left column of the seventh row, type **Select all of the bands that you enjoy from the list.** (including the period), and then press the **Tab** key to move the insertion point to the next cell.

2. In the **Forms** category of the Insert panel, click the **Select (List/Menu)** button, and then click the **OK** button in the Input Tag Accessibility Attributes dialog box. A small list box appears in the form.

3. In the Document window, select the list box, and then, in the Property inspector, type **band_list** in the Select box, click the **List** option button in the Type group, type **3** in the Height box, and check the **Allow multiple** check box in the Selections group. The NextBest Fest bands list will be three rows high, and the user can select more than one band from the list.

4. In the Property inspector, click the **List Values** button. The List Values dialog box opens. See Figure 6-38.

| Figure 6-38 | List Values dialog box |

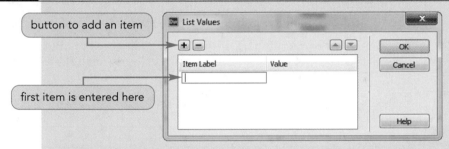

5. In the first row of the Item Label column, type **Bon-Journo**, click in the first row of the Value column, and then type **Bon-Journo**.

6. Click the **Add Item** button ⊞ to add another item, and then type **Silver Rail** in each column.

TIP

You can press the Tab key to move between columns and add another item in the List Values dialog box.

7. Repeat Step 6 to add **More Exquisite Less Dead**, **Living Dead Milkmen**, and **Wild Horses** to the list.

8. Click the **OK** button. The items appear in the list. See Figure 6-39.

| Figure 6-39 | Completed list/menu box |

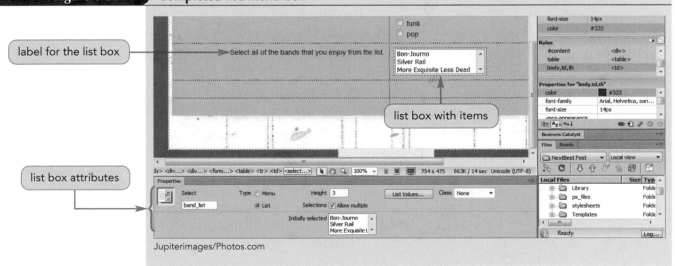

Jupiterimages/Photos.com

Adding Buttons to a Form

You must add a Submit button to a form to enable users to send the form data to the location where it will be processed. It is a good idea to add a Reset button as well so that users can clear any data they input into the form with one click and start over, if necessary. When you click the Button button in the Forms category of the Insert panel, it defaults to the Submit form action, which creates a Submit button. You can also choose the Reset Form action to create a Reset button, or you can choose None and then add other behaviors to the button. In addition to an action, you should type a name and a value for the button. The value will appear as text on the button, and the name is used to reference the button in the code.

You will add a Submit button and a Reset button to the form.

To add a Submit button and a Reset button to the contact form:

▶ **1.** Click in the left column of the eighth row. You will insert the Submit button here.

▶ **2.** In the **Forms** category of the Insert panel, click the **Button** button, and then click the **OK** button in the Input Tag Accessibility Attributes dialog box. A Submit button appears in the form.

▶ **3.** Click the **Submit** button to select it, if necessary. See Figure 6-40.

Figure 6-40	Form with one button

Jupiterimages/Photos.com

Trouble? If the button on your screen is not a Submit button, you need to adjust the button attributes. You will do this in the following steps; continue with Step 4.

▶ **4.** In the Property inspector, click the **Submit form** option button in the Action group, type **Submit** in the Button name box, and type **Submit** in the Value box, if necessary.

▶ **5.** In the Document window, click in the blank space to the right of the Submit button, and then repeat Step 2 to insert another button.

▶ **6.** If necessary, click the second **Submit** button in the Document window to select it.

▶ **7.** In the Property inspector, click the **Reset form** option button in the Action group, type **Reset** in the Button name box, and then type **Reset** in the Value box, if necessary. The Reset button is added to the form.

▶ **8.** In the All Rules pane of the CSS Styles panel, delete the **table** style.

▶ **9.** Save the page, and then save the style sheet.

▶ **10.** Switch to **Live** view to preview the form as it will appear in a browser, and then scroll down to view the new buttons. See Figure 6-41.

Figure 6-41	Live preview of the form with two buttons

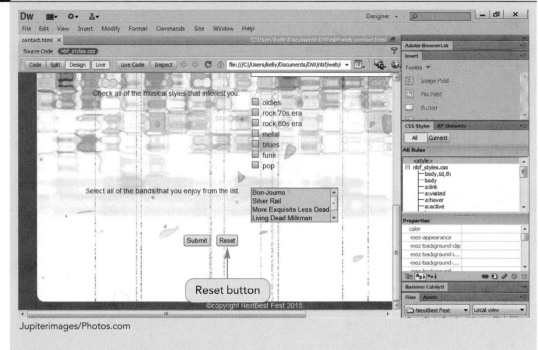

Jupiterimages/Photos.com

▶ **11.** Return to **Design** view.

Testing a Form

You should test a form to ensure that it displays properly in all of the browsers you plan to support and to ensure that the form functionality is working. You should view the form locally to verify that the form objects are laid out properly, and then you should upload the site and test the functionality of the form over the Web. It is sometimes possible to test the functionality of a form locally, but often, when the form-processing script resides on a Web server, the script will not work properly until the site is posted to the remote server. In this case, the script is located in a Web page and is set up to test the form. When you click the Submit button, the script will display the information that would be sent to the server if the script were located there.

You will test the contact form. Because the script is in a Web page, you can test the form locally. The process for testing the form is the same as it would be if you were testing the form over the Web.

To test the contact form:

1. Preview the contact.html page in a browser.
2. In the First Name text box, type your first name.
3. In the Last Name text box, type your last name.
4. In the Email Address text box, type your email address or **test@nextbestfest.com**.
5. In the Comments text area, type **testing**.
6. Check the **oldies** checkbox.
7. In the bands list, click **Bon-Journo**. See Figure 6-42.

Figure 6-42   Completed form in the contact.html page

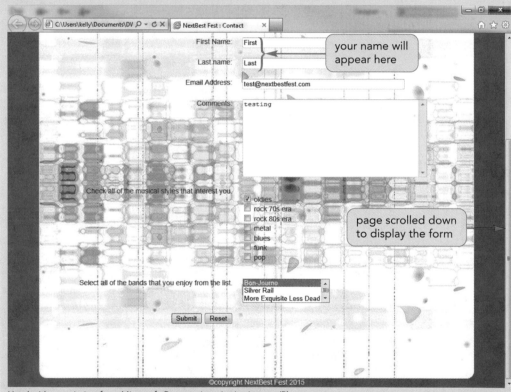

Used with permission from Microsoft Corporation; Jupiterimages/Photos.com

8. Click the **Submit** button. The test script opens another browser window with the form data that would be submitted to the server. See Figure 6-43.

Figure 6-43   Form data that would be sent to the server

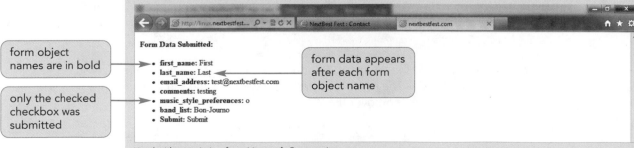

Used with permission from Microsoft Corporation

TIP

Different symbols may appear in the submitted form data (for example, "@" may appear as "%40" and spaces may appear as "%20") due to URL encoding.

9. Close the browser window with the form data, and then click the **Reset** button in the form to clear the information from the form.

10. Close the browser, and then close the contact.html page.

Updating the Web Site on the Remote Server

You will upload the site to the remote server and preview the site over the Web. This way, you can see all the changes you made to the NextBest Fest site, including the library item footer and the form.

To upload and preview the updated remote NextBest Fest site:

1. Connect to your remote host.

2. Use the **Put file(s)** button ⬆ to upload the updated pages and new dependent files to your remote site.

3. Disconnect from your remote site.

4. In your browser, open the home page of your remote NextBest Fest site.

5. Preview each of the pages, reviewing the new content and testing the footer link. The site includes all the new styles and content that you added to the local version.

6. In the contact.html page, enter information in the form to test it, and then submit the form.

7. Close the browser.

In this session, you added a form to the contact.html page site so users can submit information to the NextBest Fest.

REVIEW

Session 6.3 Quick Check

1. What is a form?
2. True or False. Forms process information entered by the user.
3. What happens when you add a form to a page?
4. What is a form object?
5. List three types of form objects.
6. Why is it important to name every form object?
7. Why must you add a Submit button to a form?
8. How should you test a form?

Practice the skills you learned in the tutorial.

PRACTICE

Review Assignments

There are no Data Files needed for the Review Assignments.

Dan wants you to create a footer library item that includes an email link to replace the existing footer in all the pages of the site. He also wants you to create a template for the antifest site that the company interns can use to create new pages for the site.

1. Open the **antifest** site you modified in Tutorial 5, and then open the **index.html** page in Design view.

2. Open the Assets panel, and then click the Library button to open the library.

3. In the Document window, select the footer text, and then drag the text to the top pane of the library.

4. Type **footer** as the library item name, and then double-click the library item to open it in the Document window.

5. Select all the text in the Document window, and then, in the Link box in the Property inspector, type **mailto:info@antifest.com** to create the email link.

6. Save the footer library item, and then click the Update button in the Update Library Items dialog box, if necessary, to update the library item in the home page.

7. Close the library item, and then save and close the home page.

8. Open the **lineup.html** page in Design view, and then delete the footer text from the page.

9. Drag the footer library item from the library in the Assets panel to the same location in the Document window of the original footer text, and then save and close the page.

10. Repeat Steps 8 and 9 to insert the footer library item in the **directions.html**, **schedule.html**, and **tickets.html** pages.

11. Open the **index.html** page in Design view, and then click the Make Template button in the Templates list in the Common category of the Insert panel.

12. In the Save As Template dialog box, select antifest as the site, type **af_template** in the Save as box, click the Save button, and then update the links. The af_template.dwt template is created.

13. Delete all the content from the content area of the page, and then create an editable region named **er1**.

14. Select the text in the editable region, type **place content here**, select the text, and then, in the Property inspector, change the format to None to remove the style from the placeholder text.

15. Save the page, preview the page in Live view to see what the page will look like in a browser, and then return to Design view.

16. Preview the page in a browser, and then close the browser and the page.

17. Upload all the pages and dependent files to your remote server, and then preview the site over the Internet, testing the form.

18. Submit the finished files to your instructor.

*Add keywords,
a meta
description, and
a contact form
to a Web site
for a skateboard
company.*

Case Problem 1

Data File needed for this Case Problem: form_test.html

Moebius Skateboards   Corey wants you to add keywords and a meta description to every page of the Moebius Skateboards site. You will create a form in the contact.html page to enable users to communicate with Corey. You will use the form_test.html file as the form action so that you can test the form.

1. Open the **Moebius Skateboards** site you modified in Tutorial 5, and then open the **index.html** page in Design view.

2. Open the Keywords dialog box, and then type **moebius skateboards, fort worth skateboarding team, moebiusskateboards.com, independent boards, indie skateboard manufacturer, decks, moebius riders, moebius** in the Keywords box. (*Hint*: Use all lowercase letters and separate each word or phrase with a comma.)

3. Copy the words in the Keywords box, click the OK button to add the keywords to the page, and then save and close the page.

4. Open each of the following pages: **about.html**, **contact.html**, **boards.html**, **events.html**, **team.html**, open the Keywords dialog box, paste the list of keywords in the Keywords box, click the OK button to add the list to the page, and then save and close the page.

5. Open the **index.html** page in Design view, open the Description dialog box, and then type **Moebius is an independent skateboard company based in Fort Worth, Texas.** in the Description box.

6. Copy the text in the Description box, click the OK button, and then save and close the page.

7. Open each of the following pages: **about.html**, **contact.html**, **boards.html**, **events.html**, **team.html**, open the Description dialog box, paste the description in the Description box, click the OK button, and then save and close the page.

8. Copy the **form_test.html** page located in the Dreamweaver6\Case1 folder included with your Data Files into the local root folder for the site.

9. Open the **contact.html** page, and then delete the "check back soon, more is on the way. . ." text.

10. Add a form to the page, and then set the following form attributes: **contact_form** as the form name, the form_test.html page as the action, GET as the method, application/x-www-form-urlencoded as the enctype, and _blank as the target. (*Hint*: Click the Browse for File button next to the Action box, navigate to the local root folder, and then double-click form_test.html.)

11. In the form area, create a table with 5 rows, 2 columns, 100% table width, 0 border thickness, 0 cell spacing, 10 cell padding, no header, and **Moebius Skateboards contact form. To contact by phone call (817) 555-1234.** as the summary.

12. Align the left column of the table to the Right and Top, and then align the right column of the table to the Left and Top.

13. In the upper-left cell, type **first name:**, move the insertion point to the next cell, insert a text field, select the text field, and then type **firstname** in the TextField box in the Property inspector. Use the default character width and maximum characters values.

14. In the left cell of the second row, type **last name:**, press the Tab key, insert a text field, select the text field, and then type **lastname** in the TextField box in the Property inspector. Use the default character width and maximum characters values.

15. Click in the left cell of the third row, type **email address:**, press the Tab key, insert a text field into the cell, select the text field, and then type **email** in the TextField box in the Property inspector.

16. Click in the left cell of the fourth row, type **comments:**, press the Tab key, insert a text area into the cell, select the text area, and then type **comments** in the TextField box in the Property inspector. Leave the other settings at the defaults.

17. In the lower-right cell, insert a Submit button, select the button, and then enter **Submit** as the button name and value in the Property inspector.

18. Insert a second button, select the button, click the Reset form option button in the Property inspector, type **Reset** in the Button name box, and then type **Reset** in the Value box, if necessary.

19. Save the page, preview the page in a browser, test the form, and then close the browser and the page.

20. Upload the site to your remote server, preview the site over the Internet, and then test the form.

21. Submit the finished files to your instructor.

Create a template and a footer library item for a Web site devoted to the work of Charles Russell.

APPLY

Case Problem 2

There are no Data Files needed for this Case Problem.

Cowboy Art Society   Members of the Cowboy Art Society have decided to make the Cowboy Charlie site a template-based site, which will make it faster to update the site. Moni wants you to create the template based on the index.html page and include a footer library item, which you also need to create. You won't add the footer library item to the existing pages because you will move their content to the template once it is approved.

1. Open the **Cowboy Charlie** site you modified in Tutorial 5, and then open the **index.html** page in Design view.

2. Click the Make Template button in the Templates list in the Common category of the Insert bar.

3. Save the new template as **charlie_main** and update links.

4. Select the page heading in the charlie_main.dwt template, insert an editable region, and then name the region **page_heading**.

5. Type **Page Heading** as placeholder text for the page heading and reapply the h1 tag formatting, if necessary.

6. Delete all the text below the page heading and navigation bar.

7. Insert an editable region, and then name the region **content**.

8. Display the library in the Assets panel.

9. Drag the footer text from the Document window to the top pane of the Assets panel to create a new library item.

10. Name the library item **footer**.

11. Save and close the template, and then create a new page from the template.

12. Type **Test Page** in the page_heading editable region, type **Test Content** in the content editable region, change the page title to **Cowboy Charlie – Template Test**, and then save the page as **template_test.html** in the local root folder.

13. Preview the page in a browser, and then close the browser and close the page.

14. Upload the site to your remote server, and then preview the site over the Internet.

15. Submit the finished files to your instructor.

APPLY

Add a meta description, keywords, and a contact form to a Web site for a life coach.

Case Problem 3

Data File needed for this Case Problem: form_test.html

Success with Tess   Tess wants you to add keywords and meta descriptions to the pages of her site so her site gets better placement in search engines. She also wants you to add a form to the contact.html page so that potential and current clients can send her an email from the Web site. You will use the form_test.html file as the form action so that you can test the form.

1. Open the **Success with Tess** site you modified in Tutorial 5, and then open the **index.html** page in Design view.

2. Add the following keywords to the home page: **success with tess, transition life coaching, executive coach, personal empowerment training, life coach, personal development, team building, family coaching**. (*Hint*: Use all lowercase letters and separate each word or phrase with a comma.)

3. Copy the entire list of keywords you added to the home page, and then save and close the page.

4. Open each of the following pages: **about_tess.html**, **coaching.html**, **contact.html**, **specials.html**, paste the list of keywords, and then save and close the page.

5. Open the **index.html** page, and then add the following meta description: **As your life coach, I can help you take control of your personal and professional life and teach you the techniques you need to create the life you've dreamed of living.**

6. Copy the meta description, and then save and close the page.

7. Open each of the following pages: **about_tess.html**, **coaching.html**, **contact.html**, **specials.html**, paste the description, and then save and close the page.

8. Open the **contact.html** page, place the insertion point after the last line of text, and then press the Enter key to create a new line in the content div.

9. Copy the **form_test.html** page located in the Dreamweaver6\Case3 folder included with your Data Files into the local root folder.

10. Add a form area in the content div, and then set the form attributes, using **contact_form** as the form name box, the form_test.html page in the local root folder as the action, GET as the method, application/x-www-form-urlencoded as the enctype, and _blank as the target.

11. In the form area, create a table with 5 rows, 2 columns, 100% table width, 0 border thickness, 0 cell spacing, 10 cell padding, no header, and **Success with Tess contact form. To contact by phone, call (817) 555-1234.** as the summary.

12. Align the left column of the table to the Right and Top, and then align the right column of the table to the Left and Top.

13. In the left cell of the first row, type **first name:**, and then add a text field in the right cell of the first row. Select the text field, and then, in the Property inspector, type **firstname** in the TextField box to name the form object. Use the default character width and maximum characters values.

14. In the left cell of the second row, type **last name:**, and then add a text field in the right cell of the second row. Enter **lastname** as the name of the form object. Use the default character width and maximum characters values.

15. In the left cell of the third row, type **email address:**, and then insert a text field in the right cell of the third row. Enter **email** as the name of the form object, and use the default values for the other settings.

16. In the left cell of the fourth row, type **comments:**, and then insert a text area in the right cell of the fourth row. Enter **comments** as the name of the form object and use the default values for the other settings.

17. In the lower-right cell, insert a Submit button.

18. Next to the Submit button, insert a Reset button, enter **Reset** as the button name, and then enter **Reset** as the value, if necessary.

19. Save the page, preview the page in a browser, test the form, and then close the browser and the page.

20. Upload the site to your remote server, preview the site over the Internet, and then test the form.

21. Submit the finished files to your instructor.

Create an online order form for a Web site for a coffee lounge.

CREATE

Case Problem 4

Data File needed for this Case Problem: form_test.html

Coffee Lounge Tommy asks you to create an online order form for the home page of the Coffee Lounge site. The coffee order form is designed to appeal to the business crowd that frequents the lounge in the early morning and during lunch hours. The form will enable customers to order coffee from their computer or smartphone and specify a pickup time. Customers must be able to specify size, quantity, temperature (hot or iced), and the drink flavor. Customers can then walk in and grab their preordered coffee with no wait at all. If the form generates enough business, Tommy will enable payment processing in the future. Because the server-side script is still being finalized, you will add the form_test.html page to the site so you can test the form.

1. Open the **Coffee Lounge** site that you modified in Tutorial 5.

2. Copy the **form_test.html** page located in the Dreamweaver6\Case4 folder included with your Data Files to the site's local root folder.

3. Open the **index.html** page in Design view, place the insertion point below the page content, and then press the Enter key to add a new line.

4. Insert a form into the page, and then, in the Property inspector, change the form's name to **order**, set the action to the form_test.html page in the site's local root folder, set the target to _blank, change the method to GET, and then set the enctype to application/x-www-form-urlencoded.

5. Type **save time and avoid waiting in line, order your coffee in advance** in the form area, apply the h2 tag, and then press the Enter key.

⊕ **EXPLORE**

6. Design your form. Use any form elements that you feel will effectively convey the information to the user. Remember that the customer must be able to specify size, quantity, temperature (hot or iced), and the drink flavor. Add any other instructions you think are necessary.

7. Insert a table inside the form to hold the form content.

8. Add form elements to the form.

9. Create a Submit button and a Reset button.

10. Create styles as needed for the form elements so they match the look and feel of the site. Apply the styles to the elements where necessary.

11. Preview the page in Live view to see how it will look on the Web.

12. Save the page, and then preview the page in a browser.

13. Upload the site to your remote server, and then preview the pages over the Internet.

14. Submit the finished files to your instructor.

TUTORIAL 7

OBJECTIVES

Session 7.1
- Learn about behaviors
- Add behaviors to a page
- Add a custom script to a page
- Add animation to a page using HTML5 and CSS3

Session 7.2
- Learn about adding media to a Web site
- Insert a Flash movie and adjust its attributes
- Insert a Shockwave movie and adjust its attributes

Session 7.3
- Learn about different sound formats
- Use HTML5 to embed a sound
- Embed a Flash movie with sound
- Create a link to an MP3 sound file
- Learn about digital video and video file formats
- Use HTML5 to embed video
- Add a Flash video to a Web page

Adding Behaviors and Rich Media

Creating Animations and Inserting Flash, Shockwave, Sound, and Video Elements

Case | *NextBest Fest*

Gage wants you to add a behavior to the contact form that will validate entries to ensure that the information received is in the correct format. For example, the behavior will validate that the user's entry in the email text field matches the standard format for an email address, such as name@domain.com. Gage also wants you to add media elements to the site and to create an animation using HTML5 and CSS3. You will add a Flash animation and a promotion for a Shockwave game that the design team is developing. You will also add audio and video clips to the page so that users can hear and see some of the bands.

STARTING DATA FILES

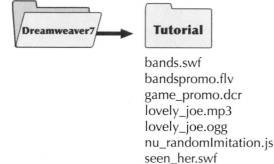

Dreamweaver7 →

Tutorial
bands.swf
bandspromo.flv
game_promo.dcr
lovely_joe.mp3
lovely_joe.ogg
nu_randomImitation.js
seen_her.swf

Review
antifest.flv
underground.mp3
underground.ogg

Case1
moebius_team.swf
nu_randomSk8.js

Case2
cr_art.swf

Case3
nu_randomSuccess.js
successbox.dcr

Case4
coffeegame.dcr
in_the_alley.mp3
sunshine.mp3

SESSION 7.1 VISUAL OVERVIEW

A behavior combines an *object* and an *event* to cause an *action*.

An object is the element in a Web page to which a behavior is attached, such as a graphic or a div.

A **CSS transition** enables you to change the value of CSS properties gradually over a specified period of time. For example, you can slowly fade between two images or make a button enlarge in size over time when a user points to it.

A preset behavior tool, like the Rollover button, is the easiest way to insert behaviors into Web pages.

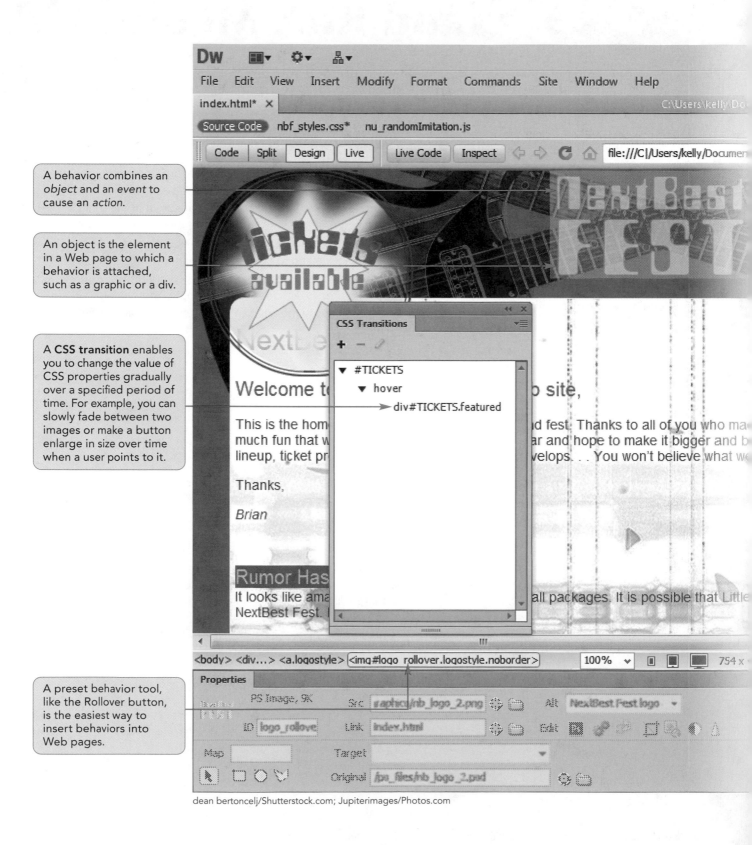

dean bertoncelj/Shutterstock.com; Jupiterimages/Photos.com

ADDING INTERACTIVITY WITH BEHAVIORS

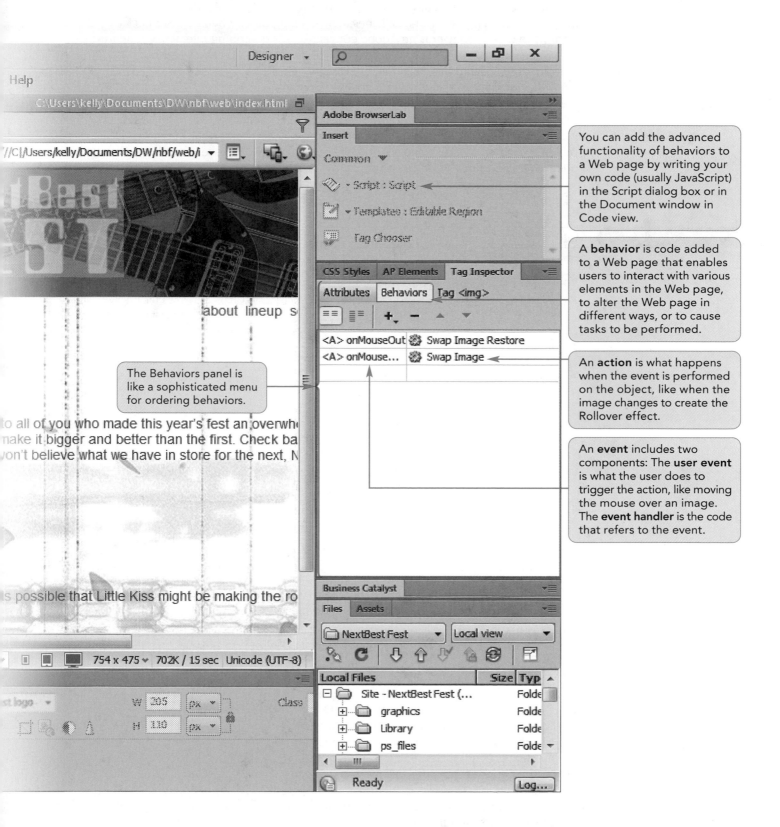

You can add the advanced functionality of behaviors to a Web page by writing your own code (usually JavaScript) in the Script dialog box or in the Document window in Code view.

A **behavior** is code added to a Web page that enables users to interact with various elements in the Web page, to alter the Web page in different ways, or to cause tasks to be performed.

The Behaviors panel is like a sophisticated menu for ordering behaviors.

An **action** is what happens when the event is performed on the object, like when the image changes to create the Rollover effect.

An **event** includes two components: The **user event** is what the user does to trigger the action, like moving the mouse over an image. The **event handler** is the code that refers to the event.

Understanding Behaviors

In Dreamweaver, a behavior is code added to a Web page that enables users to interact with various elements in the Web page, to alter the Web page in different ways, or to cause tasks to be performed. For example, you could stack two AP divs in a Web page, and then create a behavior that switches their stacking order when the user clicks a button. The word *behavior* is an Adobe convention for describing interactive functions in multimedia programs that are managed by the program and accessed through an authoring interface, in this case the Behaviors panel.

A behavior is like a mathematical equation: *object + event = action*. An object is the element in the Web page to which the behavior is attached, such as a graphic or a div. An event has two components: the user event and the event handler. The user event is what the user does to trigger the action. Common user events are moving the pointer over an object (mouseover) and clicking an object. The event handler is the code that refers to the event. For example, the code to refer to the mouseover event is onMouseOver. The action is what happens when the event is performed on the object.

Figure 7-1 describes the three ways to insert behavior functionality into Web pages.

Figure 7-1 | **Methods of inserting behaviors in Dreamweaver**

Tool	Description	You...	Dreamweaver...
Preset behavior tools	Buttons located throughout Dreamweaver to perform common tasks	Enter requested information, for example, which graphic to use, in the dialog box, if necessary	Writes the behavior and inserts it into the page
Behaviors panel	A prewritten list from which you choose an event handler and an action for a behavior	Select the elements of the behavior from lists	Writes the code and inserts it into the page
Custom scripting	Code you write usually with JavaScript in Code view or in the Script dialog box	Write and insert code in the page	Displays your code as a custom script in the Behaviors panel

© 2013 Cengage Learning

A preset behavior tool is the easiest way to insert behaviors into Web pages. You have already used preset behavior tools, including the Rollover button. When you use the Rollover button, Dreamweaver inserts a swap image behavior and a preload behavior as you insert the rollover images. The swap image behavior consists of the action (the images being swapped) triggered by a user event (the user moving the mouse to place the pointer over the image). The image is the object. The preload behavior consists of the action (the image being downloaded) triggered by a user event (the user loading the Web page into a browser window). The Web page is the object. The behaviors Dreamweaver inserted appear in the Behaviors panel when you select the object.

The Behaviors panel is like a sophisticated menu for ordering behaviors. After you select an object, you choose from lists of prewritten actions and event handlers in the Behaviors panel. Based on your selections, Dreamweaver creates the behavior and inserts the code. The Behaviors panel simplifies the process because you can choose only actions that work with the selected object, and then you can choose only event handlers that go with the selected action. For example, if the object is selected text, you cannot choose swap image as the action. If you have not selected an object, the listed actions affect the page. Also, you can limit the lists in the Behaviors panel by HTML version, browser version, or browser brand and version. In general, more complex behaviors require newer browsers.

Validating Form Data

The **Validate Form behavior** enables you to create requirements/limits that check form data before the form is submitted. When the user clicks the Submit button, the data is checked to make sure the data meets the limits/requirements set for each object in the Validate Form behavior. If information is missing or is not within the set limits, a dialog box opens, prompting the user to change incorrect information or add missing information and then click the Submit button again.

The Validate Form dialog box lists all the form objects. You select a field and then set its requirements/limits. You first set whether the selected field is required or optional. The user must enter information into a required field to submit the form. If a field is optional, the form will be submitted even if the user does not enter information in that field. You can also set the following limits for the data entered into the selected field:

- **Anything.** No limits on what the user can enter.
- **Number.** Only numeric values. This limit is often set for fields that are used to input phone numbers or zip codes.
- **Email address.** Only information that follows the format of an email address (for example, name@domain.topleveldomain). This limit ensures that the submitted address is in the correct format, but not that the user has inserted a valid email address.
- **Number from.** A range of acceptable numeric values. This limit is appropriate for a question such as, "How old is your teenager?" The numbers would range from a low of 13 to a high of 19. If a user inputs a number less than 13 or more than 19, the Validate Form behavior informs the user that the data is outside the acceptable range, and then prompts the user to input an acceptable value and resubmit the form.

REFERENCE

Adding a Behavior Using the Behaviors Panel

- In the Document window, select the object to which to add the behavior.
- In the Behaviors panel, click the Add behavior button, point to Show Events For, and then click a browser.
- In the Behaviors panel, click the Add behavior button, and then click a behavior.
- In the Behaviors panel, click the Events arrow, and then click an event.

You will use the Behaviors panel to add the Validate Form behavior to the contact form.

To add the Validate Form behavior to the contact form:

1. Reset Dreamweaver to the **Designer** workspace, minimize the **Business Catalyst** panel, open the **Files** panel, open the **NextBest Fest** site you modified in Tutorial 6, and then open the **contact.html** page in Design view.

2. In the Document window, click anywhere in the form, and then, on the status bar, click the **<form#contact>** tag to select the form. You know the form is selected because the form attributes appear in the Property inspector.

3. On the menu bar, click **Window**, and then click **Tag Inspector** to open the panel.

4. In the Tag Inspector panel group, click the **Behaviors** button to display the Behaviors panel. See Figure 7-2.

Select the specified tag so the behavior code will be applied to the correct tag; otherwise, the form validation behavior will not work.

Figure 7-2 Behaviors panel

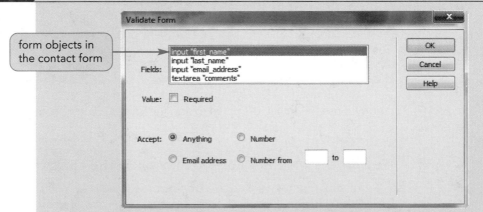

opens the
list of actions

Behaviors panel

shows set events

selected form

form tag selected

dean bertoncelj/Shutterstock.com; Jupiterimages/Photos.com

▶ **5.** In the Behaviors panel, click the **Add behavior** button [+,], and then click **Validate Form**. The Validate Form dialog box opens. See Figure 7-3.

Figure 7-3 Validate Form dialog box

form objects in
the contact form

Trouble? If the Validate Form behavior is not available, you probably selected the table, a cell, or another part of the form rather than the form itself. Click in the Document window, repeat Step 2, and then repeat Step 5.

▶ **6.** In the Fields box, click **input "first_name"** to select it, if necessary, and then click the **Required** check box to insert a check mark. The text "(R)" appears after the field name to indicate that the field is required.

▶ **7.** In the Fields box, click **input "last_name"**, and then check the **Required** check box to make the field a required field.

8. In the Fields box, click **input "email_address"**, and then check the **Required** check box to make the field a required field.

9. In the Accept group, click the **Email address** option button to set a limit requiring the data to follow the standard email format. The text "(RisEmail)" appears after the field name to indicate that the field is required and must be in the email address format.

10. Click the **OK** button. The Validate Form behavior appears in the behavior list in the Behaviors panel. See Figure 7-4.

Figure 7-4	Validate Form behavior added to the contact form

dean bertoncelj/Shutterstock.com; Jupiterimages/Photos.com

11. In the Behaviors panel, click the **Events** arrow, and then click **onSubmit**, if necessary. The behavior will run when the Submit button is clicked.

12. Save the page, and then switch to **Live** view. You will test the behavior.

13. Enter data in the form, typing the word **potato** in the email_address field, and then click the **Submit** button. A dialog box opens, stating that the email_address field must contain an email address. See Figure 7-5.

Figure 7-5	Live View Alert dialog box

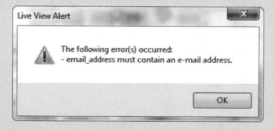

14. Click the **OK** button, return to **Design** view, and then save and close the page.

Adding a Custom Script to a Page

You can add the advanced functionality of behaviors to a Web page by writing your own code (usually JavaScript) in the Script dialog box or in the Document window in Code view. Code you write is not actually considered a behavior because it is not added to the reusable prewritten choice lists in the Behaviors panel. Instead, code you write is considered a custom script and usually appears in the Behaviors panel when you select the object to which it is attached.

Current best practices for adding custom scripts suggest that you write the script in a separate page, include that page in the local root folder, and then insert code into the page that loads the script when the page is loaded. This method is preferred because scripts are often used in more than one page of a site and this keeps the code lean and clean. Also, as with styles, when you link a script to various pages, you can update all those pages at once by editing the single script. To keep your site organized, you create a scripts folder in which to store all the scripts in the site.

INSIGHT

Writing Custom JavaScripts

If you know JavaScript, you can write your own scripts. You can also find scripts that other people have written and posted for public use. However, you will often need to fine-tune scripts that you use in Web pages, so it is a good idea to learn at least enough JavaScript so that you can debug a page. The following sites are some good basic JavaScript resources:
- webreference.com/programming/javascript
- w3schools.com/js

You will add a custom script written in JavaScript by another programmer to the home page. The script randomly selects one of the included quotations to appear in the page when the page is loaded in a browser, providing the illusion that the page has a continuous source of fresh content. The script adds a CSS class style named "quote" to the displayed quotation. You will create a quote class style and add it to the style sheet so you can customize and change the look of the quotations in the page.

To add a custom script to the home page:

1. Open the **index.html** page in Design view, place the insertion point at the end of the last line of content, and then press the **Enter** key.

2. In the Files panel, create a new folder named **scripts** in the local root folder. You will place all the custom scripts you add to the site in the scripts folder.

3. Using the Files panel, copy the **nu_randomImitation.js** script located in the **Dreamweaver7\Tutorial** folder included with your Data Files into the scripts folder you just created.

4. In the **Common** category of the Insert panel, click the **Script button arrow**, and then click the **Script** button. The Script dialog box opens.

5. Click the **Type** button, and then click **text/javascript**, if necessary.

6. Next to the Source box, click the **Browse** button 🗁, and then double-click the **nu_randomImitation.js** file in the scripts folder in the local root folder. The path to the file is added to the Source box. See Figure 7-6.

Figure 7-6   **Script dialog box**

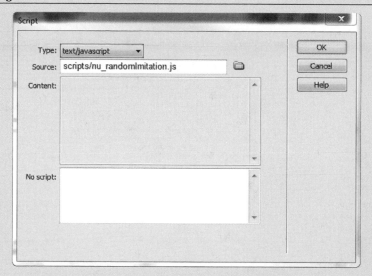

7. Click the **OK** button. This script creates the custom action of displaying one of the quotations included in the script. The action occurs when the page is loaded in the browser window (this is the event). The event handler is automatically onLoad. (The home page is the object.) You cannot see anything in Design view.

Trouble? If a dialog box opens, saying you will not see this element unless invisible elements are displayed, you might need to display invisible elements. Click the OK button to close the dialog box, click View on the menu bar, point to Visual Aids, and then click Invisible Elements, if necessary, to check the option.

8. Switch to **Code** view to see the code that was placed in the page. The code in the home page tells the browser to insert the JavaScript located in the nu_randomImitation.js page when it gets to this point in the home page. See Figure 7-7.

Figure 7-7   Code for the script added to the home page

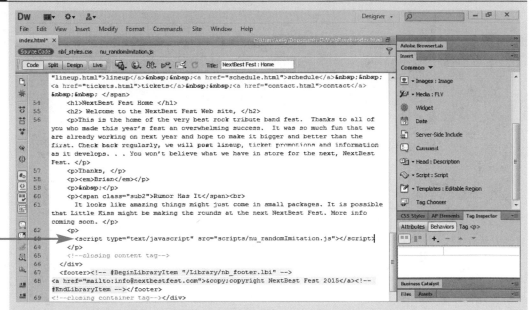

code tells the browser to insert the JavaScript in the nu_randomImitation.js page

Trouble? If the script was inserted on a different line in your page, you do not need to make any changes. The script will work correctly.

9. On the Related Files toolbar, click the **nu_randomImitation.js** button. The nu_randomImitation.js page is displayed in the Document window. See Figure 7-8.

Figure 7-8   Custom script in the nu-randomImitation.js page

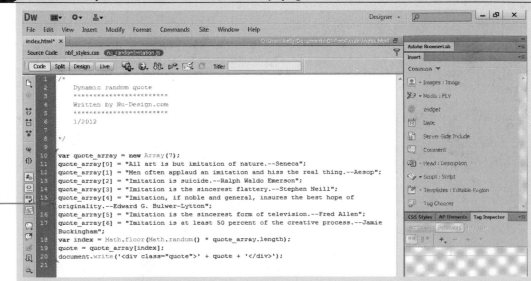

code for the custom script

10. On the Document toolbar, click the **Design** button to return to the home page, and then save the page.

11. Switch to **Live** view, and then scroll to the bottom of the home page to view the quotation. See Figure 7-9.

Figure 7-9	Quotation in the home page

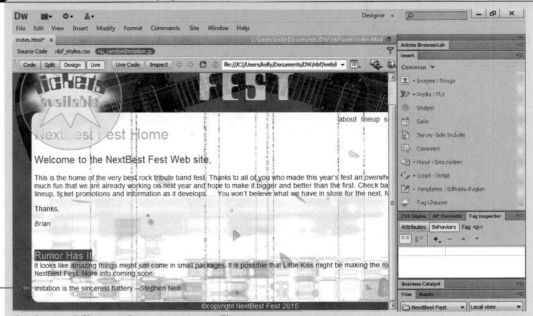

quotation from the JavaScript file (you might see a different quotation)

dean bertoncelj/Shutterstock.com; Jupiterimages/Photos.com

Because you have not defined the quote style, the quotation text is displayed in the default style for the page. You will create a CSS style.

12. Return to **Design** view, and then, using the CSS Styles panel, create a new style with the selector type **Class** named **.quote** that is defined in the **nbf_styles.css** style sheet.

13. In the **Type** category, set the color to **#663** and the font size to **20px**; in the **Box** category, set the float to **right**; and then click the **OK** button.

14. Save the page, and then save the style sheet.

15. Preview the home page in **Live** view, and then return to **Design** view.

Trouble? If the text is not fully displayed in the content area, place the insertion point at the bottom of the page after the script (you might need to look at the page in Code view to ensure that the insertion point appears after the script), press the Enter key to add an additional line to the page, save the page, and then repeat Step 15.

Now that you have finished adding behaviors and scripts to the page, you will test the behaviors in a browser. It is important to continue testing the pages in all the browsers you plan to support because new behaviors can affect the behaviors that are already in the page.

To test the behaviors in the home page:

1. Preview the page in a browser. One of the quotations that the script added appears when the page is loaded in the browser window. See Figure 7-10.

Figure 7-10   **Home page with quotation previewed in a browser**

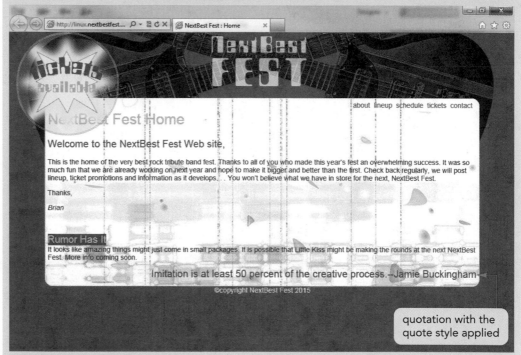

Used with permission from Microsoft Corporation; dean bertoncelj/Shutterstock.com; Jupiterimages/Photos.com

2. Position the pointer over the logo to ensure that the rollover behavior is working correctly.

3. On the browser toolbar, click the **Refresh** button. The home page is reloaded, and a different quotation appears in the page.

   Trouble? If the quotation does not change, you might need to refresh the page again to see a new quotation. This is because the quotations are loaded randomly and sometimes the same quotation will display repeatedly.

4. Refresh the page several more times to view different quotations.

5. Close the browser.

Editing and Deleting Behaviors

After a behavior has been created, you can change the event handler associated with the behavior or you can delete the behavior. If you want to change the action, you need to delete the old behavior, select the object, and then attach the new behavior. You can do this in the Behaviors panel.

Creating CSS Animations

With CSS3 comes the ability to create CSS-based animations ranging from simple fades to complex groups of movements. Before CSS-based animations, most animations were created in other programs such as Adobe Flash, and then the final code was inserted into a Web page. Now you can simply create the animation in Dreamweaver. When you create a CSS-based animation, Dreamweaver adds styles that define the movement to your style sheet and sometimes adds code to the page. In HTML5, the <canvas> tag was added as a container element, which you can use with JavaScript to draw graphics on the screen.

The simplest form of animation is a transition. CSS transitions enable you to change the value of CSS properties gradually over a specified period of time. With CSS transitions, you can do things like slowly fade between two images or specify that a button grows or shrinks in size over time when the user points to it. You can create and edit transitions from the CSS panel or from the CSS Transitions window.

Problem Solving: Creating Pages That Degrade Gracefully

Creating a site with contemporary style and functionality is particularly important if your target audience includes a younger, tech-savvy crowd. Achieving a trendy look can involve using HTML5 and CSS3 code, which is not yet the current WC3 standard and does not have unified browser support. For example, Internet Explorer 9 does not support CSS transitions at all, although Internet Explorer 10 will support CSS transitions as well as other CSS-based animation. Chrome and Firefox already support CSS transitions as well as other CSS-based animation. Because of the spotty browser support, you must carefully consider the target audience and the site goals before you add new CSS3/HTML5-based flourishes such as transitions to your pages. If the target audience will most likely view the site from browsers that do not support some CSS3/HTML5 elements, then either avoid these elements or add these elements to the site in such a way that users with older browsers can still interact with the site and experience a positive aesthetic impact. For example, you could use CSS animation to create a transition that causes the borders of a div to change colors slowly when the user mouses over it. In this case, if a user's browser does not support transitions, the user will simply see the mouseover without a slow transition, which is what the user is expecting to see. Another example is if you add rounded corners to a div. If a user's browser does not support rounded corners, the user will simply see square corners. As long as this looks natural to the user and does not interfere with the user's interaction with the site, you have created a site that gracefully degrades in older browsers. Creating a site with current code and techniques that still work well and look pleasing in older browsers enables it to degrade gracefully. In contemporary design, these are considered best practices for creating sites. Creating gracefully degrading code enables you to incorporate the latest techniques into a site while maintaining a positive user experience for everyone who visits the site.

You use the New Transitions dialog box to create a transition. First, you select a target rule to which you will add the transition. Then, you select an action from the Transition On list, which specifies what triggers the transition for the user, such as a mouseover. All transitions have a Duration, which is the amount of time the transition takes; a Delay, which specifies the amount of time that lapses between when the action occurs and the transition starts; and a Time Function, which specifies how the transaction occurs, such as getting faster or slower during the transition. Finally, you select one or more properties that the transition settings you selected earlier will affect, such as the color, border width, or font size. Each property has additional parameters that you can set, such as the ending color of the object, the ending width of the border, or the final size of the font.

Gage wants to include some contemporary flourishes in the NextBest Fest site. In addition to the rounded corners that you added to the container div and the TICKETS div, he wants transitions added to the site in a way that will not detract from the experience of users who cannot view CSS animation. You will make the border of the TICKETS div thicker so that it is easier to see, and then you will add a transition that changes the border color over 3 seconds when a user places the pointer over the div and changes back when the pointer is no longer over the div.

To create the div border color transition:

▶ **1.** In the CSS Styles panel, select the **featured** style, and then change the border property to a **6px** width.

▶ **2.** On the menu bar, click **Window**, and then click **CSS Transitions**. The CSS Transitions panel opens.

▶ **3.** In the CSS Transitions panel, click the **Create New Transition** button ⊞ . The New Transition dialog box opens.

▶ **4.** Click the **Target Rule arrow**, and then click **#TICKETS** to select the style that affects the TICKETS div.

▶ **5.** Click the **Transition On** button, and then click **hover** to set the transition to occur when the user places the pointer over the TICKETS div.

▶ **6.** In the Duration box, type **3** and then, if necessary, click the **Duration** button and click **s** to set the transition to last for 3 seconds.

▶ **7.** Click the **Timing Function arrow**, and then click **linear** to have the transition occur at the same pace throughout its duration.

▶ **8.** Click the **Add Property** button ⊞▾ , click **border-color** in the Property list, click in the **End Value** color box, and then type **#00591c** to set the border color that will appear during the transition. See Figure 7-11.

Figure 7-11 New Transition dialog box

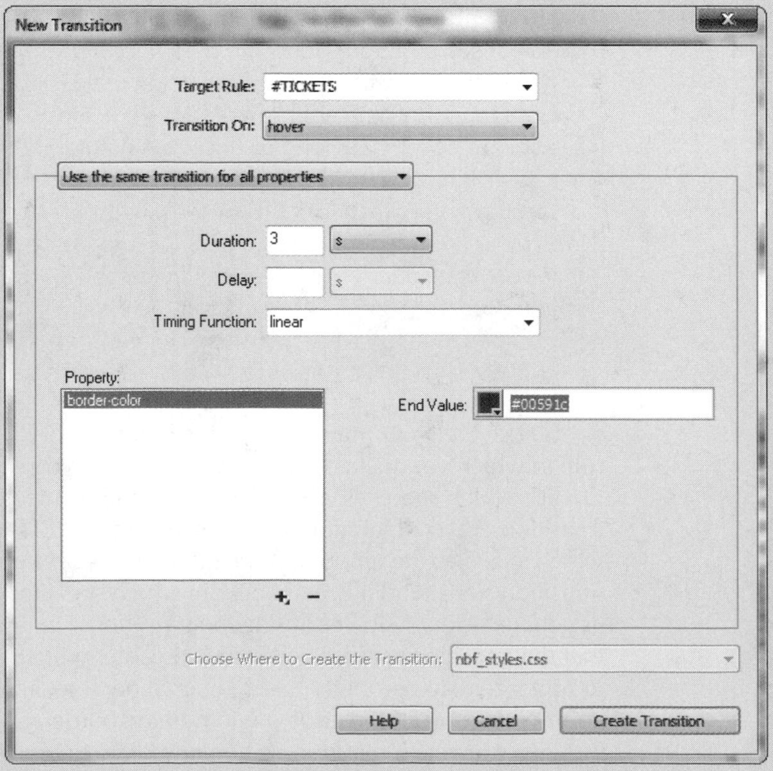

9. Click the **Create Transition** button. The transition is created and added to the TICKETS div.

10. Switch to **Live** view, and then point to the **TICKETS** div. The transition added to the #TICKETS div makes the border change to a dark green color over 3 seconds. See Figure 7-12.

| Figure 7-12 | New transition in Live view |

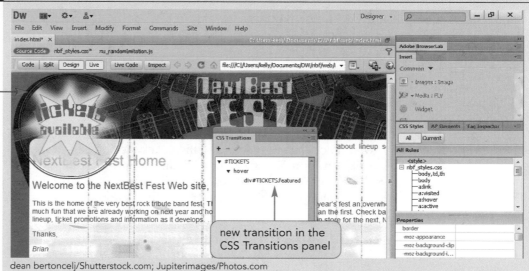

border color changes over 3 seconds when the pointer is over the div

new transition in the CSS Transitions panel

dean bertoncelj/Shutterstock.com; Jupiterimages/Photos.com

11. Move the pointer off the TICKETS div. The border color returns to the original color over 3 seconds.

12. Close the CSS Transitions panel, and then save the page and the style sheet.

Next, you will view the transition in Internet Explorer and Firefox. Because Internet Explorer 9 and earlier versions do not support CSS transitions, the border will not change color. However, the available text will still change color because that was included as part of the rollover image, which Internet Explorer does support. The transition does appear in Firefox because that browser supports CSS transitions. If you do not have Firefox installed, you can view the transition in Google Chrome or you can read but not complete Steps 4 through 7.

To view the CSS transition in different browsers:

1. View the home page in Internet Explorer.

2. Point to the **TICKETS** div. The border changes color immediately, not slowly over 3 seconds as it did in Live view. This is an example of a site degrading gracefully because the change is still aesthetically pleasing even though it did not occur over time and the user can still effectively interact with the site.

3. Close the browser.

4. Click **File** on the menu bar, point to **Preview in Browser**, and then click **Firefox**. The home page opens in Firefox.

   Trouble? If you do not have Firefox installed, you can view the transition in Google Chrome or you can read but not complete Steps 4 through 7.

▶ **5.** Point to the **TICKETS** div. The border color changes to a dark green over a 3-second period.

Trouble? If you do not see a slow transition, you may have an older version of Firefox. Update the browser to the current version, and then repeat Steps 4 and 5 to view the transition.

▶ **6.** Move the pointer off the TICKETS div. The border color returns to the original color.

▶ **7.** Close the browser.

Editing and Deleting Transitions

After a transition has been created, you can change its settings and properties or you can delete it. You can make these changes from the CSS Transitions panel or from the CSS Styles panel. In the CSS Transitions panel, you select the rule for the transition you want to change or delete, and then click the Edit Selected Transition button to open the Edit Transition dialog box or click the Remove Transition button to delete the transition. In the CSS Styles panel, you select the rule for the transition you want to change, and then edit the transition in the Transition category.

Examining the Code for a Transition

When you create a transition, Dreamweaver adds properties to the CSS rule that you selected to apply the transition to. The exact code that is added reflects the properties being changed during the transition. Because various browsers handle CSS transitions differently, Dreamweaver adds the same code on new lines for each browser. This is similar to the technique you used to add a font group, which enabled all of the different browsers and operating systems to recognize a font from the group. In this case, the new CSS code shown in Figure 7-13 was added to the TICKETS div located in the head content.

Figure 7-13   **CSS code for the new transition**

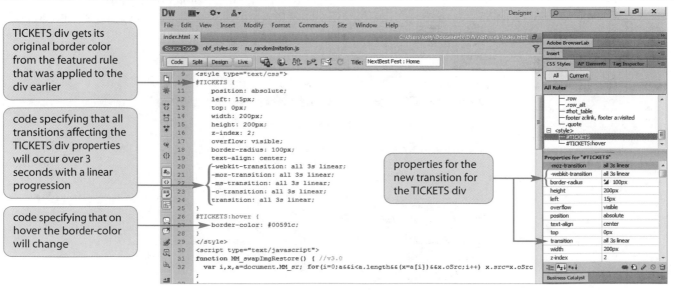

TICKETS div gets its original border color from the featured rule that was applied to the div earlier

code specifying that all transitions affecting the TICKETS div properties will occur over 3 seconds with a linear progression

code specifying that on hover the border-color will change

properties for the new transition for the TICKETS div

Notice that the code for the TICKETS div does not have a property that defines the border size, style, or color even though the TICKETS div has an aqua, double-line, 6-pixel-width border. These border properties are defined in the featured rule, which you applied to the TICKETS div. When you created the transition, the following lines of code were added to the TICKETS rule:

```
-webkit-transition: all 3s linear;
-moz-transition: all 3s linear;
-ms-transition: all 3s linear;
-o-transition: all 3s linear;
transition: all 3s linear;
```

The first line is targeted at browsers that use WebKit, which is an open source Web browser engine. WebKit-based browsers include Safari, Google Chrome, and Amazon Kindle. The second line (moz) is targeted at Mozilla Firefox. The third line (ms) is targeted at Microsoft Internet Explorer. The fourth line (o) is targeted at Opera. The fifth line is the basic line of code as it should appear when there are no adjustments or workarounds. In this code, the values are the same in all five lines, but often the values are different. In addition to the code added to the TICKETS div rule, a new style that specifies what will happen when the pointer is over the TICKETS div (called the hover state) was added to the page, which has the following code:

```
#TICKETS:hover {
    border-color: #00591C;
}
```

This rule says that on hover (or when the pointer is over an object), the border color will change to #00591c (a dark greenish color). Because the transition properties in the TICKETS div specify that any changes should occur over a 3-second period, the color changes slowly over 3 seconds when the user places the pointer over the div and then the color changes back slowly over 3 seconds when the user moves the pointer away from the TICKETS div. Being able to include CSS code that causes time-based animation of elements in your Web pages opens many possibilities in site design.

You can use HTML5/CSS3 to add other animated elements that help organize pages. For example, you could create tabs, animated drop-down menus, or accordions. You can code these advanced interactive or animated elements yourself or you can use a software package like Adobe Edge. Edge enables designers to create animated and interactive Web content using HTML5, CSS3, and JavaScript in a visual environment much like Dreamweaver enables you to create Web sites. Like Photoshop and Fireworks, Edge works with Dreamweaver so you can easily use the animations and interactivity you create in Edge in the pages of sites you create in Dreamweaver.

In this session, you added behaviors, a custom script, and a CSS transition to the NextBest Fest site. In the next session, you will add media to the site.

Session 7.1 Quick Check

REVIEW

1. What is a behavior?
2. What is an event?
3. What is an action?
4. Are all behaviors selected and assigned in the Behaviors panel?
5. True or False. You cannot change the action associated with a behavior.
6. What is a custom script?
7. What is a CSS transition?

SESSION 7.2 VISUAL OVERVIEW

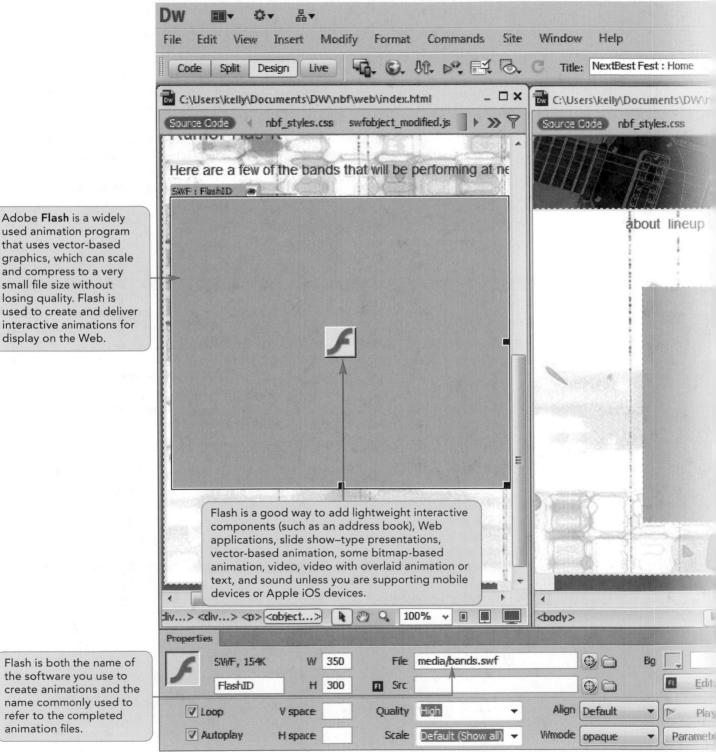

Adobe **Flash** is a widely used animation program that uses vector-based graphics, which can scale and compress to a very small file size without losing quality. Flash is used to create and deliver interactive animations for display on the Web.

Flash is a good way to add lightweight interactive components (such as an address book), Web applications, slide show–type presentations, vector-based animation, some bitmap-based animation, video, video with overlaid animation or text, and sound unless you are supporting mobile devices or Apple iOS devices.

Flash is both the name of the software you use to create animations and the name commonly used to refer to the completed animation files.

dean bertoncelj/Shutterstock.com; Jupiterimages/Photos.com

ADDING SHOCKWAVE AND FLASH MOVIES

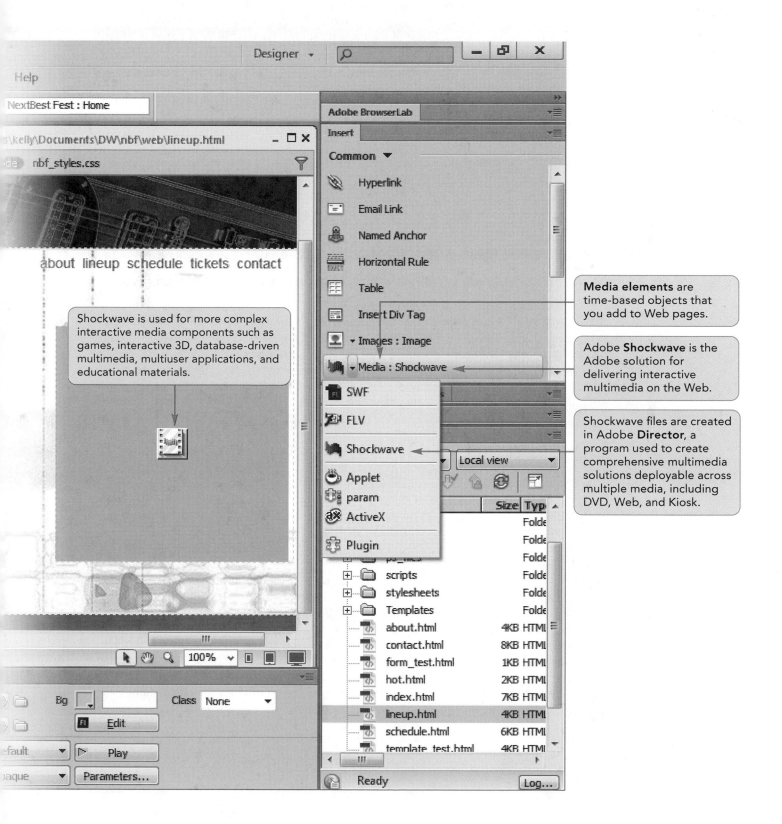

Shockwave is used for more complex interactive media components such as games, interactive 3D, database-driven multimedia, multiuser applications, and educational materials.

Media elements are time-based objects that you add to Web pages.

Adobe Shockwave is the Adobe solution for delivering interactive multimedia on the Web.

Shockwave files are created in Adobe Director, a program used to create comprehensive multimedia solutions deployable across multiple media, including DVD, Web, and Kiosk.

Adding Media to a Web Site

Media elements are time-based objects that are added to a Web page. Some media elements need a player or an application that is not part of the browser (such as plug-ins, ActiveX controls, or helper applications) to display within a browser. The terms *player* and *plug-in* are used in this tutorial to refer generally to the above-mentioned technologies. Some of the most useful media used in Web pages are Flash, Shockwave, sound, and video. You often need a special software package, separate from the player or plug-in, to create a media component. For example, you create Flash applications and animations in the Adobe Flash software. After you have created a media element, you can insert it into a Web page and users can view it. Users view Flash files that you have inserted into your Web pages with Flash Player. You can also add many media elements, like sound and video, to Web pages using only HTML5 and no players or plug-ins. This improvement standardizes the way that designers add animation, sound, and video to pages and allows users to view the added elements without downloading special players and plug-ins.

In the rest of this tutorial, you will learn about Flash, Shockwave, sound, and video, and then add each type of element to the NextBest Fest site in a variety of ways.

PROSKILLS

Decision Making: Using Media to Enhance the User's Experience

As you develop a site, you will need to decide how much media and animation to include in the pages. Too much media and animation can overwhelm a viewer and create a cluttered and aesthetically unpleasing site. So, be discriminating when you decide what media to include in a site. Make sure that each element you include in a page has a purpose. The animation, game, audio, or movie must enhance the site, contribute to the user experience, and reinforce the site goals. You do not want to overwhelm the user with too much glitz. When determining what to add to pages, consider whether the proposed element will enhance the user's ability to grasp the site goals or distract them from focusing on the message. If the element will distract the user, discard it. This might mean cutting an innovative or creative element.

Also, keep in mind the technological limitations of the target audience. Be sure that the target audience can easily access media elements that communicate necessary information. Some media require a plug-in to run on the client device. Some plug-ins are included with the latest browsers; others must be downloaded by the user. Before incorporating media into a site, learn what plug-ins users will need to view each element, determine the likelihood that users have those plug-ins, and assess how difficult it is for users to get the needed plug-ins.

Be aware that media elements can use considerable bandwidth. Evaluate the connection speed and the device speed for your target audience to determine if the user agent can display the media element effectively without prolonged delays. If users have to wait too long to view a page, they often lose interest and move to another site. Users usually wait longer for an item they perceive to be important than for an item they perceive to be unimportant. If you are asking users to wait for your site to load, make sure that the wait is worth their time.

When you add multimedia elements to the site, consider accessibility. Many media elements are not accessible to users who have impairments and rely on assistive devices. Because of this limitation, do not use multimedia elements to communicate vital content. Instead, use the elements to augment and reinforce the site content. Also, be sure to add descriptive text to alt tags for multimedia elements so impaired users can understand what those elements are communicating.

Understanding Adobe Flash

Flash was one of the first widely used animation programs that used vector-based graphics. Because vector-based graphics can scale and compress to a very small file size without losing quality, Flash was originally one of the premier solutions for creating and delivering interactive animations for display on the Web. The latest version of Flash also contains video-handling capabilities, is better at compressing bitmap-based animation, has more developed coding capabilities, and includes excellent audio capabilities. Flash is a good choice for lightweight interactive components (such as an address book), Web applications, slide show–type presentations, vector-based animation, some bitmap-based animation, video, video that has additional animation or text laid over it, and sound, if you are not supporting Apple iOS devices or mobile devices.

Viewing Flash in Apple and Mobile Devices

The Apple (iOS) operating system, which runs on devices such as iPhones, iPods, and iPads, does not currently support Flash. Although mobile devices that do not use iOS currently support Flash, Adobe does not plan to continue to develop Flash players for these mobile devices. This means that eventually Flash will not work on mobile devices unless a third party builds a player that enables mobile devices to play Flash files. (The only exception is mobile apps that are created in Flash and packaged in Adobe AIR for all of the major app stores.) Adobe announced that it has made this change because "HTML5 is now universally supported on major mobile devices, in some cases exclusively. This makes HTML5 the best solution for creating and deploying content in the browser across mobile platforms." This statement adds validity for the change in current best practices to support using HTML5 and CSS3 to create animation and add video and sound to Web sites. Because Flash remains prevalent on the Web and Adobe will continue to support Flash Player for PCs, you still need to know how to work with it in Web pages.

Flash is both the name of the software you use to create animations and the name commonly used to refer to the completed animation files. Flash files are also called Flash movies. The types of Flash files that you will see most frequently are:

- **.fla.** The source file used by the Flash program when you create a Flash movie. You edit .fla files when you want to make changes to Flash movies. These authoring files can be opened only in the Flash program. The files must be exported from Flash as .swf files to be viewed on the Web.
- **.swf.** A compressed Flash file that is viewable in a browser and can be previewed in Dreamweaver. You will use .swf Flash files in the NextBest Fest site.
- **.swt.** A Flash template file that enables you to change and replace content in the .swf file. In Dreamweaver, these files are used with the Flash button objects to enable you to update text when you add buttons to a page.
- **.swc.** A compiled clip that you work with in Flash that contains Flash symbols and ActionScript code. The components included with Flash are .swc files that enable you to incorporate mostly prebuilt Web components into pages. Like .fla files, these authoring files must be exported from Flash as .swf files to be viewed on the Web.
- **.flv and f4v.** The Flash video file format that enables you to include encoded audio and video for streaming delivery for playback through Flash Player and Adobe AIR. These are open file formats that allow other products and technologies to implement specifications.

Like every program, there are both positive and negative aspects of using Flash. Figure 7-14 lists these benefits and drawbacks.

Figure 7-14	Pros and cons of using Flash

Pros	Cons
As of July 2011, 99 percent of Internet-enabled desktops in mature markets have the Flash Player plug-in (it has a 99 percent PC penetration).	The playback speed of a Flash movie might depend on the user agent because, although there is an option to prerender certain types of frames, Flash renders at least some types of frames and movies on the user agent.
A Flash movie will look the same in all browsers and across supported platforms.	There are limitations to the amount of interactivity and control you can achieve with Flash.
Flash compresses movies to a reasonable size.	Although Flash has 99 percent browser penetration, not all users have the latest version, and problems sometimes arise in playback due to version differences. (This is usually overcome because the Flash movie checks to see which version the user has and prompts the user to download the current version, if necessary.)
You can use any font within a Flash movie without getting special Web Font licenses because Flash does not depend on fonts installed on the user agent.	While most non–Apple iOS-based devices can play Flash movies now, Adobe plans to discontinue development of Flash Player on mobile devices.
	Adobe recommends using HTML5/CSS3 to create animations and add sound and video to a site if you are supporting mobile devices rather than using Flash-based animations.

© 2013 Cengage Learning

You can find additional information and statistics about the pros and cons of using Flash on the Adobe site at *adobe.com/products/flashplayer*. The Statistics section provides current statistical data regarding Flash Player and the Benefits section provides the benefits of using Flash.

Before you add a Flash movie to the NextBest Fest site, Gage asks you to research the integration of Flash elements into a Web site. You will go to the Adobe site and review the current Flash information and statistics.

To research Flash information and statistics on the Adobe site:

1. Start your browser, type **www.adobe.com/products/flashplayer** in the Address bar, and then press the **Enter** key. The Adobe Flash Player home page opens.

   Trouble? If the Adobe Flash Player home page does not open, type www.adobe.com in the Address bar, press the Enter key to open the Adobe home page, type flash player in the Search for box, press the Enter key, click a link to Flash Player in the list of links, and then continue with Step 2.

2. Scroll down to the **Flash runtimes in depth** section, and then click the **Statistics** link. The current statistics about Flash appear in the browser window. See Figure 7-15.

Figure 7-15 **Flash Player adoption statistics**

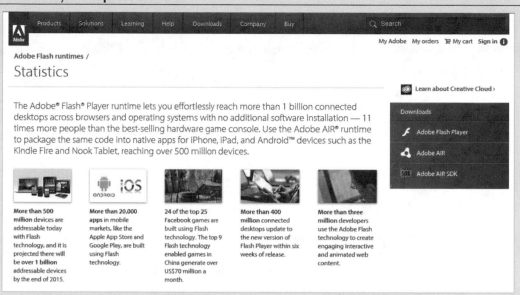

Trouble? If the statistics you see differ from Figure 7-15, Adobe has updated the data since this tutorial was published. Continue with Step 3.

3. Review the information, click the **Back** button ⬅ on the browser toolbar to return to the Adobe Flash Player home page, and then click the **Benefits** link. The Benefits for Flash Player appear in the browser window. See Figure 7-16.

Figure 7-16 **Flash Player benefits**

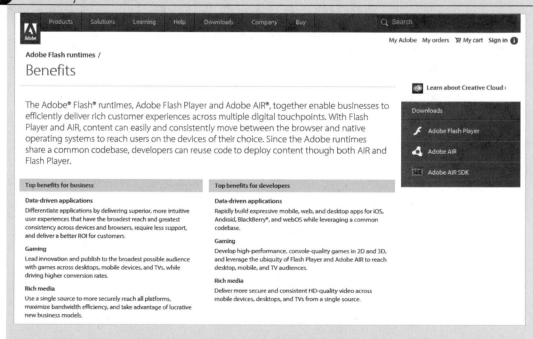

Trouble? If the data you see differs from Figure 7-16, Adobe has updated the page since this tutorial was published. Continue with Step 4.

▶ 4. Type **blogs.adobe.com/conversations/2011/11/flash-focus.html** in the Address bar, and then read the complete announcement by Adobe about the future of Flash.

Trouble? If the announcement is no longer available, Adobe has reorganized the site since this tutorial was published. Continue with Step 5.

▶ 5. Close the browser.

The statistics indicate that Flash Player has a larger share of the market than any of the competing technologies. It is included with most current browsers. As a result, most users will likely be able to view any Flash component that you add to a Web site. This is one reason that Flash is one of the most widely used media on the Web.

INSIGHT

Using the Latest Flash Player

Although Flash Player has a 99 percent browser penetration, not everyone has the latest version of the player installed. As a result, users might encounter some differences in how a Web page displays on their screen. This is generally not a big issue. If a user is connected to the Internet and does not have the latest version of Flash Player, Flash generally opens a dialog box, prompting the user to install the latest version of the player. The update is quick and easy to install.

Adding a Flash Movie to a Web Page

You will add a Flash movie with an animation that rotates the logos of bands performing at the NextBest Fest to the home page. When you insert a Flash movie, Dreamweaver places the code for the movie in the page and copies links to additional scripts to the scripts folder. Dreamweaver also prompts you to include a copy of the movie in the local root folder. You do this so that all the materials for the site are in one place. Any links to elements outside the local root folder will be incorrect after the site is uploaded to the remote server. If you are using only a few media elements in a site, you can place the files in the graphics folder. If you plan to use many media elements in a site, it is a good idea to create a new folder for each type of element so that the site remains organized and files are easy to find. You'll create a media folder to store the Flash, Shockwave, sound, and video files you add to the site.

A Flash movie appears in the Document window as a gray rectangle with the same dimensions as the Flash movie and a Flash logo in its center. The width and height of the Flash movie are determined when the movie is created, but you can adjust its width, height, scalability, and other attributes in the Property inspector. To view the Flash movie, you must preview the page in a browser or play the selected movie in the Document window.

Adding a Flash Movie to a Web Page

- In the Document window, click in the page where you want to add the Flash movie.
- In the Common category of the Insert panel, click the Media button arrow, and then click the SWF button.
- Navigate to the Flash movie file, and then double-click the file.
- Click the Yes button, navigate to the folder in which to save the file, and then click the Save button.
- In the Object Tag Accessibility Attributes dialog box, click the OK button.
- In the Document window, click the Flash movie, and then, in the Property inspector, adjust attributes as needed.

Inserting a Flash Movie

Gage wants the bands.swf movie created by another member of the design team on the home page. You will insert the new Flash movie and create a media folder in the local root folder to store the Flash movie and other media files you will add to the site. When you save the Flash movie, Dreamweaver will save the script that controls the movie in the scripts folder. You will learn more about scripts later.

To add the bands.swf Flash movie to the home page:

1. If you took a break after the previous session, make sure that the NextBest Fest site is open and the Designer workspace is reset, the Business Catalyst panel is minimized, and the Files panel is open.

2. Open the **index.html** page in Design view and close any other pages that are open, if necessary.

3. In the Document window, remove the class style from the Rumor Has It heading, and then apply the h2 tag to the heading text.

4. Delete the text below the Rumor Has It heading, type **Here are a few of the bands that will be performing at next year's fest.** (including the period), and then press the **Enter** key. You will place the Flash movie on this blank line below the new text.

   Trouble? If the new text has the H2 style, select the text, and then, in the Property inspector, click the Format arrow and click Paragraph to remove the H2 style. You might also need to select the heading text and reapply the h2 tag.

TIP

You can also drag a copy of the SWF, movie, or Shockwave file in the site from the Assets panel, clicking the corresponding button to display the objects, to the Document window.

5. In the **Common** category of the Insert panel, click the **Media button arrow**, and then click the **SWF** button. The Select SWF dialog box opens.

6. Navigate to the **Dreamweaver7\Tutorial** folder included with your Data Files, and then double-click the **bands.swf** file. A dialog box opens, prompting you to place a copy of the file in the local root folder.

7. Click the **Yes** button. The Copy File As dialog box opens.

8. Navigate to the local root folder of your NextBest Fest site, and then create a new folder in the local root folder named **media**. The media folder opens.

9. Click the **Save** button, and then click the **OK** button in the Object Tag Accessibility Attributes dialog box. A copy of the bands.swf file is placed in the media folder and a gray rectangle with the dimensions of the Flash movie appears below the Rumor Has It subheading and paragraph text. See Figure 7-17.

Figure 7-17   **Flash movie inserted in the home page**

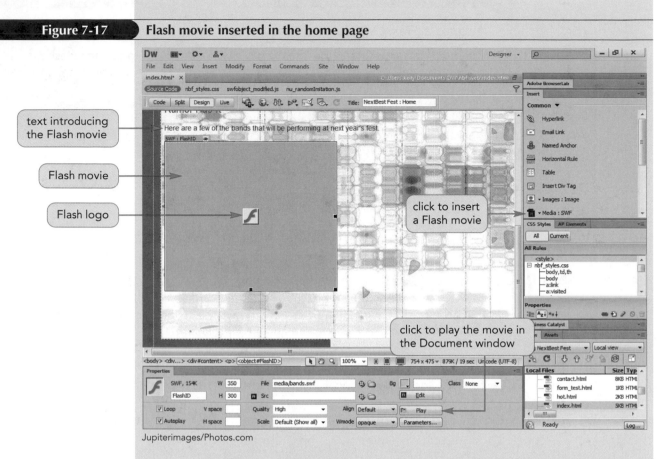

text introducing the Flash movie

Flash movie

Flash logo

click to insert a Flash movie

click to play the movie in the Document window

Jupiterimages/Photos.com

▶ **10.** Save the home page. The Copy Dependent Files dialog box opens stating that the page uses an object or behavior that requires supporting files (which have been copied to the local site).

▶ **11.** Click the **OK** button, minimize the CSS Styles panel and then, in the Files panel, expand the **scripts** folder. The new script appears in the scripts folder and on the Related Files toolbar. See Figure 7-18.

Figure 7-18   Script for the Flash movie

script to play
the Flash movie

script for the Flash
movie appears in
the scripts folder

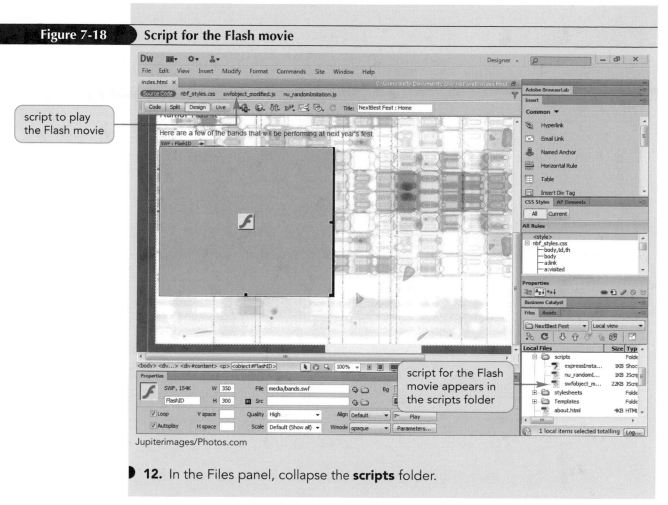

Jupiterimages/Photos.com

12. In the Files panel, collapse the **scripts** folder.

As with other elements you add to Web pages, you want to ensure the Flash movie displays as intended. You will play the Flash movie in the page, test it in Live view, and then preview it in a browser.

To test the Flash movie added to the home page:

1. In the Document window, select the **Flash movie**, if necessary, and then, in the Property inspector, click the **Play** button. The Flash movie plays. As the movie plays, the Play button in the Property inspector changes to a Stop button. See Figure 7-19.

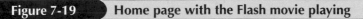

Figure 7-19   **Home page with the Flash movie playing**

Flash movie playing in the Document window

scroll to see the entire movie, if necessary

button switches between Play and Stop

Jupiterimages/Photos.com; Shumadinac/Shutterstock.com

2. In the Property inspector, click the **Stop** button when you are finished watching the movie.

3. Switch to **Live** view to see the movie as it will appear in a browser window, and then return to **Design** view.

Trouble? If you do not have the latest version of Flash Player, a Security Warning dialog box might open when you try to preview the page in a browser. Click the Yes button to update the version. After the new Flash Player is downloaded, the movie will start playing.

4. In the Property inspector, click the **Parameters** button, select the text in the first row of the value column, type **11.2.2.2** as the new value, and then click the **OK** button.

5. Save the page, preview the page in a browser, and then view the Flash movie. The movie starts after the page is loaded, as it did in Live view. See Figure 7-20.

Figure 7-20	Flash movie previewed in a browser

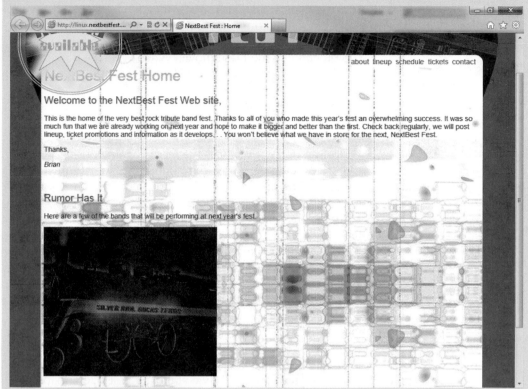

Used with permission from Microsoft Corporation; dean bertoncelj/Shutterstock.com; Jupiterimages/Photos.com; Logo/Photographs © SilverRail. Courtesy Bobby Combs.

Trouble? If you do not have the latest version of Flash Player, a Security Warning dialog box might open when you try to preview the page in a browser. Click the Yes button to update the version. After the new Flash Player is downloaded, the movie will start playing.

Trouble? If the page continues to load for an extended period of time (twice the time it would usually take), you need to download the most recent version of Flash Player. Go to the Adobe site at *www.adobe.com/downloads*, click the Adobe Flash Player button to start the download, follow the prompts to download and install the latest version of Flash Player, close the browser, and then repeat Step 5.

6. Close the browser.

Adjusting Attributes of a Flash Movie

Many attributes of Flash movies can be adjusted within Dreamweaver. You can adjust the following attributes of a Flash movie in the Property inspector when the movie object is selected:

- **FlashID.** A unique name for the movie used in scripts. The ID can contain letters and numbers, but not spaces or special characters, and it cannot start with a number.
- **W and H.** The dimensions of the Flash movie, which are set when the movie is created and measured by default in pixels. You can also measure the movie in picas (pc), points (pt), inches (in), millimeters (mm), centimeters (cm), and percentage of a parent object (%). Changing the width or height of a Flash movie can change the aspect ratio of the movie. It can cause the movie to play more slowly because every frame of the

TIP

To size a Flash movie in a unit other than pixels, type the unit abbreviation after the number in the W box.

movie must be rendered and changed on the user agent, and it can cause the movie to look distorted, especially if the movie contains a lot of text.

- **File.** The path to the Flash movie file (.swf).
- **Src.** The path to the Flash source file (.fla) for the .swf movie file; available only if Flash is installed on your local computer.
- **Edit.** The button that launches Flash and opens the .fla file specified in the Src box so you can edit the Flash movie. When you save the .fla file, Flash reexports the .swf movie file with the changes. If Flash is not installed on your local computer, the Edit button is disabled.
- **Reset size.** The button that returns the Flash movie to its original size if you have altered it; appears only if you have resized the movie.
- **Class.** A list of CSS styles that you can apply to the object.
- **Loop.** The option that plays the movie continuously as long as the page is loaded in the browser (checked) or adds code that plays the movie only once (unchecked).
- **Autoplay.** The option that, when checked, plays the movie automatically when the page is loaded in a browser.
- **V space and H space.** The number of pixels of white space inserted above and below the movie or to the left and right of the movie. If blank, no code is specified and the browser adds 0 pixels of white space around the movie.
- **Quality.** The amount of anti-aliasing that occurs when the movie is played. Movies with High anti-aliasing look best, but require more processing power to render correctly on the screen. Low emphasizes speed over appearance. Auto Low emphasizes speed, but also improves appearance when the speed is acceptable. Auto High emphasizes both appearance and speed, but sacrifices appearance for speed, if necessary. High emphasizes appearance over speed.
- **Scale.** How the Flash movie displays in the specified W and H dimensions. Default (Show all) displays the movie at the greatest size possible within the designated space while maintaining aspect ratio and showing all the content; the background color might appear on two sides of the movie. No border fits the movie into the designated space so that no border shows and the movie maintains the original aspect ratio (a portion of the movie might not be seen). Exact fit scales the movie to the exact W and H dimensions, regardless of the aspect ratio of the movie. The entire movie is seen, but it might be distorted to fit in the space.
- **Align.** The alignment of the movie in the page. The alignment options are the same as for an image: Default, Baseline, Top, Middle, Bottom, TextTop, Absolute Middle, Absolute Bottom, Left, and Right.
- **Wmode.** The setting that prevents the Flash file from having conflicts with DHTML elements. Opaque allows DHTML elements to display in front of SWF files in a browser. Transparent allows DHTML elements to appear behind SWF files and show through transparent areas in the SWF file. Window allows the SWF file to display in front of DHTML elements without the DHTML elements showing through transparent areas of the SWF file.
- **Bg.** The color specified for the background of the movie area. This color also appears in the page if the movie is not playing, such as while the page is loading.
- **Play.** The button that starts the movie in Dreamweaver. The movie plays in the Document window and the Stop button, which ends the movie, replaces the Play button.
- **Parameters.** The button that opens a dialog box for entering parameters that are passed to a movie if the movie was designed to receive them. Parameters entered in the Parameters dialog box are placed in the appropriate places in the page code.

Gage wants you to name the Flash movie, and turn on Loop and Autoplay.

To adjust the attributes of the Flash movie in the home page:

1. In the Document window, click the **Flash movie** to select it, if necessary, and then, in the Property inspector, replace FlashID in the SWF box with **nbf_bands**. The Flash movie is named.

▶ **2.** If necessary, in the Property inspector, click the **Loop** and **Autoplay** check boxes to insert check marks. The movie will play continuously and start as soon as the page is loaded in a browser window.

▶ **3.** In the Property inspector, click the **Play** button. The bands.swf Flash movie plays in the Document window. The movie restarts from the beginning after it reaches the end. This continues until you click the Stop button.

▶ **4.** In the Property inspector, click the **Stop** button. The movie ends and the Play button reappears.

▶ **5.** Save and close the home page.

Understanding Adobe Shockwave

Shockwave is the Adobe solution for delivering interactive multimedia on the Web. You use Shockwave for more complex interactive media components such as games, interactive 3D, database-driven multimedia, multiuser applications, and educational materials.

Unlike Flash files, which are created in the Flash program, Shockwave files are created in Adobe Director. Director is a program that is used to create comprehensive multimedia solutions deployable across multiple media, including DVD, Web, and Kiosk. Some packaged multimedia is produced in Director, and many casual Web games are distributed in Shockwave.

Several file extensions are associated with Director, including:

- **.dcr (Shockwave).** A compressed Director file that is viewable in a browser and can be previewed in Dreamweaver. You will use .dcr files in the NextBest Fest site for Shockwave movies.
- **.dir.** The source files used by Director when you are creating movies. These authoring files can be opened in Director. Unlike Flash authoring files, .dir files can be called by Director projectors for playback. (A **Director projector** is a stand-alone executable file that does not need any software or plug-in to run on a user agent.) Files that are going to be viewed on the Web are usually exported from Director as .dcr files.
- **.dxr.** Director files that are locked for distribution. A **locked file** cannot be opened in the authoring environment. Usually, .dxr files are used with Director projectors to deliver material via DVD.
- **.cst.** Cast files that contain additional information used in a .dir or .dxr file.
- **.cxt.** The .cst files that are locked for distribution.

Although Flash and Shockwave files are often used in similar ways, there are some marked differences between them. Because Director movies are prerendered, Shockwave files are less dependent on the processing speed of the user agent for playback speed than Flash files, which are fully or partially rendered on the user agent. For this same reason, the file size of a Flash movie with vector graphics is usually smaller than the file size of a Director movie with the same content. Shockwave movies tend to process complex coding faster than Flash movies. Shockwave movies can display a wider range of media formats. For example, all Flash video is converted to the .flv video file format, which uses the H.264, the On2 VP6, or the Sorenson Spark codec, whereas Shockwave can display video in a wide range of native formats. Finally, Shockwave Player must be installed on the user agent for Shockwave movies to be displayed. Unlike the Flash Player plug-in, Shockwave Player is generally not distributed with current browsers and must be downloaded separately by users.

Some positive and negative aspects of using Shockwave are listed in Figure 7-21.

Figure 7-21 Pros and cons of using Shockwave

Pros	Cons
Shockwave files are less dependent on the processing speed of the end user's computer for playback speed.	As of July 2011, only 41.0 percent of users have the Shockwave Player plug-in.
Shockwave movies tend to process complex code faster than Flash movies and are sometimes used for 3D games and highly interactive applications.	The Shockwave Player plug-in is not included with the latest versions of Microsoft Internet Explorer and Mozilla Firefox; it must be downloaded by the end user.
Shockwave movies can display a wide range of media formats.	Shockwave file size might be larger than Flash files because the files are prerendered.
Shockwave movies look the same across browsers and across platforms.	
You can use any font within a Shockwave movie because Shockwave is not dependent on the fonts on the user agent.	

© 2013 Cengage Learning

You can find additional information and statistics about Shockwave on the Adobe site at *www.adobe.com/products/shockwaveplayer*. The Adobe site also provides a Flash and Director comparison and a Shockwave/Flash movie comparison at *www.adobe.com/products/director/resources/integration*.

In preparation for adding Shockwave elements to the NextBest Fest site, you will go to the Adobe site and review the current Shockwave information and statistics.

To research current Shockwave information and statistics:

1. Start your browser, type **www.adobe.com/products/shockwaveplayer** in the Address bar, and then press the **Enter** key. The Adobe Shockwave Player home page opens in the browser window. See Figure 7-22.

Figure 7-22 Adobe Shockwave Player home page

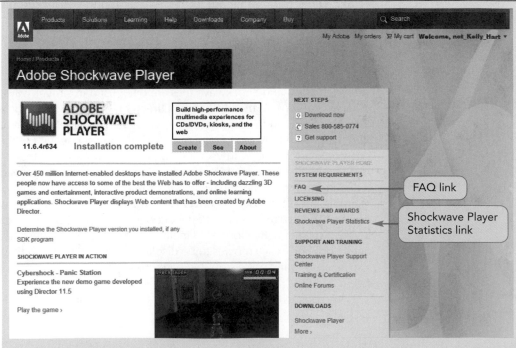

Trouble? If you do not have the latest version of Shockwave Player installed on your computer, a dialog box may open asking for permission to install the player on your machine. Install the player, and then the Adobe Shockwave Player home page will display.

Trouble? If the Adobe Shockwave Player home page does not open, you need to download the latest version of Shockwave Player. Go to the Adobe site at *www.adobe.com/downloads*, click the Get Adobe Shockwave Player button to start the download, follow the prompts to download and install the latest version of Shockwave Player, close the browser, and then repeat Step 1.

▶ **2.** In the right column of the Adobe Shockwave Player page, click the **FAQ** link to open a page of frequently asked questions, and then read the FAQs.

▶ **3.** Click the **Back** button ◀ on the browser toolbar to return to the Adobe Shockwave Player home page.

▶ **4.** Click the **Shockwave Player Statistics** link, and then read the adoption statistics.

▶ **5.** Click the **VERSION PENETRATION** link to view browser penetration statistics. See Figure 7-23.

| Figure 7-23 | Shockwave Player version penetration |

Shockwave Player version penetration statistics

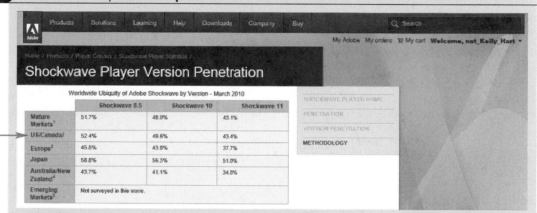

Trouble? If the data you see differs from Figure 7-23, Adobe has updated the data since this tutorial was published. Continue with Step 6.

▶ **6.** Close the browser.

Adding Shockwave Movies to Web Pages

Adding a Shockwave movie to a Web page is very similar to adding a Flash movie to a Web page. When you insert a movie, Dreamweaver places the code for the movie into the page. When you add a Shockwave movie that is located outside of the site's local root folder to a page, Dreamweaver prompts you to include a copy of the file in the local root folder. You should place a copy of the file in the media folder in the local root folder so that all the materials for the site are located in one place.

After the Shockwave movie has been added to a page, a small gray rectangle with the Shockwave logo appears in the page. The gray rectangle is 32 × 32 pixels, regardless of the size at which the Shockwave movie was created. (This occurs because a bug in the Shockwave code prevents the program from seeing the correct dimensions of the movie.) You must enter the correct width and height for the movie in the Property inspector to see the movie in a browser or to play the movie from within Dreamweaver. In addition, the Play button in the Property inspector might not start the movie; you might need to preview the page in a browser to see the movie. If you do not see the movie, you might need to install Shockwave Player.

REFERENCE

Adding a Shockwave Movie to a Web Page

- In the Document window, click in the page where you want to add the Shockwave movie.
- In the Common category of the Insert panel, click the Media button arrow, and then click the Shockwave button.
- Navigate to the Shockwave movie file, and then double-click the file.
- Click the Yes button, navigate to the folder in which you want to save the file, and then click the Save button.
- Click the OK button in the Object Tag Accessibility Attributes dialog box.
- In the Property inspector, adjust Shockwave movie attributes as needed.

Gage wants to add an interactive game to the lineup.html page. The new game will be a Shockwave movie. The game is still in production, but the game group has provided an animated promo for the game in the Shockwave format. Although the preview is animation without interactivity and could be delivered as a Flash movie, the team wants to deliver the preview as a Shockwave movie to test for problems that might arise. It is a good idea to use the intended final technology when making placeholder objects because you can test the technology in advance.

You will add the Shockwave movie game placeholder to the lineup.html page in a new div, and then you will create a CSS style to position the movie in the page.

To insert the Shockwave movie into the lineup.html page:

1. Open the **lineup.html** page in Design view, delete the **what's hot** graphic from the page, and then press the **Enter** key twice to add two new lines and press the **Up** arrow twice to position the insertion point where you want to insert the Shockwave movie.

2. Insert a div tag at the insertion point, and then create a new CSS rule from within the Insert Div Tag dialog box to create a style for the div.

   Trouble? If the closing div tag is located below the closing content div, drag it above the closing content div to avoid display problems.

3. Create an **ID** style named **game** and defined in the **nbf_styles.css** style sheet.

4. In the **Box** category, set the float to **right**, and then click the **OK** button in each dialog box. The game div is inserted into the page.

5. Click in the **game** div, delete the placeholder text, and then, in the Property inspector, click the **Div ID arrow** and select **game**, if necessary.

TIP

You can also click Insert on the menu bar, point to Media, and then click Shockwave to insert a Shockwave movie.

6. In the **Common** category of the Insert panel, click the **Media button arrow**, and then click the **Shockwave** button. The Select File dialog box opens.

7. Double-click the **game_promo.dcr** file located in the **Dreawmweaver7\ Tutorial** folder included with your Data Files, click the **Yes** button in the message dialog box, and then save a copy of the file in the **media** folder in the local root folder. The Object Tag Accessibility Attributes dialog box opens.

8. In the Title box, type **Promo animation for a shockwave game that is coming soon.** (including the period), and then click the **OK** button. The game_promo.dcr Shockwave movie is inserted into the game div, as you can see from the small gray rectangle with the Shockwave logo. See Figure 7-24.

| Figure 7-24 | Shockwave movie added to the lineup.html page |

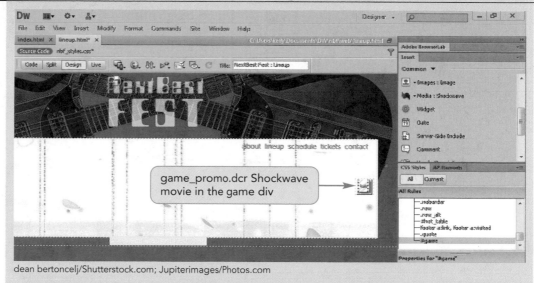

dean bertoncelj/Shutterstock.com; Jupiterimages/Photos.com

Trouble? If the size of your game div differs from the one shown in Figure 7-24, continue with the tutorial. You will adjust the size of the game div in the next set of steps.

9. Save the page, and then save the style sheet.

Adjusting Attributes of a Shockwave Movie

Shockwave movies have some of the same attributes as Flash movies: ID, W, H, File, Bg, Class, V Space, H Space, Play, Align, and Parameters. For descriptions of these attributes, refer to the "Adjusting Attributes of a Flash Movie" section. You can adjust the attributes in the Property inspector when the Shockwave movie is selected.

The Shockwave movie embedded in the lineup.html page is not at the proper size and will not play. You will change the width and height of the Shockwave movie to its original creation size so that it will display properly in the browser.

To adjust the attributes of the game_promo.dcr Shockwave movie:

▶ **1.** In the Document window, select the Shockwave movie, if necessary.

▶ **2.** In the Property inspector, type **240** in the W box, type **240** in the H box, and then press the **Enter** key. The gray square increases in size. See Figure 7-25.

Figure 7-25   **Edited Shockwave movie**

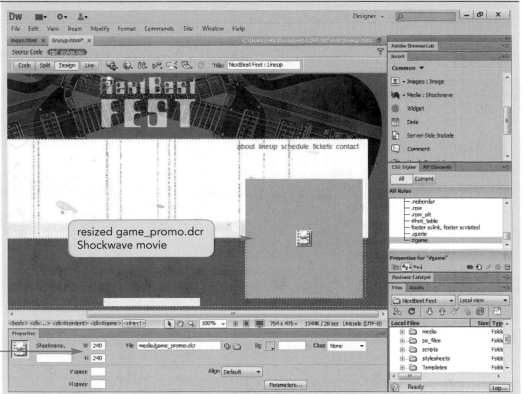

new dimensions for the Shockwave movie

resized game_promo.dcr Shockwave movie

dean bertoncelj/Shutterstock.com; Jupiterimages/Photos.com

▶ **3.** Select the **div#game** tag in the status bar, press the **Right** arrow key to move past the div, and then press the **Enter** key five times to add extra spaces to the content div. This ensures that the content div background displays behind the entire Shockwave movie.

▶ **4.** Save the page, and then preview the page in a browser. See Figure 7-26.

Figure 7-26 | **Shockwave movie in the lineup.html page previewed in a browser**

Used with permission from Microsoft Corporation; dean bertoncelj/Shutterstock.com; Jupiterimages/Photos.com

Trouble? If a dialog box opens or an icon appears, prompting you to install the latest version of Shockwave Player, you must install the latest version of the player to view the Shockwave movie. Click the Yes button, deselect the option to install a free version of unrelated software, click the Next button to install the player, and then preview the page in the browser.

Trouble? If the movie displays poorly (the words are split between lines and so forth), you are probably viewing the Shockwave movie in the wrong font. You are probably logged in to your computer as a restricted user and do not have access to some system folders that are necessary to view the movie in the correct font. This is a potential drawback of using media elements in a Web site. Continue with Step 5.

▶ **5.** Close the browser, and then close the page and the style sheet.

In this session, you added Flash and Shockwave movies to the NextBest Fest site. In the next session, you will insert audio in some of the pages of the site.

Session 7.2 Quick Check

1. What are media elements?
2. What might a user need to view media elements in a browser?
3. What is the file extension for Flash movies that you place in Web pages?
4. True or False. Flash Player is included with the latest versions of Internet Explorer and Firefox.
5. True or False. Apple iOS devices support Flash Player.
6. True or False. Shockwave files are created in Adobe Flash.
7. What is the Shockwave file extension?

SESSION 7.3 VISUAL OVERVIEW

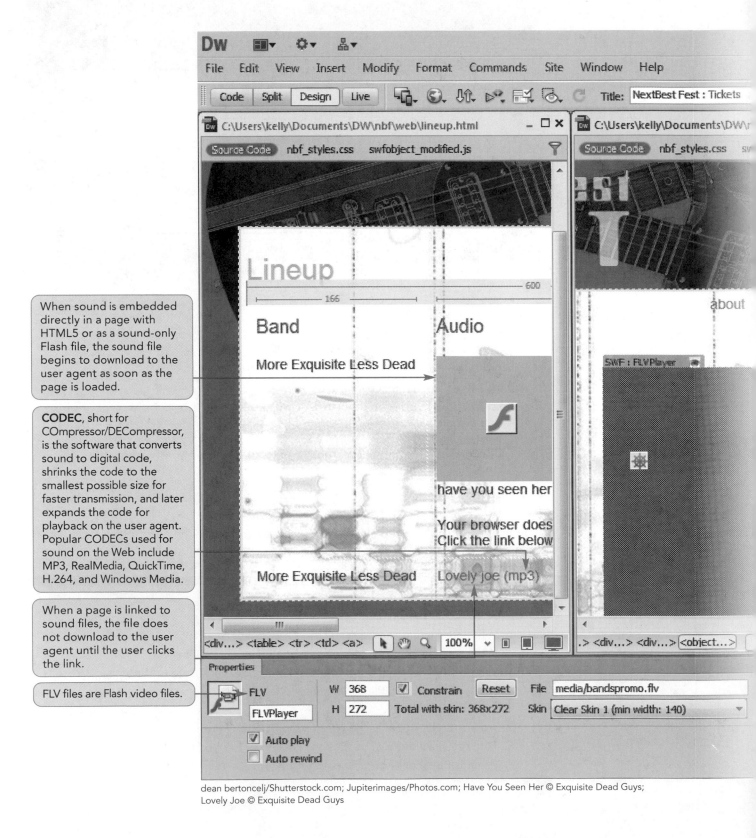

When sound is embedded directly in a page with HTML5 or as a sound-only Flash file, the sound file begins to download to the user agent as soon as the page is loaded.

CODEC, short for COmpressor/DECompressor, is the software that converts sound to digital code, shrinks the code to the smallest possible size for faster transmission, and later expands the code for playback on the user agent. Popular CODECs used for sound on the Web include MP3, RealMedia, QuickTime, H.264, and Windows Media.

When a page is linked to sound files, the file does not download to the user agent until the user clicks the link.

FLV files are Flash video files.

dean bertoncelj/Shutterstock.com; Jupiterimages/Photos.com; Have You Seen Her © Exquisite Dead Guys; Lovely Joe © Exquisite Dead Guys

INSERTING AUDIO AND VIDEO

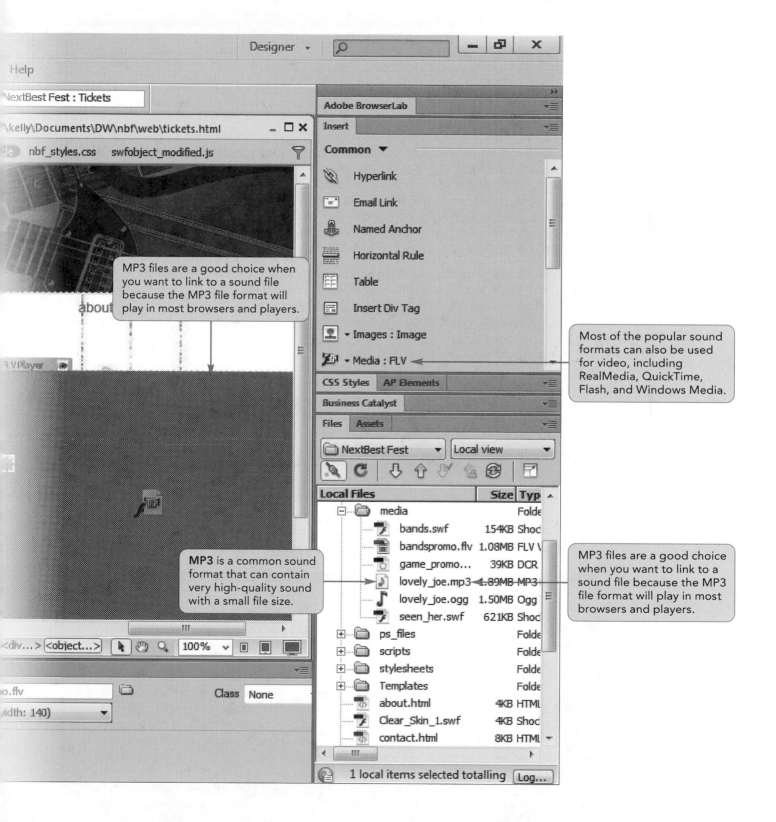

MP3 files are a good choice when you want to link to a sound file because the MP3 file format will play in most browsers and players.

Most of the popular sound formats can also be used for video, including RealMedia, QuickTime, Flash, and Windows Media.

MP3 is a common sound format that can contain very high-quality sound with a small file size.

MP3 files are a good choice when you want to link to a sound file because the MP3 file format will play in most browsers and players.

Understanding Digital Audio

As you create more advanced Web sites, you might want to include sound on some pages. Some common uses of sound on the Web are music, narration, and sounds paired with user actions, such as sound that plays when the pointer is positioned over a button or other element. You can use the following methods to add sound to a site:

- You can embed sound directly in a page using HTML5 and then write code that causes the sound to download, play, rewind, and so forth or that tells the browser to use its default controls to play, rewind, and so forth.
- You can embed sound in a page using standard methods, which causes the sound to be played in an outside player or plug-in. Plug-ins and players are additional software that interpret the sound format and convert the code back to sound.
- You can embed a player in a page and then write code that instructs the player when to download the sound files. For example, if a page includes many sound clips, you can program the player to download the sound file only when the user tells the player that he or she wants to hear the sound.
- You can include a link to a sound file. This is done infrequently because the way that the sound is opened and played depends entirely on the user agent configuration and preferences, which gives the designer little control. For example, the sound file might play in a player that opens in a separate Web page, taking the user away from the site.

With most sound formats, sound streams to the user agent. **Streaming** means that sound can begin to play after only a small portion downloads and will continue to play while the rest of the file is downloading. Streaming is especially helpful to users with slow connections because they can begin to hear the sound without waiting for large files to download completely.

When sound is embedded directly in a page, the sound files usually begin to download to the user agent as soon as the page is loaded. Embedded sound files can start automatically or can be set to start when the user clicks a button. Either way, the embedded file often begins to download as soon as the page loads, allowing relatively quick automatic playback or preloading so that it plays as soon as the user clicks the button. However, beginning to download many files a user might not even play wastes the user's time and consumes unnecessary bandwidth. If you intend to include a lot of sound files in a page using HTML, you can write code that designates when and under what circumstances each sound file will begin to download. Another option is to embed a more sophisticated audio player in the page and program it to handle download and streaming of audio files intelligently based on parameters you set. This enables you to create responsive playback that minimizes the time the user waits for the sound to play while minimizing the amount of bandwidth used for download.

INSIGHT

Choosing When to Add Sound to a Site

Sound can add richness and depth to Web sites when used wisely. The sound you add to a site should reinforce the site goals and enhance the user's experience. When deciding whether to add sound to a site, consider whether the target audience even has sound playback hardware and capabilities. For example, students who use a computer lab or people who use computers in public spaces often have limited access to sound. It is also important to think about issues such as user connection speed and user agent speed, which can be problematic for users who will view the site on a mobile device. You must also determine whether sound is appropriate to the site goals and whether it truly adds value to the site for the users. Audio elements can also present accessibility issues. To make a site accessible, you should use audio files to reinforce information that is presented in other, more accessible ways and not as the only way to present important information.

Sound files are created or recorded with programs outside of Dreamweaver, such as Audition, Audacity, or Pro Tools. You can add sound files to Web pages and, in some cases, preview them within Dreamweaver.

Many formats can be used to store and play sound on a computer. Some formats can only be played using a specific player or plug-in, whereas other formats can be used to embed sound with HTML5 or can be played on several different players. Sound files can be fairly large and, like graphics, must be compressed to be delivered over the Web. Each type of compression used for sound is often called a **sound format**. Each sound format uses a different CODEC as the sound is compressed for delivery and decompressed for playback. CODEC, short for COmpressor/DECompressor, is the software that converts sound to digital code, shrinks the code to the smallest possible size for faster transmission, and later expands the code for playback on the user agent. Popular CODECs used for sound on the Web include MP3, RealMedia, QuickTime, H.264, and Windows Media. In the past, each format was better for some types of sound and worse for others. Today, all the formats provide high-quality sound for nearly any application.

For a user agent to play sound, some sound formats require the user to download a plug-in or a player. When a user installs plug-in or player software, it often includes both browser integration (sound that plays from within the browser) as well as a stand-alone player with its own interface and controls. Most users have several players installed on their systems, and most players work with a wide range of sound formats. For example, the QuickTime Player will work with QuickTime formats as well as with MP3 and wave formats. When you add sound using HTML5, you can write code that tells the sound file to download, play, pause, stop, rewind, and so forth without using an outside player or plug-in. This is a great advancement because it enables designers to standardize the way that sound is delivered over the Web. Because this method of delivery is new, it has its own set of problems, discussed in the ProSkills box.

PROSKILLS

Problem Solving: Creating a Consistent Sound Experience for All Users

Making sound work the same on all users' systems is complex and sometimes impossible. The inability to control a user's experience with sound is one of the challenges of adding sound to a Web page. The difficulties depend on the user's browser, browser version, installed players, and hardware configuration. For example, a single user might have the RealMedia, QuickTime, and Windows Media players installed on his or her system. When the user visits a site that includes an mp3 Audio clip, any of the installed players might handle the sound. And, depending on configuration, the sound might just play, or a separate player window with sound controls (and ads) might pop up, which is often not desirable. Also, depending on the configuration, the sound can either start automatically or require the user to click the Play button on the launched player. Another user who has the same players installed might have a different player respond to the audio clip, leading to a completely different experience.

With care, however, you can make sure that sound will work for the majority of the target audience. One way to alleviate player confusion and to ensure the same sound experience for all site visitors is to use the Flash format to add sound to Web pages, but remember, this will not work for users with Apple iOS devices and, in the future, users with mobile devices. Most player problems and inconsistencies can be solved by adding sound to a site using HTML5. However, this creates another set of problems: Older browsers do not support HTML5. Although most new browsers support adding audio with HTML5, different browsers support different file formats. This means that you must add sound using multiple formats much like you did when you added fonts to the page.

Embedding a Flash Movie with Sound

Although Flash is more often used to add animation to Web sites, it is also a very consistent and reliable method for adding sound to Web pages. Because Flash Player is widely installed and does not open a separate application to play sound, Flash delivers sound without disrupting the aesthetic of Web pages. However, keep in mind that users of Apple iOS devices cannot access the Flash movies and that users of mobile devices might not be able to access them in the future. Despite this limitation, many sites still use Flash to deliver sound and video even though using HTML5 and CSS3 to add sound to Web pages is the current best practice. For example, many sites that offer training, business services, or professional services believe the users they are targeting will access their site on computers, not mobile devices. In addition, people are often slow to transition to new development due to expense, time, and knowledge. Therefore, it is important to understand how to embed and work with Flash sound.

When you use Flash to add sound to a page, you are simply adding a Flash movie that contains sound with or without images. This means that the formats you can use for Flash sound files are the same formats that you used for Flash movies. The process for adding the Flash movie to a page is the same whether the Flash movie contains sound and images or only sound. A Flash movie that contains only sound is generally created at a size of 1 × 1 pixel and with the same background color as the page.

Sound-inclusive Flash movies can either prevent automatic play or play automatically when the page loads. (When creating a Flash movie, a stop action added to the first frame prevents automatic play, omitting this action allows automatic play.) Flash movies that play automatically are used to add background sound to pages. For example, a Web page that loads music when the home page loads in the browser might use a Flash movie that includes only sounds and plays automatically. Flash movies that do not play automatically are often used to provide sounds that the user can activate by clicking a button. You can include the button that starts the audio contained in the Flash movie. For example, when you include multiple Flash movies that contain audio in a page, you can create a Play button in each movie that the user can click to play the audio in that particular movie.

REFERENCE

Adding a Flash Movie with Sound to a Web Page

- In the Document window, click the location where you want to add the Flash movie.
- In the Common category of the Insert panel, click the Media button arrow, and then click the SWF button.
- Navigate to the Flash movie file, and then double-click the file.
- Click the Yes button, navigate to the folder in which you want to save the file, and then click the Save button.
- Click the OK button in the Object Tag Accessibility Attributes dialog box.
- In the Property inspector, adjust Flash movie attributes as needed.

Gage wants to add audio files he received from More Exquisite Less Dead—an Exquisite Dead Guys tribute band that is playing at the next fest—to the lineup.html page. You will add a Flash movie with sound to the page that does not play automatically. The movie will contain a button that users click to start the audio. You will use a table to structure this content so that other band names and audio files can easily be added to the page.

To add a Flash movie with sound to the lineup.html page:

1. If you took a break after the previous session, make sure that the NextBest Fest site is open, the Business Catalyst panel is minimized, the Files panel is open, and the Designer workspace is reset.

2. Open the **lineup.html** page in Design view. You will create a table to hold the new content.

3. Below the Lineup heading text, create a table that has **4** rows, **3** columns, **600 pixels** width, **0** border thickness, **10** cell padding, **0** cell spacing, no header, and type **The left column of the table contains the names of bands who will be playing at the next fest and logo artwork, when possible. The right column contains sound clips for those bands.** as the summary.

4. Set all three columns to have a horizontal alignment of **Left** and a vertical alignment of **Top**.

5. Click in the first cell in the first row, type **Band**, press the **Tab** key, type **Audio**, press the **Tab** key, type **Info**, and then format the first row with **Heading 2**. See Figure 7-27.

Figure 7-27 | Table in the lineup.html page

three-column table for the audio content

dean bertoncelj/Shutterstock.com; Jupiterimages/Photos.com

6. Click in the first cell in the second row, type **More Exquisite Less Dead**, and then press the **Tab** key to move to the next cell.

7. In the **Common** category of the Insert panel, click the **Media button arrow**, and then click the **SWF** button. The Select SWF dialog box opens.

8. Double-click the **seen_her.swf** movie located in the **Dreamweaver7\Tutorial** folder included with your Data Files, click the **Yes** button, save a copy of the Flash movie in the **media** folder, and then click the **OK** button in the accessibility dialog box. A Flash placeholder image appears in the cell. See Figure 7-28.

TIP

You can also click Insert on the menu bar, point to Media, and then click SWF, FLV, or Shockwave to insert the corresponding media file.

Figure 7-28   Flash movie with sound in the lineup.html page

selected Flash movie
in the Audio column

dean bertoncelj/Shutterstock.com; Jupiterimages/Photos.com

9. Click the **Parameters** button, select the text in the top cell of the value column, type **11.2.2.2**, and then click the **OK** button.

10. Press the **Right** arrow key to deselect the Flash movie, press the **Shift+Enter** keys to move the insertion point below the movie, and then type **have you seen her**.

11. Drag the left border of the second column to the left until only a small space is between the band name and the border, and then delete the additional lines below the table.

12. Save the page, and then preview the page in a browser.

13. Click the **Flash sound** button to play the Flash movie. See Figure 7-29.

Figure 7-29   Flash movie with sound in the lineup.html page previewed in a browser

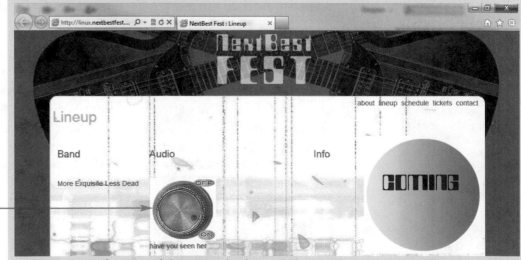

Flash movie with
sound will play
when clicked

Used with permission from Microsoft Corporation; dean bertoncelj/Shutterstock.com; Jupiterimages/Photos.com;
Have You Seen Her © Exquisite Dead Guys; © NU, Inc.

14. Close the browser.

Adjusting Attributes of a Flash Movie

After you have added a Flash movie to a Web page, you might need to set some of its attributes in the Property inspector. Most of the settings affect the visual aspects of the Flash movie and do not apply to Flash movies that include only sound. Only the Loop and Autoplay attributes affect the sound of a Flash movie. When using a movie that is designed to prevent automatic play, checking the Loop and Autoplay check boxes has no effect, but they function as usual with a movie that is designed to allow automatic play when the page loads.

You do not need to set any attributes for the Flash movie in the lineup.html page.

Embedding Other Sound Formats Using Plug-Ins and Players

Embedding other types of sound files (such as MP3 and RealMedia) using traditional players and plug-ins is a bit more difficult than embedding a Flash movie because Dreamweaver does not have a custom control for embedding the other types of files. You can use the generic Plugin button in the Media list in the Common category of the Insert panel, but you must type many parameters to make the sound work, or you must download an extension from Adobe Exchange. After you have downloaded an extension, embedding other types of sound files follows the same basic process as embedding a Flash movie.

Embedding Sound Using HTML5

You can embed a sound file in a page using HTML5. Currently Dreamweaver does not have a mechanism to create the code for you but you can write the code yourself. To add sound, you use the <audio> tag, which is a new tag in HTML5. The audio tag has a number of attributes, including those listed in Figure 7-30.

| Figure 7-30 | Audio tag attributes |

Attribute	Value	Description
autoplay	autoplay	Makes the audio start playing as soon as enough of the file is downloaded
controls	controls	Displays audio controls such as play/pause and so forth
loop	loop	Starts the audio over again every time it has finished playing
preload	auto metadata none	Specifies how the audio is loaded: auto lets the browser decide how to preload the file, metadata loads only information about the audio like the duration, none does not perform any preloading
src	URL	Specifies the URL of the audio file

© 2013 Cengage Learning

When adding audio with HTML5, be aware that different browsers support different audio file formats, as listed below:

- **WAV**—Firefox, Safari, Opera, Chrome
- **MP3**—Safari, Internet Explorer 9, Chrome
- **MP4**—Safari, Internet Explorer 9, Chrome
- **AAC**—Safari, Internet Explorer 9, Chrome
- **OGG Vorbis**—Firefox, Opera, Chrome

If you include the MP3 and OGG Vorbis file formats, audio should play in all of the browsers that support HTML5. However, to create a site that degrades gracefully, you should also include code that enables older browsers to access the audio file by including a link to the MP3 file as well. Including access to the MP3 file with HTML5 as well as a link ensures that all users can listen to the audio, whether they are using a newer or older browser.

You will add another song from More Exquisite Less Dead using HTML5 to embed the file in the page, and then you will add a link to the MP3 file.

To embed the Lovely Joe audio file using HTML5:

1. Copy the **lovely_joe.ogg** file and the **lovely_joe.mp3** file located in the **Dreamweaver7\Tutorial** folder included with your Data Files to the **media** folder in the NextBest local root folder.

2. Click in the second cell of the third row of the table.

3. Switch to **Code** view, select the code for the nonbreaking space tag ( ), and then delete the selected code.

4. Type the following code to place the audio files in the lineup.html page, as shown in Figure 7-31:

```
<audio controls>
    <source src="media/lovely_joe.ogg" type="audio/ogg" />
    <source src="media/lovely_joe.mp3" type="audio/mp3" />
    Your browser does not support the audio tag. Click the link
    below to hear the audio file.
</audio>
```

Figure 7-31 **Code to insert audio into the lineup.html page**

5. Save the page, switch to **Live** view, and then scroll down the page to see the effect of the audio tag you just entered. See Figure 7-32. The text is displayed because Live view does not support this feature. This is what users will see if they are viewing the site in a browser that does not support HTML5.

Figure 7-32   Live view of page with the audio file

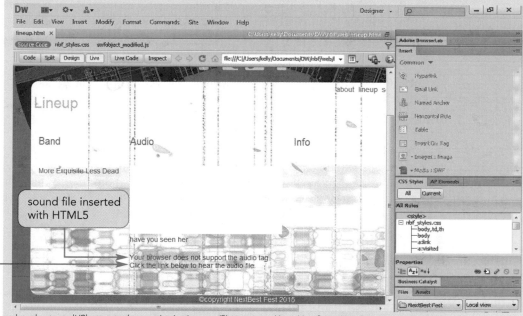

dean bertoncelj/Shutterstock.com; Jupiterimages/Photos.com; Have You Seen Her © Exquisite Dead Guys

6. Return to **Design** view, and then preview the page in a browser. See Figure 7-33.

Figure 7-33   Audio with default browser controls displayed

Used with permission from Microsoft Corporation; dean bertoncelj/Shutterstock.com; Jupiterimages/Photos.com; Have You Seen Her © Exquisite Dead Guys; © NU, Inc.

7. Close the browser.

Creating a Link to an MP3 Sound File

MP3 is a common sound format that can contain very high-quality sound with a small file size. This is perfect for sending sound over the Web, especially when the user has a slow connection. It is such a popular format that most user agents come preconfigured with a player that will play MP3 files, avoiding the need to download additional software. MP3 files are a good choice when you want to link to a sound file instead of embedding the file in a page because the sound will very likely play as expected even though many different players might handle MP3 on a user agent. Using a link, instead of embedding, ensures that whatever player handles MP3 does not display its own sound control interface in the Web page, potentially interfering with the page's design.

Gage wants to provide users with a choice of sound formats. You already added sound to the page by embedding the sound using HTML5. Now you will create a link to an MP3 file that contains the same sound content to provide users with older browsers with an alternate way to hear the audio. When the user clicks the link, the sound file will begin to download and will be played back by whatever player is configured to handle MP3s on the user agent.

To link an MP3 sound file to the lineup.html page:

▸ **1.** In the Document window, click in the first cell in the fourth row of the table, and then type **More Exquisite Less Dead** to enter the band's name.

▸ **2.** Press the **Tab** key to move the insertion point to the second cell in the fourth row, type **lovely joe (mp3)** to enter the song name and format, and then select the text you just typed.

▸ **3.** In the Property inspector, next to the Link box, click the **Browse for File** button ☐. The Select File dialog box opens.

▸ **4.** Double-click the **lovely_joe.mp3** file located in the **media** folder in the local root folder. A link is created from the new text to the lovely_joe.mp3 file.

▸ **5.** Save the page, and then preview the page in a browser.

▸ **6.** Click the **lovely joe (mp3)** link. Sound plays and, depending on which player is playing the sound, a number of things could happen: A player could appear in the browser, a player could appear outside the browser, or the sound might simply begin to play without any player opening. Figure 7-34 shows the lovely_joe.mp3 file playing in the Windows Media Player.

Figure 7-34   **Windows Media Player**

Used with permission from Microsoft Corporation

Trouble? If a File Download dialog box opens, click Open and continue with the next step.

Trouble? If a player opens and no sound plays, you probably need to click the Play button in the player to start the sound. If that doesn't start the sound, you might need to view the page over the Web to hear the sound; sometimes MP3 files do not play locally.

Trouble? If a Media Bar Settings dialog box opens, asking whether Internet Explorer should play this link in its own window so it will be easier to see and hear, you need to determine where you want the player to appear. Click the Yes button to open a side panel with the player in your browser, or click the No button to have the player open in its own window.

Trouble? If a dialog box opens, prompting you to update your media player, a newer version might be available. Click the Yes button to update your media player, or click the No button if you do not want to update the player.

7. Close the browser, close the player and panel, if necessary, and then close the page.

Creating Links to Other Sound Files

You can create a link to any of the other commonly used sound file formats, including MP3, RealMedia, QuickTime, and Windows Media. (Generally, it is not a good idea to link directly to Flash movies with only sound; instead, embed these Flash movies in a page so that they play reliably.) You link to the other types of sound files in the same way that you link to an MP3 file. Simply add a button to the page, create a link to the sound file, and save a copy of the sound file in the media folder in the site's local root folder. One file format will basically work as well as another, and the CODECs needed to play each format are included in all the popular media players.

Understanding Digital Video

Video files, like sound files, must be compressed to make them small enough to deliver over the Web. Several major factors affect the file size of a digital video clip, including frame size, playback quality, and sound parameters. Some common video frame sizes used on the Web are 368 × 272 pixels, 640 × 480 pixels, and 720 × 480 pixels—the smaller frame size creates a smaller video file. While you can create video at many different frame sizes, all of the sizes are either a standard-screen aspect ratio (4:3) or a wide-screen aspect ratio (16:9). **Aspect ratio** refers to the width of the frame of video in relation to the height. Standard-screen aspect ratio is the aspect ratio of standard television screens and computer monitors, whereas wide-screen aspect ratio is the newer aspect ratio seen in wide-screen televisions and computer monitors. In the previously listed frame sizes, 720 × 480 is a wide-screen aspect ratio.

Playback quality for digital video is often adjusted to match the target connection speed and is usually measured in the amount of data that needs to be downloaded per second. For example, 0.5 Megabits per second (Mbps) is a standard minimum required broadband connection speed for streaming video, 3.0 Mbps is recommended for streaming DVD quality video, and 5.0 Mbps is recommended for streaming HD quality video.

TIP

You can also upload a video to a free Web site such as YouTube.com and then include a link to the site instead of adding video directly to the page if you have limited server space or bandwidth for your Web site.

Video quality affects the amount of detail and motion in the video image. Higher-quality video contains cleaner, more detailed images and smoother movement than lower-quality video. Sound parameters in digital video include the choice of stereo or mono and the resolution or clarity of the sound. Stereo and higher resolution occupy more file space than mono and lower resolution. Because the average home broadband connection speed in the United States for download is 6 Mbps, you must carefully consider when and how you will use video in a site. It is important to maximize the impact that the video has on your users while minimizing the inconvenience they experience by waiting for the video to download and play.

To ensure continuous playback of a video clip, it must be **buffered**, which means that the first 5 or 10 seconds of the clip are downloaded before it begins to play. After the clip begins to play, as long as the current download is at or past the current clip playback location, the playback will continue without interruption. A user who has a fast, consistent connection is more likely to be able to download enough of the clip each second to view a continuous playback. If the download does not keep up with the playback (that is, if the next piece of needed file has not completed downloading yet), the video playback will be interrupted. The user might see any of a number of things: The video might stop until the download catches up, the video might become jittery and chunks of it might not play, and sometimes a warning appears telling the user that the download is being interrupted. Any of these things can be annoying and cause the user to leave the page without viewing the entire video clip.

Web sites that include digital video use several solutions to minimize playback interruptions and maximize the user's viewing experience. These solutions include multiple clip options, multiple formats, and specialized video servers. By offering the same digital video clip in multiple file sizes, a site can satisfy a wide range of visitors. Sites taking this approach often offer each clip in low, medium, and high resolutions. They sometimes instead offer dial-up and broadband sizes, which means that they have used the compression parameters discussed earlier to offer the same clip in a lower-quality/smaller-frame size for users with slower dial-up connections and in a higher-quality/larger-frame size for users with faster broadband connections.

Video, like sound, is compressed using different CODECs and offered in different file formats. Some file formats are proprietary and only play in certain players, whereas other file formats will play in many different players. Some sites offer a variety of format options because some users prefer the QuickTime format and player, whereas others might choose RealMedia, Flash video, or Windows Media. In addition, bigger-budget Web sites might use a specialized video server to monitor a user's connection and adjust the video quality to compensate for slowdowns, increasing the likelihood that the user can view the video clip without interruption. Another benefit provided by a video server is the ability to allow thousands of users to view the same clip simultaneously, which is impossible when including video on a standard Web server.

Video files are created or recorded with programs outside of Dreamweaver, such as Avid, Apple Final Cut, and Adobe Premiere, and can be added to Web pages in Dreamweaver.

INSIGHT

Choosing When to Include Video in a Site

Video can add excitement to a Web page and greatly enhance the experience of site visitors. However, even with compression, video files are relatively large and might be slow to download. Because video includes moving images and often sound, it requires more focused attention from site visitors. This can be both good and bad. Video can really reinforce what you are trying to say and users tend to pay attention, so it is a good way to drive home an important message. But, it is easy to overload users with too many messages or too much motion in a page. Video then becomes a distraction and can detract from the site's effectiveness rather than reinforce it. Because of the steeper user requirements (more time to download and more focused attention from the user), include video in a site only when it is truly appropriate for the site goals and the target audience.

When deciding whether to use video in a site, keep in mind that when site visitors must wait for something large to download, their expectations are raised. Or, put another way, site visitors wait for downloads only when they perceive that the content is something worth waiting for.

As with other media elements, assistive devices usually cannot interpret video content. This means that video content will not be accessible to users who require these devices. Because of this, do not use video as the primary source to convey important information. Instead, use video to augment the accessible content in your site.

Reviewing Video File Formats

Digital video can have many different formats. Most of the popular sound formats can also be used for video, including RealMedia, QuickTime, Flash, and Windows Media. As with audio formats, earlier versions of these video formats were preferred for different uses. Although differences still exist, all of these formats provide excellent video performance with a wide range of materials. Today, Web sites that include video often offer the user a choice of formats. On the Web, these formats are identified by their file extensions. Some of the most common extensions are:

- **.mov.** A QuickTime movie that can contain sound, video, and animation tracks. QuickTime is a very popular cross-platform format from Apple used for both Web and DVD.
- **.rm.** A RealMedia movie, which is another popular format for Web and intranet streaming video.
- **.wmv.** A Windows Media File, which is a format for Web- and DVD-based digital video made popular by Microsoft.
- **.avi.** An earlier Microsoft format designation that has largely been replaced by the Windows Media format (.wmv).
- **.mpg.** A format created by the Moving Picture Experts Group that is generally used for DVDs, download, and multimedia pieces rather than for Web distribution.
- **.flv/f4v.** The Flash video formats.
- **.mp4/H.264.** A format that uses MPEG-4 compression, which is a standard developed by the Moving Picture Experts Group and is commonly used for sharing video files on the Internet. Apple iOS devices prefer this format. The actual file format is MP4 and the CODEC that is often used to compress MP4 files is the H.264 CODEC. However, people often refer to files in the MP4 file format as H.264s.
- **.oog/.ogv.** A free and open format for providing efficient streaming and manipulation of high-quality digital multimedia including audio, video, text (subtitles), and metadata. It was created and is maintained by the Xiph.Org Foundation.
- **.vp8.** A video compression format focused on more compact storage for more efficient transmission over networks. VP8 is owned by Google, which released it for use under the Creative Commons Attribution 3.0 license for royalty-free use and distribution.

You can add video directly to Web pages using HTML5, just like you did with HTML5 audio. You can also use one of the popular players to view the video. Most of the popular players play back both sound and video. The makers of the RealMedia, QuickTime, and Windows Media formats each provide a free player that can be downloaded. And, as with sound, the players include both stand-alone player functionality as well as browser integration, which allows the browser to play video embedded directly in a Web page. Flash video is played in the latest version of Flash Player, which is included with recent versions of popular browsers. However, Flash Player is not supported by Apple iOS devices and, in the future, will not be supported on other mobile devices. Users who have older browsers can download the most recent version of Flash Player.

Adding Video to a Web Page Using HTML5

When you add video to a Web page using HTML5, you write code that tells the video file to download and use the device's native controls to play, pause, stop, rewind, and so forth without using an outside player or plug-in, just like you did when you added audio using HTML5. This enables all users who have HTML5-compatible browsers to view the video, including users who own Apple iOS devices that do not support Flash. In addition, the native video controls are keyboard accessible. You can also create text transcripts/captions for the video, which makes it more accessible for users who are disabled or who need assistive devices. Using HTML5 to add video makes the video more searchable and indexable, which makes it more likely to be discovered by search engines. As with audio, when you add video, you should include multiple formats to ensure that all browsers will be able to display the video. Currently, your video should run on all browsers that support HTML5 if you include .mp4 and .ogg/.ogv. In the future, the .vp8 format may be a better choice.

The process for adding video to a Web page using HTML5 is similar to the process you used to add audio to the lineup.html page in the NextBest Fest site: You write code that tells the various browsers to play the video, you include a copy of the video file in the media folder of the site, and you provide the video in another format for users who are viewing the page in an older browser that does not support HTML5 video. However, video has a visual component in addition to an audio component, which means that the <video> tag has many more attributes than the <audio> tag, including those shown in Figure 7-35.

Figure 7-35 Video tag attributes

Attribute	Value	Description
autoplay	autoplay	Specifies that the video will start playing as soon as it has downloaded
controls	controls	Specifies that the browser's default video controls will be displayed
height	pixels	Sets the height of the video player
loop	loop	Specifies that the video will restart after it has finished playing
muted	muted	Specifies that any audio output of the video will be muted
poster	URL	Specifies an image to be displayed while the video is downloading or until the user clicks the play button
preload	auto metadata none	Specifies how the audio is loaded: auto lets the browser decide how to preload the file, metadata loads only information about the video like the duration, none does not perform any preloading
src	URL	Specifies the URL of the video file
width	pixels	Sets the width of the video player

© 2013 Cengage Learning

Because of the additional attributes for video and because different browsers support different video file formats, the code you must write to embed video using HTML5 is more complex than the code you wrote to add audio, as shown in the following code:

```
<video width="320" height="240" controls="controls">
  <source src="movie.mp4" type="video/mp4" />
  <source src="movie.ogg" type="video/ogg" />
  Your browser does not support the video tag.
</video>
```

As you did with audio, you must write the code for adding video with HTML5 or you can download a widget from Adobe Exchange that will write some of the code for you. **Widgets** are pieces of HTML, CSS, and JavaScript code that create complex Web page components. They are usually written and shared by other designers who are using Dreamweaver to create Web sites. Adobe Exchange is the part of the Adobe Web site that enables developers to exchange widgets and ideas. To download widgets, you must register with Adobe Exchange, agree to the terms of use, and get a login ID and password. Then you can use the Adobe Widget Browser to browse for widgets, configure the widget you select, and save the code so you can integrate the widget into Web pages. Because of the complexity, Gage does not want you to add video to the page using HTML5.

REFERENCE

Selecting, Configuring, and Inserting Widgets

- On the menu bar, click Insert, and then click Widget to open the Widget dialog box.
- Click the Widget Browser link at the bottom of the Widget dialog box to open the Widget Browser. (If you do not have an Adobe Exchange account, follow the steps to create an account and enable the Widget Browser link.)
- Sign in to your Adobe Exchange account, click the Adobe Exchange link to view a list of popular widgets, and then point to a widget to see detailed information about that widget.
- Type *video* or another keyword into the Filter box, and then press the Enter key to narrow the list of widgets. Click a widget to see detailed information and a working preview of that widget.
- Click Add to My Widgets to add the selected widget to your widget list.
- Click the My Widgets link, select the widget in the list, and then click Configure to configure the widget and view the code.
- Click Save Preset when you have finished configuring the widget, and then close the widget browser.
- In Dreamweaver, click Insert on the menu bar, and then click Widget. A list of the widgets that you have downloaded appears in the Widget dialog box.
- In the Widget list, click the widget you want to add to the page, and then click the OK button to add the code to your page.

Adding Flash Video to a Web Page

TIP

In Dreamweaver on a Macintosh, you must use an absolute path if the Flash video file is in a directory two or more levels up from the page in which you are inserting it.

The process for adding Flash video to a Web site is similar to the process for adding other Flash elements to the site. When you add a Flash video clip to a site, you set some attributes that are only applicable to video. Some of these parameters can be set from the Property inspector or the Insert FLV dialog box. Others can be set only in the Insert FLV dialog box when you insert the video clip into the page. Flash video parameters include:

- **Video type.** The choice between progressive download video and streaming video. Unless you have a streaming video server, select progressive download video.
- **URL.** The path to the video clip.

- **Skin.** A predefined look that you select for the control bar, which lets users play, stop, pause, mute, and control the video volume, and is included with the video file when you insert the Flash video in a page. A sample of the skin you select appears below the Skin box. Some skins require the video clip to be a certain minimum width to accommodate the width of the control bar. The minimum width requirements are listed at the right of the selection.
- **Width and Height.** The dimensions of the video clip. You can specify the video clip's width and height or have Dreamweaver detect them.
- **Auto play.** The option to start playing the video clip automatically when the page is loaded into a browser.
- **Auto rewind.** The option to rewind the video clip to the first frame automatically after it has played.

REFERENCE

Adding a Flash Video Clip to a Web Page

- In the Document window, click in the page where you want to add the video.
- In the Common category of the Insert panel, click the Media button arrow, and then click the FLV button.
- Click the Browse button, navigate to the video file, and then double-click the file.
- Click the Yes button, navigate to the folder in which you want to save the file, and then click the Save button.
- Insert the width and height of the video (or click the Detect Size button), and then adjust any other video clip attributes as needed.
- Click the OK button.

You will add a Flash video clip with audio that contains a promo for the NextBest Fest featuring some of the bands that will be playing. The movie does not loop, so it will play only once in the browser.

To add the promotional Flash video clip to the tickets.html page:

1. Open the **tickets.html** page in Design view, and then, below the heading, click to the left of the first line of text. You will add the div for the video clip here.

2. Insert a div at the insertion point, select **game** from the ID list, and then click the **OK** button. The div appears at the right side of the page with the game style applied.

3. Delete the placeholder text from the div. You'll insert the Flash video clip in the div.

4. In the **Common** category of the Insert panel, in the **Media** list, click the **FLV** button. The Insert FLV dialog box opens.

5. If necessary, click the **Video type** button, and then click **Progressive Download Video**.

6. Next to the URL box, click the **Browse** button, double-click the **bandspromo.flv** file located in the **Dreamweaver7\Tutorial** folder included with your Data Files, click the **Yes** button, and then save a copy of the file in the **media** folder in the local root folder.

7. If necessary, click the **Skin** button, and then click **Clear Skin 1**. The preview of the skin appears below the Skin box.

TIP

You can also insert a Flash video clip by clicking Insert on the menu bar, pointing to Media, and then clicking FLV.

8. Click the **Detect Size** button. Dreamweaver determines the video's width and height (368 and 272) and enters the values in the Width and Height boxes.

9. Click the **Auto play** check box to insert a check mark. See Figure 7-36.

Figure 7-36   **Insert FLV dialog box**

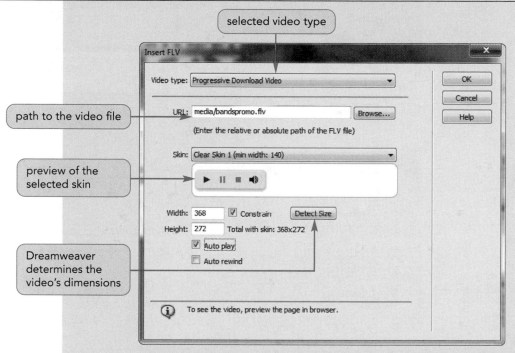

10. Click the **OK** button. A gray square with the Flash video logo appears in the div and the Clear_Skin_1.swf and FLVPlayer_Progressive.swf files are added to the local root directory. (Collapse the CSS Styles panel, if necessary, to view the new files.) These files enable the Flash video to play and must be in the top level of the root directory. Do not move them to the media folder. See Figure 7-37.

Figure 7-37   **Flash video in the tickets.html page**

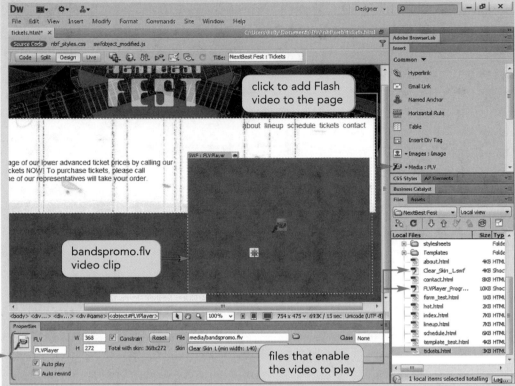

dean bertoncelj/Shutterstock.com; Jupiterimages/Photos.com

11. Click after the text at the end of the page, and then press the **Enter** key until the content area background extends below the video clip.

12. Save the page, and then preview the page in a browser. See Figure 7-38.

Figure 7-38   tickets.html page with the video clip previewed in a browser

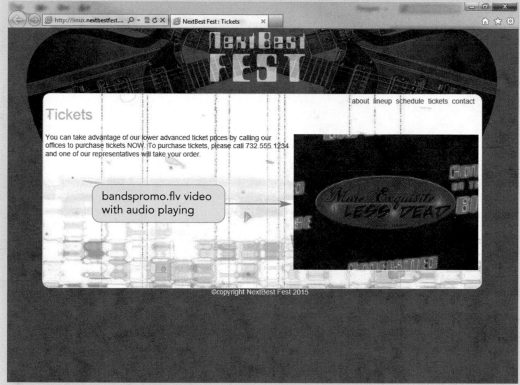

Used with permission from Microsoft Corporation; dean bertoncelj/Shutterstock.com; Jupiterimages/Photos.com

Trouble? If a dialog box opens prompting you to download a newer version of Flash Player, click the Yes button and update Flash Player to its most current version.

13. Close the browser.

Reviewing the Files Added with Flash Video Clips

When you add a Flash video clip to a page using the Insert FLV button, two additional files are added to the site's local root folder. In the Files panel, a Flash file with the name of the skin you selected (Clear_Skin_1.swf) was added to the local root folder. This file contains the information for the look you selected for the control bar that was inserted in the Flash video. The second file inserted into the site's local root folder is the FLVPlayer_Progressive.swf file, which enables the page to play the Flash video file.

You will review these files now.

To review the files inserted with the Flash video:

1. In the Files panel, locate the two files that were added to the local root folder. See Figure 7-39.

Figure 7-39	Files added to the local root folder with the Flash video

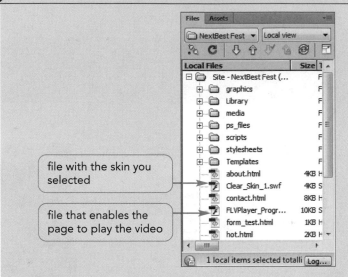

file with the skin you selected

file that enables the page to play the video

Trouble? If you do not see the new files in the Files panel, click the Refresh button on the Files panel toolbar to update the files list.

In addition to the files, Dreamweaver adds some extra code when a Flash video file is inserted into the page using the FLV button. A CheckFlashVersion script detects the version of Flash Player and determines if it is the correct version of Flash Player.

Deleting Flash Video

If you no longer want a Flash video in a Web page, you can select and delete the video from the div. However, deleting the Flash video does not delete the additional files that were added to the site. If you delete all the Flash video from a site, you should also delete the extra files to prevent the site from becoming cluttered or unnecessarily large.

Adding Mark of the Web

Sometimes Internet Explorer (version 6 and above) prevents you from previewing pages with active content in them or warns that it has restricted the file from showing active content. **Active content** is JavaScript or anything that requires an ActiveX control, such as Flash Player. Originally, this was intended to tighten security because attackers were attempting to take advantage of the fact that active content is displayed in the Local Machine zone by default when run from a local computer (and not over the Web). Because it is inconvenient to upload pages that contain active content every time you want to view those pages in a browser, you can solve the problem by adding code called Mark of the Web to your pages with active content to enable you to safely preview the pages locally. **Mark of the Web** is a special comment that you insert into the head area of the Web page code to enable Internet Explorer to display active content from a local file without a warning. It is safe because it tells the active content to display in the Internet zone and not in the Local Machine zone. The comment tag that adds Mark of the Web to a page is:

```
<!-- saved from url=(0014)about:internet -->
```

You type this code in the head content of each page directly in Code view.

Adding Mark of the Web to a Web Page

- Open the page to which you want to add Mark of the Web in Code view.
- Type `<!-- saved from url=(0014)about:internet -->` in the head content.
- Save the page, and then preview the page in a browser to confirm that the page displays without warnings.

You will add Mark of the Web to the pages of the NextBest Fest site.

To add Mark of the Web to the NextBest Fest pages:

1. Switch to **Code** view, position the pointer before the closing head tag, and then press the **Enter** key to move the tag down one line in the code.

2. In the blank line above the closing head tag, type `<!-- saved from url=(0014)about:internet -->` to enter the code for Mark of the Web to the head content.

3. Save the page, and then close the page.

4. Open each of the following pages, and then repeat Steps 1 through 3 to add the Mark of the Web to the other pages in the NextBest Fest site: **about.html**, **contact.html**, **index.html**, **lineup.html**, and **schedule.html**.

Updating the Web Site on the Remote Server

As a final test of the media elements you have added to the NextBest Fest site, you will view the pages over the Web. You will upload the pages you changed and the media folder to your remote server, and then view the site over the Web.

To upload and preview the updated remote NextBest Fest site:

1. Connect to your remote host.

2. Use the **Put file(s)** button ⬆ to upload the updated pages and new dependent files to your remote site.

3. Disconnect from your remote site.

4. In your browser, open the home page of your remote NextBest Fest site.

5. Preview each of the pages, reviewing the new content (the movies, the sounds, and the video). The site includes all the new styles and content that you added to the local version. Also note that no warnings appear about viewing active content.

6. Close the browser.

In this session, you explored a variety of ways to insert video into Web pages. You added video to the NextBest Fest site, and then examined the code that is inserted in the page when you insert Flash video. You added Mark of the Web to all of the pages in the NextBest Fest site. Finally, you uploaded the site to your remote server and viewed the pages over the Web.

REVIEW

Session 7.3 Quick Check

1. What are two ways to include sound in a page?
2. Define the term *streaming*.
3. What is CODEC?
4. _____ is a common sound format that can contain very high-quality sound with a small file size.
5. List three things that might affect the file size of a video clip.
6. Why must a video clip be buffered?
7. True or False. Most of the popular sound formats can also be used for video.
8. True or False. Installing a video player on your user agent enables all other users to view the video on their user agents.

Review Assignments

Data Files needed for the Review Assignments: antifest.flv, underground.mp3, underground.ogg

Dan wants you to add some media elements to the antifest site to increase interest in the fest and to get exposure for the bands that will be appearing at the fest. First, you will add a movie to the home page that promotes the bands playing at next year's fest. Then, you will add a sound to the lineup.html page so users can hear a sample of a sloth child song. You will add the sound file using HTML5 as well as a link so that users with older browsers will have access to the file as well.

1. Open the **antifest** site you modified in Tutorial 6, and then open the **index.html** page in Design view.
2. To the left of the first line of content under the news subheading, insert a new div at the insertion point, and then create a new style for the div from the Insert Div Tag dialog box.
3. Create an ID style named **#promo** in the antistyles.css style sheet. In the Box category, set the float to right and set the margins to 5.
4. Delete the placeholder content from the promo div, and then insert the **antifest.flv** file located in the Dreamweaver7\Review folder included with your Data Files, saving a copy of the antifest.flv file in a **media** folder you create in the local root folder.
5. Select Halo Skin 2 as the skin, have Dreamweaver detect the size, set the movie to autoplay, and autorewind. If a dialog box opens, asking to include additional scripts, click the Yes button to add those scripts to the root folder.
6. Preview the page in Live view. The movie plays automatically, but looks too large in the page and squishes the text that flows around it.
7. Return to Design view, select the movie, and then, in the Property inspector, check the Constrain check box, if necessary, and enter **200** in the H box. The movie's height shrinks to 200px and its width adjusts proportionally.
8. Save the page, copying dependent files as needed, save the style sheet, preview the page in a browser, and then close the browser.
9. Open the **lineup.html** page in Design view. In the sloth child row, in the right column, click before the text, press the Enter key to move the text to the next line, press the Up arrow key to move the insertion point to the blank line, type **song samples:** (including the colon), and then press the Enter key to move to the next line.
10. Switch to Code view, delete the nonbreaking space, and then type the following code at the location of the insertion point:

```
<audio controls>
    <source src="media/underground.ogg" type="audio/ogg" />
    <source src="media/underground.mp3" type="audio/mp3" />
    Your browser does not support the audio tag. Click the link
    below to hear the audio file.
</audio>
```

11. Copy the **underground.mp3** and the **underground.ogg** files located in the Dreamweaver7\Review folder to the media folder in the local root folder.
12. In Design view, move the insertion point to the line below the text, type **underground mp3**, link the text to the underground.mp3 file, and target the link to open in a blank page.
13. Save the page, preview the page in a browser, click the audio controls and listen to the sound, click the underground.mp3 link to test it, close the new page, and then close the browser.
14. Upload all the pages and dependent files to your remote server, and then preview the site over the Internet, testing the media elements.
15. Submit the finished files to your instructor.

Add a Flash animation and add a custom script that displays quotes from skaters.

APPLY

Case Problem 1

Data Files needed for this Case Problem: moebius_team.swf, nu_randomSk8.js

Moebius Skateboards   Corey created a short Flash animation to promote the members of the Moebius skateboard team. In addition, a member of the design team created a custom script that randomly displays quotations from various skaters. Corey wants you to add both of these elements to the home page of the site to add more interest to the page.

1. Open the **Moebius Skateboards** site you modified in Tutorial 6, and then open the **index.html** page in Design view.

2. Click to the left of the Check Out Team Moebius heading, insert a div at the insertion point, and then create a new style for the div.

3. Create an ID style named **team** in the moebius.css style sheet. In the Box category, set the float to right and set the margins to 5.

4. Delete the placeholder text from the team div, and then insert the **moebius_team.swf** file located in the Dreamweaver7\Case1 folder included with your Data Files, saving a copy of the animation in a **media** folder that you create in the local root folder of the Moebius Skateboards site and adding **Promotional animation featuring members of the Moebius Skate Team** as the animation's title.

5. Select the movie in the Document window, if necessary, and then uncheck the Loop check box in the Property inspector. Click the Parameters button, select the text in the first cell of the Value column, type **11.2.2.2** to change the value, and then click the OK button.

6. If necessary, move the insertion point after the last content in the page, and then press the Enter key until the content background is displayed behind the entire animation.

7. Add the Mark of the Web to all of the pages in the site.

8. Preview the animation in the home page by selecting the movie, and then clicking the Play button. When you have viewed the entire animation, click the Stop button.

9. At the top of the index.html page, delete the quotation, and then insert the **nu_randomSk8.js** script located in the Dreamweaver7\Case1 folder, adding a copy of the script to the Scripts folder in the local root folder. (*Hint*: Dreamweaver created the Scripts folder when you added the Flash animation to the site.)

10. Save the page and the style sheet, preview the page in a browser, view the animation you added to the page and reload the page several times to ensure that different quotations appear at the top of the page, and then close the browser and the page.

11. If the animation is over the bottom green band when viewed in the browser, add additional space after the text in the content div, and then save and preview the page again.

12. Upload the site to your remote server, and then preview the site over the Internet, testing the new elements.

13. Submit the finished files to your instructor.

Add an animation and a behavior so that a user mouses over a painting in the animation to display a description of that painting.

CHALLENGE

Case Problem 2

Data File needed for this Case Problem: cr_art.swf

Cowboy Art Society   Moni wants you to insert an animation that displays some of Charles Russell's artwork into the home page of the Cowboy Charlie site. In addition, you will add a prewritten behavior to the artwork.html page that displays the text from the second column of the table in a div when a user mouses over a painting image in the first column. Moving the text from the second column to the div frees up more space for the third column.

1. Open the **Cowboy Charlie** site you modified in Tutorial 6, and then open the **artwork.html** page in Design view.

2. Click the first painting (Cowpunching Sometimes Spells Trouble), press the Right arrow key, and then insert a new div at the insertion point.

3. Create an ID style for the div named **#paint1** defined in the cowboy.css style sheet. The style should provide a 5-pixel margin and a 160px width for the div.

4. Delete the placeholder text from the div, and then open the Behaviors panel in the Tag Inspector.

⊕ **EXPLORE**

5. Select the text in the second cell of the first row of the table, switch to Code view, copy all the code in the cell, and then return to Design view. (*Hint*: Copy all the code between the opening and closing td tags.)

6. Select the cowpunching.jpg graphic.

⊕ **EXPLORE**

7. Add the Set Text of Container behavior. (*Hint*: Click the Add behavior button, point to Set Text, and then click Set Text of Container.)

⊕ **EXPLORE**

8. In the Set Text of Container dialog box, click the Container button, click div "paint1", and then, in the New HTML box, paste the code you copied.

9. In the left column of the Behaviors panel, select <A> onMouseOver so that when the user mouses over the utica.jpg image, the text is displayed in the new div.

10. Delete the text in the second column of the first row and remove any formatting from the cell, and then merge the second and third cells in the row.

11. Save the page and the style sheet, preview the page in a browser, mouse over the image to display the text in the div, and then close the browser.

12. Repeat Steps 2 through 11 for the utica.jpg, grubpile.jpg, and bucker.jpg images, using **#paint2** and the content from the second cell in the second row of the table for the second div, **#paint3** and the content from the second cell in the third row for the third div, and so on.

13. Open the **index.html** page in Design view, and then, at the end of the last line of content before the closing paragraph tag, insert the **cr_art.swf** file located in the Dreamweaver7\Case2 folder included with your Data Files, saving a copy of the file in a **media** folder you create in the local root folder. Use **Charles M Russell paintings** as the title.

14. Top align the Flash movie in the page, and then change the version number to **11.2.2.2** in the Parameters in the Property inspector.

15. Save the page, preview the page in a browser, view the animation, and then close the browser and the page.

16. Upload the site to your remote server, and then preview the site over the Internet.

17. Submit the finished files to your instructor.

Insert an interactive game and add a custom script that generates motivational statements.

APPLY

Case Problem 3

Data Files needed for this Case Problem: successbox.dcr, nu_randomSuccess.js

Success with Tess   Tess wants to add some interactive elements to the Success with Tess site. Another team member has created an interactive success game that will increase user involvement in the site. A third team member has created a custom script that randomly generates motivational sayings. Tess wants you to add the Shockwave game and script to the site.

1. Open the **Success with Tess** site you modified in Tutorial 6, and then open the **index.html** page in Design view.

2. To the left of the first line of content after the TESS-timonials subheading, insert the **successbox.dcr** Shockwave movie file located in the Dreamweaver7\Case3 folder

included with your Data Files, copying the file to a **media** folder that you create in the local root directory of the site, and typing **An interactive success game** as the title.

3. Select the movie, if necessary, and then, in the Property inspector, change the width of the movie to **500**, change the height of the movie to **400**, and set the alignment to right. In the page, add extra spaces to extend the page background below the movie.

4. Save the page, and then preview the page in a browser. When the clover appears, click a leaf, read the statement, click that statement, and then repeat until the full clover is revealed. Close the browser and the page.

5. Open the **contact.html** page in Design view, place the insertion point after the "Please call for a complimentary Q&A / mini-coaching session to experience Success with Tess!", and then press the Enter key to move to the next line.

6. Insert the **nu_randomSuccess.js** script located in the Dreamweaver7\Case3 folder, saving a copy of the script in a **scripts** folder that you create in the local root folder.

7. Save the page, preview the page in Live view, switching between Design view and Live view several times to view some of the quotations, and then return to Design view.

8. On the Related Files toolbar, click the nu_randomSuccess.js button, scroll through the page to view the code, and then close the page.

9. Upload the site to your remote server, and then preview the site over the Internet.

10. Submit the finished files to your instructor.

Case Problem 4

Add a Shockwave movie and a sound clip to a Web site for a coffee lounge.

CREATE

Data Files needed for this Case Problem: coffeegame.dcr, in_the_alley.mp3, sunshine.mp3

Coffee Lounge   Tommy wants to add a Coffee Cup/Shell Game to the Coffee Lounge site. The game will be a Shockwave movie that emails the user a $1 off coupon if the user finds the coffee bean hidden under the cup. Tommy also wants you to add a sound clip of a band that will be playing this weekend. The sound file is an MP3 file.

1. Open the **Coffee Lounge** site you modified in Tutorial 6.

2. Find an appropriate location to add the game to the site (for example, you might place the game in the contact.html page or the home page), and then insert the **coffeegame.dcr** Shockwave movie located in the Dreamweaver7\Case4 folder included with your Data Files, saving a copy of the game in a **media** folder you create in the local root folder. Add an appropriate title for the element.

3. Change the dimensions of the Shockwave movie to a width of **500** and a height of **330**.

4. Save the page, copying the dependent files as needed, preview the page in a browser, play the game, and then close the browser and the page.

5. Find an appropriate location for the sound clip (for example, at the end of the events.html page).

6. On a new line, type **indigNATION will be playing at the Lounge on Wed. nights. Check out one of their songs.** (including the period if it fits your style), and then add a heading and apply styles as needed.

7. On the next line, type **in the alley**, and then copy the **in_the_alley.mp3** file located in the Dreamweaver7\Case4 folder into the media folder in the local root folder.

8. Create a link from the "in the alley" text to the MP3 file in the media folder that is targeted to open in a blank browser window.

9. Repeat Steps 7 and 8 using the **sunshine.mp3** file located in the Dreamweaver7\Case4 folder.

10. Save the page, preview the page in a browser, and then close the browser and the page.

11. Upload the site to your remote server, and then preview the site over the Internet.

12. Submit the finished files to your instructor.

OBJECTIVES

Session 8.1
- Learn about responsive design
- Create a Web page using the Fluid Grid Layout
- Use media queries to define different layouts for the content
- Add fluid grid div tags
- Adjust a Fluid Grid Layout
- Examine HTML code for a fluid grid page
- Insert content into a fluid grid page

Session 8.2
- Create a mobile site with jQuery Mobile
- Use a jQuery Mobile starter page
- Update the jQuery Mobile files
- Add pages to a jQuery Mobile site
- Adjust themes to style a jQuery Mobile site
- Add functionality to a jQuery Mobile site

Session 8.3
- Learn about mobile apps
- Create a PhoneGap account
- Create a mobile app with PhoneGap

Creating Responsive Sites, Mobile Sites, and Apps

Using Fluid Grid Layouts, Media Queries, jQuery Mobile, and PhoneGap

Case | *NextBest Fest*

Gage wants to continue to drum up excitement about NextBest Fest and engage with attendees both before and during the fest. To accomplish this, he is developing an additional site to provide information about what bands are playing on each stage. During the fest, the start and stop times will be continuously updated, enabling attendees to maximize their viewing experience and stay connected. This site will complement—not replace—the main NextBest Fest site. The goal for this secondary site is to provide attendees with useful information that they can access easily with mobile and tablet devices.

Gage anticipates that most attendees will access the site via mobile devices and tablets. Because of this, he wants you to design a responsive site that changes based on the user's screen size, platform, and device orientation. You will create two versions of the site as well as a mobile app for Gage to evaluate. The mobile app will also provide fans with branded souvenir pictures of the fest. The app will process pictures taken with a mobile device's camera so that the pictures are displayed in a frame with the NextBest Fest logo over it.

STARTING DATA FILES

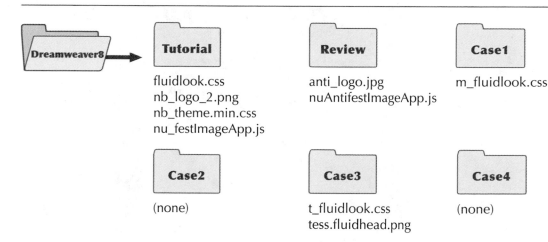

Dreamweaver8 →

Tutorial
fluidlook.css
nb_logo_2.png
nb_theme.min.css
nu_festImageApp.js

Review
anti_logo.jpg
nuAntifestImageApp.js

Case1
m_fluidlook.css

Case2
(none)

Case3
t_fluidlook.css
tess.fluidhead.png

Case4
(none)

SESSION 8.1 VISUAL OVERVIEW

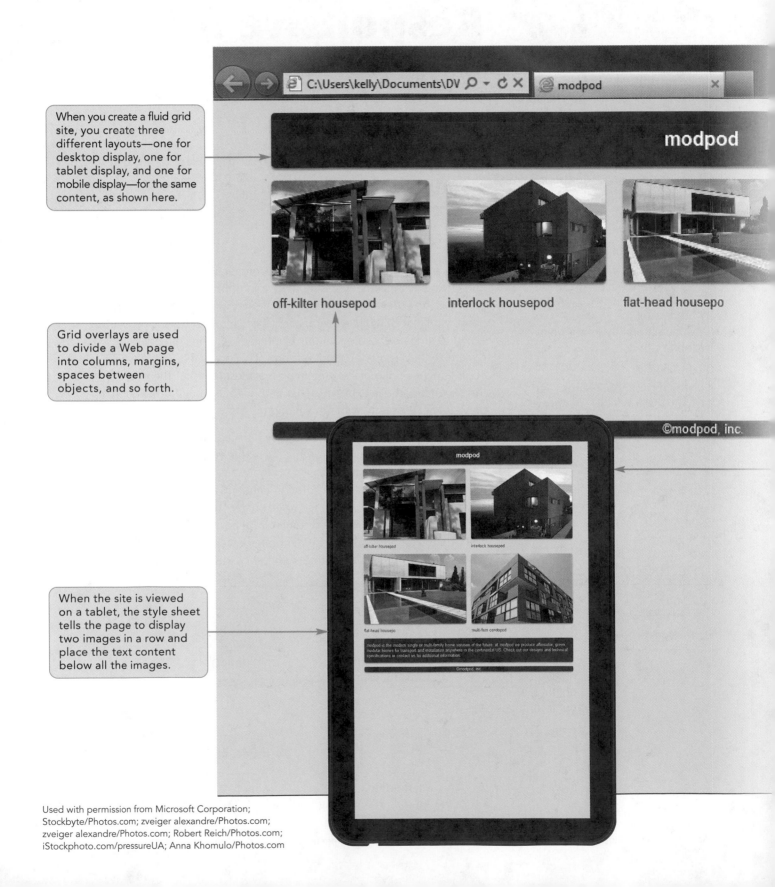

When you create a fluid grid site, you create three different layouts—one for desktop display, one for tablet display, and one for mobile display—for the same content, as shown here.

Grid overlays are used to divide a Web page into columns, margins, spaces between objects, and so forth.

When the site is viewed on a tablet, the style sheet tells the page to display two images in a row and place the text content below all the images.

off-kilter housepod   interlock housepod   flat-head housepo

©modpod, inc.

FLUID GRID SITE

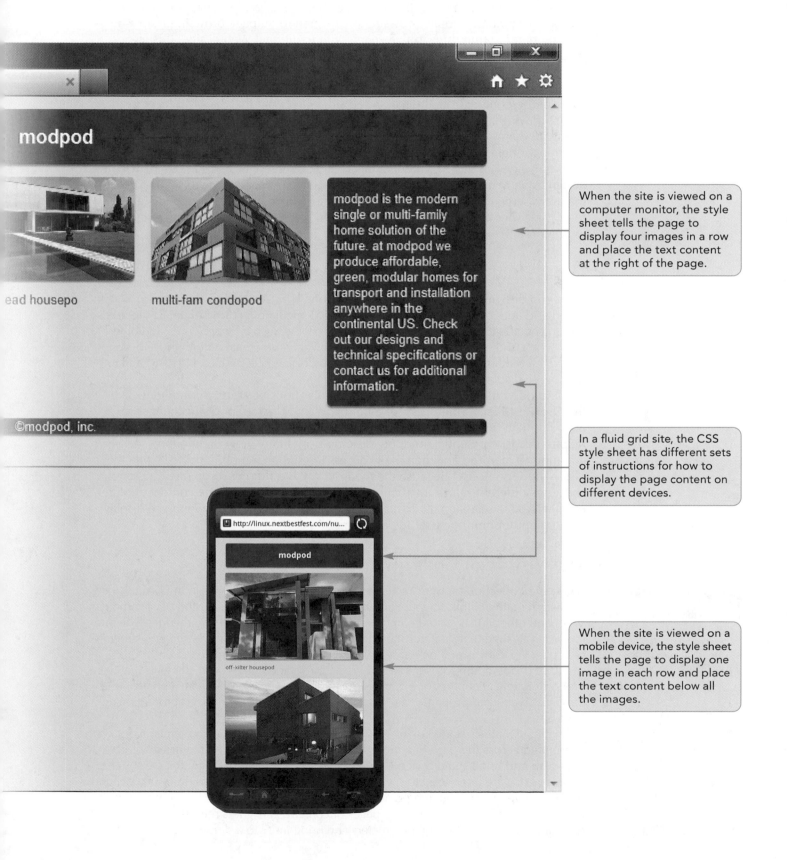

When the site is viewed on a computer monitor, the style sheet tells the page to display four images in a row and place the text content at the right of the page.

In a fluid grid site, the CSS style sheet has different sets of instructions for how to display the page content on different devices.

When the site is viewed on a mobile device, the style sheet tells the page to display one image in each row and place the text content below all the images.

Designing a Responsive Web Site

Creating a Web site has become more difficult and costly because most clients want users to have an engaging experience whether they view the site on a computer, a tablet, or a phone and whether they view the site in landscape orientation or portrait orientation. Mobile browsing is expected to outpace browsing from a desktop computer within three to five years. With traditional Web design, this means creating more versions of a site to accommodate the growing number of viewing scenarios. For example, many companies have a main Web site targeted to display on a computer monitor as well as an additional mobile Web site that presents some of the content from the main Web site in a format that is easy to access on mobile devices.

An approach that is simpler to maintain and more cost effective to create is to develop a single site that can customize display for endless varieties of user devices. Responsive design has grown out of this need. **Responsive design** (also called **adaptive design**) is an approach to Web design that creates sites that change to accommodate the user's screen size, platform, and device orientation. Two approaches to creating responsive sites are fluid grid design (discussed next) and jQuery Mobile (discussed in Session 8.2).

Using Fluid Grid Design

Fluid grid design enables designers to create one Web site using a fluid, proportion-based grid and style sheets that rely on the CSS3 media query rule to detect the user's device specifications and to adapt the page layout, text size, image sizes, and other elements based on the viewing environment. When you create a fluid grid site, you create three different layouts—one for desktop display, one for tablet display, and one for mobile display—for the same content.

Modpod, a manufacturer of modern modular housing structures and one of the NextBest Fest's sponsors, uses a fluid grid site. The modpod site changes to accommodate display on monitors, tablets, and mobile devices. This is especially helpful because potential modpod customers originally view the modpod site on a computer monitor, and then many access the site on a mobile device while they visit a modpod house. Because the modpod site is a fluid grid site, the CSS style sheet has different sets of instructions for how to display the page content on different devices. The Session 8.1 Visual Overview shows how the modpod site displays on a computer monitor, a tablet, and a mobile device.

The History of Grids in Art

TIP

To see this famous example of early grid overlay in art, search the Web for images of da Vinci's Vitruvian Man.

A grid is a collection of evenly spaced vertical and horizontal lines. In the Renaissance era, when mathematics, science, and art were emerging as areas of study, Leonardo da Vinci and other artists started combining mathematical and scientific theories with art. It was at this time that da Vinci started overlaying a mathematically based grid structure on a page (or canvas or block of stone) to divide it into evenly spaced chunks. This structure enabled him to visualize and create forms and figures with elements that were proportionately accurate. For example, the grid made it easier to create a body with a torso that was sized proportionately to its legs, and legs that were sized proportionately to its arms.

Eventually, artists started using a grid to create compositions with elements that were distributed across the page in a more structured way. They also began using a grid to play with and understand concepts such as white space and balance that we still use. In print, grids are often used to divide a page into columns, margins, lines of type, and spaces between type and images. Magazines and other modern publications often use templates based on grids to lay out pages of content. Designers rely on these templates to maintain consistent layout parameters and bring unity to a document.

Today, designers are using grid overlays to create Web sites. Grids work well for responsive design layout because their lines remain proportionately consistent when they are resized. As a result, elements in sites that have a design based on a grid structure can be repositioned on the screen based on the relative size of the grid on the user's screen. Figure 8-1 shows an example of the grid applied to the modpod Web site.

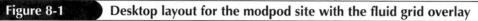

Figure 8-1   **Desktop layout for the modpod site with the fluid grid overlay**

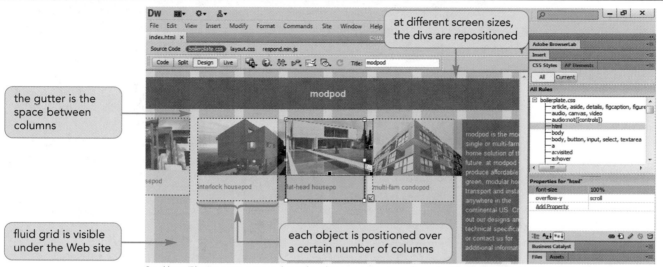

Stockbyte/Photos.com; zveiger alexandre/Photos.com; zveiger alexandre/Photos.com; Robert Reich/Photos.com

Creating a Fluid Grid Page

Dreamweaver Fluid Grid Layouts make designing for multiple user devices simpler. The Dreamweaver system is based on the work of Ethan Marcotte (*www.alistapart.com/articles/responsive-web-design*) and Joni Korpi's Golden Grid system (*goldengridsystem.com*). The Golden Grid system splits the screen into 18 even columns that are separated by margins, or gutters. The two outer columns are used as outer margins, leaving the designer up to 16 columns to use in design. Because 16 columns might be too many when designing for smaller screens, the columns can be folded, or combined. Dreamweaver defaults to 10 columns for desktop layouts, 8 columns for tablet layout, and 5 columns for mobile layout, but you can change the number of columns to suit your needs. Dreamweaver also specifies the percentage of the screen that will be filled with the site for each device, although you can change these as well. When you create a fluid grid site, you create three different layouts—one for desktop display, one for tablet display, and one for mobile display—for the same content.

REFERENCE

Creating a Web Page Using the Fluid Grid Layout

- On the menu bar, click File, and then click New Fluid Grid Layout.
- Set the number of columns for each device, if needed.
- Click the Create button.
- Name and save the style sheet in the local root folder or in a subfolder of the local root folder.
- Save the page and save a copy of the associated files.
- Add fluid grid div tags and content, and then adjust the layout for mobile, tablet, and desktop displays.

You will create a new Web page based on the fluid grid. You will store the page in a new folder to keep it separate from the main site. You will name the page index.html so the server will automatically display the page when fest attendees navigate to the site.

To create a fluid grid–based page:

1. Reset Dreamweaver to the Designer workspace, minimize the Business Catalyst panel, open the Files panel, and then open the **NextBest Fest** site you modified in Tutorial 7.

2. In your site's local root folder, create a new folder named **fluid**. You will store the fluid grid–based page and the style sheet in this folder.

3. Click **File**, and then click **New Fluid Grid Layout**. The New Document dialog box opens with the Fluid Grid Layout displayed. Although you can change the number of columns included for each of the three devices, you will use the default. See Figure 8-2.

Figure 8-2 **Fluid Grid Layout in the New Document dialog box**

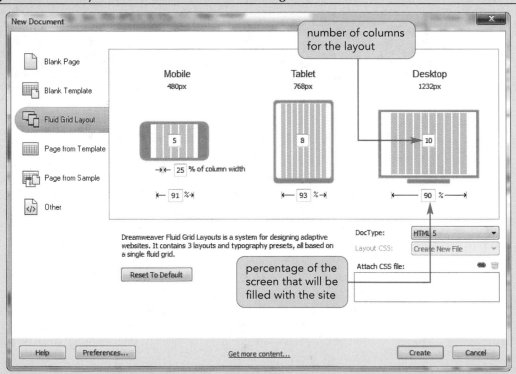

4. Click the **Create** button to create the site.

5. Save the new CSS style sheet as **fluidlayout.css** in the fluid folder. The style sheet is saved, and the new page opens in the Document window. Dreamweaver creates several additional files related to the fluid grid page.

6. In the All Rules pane of the CSS Styles panel, collapse the **boilerplate.css** file if necessary to see the list of files. See Figure 8-3.

Figure 8-3 | Fluid grid page in Mobile Size view

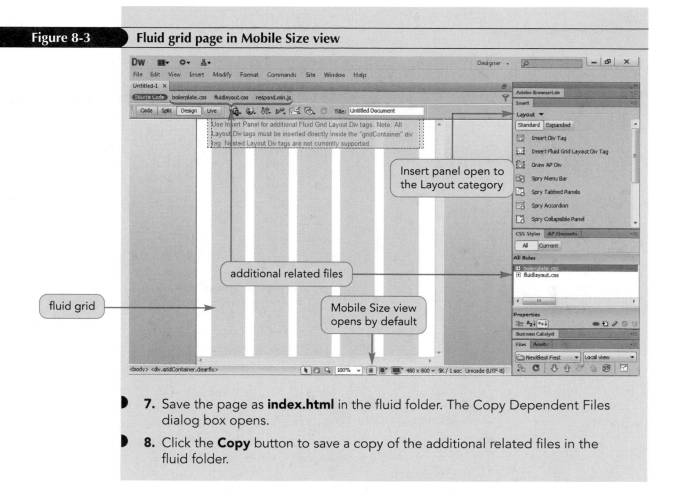

7. Save the page as **index.html** in the fluid folder. The Copy Dependent Files dialog box opens.

8. Click the **Copy** button to save a copy of the additional related files in the fluid folder.

Viewing a Fluid Grid Page at Different Sizes

Using a fluid grid means that you can see the page as it will appear on different devices as you create it. You can display the fluid grid page as it will display on desktop, tablet, or mobile devices, or you can use Multiscreen Preview to view all three layouts at one time. You can also hide the Fluid Grid Layout guides so that you can better see how the page will look to the end user. Asterisks appear next to the Tablet Size and Desktop Size buttons on the status bar until you view the page in that layout.

To view the fluid grid page in different layouts:

1. On the status bar, click the **Tablet Size** button ▣. The page is displayed as it will appear on a tablet screen. See Figure 8-4.

Figure 8-4   Fluid grid page displayed in the Tablet Size view

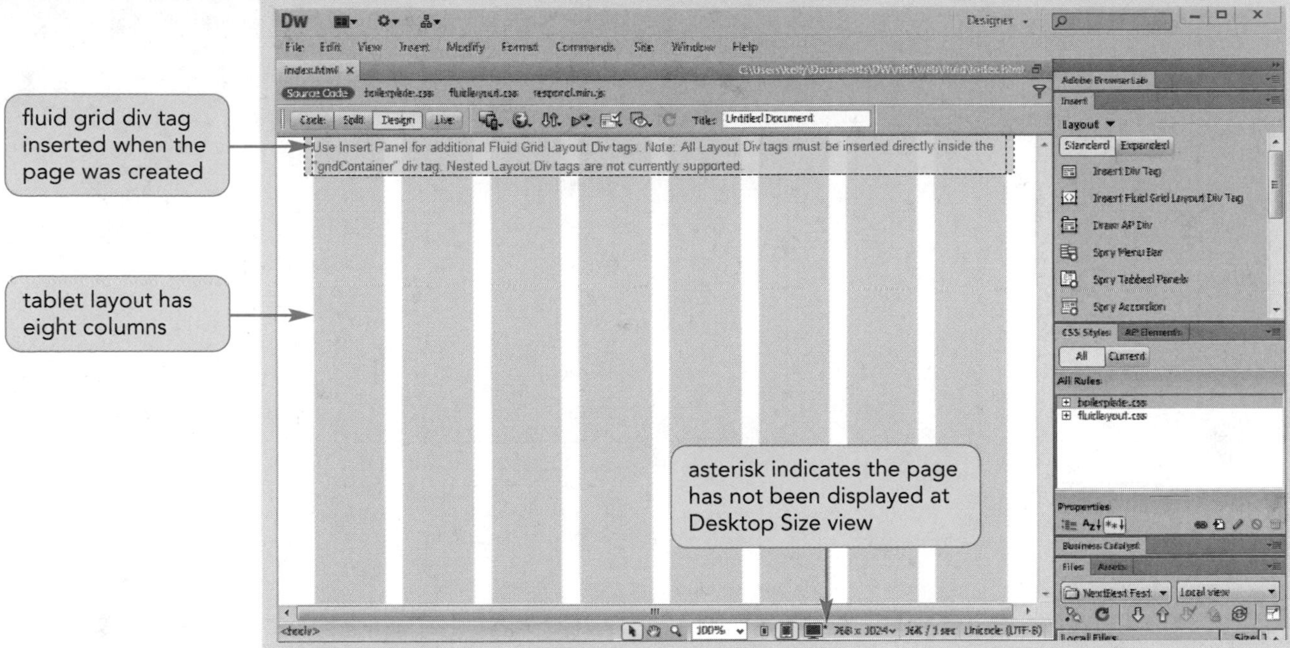

fluid grid div tag
inserted when the
page was created

tablet layout has
eight columns

asterisk indicates the page
has not been displayed at
Desktop Size view

2. Click the **Desktop Size** button [icon] to view the page as it will display on a computer monitor.

3. On the Document toolbar, click the **Visual Aids** button [icon], and then click the **Fluid Grid Layout Guides** check box to uncheck it. The guides disappear.

4. On the Document toolbar, click the **Visual Aids** button [icon], and then click the **Fluid Grid Layout Guides** check box to check it again. The guides reappear.

5. On the Document toolbar, click the **Multiscreen Preview** button [icon], and then click **Multiscreen Preview**. The Multiscreen Preview panel opens with the page displayed in the mobile, tablet, and desktop layouts. You can scroll each layout to view any parts that are hidden. See Figure 8-5.

| Figure 8-5 | Multiscreen Preview of the fluid grid page |

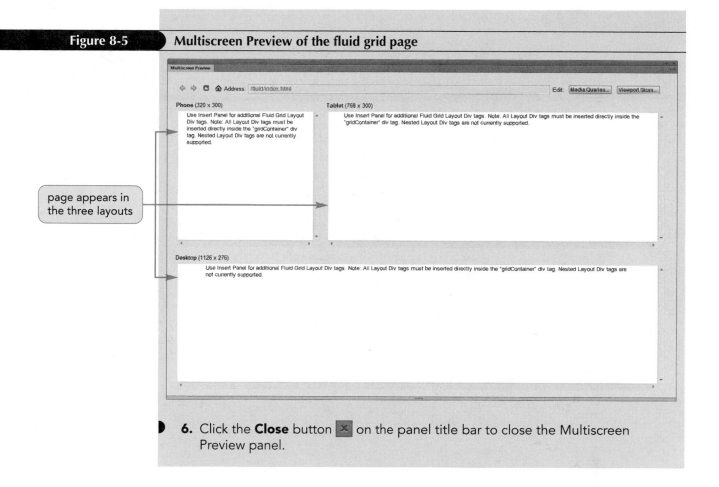

page appears in the three layouts

6. Click the **Close** button ☒ on the panel title bar to close the Multiscreen Preview panel.

Understanding CSS3 Media Queries

Professional Web designers control the way pages display across media so that the target audience has a positive experience with the site no matter how they view or interact with the site. With a style sheet, you can specify how a page is displayed on different media, such as how the page looks when viewed on a screen or when printed on paper. Some properties are only applicable to certain media types. For example, the voice-family property is applicable only for aural user agents. Other properties are shared by several media types but require different values for each media type. For example, a good font size for the general page content is 14 pixels when viewed on a screen but 10 pixels when viewed on a printed page. Designers use the media types described in Figure 8-6 to specify which styles apply when a Web page is displayed on or output to certain media. If no media type is defined in a style sheet, the styles apply to all media types for which they are applicable.

Figure 8-6	Media types

Media Type	Device Type
all	All media type devices
speech	Speech and sound synthesizers
braille	Braille devices
embossed	Paged Braille printers
handheld	Small or handheld devices
print	Printers
projection	Projected presentations
screen	Computer screens
tty	Media using a fixed-pitch character grid, like teletypes and terminals
tv	Television-type devices

© 2013 Cengage Learning

CSS2 included the @media rule, which you use to specify media dependencies for style sheets. In other words, you can place styles in a section of the style sheet where they will affect only the specified media type. This is done by placing the @media rule and a specified media type around a set of rules, as shown in the following example:

```
@media screen {

 body {

  font-size: 14px;

 }

}

@media print {

 body {

  font-size: 10px;

 }

}
```

TIP

You can use the media attribute of the link rule to specify a separate style sheet for a specific media type.

This code specifies that the text will be displayed using a 14px font when the page is viewed on a screen, and the text will be output using a 10px font when the page is printed. All of the styles between the opening and closing brackets of the @media rule will apply only to the media type specified.

Because users interact with sites on a variety of user agents, designers need a way to determine some parameters of the device that the site will be viewed on or output to so that they can customize pages for display on or output to that device and create responsive sites. HTML5/CSS3 expanded the functionality of media types to enable them to check the user agent (or output device because a printer is not really a user agent) to determine particular media features such as width and height. Figure 8-7 describes the current media features.

Figure 8-7	**Media features**

Value	Description
width	The distance across the targeted display area, and optionally the minimum or maximum measurement
height	The distance from the bottom to the top of the targeted display area, and optionally the minimum or maximum measurement
device-width	The distance across the target display/paper, and optionally the minimum or maximum measurement
device-height	The distance from the bottom to the top of the target display/paper, and optionally the minimum or maximum measurement
orientation	The orientation of the target display/paper with possible values of "portrait" or "landscape"
aspect-ratio	The width/height ratio of the targeted display area, and optionally the minimum or maximum measurement
device-aspect-ratio	The device-width/device-height ratio of the target display/paper, and optionally the minimum or maximum value
color	The bits per color of the targeted display, and optionally the minimum or maximum value
color-index	The number of colors that the target display can handle, and optionally the minimum or maximum value
monochrome	The bits per pixel in a monochrome frame buffer, and optionally the minimum or maximum value
resolution	The pixel density (dpi or dpcm) of the target display/paper, and optionally the minimum or maximum value
scan	The scanning method of a TV display, and optionally progressive or interlace
grid	The output device type as grid or bitmap with a value of 1 for grid or 0 for other

© 2013 Cengage Learning

When you use code to ask for information, it is called a **query**. Because media types enable designers to ask true or false questions regarding the user agent/output device media features, they are called **media queries**. According to W3C, "A media query consists of a media type and zero or more expressions that check for the conditions of particular media features." Designers use media queries to tailor the presentation of a page for specific user agents or output devices.

The following code shows a media query in a style sheet using the @media rule:

```
@media screen (min-width: 500px, orientation: portrait) {

 body {

  font-size: 14px;

 }

}
```

In this code, the font-size style with a value of 14px will be applied when the user views the site on a screen that is wider than 500px and the orientation of the screen is portrait. The style sheet knows that these conditions have been met by the user agent because the code essentially asks:

1. True or False: The media type is screen? If True, continue; if False, move past the styles inside the @media rule and do not use them.
2. True or False: The screen is at least 500px in width? If True, continue; if False, move past the styles inside the @media rule and do not use them.

3. True or False: The device is in portrait view? If True, continue and use the styles inside this @media rule to lay out and style the elements in the page; if False, move past the styles inside the @media rule and do not use them.

Media queries are powerful tools because you can place any style inside of them. You can even use media queries to specify that the position of a div is different when a media type has different media features. For example, if you place the site's navigation in a div named nav, you can use media queries to position the div at the left of the screen when the page is displayed on a desktop, at the top of the screen when the page is displayed on a tablet, and in the middle of the screen when the page is viewed on a mobile device.

Reviewing the Code for Fluid Grid Layout Pages

You will create three separate layouts for the fluid grid site: a mobile layout, a tablet layout, and a desktop layout. Using media queries, you can create styles that apply only to one layout and specify different values for a style when it is used in more than one layout. Styles that remain the same in all of the layouts are placed outside of the media queries. For example, the monopod site uses a style to create a content div (the div that holds the text that is displayed in the page). In the mobile layout, the content div is displayed at the bottom of the page, whereas in the desktop layout, the content div is displayed at the right side of the page. The content div appears in different locations because its style is included in the mobile layout media query and in the desktop layout media query with different values specified for the style in each section. Conversely, styles that are consistent across all of the layouts, such as the headings and the body text, are placed outside of the media queries.

The media queries and other code that makes the Fluid Grid Layout page work are included in the following related documents that Dreamweaver added when you created the new Fluid Grid Layout page:

- **fluidlayout.css**—A CSS style sheet you named and saved in the fluid folder. This style sheet includes three media queries, which are where you will create styles that affect the layout of the page at different sizes.
- **boilerplate.css**—A second CSS style sheet that provides CSS styles that will fix common bugs and display differences to produce a consistent, cross-browser display of pages. In this style sheet, you will customize the look of tags, such as the body tag, and add styles that affect the page consistently regardless of the display size.
- **respond.min.js**—A JavaScript file that provides code that makes media queries work with browsers that do not support media queries.

You will view the code for the fluidlayout.css page. You will read the comments included to help designers understand the code, and then examine the media query with styles that affect desktop layout. The media type for this query is only screen and the specified media feature is a minimum width of 769 pixels.

To examine the media query that defines the styles for the desktop layout:

▶ 1. Switch to **Code** view, and then click the **fluidlayout.css** button on the Related Files toolbar.

▶ 2. Scroll down to Line 63 in the code, and then read the comment about the desktop layout media query. See Figure 8-8.

Figure 8-8   Media query with desktop layout styles

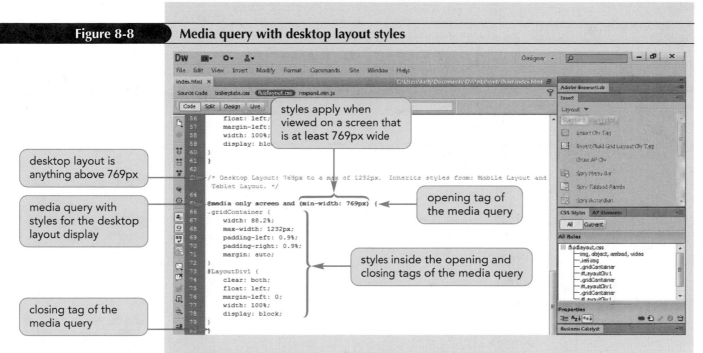

desktop layout is anything above 769px

media query with styles for the desktop layout display

closing tag of the media query

styles apply when viewed on a screen that is at least 769px wide

opening tag of the media query

styles inside the opening and closing tags of the media query

3. Read the media query and styles that begin on Line 65 and end on Line 80. Notice that the media query contains only styles that control page layout at the desktop screen size.

Next, you will view the media query with styles for tablet layout. The media type for this media query is also only screen and the specified media feature is a minimum width of 481 pixels. This is the default width for desktop layout when you create a Fluid Grid Layout page. If you specify a different width when you create a Fluid Grid Layout page, that width will appear in the media query. Because the desktop layout media query has a specified minimum width of 769, the styles in this media query will only affect screen sizes from 481px to 768px.

To examine the media query that defines the styles for the tablet layout:

1. Scroll up to Line 46 in the code and read the comment.

2. Read the code for the media query that starts on Line 48 and ends on Line 61.

3. Minimize the Insert panel to display all of the styles in the CSS Styles panel. The same styles are included in the media query that affects desktop layout and the media query that affects tablet layout. This is done so that you can change the values of the styles to customize the display at that screen size. See Figure 8-9.

Figure 8-9   Tablet layout media query

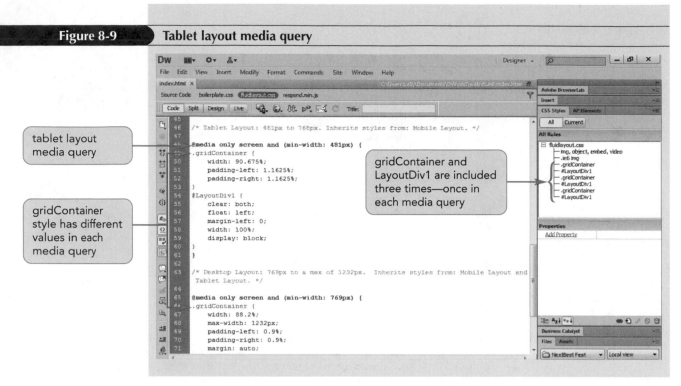

Next, you will view the styles that affect the mobile layout. The same styles are in this section as well. These styles are not in a media query because it is not necessary. The desktop layout media query affects screen widths above 768, and the tablet layout media query affects screen widths from 481px to 768px. Styles that are not in either of those media queries will affect screens widths below 481 and all other devices for which they are applicable.

To examine styles that affect mobile layout:

1. Scroll up to Line 29 in the code and read the comment.

2. Read the code for the styles that starts on Line 31 and ends on Line 44. There is no media query because these styles will apply to any screen that does not match the widths in the desktop layout and tablet layout media queries.

3. In the All Rules pane of the CSS Styles panel, click the top **.gridContainer** style, and then view its properties in the Properties pane.

   Trouble? If you cannot see all of the styles in the Properties pane, you need to resize the pane. Drag the top of the panel up until all of the styles are displayed.

4. Compare these properties with the properties of the .gridContainer style in the mobile layout section of the style sheet. The values are the same. See Figure 8-10.

Figure 8-10   Mobile layout section of the style sheet

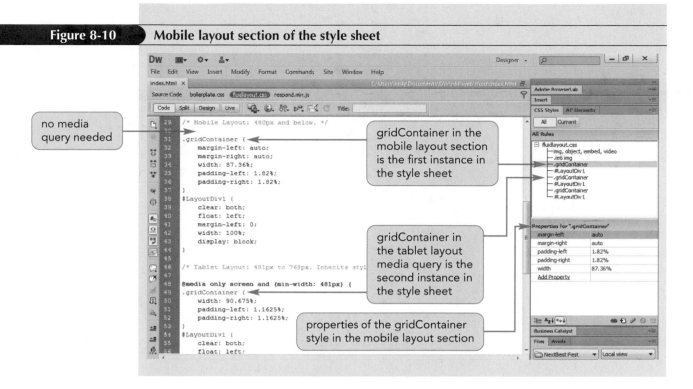

Adding Fluid Grid Div Tags

You have already used divs to structure the layout of regular Web pages. Similarly, you can use Fluid Grid Layout div tags to structure the content of Fluid Grid Layout pages. When you add a Fluid Grid Layout div tag, Dreamweaver adds a copy of the div to the tablet layout media query, the desktop layout media query, and the mobile layout section of the style sheet so that you can specify different values for each layout.

When you add a new div to the page, the Start a new row check box is checked. As a result, the div appears on its own row in the Document window. In the CSS code, the clear property is set to both, preventing other divs from displaying next to it. Also, the margin-left property is set to 0 so that its left border is flush with the left of the gridContainer div. When you uncheck the Start a new row check box, the div is indented in the page and a yellow line appears around the border in the Document window. In the code, the clear property is set to none, enabling another div to occupy the same row, and the margin-left property is set to 2.0408%, which is the size of the gutter between columns. You must add divs inside the gridContainer style to ensure that the fluid grid styles are applied.

You will add a new Fluid Grid Layout div to the page and name it head.

To add a Fluid Grid Layout div to the page:

1. Switch to **Design** view, scroll to the right, click in the fluid grid div, click **<div#LayoutDiv1>** in the status bar to select the div in the Document window, and then press the **Right** arrow key to deselect the div and move the insertion point to its right.

2. In the **Layout** category of the Insert panel, click the **Insert Fluid Grid Layout Div Tag** button. The Insert Fluid Grid Layout Div Tag dialog box opens.

3. Type **head** in the ID box, click the **Start new row** check box, if necessary, to insert a check mark, and then click the **OK** button. The new head div is added to the page.

4. Minimize the Files panel, and then click the **fluidlayout.css** style sheet in the CSS Styles panel to open the style sheet in the All Rules pane of the CSS Style panel. See Figure 8-11.

Figure 8-11 **Fluid Grid Layout page with head div**

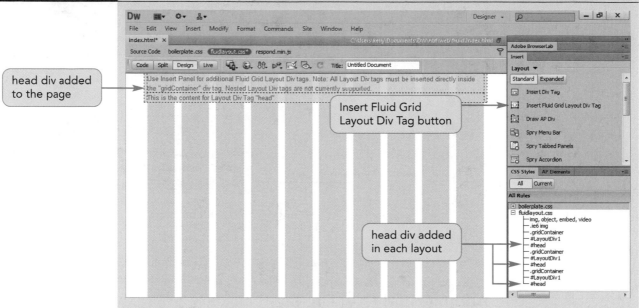

5. Click in the **head** div in the Document window to display its tag in the status bar, click **<div#head>** in the status bar, and then press the **Right** arrow key to move past it.

6. Click the **Insert Fluid Grid Layout Div Tag** button, type **stages** in the ID box, click the **Start new row** check box, if necessary, to check it, and then click the **OK** button.

7. Repeat Steps 5 and 6, selecting and moving past the previously created div and using the following IDs and settings:

Move past	ID	Start new row check box
<div#stages>	**main_stage**	Checked
<div#main_stage>	**starlight_stage**	Unchecked
<div#starlight_stage>	**satellite_stage**	Unchecked
<div#satellite_stage>	**neon_stage**	Unchecked
<div#neon_stage>	**content**	Unchecked
<div#content>	**footer**	Checked

8. Press the **Right** arrow key to deselect the div. See Figure 8-12.

Figure 8-12   New fluid grid div tags added to the page

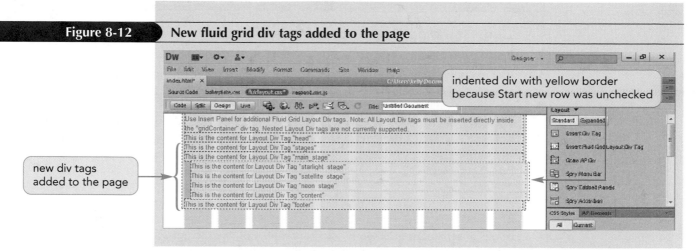

new div tags added to the page

indented div with yellow border because Start new row was unchecked

Next, you will delete the LayoutDiv1 from the page. This is the default div that Dreamweaver included when you created the page. Because the div is in the style sheet in three places, you must remove the div from the HTML code, and you must remove all three instances from the CSS.

To remove the default Fluid Grid Layout div:

▶ **1.** In the Document window, click in the **LayoutDiv1** div, click the div tag in the status bar, and then press the **Delete** key. The LayoutDiv1 div is removed from the HTML code of the index.html page.

▶ **2.** In the All Rules pane of the CSS Styles panel, select the first instance of the **#LayoutDiv1**, and then press the **Delete** key.

▶ **3.** Repeat Step 2 to remove the other two instances from the fluidlayout.css style sheet.

▶ **4.** Save the style sheet, and then save the page.

Visually Adjusting a Fluid Grid Layout

The Fluid Grid Layout was designed to enable you to adjust responsive pages visually while Dreamweaver writes the code, instead of having to modify the code yourself. This is a big step forward in making responsive design quick and accessible to all designers. You adjust the layout for each display size—desktop, tablet, and mobile—by selecting that size in the status bar and then dragging elements in the Document window. When you make adjustments in the Document window, Dreamweaver changes the code for the instance of the selected div in the media query that is associated with the size you are viewing. For example, if you have the desktop layout displayed in the Document window, the instance of the selected div in the desktop layout media query will be affected by the changes. When you reposition elements, all of the elements must stay inside the gridContainer div for the Fluid Grid Layout to work.

Understanding Proportional Measurements

When creating a responsive site, designers rely on proportional measurements rather than creating elements at a fixed size. This enables the style sheet to adjust the size and placement of elements on a screen based on the size and other parameters of the device on which you display (or output) the site. So a div might be set with a 100% width instead of at 800px because 100% of a 480px width screen is much different than 100% of a monitor set at 1024px width. In addition to percentage, designers frequently use the em unit of measurement. In typography, the em is used to measure horizontal widths. In CSS, the em is usually used to measure both horizontal and vertical lengths. When used to specify font size, one em is equal to the base font size for the parent of the element on which it is used. For example, if you are setting the size of the H1 tag, one em equals the font size of the body tag. Because of the cascading effect of style sheets, when an element does not have a font-size value defined, the value is inherited from farther up the document tree or from the default style sheet supplied by the user agent if no value is specified by the author. (HTML documents are hierarchical. To understand the relationship of elements, it may help to visualize the document as a tree: The HTML tag is the root, the next elements branch off from the root, the subsequent elements branch off from those elements, and so forth, creating a treelike structure in which the elements that are farther away from the root inherit the characteristics of their parent elements.) So, if the body tag has no set font size, the browser will look in the user settings for normal font size or it will use the browser default size.

When creating responsive sites, designers often refrain from using fixed font sizes so that all em-based elements are sized based on the user settings or browser defaults. For example, a designer may make the font size of the body tag 1em, the h2 tag 1.5em, and the h1 tag 2em so that the text will get proportionally bigger for headings, but will be based on the device's defaults for display. Using ems in this way also ensures that sites are accessible because users who need to view text larger can do so without problem. In addition to text, ems can also be used as a unit of proportional measurement throughout the style sheet. For example, designers sometimes use em units to set things like margin-width, padding, and indention to ensure that these will scale with the font size. Percentages and ems are the most frequently used units when creating responsive sites.

Adjusting Div Width and Layout

In a Fluid Grid Layout, all divs are inserted at a default size. To make them useful for displaying content, you need to adjust their widths. You can do this by dragging the right resize handle of a selected div. As you drag, a tooltip indicates the number of fluid grid columns in the new width of the div when you release the mouse button. The minimum width for a div is one column and the maximum width is the number of columns specified for the layout. You cannot select partial columns. When you adjust the width of a div, Dreamweaver calculates the percentage of the layout that the new width will take up and adds that percentage to the CSS style. The height of a div is dictated by the content in the div so you cannot adjust the height manually. The placement of the div in the page when you adjust the width of a column depends on the CSS properties set for the div when it was added to the page. If the Start new row check box was checked, the div will change width but will remain on its own row due to the both value for the clear property; if the box was unchecked, the div will move up in the page when there is sufficient room.

You will lay out the desktop display of the site. The head and stages divs will be the page width and on their own lines. The main_stage, starlight_stage, satellite_stage, neon_stage, and content divs will each be two columns in width and displayed on the following line. The footer div will be the page width and follow on its own line. You will start by adjusting the widths of the divs that need to be two columns wide.

To adjust the width of Fluid Grid Layout divs:

▸ 1. In the Document window, select the **main_stage** div and point to the right resize handle.

▸ 2. Drag the right resize handle to the left until the tooltip reads **columns:2**, and then release the mouse button. The main_stage div changes size. See Figure 8-13.

Figure 8-13	The main_stage div resized

arrow button moves the div up a row

left resize handle increases the div's left margin

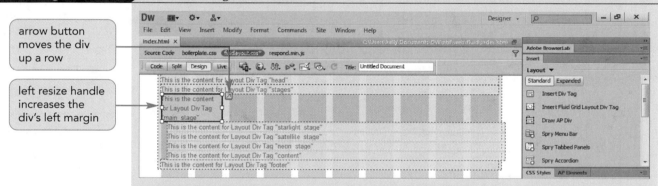

▸ 3. In the Document window, select the **starlight_stage** div, and then drag the right resize handle to the left until the tooltip reads **columns:2**.

▸ 4. Repeat Step 3 to resize the **satellite_stage**, **neon_stage**, and **content** divs. See Figure 8-14.

Figure 8-14	Resized fluid grid divs

resized divs moved up because the Start new row check box was unchecked

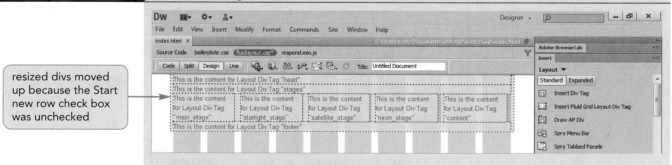

▸ 5. Save the fluidlayout.css style sheet.

Next, you will switch to Tablet Size view and repeat the process to create the tablet layout. On a tablet, the head and stages divs will remain in their original placement. The main_stage and starlight_stage divs will occupy the next line, and the satellite_stage and neon_stage divs will be displayed on the following line. The content and the footer divs will each occupy an entire line and be displayed at the bottom of the page.

To resize the divs for the tablet layout:

1. On the status bar, click the **Tablet Size** button (🔲), click the **main_stage** div in the Document window to select it, and then drag the right resize handle to the left until the width is 4 columns.

2. Select the **starlight_stage** div, and then drag the right resize handle to the left until the width is 4 columns. The starlight_stage div moves to the same row as the main_stage div.

3. Select the **satellite_stage** div, and then click the **Click to align DIV with grid** button ◀ that appears at the left of the div to set the margin-left property to 0 and the clear property to both.

4. Drag the div's right resize handle to the left until its width is **4** columns.

5. Select the **neon_stage** div, and then resize the div's width to **4** columns.

6. Select the **content** div, click the **Click to align DIV with grid** button ◀, and then click outside of the divs to deselect them. Figure 8-15 shows the new tablet layout.

Figure 8-15 ▶ **Layout for the tablet display**

resized divs are 4 columns wide

7. Save the fluidlayout.css page.

Finally, you will lay out the mobile display. On mobile devices, each div will occupy a full row. You do not need to adjust the width of the divs for this display, but you do need to change the alignment of the divs that were not set to display on their own line.

To realign the divs for the mobile layout and preview the site in a browser:

1. In the status bar, click the **Mobile Size** button (🔲) to display the mobile layout.

2. Click in the **starlight_stage** div to select it, and then click the **Click to align DIV with grid** button ◀.

3. Repeat Step 2 to realign the **satellite_stage**, **neon_stage**, and **content** divs. See Figure 8-16.

Figure 8-16   **Layout for the mobile display**

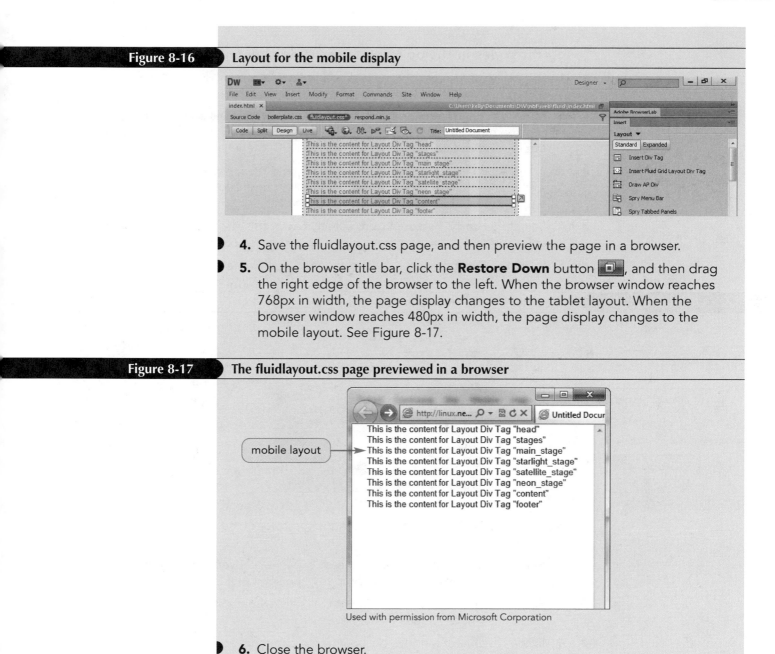

4. Save the fluidlayout.css page, and then preview the page in a browser.

5. On the browser title bar, click the **Restore Down** button ⬜, and then drag the right edge of the browser to the left. When the browser window reaches 768px in width, the page display changes to the tablet layout. When the browser window reaches 480px in width, the page display changes to the mobile layout. See Figure 8-17.

Figure 8-17   **The fluidlayout.css page previewed in a browser**

mobile layout →

> This is the content for Layout Div Tag "head"
> This is the content for Layout Div Tag "stages"
> This is the content for Layout Div Tag "main_stage"
> This is the content for Layout Div Tag "starlight_stage"
> This is the content for Layout Div Tag "satellite_stage"
> This is the content for Layout Div Tag "neon_stage"
> This is the content for Layout Div Tag "content"
> This is the content for Layout Div Tag "footer"

Used with permission from Microsoft Corporation

6. Close the browser.

Creating Styles for the Site

With all of the divs in place, the next step is to customize the styles that apply to the entire site. When you created the Fluid Grid Layout page, Dreamweaver defined styles for the site in the boilerplate.css style sheet. The boilerplate.css style sheet already includes fixes that enable the site to display uniformly across browsers, operating systems, and so forth, as well as styles for the body tag, h1 tag, and other elements that are common to all layouts of the page. You will adjust these CSS styles to match the styles in the main NextBest Fest site. The process for customizing styles in a fluid grid page is the same as customizing styles for a regular site.

To edit styles in the boilerplate.css style sheet:

▶ **1.** On the Related Files toolbar, click the **boilerplate.css** style sheet, and then switch to **Code** view.

▶ **2.** Minimize the Insert panel, and then resize the CSS Styles panel so that you can see most of the styles in the All Rules pane and most of the properties in the Properties pane.

▶ **3.** In the All Rules pane, click the **body** style, and then, in the Properties pane, add a background-color of **#666**. The background color is added to the entire page.

▶ **4.** Select the **body, button, input, select, textarea** style, and then change the color to **#666** to change the color of the text in the page.

▶ **5.** Switch to **Design** view to see the changes. See Figure 8-18.

Figure 8-18	Edited styles in the boilerplate.css style sheet

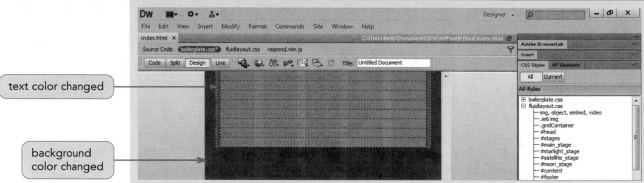

text color changed

background color changed

▶ **6.** Switch to **Code** view, and then change the color of the a and a:visited tags to **#666**.

▶ **7.** Select the **a:hover** tag, change the color of the a:hover tag to **#666**, and then add the **text-decoration** property and set its value to **underline**.

▶ **8.** Scroll down to locate the comment that says **primary styles Author:**. This section is where you can create new styles.

▶ **9.** In the Document window, click below the comment area, and then type the following code, as shown in Figure 8-19:

```
.align_center {
    text-align: center;
}
```

Figure 8-19   **New style in Code view**

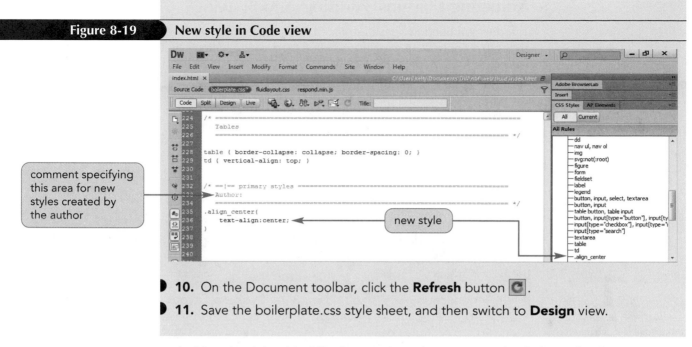

comment specifying this area for new styles created by the author

new style

▶ **10.** On the Document toolbar, click the **Refresh** button 🗘.

▶ **11.** Save the boilerplate.css style sheet, and then switch to **Design** view.

At this point, it is a bit difficult to see how the content is divided into the divs because the individual divs do not have styles. Although you could continue to create new styles for the divs in the boilerplate.css style sheet, Gage had a designer create a new style sheet named fluidlook.css that contains all of the CSS styles you need for the site. Designers often create separate style sheets for different types of styles to keep the site organized and to keep style sheets uncluttered and manageable. For example, you might keep all of the styles that affect page layout in one style sheet and all of the styles that affect the look of elements, such as colors, in another style sheet. This is particularly true when a team of people is working on a site and team members are responsible for different parts of the site. You will place a copy of the fluidlook.css style sheet in the fluid folder, and then you will attach the page to the new style sheet.

To connect the page to the new style sheet:

▶ **1.** Copy the **fluidlook.css** file located in the Dreamweaver8\Tutorial folder included with your Data Files into the fluid folder in the site's local root folder.

▶ **2.** Attach the **fluidlook.css** style sheet to the page.

▶ **3.** Save the page, and then preview the page in a browser to view the styles. Some divs have background colors with a bit of opacity, rounded edges, and drop shadows. The gridContainer div has the same background image, rounded corners, and border colors as the main site. See Figure 8-20.

Figure 8-20   **Page attached to the new fluidlook.css style sheet**

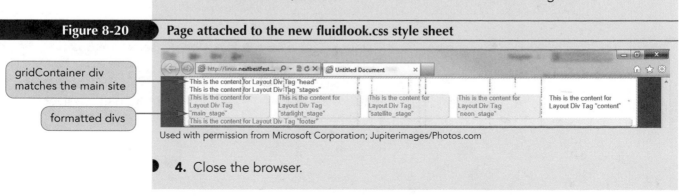

gridContainer div matches the main site

formatted divs

Used with permission from Microsoft Corporation; Jupiterimages/Photos.com

▶ **4.** Close the browser.

Adjusting Margins, Padding, and Spacing

The divs still need to be better placed in the page. You will fix this by adjusting the styles that control the margins, padding, and other elements that are specific to each layout (desktop, tablet, and mobile) of the fluid grid site. When you make changes that fine-tune the display of a site, it is a good idea to frequently preview the page in a browser to ensure that the layout displays exactly as you intended.

You will begin by changing the style for the divs in the media query for the desktop layout. You will add 1em top and bottom margins to the header, stages, and footer divs to create space between the divs.

To add margins to divs in the desktop layout:

1. On the Related Files toolbar, click the **fluidlayout.css** style sheet. The page opens in Split view and the fluidlayout.css styles are displayed in the All Rules pane of the CSS Styles panel.

2. On the status bar, click the **Desktop Size** button 🖥.

There are three instances of the #head div, so be sure you are in the desktop layout section of the style sheet.

3. In the Code pane, scroll down to the **Desktop Layout** section of the page, and then select the **#head** div. That instance of the head div style is selected in the All Rules pane of the CSS Styles panel and its properties are displayed in the Properties pane. See Figure 8-21.

| Figure 8-21 | The head div selected in the desktop layout |

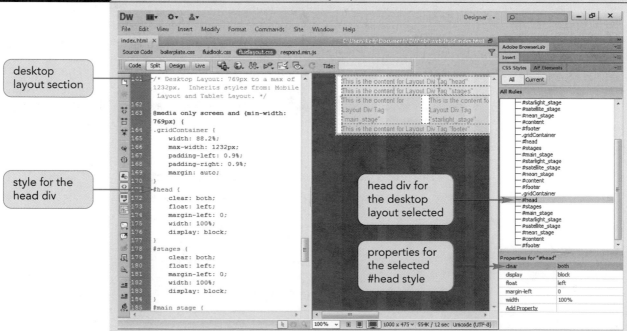

4. In the CSS Styles panel, click the **Edit Rule** button 🖉, select the **Box** category, under Margin, type **1** and select **em** as the unit of measure for the Top and Bottom margins, and then click the **OK** button.

5. Repeat Steps 3 and 4 for the **stages** div and the **footer** div in the desktop layout media query. The three styles have margins to better space the divs in the page.

6. Save the style sheet, and then switch to **Design** view to see the page. See Figure 8-22.

Figure 8-22   **Desktop layout with margins added**

margins add space between the divs

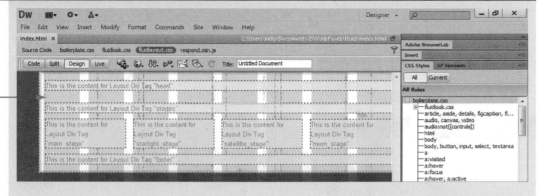

7. Preview the page in a browser to ensure that the styles display correctly. See Figure 8-23.

Figure 8-23   **Desktop layout with margins added previewed in a browser**

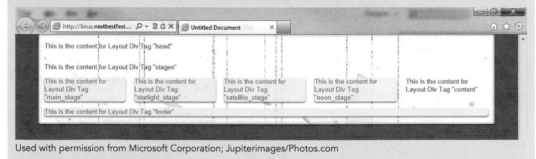

Used with permission from Microsoft Corporation; Jupiterimages/Photos.com

8. Close the browser.

Next, you will adjust the margins for the tablet layout of the page. You will add margins to the top and bottom of the head, stages, and footer divs, as you did for desktop layout. You will also add margins to the top and bottom of the satellite_stage and neon_stage divs to create space between the images.

To add margins to divs in the tablet layout:

1. On the Related Files toolbar, click the **fluidlayout.css** style sheet. The page opens in Split view and the fluidlayout.css styles are displayed in the CSS Styles panel.

2. On the status bar, click the **Tablet Size** button 🔲.

3. In the Code pane, scroll to the **Tablet Layout** section of the page, and then select the **#head** div. That instance of the head div style is selected in the All Rules pane of the CSS Styles panel and its properties are displayed in the Properties pane.

4. In the CSS Styles panel, click the **Edit Rule** button , select the **Box** category, under Margin, type **1** and select **em** as the unit of measure for the Top and Bottom margins, and then click the **OK** button.

5. Repeat Steps 3 and 4 for the **stages**, **satellite_stage**, **neon_stage**, and **footer** divs in the tablet layout media query.

6. Save the style sheet, and then switch to **Design** view to see the page.

7. Preview the page in a browser, click the **Restore Down** button on the title bar, and then drag the right border to the left until you can see the tablet layout. See Figure 8-24.

| Figure 8-24 | Tablet layout with margins added previewed in a browser |

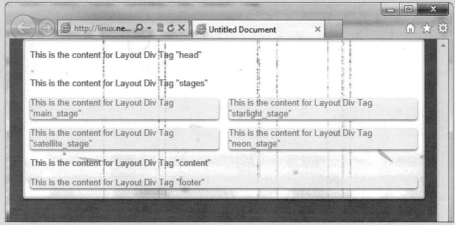

Used with permission from Microsoft Corporation; Jupiterimages/Photos.com

Trouble? If the new styles are not applied in the browser, you might need to update the display. Click the Refresh button in the Address bar.

8. Close the browser.

Finally, you will add margins to the mobile layout of the page. In mobile layout, each div occupies a full line so you will add top and bottom margins to every div. You will add a 1em margin to the top of the head div and to the bottom of the footer div, and you will add .5em top and bottom margins to the remaining divs to keep the spacing consistent throughout the page.

To add margins to divs in the mobile layout:

1. On the Related Files toolbar, click the **fluidlayout.css** style sheet. The page opens in Split view and the fluidlayout.css styles are displayed in the CSS Styles panel.

2. On the status bar, click the **Mobile Size** button .

3. In the Code pane, scroll to the **Mobile Layout** section of the page, and then select the **#head** div. That instance of the head div style is selected in the All Rules pane of the CSS Styles panel and its properties are displayed in the Properties pane.

TIP

You can copy those properties in a style and paste them in other styles in the style sheet to speed up the process.

4. In the CSS Styles panel, click the **Edit Rule** button ✐, select the **Box** category, under Margin, type **1** and select **em** as the unit of measure for the Top margin, type **.5** and select **em** as the unit of measure for the Bottom margin, and then click the **OK** button.

5. Repeat Steps 3 and 4 for the **stages**, **main_stage**, **starlight_stage**, **satellite_stage**, **neon_stage**, and **content** divs in the Mobile Layout section using **.5em** for the Top and Bottom margins.

6. Repeat Steps 3 and 4 for the **footer** div in the Mobile Layout section using **.5em** for the Top margin and **1em** for the Bottom margin.

7. Save the style sheet, and then switch to **Design** view to see the page.

8. Preview the page in a browser, click the **Restore Down** button 🗗 on the title bar, and then drag the right border to the left until you can see the mobile layout. See Figure 8-25.

Figure 8-25 | **Mobile layout with margins added previewed in a browser**

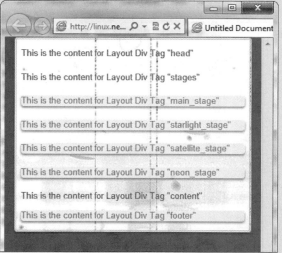

Used with permission from Microsoft Corporation; Jupiterimages/Photos.com

Trouble? If the new styles are not applied in the browser, you might need to update the display. Click the Refresh button in the Address bar.

9. Close the browser.

Examining the HTML Code for the Fluid Grid Page

Although you have three instances of the styles that control each div tag, the actual div is only added to the page one time. This means that you add content to the page once and it is restyled based on which device it is being viewed with. You will examine the HTML for the page.

To examine the HTML code for the fluid grid page:

1. Switch to **Code** view, click the **Source Code** button on the Related Files toolbar, and then minimize the Property inspector.

2. At the top of the page, review the code in the head section. Notice the links to the three style sheets and the script that tells the page to locate and run the respond.min.js JavaScript. See Figure 8-26.

Figure 8-26 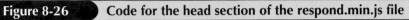 **Code for the head section of the respond.min.js file**

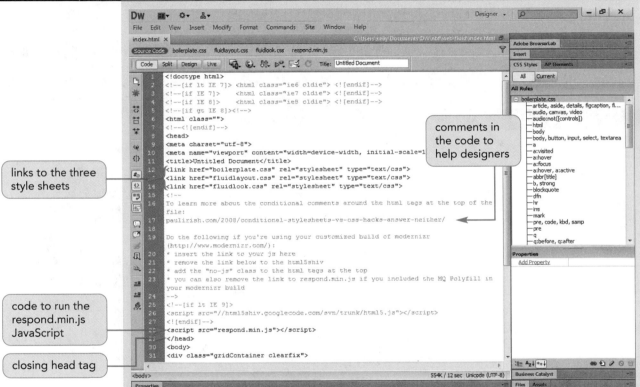

3. Scroll down to review the remaining code in the page. Notice the opening and closing tags for the gridContainer div as well as the head, stages, main_stage, starlight_stage, satellite_stage, neon_stage, content, and footer divs. See Figure 8-27.

Figure 8-27 Code for the body section of the respond.min.js file

opening tag of the gridContainer div that surrounds the other divs

remaining divs in the page

closing tag for the gridContainer div

content in the head div

closing tag for the head div

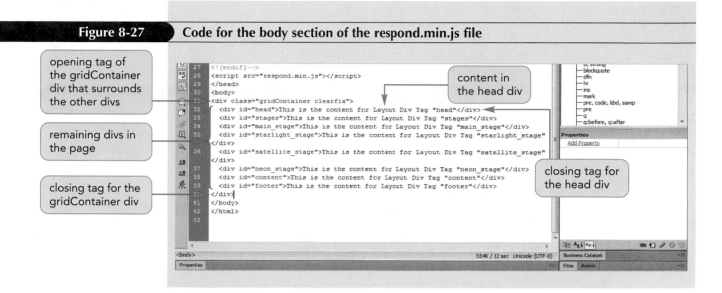

Problem Solving: Adding Fixed-Width Elements to a Responsive Site

You have seen how variable-width elements like divs and text can be made to flow flexibly in a responsive site. But, how do you overcome the limitations of fixed-width elements like images when you are creating a responsive site? Using proportional measurements to insert an image into the page makes the image display at a percentage of its original size, but it will not cause the image to scale when the viewing area changes size. Without the ability for these elements to scale, responsive design can at best be used only for sites that have no graphics, images, or video. Fortunately, Ethan Marcotte and other designers who are pushing the boundaries of responsive design discovered a solution: proportional measurements. When you create a Fluid Grid Layout page, Dreamweaver adds a style to the top of the style sheet specifying that images, objects, embedded elements, and video display at a max-width of 100%. With this style in place, you can insert fixed-width elements such as an image. If you do not specify a width or height within the element, the browser will display the element at 100% unless there is not enough space. When there is not enough space, the browser will scale the element, making it small enough to fit into the available space. This style scales the fixed-width elements that you include in the pages of a responsive site.

Adding Content to a Fluid Grid Layout Page

You insert content into a fluid grid page in the same way that you insert content into other pages because a fluid grid page is just a regular page. A fluid grid page is only different in that its layout is customized for display on different sized devices. But, this is controlled by the attached style sheets, not the HTML page. When inserting text in the Document window, you can be in any view—Desktop Size, Tablet Size, or Mobile Size—because the content is added once. No matter in which layout the page is being viewed, the content comes from the actual HTML page.

You are ready to add content to the page. The schedule for each stage will be displayed in its corresponding div and important, ongoing updates will be displayed in the content div. Because the site will not be used until shortly before the fest begins, the content is not ready yet so you will leave the placeholder text already in the divs. For now, you will add a footer to the bottom of the page. You will also add two graphics at the top of the page—the NextBest Fest logo to the head div and the fest map to the stages div. When you add the images, you will not specify a width or height because Dreamweaver added a style to the top of the fluidlayout.css style sheet that tells browsers to display images at 100% width. This means that the images will display at 100% width when possible and scale to a smaller size when it is not. After the final content is ready, Gage will have another team member create hotspots over the stages on the fest map and create links from the hotspots to the heading text that will be placed at the top of each stage div.

To add text and graphics to the page:

1. Switch to **Design** view, and then, on the status bar, click the **Desktop Size** button (🖥). You will add the page content in Desktop Size view so you can more easily see the content.

2. Select the **footer** div, open the Property inspector, and then apply the **align_center** style, which you created earlier. The text is aligned to the center of the div.

3. Click in the **footer** div, delete the placeholder text, insert the copyright symbol, press the **Spacebar**, and then type **NextBest Fest**. The footer is added to the page.

4. Click after the text in the head div, insert the **nb_logo_2.png** file located in the graphics folder of the NextBest Fest site with no alt text, and then delete the placeholder text from the div.

5. Select the **head** div, and then apply the **align_center** style. The content in the div is aligned to the center of the div.

6. Repeat Steps 4 and 5 to insert the **fest_map.png** graphic into the stages div. See Figure 8-28.

Figure 8-28 **Content added to the fluid grid site**

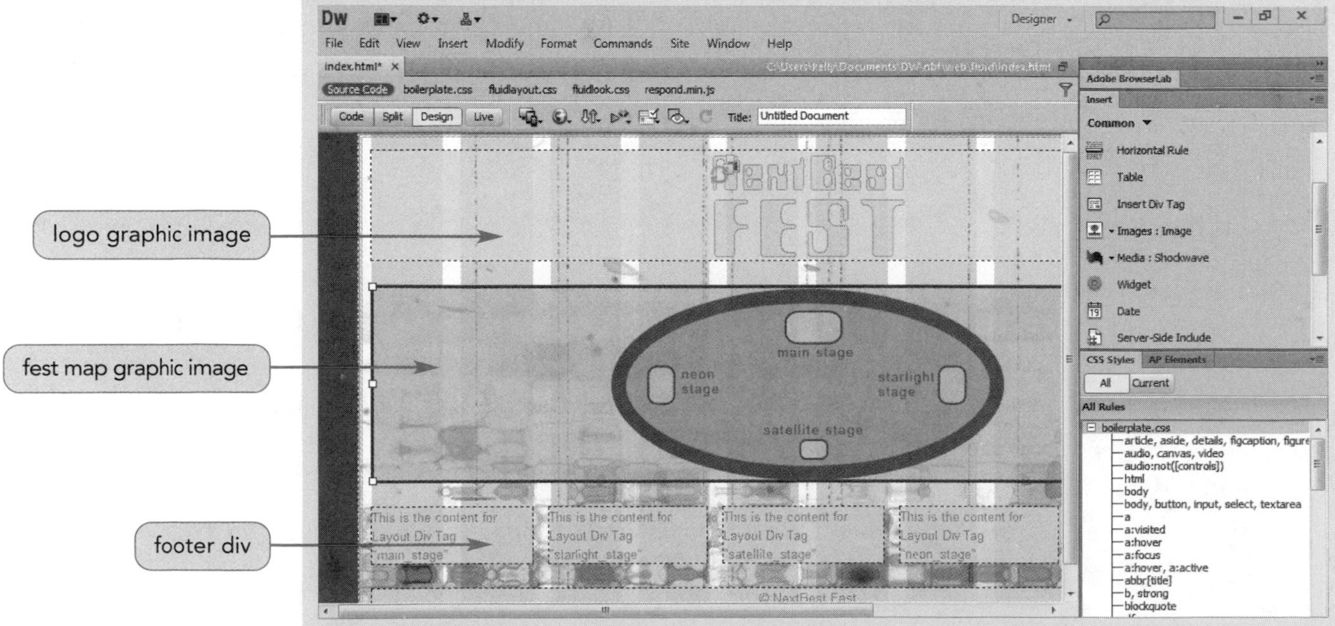

logo graphic image

fest map graphic image

footer div

Jupiterimages/Photos.com

7. Save the page, and then preview the page in a browser.

8. Resize the browser window until the tablet layout is displayed. See Figure 8-29.

Figure 8-29 **Page with content previewed in a browser at tablet layout**

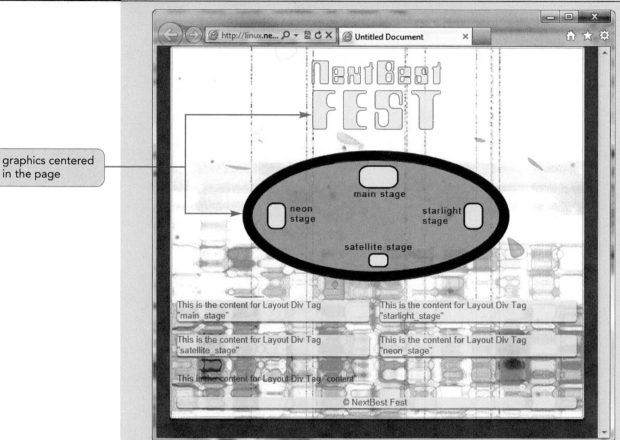

graphics centered in the page

Used with permission from Microsoft Corporation; Jupiterimages/Photos.com

9. Resize the browser window as far to the left as it will go. The graphics scale to fit in the window. See Figure 8-30.

Figure 8-30   **Page with content previewed in a browser at mobile layout**

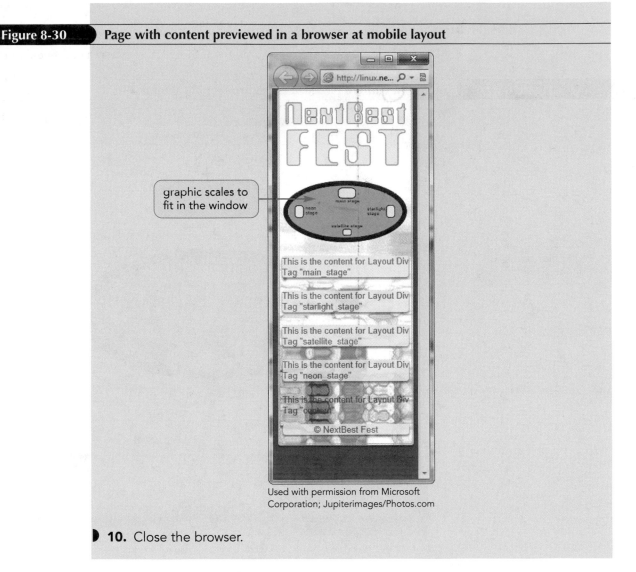

graphic scales to fit in the window

Used with permission from Microsoft Corporation; Jupiterimages/Photos.com

▶ **10.** Close the browser.

Testing a Mobile Site over the Web

You will not upload the site to the remote server and test it until Gage decides whether he will use the responsive site, the jQuery Mobile site, or a mobile app. Once he makes a decision, you should test that site on your remote server using all of the devices that the site is intended to be displayed on. This testing is important because mobile sites are still Web sites, and problems often occur when you view a site over the Web that were not present when you viewed the site locally.

INSIGHT

Demystifying the Grid

Now that you understand grid-based layout and responsive design, there is a secret to unveil: There is no grid. When you create Fluid Grid Layout pages in Dreamweaver, you use the grid convention to help you rapidly develop pages, but no extra code that defines the grid is added to the page. The only difference between a regular page and a responsive page is that you used proportional measurements and media queries to create a responsive design. Dreamweaver provided CSS styles and JavaScript that fixes all the problems you would have encountered had you made a responsive site on your own. The grid guides make the concepts easier to visualize and use.

So far you have created a responsive site using the Fluid Grid Layout. You used media queries to define different layouts for the content, you added fluid grid div tags, you adjusted the layout, and then you inserted content into the fluid grid page. In the next session, you will create a mobile site using jQuery Mobile.

REVIEW

Session 8.1 Quick Check

1. What is responsive design?
2. Describe fluid grid design.
3. Why do designers use media queries?
4. What happens when you add a Fluid Grid Layout div tag to a Fluid Grid Layout page?
5. Why are there three instances of a style in the style sheet for a fluid grid site?
6. How do you add content into a fluid grid page?
7. Is there extra code that defines the grid added to a fluid grid page?
8. What is the difference between a regular page and a responsive page?

SESSION 8.2 VISUAL OVERVIEW

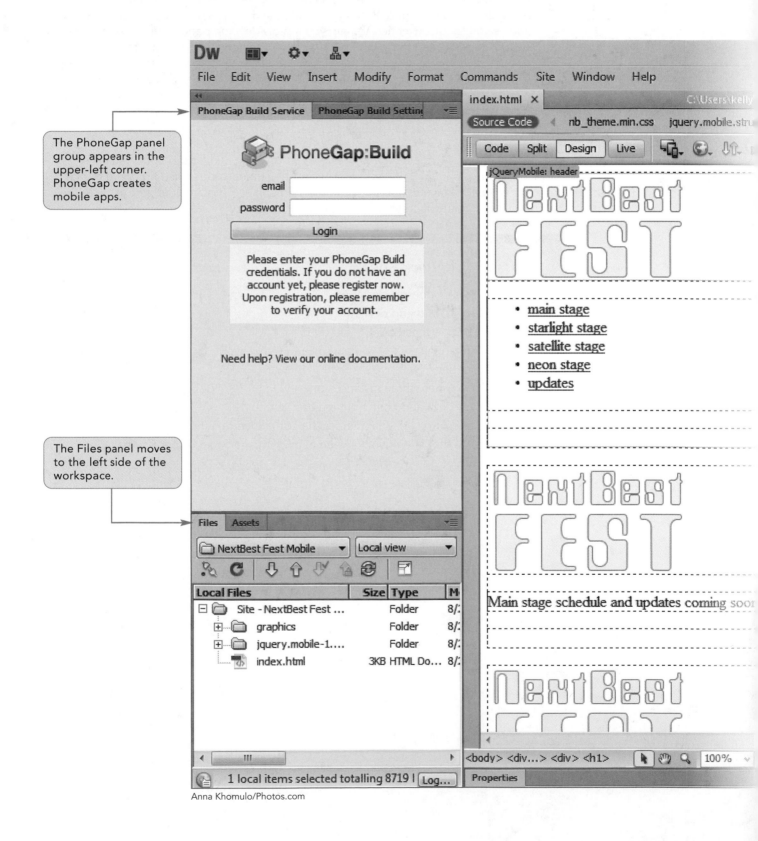

The PhoneGap panel group appears in the upper-left corner. PhoneGap creates mobile apps.

The Files panel moves to the left side of the workspace.

Anna Khomulo/Photos.com

JQUERY MOBILE SITE

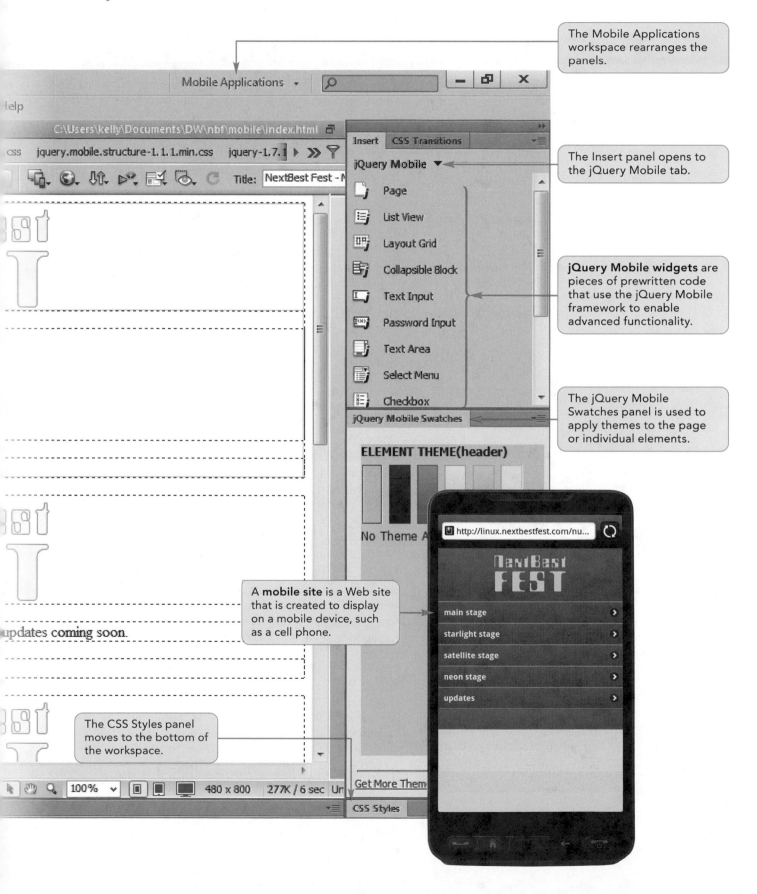

The Mobile Applications workspace rearranges the panels.

The Insert panel opens to the jQuery Mobile tab.

jQuery Mobile widgets are pieces of prewritten code that use the jQuery Mobile framework to enable advanced functionality.

The jQuery Mobile Swatches panel is used to apply themes to the page or individual elements.

A **mobile site** is a Web site that is created to display on a mobile device, such as a cell phone.

The CSS Styles panel moves to the bottom of the workspace.

Creating a Mobile Site with jQuery Mobile

Although you can create a mobile site on your own, jQuery Mobile makes it simpler. jQuery Mobile is based on **jQuery** (a JavaScript framework), which makes it easier to develop Web sites and Web apps that use JavaScript functionality. A **framework** is a cohesive library of code that structures and simplifies programming in whatever programming language you are using. So, jQuery is more than just some JavaScripts; it provides a simple and structured way to access advanced functionality without having to write complex code on your own. **jQuery Mobile** is a touch-optimized mobile framework used to create Web sites that will work on current tablets and smartphones.

INSIGHT

APIs

An important advantage to using a framework like jQuery is that a team of coders constantly updates and maintains the library, fixing bugs and problems that are introduced as Web technology changes. Also, if you use the framework as intended, as technology and standards change over time, changes and updates that keep the framework current should not break older code in Web sites you created in the past. That is often not the case when you write everything yourself. To learn how to use a framework properly, you need to read the API documentation—in this case, on the jQuery Mobile Web site. An **API (application programming interface)** is the specific set of methods prescribed by the framework's authors by which a programmer can utilize features of the framework.

The concept of an API can be difficult to grasp because the word *interface* is most commonly heard in connection with a GUI (Graphical User Interface), which is a computer interface that is designed for human interaction. GUIs use graphics, windows, icons, and so forth so nonprogrammers can navigate and interact with the computer in a nontechnical environment. The GUI is what you see when you open Dreamweaver and view the workspace or lay out a page that enables a user to interact with a site and its content. An interface does not need to have a graphic component nor does it need to be targeted at an end user. In actuality, an **interface** is simply a point of interaction. This definition makes it easier to understand that an API is a set of instructions, code, and standards that a programmer uses to facilitate interaction between what he or she is creating and the framework or software with which he or she wants to communicate. For example, Google Maps publishes an API that provides programmers with standards and instructions that will enable them to write code to include Google Maps in any Web site. The API does not give all of the code that the authors used to create Google Maps. Instead, it provides lines of code the programmers can customize and place in their sites that will communicate with Google Maps and include a Google Map in their sites. The API also provides instructions and standards for including the code in their sites. For jQuery, the API provides documentation that explains what pieces of code the programmer can use to access various advanced functionality and it provides instructions on how to approach coding.

Most jQuery sites are designed to look like a mobile app. They have built-in functionality that mobile users are familiar with. For example, you can use the jQuery Mobile framework to easily add functionality that enables users to swipe a page or move it when a button is pressed, or to set the transition so that the page slides out/in, fades out/in, and so forth. All of this functionality is created using JavaScript and CSS.

Decision Making: Determining When to Create a Mobile Site

Clients might want you to create a mobile site for a variety of reasons. Responsive Web design is a relatively new concept, and clients frequently do not want one site that is designed to adapt its display to the user agent. It might be because they are used to the idea of creating a separate mobile experience, or because responsive sites can be slower because all of the CSS for the entire site is downloaded even when only the pared-down mobile version displays. Sometimes clients have a traditional site in place and want to create a separate site to display on mobile (and sometimes tablet) devices. Other times clients believe that users who view the site from a mobile device have different needs than users who view the site from a home computer, and want to create a separate site designed specifically to target mobile users.

Clients often expect a mobile site to have the look and feel of a mobile app. You can create a mobile site from scratch, doing all of the coding and design yourself. Or, you can take advantage of the jQuery Mobile framework to help create the site and then focus your energy on customizing the user experience to create a dynamic site that works with the client's other materials and fulfills the site goals. Because jQuery Mobile sites are targeted specifically to mobile users, they have the look of a mobile app that you might download from an app store.

Gage wants you to create a jQuery Mobile version of the fluid grid site you created in the previous session. You will duplicate the NextBest Fest site and use the copy for the mobile site. You will create the local and remote folders because it is good practice to do so. The mobile site will be located in a mobile folder inside of the nbf folder on your computer and in a mobile folder on the remote server. This way, you can keep the sites separate while using one domain. You will begin by creating the folder on the remote server and duplicating the NextBest Fest site.

To create a folder on the remote server and duplicate the NextBest Fest site:

1. If you took a break after the previous session, make sure your NextBest Fest site is open, the Designer workspace is reset, the Business Catalyst panel is minimized, and the Files panel is open.

2. On the Files panel toolbar, click the **Expand to show local and remote sites** button, and then click the **Connect to Remote Server** button. Dreamweaver connects to your remote server and the remote files are displayed in the left pane.

3. Right-click a blank area of the left pane, click **New Folder** on the context menu, type **mobile** as the new folder name, and then press the **Enter** key. The mobile folder is created on the remote server.

4. On the Files panel toolbar, click the **Collapse to show only local or remote site** button.

5. On the Files panel toolbar, click the **site arrow**, and then click **Manage Sites**. The Manage Sites dialog box opens.

6. In the Your Sites list, click **NextBest Fest** to select it, and then click the **Duplicate currently selected site(s)** button. A NextBest Fest copy is created in the Files panel.

7. Select the **NextBest Fest copy**, if necessary, and then click the **Edit the currently selected site** button to edit the site.

▶ **8.** In the Site Name box, select the text and type **NextBest Fest Mobile** to rename the site, and then click the **Browse** button 🗀 to the right of the Local Site Folder box. The Choose Root Folder dialog box opens.

▶ **9.** Click the **Up one level** button 🔼 to move out of the web folder, click the **Create new folder** button 📁, type **mobile** as the name of the new folder, click the **Open** button, and then click the **Select** button. The path in the Local Site Folder box includes the mobile folder instead of the web folder.

▶ **10.** Click the **Advanced Settings** tab, select **web** in the path shown in the Default Images Folder box, and then type **mobile**. The folder path is updated.

▶ **11.** Click the **Servers** tab, select your server, and then click the **Edit existing Server** button. The Servers panel opens and you can edit your server information.

▶ **12.** In the Root Directory box, type **mobile** at the end of the file path, and then, in the Web URL box, type **mobile** at the end of the file path.

▶ **13.** Click the **Test** button to confirm that the connection to the new remote folder works.

   Trouble? If the test is not successful, check your information to ensure that you have typed it correctly, and then try again. If the test is still unsuccessful, check with your instructor, IT department, or ISP to make sure the information you entered is correct.

▶ **14.** Click the **Save** button in each dialog box, and then click the **Done** button in the Manage Sites dialog box. The new site is created and appears in the Files panel.

▶ **15.** In the Files panel, expand the **mobile** folder. The folder is empty.

Using a jQuery Mobile Starter Page

Dreamweaver has jQuery Mobile starter pages that provide the HTML, CSS, JavaScript, and image files needed to create a basic site. Most often, jQuery Mobile sites consist of only one page. This keeps the site lean, making it faster to download to a mobile device. To provide the illusion of separate pages, content is placed into divs that are shown or hidden based on which button the user presses. So, you can use one jQuery Mobile starter page to create an entire jQuery Mobile site. You can choose one of the following three starter pages:

• **JQuery Mobile (CDN).** This starter page uses a Content Delivery Network (CDN) to provide the required jQuery files (jquery, jquerymobile, css, and images). In this scenario, you host your Web site and you link to the jQuery Mobile files that are hosted by jQuery free of charge. Programmers sometimes prefer this method because it decreases the load on their Web server and may increase the speed with which the files load on the client device.

• **JQuery Mobile (Local).** This starter page adds the required jQuery files directly to the site's local root folder so you can host the files yourself or include them with an application that does not require an Internet connection.

• **JQuery Mobile with theme (Local).** This starter page adds the required jQuery files directly to the site's local root folder so you can host the files yourself or include them with an application that does not require an Internet connection. It also separates the CSS into two files: one for styles that affect layout and structure, and one for styles that affect the look or theme. This enables you to use Dreamweaver tools to customize the look (or theme) of the site, and it enables you to create and download custom themes from the jQuery Mobile site.

Figure 8-31 shows the basic jQuery Mobile with theme (Local) starter page. When a user views the site from a mobile device, the site will be displayed in a browser. In mobile devices, the browser's default setting has the site fill the user's entire screen. As a result, the site will not look like it is in a browser window or only a small search bar appears across the top of the screen.

Figure 8-31   **jQuery Mobile starter page**

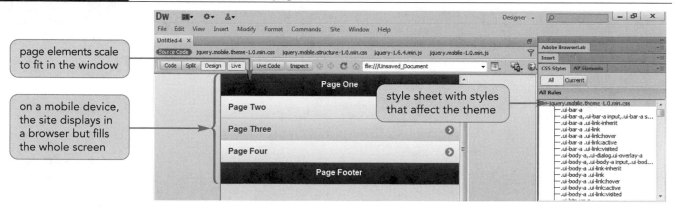

- page elements scale to fit in the window
- on a mobile device, the site displays in a browser but fills the whole screen
- style sheet with styles that affect the theme

After you save a starter page, you can add content and customize the site's look and functionality. The site includes divs that can be hidden to organize the page content, as well as styles that set the structure and look of the site. You can insert jQuery Mobile widgets from the jQuery Mobile tab of the Insert panel to provide additional functionality. You can also use the jQuery Mobile Swatches panel to add themes that quickly restyle the site and page elements.

You will create a jQuery Mobile site from the jQuery Mobile with theme starter page so that you can use the jQuery Mobile Swatches panel to style the page.

To create a jQuery Mobile site from a starter page:

1. On the menu bar, click **File**, and then click **New**. The New Document dialog box opens.

2. Click **Page from Sample** in the main list, click **Mobile Starters** in the Sample Folder list, click **jQuery Mobile with theme (Local)** in the Sample Page list, and then click the **Create** button. The new jQuery Mobile site is created, and the Document window changes to Split view.

3. Switch to **Design** view to view the page. The site includes four divs. The first div includes links to the other three divs in which you can enter content and that you can show or hide. The styles for the site's theme and structure are added to the CSS Styles panel.

4. Save the page as **index.html** in the local root folder. The Copy Dependent Files dialog box opens.

5. Click the **Copy** button to copy the files to the local root folder. Dreamweaver creates a jquery.mobile folder in the root folder. See Figure 8-32.

Figure 8-32 jQuery Mobile starter page

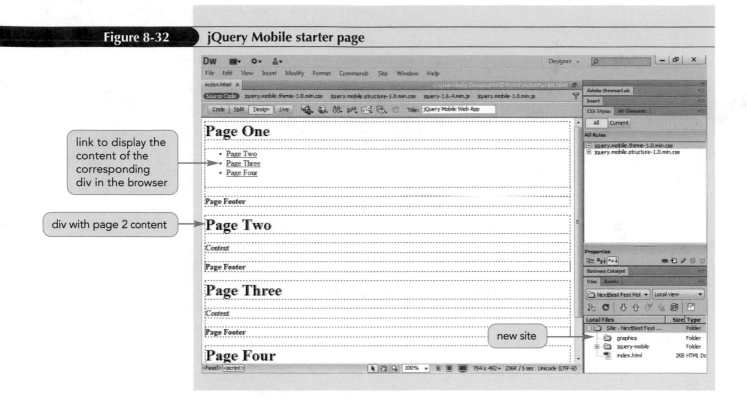

link to display the content of the corresponding div in the browser

div with page 2 content

new site

Updating the jQuery Mobile Files

The jQuery Mobile framework is constantly being updated. As a result, the jQuery Mobile files included with Dreamweaver are probably not the current versions. You should create sites using the most recent versions of the files to ensure that the latest bug fixes and features are being used.

You will download the current version of the jQuery Mobile files from the jQuery Mobile site.

To download the current jQuery Mobile files:

Throughout the tutorial, replace *x.y.z* with the current version numbers.

1. Open a browser, navigate to the **jquerymobile.com** Web site, and then click the **Latest stable version-x.y.z** link (where **x.y.z** are the numbers for the latest version).

2. Scroll to locate the Requires jQuery core file, and then write down the version numbers of the files. If two numbers are listed, write both numbers down. You will need to get that file after you have downloaded the jQuery Mobile files. See Figure 8-33.

| Figure 8-33 | Download new jQuery Mobile files |

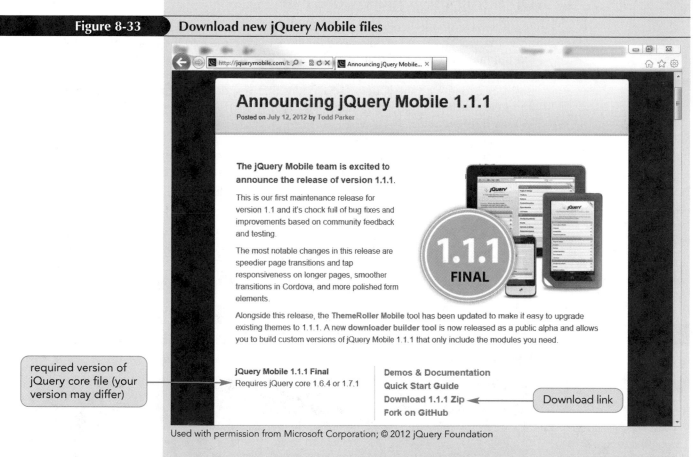

required version of jQuery core file (your version may differ)

Announcing jQuery Mobile 1.1.1

Posted on July 12, 2012 by Todd Parker

The jQuery Mobile team is excited to announce the release of version 1.1.1.

This is our first maintenance release for version 1.1 and it's chock full of bug fixes and improvements based on community feedback and testing.

The most notable changes in this release are speedier page transitions and tap responsiveness on longer pages, smoother transitions in Cordova, and more polished form elements.

Alongside this release, the **ThemeRoller Mobile** tool has been updated to make it easy to upgrade existing themes to 1.1.1. A new downloader builder tool is now released as a public alpha and allows you to build custom versions of jQuery Mobile 1.1.1 that only include the modules you need.

jQuery Mobile 1.1.1 Final
Requires jQuery core 1.6.4 or 1.7.1

Demos & Documentation
Quick Start Guide
Download 1.1.1 Zip
Fork on GitHub

Download link

Used with permission from Microsoft Corporation; © 2012 jQuery Foundation

3. Click the **Download *x.y.z* Zip** link to download a zip file that contains all of the JavaScript, CSS, and image files you will need.

   Trouble? If the name of the file you are downloading is different from the name of the file shown in Figure 8-33, the file has been updated since this tutorial was published. You are downloading the most recent stable version of jQuery Mobile.

4. Click the **Save** button, and then save a copy of the file in the **Dreamweaver8\Tutorial** folder.

5. Start Windows Explorer, right-click the **jquery.mobile-*x.y.z*.zip** file, and then click **Extract to here** to extract the zip files. The files extract to a jquery.mobile-*x.y.z* folder.

   Trouble? If you don't see the Extract to here option, you are probably using different extraction software. Click Extract All or something similar to extract the files into a jquery.mobile-*x.y.z* folder.

You now have the latest jQuery Mobile files, which you will use to replace files that Dreamweaver added to your root folder, but first you must download the latest version of the jQuery core file.

Updating the jQuery Core File

The jQuery core file is not included with the jQuery Mobile files that you just downloaded. You need to download the jQuery core file into the jquery.mobile folder, but the latest version of the file may be too recent for the files you just downloaded. If this is the case, you will locate and then download the version that you need. This file is not included with the jQuery Mobile files that you downloaded because the jQuery framework is being updated continuously and is often "out of sync" with the jQuery Mobile framework.

You determine the latest version of the core jQuery file that will work with the jQuery Mobile framework by looking at the Required jQuery core file version numbers that you just wrote down. If the latest version number is higher than the version number you just wrote down, you will navigate to the Download page, locate the version number that you wrote down, and download that file.

To download the jQuery core file:

▶ 1. Start your browser, and then navigate to the **jquery.com** Web site. See Figure 8-34.

Figure 8-34   **jQuery page to download new jQuery core files**

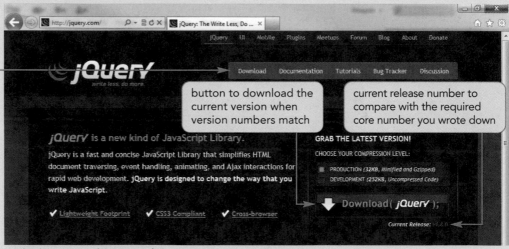

link to the Download page to download an earlier version if the current release number is higher

button to download the current version when version numbers match

current release number to compare with the required core number you wrote down

Used with permission from Microsoft Corporation; © 2012 jQuery Foundation

Be sure to check the current release number against the required core number to determine whether to download the jQuery core file.

▶ 2. If the current release number matches or falls between the required jQuery core numbers that you wrote down from the jQuery Mobile site, click the **Download (jQuery);** button, save the file in the **jquery.mobile** folder located in the Dreamweaver8\Tutorial folder, and then continue with Step 4. If the current release number is higher than the required jQuery core numbers you wrote down, continue with Step 3.

▶ 3. Click the **Download** link on the navigation bar to open the Download page, scroll down to the Past Releases section (which contains a clickable list of older versions of the files), locate the latest version number you can use (which is the highest number that you wrote down), click the **Minified** link next to the version number you want to download, and then save the file in the **jquery.mobile** folder located in the Dreamweaver8\Tutorial folder.

▶ 4. In Windows Explorer, navigate to the **jquery.mobile** folder located in the Dreamweaver8\Tutorial folder to view the file that you downloaded.

Deleting Unnecessary Files

Dreamweaver does not use all of the downloaded files that are in the jquery.mobile folder. The folder contains two versions of most of the files: (1) the regular version, which is readable by humans, that is provided so developers can easily change and modify the code, and (2) a minified version of the file. A **minified file** is a file that has been compressed by removing comments and extra white space that are not needed by Web browsers to reduce the file size. The minified file is usually included when you upload the file to the remote server because this version has a smaller file size, which helps the site load in the user's device faster. Many programs are available that will minify files. If you decide to start from the regular version of the file and modify the JavaScript yourself, you can use a program to create a minified version of the file to upload to the remote server. In this tutorial, you will not modify the JavaScript by hand so you do not need the regular versions of the files.

You will delete the files and folders that you do not need from the jquery.mobile folder to keep the root folder uncluttered.

To delete the unnecessary files from the jquery.mobile folder:

1. In Windows Explorer, make sure the Dreamweaver8\Tutorial\jquery.mobile-x.y.z folder is displayed. See Figure 8-35. You will delete the files that are highlighted in yellow in the figure.

Figure 8-35   Downloaded files in the jquery.mobile folder

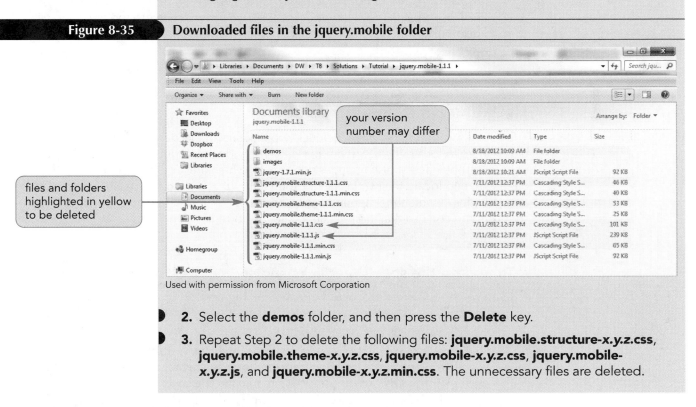

Used with permission from Microsoft Corporation

2. Select the **demos** folder, and then press the **Delete** key.

3. Repeat Step 2 to delete the following files: **jquery.mobile.structure-x.y.z.css**, **jquery.mobile.theme-x.y.z.css**, **jquery.mobile-x.y.z.css**, **jquery.mobile-x.y.z.js**, and **jquery.mobile-x.y.z.min.css**. The unnecessary files are deleted.

Replacing the jquery.mobile Folder

Advanced sites, such as jQuery Mobile sites, routinely require much more hands-on code work and file replacement. This is because the files are constantly being updated by a team of people and must be replaced for the mobile site to remain current. If you do not update the files, you will not be able to use the latest features of the framework.

All of the files you need to proceed are located in the jQuery Mobile folder with your Data Files. Before you begin working on the files, you will create a copy of the folder in the root folder of your NextBest Fest site. You will keep a copy of the folder with the original files in the Dreamweaver8\Tutorial folder as you work on the mobile site for Gage. This way, if the changes you make do not work as expected, you can compare the files you modified within Dreamweaver with original files to help you troubleshoot the problems or you can restart using the original versions of the files.

Next, you will copy the jquery.mobile-*x.y.z* folder into the local root folder for your NextBest Fest site, and then delete the jquery.mobile folder that was created with the jQueryMobile starter page. You will not update links when you are asked because you will be replacing the links shortly.

To replace the jquery.mobile folder in the local root folder:

1. In the Files panel, copy the **jquery.mobile-x.y.z** folder located in the Dreamweaver8\Tutorial folder.

2. Paste a copy of the **jquery.mobile-x.y.z** folder in the local root folder for your NextBest Fest mobile site.

3. In the Files panel, delete the **jquery.mobile** folder located in the root folder of your NextBest Fest Mobile site.

   Trouble? If a dialog box opens indicating that the index.html file has links to the files that you are deleting, click the Yes button to delete the files. You will update the link tags and scripts in the next section.

4. Save the page, if necessary.

Updating Link Tags and Scripts

The jQuery Mobile starter page includes two link tags in the HTML code that tell the page where to locate the CSS style sheets that provide the layout (structure) and style (theme) for the page. It also includes two scripts, which are JavaScript code that tell the page where to locate the two JavaScript source files that it needs. Because you created a new folder in which the mobile site will be stored, you must update the links and the scripts in the code so that the site can locate the current external files.

To update the style sheet links and source files for the JavaScript:

1. Switch to **Code** view, locate the first link tag on Line 6 of the code, and then click in the text within quotation marks after href=. The link to the old jQuery Mobile theme style sheet is displayed in the Property inspector.

2. Click the **Browse** button 🗀, navigate to the **jquery.mobile-x.y.z** folder in your site's local root folder, click **jquery.mobile.theme-x.y.z.min.css**, and then click the **OK** button to update the link in the code.

3. Repeat Steps 1 and 2 for the link tag in Line 7, using **jquery.mobile.structure-x.y.z.min.css** for the file.

4. Right-click anywhere in the red script tag in Line 8, and then click **Edit Tag <script>** on the context menu. The Tag Editor opens. See Figure 8-36.

Figure 8-36   Tag Editor – script dialog box

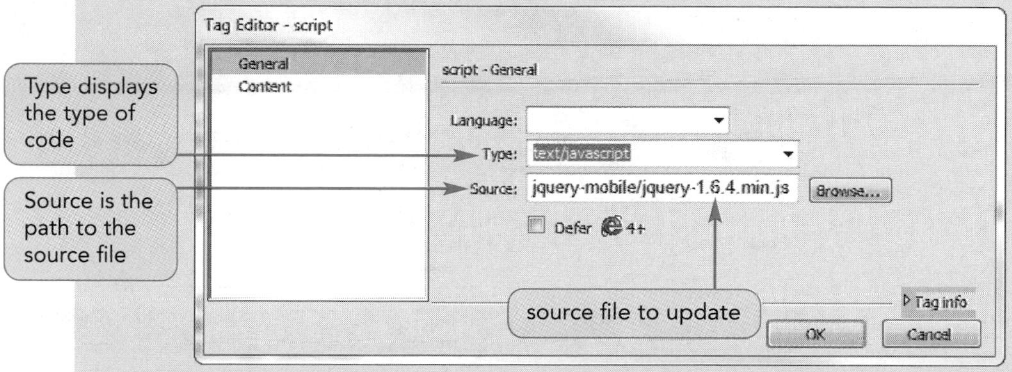

Type displays the type of code

Source is the path to the source file

```
Tag Editor - script

    General          script - General
    Content

                     Language: [                  ▼ ]

                     Type:  [text/javascript          ▼ ]

                     Source: [jquery-mobile/jquery-1.6.4.min.js]  [Browse...]

                     ☐ Defer  🌐 4+

                                              source file to update

                                                              ▷ Tag info
                                              [ OK ]   [ Cancel ]
```

source file to update

5. Click the **Browse** button to open the Select File dialog box, double-click the **jquery-x.y.z.min.js** file located in the jquery.mobile-x.y.z folder in your site's local root folder to update the source file, and then click the **OK** button. The src (or Source) is updated with the path to the new file.

6. Repeat Steps 4 and 5 in Line 9 using **jquery.mobile-x.y.z.min.js** for the file to update the source file for the second JavaScript. The code is updated. See Figure 8-37.

Figure 8-37   Updated code for the jQuery Mobile site

lines of code you updated

```
1   <!DOCTYPE html>
2   <html>
3   <head>
4   <meta charset="utf-8">
5   <title>jQuery Mobile Web App</title>
6   <link href="jquery.mobile-1.1.1/jquery.mobile.theme-1.1.1.min.css" rel="stylesheet"
    type="text/css"/>
7   <link href="jquery.mobile-1.1.1/jquery.mobile.structure-1.1.1.min.css" rel=
    "stylesheet" type="text/css"/>
8   <script src="jquery.mobile-1.1.1/jquery-1.7.1.min.js" type="text/javascript"></script
    >
9   <script src="jquery.mobile-1.1.1/jquery.mobile-1.1.1.min.js" type="text/javascript">
    </script>
10  </head>
```

7. Save the page, return to **Design** view, switch to **Live** view, and then make sure the page is linked to the new files and displays correctly. See Figure 8-38.

Figure 8-38   Updated page in Live view

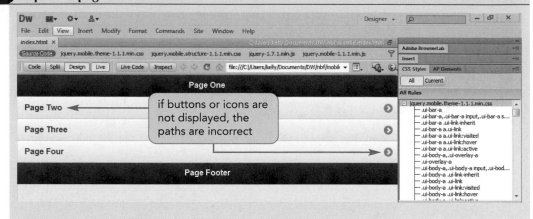

Now that you have the new files in place, you will add content.

INSIGHT

Designing Sites with a Mobile First Approach

As the Web audience that views sites on mobile devices continues to increase, designers are struggling with how they should approach site design. Traditionally, designers created the largest, most elaborate version of the site for view on a computer monitor, and then adjusted the site for tablet and mobile display, eliminating unnecessary content and high-bandwidth items. In 2010, Google announced that mobile first would be its new approach to design. A **mobile first approach** means that designers start by creating the mobile version of the site and then add content and complexity to the site targeted to tablets and desktop computers. Google CEO Eric Schmidt said, "I think it's now the joint project of all of us to make mobile the answer to pretty much everything" (*www.pcmag.com/article2/0,2817,2359752,00.asp*). Since then, many designers have started using a mobile first approach to Web design.

This switch to a mobile first approach has occurred for several reasons. First, the mobile market is growing and will eventually overtake the PC market. Currently, 25 percent of U.S. mobile Web users are mobile-only, meaning they rarely access the Web via desktop computer. Second, creating the mobile site first forces designers to identify and concentrate on the most important content and user interactions, saving the "nice-to-have" enhancements for the tablet and desktop versions of the site, providing users with a better experience. Third, mobile platforms are introducing new capabilities that are leaving PC-based Web browsers in the dust. Creating the mobile site first, instead of as an adapted afterthought, encourages designers to include cutting-edge features such as GPS location or multitouch input from one or more simultaneous gestures in the mobile site, providing mobile users with a better experience.

Adding New Pages to the jQuery Mobile Site

Remember that most jQuery Mobile sites are actually one page that contains page divs with what would be page content in a traditional site. Usually, jQuery Mobile sites include one page div for every page in the site. Each page div contains a header div, a content div, and a footer div, so that the page content can be split into areas that are standard for mobile apps. When the user navigates to a different page in the jQuery Mobile site, the link is a path to the div in the page and clicking the link displays the page div containing the header, content, and footer for that page and hides the other page divs. Because the site is one page, the mobile device downloads the content for the entire site when the user loads the home page, enabling faster, more reliable user interaction with the site. This provides users a better experience with the site because mobile devices have less consistent and stable Internet connectivity. You add new page divs to the site using the Page button in the jQuery Mobile category on the Insert panel.

Using Site Maps

A site map can be helpful for locating information in a complex site that has a variety of components including a mobile site. A site map is also accessible to spiders and crawlers that search engines use to index Web sites.

The NextBest Fest jQuery Mobile site includes a home page, pages that display the latest schedule for each stage, and a page with important festival updates and information. The starter page contains links to three pages, so you need to create two more links and two more pages. You will switch to the Mobile Applications workspace, which provides a better layout for working on mobile sites and mobile applications.

To add new pages to the mobile site:

1. Click the **workspace switcher** button, and then click **Mobile Applications** to change the workspace to the layout that is better for working on mobile sites and apps. Refer to the Session 8.2 Visual Overview.

2. Switch to **Design** view, and then click the **Mobile Size** button 🔲 on the status bar, if necessary.

3. Click the **Page Four** div to select it, and then press the **Right** arrow key until the <div #page4> tag is no longer listed in the status bar.

4. In the jQuery Mobile category on the Insert panel, click the **Page** button. The jQuery Mobile Page dialog box opens.

5. Select the text in the ID box, type **neon_stage**, click the **header** and **footer** check boxes, if necessary, to check them, and then click the **OK** button to add the new div to the page. See Figure 8-39.

Figure 8-39	New div in the Mobile Applications workspace

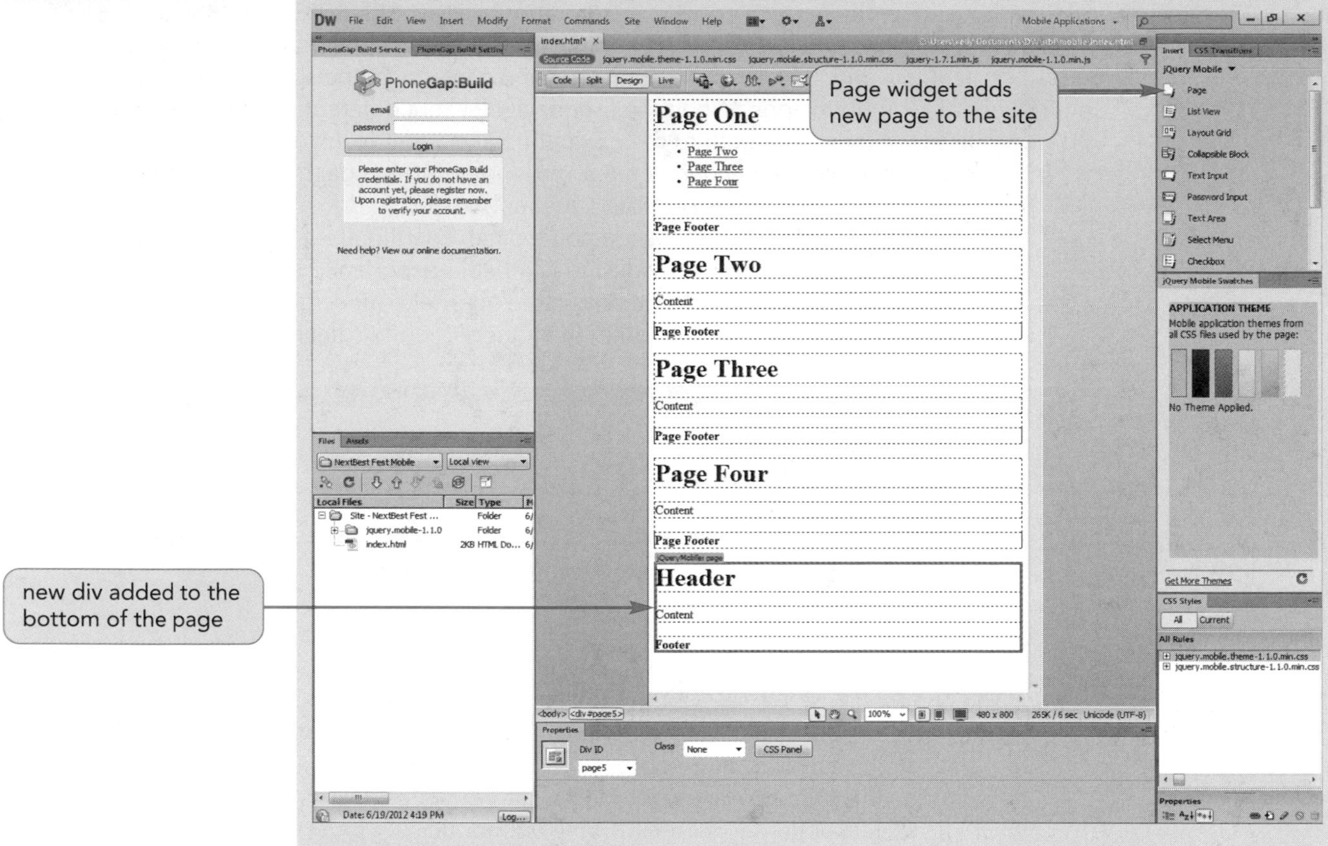

new div added to the bottom of the page

Page widget adds new page to the site

6. Repeat Steps 3 through 5 to create the Page Six div, typing **updates** in the ID box in Step 5.

7. Save the page.

In Design view, the Page One div includes a bulleted list of links to the other pages in the site. These links appear as buttons in Live view or a browser. You will rename the existing items in the bulleted list and links as well as the Div ID to which they link, then you will create list items for the new page, rename the new Div IDs, and create links from the new list items to the new divs. Because the links are all to divs that are actually in the same page, the path to the link is simply #div id name.

To update the links and create new links:

1. In the Page One div, click to the right of the Page Four bullet item, press the **Enter** key to move the pointer to the next line and create a new bullet, and then type **neon stage**. The new bullet item is added.

2. Press the **Enter** key to move the pointer to the next line and create a new bullet, and then type **updates**. The new bullet item is added.

3. In the Page One div, select the **Page Two** link in the first bullet, type **main stage** as the new link text, double-click the Property inspector, if necessary, to show it, select the text in the Link box, and then type **#main_stage**. The link in the bulleted list is linked to the main_stage div, whose ID you will set next.

4. Select the **Page Two** div, and then, in the Property inspector, select the text in the Div ID box and type **main_stage**. The Page Two Div ID is reset, which you can see in the div tab. See Figure 8-40.

Figure 8-40   **Link and Div ID updated**

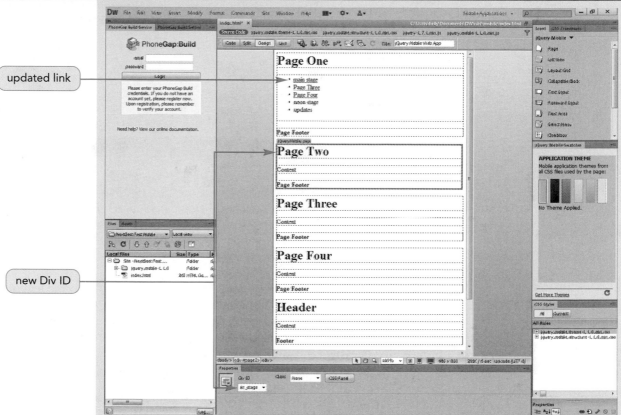

updated link

new Div ID

Trouble? If you have trouble selecting the div in the Document window, you can use the tag to select it. Click in the div in the Document window, and then select the div tag in the status bar.

5. Repeat Steps 3 and 4 to rename the Page Three bulleted list item as **starlight stage**, change the link from #page3 to **#starlight_stage**, and then change the Div ID to **starlight_stage**.

6. Repeat Steps 3 and 4 to rename the Page Four bulleted list item as **satellite stage**, change the link from #page4 to **#satellite_stage**, and then change the Div ID to **satellite_stage**.

7. Repeat Steps 3 and 4 to set the link in the neon stage bulleted list item to **#neon_stage**.

8. Repeat Steps 3 and 4 to set the link in the updates bulleted list item to **#updates**.

9. Save the page, and then turn on **Live** view. The page appears as it will for a user. See Figure 8-41.

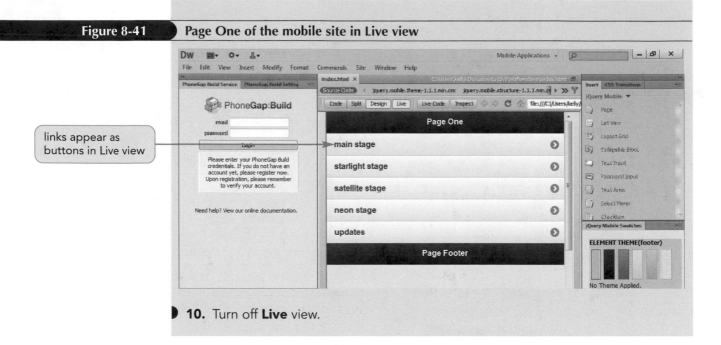

Figure 8-41   **Page One of the mobile site in Live view**

> **10.** Turn off **Live** view.

Adding and Editing Text and Images

You add and edit text and images in jQuery Mobile pages using the same techniques and tools as you do to add and edit them in regular Web pages. The only difference is that the content for each page is added to its corresponding div. As you work on the content, you should frequently examine the page in Live view and preview the page in a browser to see what each page will look like in a browser.

You will add placeholder text for each page in the page divs.

To add text to the pages in the jQuery Mobile site:

> **1.** In the main stage div, in the content div, select the **Content** text, and then type **Main stage schedule and updates coming soon.** (including the period). The content div is updated.

> **2.** Repeat Step 1 for the next three content divs, replacing "Main stage" with **Starlight stage**, **Satellite stage**, and **Neon stage**, respectively.

> **3.** In the updates div, select the text in the content div, and then type **Updates coming soon.** (including the period).

> **4.** In all six divs, delete the text from the header and footer divs. See Figure 8-42.

Figure 8-42   Text added to the jQuery Mobile site

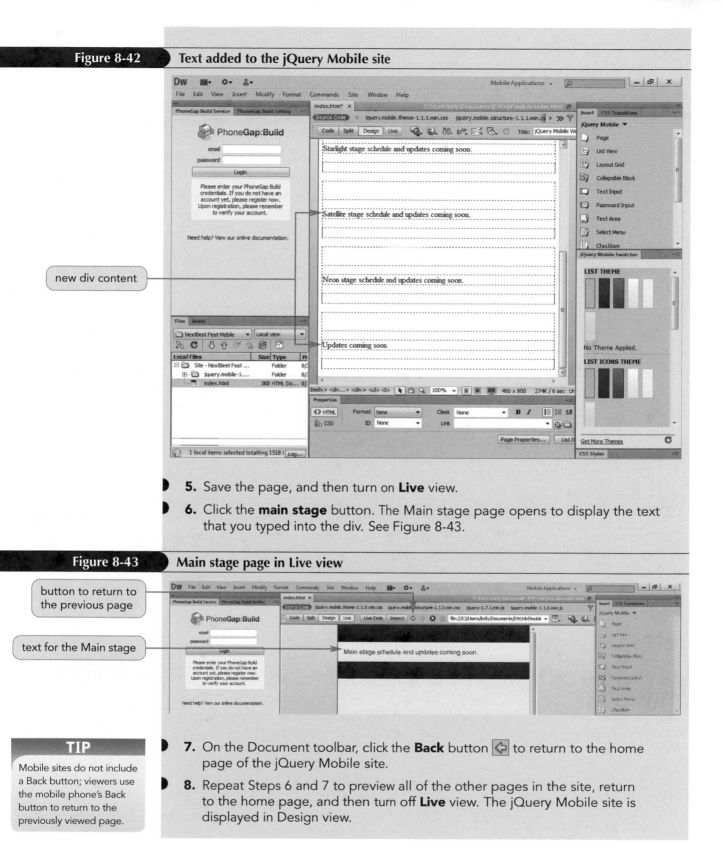

new div content

5. Save the page, and then turn on **Live** view.

6. Click the **main stage** button. The Main stage page opens to display the text that you typed into the div. See Figure 8-43.

Figure 8-43   Main stage page in Live view

button to return to the previous page

text for the Main stage

TIP

Mobile sites do not include a Back button; viewers use the mobile phone's Back button to return to the previously viewed page.

7. On the Document toolbar, click the **Back** button to return to the home page of the jQuery Mobile site.

8. Repeat Steps 6 and 7 to preview all of the other pages in the site, return to the home page, and then turn off **Live** view. The jQuery Mobile site is displayed in Design view.

Next, you will add the NextBest Fest logo to the header area of each page. You will add a CSS style that displays images at max-width 100% to make images scalable as you did in the fluid grid site. This will ensure that the image scales to fit on a variety of mobile devices.

To add images to the pages in the jQuery Mobile site:

1. Switch to **Code** view, click to the left of the closing </head> tag, and then press the **Enter** key to create a blank line.

2. Click in the new blank line, and then type the following code to create a new style that displays images at max-width 100%, which makes the images scalable:

```
<style type="text/css">

img, object, embed, video {

 max-width: 100%;

}

</style>
```

3. Insert the **nb_logo_2.png** image located in the Dreamweaver8\Tutorial folder included with your Data Files into the header div of the page div, placing a copy of the image in the graphics folder you just created. Because you created the new style for images, the image will be inserted without a width or height property.

4. Insert the **nb_logo_2.png** graphic into the header div of the remaining five page divs in the site.

5. Save the page, preview the page in a browser, click the **Restore Down** button ▣ , and then drag the right edge of the browser to the left to resize the window and see the image scaling in the page. See Figure 8-44.

Figure 8-44	Mobile site previewed in Internet Explorer

Image scales to fit into the available space

Used with permission from Microsoft Corporation

6. Use the buttons on the home page to preview the other pages of the site, and then close the browser.

7. Change the page title to **NextBest Fest - Mobile**, and then save the page.

Once you have finished adding content to a site, you can change how it looks.

Adjusting Themes to Style Pages

Dreamweaver includes six themes that you can use to change the look of a jQuery Mobile site. The available themes are listed in the jQuery Mobile Swatches panel. You can apply a theme to the entire site, a page, or an element in a page. When you select an item in the Document window, the themes that you can apply to that item are listed in the jQuery Mobile Swatches panel. If the selected item has an icon such as the buttons in the home page or another element you can apply a theme to, the available icon themes appear at the bottom of the panel. When working with themes, it is helpful to switch to Split view and turn on Live view so that you can view the code and the themed elements at the same time.

You will apply themes to the jQuery Mobile site.

To apply themes to the jQuery Mobile site:

1. Switch to **Split** view, turn on **Live** view, and then, in the Code pane, select the opening div tag for the first div. The first page is selected in the code.

2. In the jQuery Mobile Swatches panel, click the **yellow** swatch. Theme 'e' is applied to the page. See Figure 8-45.

Figure 8-45   **Theme applied to the home page**

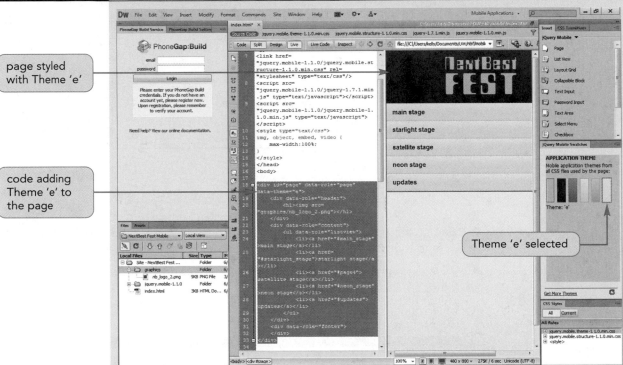

page styled with Theme 'e'

code adding Theme 'e' to the page

Theme 'e' selected

3. In the jQuery Mobile Swatches panel, click the **black** swatch to apply Theme 'a' to the page.

4. In the Code pane, select the unordered list (from the opening <ul> tag to the closing </ul> tag).

5. In the jQuery Mobile Swatches panel, click the **blue** swatch in the LIST THEME section to apply Theme 'b' to the items in the unordered list. The rest of the page remains styled with Theme 'a'. See Figure 8-46.

Figure 8-46	Page with two themes

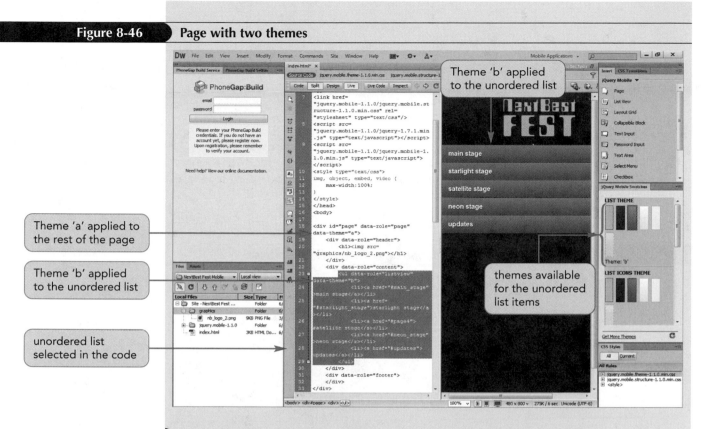

Theme 'a' applied to the rest of the page

Theme 'b' applied to the unordered list

unordered list selected in the code

Theme 'b' applied to the unordered list

themes available for the unordered list items

6. In the jQuery Mobile Swatches panel, click the **No Theme** swatch in the LIST THEME section to remove Theme 'b' from the list.

7. Scroll to the bottom of the jQuery Mobile Swatches panel to view the icons that are available for display. You will leave the default icon in place.

8. Click the **main stage** button, select the code for the main_stage div in Code view, and then apply Theme 'a' to the page.

9. Repeat Step 8 to apply Theme 'a' to the remaining page divs.

10. Save the page, preview the page in a browser, clicking each link to verify that the theme was applied to every page, and then close the browser.

If the built-in themes do not match the site design outlined in the site plan, you can create a custom theme that better fits the look and feel you want for the site. To create a custom theme, you use ThemeRoller, which is a tool available on the jQuery Mobile site. ThemeRoller enables you to create custom themes with a simple graphical user interface. When the custom theme is complete, you download the file and replace the current jquery.mobile.theme-*x.y.z*.min.css file with the custom theme file and update the link tag.

Another member of the NextBest Fest Web design team has created a custom theme for the jQuery Mobile site. You will replace the current file with the new file to update the theme.

To use a custom theme in the jQuery Mobile site:

1. Copy the **nb_theme.min.css** file located in the Dreamweaver8\Tutorial folder included with your Data Files.

▶ **2.** Paste a copy of the file in the jquery.mobile-*x.y.z* folder located in the local root folder for your NextBest Fest Mobile site.

▶ **3.** Delete the **jquery.mobile.theme-x.y.z.min.css** file from the jquery.mobile.*x.y.z* folder.

▶ **4.** Switch to **Code** view, locate the first link tag located around Line 6, and then click in the tag.

▶ **5.** In the Property inspector, click the **Browse** button ◻ next to the Href box, select the **nb_theme.min.css** file located in the jquery.mobile.*x.y.z* folder in your NextBest Fest Mobile site's local root folder, and then click the **OK** button.

▶ **6.** Turn on **Live** view to see the site with the new theme. See Figure 8-47.

| Figure 8-47 | Custom theme applied to the jQuery Mobile site |

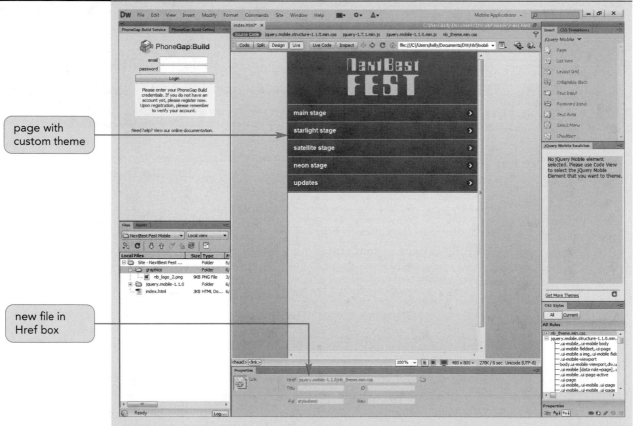

▶ **7.** View each page of the mobile site, and then save the page.

Adding Functionality to a jQuery Mobile Site

The jQuery Mobile framework enables you to quickly add functionality to a site. You can use the jQuery Mobile widgets that are built in to Dreamweaver to do such things as add forms or add collapsible blocks of content, or you can use the jQuery Mobile framework to write code that enables your site to do such things as create columns of content or add thumbnail images to buttons.

Adding Functionality with Widgets

The jQuery Mobile category of the Insert panel includes widgets that you can add to a page to create additional functionality. A **widget** is a reusable prebuilt page element that enables user interaction. You have already used the Page widget to add more page divs to the site. Figure 8-48 describes the other widgets available in Dreamweaver.

| Figure 8-48 | jQuery Mobile widgets |

TIP

You can download additional jQuery Mobile widgets from the Adobe Exchange for Dreamweaver Web site.

Name	Description
Page	Inserts an additional div that acts as a page. By default, the ID is the next page number. Including a header or footer is optional.
List View	Displays navigation or selection controls, data, or results. Options include list type, number of items in the list, space between the list and the outer container, a bold title and descriptive text for each item, and a counter that displays the number of items each list item links to.
Layout Grid	Divides the content into 1 to 5 rows and/or columns with no padding, margins, borders, or color at 100% width.
Collapsible Block	Inserts three collapsible blocks, each of which includes a header with a + icon that opens the content portion of the collapsible block.
Text Input	Inserts a labeled single-line text input that is highlighted when selected.
Password Input	Inserts a labeled single-line text input that is highlighted when selected and uses bullets for each letter typed, keeping the password hidden.
Text Area	Inserts a labeled multiline text input that is highlighted when selected and expands vertically as it is filled with text.
Select Menu	Inserts a form select (drop-down) menu with a label. Item labels and values can be edited and reordered.
Checkbox	Creates a checkbox group with 1 to 10 check boxes in a horizontal or vertical layout.
Radio Button	Creates a radio button group with 2 to 10 radio buttons in a horizontal or vertical layout.
Button	Inserts 1 to 10 buttons. Options include button type, position, layout, and icons to add to the buttons.
Slider	Inserts a button that is draggable within a horizontal track with the value increasing from 0 to 100 as the button reaches the rightmost edge of the track.
Flip Toggle Switch	Inserts a button within a track that changes between off and on.

© 2013 Cengage Learning

Adding Functionality Yourself

In addition to the jQuery Mobile functionality integrated into Dreamweaver, many advanced options, settings, and transitions are built in to jQuery Mobile that are not accessible through Dreamweaver. You can learn about additional options, settings, functionality, and transitions at *jquerymobile.com*. You can also read articles about jQuery Mobile functionality to extend your knowledge. After you know what you want to add to a jQuery Mobile site, you can write the appropriate code yourself or you can copy the code from a sample file, paste it into the page, and then adapt it for your needs. The demo pages on the *jquerymobile.com* site are particularly useful for this.

You will research transitions on the jQuery Mobile site, and then you will add transitions to your NextBest Fest Mobile site.

To research and add new transitions to the NextBest Fest Mobile site:

▶ **1.** Start your Web browser, and then open the **jquerymobile.com** site.

▶ **2.** Click the **Docs** button in the navigation bar, click the **Pages and dialogs** button in the Components section, click the **Page transitions** button, and then read the page to learn about transitions.

▶ **3.** Once you have read the page and have an understanding of what you can do with transitions and how you might add code to the page to create a transition, close the browser.

▶ **4.** In Dreamweaver, switch to **Code** view.

▶ **5.** In the first list item in the code in Line 24, click to the left of the > in the opening <a> tag, press the **Spacebar**, and then type **data-transition="slidefade"**. This code adds a transition so that when a user presses the button, the new page will slide in from the right and fade in. See Figure 8-49.

Figure 8-49   **New transition added to the <a> tag**

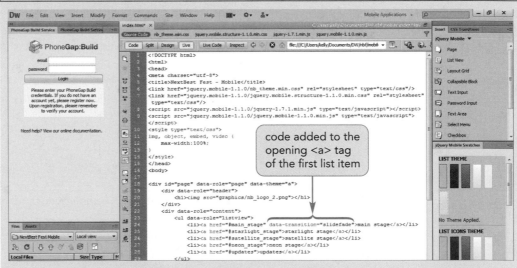

▶ **6.** Save the page, switch to **Design** view and turn on **Live** view, if necessary, and then click the **main stage** button to watch the new transition. The new page slides in from the right and fades in.

▶ **7.** Repeat Steps 4 through 6 for the remaining list items.

In this session, you created a jQuery Mobile site from a starter page, you updated the jQuery files and updated the links to see the new pages, you added pages to the site using a widget, you added themes to the site, and you researched and added new transitions to the site. In the next session, you will add new functionality to the site that requires access to the user's mobile device and you will turn the site into a mobile app using PhoneGap.

REVIEW

Session 8.2 Quick Check

1. What is a jQuery Mobile?
2. Explain what an API is.
3. How does a jQuery Mobile site that is one page provide the illusion of separate pages?
4. What do you use jQuery Mobile widgets for?
5. Why should you create sites using the most recent versions of the jQuery Mobile files?
6. What is a minified file?
7. What is a mobile first approach?
8. What is a widget?

SESSION 8.3 VISUAL OVERVIEW

PhoneGap is an HTML5-based app platform that allows designers to use Web technologies to author native mobile applications that can access native device features and can be placed in the app stores. In other words, PhoneGap is used as the interface between the code that you write and the mobile device.

A **mobile application** (or **app**) is self-contained software that runs on a mobile device without needing any additional software or components.

An app has access to the mobile device's native features and systems through the device's API. This means that you can write something that interacts with the mobile device's camera.

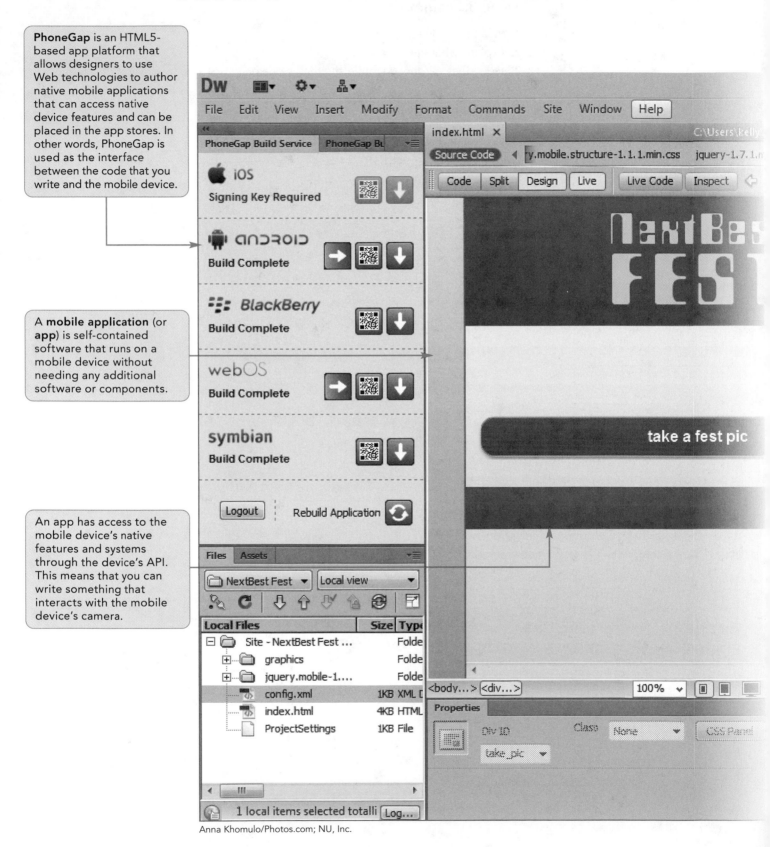

Anna Khomulo/Photos.com; NU, Inc.

MOBILE APPS AND PHONEGAP

The take a fest picture functionality returns a photo with a frame and NextBest Fest logo over the image.

Understanding Mobile Apps

A mobile application (or app) is self-contained software that runs on a mobile device without needing any additional software or components. Apps fall into two categories: native and Web-based. **Native apps** do not use Web technologies; instead they are written in languages such as Java or C++ and use technologies that are part of the mobile device's operating system to display the application. **Web-based apps** are written in traditional Web authoring languages, such as JavaScript, HTML, and CSS, and they use the Web display technology included in the default Web browser that comes with the device's operating system to display the app, but they do not use the browser's graphical user interface.

Although some mobile Web sites look a lot like mobile apps, there are differences between them. One difference is that a Web site, unlike an app, is code that you create to display in a software application—namely, a browser.

Another difference is that an app has access to the mobile device's native features and systems through the device's API. Recall that a device's API is the code, instructions, and specifications that programmers use to access and interact with native features and systems of the device. This means that you can write something that interacts with the mobile device's camera, contact list, or accelerometer. A Web site cannot access the device's features and systems due to security restrictions. As a result, apps are more robust than Web sites, and users have come to expect apps to provide more interactivity and functionality than Web sites.

A third difference is how apps and mobile Web sites appear on a device's screen. It is impossible to ensure that a mobile Web site will always display without any browser chrome, but this is not a problem for apps. Native apps are not displayed in a browser so the user interface can take over the entire screen of the mobile device. Web-based apps use Web technologies including browser technology to run, but they do not use the browser interface. You can think of a Web-based app as running in a chromeless browser that takes over the entire screen of the mobile device and looks just like a native app.

Finally, unlike Web sites, apps must be downloaded, usually from an app store, which means that you must create a version of the app for every type of mobile device that you will support. In addition, you must also get the app placed in the corresponding app stores—Google Play Store, Apple Store, Windows Marketplace for Mobile, and so forth. On the other hand, any user can access a Web site by typing a URL into a browser.

PROSKILLS

Decision Making: Deciding When to Create a Mobile App

Although mobile apps are trendy, not all mobile sites need to be apps. In fact, some should not be apps.

Before deciding to turn a mobile site into an app, be sure to consider the advantages and disadvantages of creating an app. Apps provide access to advanced features of mobile devices through their APIs so you can create advanced functionality and interactions. They provide a standard experience across devices even if the devices have different operating systems and settings. Apps can be perceived as more professional or high end than sites. However, apps are more costly to create and to update. They usually must be hosted at the app store for each mobile operating system and, therefore, may reach a smaller audience. They require installation (users cannot just type a URL into a browser and access the app). Users have higher expectations of and expect advanced functionality from apps, and can become annoyed about installing an app that provides nothing more than a Web site. If the advantages of creating an app outweigh the disadvantages, then you should move forward.

The next step in determining whether a mobile site should be an app is to evaluate the project by answering the following questions:

- Does the project need to interact with the API? If so, what will these interactions cost the client (both in time and money), what value will they provide to the end user, and are the benefits worth the costs?
- What is the goal of the project? Can the goal be better achieved with an app or a mobile site?
- Will the hassle of downloading and installing an app negatively impact the project? Is the target audience likely to spend the time to download the app? If they download the app, will it fulfill their expectations?

The answers to these questions should help you determine whether the project is best suited as a mobile site or an app.

Be sure to include the client in the entire decision-making process to ensure that the choice you make will best suit the client's needs and will provide the outcome that he or she is expecting.

Mobile apps come in all shapes and sizes. Some apps are games, such as *Angry Birds;* others are utilities, such as TeleNav's GPS navigator; and some function more like mini Web sites that provide a few advanced features that a regular Web site would not include. This third type of app is often created by institutions like museums or theme parks to promote their organization by providing the user with fun bonus material. You will create this type of app for NextBest Fest. You will add a new feature to the mobile Web site you created in Session 8.2. The new feature will enable users to take a photo at the fest that is uploaded to a remote server and processed, and then returned to the user in a commemorative frame that has the fest logo over it. Because the new feature requires the site to interact with the camera, which is part of the device's native feature set, you must turn the entire site into an app.

In this case, turning the mobile site into an app is a good idea because it allows NextBest Fest to provide current information and advanced functionality to festival attendees. The new feature will be appealing to the attendees who will post the souvenir photos on Facebook and other social media sites, enhancing the branding and PR efforts of NextBest Fest.

Creating a Basic App

In Dreamweaver, you create mobile apps using HTML, jQuery Mobile, PhoneGap, and JavaScript. The exact process for creating an app changes depending on what functionality the app will include. For example, the process for creating an interactive game is very different from the process for creating a mini Web site with few features that interact directly with the mobile device.

In general, HTML is used to write basic page functionality and CSS is used to style page elements. For example, the jQuery Mobile site includes HTML pages that use div tags to hold page content, and the theme used to style the pages was created using CSS styles. jQuery Mobile is responsible for converting the code into something that works on mobile devices. For example, jQuery Mobile changes links into pressable buttons and intelligently scales the content for display on the mobile device. You use JavaScript to write code that enables your app to do things that HTML cannot do, such as calculate numbers, enable user input to change or move onscreen elements, or change onscreen information without loading a new page. Often, the way that this works is that jQuery Mobile and PhoneGap code is incorporated into custom JavaScript code to create advanced functionality. PhoneGap is an HTML5-based app platform that allows designers to use Web technologies to author native mobile applications that can access native device features and can be placed in the app stores. In simpler English, PhoneGap is used as the interface between the code you write and the mobile device. It works in two ways: One, it packages the code and turns it into an app that runs on a mobile device; and two, it enables the app to interact with the device's native features, such as a camera.

Gage wants to turn the jQuery Mobile site you created into an app that will provide NextBest Fest attendees with a new feature that enables them to take a photograph at the fest (by interfacing with the camera functionality built in to their mobile device) and upload the photo to a Web server, processes and crops the image, places a frame around the image and the NextBest Fest logo over the image, and then returns the processed image to the attendee, creating a unique souvenir photo. Because the new feature will need to access the device's native features (the camera), you will convert the site into an app.

REFERENCE

Creating a Basic App

- Use jQuery Mobile to create the pages of the app, add content to the pages, and style the pages.
- Write an external JavaScript file (or files) to create advanced functionality. (Use the jQuery Mobile and PhoneGap APIs to include code that will enable the advanced interaction to take place.)
- Copy the JavaScript file to the jquery.mobile folder in your site's local root folder.
- Add a script to the head of the jQuery Mobile page that tells where to find the external JavaScript file.
- Add whatever code is needed to the pages of the app to enable users to interact with the advanced features or enable the page to display advanced content.
- Insert a line of code into the head to fix a bug in the current version of PhoneGap.
- Set up or log in to a PhoneGap account, set up a new project, and then create a build that creates the app for a variety of platforms.
- Update the config.xml file with your information and information about the app. This file is used to provide the information that will appear in app listings when the app is installed, checked, or added to an app store.
- Download and test each version of the app you will support.
- Make any needed changes; upload the revised app to PhoneGap; and then rebuild, download, and test each version of the app. Repeat until the app is error free.
- Place the app in app stores.

Inserting the JavaScript File

You already created the jQuery Mobile site that you will turn into an app. Now you will add the JavaScript file to the site and you will examine the JavaScript file to see how it works.

A NextBest Fest programmer created the branded photo functionality in an external JavaScript file. The programmer used the jQuery Mobile and PhoneGap APIs to find the code that he needed to insert into the JavaScript to make the app work on mobile devices and communicate with the device's camera. Writing good JavaScript code takes a lot of practice. A good first step to becoming a proficient coder is to examine existing code.

You will copy the JavaScript file with the code that will enable the branded photo functionality to occur into the jquery.mobile folder, you will insert a script that tells the page where to find the new file, and then you will examine the code.

To copy and open the JavaScript file:

1. If you took a break after the previous session, make sure the NextBest Fest Mobile site is open, the Mobile Applications workspace is reset, and the index.html page is open in Code view.

2. Turn off **Live** view if necessary.

3. Copy the **nu_festImageApp.js** file located in the Dreamweaver8\Tutorial folder into the jquery.mobile-x.y.z folder in your site's local root folder.

4. In the head of the page, click after the last closing JavaScript tag, </script>, press the **Enter** key to create a blank line, and then place the insertion point in the blank line.

5. In the **Common** category of the Insert panel, click **Script**. The Script dialog box opens.

6. Click the **Type arrow**, click **text/javascript**, click the **Browse** button 📁 to the right of the Source box, navigate to the **jquery.mobile-x.y.z** folder, and then double-click **nu_festImageApp.js**.

7. Click the **OK** button in the Script dialog box. The script that tells Dreamweaver to load the file into the page is inserted. See Figure 8-50.

Figure 8-50   New script inserted in the head of the page

```
1   <!DOCTYPE html>
2   <html>
3   <head>
4   <meta charset="utf-8">
5   <title>NextBest Fest - Mobile</title>
6   <link href="jquery.mobile-1.1.1/nb_theme.min.css" rel=
    "stylesheet" type="text/css"/>
7   <link href=
    "jquery.mobile-1.1.1/jquery.mobile.structure-1.1.1.min.css"
    rel="stylesheet" type="text/css"/>
8   <script src="jquery.mobile-1.1.1/jquery-1.7.1.min.js" type=
    "text/javascript"></script>
9   <script src="jquery.mobile-1.1.1/jquery.mobile-1.1.1.min.js"
    type="text/javascript"></script>
10  <script type="text/javascript" src=
    "jquery.mobile-1.1.1/nu_festImageApp.js"></script>
11
```

script tells Dreamweaver to load the JavaScript file into the page

8. On the Related Files toolbar, click the **nu-festImageApp.js** file to view the code of the JavaScript file. See Figure 8-51.

Figure 8-51 Code for nu_festImageApp.js file

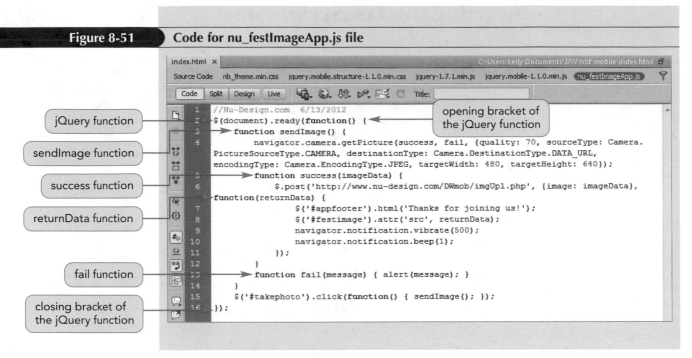

Each line of the code in the JavaScript file has a purpose. As you read the following descriptions, refer back to the code shown in Figure 8-51 or displayed on your screen. Line 1 of the code contains a comment that identifies the programmer and the date the code was created. It is considered good practice to identify the programmer and the date so that anyone who is viewing the code knows who created the code and when it was created. The actual JavaScript code starts on Line 2.

JavaScript code can have pieces of code that wrap around other pieces of code, just like an HTML div tag surrounds the other tags and content that are contained in the div. In this case, the first piece of code lets the device know that this file will be using the jQuery framework. The jQuery syntax is specifically made for selecting HTML elements and performing an action on the elements. Basic jQuery syntax is

`$(selector).action()`

The $ indicates that what follows uses the jQuery framework. The *selector* tells the code what HTML element to find or use. The *action* defines what jQuery action will be performed on the HTML element identified as the selector.

Look at Line 2 of the code: `$(document).ready(function() {`
The first character is $, which indicates that what follows uses the jQuery framework. The programmer knew to use this symbol from the API documentation on the jQuery Mobile Web site. The selector *(document)* is the HTML document—the index.html page. The jQuery action *.ready(function()* says wait until the document has finished loading and is ready to begin performing the code inside the opening and closing brackets, { }. The opening bracket is at the end of Line 2. The closing bracket is the first bracket on Line 16, which means that this code wraps around all of the other code.

The code on Lines 3 through 15 is indented so you can quickly see that the code from Line 2 wraps around all of the other code. Each indented line (or lines) of code is a visual indication that the previous line of code wraps around the indented code. The indented line of code extends to the left margin only when the code is too long to fit on one line and it wraps to the next line, as in Lines 4 and 6. In these instances, only the first line of wrapped code is indented because the line will break in different places depending on the size of the user's screen. Notice that the unindented lines of wrapped code are not numbered to help you track specific lines of code. These visual cues help you interpret complex code.

A lot of programming is actually mathematical equations that are wrapped in syntax that is defined by the language and framework in which you are coding. For example, the word *function* in Line 2 indicates that this code is a mathematical function. The word *function* appears frequently in code because mathematical functions are used repeatedly. A **function** is a relationship between a set of inputs and a set of potential outputs where each input has exactly one output. Programmers use functions to do a variety of things, such as drawing graphics on a screen, getting information from a server, or doing numeric calculations.

Line 3 of the code, `function sendImage() {`, begins the sendImage function, which is contained in the jQuery function. The closing tag for the sendImage function is at the beginning of Line 16. All of the code between the sendImage function opening and closing brackets is indented to indicate that it is contained in the sendImage function.

Line 4 of the code came from the PhoneGap API documentation:

```
navigator.camera.getPicture(success, fail, {quality: 70,
sourceType: Camera.PictureSourceType.CAMERA, destinationType:
Camera.DestinationType.DATA_URL, encodingType:
Camera.EncodingType.JPEG, targetWidth: 480, targetHeight: 640 });
```

The code *navigator.camera.getPicture* tells the app to retrieve a picture using the attributes defined in the parentheses. The sourceType attribute has the value *Camera.PictureSourceType.CAMERA* that tells the app to get the picture from the camera, which means use the device's camera to take a picture rather than retrieve a picture from a file. The *DestinationType* attribute has the value *Camera.DestinationType.DATA_URL*, which tells the app that the data (ImageData) that is the output of this function will be sent to a URL that you will specify later. Notice that the ImageData, a picture, will be a JPEG file with a width of 480, a height of 640, and a quality of 70. Finally *success, fail* at the beginning of the opening parentheses tells the JavaScript to run the success function that starts on Line 5 if it gets the picture from the phone, or to run the fail function on Line 13 if it fails to get the picture from the phone.

Line 5 of the code, `function success(imageData) {`, creates a function named *success*, and *(ImageData)* says to get the image data that the last function produced and use it in this function.

Line 6 of the code, `$.post('http://www.nu-design.com/DWmob/imgUpl.php', {image: imageData}, function(returnData) {`, indicates what to do with the image. The *$* specifies that the jQuery framework is being used. *Post* says to upload the image data to the URL contained in the (). The Web server will then take over, processing the image using server-side code and outputting the processed image back to the phone as *returnData* (the photo that the user took with a frame and the NextBest Fest logo on it). Once returnData is returned to the phone, the function(returnData) function will run using the returnData.

Line 7 of the code, `$('#appfooter').html('Thanks for joining us!');`, changes the text displayed in the footer div. The *$* specifies that the jQuery framework is being used. The *('#appfooter')* code looks for something with an appfooter ID in the HTML of the index.html page. You will enter appfooter as the ID for the footer div in the page so that this will find the correct footer div. The *.html('Thanks for joining us!')* code changes the content of the div with the appfooter ID to display the specified text: *Thanks for joining us!*

Line 8 of the code, `$('#festimage').attr('src', returnData);`, displays the commemorative photo in the page. The *$* specifies that the jQuery framework is being used. The *('#festimage')* code finds something with an ID of festimage. You will place an image tag with an ID of festimage in the page. The *.attr('src', returnData)* code puts the returnData in the thing with the festimage ID, so that the modified image will be displayed in the page.

Line 9 of the code, `navigator.notification.vibrate(500);`, came from the PhoneGap API documentation. It tells the device to vibrate for .5 seconds when the image data is returned to the phone.

Line 10 of the code, `navigator.notification.beep(1);`, also came from the PhoneGap API documentation. It tells the device to beep once when the image data is returned to the phone.

Line 13 of the code, `function fail(message) { alert(message); },` is the function that runs if the device failed to take a picture. The fail function displays an alert with the error message that the device returns if it fails to take a picture.

Finally, although this code is at the bottom of the page, Line 15 of the code, `$('#takephoto').click(function() { sendImage(); });`, is the code that gets things started because it tells the app what to do when the user clicks the button in the app. The *$* specifies that the jQuery framework is being used. The *('#takephoto')* code finds something with an ID of takephoto. You will place a button in the page with an ID of takephoto. The *.click(function() { sendImage(); }* code runs the sendImage function in Line 3 when the object with the takephoto ID is clicked. It does not matter that this code is close to the bottom of the page. JavaScript code is not always linear. In this case, all of the code is triggered by a user interaction, a button press, and this function defines what happens when the user presses that button. All of the other code between Line 3 and Line 14 is in the sendImage function, so none of that code will run until the user clicks the button.

Modifying the jQuery Mobile Site

Now that you have a basic understanding of what the new feature of the app will do, you will adjust the code for the existing jQuery Mobile site. You will change the updates page to the take a pic page, where the new app will run. The updates will now be displayed in the home page. In the home page, you will change the updates link to take a pic, so it matches the content of the modified page. Then you will add the update text below the unordered list of links being used for navigation.

To adjust the home page:

▶ **1.** Switch to **Design** view, and then, in the Document window, select the **updates** link, type **take a pic**, and then select the text you just typed.

▶ **2.** In the Property inspector, select the text in the Link box, and then type **#take_pic**.

▶ **3.** In the Document window, click after the take a pic text, and then press the **Right** arrow key until the <ul>, <li>, and <a> tags are no longer displayed in the status bar.

▶ **4.** Press the **Enter** key, and then type **Important updates will be displayed here during the fest.** (including the period). See Figure 8-52.

| Figure 8-52 | Updated home page |

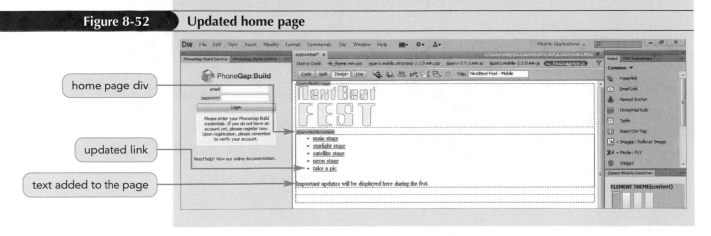

The next modifications you will make to the site are in the updates page. You will change the ID of the updates div to take_pic so that the navigation can locate it. Then, you will insert an empty image tag, which has "" for the source, with an ID of festimage in the page. When the image data is returned to the device, the app will locate the festimage ID and display the updated image in the page. Next, you will insert a button below the image tag in the content area of the page that has an ID of takephoto and is styled using CSS. The user will click the button to start the app functionality. Finally, you will select the footer div and give it an ID of app_footer. When the updated image is displayed in the page, "Thanks for joining us!" will appear in the footer div.

To modify the updates page:

1. Click in the **updates** div, and then click the **updates** div tag in the status bar to select the div.

2. In the Property inspector, type **take_pic** in the Div ID box, and then press the **Enter** key to give the div a new ID.

3. In the Document window, delete the **Updates coming soon.** text from the div.

4. Switch to **Code** view, and then click the **Source Code** button on the Related Files toolbar. The pointer is in the content div located within the take_pic div.

5. Type **<img src="" id="festimage">** to insert an empty image tag in the page. When the image data is returned from the server, it will look for the empty image tag with the festimage ID and will use it to display the returned image.

6. Switch to **Design** view, and then press the **Enter** key to create a new line for the button.

   Trouble? If a gray square or broken link image appears in Design view, don't worry. It will not display when you view the page in Live view or in the final app.

7. In the **jQuery Mobile** category of the Insert panel, click **Button** to open the jQuery Mobile Button dialog box.

8. Select **1** from the Buttons list, select **Button** from the Button Type list, select **None** from the Icon list, and then click the **OK** button to insert the button into the page.

9. In the Document window, replace the Button text with **take a fest pic**, select the **button** tag in the status bar, type **takephoto** in the ID box in the Property inspector, and then press the **Enter** key. The button label and ID are updated. When the user clicks the button, the app will start the process described when you examined the JavaScript.

10. In the Document window, click in the **footer** div located inside of the take_pic div, type **app_footer** in the Div ID box in the Property inspector, and then press the **Enter** key. The footer div ID is updated to match the ID referenced in the JavaScript code.

11. Save the page, turn on **Live** view, switch to **Mobile Size** view and click the **take a pic** button to display the page as it will look on a mobile phone, and then click the **take a fest pic** button. See Figure 8-53.

Figure 8-53	Updated take a pic page

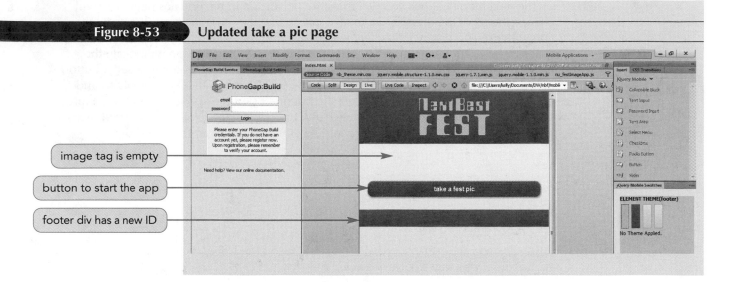

image tag is empty

button to start the app

footer div has a new ID

Fixing a PhoneGap Bug

The current version of PhoneGap does not add a line of code to the head of the page that must be included for the app to function correctly. You will add the new script to the page.

Note that this bug might be fixed in future versions of PhoneGap. If the app does not work when you test it, open the source code for the page to see if the line of code was inserted twice. If this happens, delete one of the duplicate lines of code, and then rebuild the app. The app should work correctly.

To add a script to the head of the page:

1. Switch to **Code** view.

2. In Line 10, click before the `<script type="text/javascript" src="jquery.mobile-1.1.0/nu_festImageApp.js"></script>` code, and then press the **Enter** key to create a new blank line.

3. In the blank line, type the following script: `<script src="phonegap.js" type="text/javascript"></script>`. This code fixes the current PhoneGap bug. See Figure 8-54.

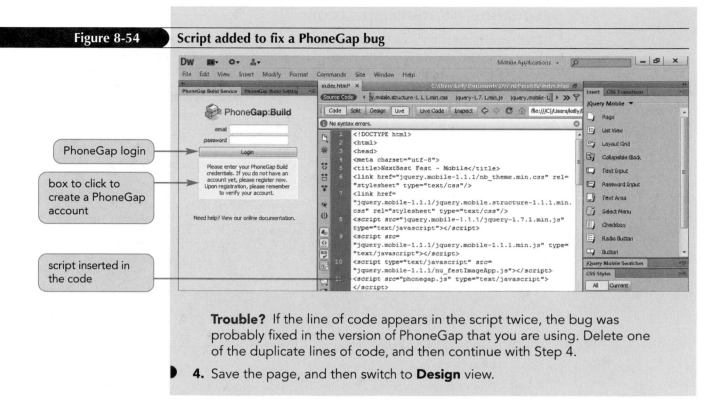

Figure 8-54   Script added to fix a PhoneGap bug

Trouble? If the line of code appears in the script twice, the bug was probably fixed in the version of PhoneGap that you are using. Delete one of the duplicate lines of code, and then continue with Step 4.

4. Save the page, and then switch to **Design** view.

Building an App in PhoneGap

The next phase of app development is to create a PhoneGap build. In other words, you will use PhoneGap to create (or build) a version of the app for every platform that you will support. Creating a build is a multiphase process that includes the following:

- Create a PhoneGap account, if necessary, and then log in to PhoneGap from the PhoneGap panel in Dreamweaver.
- Create a new project or select an existing project.
- Modify one of the files that PhoneGap creates.
- Click Build the Application, which uploads the source files and provides you with completed apps.

Although Adobe owns PhoneGap and Dreamweaver includes a PhoneGap panel, PhoneGap is not part of Dreamweaver. To complete the steps in this section, you must have Internet access and you must be able to create a PhoneGap account. If you do not have Internet access or you cannot create a PhoneGap account, you will not be able to build the application. If that is the case, then read the rest of the tutorial, but do not perform any of the steps.

TIP

When this tutorial was written, PhoneGap was still in beta, which means that Adobe is still testing the program's functionality and fixing bugs.

INSIGHT

Commercial Use of PhoneGap

According to the PhoneGap Web site, at some point there will be a charge to use PhoneGap on commercial projects. This means that you will, most likely, not be able to update commercial apps that you build using PhoneGap without paying to use the platform. You can find more information at *https://build.phonegap.com/docs/faq*.

Creating a PhoneGap Account

Before you can use PhoneGap, you must have a PhoneGap account. If you do not have a PhoneGap account, you must create one in order to use PhoneGap. You need an Adobe ID to create a PhoneGap account. If you already have a PhoneGap account, continue with the next set of steps.

To create a PhoneGap account:

▶ **1.** In the PhoneGap panel, click in the yellow note area below the Login button. The PhoneGap site opens, and the Register page appears in a browser window.

▶ **2.** Click the **with Adobe ID** button to open the Sign in page, and then enter the email address and password you used to create your Adobe ID account.

   Trouble? If you do not have an Adobe ID account, you must create one before you can complete these steps. Click Complete/Update Adobe ID Profile from the Help menu, complete the steps to create an Adobe ID, and then repeat Step 2.

▶ **3.** Click the **Sign In** button. PhoneGap uses your Adobe ID to create a PhoneGap account, and then displays the Welcome to PhoneGap Build page. You do not need to enter additional information because you are using Dreamweaver to create the app.

▶ **4.** Close the browser. You will log in to PhoneGap through the PhoneGap panel in Dreamweaver.

▶ **5.** In the PhoneGap panel in Dreamweaver, type the Adobe ID and password you used to create your PhoneGap account in the email and password boxes, respectively, and then click the **Login** button. You are logged in to PhoneGap through Dreamweaver. See Figure 8-55.

Figure 8-55   **PhoneGap panel after logging in**

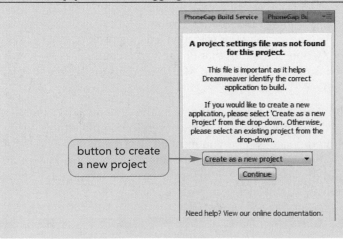

Creating a PhoneGap Project

If you were creating an app through the PhoneGap Web site, you would need to provide information about your site and your files. Because PhoneGap integrates with Dreamweaver, the process is much simpler. You simply create a new project and Dreamweaver provides all of the necessary information. PhoneGap can then build a version of the app for every mobile platform you specify, including the following:

- **iOS.** The Apple platform for mobile devices. You must provide a signing key from Apple before the iOS build can be generated. To obtain a signing key, you must sign up and pay a fee to become an Apple developer, then you must request a key, and finally, you add it to the project.
- **Android.** The Google platform for mobile devices used by many different manufacturers of mobile devices.
- **BlackBerry.** The Research In Motion (RIM) platform used on BlackBerry devices.
- **webOS.** The Palm platform used on most Palm devices.
- **Symbian.** The Nokia platform used on many Nokia mobile devices.

You will create a new PhoneGap project for the take a picture app.

To create a new PhoneGap project:

1. Make sure **Create as a new project** appears in the projects list button. If you have existing PhoneGap projects, they will also appear in the projects list.

2. Click the **Continue** button. PhoneGap creates a new project and builds an app for each device operating system that is supported. See Figure 8-56.

Figure 8-56 New project created

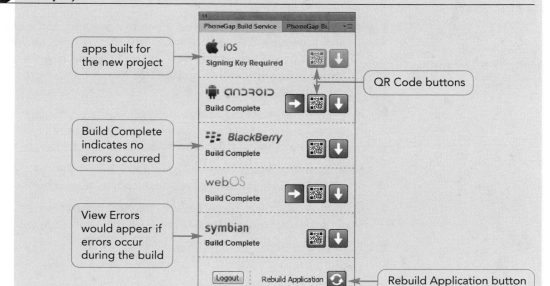

When you build a project, Dreamweaver inserts two files into the local root directory: ProjectSettings and config.xml. The ProjectSettings file enables Dreamweaver and PhoneGap to understand the parameters of the project. The config.xml file provides information about the app that will appear in app listings when the app is installed, checked, or added to an app store.

You will open the config.xml file and add information, and then you will rebuild the project.

To update the config.xml file:

▶ **1.** In the Files panel, double-click the **config.xml** file to open the file. See Figure 8-57.

Figure 8-57 The config.xml page

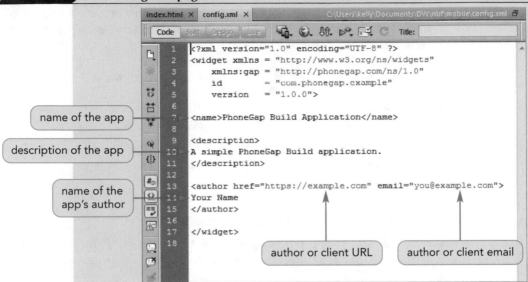

name of the app

description of the app

name of the app's author

author or client URL

author or client email

▶ **2.** In Line 7, select **PhoneGap Build Application**, and then type **NextBest Fest App. version 1** to enter the name and current version number of the app you are creating.

▶ **3.** In Line 10, select the text between the opening and closing description tags, and then type **This app will provide fest attendees with updates and current stage schedules during the fest and it will enable them to take funky commemorative pictures of the event.** as a description of the app you are creating.

▶ **4.** In Line 13, locate the href parameters of the author tag, select the text between the opening and closing quotes, and then type **http://nextbestfest.com** as the name of the app's author.

▶ **5.** In Line 13, locate the email parameter, select the text between the quotes, and then type **info@nextbestfest.com** as the author's email.

▶ **6.** In Line 14, select **Your Name** between the opening and closing author tags, and then type **NextBest Fest** as the name of the app's author.

▶ **7.** Save the page, and then close it.

Testing Builds of an App

You should test and download the builds for all of the devices that you plan to support. Testing is the final phase in the process of creating an app. Testing is considered a phase because it includes several steps. First, you download the app. Second, you test the functionality of the app. Third, you fix any bugs and problems you encounter. Finally, you create a new build and repeat Steps 1 through 3 to retest the app. Whenever you make a change to the app, you must retest the app on all of the platforms you will support. You will probably complete these steps many times before the project is finalized and ready for distribution.

The three main methods for testing the functionality of an app before it is placed in an app store for download are QR Code, software development kits, and download to computer.

You can use the QR Code button 🈁 to display a QR Code that any QR Code reader can read. When your mobile device reads the QR Code, it will install the app on your mobile device and you can then test it. This method requires that you have a QR Code app installed on your phone. You can download free QR Code apps from all the different app stores. A good, free app that is available on most stores is QuickMark (*http://quickmark.cn/En/basic/index.asp*). You must also have a device from each supported platform on which to test the app. You will use this method to test the app you created in this session on an Android device. On Android devices, you must change the settings to allow installation of non-Market applications, which is not the default setting for devices.

Some platforms provide software development kits (SDKs) that you can download and install on your computer. SDKs provide an emulator that enables you to test the functionality of the app on something that resembles and emulates the functionality of a mobile device on your computer. You can use the Android and webOS SDKs on a PC. On a Mac, you can use the Android, webOS, or iOS SDKs. After you download an SDK, you specify where it is located on the PhoneGap Build Settings tab in the PhoneGap panel. Then you can use the SDK to test a build by clicking the Emulate Build button ➡ next to that build. Although SDKs are great for testing apps, they are somewhat limited in functionality. For example, you cannot test camera functionality using an SDK, so downloading SDKs would not be helpful for testing this app. Because this method will not work for testing the picture app you created in this session, you will not use this method.

The final method for testing is to download the app to your computer, and then use your computer to transfer it to a mobile device. You can do this in a variety of ways depending on how your computer and mobile device are set up. Some mobile devices have Bluetooth connections to the computer, and most mobile devices will connect to a computer with a cord. Because so many variations for connection and installation exist, you will not use this method.

You will test the app using the QR Code method. If you have an Android device, complete the next set of steps. If you do not have an Android device, you can test the app on your own with a mobile device that uses a supported platform other than the iOS platform, which requires a developer account and sign-in key, as mentioned earlier. If you do not have a device on which to test the app, read but do not perform these steps.

To test the app with an Android device using the QR Code method:

▶ 1. In the PhoneGap panel, click the **QR Code** button 🈁 for the Android build to display a larger QR Code. See Figure 8-58.

Figure 8-58   **Large QR Code for the Android build**

2. On your Android mobile device, press the **Unknown sources** check box on the Applications tab of the Settings menu to check it. This enables download of apps from places other than the Play Store.

3. Open a QR Code app, and then use it to scan or take a picture of the QR Code and download the app to your phone. Depending on your QR Code app, you might need to click the URL that is displayed to begin app download.

   Trouble? If you do not have a QR Code app on your phone, you can download one from the Play Store and then repeat Step 3. You can locate a QR Code app by typing QuickMark or QR into the search box at the top of the screen.

   The exact process for installing the app may differ slightly for various devices, but follow this general process.

4. After the app is completely downloaded, locate the app (you will usually receive a notification in the status bar at the top of the screen of your mobile device) and press it, press the **Install** button, and then, once the installation is complete, press **Open** to view the app on your phone. See Figure 8-59.

Figure 8-59   **NextBest Fest mobile app in a mobile device**

link to the take a pic feature

Anna Khomulo/Photos.com

5. Press the **take a pic** button, and then press the **take a fest pic** button. The app opens your device's camera so you can take a picture.

6. Take a picture, and then press the **Done** button. The image is sent to the server, processed, and then returned to you. Your device will vibrate and beep once, indicating the updated image was returned.

7. If necessary, swipe your device to make the screen active. The take a pic page is displayed on the screen and the new, processed image is displayed in the page. See Figure 8-60.

| Figure 8-60 | Take a pic page displayed on an Android mobile device |

processed image is returned with a frame and NextBest Fest logo

Anna Khomulo/Photos.com; NU, Inc.

8. Use the **Back** button on your device to return to the home page, and then view the other pages in the site.

At this point, you would test the app on the other platforms that you will support. If you found errors, you would correct them, rebuild the app, and then begin the testing process again. Once the app worked as expected, you would show it to the client and obtain sign-off before submitting the app to the app stores for all the platforms that you will support.

Submitting an App to an App Store

Each platform has its own app store where users can download the latest apps. Generally, the steps for submitting an app to the different stores are somewhat similar. First, go to the store Web site, locate the developer section, and create a developer account for that store/platform. Usually this process also requires you to sign some sort of developer agreement where you agree to the rules and terms of the store. You may have to pay a fee as part of this process. Next, you submit the app for approval and inclusion in the store. This usually involves filling out an online form that provides the name of the app and information about the app as well as uploading a copy of the app. Finally, you are notified of acceptance or exclusion. If accepted, you are provided with back-end tools that enable you to monitor downloads, answer user support questions, view user reviews, and so forth.

Most stores will not accept multiple versions of the same app. Therefore, you will not submit this app to a store as part of the tutorial. However, the authors have followed the process outlined previously to submit the app in the Android Play Store. If you have an Android device, complete the following steps to download the app from the store. If not, then read but do not perform the following steps.

To download the app from the Android Play Store:

▶ **1.** On your Android mobile device, open the **Play Store**.

▶ **2.** Type **nextbest fest** into the search box at the top of the screen.

▶ **3.** Select the **nextbest fest** app, press the **Install** button, and then press **Accept & download** to download the app to your device.

▶ **4.** After the app has downloaded, press **Open** to start the app.

▶ **5.** Press the **take a pic** button to display the take a pic page.

▶ **6.** Press the **take a fest pic** button on the page. The device will open the camera.

▶ **7.** Frame your shot and press the button that your device uses to take a picture, and then press **Done** to return to the app. The photo will be sent to the remote server for processing automatically, and the device will shake and buzz when the adjusted image is returned.

▶ **8.** Make the phone active, if necessary. The image will be displayed in the take a pic page with the frame and logo over it.

After reviewing the fluid grid site, the mobile site, and the mobile app you created, Gage has decided to move forward with the mobile app. The mobile app enables fest attendees to take branded souvenir photos that will enhance their experience as well as works with the festival's other marketing efforts to increase brand recognition. The app is also a good choice because it targets a very specific set of users—festival attendees—and it provides them with useful benefits: up-to-date information about stage schedules, pertinent NextBest Fest information, and a branded souvenir photo.

In this session, you learned to create a mobile app using HTML/CSS, JavaScript, jQuery Mobile, and PhoneGap. In the next tutorial, you will add database functionality in the NextBest Fest site.

Session 8.3 Quick Check

REVIEW

1. What is a mobile app?
2. What is PhoneGap?
3. In the basic jQuery syntax `$(selector).action()`, what does the $ indicate?
4. For which mobile platforms can PhoneGap build a version of an app?
5. What is the config.xml file that Dreamweaver inserts into the local root directory when you build a PhoneGap project used for?
6. What are the general steps for testing the builds of an app?
7. True or False. Most app stores will accept multiple versions of the same app.

Practice the skills you learned in the tutorial.

PRACTICE

Review Assignments

Data Files needed for the Review Assignments: anti_logo.jpg, nu_AntifestImageApp.js

Dan wants you to create an app that will be targeted at festival attendees, providing them with the latest information about stage schedules, breaking news, and the ability to take a branded photo at the fest. You will create the pages of the app using a jQuery Mobile starter page, you will add the advanced functionality, and then you will build the app using PhoneGap.

1. Open the **antifest** site you modified in Tutorial 7, reset the workspace to Mobile Applications, and then expand the Files panel to show local and remote sites.

2. Connect to the remote server, create a mobile folder in the root folder for your site on the remote server, and then collapse the Files panel to show only remote or local site.

3. Open the Manage Sites dialog box, select and duplicate the antifest site, and then edit the antifest copy site, renaming the site **antifest mobile** and setting the local root folder to be a new folder named **mobile** that is in the anti folder.

4. Set the default images folder to be a new folder named **graphics** that is in the mobile folder you just created.

5. Select your server in the Servers tab, edit the settings by typing **mobile** at the end of the file path in the Root Directory box, click the **Test** button to confirm that the connection to the new remote folder works, and then click the Save button in the dialog boxes and click the Done button in the Manage Sites dialog box.

6. Create a new jQuery Mobile site using the jQuery Mobile with theme (Local) sample page in the Mobile Starters Sample Folder in the Page from Sample tab of the New Document dialog box, and then save the page as **index.html** and copy the dependent files.

7. Download the latest version of the jQuery Mobile files from the jQuery Mobile Web site, write down the version numbers of the Requires jQuery core files that you will need, and then go to the jQuery Web site and download the latest version that will work with your jQuery Mobile files, placing a copy in the new jquery.mobile-x.y.z folder.

8. Delete the demo folder and the jquery.mobile.structure-x.y.z.css, jquery.mobile.theme-x.y.z.css, jquery.mobile-x.y.z.css, jquery.mobile-x.y.z.js, and jquery.mobile-x.y.z.min.css files.

9. Place a copy of the new jquery.mobile-x.y.z folder in the local root folder of your mobile site, delete the existing jquery mobile folder, and then update the links and scripts in the head of your index.html page with the new file information.

10. Select each of the following divs in the status bar, and then click Theme 'a' in the jQuery Mobile Swatches panel to apply the theme to the site: page, page2, page3, page4, take_pic.

11. Click after the page4 div, add a new page div, type **take_pic** in the ID box, check the Header and Footer check boxes, and then click the OK button to create the page div.

12. Switch to Code view, click the Source Code button on the Related files toolbar, add a blank line above the closing </head> tag, and then type the following code to create a new style that displays images at max-width 100%, which makes the images scalable:

```
<style type="text/css">
img, object, embed, video {
    max-width: 100%;
}
</style>
```

13. In the page div, delete the text from the heading div, and then insert the **anti_logo.jpg** file located in the Dreamweaver8\Review folder with no alt text. Repeat for the following divs: page2, page3, page4, and take pic.

14. Delete the placeholder text from the footer divs in the following page divs: page, page2, page3, page4, and take_pic.

15. Use the jQuery Mobile Swatches panel to add themes to pages or page elements, or create your own custom theme using ThemeRoller on the jQuery Mobile site.

16. In the page div, select the Page Two text from the unordered list, and then type **Stage Two**. The text is still linked to #page2 because you did not rename the div. Repeat to change Page Three to **Stage Three** and Page Four to **Stage Four**.

17. Place the pointer after the last item in the list, press the Enter key to add another item to the unordered list, type **Take a Pic**, select the text, and then type **#take_pic** in the Link box in the Property inspector to create a link to the take a pic page.

18. In the page2 div, select the Content placeholder text, and then type **Info coming soon.** (including the period). Repeat in the page3 and page4 divs.

19. In the take_pic div, delete the Content text from the div, switch to Code view, click the Source Code button on the Related Files toolbar, make sure the pointer is in the content div located within the take_pic div, and then type **<img src="" id="festimage">** to insert an empty image tag in the page.

20. Switch to Design view, and then press the Enter key to create a new line. In the jQuery Mobile category of the Insert panel, click the Button button, select 1 from the Button list, select Button from the Button Type list, select None from the Icon list, and then click the OK button to insert the button into the page.

21. Select the button text in the Document window, type **Take a Fest Pic**, select the button tag in the status bar, type **takephoto** in the ID box in the Property inspector, and then press the Enter key to update the label and ID.

22. In the Document window, click in the footer div located in the take_pic div, type **app_footer** in the Div ID box in the Property inspector, press the Enter key to update it to match the ID referenced in the JavaScript code you will add, and then save the page.

23. Copy the **nu_AntifestImageApp.js** file located in the Dreamweaver8\Review folder to the jquery.mobile-*x.y.z* folder in the local root folder of your mobile site. In Code view, in the head of the page, click after the last closing JavaScript tag, </script>, press the Enter key to create a blank line, and then place the insertion point in the blank line.

24. In the Common category of the Insert panel, click Script. Select text/javascript as the type, set the source to the nu_AntifestImageApp.js file located in the jquery.mobile-*x.y.z* folder, and then click the OK button in the Script dialog box. The script tells Dreamweaver to load the file into the page.

25. Scroll below the scripts in the head of the page, create a blank line, and then type the following script to fix the current PhoneGap bug in the blank line: **<script src="phonegap.js" type="text/javascript"></script>**.

26. Save the page, upload the entire mobile site to the remote server, view the site in a browser, press each button to ensure that the functionality works, and then close the browser. (*Hint*: You cannot test the take a pic functionality over the Internet.)

27. In the PhoneGap Build Service panel, if you are not logged in, enter your email and password, and then click the Login button.

28. Select Create as a new project from the Project settings list, and then click Continue to create a new PhoneGap project.

29. If you have an Android device, when the Android build is complete, click the View QR Code button, use the QR Code reading app you used in the tutorial to download the antifest mobile site to your Android device, and then test the site.

30. Submit the finished files to your instructor. (*Hint*: The config.xml file will not be updated until the app is ready to be uploaded to the app store.)

Create a responsive site to replace the existing site.

APPLY

Case Problem 1

Data File needed for this Case Problem: m_fluidlook.css

Moebius Skateboards   Corey is considering replacing the Moebius Skateboards site with a responsive site. He wants you to create the home page of the responsive site so that he can test it and get feedback from some clients. You will use the Fluid Grid Layout to make a responsive site that you will store in a fluid folder that you create in the main site. Corey will maintain the current site while you work on the new site.

1. Open the **Moebius Skateboards** site you modified in Tutorial 7, and then create a folder named **fluid** in the local root folder of your site.

2. Create a new Fluid Grid Layout page, using the default settings. Save a copy of the style sheet in the fluid folder with the name **m_fluidlayout.css**, save the page in the fluid folder with the name **index.html**, and then save a copy of the dependent files boilerplate.css and respond.min.js in the fluid folder.

3. After the LayoutDiv1, insert the following Fluid Grid Layout div tags inside the gridContainer: **nav** (check Start new row), **content** (check Start new row), and **logo** (check Start new row).

4. Select the LayoutDiv1 tag in the status bar, delete the div from the page, open the **m_fluidlayout.css** page in the All Rules pane of the CSS Styles panel, and then delete all three instances of the LayoutDiv1 tag from the style sheet.

5. Place a copy of the m_fluidlook.css style sheet from the Dreamweaver8\Case1 folder into the fluid folder and attach the new style sheet to the new fluid grid page.

6. In Code view, copy the navigation (all the code in the nav div) from the main site, paste it into the nav div in the fluid site, and then delete the placeholder text. (*Hint*: The nav links will not work until you create the rest of the pages in the site.)

7. Copy the text (but not the Flash movie) from the home page of the existing site (starting with the h2 tag "Check Out Team Moebius"), paste it into the content div in the fluid grid page, and then delete the placeholder text. To the left of the heading text, insert the asher.png image from the graphics folder of the main site. Do not add alt text for now. Use Apply multiple classes to apply the noborders and the right_with_space styles to the image.

8. In the logo div, insert an image rollover named **m_roll** using the m_logo.jpg and m_logo_over.jpg graphics located in the graphics folder of the main site and linking to the new fluid grid home page; apply the align-center style to the rollover.

9. Open the **m_fluidlayout.css** file in Split view, and then adjust the following mobile layout styles:

   - Select the .gridContainer style, and then disable the padding-left and padding-right properties.
   - Select the #nav style, and then add the following properties and values: border-bottom-color = #d9f666, border-bottom-style = dashed, border-bottom-width = medium.
   - Select the #content style, and then change the value for margin-left to 1.82% and add margin-right = 1.82%.

10. Adjust the following tablet layout styles:
    - Select the .gridContainer style, and then disable the padding-left and padding-right properties.
    - In Design view, resize the #nav div to 3 columns in width by dragging the right resize handle. Return to Split view, and then change the float property to right, change the margin-left value to .5em, set margin to Same for all, and add border = medium dashed #d9f666.
    - Select the #content style, and then change the width value to 97%, change the margin-left value to 1.1625%, and add margin-right = 1.1625%.

11. Adjust the following desktop layout styles:
    - Select the .gridContainer style, and then disable the padding-left and padding-right properties.
    - In Design view, resize the #nav div to 5 columns in width by dragging the right resize handle. Return to Split view, and then change the float property to right, change the margin-left value to .5em, set margin to Same for all, and add border = medium dashed #d9f666.
    - Select the #content style, and then change the width value to 97%, change the margin-left value to .9%, and add margin-right = .9%.

12. Upload the site to your remote server, and then preview the site over the Internet, testing the new elements.

13. Submit the finished files to your instructor.

Create a jQuery Mobile site to augment the main Cowboy Charlie site.

APPLY

Case Problem 2

There are no Data Files needed for this Case Problem.

Cowboy Art Society Moni wants you to create a jQuery Mobile site targeted to mobile users that will have the same pages as the regular Cowboy Charlie site: home, Charles M. Russell, Artwork, and Poetry.

1. Open the **Cowboy Charlie** site you modified in Tutorial 7, reset the workspace to Mobile Applications, and then expand the Files panel to show local and remote sites.

2. Connect to the remote server, create a mobile folder in the root folder for your site on the remote server, and then collapse the Files panel to show only remote or local site.

3. In the Manage Sites dialog box, duplicate the Cowboy Charlie site, rename the duplicate site **Cowboy Charlie Mobile**, and then create a new local root folder named **mobile** in the charlie folder.

4. Create a new default images folder for the site named **graphics** in the mobile folder you just created.

5. In the Servers tab, edit your server settings by typing **mobile** at the end of the file path in the Root Directory box and the Web URL box, and then click the **Test** button to confirm that the connection to the new remote folder works.

6. Create a new jQuery Mobile site using the jQuery Mobile with theme (Local) sample page from the Mobile Starters Sample Folder in the Page from Sample tab of the New Document window. Save the page as **index.html** and copy the dependent files.

7. Download the latest version of the jQuery Mobile files from the jQuery Mobile Web site, write down the versions of the jQuery core files that you will need, go to the jQuery Web site and download the latest version that will work with your jQuery Mobile files, and then place a copy in the new jquery.mobile-*x.y.z* folder.

8. Delete the demo folder and the following files: jquery.mobile.structure-*x.y.z*.css, jquery.mobile.theme-*x.y.z*.css, jquery.mobile-*x.y.z*.css, jquery.mobile-*x.y.z*.js, and jquery.mobile-*x.y.z*.min.css.

9. Place a copy of the new jquery.mobile-*x.y.z* folder in the local root folder of your mobile site, delete the existing jquery.mobile folder, and then update the links and scripts located in the head of the index.html page with the new file information.

10. Select each of the following divs in the status bar, and apply Theme "b" in the jQuery Mobile Swatches panel: page, page2, page3, and page4.

11. Switch to Code view, open the Source Code, add a blank line above the closing </head> tag, and then type the following code to create a new style that displays images at max-width 100%, which makes the images scalable:

```
<style type="text/css">
img, object, embed, video {
    max-width: 100%;
}
</style>
```

12. In the page div, delete the text from the heading div, type **Cowboy Charlie**, and then apply the H1 tag. Repeat for the page2, page3, and page4 divs.

13. In the page, page2, page3, and page4 divs, delete the placeholder text from the footer divs and insert a nonbreakable space.

14. In the page div, select the Page Two text from the unordered list and type **Charles M. Russell**. The text is still linked to #page2 because you did not rename the div.

15. In the unordered list, change Page Three to **Artwork**, and then change Page Four to **Poetry**.

16. In page, click after the text in the last item of the unordered list press the Right arrow key until the unordered list tag is not displayed in the status bar, and then press the Enter key to move down a line.

17. Copy the content from the home page of the main site (do not include the Shockwave movie) and paste it into the home page of the new site. (*Hint*: Copy and paste in Code view to ensure that you include the surrounding tags that style the text.)

18. In the content div in the page2 div, select the placeholder text, and then type **Charlie's bio will be here soon.** (including the period). In the content div in the page3 div, select the placeholder text, and then type **Charlie's art will be here soon.** (including the period). In the content div in the page4 div, select the placeholder text, and then type **Charlie's poetry will be here soon.** (including the period).

19. Save the page and the style sheets, upload the site to your remote server, view the site in a browser, click each page to ensure that the site is functioning, and then close the browser.

20. Submit the finished files to your instructor.

Create a responsive Web site to replace the existing site.

APPLY

Case Problem 3

Data Files needed for this Case Problem: t_fluidlook.css, tess_fluidhead.png

Success with Tess Tess wants to replace the current site with a more contemporary, responsive site. This will enable her to optimize the experience for desktop, tablet, and mobile display. She wants you to create a home page for the new site using Fluid Grid Layout. After she has reviewed the design and signed off on the new layout, the rest of the site will be created.

1. Open the **Success with Tess** site you modified in Tutorial 7, and then create a folder named **fluid** in the root folder.

2. Create a new Fluid Grid Layout page, using the default settings. Save a copy of the style sheet in the fluid folder with the name **t_fluidlayout.css**, save the page in the fluid folder with the name **index.html**, and then save a copy of the dependent files boilerplate.css and respond.min.js in the fluid folder.

3. Change the title to **Success with Tess – Home**. After the LayoutDiv1, insert the following Fluid Grid Layout div tags in the gridContainer, checking the Start on new row check box: **head**, **nav**, **content**, **tess-timonials**, and **footer**.

4. Delete the LayoutDiv1 div from the page, and then the three instances of the LayoutDiv1 style from the m_fluidlayout.css page.

5. Copy the **t_fluidlook.css** style sheet located in the Dreamweaver8\Case3 folder included with your Data Files into the fluid folder, and then attach the style sheet to the fluid grid page.

6. Place a copy of the **tess_fluidhead.png** file located in the Dreamweaver8\Case3 folder included with your Data Files into the main graphics folder. The image is added at the top of the page.

7. In Code view, copy the navigation from the main site (everything inside of the nav div except the paragraph tag that surrounds the nav), paste it into the fluid nav div copy, delete the placeholder text, and then apply the align-center style to the nav div. (*Hint*: The nav links will not work until you create the rest of the pages in the site.)

8. In the boilerplate.css style sheet, change the value for the following tags as indicated: a = fff, a:visited = fff, a:hover = 06c.

9. Copy the first heading and the following two paragraphs of text from the home page of the existing site, paste it into the content div in the fluid grid page, and then delete the placeholder text. Copy the second heading (TESS-timonials) and the following text from the home page of the existing site, paste it into the tess-timonials div in the fluid grid page, and then delete the placeholder text. (*Hint*: Use Code view to ensure you include the tags that surround the text.) Do not copy the Shockwave movie.

10. Copy the text in the footer div of the main site, paste it into the footer div in the fluid site, and then delete the placeholder text. Save the page and style sheets.

11. In the head div, insert an image rollover named **t_roll** using the tess_logo.png and tess_logo_over.png graphics located in the main site's graphics folder and linking to the new fluid grid home page. Use Apply Multiple Classes to apply the align-right-pad style and the no borders style to the images.

12. Open the **m_fluidlayout.css** file in Split view, and then use the style sheet and the CSS Styles panel to adjust the following mobile layout styles:
    - In the .gridContainer style, disable the padding-left and padding-right properties.
    - In the #content and #tess-timonials styles, change the value for width to 97% and add padding-left = 1.5%, padding-right = 1.5%.

13. Adjust the following tablet layout styles:
    - In the .gridContainer style, disable the padding-left and padding-right properties.
    - In Design view, resize the #content div to 3 columns.
    - In Design view, resize the #tess-timonials div to 4 columns, and then click the Move up a row button to enable the div to move to the same line as the #content div.

14. Adjust the following desktop layout styles:
    - In the .gridContainer style, disable the padding-left and padding-right properties.
    - In Design view, resize the #content div to 6 columns.
    - In Design view, resize the tess-timonials div to 3 columns, click the Move up a row button to enable the div to move to the same line as the content div, and then add background-color = #06C, margin-top = .5em, and margin-bottom = .25em.

15. Upload the site to your remote server, and then preview the site over the Internet, testing the new elements.

16. Submit the finished files to your instructor.

Create a coffee ordering app for a coffee lounge.

CREATE

Case Problem 4

There are no Data Files needed for this Case Problem.

Coffee Lounge   Tommy wants to create an app that generates some buzz about the Coffee Lounge. The app should have some advanced functionality that will engage users or provide them with some benefit that they cannot get from the regular Web site. In order to complete this Case Problem, you must use JavaScript, jQuery Mobile, and PhoneGap to create your own advanced functionality.

1. Create a new mobile folder on your remote server.

2. Create a duplicate of your existing Coffee Lounge site, and then rename the copy of the site **Coffee Lounge Mobile**.

3. Create a new local root folder named **mobile** in the Coffee folder for the new app.

4. Update the path in the Default Images Folder box from web to **mobile**.

5. In the Servers tab, edit your server settings by typing **mobile** at the end of the file path in the Root Directory box, and then click the Test button to confirm that the connection to the new remote folder works.

6. Create a new jQuery Mobile site using the jQuery Mobile with theme (Local) sample page from the Mobile Starters Sample Folder in the Page from Sample tab of the New Document dialog box, save the page as **index.html**, and then copy the dependent files.

7. Download the latest version of the jQuery Mobile files from the jQuery Mobile Web site, write down the versions of the jQuery core files that you will need, and then download the latest version that will work with your jQuery Mobile files from the jQuery Web site.

8. Delete the demo folder and the jquery.mobile.structure-*x.y.z*.css, jquery.mobile.theme-*x.y.z*.css, jquery.mobile-*x.y.z*.css, jquery.mobile-*x.y.z*.js, and jquery.mobile-*x.y.z*.min.css files.

9. Place a copy of the new jquery.mobile-*x.y.z* folder in your local root folder, delete the existing jquery.mobile folder, and then update the links and scripts located in the head of the index.html page with the new file information.

10. Add pages and content to the app as needed.

11. Use the jQuery Mobile Swatches panel to add themes to pages or page elements as needed, or create your own custom theme using ThemeRoller on the jQuery Mobile site.

12. Create and add the advanced functionality to the site.

13. Add the following script below the other scripts in the head of the page to fix the PhoneGap bug, and then save the page and the related files as necessary:

    ```
    <script src="phonegap.js" type="text/javascript"></script>
    ```

14. Create a new PhoneGap project and build the apps for the platforms that you will support.

15. Update the config.xml file with your app information.

16. Test the app on the platforms that you will support, fix any problems, rebuild the app, and then retest until you are satisfied that the app is finished.

17. Upload the app to the app store(s) for the platform(s) that you will support.

18. Submit the finished files to your instructor.

Adding Database Functionality

Collecting and Viewing Form Data in a Database

OBJECTIVES

Session 9.1
- Learn about creating dynamic database content for Web pages
- Create database-driven pages using MySQL and PHP for a Linux server
- Create a database on a remote Linux server
- Connect a Web site to a database
- Add server behaviors to Web pages
- Create pages to view data in a database
- Create a login page

Session 9.2
- Create database-driven pages using Access and ASP for a Windows server
- Upload a database to a remote Windows server
- Connect a Web site to a database
- Add server behaviors to Web pages
- Create pages to view data in a database
- Create a login page

Case | *NextBest Fest*

Gage thinks the NextBest Fest site could benefit from the collection of some user data. He thinks it would be helpful to collect the data that is received from users who complete and submit the form in the contact.html page. You will create a database to store the information collected from the form and connect the form in the contact page to the database. You will also create pages that enable you to view the data collected in the database. Finally, you will create a login page and connect the pages that display collected database information to the login page so that users must have a valid login and password to view the data.

STARTING DATA FILES

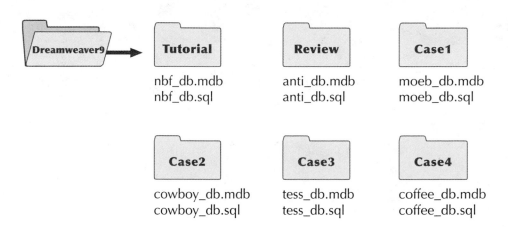

Dreamweaver9 → Tutorial
nbf_db.mdb
nbf_db.sql

Review
anti_db.mdb
anti_db.sql

Case1
moeb_db.mdb
moeb_db.sql

Case2
cowboy_db.mdb
cowboy_db.sql

Case3
tess_db.mdb
tess_db.sql

Case4
coffee_db.mdb
coffee_db.sql

Adobe product screenshot(s) reprinted with permission from Adobe Systems Incorporated.

DMR 535

SESSION 9.1 VISUAL OVERVIEW

A **database-driven Web site** is a Web site that uses a database to gather, display, or manipulate information.

A **database** is a collection of information that is arranged for ease and speed of search and retrieval, and is usually associated with a specific software package such as Microsoft Access or a specific database server such as MySQL.

MySQL is a free open source database engine that was designed specifically for Web use.

A **recordset** is a temporary collection of data retrieved from a database and stored on the application server that generates the Web page when that page is loaded in a browser window.

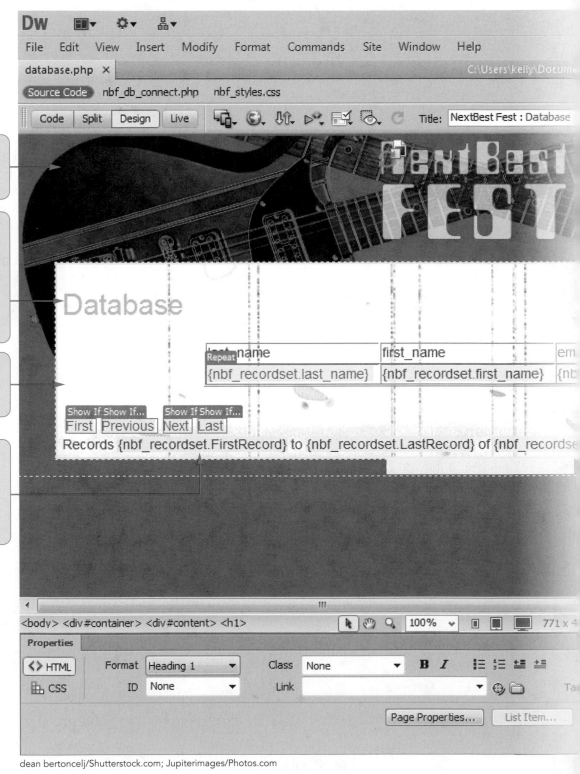

dean bertoncelj/Shutterstock.com; Jupiterimages/Photos.com

ADDING DATABASE FUNCTIONALITY

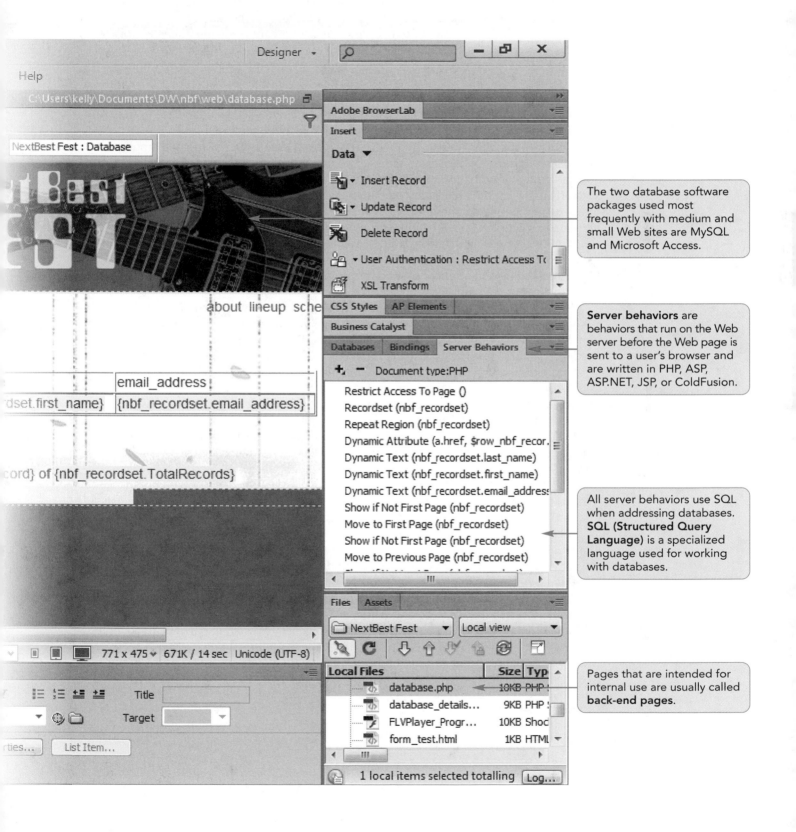

The two database software packages used most frequently with medium and small Web sites are MySQL and Microsoft Access.

Server behaviors are behaviors that run on the Web server before the Web page is sent to a user's browser and are written in PHP, ASP, ASP.NET, JSP, or ColdFusion.

All server behaviors use SQL when addressing databases. **SQL (Structured Query Language)** is a specialized language used for working with databases.

Pages that are intended for internal use are usually called **back-end pages**.

Exploring Databases and Dynamic Page Content

One of the best ways to extend the functionality of a Web site is to connect the site to a database. A database is a collection of information that is arranged for ease and speed of search and retrieval and is usually associated with a specific software package such as Microsoft Access or a specific database server such as MySQL. A database can be a simple list of people's names or it can be a large collection of complex information such as product inventory. A database-driven Web site is a Web site that uses a database to gather, display, or manipulate information. For example, e-commerce sites often use a database to store online orders and billing information, and weather sites often retrieve current weather conditions from a database and display the reports in a Web page. The NextBest Fest site will use a database to store the information collected from a form in the contact.html page.

There are different ways to create database-driven Web sites. The method employed depends on the amount of data being served out, the number of users potentially accessing that information simultaneously, the budget available, and the technology already being used. Some large companies, such as Panasonic and LG Electronics, Inc., use expensive database software like Oracle or DB2 to serve out massive amounts of data to multiple users. If you plan to serve out massive amounts of information to thousands of users simultaneously and have access to a large budget, this is a great solution. However, even many large companies are turning to other solutions, and if you are creating a medium or small database-driven site, these other database software solutions are more realistic for your needs.

The two database software packages used most frequently with medium and small Web sites are MySQL and Microsoft Access. MySQL is a free, open source database engine that was designed specifically for Web use. Both Google and Yahoo! use MySQL as their database engine. It is usually installed by default on Linux servers. MySQL can also be installed on Windows servers. Additional information about MySQL is available at *mysql.com*. Access is a database management program that is part of the Microsoft Office suite. Windows servers can serve out Access files by default if the permissions are set correctly for the database file.

In addition to selecting a database, you must also select the programming or scripting language that you will use to create server behaviors. Server behaviors are behaviors that run on the Web server before the Web page is sent to a user's browser and are written in PHP, ASP, ASP.NET, JSP, or ColdFusion. You will use server behaviors to communicate with a database (send data and retrieve data) and to turn data into plain HTML that can be displayed in a browser as part of a Web page.

All server behaviors use SQL when addressing databases. SQL (Structured Query Language) is a specialized language used for working with databases. When Web pages display data stored in a database, they are said to be **dynamically generated**. You will use server behaviors to process data collected from the form in the contact.html page and stored in the database to create HTML code. This code will display an overview of the data stored in the database and will display the details of selected records from the database_details page. Using server behaviors to generate dynamic pages is much more efficient than updating content manually each time the information changes.

This tutorial provides two methods for creating the database-driven pages in the NextBest Fest site. If you are working with a Linux server, you will use a MySQL database and PHP to create the database-driven pages. If you are working with a Windows server, you will use an Access database and ASP to create the pages. Each method requires different steps and methodologies, both of which are provided in this tutorial.

Regardless of which method you use, the general process for creating the database-driven pages in the NextBest Fest site is:

- Adjust the form in the contact.html page.
- Create the Web pages you will need.
- Place or create the database on the remote server.
- Add server behaviors to the form to connect the database.
- Add server behaviors to view the data collected in the database from within the designated Web pages.
- Format the login page.
- Set the database pages to display only when a user has logged in.

If you are working on a Linux server with MySQL and PHP, continue with the rest of Session 9.1. If you are working on a Windows server with Access and ASP, continue with Session 9.2. If you are unsure which type of server you are using or if you do not have access to a server, check with your instructor or technical support person before continuing with this tutorial.

Creating Database-Driven Pages Using MySQL and PHP

Adding database functionality to a Web site can be quite complex. Just as it is a good practice to make a plan prior to creating a Web site, it is also a good practice to plan the database-driven portion of the site in advance. Gage created a site plan for the new portion of the NextBest Fest site.

Based on Gage's plan, the technical team will create the SQL for a database that stores the information collected from the form in the contact.html page. You will modify the form to work with the database. You will create the pages for the new portion of the site: thankyou.html, access_denied.html, database.php, database_details.php, and login.php. You will create the database on the remote server using the SQL provided by the technical team, and then you will connect the site to the database. Next, you will add server behaviors to the pages you created so that the form data can be sent to and stored in the database and so that the database.php and database_details.php pages display the information stored in the database. Finally, you will create a login.php page and add code to the back-end pages to prevent unauthorized users from viewing the content of those pages.

When the database-driven pages are complete, the information received from users who completed the form in the contact.html page will be stored in a database that only authorized users can access.

REFERENCE

Creating Database-Driven Pages for a Linux Server

- Create the Web pages you need.
- Create a database on your remote server.
- Add server behaviors to connect the site to the database.
- Add server behaviors to store submitted data in the database and to view the data collected in the database from within designated Web pages.
- Create a login page.
- Add code to the back-end pages to prevent unauthorized users from viewing the content of those pages.

Modifying the Form

Before you create the database-driven pages of the NextBest Fest site, you will modify the form in the contact.html page to work with the database that you will create on your remote server. You will delete the list box with the band names from the form, and then create a series of check boxes to collect this same information. You are replacing the list box with the check boxes to keep things simpler because a list box as the storage element requires more steps and custom scripts to process data.

To modify the form in the contact.html page:

▸ **1.** Reset Dreamweaver to the **Designer** workspace, minimize the **Business Catalyst** panel, open the **Files** panel, open the **NextBest Fest** site you modified in Tutorial 8, and then open the **contact.html** page in Design view.

▸ **2.** In the right column near the bottom of the form, select the list box, and then press the **Delete** key. The list box is removed from the form.

▸ **3.** In the same location as the deleted list box, insert a **checkbox group**. The Checkbox Group dialog box opens.

▸ **4.** Type **band_list** in the Name box, and then add the following labels and values for the check boxes: **Bon-Journo / bj**, **Silver Rail / sr**, **More Exquisite Less Dead / meld**, **Undead Milkmen / um**.

▸ **5.** Click the **Line breaks** option button, if necessary, and then click the **OK** button. The checkbox group is added to the form.

▸ **6.** Select the sentence in the left column next to the new checkbox group, and then type **Check all of the bands that you enjoy.** (including the period). See Figure 9-1.

Figure 9-1	Modified form

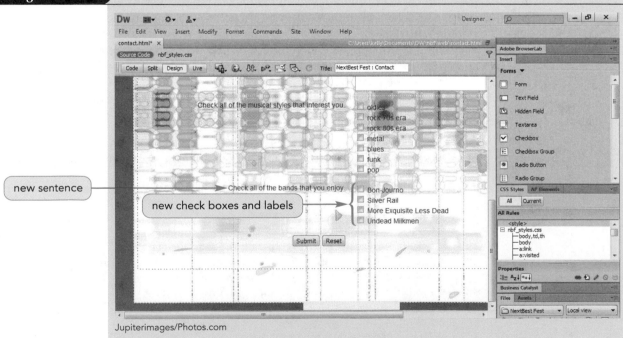

Jupiterimages/Photos.com

▸ **7.** Save and close the contact.html page, and then upload the page to your remote server.

Creating New Pages

You need five pages for the database-driven portion of the NextBest Fest site. You will create all of these pages now so that they are available when you need them. According to Gage's plan for the database-driven portion of the site, you will create the following pages:

- **thankyou.html.** A page thanking the user for his or her submission that appears when the user submits the form in the contact.html page.
- **access_denied.html.** A page informing the user that the wrong username or password has been entered that appears when a user attempts to log in on the login.php page with incorrect information or if a user attempts to access a password-protected page without logging in. After a four-second delay, the user is returned to the login.php page.
- **database.php.** A page showing an overview of the data stored in the database. After the login.php page is created, users cannot access this page unless they log in.
- **database_details.php.** A page showing the details of a selected record that appears when a user clicks a record in the database.php page. After the login.php page is created, users cannot access this page unless they log in.
- **login.php.** A page in which a user enters his or her username and password and then clicks the Login button. If the information is correct, the database.php page appears; if the information is incorrect, the access_denied.html page appears.

Three of the pages you will create are PHP pages. You can create a PHP page by typing .php as the file extension when you name the page.

TIP

You can press the Ctrl+D keys to duplicate the selected page.

To create the pages for the database-driven portion of the NextBest Fest site:

1. In the Files panel, duplicate the **contact.html** page. A new page named contact – Copy.html appears at the bottom of the files list.

2. In the Files panel, rename the Copy of contact.html page as **thankyou.html**.

3. Open the **thankyou.html** page in Design view, and then edit the page title to replace the word *Contact* with **Thank You**. The new page title appears.

4. Change the page heading to **Thank You**.

5. Delete all the content below the heading and above the footer, type **Thank you for submitting your information.** (including the period) in the line below the heading text, and then make sure the sentence is in the **Paragraph** format. See Figure 9-2.

Figure 9-2	New thankyou.html page

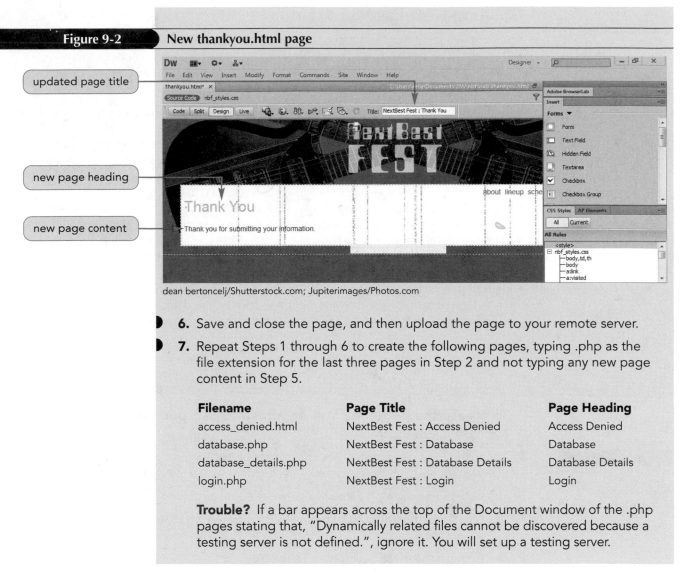

updated page title

new page heading

new page content

dean bertoncelj/Shutterstock.com; Jupiterimages/Photos.com

6. Save and close the page, and then upload the page to your remote server.

7. Repeat Steps 1 through 6 to create the following pages, typing .php as the file extension for the last three pages in Step 2 and not typing any new page content in Step 5.

Filename	Page Title	Page Heading
access_denied.html	NextBest Fest : Access Denied	Access Denied
database.php	NextBest Fest : Database	Database
database_details.php	NextBest Fest : Database Details	Database Details
login.php	NextBest Fest : Login	Login

Trouble? If a bar appears across the top of the Document window of the .php pages stating that, "Dynamically related files cannot be discovered because a testing server is not defined.", ignore it. You will set up a testing server.

Now that you have modified the form and created the new pages, you are ready to create the database on your remote server.

Creating a Database on a Remote Server

You must create the database on the remote server so that it can send data to and receive data from Web pages or Web applications. For example, in the NextBest Fest site, the form in the contact.html page will send data to the database that you create on the remote server.

If your instructor has already created the database on your remote server, you should read but not complete the next set of steps. In this case, you will be sharing the same database with your classmates, so you might see data that you did not add in the database or you might observe that data you added is removed. If you are creating the database on your remote server, you need to contact your ISP (or your IT Department) and have a technical support person create an empty MySQL database, name the empty database "nbf_db," and provide you with access information. After the empty database is available on your remote server, you will use the administrative tools your host provides to do the following:

• Log in to the database management interface (use the information and steps provided by your ISP or IT Department).

• Run the statements that are provided as SQL in the nbf_db.sql file located in the Dreamweaver9\Tutorial folder included with your Data Files. (The steps will vary depending on the system your ISP or IT Department uses.) Running the statements will create the database that will be used in this tutorial by filling the empty database on the remote server with the structure and content that the NextBest Fest technical team provided.

The author's ISP provided the following steps to log in to the empty database and run the nbf_db.sql file using phpMyAdmin as the database management interface. phpMyAdmin is the most frequently used database management interface for MySQL databases. If your ISP or IT Department uses a different interface or if the interface is configured differently, your steps will differ slightly; contact your ISP or IT Department for the exact steps you should follow. If your instructor has already created the database for you, read the following steps, and then continue working in the "Connecting a Web Site to a Database" section.

To log in to the database management interface and run the SQL file:

1. Open a browser window, type the URL provided by your ISP or IT Department in the Address bar, and then press the **Enter** key. A page or dialog box opens in which you enter login information.

2. Type the username and password information provided by your ISP or IT Department in the appropriate boxes, and then click the **OK** button. The default page of the database management interface that your ISP or IT Department uses appears in the browser window. Figure 9-3 shows the default page for the phpMyAdmin database management interface.

| Figure 9-3 | phpMyAdmin default page |

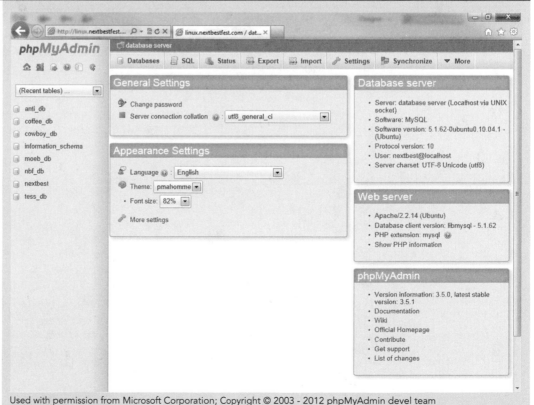

Used with permission from Microsoft Corporation; Copyright © 2003 - 2012 phpMyAdmin devel team

Trouble? If your screen does not match Figure 9-3, your ISP or IT Department uses a different interface or has phpMyAdmin configured differently. The same general steps should work. However, if you have difficulty, ask your instructor, technical support person, ISP, or IT Department for instructions.

3. Click the **Databases** tab, and then click **nbf_db** from the list of databases. The nbf_db detail page is displayed. See Figure 9-4.

Figure 9-4   **nbf_db detail page**

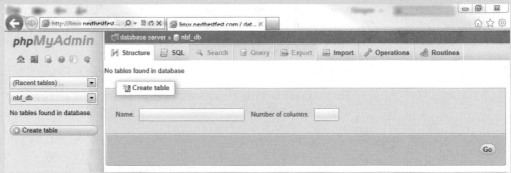

Used with permission from Microsoft Corporation; Copyright © 2003 - 2012 phpMyAdmin devel team

4. Click the **SQL** tab at the top of the page. The SQL page opens in the browser window.

> You must run the SQL file; otherwise, the database will not be created properly.

5. Using Notepad or another text editor, open the **nbf_db.sql** file located in the Dreamweaver9\Tutorial folder included with your Data Files, copy all of the content, and then paste it into the **Run SQL query/queries on database nbf_db** text area.

6. Click the **Go** button. The database management interface runs the SQL, the database structure is created, and a list of the tables in the database appears at the left of the browser window below the database name. See Figure 9-5.

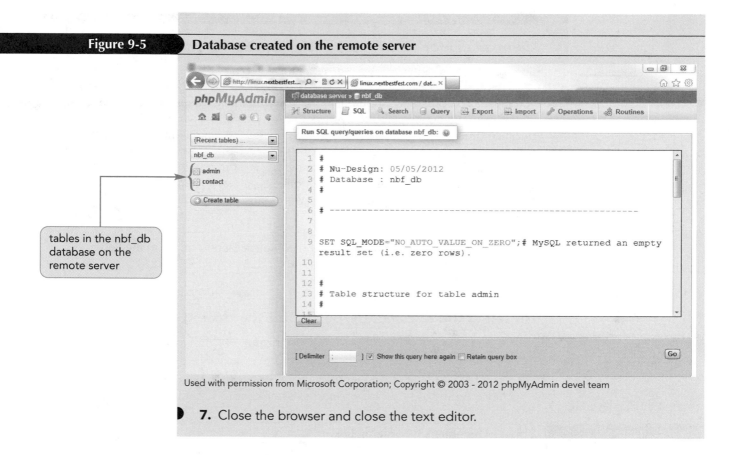

Figure 9-5 **Database created on the remote server**

Used with permission from Microsoft Corporation; Copyright © 2003 - 2012 phpMyAdmin devel team

▶ **7.** Close the browser and close the text editor.

Connecting a Web Site to a Database

The database is created on the remote Web server, and you are ready to connect the site to the database. When you open a Web page in the Document window that is not connected to the database, the Server Behaviors panel displays an interactive list of steps for setting up Dreamweaver to connect the site to the database. Clicking the linked text in each step opens the dialog boxes needed to complete that step. A check mark appears at the left of each step to indicate that all the necessary information has been entered and the step is completed.

The three main steps for connecting a Web page to the database are:

1. **Create a site for this file.** This step is checked because you have already set the local and remote information for the site when you created the site definition.
2. **Choose a document type.** In this step, you specify which document type you are using to create server behaviors. When you click the link text in Step 2, the Choose Document Type dialog box opens, and you can select ASP JavaScript, ASP VBScript, ASP.NET C#, ASP.NET VB, ColdFusion, JSP, or PHP MySQL as the document type. For the NextBest Fest site, you will use PHP.
3. **Set up the site's testing server.** In this step, you specify the testing server in the site definition. You cannot preview dynamic pages from within Dreamweaver until you specify a folder in which the dynamic pages can be processed. Dreamweaver uses this folder to generate dynamic content and to connect to the database while you work. For the NextBest Fest site, you will use the root folder you created on your remote server for your NextBest Fest site because the server usually runs an application server that can handle the dynamic pages. You can, however, specify a different location for the testing server as long as it can handle dynamic pages. When you set up the testing server for a professional site that is already live, you might designate a separate folder on another server where you can test the pages without affecting the live site.

Comparing Modified Times of Local and Server Files

Some of the files required for server-side processing are located outside of the Web page. Therefore, whenever you upload pages to the remote or testing server, you must also upload dependent files. As you upload files, a dialog box might open, indicating that you are trying to overwrite newer files with older files. This occurs because Dreamweaver has a feature that compares the modified time of local files with the modified time of server files. If the time on either the server or your computer is inaccurate and your local computer time is behind the server time, Dreamweaver sees the file on the server as newer and notifies you that you are overwriting a newer file with an older file. Click the OK button each time you see this message.

You will open the contact.html page and complete Steps 2 and 3 in the Server Behaviors panel.

To select the document type and set the testing server:

1. Open the **contact.html** page in Design view, and then open the Server Behaviors panel.

2. In the Server Behaviors panel, click the **document type** link. The Choose Document Type dialog box opens. See Figure 9-6.

Figure 9-6 Choose Document Type dialog box

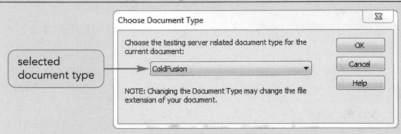

Trouble? If the document type in your list is different from the document type in the figure, your default is set differently. You will select the document type in Step 3.

3. Click the **document type** button, click **PHP**, and then click the **OK** button. The Update Files dialog box opens. You will update the links in all the listed files.

4. Click the **Update** button to update the links. The file extension for the contact page changes to .php, and the Update Files dialog box opens, indicating that the contact.php page could not be updated. You will update the link in the contact.php page yourself.

5. Click the **OK** button. A check mark appears in the Server Behaviors panel beside Step 2 to indicate that this step is complete (the check mark might not appear immediately).

Trouble? If a bar appears at the top of the Document window indicating that the dynamically related files cannot be discovered, ignore it. This problem will be corrected when you set up the testing server.

6. In the Document window, select **contact** in the navigation text, and then, in the Property inspector, delete **.html** from the Link box and type **.php**. The contact link is updated.

   Trouble? If a bar appears at the top of the Document window indicating that the dynamically related files cannot be discovered because a testing server is not defined, ignore it; you will set up the testing server in Step 8.

7. Save the page, and then upload the page to your remote server, including the dependent files. (The contact.html page remains in the site's root folder but is no longer used.)

8. In the Server Behaviors panel, click the **testing server** link in Step 3. The Site Setup for NextBest Fest dialog box opens with the Servers tab displayed.

9. Click the **Testing** check box for your remote server, and then click the **Edit** button.

10. In the Web URL box, delete all the file path information, and then type the Web URL for your remote site.

11. Click the **Advanced** button at the top of the dialog box, and then select **PHP MySQL** from the Server Model list. See Figure 9-7.

Figure 9-7	Completed Testing Server information

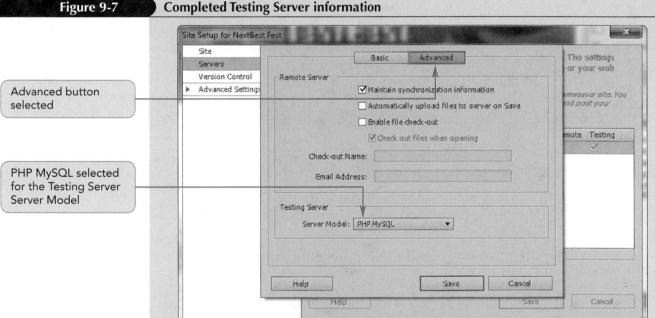

Advanced button selected

PHP MySQL selected for the Testing Server Server Model

12. Click the **Save** button to save the settings, and then click the **Save** button to close the Site Setup for NextBest Fest dialog box. The Testing Server information is set, and a check mark appears beside Step 3 in the Server Behaviors panel.

   Trouble? If a dialog box opens, stating that the site URL prefix for the testing server does not match the site URL prefix specified in the HTTP address for the site, your server includes a public_html directory that stores all the content viewers can access with a Web browser. However, when visitors view the Web site, the URL they enter does not include the public_html directory. Therefore, these paths are different. Click the OK button now and whenever this dialog box appears.

▶ **13.** Click the **Setup** link that appears in the banner at the top of the Document window, if necessary. The Site Setup for NextBest Fest dialog box opens and green check marks are displayed indicating that the testing server has been set up successfully.

▶ **14.** Click the **Cancel** button to close the dialog box, click the **Discover** link that appears in the banner, and then click the **Yes** button to discover any dynamically related files.

Adding Server Behaviors

Dreamweaver provides a list of prewritten server behaviors in the Server Behaviors panel once the page is connected to the database. You include these server behaviors in the page to extend the functionality of the page and to enable you to retrieve and display the data from the database. You will include two server behaviors in the contact.php page: Recordset and Insert Record.

The Recordset behavior enables you to specify which data you want to retrieve from the database and display in the Web page. A recordset is a temporary collection of data retrieved from a database and stored on the application server that generates the Web page when that page is loaded in a browser window. You specify the database and the records (or data) to include in the recordset when you set the parameters for the behavior. A recordset can include all the data in the database or a subset of the data. You must add the server-side behaviors that will create the recordset in which to store and retrieve data before you can use a database as a content source for a dynamic Web page. The server discards the recordset when it is no longer needed.

The Insert Record behavior enables you to specify what will happen to the information collected from the Web page (in this case, when the form is submitted). You can specify in which database the data will be placed, where the data will be stored in the database, what columns will be included, and so on. It also lets you select the page that appears in the browser window after the form is submitted.

You will create a recordset for the contact.php page.

To create the recordset for the contact.php page:

▶ **1.** At the top of the Server Behaviors panel, click the **Add behavior** button ⊞, and then click **Recordset**. The Recordset dialog box opens. See Figure 9-8.

Figure 9-8   Recordset dialog box

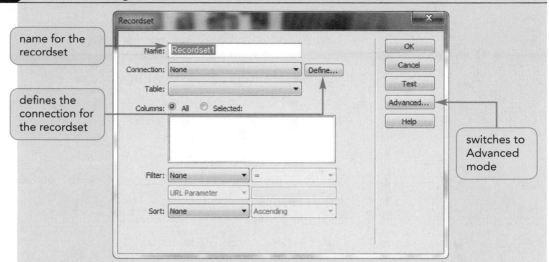

name for the recordset

defines the connection for the recordset

switches to Advanced mode

2. Click the **Advanced** button to switch the Recordset dialog box to Advanced mode, and then click the **Define** button next to the Connection box. The Connections for Site 'NextBest Fest' dialog box opens.

3. Click the **New** button. The MySQL Connection dialog box opens. See Figure 9-9.

Figure 9-9   MySQL Connection dialog box

4. In the Connection name box, type **nbf_db_connect**. This is an internal name that is visible only when you are working in Dreamweaver.

5. In the MySQL server box, type **localhost** if your database server is on the same server as your Web server or type the database server's URL provided by your ISP when you requested access information.

   Trouble? If you are using a different testing server than the remote server, you will need different information for this step. Ask your instructor or technical support person for help.

6. In the User name box, type your database username, and then, in the Password box, type your database password. You will need to obtain this information from your instructor, technical support person, ISP, or IT Department.

7. Click the **Select** button next to the Database box. Dreamweaver connects to the remote server, the Select Database dialog box opens, and the names of all the databases on the remote server to which you have access appear in the Select Database box.

Trouble? If an error message appears, Dreamweaver cannot connect to the database on the remote database server. Check the information you typed in the Testing Server category of the site definition and in the MySQL Connection dialog box, and then repeat Step 7. If you still have trouble, ask your instructor or technical support person for help.

8. In the Select Database box, click **nbf_db** to select it, if necessary.

9. Click the **OK** button in the Select Database dialog box, click the **OK** button in the MySQL Connection dialog box, and then click the **Done** button in the Connections for Site 'NextBest Fest' dialog box. The dialog boxes close.

10. In the Recordset dialog box, type **nbf_recordset** in the Name box.

11. Click the **Connection** button, and then click **nbf_db_connect** in the list.

12. In the Database items box, expand the **Tables** list, click **contact** to select the database table, and then click the **SELECT** button.

13. Click the **OK** button. The Recordset behavior is added to the page and appears in the Server Behaviors panel. See Figure 9-10.

| Figure 9-10 | Recordset behavior added to the contact.php page |

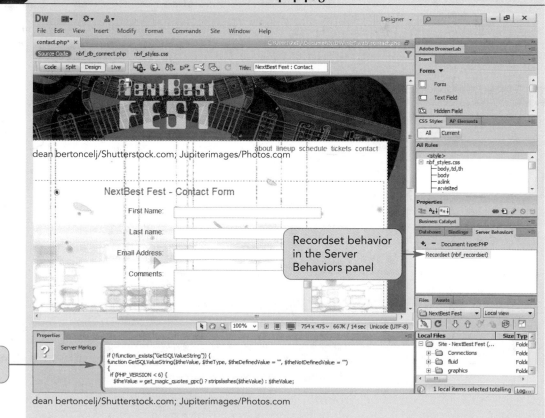

dean bertoncelj/Shutterstock.com; Jupiterimages/Photos.com

Next, you will add the Insert Record behavior to the page.

To add the Insert Record behavior:

1. At the top of the Server Behaviors panel, click the **Add behavior** button [+▾], and then click **Insert Record**. The Insert Record dialog box opens.

2. Click the **Submit values from** button, and then click **contact**, if necessary, to select the contact table in the database.

3. Click the **Connection** button, and then click **nbf_db_connect** to select the connection to the database, if necessary.

4. Click the **Insert table** button, and then click **contact**. The columns in the contact table are displayed in the Columns box. See Figure 9-11.

Figure 9-11   **Insert Record dialog box**

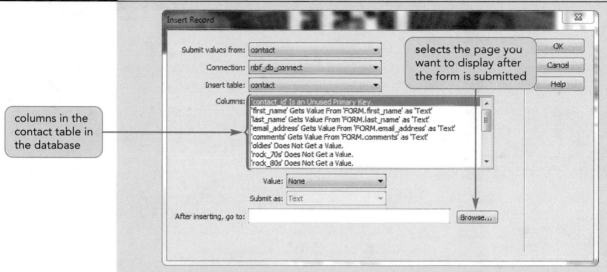

columns in the contact table in the database

selects the page you want to display after the form is submitted

5. Click the **Browse** button next to the After inserting, go to box. The Select a redirect file dialog box opens.

6. Click the **thankyou.html** page in the site's local root folder, and then click the **OK** button. The Select a redirect file dialog box closes, and the page filename appears in the After inserting, go to box.

7. In the Insert Record dialog box, click the **OK** button. The Insert Record behavior is added to the page and appears in the Server Behaviors panel.

8. If necessary, click **Discover** on the bar that appears across the top of the Document window to enable Dreamweaver to discover any dynamically related pages. See Figure 9-12.

Figure 9-12   **Insert Record behavior added to the contact.php page**

Insert Record behavior in the Server Behaviors panel

code for the Insert Record behavior

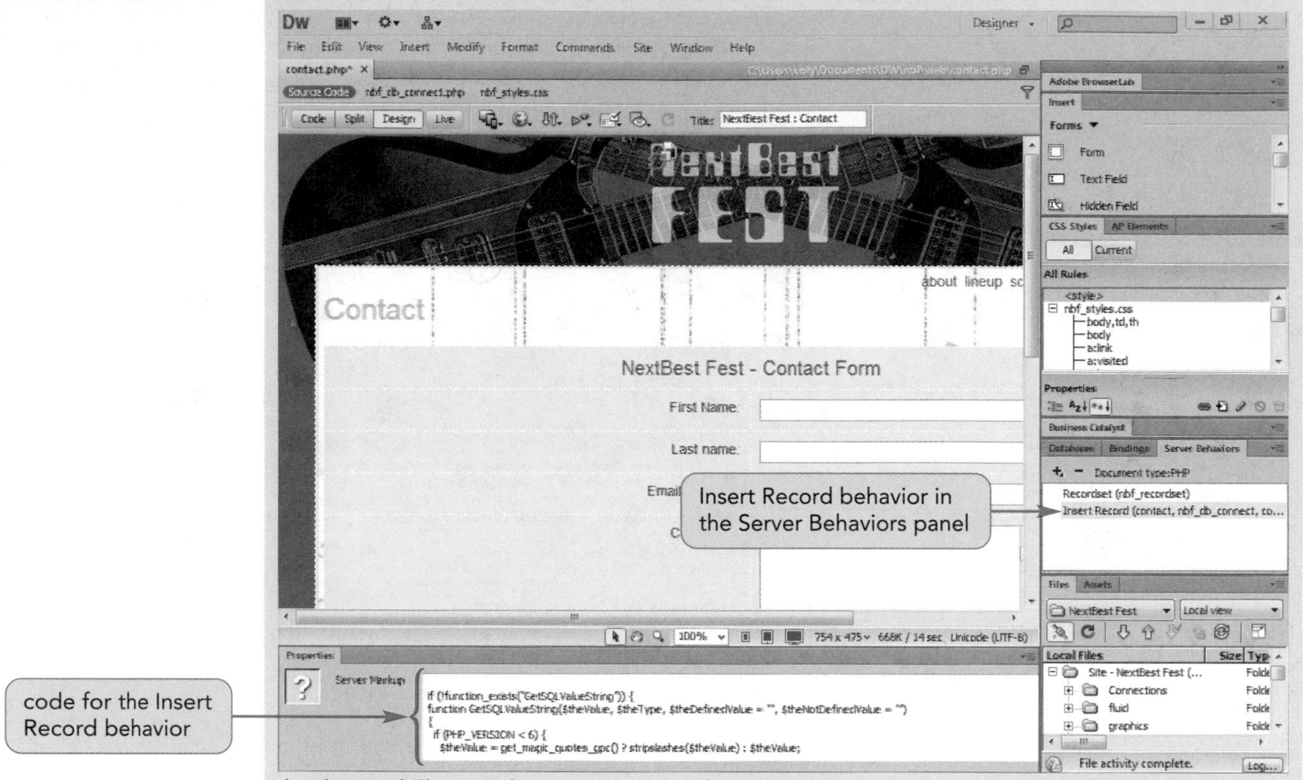

dean bertoncelj/Shutterstock.com; Jupiterimages/Photos.com

Before continuing, you will test the Insert Record behavior you added to the contact.php page. You will upload the page to the remote server, preview the page in a browser, and then complete and submit the form. The thankyou.html page should then display.

To test the Insert Record behavior:

1. Save the page, and then upload the page to the remote server. The Dependent Files dialog box opens.

2. Click the **Yes** button to update the dependent files.

3. Preview the contact.php page in a browser. The Update Copy on Testing Server dialog box opens.

4. Click the **Yes** button to update the file on the testing server, and then click the **Yes** button in the Dependent Files dialog box, if necessary.

5. Scroll down to view the contact form, enter appropriate information in the form, and then click the **Submit** button to submit the form. The thankyou.html page appears in a new browser window.

6. Close the browser.

The page is connected to the database and the behaviors have been added to the page. Next, you will create back-end pages to view the data collected in the database.

Creating Back-End Pages for Viewing Data in a Database

Pages that are intended for internal use are usually called back-end pages. For the NextBest Fest site, the database.php and database_details.php pages are back-end pages. You will set the database.php and database_details.php pages to display the data that you collect in the database.

The Master Detail Page Set button in the Data category of the Insert panel enables you to create a set of pages that presents information in two levels of detail. The master page (in this case, the database.php page) lists all the records in the recordset that you create for the page. The detail page (in this case, the database_details.php page) displays the detail of the selected record. You determine which fields of information are displayed in the master page and which fields of information are displayed in the detail page when you set the parameters for the pages.

In addition to creating all the code needed to display the dynamic content in the pages, Dreamweaver also adds server behaviors to create a page navigation bar so you can move between the dynamic records if more records are in the database than are displayed in the page. The navigation bar includes First Page, Last Page, Previous Page, and Next Page buttons. The pages also include Display Record Count server behaviors to indicate which records are visible in the page and the total number of records in the database (Records *x* to *y* of *z*).

To create the master page:

▶ 1. In the Server Behaviors panel, click **Recordset**, right-click the selected behavior, and then click **Copy** on the context menu.

▶ 2. Open the **database_details.php** page in Design view, right-click in the Server Behaviors panel, and then click **Paste** on the context menu. The Recordset behavior is pasted in the database_details.php page.

▶ 3. Place the insertion point in the heading line after the heading text, press the **Right** arrow key to move the insertion point past the heading text and the h1 tag and to the next line.

▶ 4. Click the **Discover** text in the bar at the top of the Document window, and then click the **Yes** button in the Script warning dialog box to enable Dreamweaver to discover any dynamically related files. If another bar appears indicating that the page has server processing directives that Design view cannot display, close it.

▶ 5. Open the **database.php** page in Design view, right-click in the Server Behaviors panel, and then click **Paste** on the context menu to paste the Recordset behavior into the page.

▶ 6. Place the insertion point in the heading line, press the **Right** arrow key to move the insertion point past the heading text and past the h1 tag, and then press the **Enter** key, if necessary, to move the insertion point to the next line.

▶ 7. Click the **Discover** text in the bar at the top of the Document window, then click the **Yes** button in the Script warning dialog box to enable Dreamweaver to discover any dynamically related files. If another bar appears indicating that the page has server processing directives that Design view cannot display, close it. Repeat this step, as needed, whenever the bar appears in the Document window.

▶ 8. In the **Data** category of the Insert panel, click the **Master Detail Page Set** button. The Insert Master-Detail Page Set dialog box opens. See Figure 9-13.

Figure 9-13 **Insert Master-Detail Page Set dialog box**

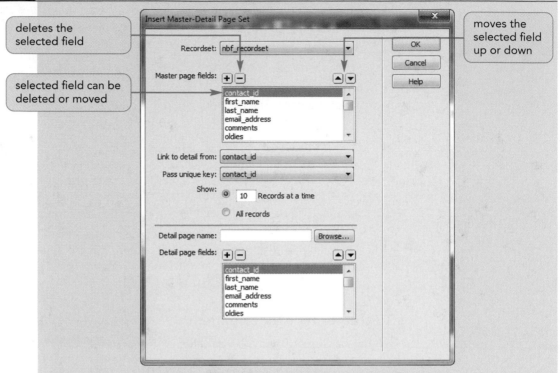

You will remove the fields from the Master page fields box that you do not want to display in the master page. You will also change the field order so that the last name appears in the first column.

▶ **9.** In the Master page fields box, click **contact_id**, if necessary, and then click the Master page fields **Remove Item** button ⊟. The selected field name is removed from the list.

▶ **10.** Repeat Step 9 to remove the following field names: **comments**, **oldies**, **rock_70s**, **rock_80s**, **metal**, **blues**, **funk**, **pop**, **bj**, **sr**, **meld**, and **um**. Only the names of fields that will be visible in the database.php page appear in the Master page fields box.

▶ **11.** In the Master page fields box, click **last_name**, and then click the Master page fields **Move item up in list** button ▲ until the last_name field is at the top of the list. The fields will display in the page in the same order they appear in the list.

▶ **12.** Click the **Link to detail from** button, and then click **last_name**. The data from the last_name field in the database.php page is now linked to the record details, which will display in the database_details.php page.

You will set the record details to display in the database_details.php page. As with the master page, you will delete unneeded fields and change the field order for the detail page.

To create the detail page:

1. Click the **Browse** button next to the Detail page name box, click the **database_details.php** page in the Select Detail Page dialog box, and then click the **OK** button. The page name appears in the Detail page name box.

2. In the Detail page fields list, click **contact_id**, if necessary, and then click the **Remove Item** button ⊟. The field name is removed from the list and will not be displayed in the database_details.php page. See Figure 9-14.

Figure 9-14   **Completed Insert Master-Detail Page Set dialog box**

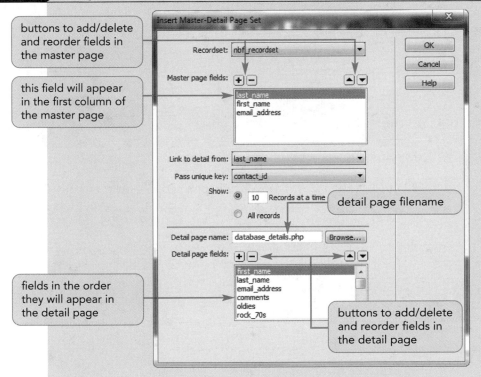

buttons to add/delete and reorder fields in the master page

this field will appear in the first column of the master page

detail page filename

fields in the order they will appear in the detail page

buttons to add/delete and reorder fields in the detail page

3. Click the **OK** button. The dialog box closes, and the master/detail pages are complete.

Dreamweaver adds elements to the pages so you can view the data collected in the database as well as the details of selected records. Before continuing, you will upload the pages to the remote server and preview the pages in a browser.

To view the database_details.php page:

1. In Design view or Code view, move all the additional content inserted into the database.php page into the content div, below the heading, if necessary, and delete any extra blank lines between the heading text and the content.

2. Close the CSS Styles panel so that you can see more of the information in the Server Behaviors panel.

3. Save the database.php page, and then upload the page and dependent files to your remote server. Dreamweaver added elements to the page so you can view the data collected in the database. See Figure 9-15.

Figure 9-15 database.php page

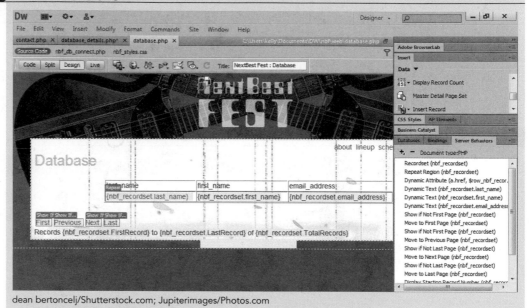

dean bertoncelj/Shutterstock.com; Jupiterimages/Photos.com

▶ **4.** Click the **database_details.php** tab to view the page. Dreamweaver also added elements to this page so you can view the details of records selected in the database.php page.

▶ **5.** In Design view or Code view, move all the new content into the content div, below the heading, if necessary, and delete any extra blank lines from the page. See Figure 9-16.

Figure 9-16 database_details.php page

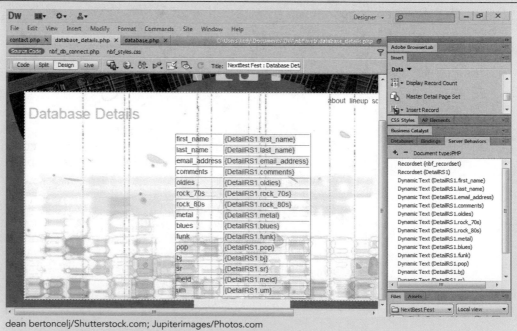

dean bertoncelj/Shutterstock.com; Jupiterimages/Photos.com

▶ **6.** Save the database_details.php page, and then upload the page and dependent files to your remote server.

7. Click the **database.php** tab, and then preview the page in a browser, clicking the **No** button when Dreamweaver prompts you to update the files on the testing server because you have already done that. The data you collected from the form in the contact.php page appears in the browser window. See Figure 9-17.

Figure 9-17 | database.php page previewed in a browser

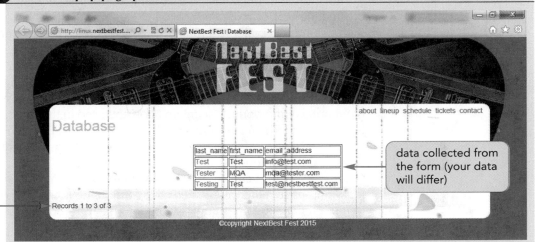

you might see a different number of records

Used with permission from Microsoft Corporation; dean bertoncelj/Shutterstock.com; Jupiterimages/Photos.com

> **Trouble?** If you see more than the one record you entered into the contact form, you are sharing the database with classmates and the database will include all the entries that have been submitted. In a professional environment, this would probably not be the case.

8. Click a link to view the details of a record. The details are displayed in the database_details.php page.

9. On the browser toolbar, click the **Back** button to return to the database.php page, and then click another record, if available.

10. Close the browser, and then close all of the pages.

Next, you will create a form in the login.php page in which users can enter their username and password to gain access to the database.php page.

Written Communication: Copying and Pasting Code

PROSKILLS

As you use more advanced techniques, you will begin to work with code more frequently. When you want the same functionality in two different places, a good technique is to copy the code from one location and paste it in the other location. Not only does this technique save you time, it also eliminates the chance of mistyping the code. It is also an acceptable technique to copy and paste code from other code sources that are "available to the public" such as sample code sites and books that teach coding techniques. When copying and pasting code from one source to another, paste the copied code into a style-free text editor such as TextPad or Notepad and remove any formatting from the text before pasting it into the code of your Web pages. This prevents hard-to-trace code errors that arise from pasting formatted text in code.

Creating a Login Page to Protect Back-End Pages

Data collected from a Web site and stored in a database is often displayed in Web pages. This convenience enables you to view the data from any computer that is connected to the Internet. However, most businesses do not want the general public to have access to this type of proprietary information. One way to restrict the access to Web pages is to require users to log in before they can view the pages. This protects the data from unauthorized access. To add this functionality, you must:

- **Create a table in the database that holds usernames and passwords.** The team that created the SQL you used to create the database included an administrative table with columns to collect usernames and passwords. They also added one username (nextbest) and one password (zergrush) in the table. You will use the username and password included in the database to create and test the login.php page.
- **Create a page that enables users to create accounts by entering a unique username and password.** Because only one member of the NextBest Fest staff is in charge of monitoring and reporting the information collected in the database, you will not create this page now. The team member will use the supplied username and password to log in to protected pages. At another point, the team will create additional pages to enable users to create unique usernames and passwords.
- **Create a page that enables users to log in to the site.** You have already created the login.php page. Now you will create a form in the login.php page that allows users to input their username and password information. You will add the Log In User server behavior to the page, which will check the database when a user submits the form to ensure that the username and password are valid. If login is successful, the database.php page will appear in the user's browser window. If login is unsuccessful, the access_denied.html page will be displayed in the browser window.
- **Restrict access to the pages.** You add the Restrict Access To Page server behavior to the pages that you want to protect; in this case, the database.php and database_details.php pages. After this behavior is added to the pages, users who are not logged in will be sent to the access_denied.html page.

You will create the form in the login.php page, and then add the Log In User server behavior to the page.

To add content to the login.php page:

▶ 1. Open the **login.php** page in Design view, place the insertion point at the right of the heading text after the closing h1 tag, and then press the **Right** arrow key or the **Enter** key as needed to move the insertion point to the next line.

▶ 2. Insert a form in the page, and then, in the Property inspector, type **loginform** in the Form ID box. For this form, it is not necessary to enter information for the other attributes in the Property inspector because you will add behaviors to control the form.

▶ 3. Click inside of the form area (the dotted red lines), and then insert a table with **3** rows, **2** columns, **80%** table width, **2** cell padding, **0** border thickness, **2** cell spacing, and no header. A table with three rows and two columns is inserted into the form.

▶ 4. Set the alignment of the left column of the table to **Right** and **Top**, and then set the alignment of the right column of the table to **Left** and **Top**.

▶ 5. Click in the first cell of the table, type **User name:** (including the colon), press the **Tab** key to move the insertion point to the upper-right cell, and then insert a text field.

▶ 6. Click the **OK** button to close the Input Tag Accessibility Attributes dialog box, and then select the text field.

7. In the Property inspector, type **username** as the ID, set the Char width to **40**, and then set Max chars to **20**.

8. Click in the middle-left cell of the table, type **Password:** (including the colon), press the **Tab** key to move the insertion point to the next cell, and then insert a text field with **password** as the ID, **40** Char width, and **20** Max chars.

9. Click in the lower-right cell of the table, insert a button, and then set the button name and value to **Login**. See Figure 9-18.

Figure 9-18 ▶ **Form in the login.php page**

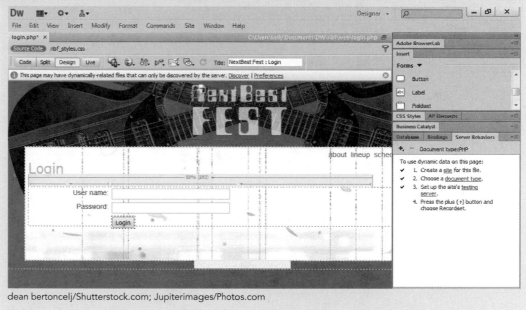

dean bertoncelj/Shutterstock.com; Jupiterimages/Photos.com

Next, you will add the Log In User server behavior to the page, which will verify the submitted username and password.

To add server behaviors to the login.php page:

1. Select the **Login** button in the form.

2. In the **Data** category of the Insert panel, click the **User Authentication button arrow**, and then click **Log In User**. The Log In User dialog box opens.

3. Click the **Validate using connection** button, and then click **nbf_db_connect**.

4. Click the **Table** button, and then click **admin**.

5. Click the **Username column** button, and then click **username**.

6. Click the **Password column** button, and then click **password**.

7. Click the **Browse** button next to the If login succeeds, go to box, click the **database.php** page in the Select File dialog box, and then click the **OK** button. This sets the database.php page to display in the browser window if the submitted username and password are listed in the database.

8. Click the **Browse** button next to the If login fails, go to box, click the **access_denied.html** page in the Select File dialog box, and then click the **OK** button. This sets the access_denied.html page to display in the browser window if the submitted username and password are not listed in the database. See Figure 9-19.

Figure 9-19   **Log In User dialog box**

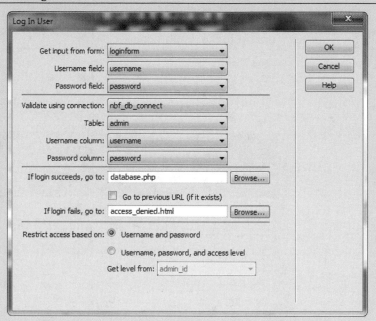

9. Click the **OK** button. The Log In User server behavior is added to the page.

10. Save the page, and then upload the page and the dependent files to your remote server.

You will add a meta refresh tag to the access_denied.html page, which tells the browser to automatically refresh the page (by reloading the current page or going to a different page) after a certain amount of time. You will also add text to indicate that access was denied to that user.

To add a meta refresh tag and content to the access_denied.html page:

1. Open the **access_denied.html** page in Design view.

2. In the **Common** category of the Insert panel, click the **Head button arrow**, and then click **Refresh**. The Refresh dialog box opens.

3. In the Delay box, type **4**, and then, in the Go to URL box, type **login.php**. See Figure 9-20.

Figure 9-20	Refresh dialog box

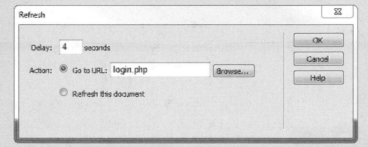

4. Click the **OK** button.

5. Place the insertion point after the heading text and after the closing h1 tag, press the **Right** arrow key or the **Enter** key, if necessary, to move the insertion point to the next line, and then type **Your access was denied. Please enter your login ID and password again.** (including the period).

6. Save the page, and then upload the page and the dependent files to your remote server.

Before you continue, you will test the login.php page.

To test the login.php page:

1. Preview the login.php page in a browser. The Update Copy on Testing Server dialog box opens.

2. Click the **Yes** button to ensure that the most recent copy of the page is on both the testing and remote servers. The Dependent Files dialog box opens.

3. Click the **Yes** button to ensure that all the dependent files are current on both the testing and remote servers. The login.php page appears in the browser window. You will enter an invalid username and password.

   Trouble? If the message, "Warning: session_start():" followed by a file path and "failed: Permission denied" appears when you test the page on your remote server, you might need to adjust the permissions on your Web server's temporary directory (usually tmp) so that it is writable by the server. Contact your ISP or technical support person for assistance.

4. Type **test** in the User name box, type **random** in the Password box, and then click the **Login** button. The login information is invalid, so the access_denied.html page is displayed in the browser window. After four seconds, the login.php page is redisplayed. Now, you will enter a valid username and password.

5. Type **nextbest** in the User name box, type **zergrush** in the Password box, and then click the **Login** button. The database.php page is displayed in the browser window.

6. Close the browser, and then close the pages.

Finally, you will protect the database.php and database_details.php pages from unauthorized access by adding the Restrict Access server behavior to the pages.

To restrict access to the database.php and database_details.php pages:

1. Open the **database.php** page in Design view.

2. In the **Data** category of the Insert panel, click the **User Authentication button arrow**, and then click **Restrict Access To Page**. The Restrict Access To Page dialog box opens.

3. In the If access denied, go to box, type **access_denied.html**. See Figure 9-21.

Figure 9-21	Restrict Access To Page dialog box

4. Click the **OK** button, save the page, and then upload the page and the dependent files to your remote server and update the copy on the testing server if asked.

5. Open the **database_details.php** page in Design view, and then repeat Steps 2 through 4 to restrict access to that page. You will test the behavior you added to the pages.

6. Preview the database.php page in a browser. Because you are not logged in, the database.php page does not display in the browser window. Instead, the access_denied.html page is displayed for four seconds, and then the login.php page is displayed.

    Trouble? If the database.php page does appear, you did not close the browser window after you logged in and you are still logged in. Close any open browser windows, and then repeat Step 6.

7. Close the browser, and then close the pages.

In this session, you created database-driven Web pages for the NextBest Fest site using MySQL and PHP for a Linux server. The database functionality will enable Gage to collect data about the preferences of NextBest Fest's customers. Analyzing this data will help shape future marketing plans for NextBest Fest.

REVIEW

Session 9.1 Quick Check

1. What is a database?
2. What are two popular databases used by medium and small Web sites?
3. In addition to selecting a database, you must also select a(n) _____ that you will use to create server behaviors.
4. What language do you use to create server behaviors when you use a MySQL database?
5. What is a server behavior?
6. Why do you need the Recordset behavior?
7. Why would you create a login page?
8. What is the purpose of the meta refresh tag?

SESSION 9.2 VISUAL OVERVIEW

A **database-driven Web site** is a Web site that uses a database to gather, display, or manipulate information.

A **database** is a collection of information that is arranged for ease and speed of search and retrieval, and is usually associated with a specific software package such as Microsoft Access or a specific database server such as MySQL.

A **recordset** is a temporary collection of data retrieved from a database and stored on the application server that generates the Web page when that page is loaded in a browser window.

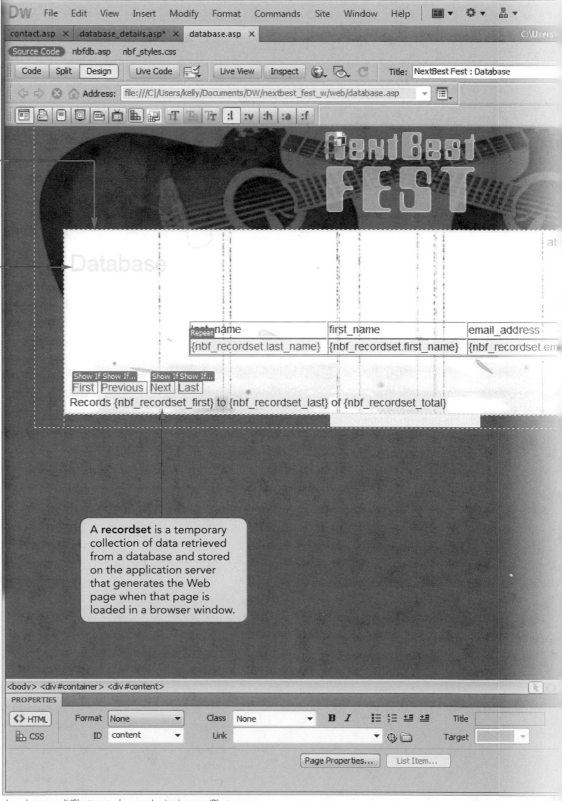

dean bertoncelj/Shutterstock.com; Jupiterimages/Photos.com

ADDING DATABASE FUNCTIONALITY

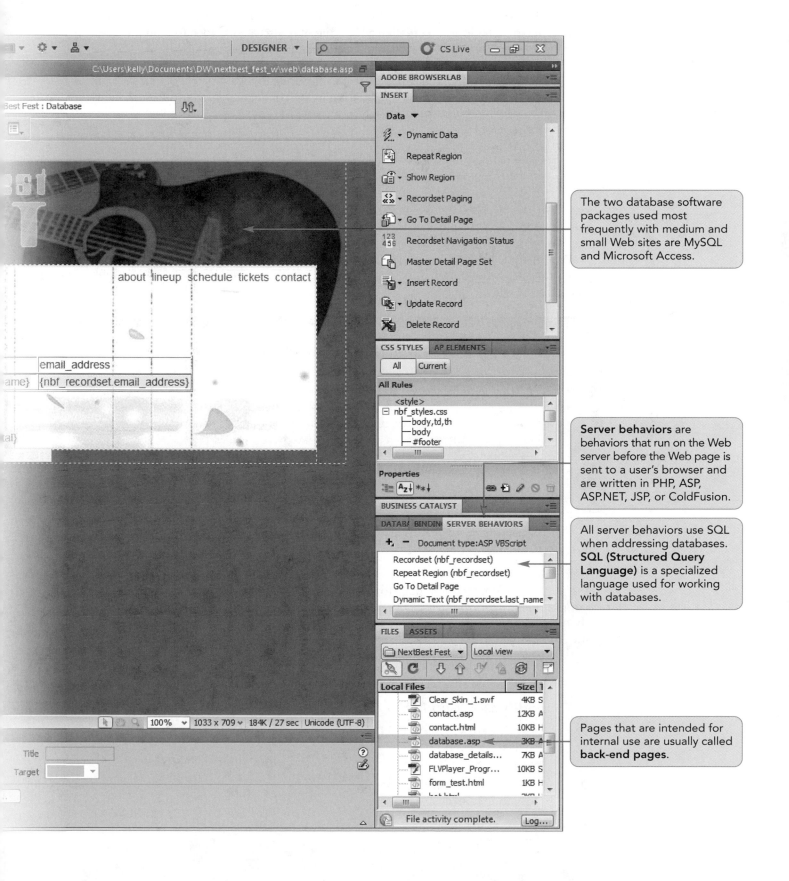

The two database software packages used most frequently with medium and small Web sites are MySQL and Microsoft Access.

Server behaviors are behaviors that run on the Web server before the Web page is sent to a user's browser and are written in PHP, ASP, ASP.NET, JSP, or ColdFusion.

All server behaviors use SQL when addressing databases. **SQL (Structured Query Language)** is a specialized language used for working with databases.

Pages that are intended for internal use are usually called **back-end pages**.

Creating Database-Driven Pages Using Access and ASP

Adding database functionality to a Web site can be quite complex. Just as it is a good idea to make a plan prior to creating a Web site, it is also a good idea to plan the database-driven portion of the site in advance. Gage created a site plan for the new portion of the NextBest Fest site.

Based on Gage's plan, the NextBest Fest technical team will create a database to store the information collected from the form in the contact.html page. You will modify the form to work with the database. You will create the pages that you will need for the new portion of the site: thankyou.html, access_denied.html, database.asp, database_details.asp, and login.asp. You will upload the database file provided by the technical team to the remote server, and then you will connect the site to the database. Next, you will add server behaviors to the pages you created so that the form data can be sent to and stored in the database and so that the database.asp and database_details.asp pages display the information stored in the database. Finally, you will create a login.asp page and add code to the back-end pages to prevent unauthorized users from viewing the content of those pages.

When the database-driven pages are complete, the information received from users who completed the form in the contact.html page will be stored in a database that only authorized users can access.

REFERENCE

Creating Database-Driven Pages for a Windows Server

- Create the Web pages you need.
- Upload to your remote server a database file in which to store data.
- Add server behaviors to connect the site to the database.
- Add server behaviors to store submitted data in the database and to view the data collected in the database from within designated Web pages.
- Create a login page.
- Add code to the back-end pages to prevent unauthorized users from viewing the content of those pages.

Modifying the Form

Before you create the database-driven pages of the NextBest Fest site, you will modify the form in the contact.html page to work with the database that you will place on your remote server. You will delete the list box with the band names from the form, and then create a series of check boxes to collect this same information. You are replacing the list box with the check boxes to keep things simpler because the list box, as the database storage element, requires more steps and custom scripts to process data.

To modify the form in the contact.html page:

▶ **1.** Reset Dreamweaver to the **Designer** workspace, minimize the Business Catalyst panel, open the Files panel, open the **NextBest Fest** site you modified in Tutorial 8, and then open the **contact.html** page in Design view.

▶ **2.** In the right column near the bottom of the form, select the list box, and then press the **Delete** key. The list box is removed from the form.

▶ **3.** In the same location as the deleted list box, insert a **checkbox group**. The Checkbox Group dialog box opens.

4. Type **band_list** in the Name box, and then add the following labels and values for the check boxes: **Bon-Journo / bj**, **Silver Rail / sr**, **More Exquisite Less Dead / meld**, **Undead Milkmen / um**.

5. Click the **Line breaks** option button, if necessary, and then click the **OK** button. The checkbox group is added to the form.

6. Select the sentence in the left column next to the new checkbox group, and then type **Select all of the bands that you enjoy.** (including the period). See Figure 9-22.

Figure 9-22	Modified form

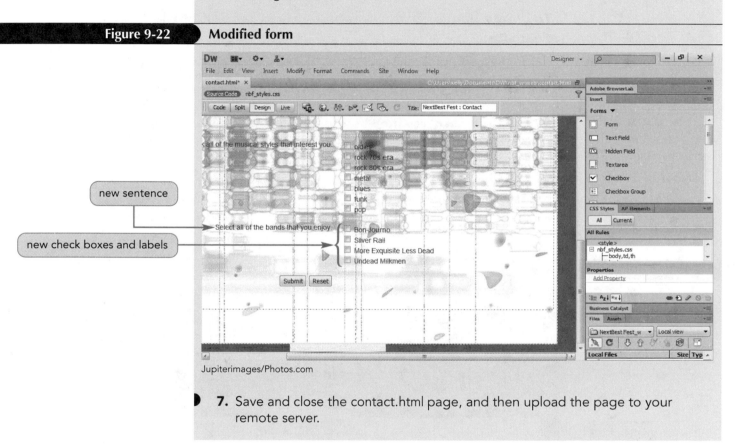

new sentence

new check boxes and labels

Jupiterimages/Photos.com

7. Save and close the contact.html page, and then upload the page to your remote server.

Creating New Pages

You need five pages for the database-driven portion of the NextBest Fest site. You will create all of these pages now so that they are available when you need them. According to Gage's plan for the database-driven portion of the site, you will create the following pages:

- **thankyou.html.** A page thanking the user for his or her submission that appears when the user submits the form in the contact.html page.
- **access_denied.html.** A page informing the user that the wrong username or password has been entered that appears when a user attempts to log in on the login.asp page with incorrect information or if a user attempts to access a password-protected page without logging in. After a four-second delay, the user will be returned to the login.asp page.
- **database.asp.** A page showing an overview of the data stored in the database. After the login.asp page is created, users cannot access this page unless they log in.

- **database_details.asp.** A page showing the details of a selected record that appears when a user clicks a record in the database.asp page. After the login.asp page is created, users cannot access this page unless they log in.
- **login.asp.** A page in which a user enters his or her username and password and then clicks the Login button. If the information is correct, the database.asp page appears; if the information is incorrect, the access_denied.html page appears.

Three of the pages you will create are ASP pages. You can create an ASP page by typing .asp as the file extension when you name the page.

To create pages for the database-driven portion of the NextBest Fest site:

TIP

You can press the Ctrl+D keys to duplicate the selected page.

1. In the Files panel, duplicate the **contact.html** page. A new page named contact - Copy.html appears at the bottom of the files list.

2. In the Files panel, rename the contact - Copy.html page as **thankyou.html**.

3. Open the **thankyou.html** page in Design view, and then edit the page title to replace the word *Contact* with **Thank You**. The new page title appears.

4. Change the page heading to **Thank You**.

5. Delete all the content below the heading and above the footer, type **Thank you for submitting your information.** (including the period) in the line below the heading text, and then make sure the sentence is in the **Paragraph** format. See Figure 9-23.

Figure 9-23   New thankyou.html page

dean bertoncelj/Shutterstock.com; Jupiterimages/Photos.com

6. Save and close the page, and then upload the page to your remote server.

7. Repeat Steps 1 through 6 to create the following pages, typing .asp as the file extension for the last three pages in Step 2 and not typing any new page content in Step 5:

Filename	Page Title	Page Heading
access_denied.html	NextBest Fest : Access Denied	Access Denied
database.asp	NextBest Fest : Database	Database
database_details.asp	NextBest Fest : Database Details	Database Details
login.asp	NextBest Fest : Login	Login

Trouble? If a bar appears across the top of the Document window of the .asp pages stating that, "Dynamically related files cannot be discovered because a testing server is not defined.", ignore it. You will set up a testing server.

Now that you have modified the form and created the new pages, you are ready to upload the database to your remote server.

Uploading a Database to a Remote Server

You must upload the database for the NextBest Fest site to your remote server so that it can send data to and receive data from Web pages or Web applications. For example, in the NextBest Fest site, the form in the contact.html page will send data to the database that you place on the remote server.

If your instructor has already uploaded the database to your remote server, you should read but not complete the next set of steps. In this case, you will be sharing the same database with your classmates, so you might see data that you did not add in the database or you might observe that data you added is removed. If you are uploading the database on your remote server, you need to contact your ISP (or your IT Department) and have a technical support person create a directory named "Database" on the remote server and provide you with the exact file path to the directory as well as the FTP host, host directory, login, and password you should use. The directory must be writable by the IUSR_SERVER account. (Instructors should verify that the new directory is accessible to all their students.) After the database directory has been created, you can then upload the nbf_db.mdb file located in the Dreamweaver9\Tutorial folder included with your Data Files to the database directory on the remote server.

The following steps show how to use Dreamweaver to FTP the database file to your remote server. To do this, you will need to add a server to the NextBest Fest site because the database will, most likely, be located outside of the root folders that you designated for the NextBest Fest site on your Web server. The new server will be set up to upload the database to the correct folder on your remote Web server. If your instructor has already uploaded the database for you, read the following steps and then continue working in the "Connecting a Web Site to a Database" section.

To upload the database to the Web server:

1. On the menu bar, click **Site**, and then click **Manage Sites**. The Manage Sites dialog box opens.

2. Click the **NextBest Fest** site, and then click the **Edit** button 🖉. The Site Setup for NextBest Fest dialog box opens.

3. Click the **Servers** tab, and then click the **Add new Server** button ➕ to open the Servers Basic settings. See Figure 9-24.

Figure 9-24 **Site Setup dialog box opened to the Servers Basic tab**

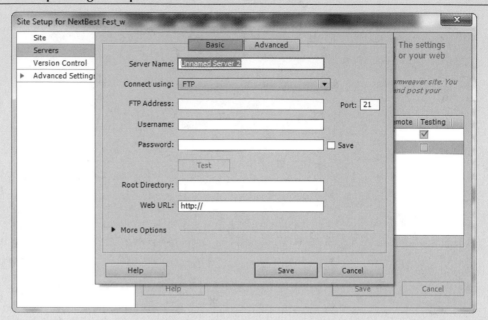

4. Type **remote_database_ftp** in the Server Name box, click the **Connect using** button and click **FTP**, if necessary, and then type the FTP host, host directory, login, and password that your ISP provided into the appropriate boxes (make sure the root directory ends with /Database/).

5. Click **More Options**, if necessary, and then click the **Use passive FTP** check box to insert a check mark, and then click the **Save** button in the dialog box. The new server is added to the list of servers for the site. See Figure 9-25. You must uncheck the Testing check box and check the Remote check box for the new server.

Figure 9-25 **New remote_database_ftp server added to the server list**

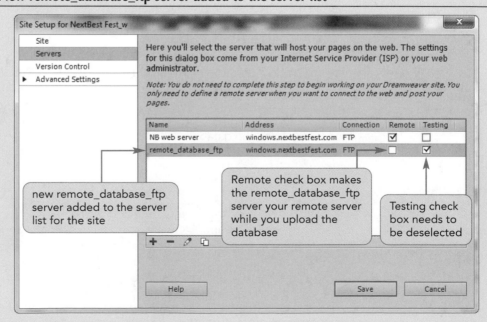

6. Click the **Testing** check box for the remote_database_ftp server to uncheck the box, and then click the **Remote** check box for the remote_database_ftp server to select it. This unchecks the Remote check box for the NB web server; you will switch it back after you have finished uploading the database.

7. Click the **Save** button, click the **OK** button to re-create the cache, if necessary, and then click the **Done** button to close the Manage Sites dialog box.

Be sure to copy the database file to the specified location so that it will function properly.

8. Navigate to the **Dreamweaver9\Tutorial** folder included with your Data Files, copy the **nbf_db.mdb** file, and then place a copy of the file in the root folder for the site.

9. Select the copied file in the Files panel and upload the file to the new site. Because you are using the new server, the file is uploaded to the database folder. Now you can reset the NB web server as the remote server.

10. Open the Manage Sites dialog box, edit the **NextBest Fest** site, click the **Remote** check box for the NB web server in the Servers list to select it, click the **Save** button, click the **OK** button to re-create the cache, and then close the Manage Sites dialog box.

Connecting a Web Site to a Database

The database is copied to the remote server, and you are ready to connect the site to the database. When you open a Web page in the Document window that is not connected to the database, the Server Behaviors panel displays an interactive list of steps for setting up Dreamweaver to connect the site to the database. Clicking the linked text in each step opens the dialog boxes needed to complete that step. A check mark appears at the left of each step to indicate that all the necessary information has been entered and the step is completed.

The following are the three main steps for connecting a page to the database:

1. **Create a site for this file.** This step is checked because you already set the local and remote information for the site when you created the site definition.

2. **Choose a document type.** In this step, you specify which document type you are using to create server behaviors. When you click the link text in Step 2, the Choose Document Type dialog box opens, and you can select ASP JavaScript, ASP VBScript, ASP.NET C#, ASP.NET VB, ColdFusion, ColdFusion component, JSP, or PHP as the document type. For the NextBest Fest site, you will use ASP VBScript. If your instructor or IT Department informs you that you will be using a different document type, your steps might differ somewhat from the remaining steps in this section. If this is the case, ask your instructor or IT Department for help.

3. **Set up the site's testing server.** In this step, you specify the testing server in the site definition. You cannot preview dynamic pages from within Dreamweaver until you specify a folder in which the dynamic pages can be processed. Dreamweaver uses this folder to generate dynamic content and connect to the database while you work. For the NextBest Fest site, you will use the root folder you created on your remote server for your NextBest Fest site because the server usually runs an application server that can handle the dynamic pages. You can, however, specify a different location for the testing server as long as it can handle dynamic pages. When you set up the testing server for a professional site that is already live, you might designate a separate folder on another server where you can test the pages without affecting the live site. When you click the link text in Step 3, the Site Definition dialog box opens to the Testing Server category. The information for the remote server is displayed by default, but you might need to delete the first part of the file path in the URL prefix box.

INSIGHT

Comparing Modified Times of Local and Server Files

Some of the files required for server-side processing are located outside of the Web page. Therefore, whenever you upload pages to the remote or testing server, you must also upload dependent files. As you upload files, a dialog box might open indicating that you are trying to overwrite newer files with older files. This occurs because Dreamweaver has a feature that compares the modified time of local files with the modified time of server files. If the time on either the server or your computer is inaccurate and your local computer time is behind the server time, Dreamweaver sees the file on the server as newer and notifies you that you are overwriting a newer file with an older file. Click the OK button each time you see this message.

You will open the contact.html page and complete Steps 2 and 3 in the Server Behaviors panel.

TIP

You can press the Ctrl+F9 keys to open and close the Server Behaviors panel.

To select the document type and set the testing server:

1. Open the **contact.html** page in Design view, open the Server Behaviors panel, and then collapse the CSS Styles panel.

2. In the Server Behaviors panel, click the **document type** link. The Choose Document Type dialog box opens. See Figure 9-26.

Figure 9-26 Choose Document Type dialog box

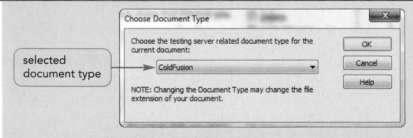

Trouble? If the document type in your list is different from the document type in the figure, your default is set differently. You will select the document type in Step 3.

3. Click the **document type** button, select **ASP VBScript**, and then click the **OK** button. The Update Files dialog box opens. You will update the links in all the listed files.

4. Click the **Update** button to update the links. The page extension for the contact page changes to .asp and the Update Files dialog box opens, indicating that the contact.asp page could not be updated. You will update the link in the contact.asp page yourself.

5. Click the **OK** button. A check mark appears in the Server Behaviors panel beside Step 2 to indicate this step is complete (the check mark might not appear immediately).

Trouble? If the background image disappears from the pages of your site when you view them in Dreamweaver, don't worry. The background image will be visible when you preview the page in a browser and when you view the pages over the Internet.

Trouble? If your instructor or IT Department informed you that you will be using something other than the ASP VBScript document type, you will select that document type and your steps might differ somewhat from the remaining steps in this section. If this is the case, ask your instructor or IT Department for help.

6. In the Document window, select **contact** in the navigation text, and then, in the Property inspector, delete **.html** from the Link box and type **.asp**. The contact link is updated.

7. Save the page, and then upload the page to your remote server, including the dependent files. (The contact.html page remains in the site's root folder but is no longer used.)

8. In the Server Behaviors panel, click the **testing server** link in Step 3. The Site Setup for NextBest Fest dialog box opens with the Servers tab displayed.

9. Click the **Testing** check box for the NB web server. The Remote check box is already checked. See Figure 9-27.

Figure 9-27   Completed Testing Server information

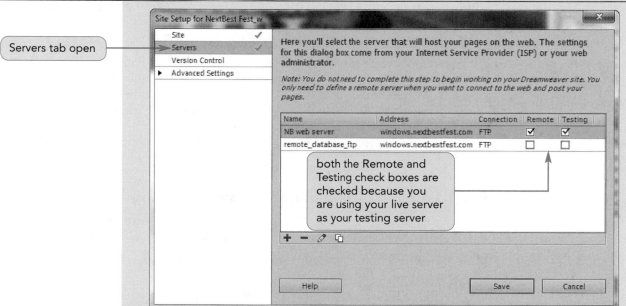

Servers tab open

both the Remote and Testing check boxes are checked because you are using your live server as your testing server

10. Click the **Save** button. The Testing Server information is set, and a check mark appears beside Step 3 in the Server Behaviors panel.

Trouble? If a dialog box opens, stating that the site URL prefix for the testing server does not match the site URL prefix specified in the HTTP address for the site, your server includes a public_html directory that stores all the content that viewers can access with a Web browser. However, when visitors view the Web site, the URL they enter does not include the public_html directory. Therefore, these paths are different. Click the OK button now and whenever this dialog box appears.

Adding Server Behaviors

Dreamweaver provides a list of prewritten server behaviors in the Server Behaviors panel once the page is connected to the database. You include these server behaviors in the page to extend the functionality of the page and to enable you to retrieve and display the data from the database. You will include two server behaviors in the contact.asp page: Recordset and Insert Record.

The Recordset behavior enables you to specify which data you want to retrieve from the database and display in the Web page. A recordset is a temporary collection of data retrieved from a database and stored on the application server that generates the Web page when that page is loaded in a browser window. You specify the database and the records (or data) to include in the recordset when you set the parameters for the behavior. A recordset can include all the data in the database or a subset of the data. You must add the server-side behaviors that will create the recordset in which to store and retrieve data before you can use a database as a content source for a dynamic Web page. The server discards the recordset when it is no longer needed. When you use ASP and an Access database, you must input a custom connection string that Dreamweaver inserts into the page's server behaviors to set up the recordset. A **connection string** is all of the information that a Web application server needs to connect to a database. The connection string begins and ends with quotation marks. The connection string has two parts:

- **Provider.** The name of the interface that provides ASP pages with access to the specific type of database you are using.
- **Data source.** The complete path to the database on the server.

The Insert Record behavior enables you to specify what will happen to the information collected from the Web page (in this case, when the form is submitted). You can specify in which database the data will be placed, where the data will be stored in the database, what columns will be included, and so on. It also lets you select the page that appears in the browser window once the form is submitted.

You will create a recordset for the contact.asp page.

To create the recordset for the contact.asp page:

1. At the top of the Server Behaviors panel, click the **Add behavior** button ⊞, and then click **Recordset (Query)**. The Recordset dialog box opens. See Figure 9-28.

Figure 9-28   Recordset dialog box

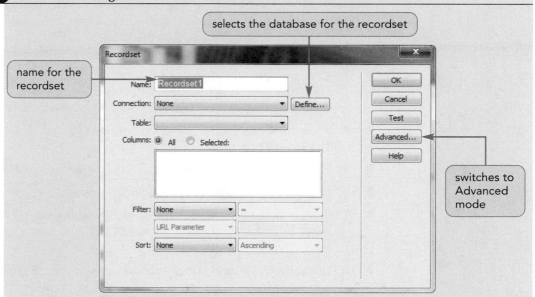

selects the database for the recordset

name for the recordset

switches to Advanced mode

> **2.** Click the **Advanced** button to switch the Recordset dialog box to Advanced mode, and then click the **Define** button next to the Connection box. The Connections for Site 'NextBest Fest' dialog box opens.

> **3.** Click the **New** button, and then click **Custom Connection String**. The Custom Connection String dialog box opens. See Figure 9-29.

Figure 9-29   Custom Connection String dialog box

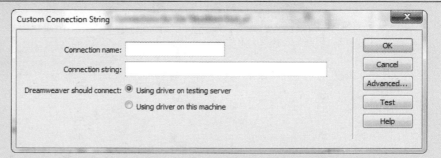

> **4.** In the Connection name box, type **nbfdb**. This is an internal name that is visible only when you are working in Dreamweaver.

> **5.** In the Connection string box, type **Provider=Microsoft.Jet.OLEDB.4.0; Data Source=** followed by the exact file path to your database, and then type **;** (a semicolon).

> **6.** Click the **Using driver on testing server** option button, if necessary, and then click the **Test** button. A dialog box opens, stating that the connection was made successfully.

> **Trouble?** If error messages appear when you click the Test button, you probably mistyped the connection string. Click the OK button to close the message dialog box, delete the text in the Connection string box, retype the information, and then repeat Step 6. If the test is still unsuccessful, verify the file path for your database with your instructor or technical support person and verify the information in the Testing Server category in the Site

Definition dialog box. If you still are having trouble, use an outside FTP program to upload the _mmServerScripts folder to the root directory on your remote server and on your testing server if you are using a separate testing server. In addition, verify that the IUSR_SERVER has been given written permission to the database.

7. Click the **OK** button to close the message dialog box, and then click the **OK** button to close the Custom Connection String dialog box. The database name appears in the Connections for Site 'NextBest Fest' dialog box.

8. Click the **Done** button in the Connections for Site 'NextBest Fest' dialog box. The dialog box closes.

9. In the Recordset dialog box, type **nbf_recordset** in the Name box.

10. If necessary, click the **Connection** button, and then click **nbfdb** in the list.

11. In the Database items box, expand the **Tables** list, click **contact** to select the database table, and then click the **SELECT** button to add the information to the SQL box.

12. Click the **OK** button. The Recordset behavior is added to the page and appears in the Server Behaviors panel. See Figure 9-30.

| Figure 9-30 | **Recordset behavior added to the contact.asp page** |

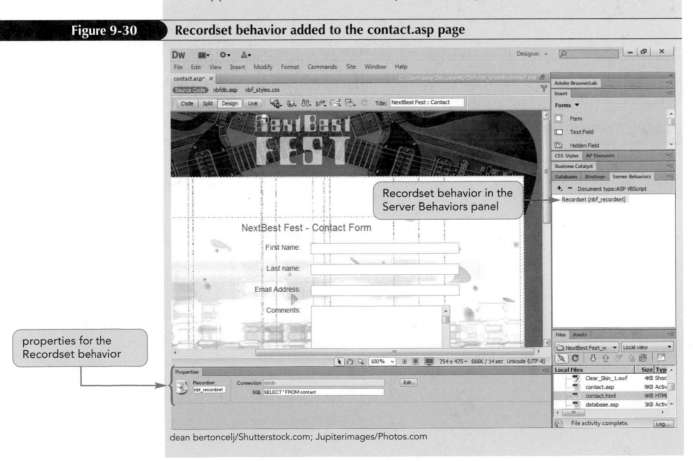

dean bertoncelj/Shutterstock.com; Jupiterimages/Photos.com

Next, you will add the Insert Record behavior to the page.

To add the Insert Record behavior:

1. At the top of the Server Behaviors panel, click the **Add behavior** button ![+], and then click **Insert Record**. The Insert Record dialog box opens.

2. Click the **Connection** button, and then click **nbfdb** to select the connection to the database.

3. Click the **Insert into table** button, and then click **contact** to select the contact table in the database.

4. Click the **Browse** button next to the After inserting, go to box. The Select File dialog box opens.

5. Click **thankyou.html** in the site's local root folder, and then click the **OK** button. The Select File dialog box closes, and the page filename appears in the After inserting, go to box.

6. Click the **Get values from** button, and then click **contact**, if necessary. The contact form's elements appear in the Form elements box, and the column headings in the contact table are displayed in the Column list. See Figure 9-31.

Figure 9-31   **Insert Record dialog box**

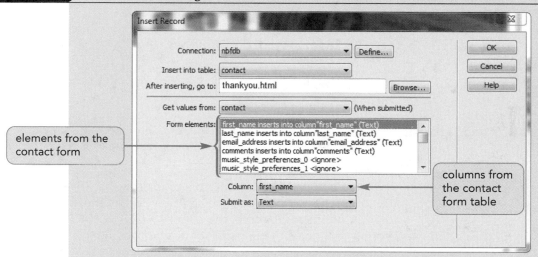

elements from the contact form

columns from the contact form table

7. In the Insert Record dialog box, click the **OK** button. The Insert Record behavior is added to the page and appears in the Server Behaviors panel. See Figure 9-32.

Figure 9-32 **Insert Record behavior added to the contact.asp page**

Insert Record behavior in the Server Behaviors panel

NextBest Fest - Contact Form

dean bertoncelj/Shutterstock.com; Jupiterimages/Photos.com

Before continuing, you will test the Insert Record behavior you added to the contact.asp page. You will upload the page to the remote server, preview the page in a browser, and then complete and submit the form. The thankyou.html page should then display.

To test the Insert Record behavior:

1. Save the page, and then upload the page and the dependent files to your remote server (update the page on the testing server, if necessary).

2. Preview the contact.asp page in a browser.

3. Enter appropriate information in the form, and then click the **Submit** button to submit the form. The thankyou.html page appears in a new browser window.

   Trouble? When you save .html files as .asp pages, Dreamweaver does not insert code that might be necessary to identify the ASP scripting language at the top of the page. If you have an ASP VBScript site, an .asp file requires the following code at the top of the page: <%@LANGUAGE="VBSCRIPT"%>. Without this code, the page might not function on the server, and Dreamweaver might not recognize or add server behaviors correctly. Close the browser, switch the contact.asp page to Code view, type the missing code at the top of the page, save and close the page, reopen the contact.asp page in Dreamweaver, and then repeat Steps 1 through 3.

4. Close the browser.

The page is connected to the database and the behaviors have been added to the page. Next, you will create back-end pages to view the data collected in the database.

Creating Back-End Pages for Viewing Data in a Database

Pages that are intended for internal use are usually called back-end pages. For the NextBest Fest site, the database.asp and database_details.asp pages are back-end pages. You will set the database.asp and database_details.asp pages to display the data that you collect in the database.

The Master Detail Page Set button in the Data category of the Insert panel enables you to create a set of pages that presents information in two levels of detail. The master page (in this case, the database.asp page) lists all the records in the recordset that you create for the page. The detail page (in this case, the database_details.asp page) displays the detail of the selected record. You determine which fields of information are displayed in the master page and which fields of information are displayed in the detail page when you set the parameters for the pages.

In addition to creating all the code needed to display the dynamic content in the pages, Dreamweaver also adds server behaviors to create a page navigation bar so you can move between the dynamic records if more records are in the database than are displayed in the page. The navigation bar includes First Page, Last Page, Previous Page, and Next Page buttons. The pages also include Display Record Count server behaviors to indicate which records are visible in the page and the total number of records in the database (Records *x* to *y* of *z*).

To create the master page:

1. In the Server Behaviors panel, click **Recordset**, right-click the selected behavior, and then click **Copy** on the context menu.

2. Open the **database_details.asp** page in Design view, right-click in the Server Behaviors panel, and then click **Paste** on the context menu. The Recordset behavior is pasted in the database_details.asp page.

3. Place the insertion point in the heading line after the heading text, and then press the **Right** arrow key to move the insertion point past the heading text to the next line.

4. Open the **database.asp** page in Design view, right-click in the Server Behaviors panel, and then click **Paste** on the context menu to paste the Recordset behavior into the page.

5. Place the insertion point in the heading line, and then press the **Right** arrow key to move the insertion point past the heading text to the next line.

6. In the **Data** category of the Insert panel, click the **Master Detail Page Set** button. The Insert Master-Detail Page Set dialog box opens. See Figure 9-33.

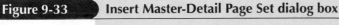

Figure 9-33   Insert Master-Detail Page Set dialog box

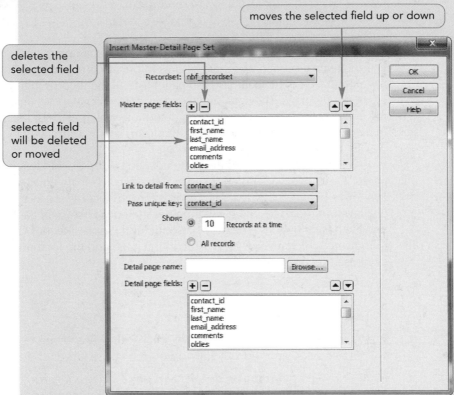

You will remove the fields from the Master page fields box that you do not want to display in the master page. You will also change the field order so that the last name will appear in the first column.

7. In the Master page fields box, click **contact_id**, and then click the Master page fields **Remove item** button ⊟. The selected field name is removed from the list.

8. Repeat Step 7 to delete the following field names: **comments**, **oldies**, **rock_70s**, **rock_80s**, **metal**, **blues**, **funk**, **pop**, **bj**, **sr**, **meld**, and **um**. Only the names of fields that will be visible in the database.asp page appear in the Master page fields box.

9. In the Master page fields box, click **last_name**, and then click the Master page fields **Move item up in list** button ▲ until the last_name field is at the top of the list. The fields will display in the page in the same order they appear in the list.

10. Click the **Link to detail from** button, and then click **last_name**. The data from the last_name field in the database.asp page is now linked to the record details, which will display in the database_details.asp page.

You will set the record details to display in the database_details.asp page. As with the master page, you will delete unneeded fields and change the field order for the detail page.

To create the detail page:

1. Click the **Browse** button next to the Detail page name box, click the **database_details.asp** page in the Select detail page dialog box, and then click the **OK** button. The page name appears in the Detail page name box.

2. In the Detail page fields list, click **contact_id**, if necessary, and then click the **Remove item** button ⊟. The field name is removed from the list and will not be displayed in the database_details.asp page. See Figure 9-34.

Figure 9-34   Completed Insert Master-Detail Page Set dialog box

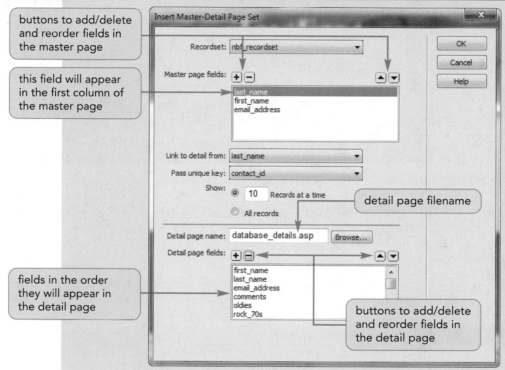

buttons to add/delete and reorder fields in the master page

this field will appear in the first column of the master page

detail page filename

fields in the order they will appear in the detail page

buttons to add/delete and reorder fields in the detail page

3. Click the **OK** button. The dialog box closes, and the master/detail pages are complete.

Dreamweaver adds elements to the pages so you can view the data collected in the database as well as the details of selected records. Before continuing, you will upload the pages to the remote server and preview the pages in a browser.

To view the database_details.asp page:

1. In Design view or Code view, move all the additional content inserted into the database.asp page into the content div, below the heading, if necessary, and remove any extra blank lines between the heading text and the content.

2. Save the database.asp page, and then upload the page to your remote server. Dreamweaver added elements to the page so you can view the data collected in the database. See Figure 9-35.

Figure 9-35 database.asp page

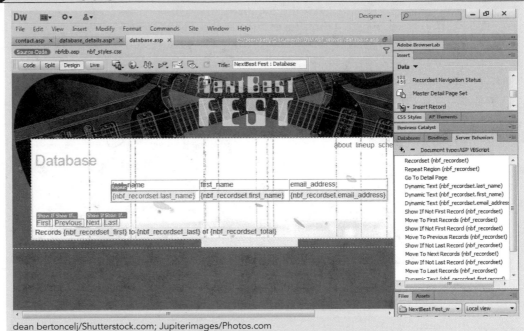

dean bertoncelj/Shutterstock.com; Jupiterimages/Photos.com

3. Click the **database_details.asp** tab to view the page. Dreamweaver also added elements to this page so you can view the details of records selected in the database.asp page.

4. In Design view or Code view, move all the new content into the content div, below the heading, if necessary, and remove any extra blank lines between the heading text and the content. See Figure 9-36.

Figure 9-36 database_details.asp page

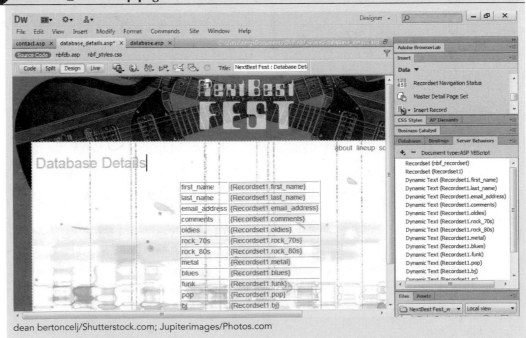

dean bertoncelj/Shutterstock.com; Jupiterimages/Photos.com

5. Save the database_details.asp page, and then upload the page to your remote server.

6. Click the **database.asp** tab, and then preview the page in a browser, clicking the **No** button when Dreamweaver prompts you to upload the changes to the testing server because you have already done that (remember, your testing server and remote server are the same). The data you collected from the form in the contact.asp page appears in the browser window. See Figure 9-37.

Figure 9-37 | **The database.asp page previewed in a browser**

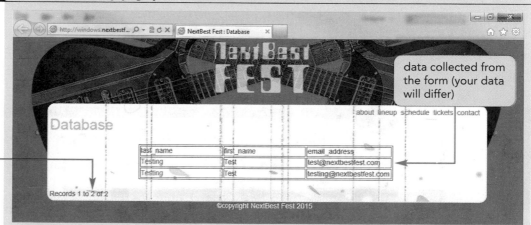

you might see a different number of records

Used with permission from Microsoft Corporation; dean bertoncelj/Shutterstock.com; Jupiterimages/Photos.com

Trouble? When you save .html files as .asp pages, sometimes Dreamweaver does not insert code that might be necessary to identify the ASP scripting language. If you have an ASP VBScript site, all the .asp files require the following code at the top of the page: <%@LANGUAGE="VBSCRIPT"%>. Without this code, the pages might not function on the server, and Dreamweaver might not recognize or add server behaviors correctly. Close the browser, switch to Code view, type the missing code at the top of the file, save and close the page, reopen it in Dreamweaver, and then repeat Steps 2 and 6.

Trouble? If you see more than the one record you entered into the contact form, you are sharing the database with classmates and the database will include all the entries that have been submitted. In a professional environment, this would probably not be the case.

7. Click a link to view the details of a record. The details are displayed in the database_details.asp page.

Trouble? If the database_details.asp page does not display in your browser window, Dreamweaver may have inserted the include file code in the wrong location, or it may have inserted the include file code in the page two times. To correct this, open the Database Details page in Dreamweaver in Code view, scroll to the top of the source code, and then locate the include file code <!--#include file="Connections/nbfdb.asp" -->. It should be inserted in the code one time on Line 2, after the <%@LANGUAGE="VBSCRIPT"%> and before the <% on Line 3, and should look like this in the page:

```
<%@LANGUAGE="VBSCRIPT"%>
<!--#include file="Connections/nbfdb.asp" -->
<%
```

If it is included twice, delete the second instance and save the page. If not, in the second line scroll down and find where it is located in the page (possibly around Line 36 or 37), select the code and drag it to the second line so that it looks like the preceding example, and then save the page and repeat Steps 5 through 7.

▶ **8.** On the browser toolbar, click the **Back** button to return to the database.asp page, and then click another record, if available.

▶ **9.** Close the browser, and then close all of the pages.

Next, you will create a form in the login.asp page in which users can enter their username and password to gain access to the database.asp page.

PROSKILLS

Written Communication: Copying and Pasting Code

As you use more advanced techniques, you will begin to work with code more frequently. When you want the same functionality in two different places, a good technique is to copy the code from one location and paste it in the other location. Not only does this technique save you time, it also eliminates the chance of mistyping the code. It is also an acceptable technique to copy and paste code from other code sources that are "available to the public" such as sample code sites and books that teach coding techniques. When copying and pasting code from one source to another, paste the copied code into a style-free text editor such as TextPad or Notepad and remove any formatting from the text before pasting it into the code of your Web pages. This prevents hard-to-trace code errors that arise from pasting formatted text in code.

Creating a Login Page to Protect Back-End Pages

Data collected from a Web site and stored in a database is often displayed in Web pages. This convenience enables you to view the data from any computer that is connected to the Internet. However, most businesses do not want the general public to have access to this type of proprietary information. One way to restrict access to Web pages is to require users to log in before they can view the pages. This protects the data from unauthorized access. To add this functionality to pages, you must:

- **Create a table in the database that holds usernames and passwords.** The team that created the database included an administrative table with columns to collect usernames and passwords. They also added one username (nextbest) and one password (zergrush) in the table. You will use the username and password included in the database to create and test the login.asp page.
- **Create a page that enables users to create accounts by entering a unique username and password.** Because only one member of the NextBest Fest staff is in charge of monitoring and reporting the information collected in the database, you will not create this page now. The team member will use the supplied username and password to log in to protected pages. At another point, the team will create additional pages to enable users to create unique usernames and passwords.

- **Create a page that enables users to log in to the site.** You have already created the login.asp page. Now you will create a form in the login.asp page that allows users to input their username and password information. You will add the Log In User server behavior to the page, which will check the database when a user submits the form to ensure that the username and password are valid. If login is successful, the database.asp page will appear in the user's browser window. If login is unsuccessful, the access_denied.html page will be displayed in the browser window.
- **Restrict access to the pages.** You add the Restrict Access To Page server behavior to the pages that you want to protect; in this case, the database.asp and database_details.asp pages. After this behavior is added to the pages, users who are not logged in will be sent to the access_denied.html page.

You will create the form in the login.asp page, and then add the Log In User server behavior to the page.

To add content to the login.asp page:

▶ 1. Open the **login.asp** page in Design view, place the insertion point at the right of the heading text after the closing h1 tag, and then press the **Right** arrow key. The insertion point moves to the next line.

▶ 2. Insert a form into the page, and then, in the Property inspector, type **loginform** in the Form ID box. For this form, it is not necessary to enter information for the other attributes in the Property inspector because you will add behaviors to control the form.

▶ 3. Click inside of the form area (the dotted red lines), and then insert a table with **3** rows, **2** columns, **80%** table width, **2** cell padding, **0** border thickness, **2** cell spacing, and no header. A table with three rows and two columns is inserted into the form.

▶ 4. Set the alignment of the left column of the table to **Right** and **Top**, and then set the alignment of the right column of the table to **Left** and **Top**.

▶ 5. Click in the first cell of the table, type **User name:** (including the colon), press the **Tab** key to move the insertion point to the upper-right cell, and then insert a text field.

▶ 6. Click the **OK** button to close the Input Tag Accessibility Attributes dialog box, and then select the text field.

▶ 7. In the Property inspector, type **username** as the ID, set the Char width to **40**, and then set Max chars to **20**.

▶ 8. Click in the middle-left cell of the table, type **Password:** (including the colon), press the **Tab** key to move the insertion point to the next cell, and then insert a text field with **password** as the ID, **40** Char width, and **20** Max chars.

▶ 9. Click in the lower-right cell of the table, insert a button, and then set the button name and value to **Login**. See Figure 9-38.

Figure 9-38   **Form in the login.asp page**

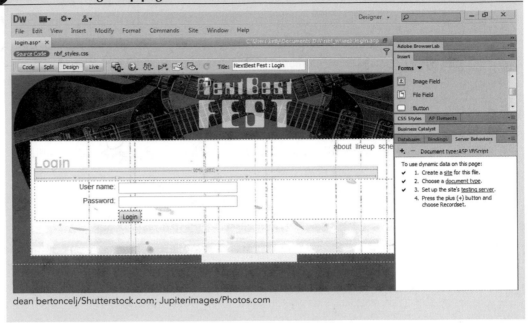

dean bertoncelj/Shutterstock.com; Jupiterimages/Photos.com

Next, you will add the Log In User server behavior to the page, which will verify the submitted username and password.

To add server behaviors to the login.asp page:

1. Select the **Login** button in the form.

2. In the **Data** category of the Insert panel, click the **User Authentication button arrow**, and then click **Log In User**. The Log In User dialog box opens.

3. Click the **Validate using connection** button, and then click **nbfdb**.

4. Click the **Table** button, and then click **admin**, if necessary.

5. Click the **Username column** button, and then click **username**.

6. Click the **Password column** button, and then click **password**.

7. Click the **Browse** button next to the If login succeeds, go to box, click the **database.asp** page in the Select File dialog box, and then click the **OK** button. This sets the database.asp page to display in the browser window if the submitted username and password are listed in the database.

8. Click the **Browse** button next to the If login fails, go to box, click the **access_denied.html** page in the Select File dialog box, and then click the **OK** button. This sets the access_denied.html page to display in the browser window if the submitted username and password are not listed in the database. See Figure 9-39.

Figure 9-39   Log In User dialog box

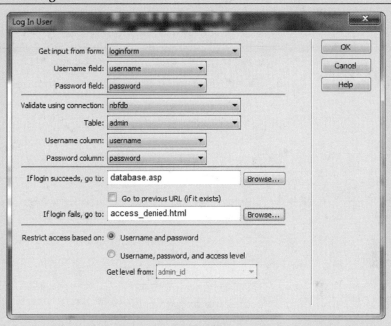

9. Click the **OK** button. The Log In User server behavior is added to the page and appears in the Server Behaviors panel.

10. Save the page, and then upload the page to your remote server.

You will add text and a meta refresh tag to the access_denied.html page, which tells the browser to automatically refresh the page (by reloading the current page or going to a different page) after a certain amount of time. You will also add text to indicate that access was denied to that user.

To add content and a meta refresh tag to the access_denied.html page:

1. Open the **access_denied.html** page in Design view.

2. In the **Common** category of the Insert panel, click the **Head button arrow**, and then click **Refresh**. The Refresh dialog box opens.

3. In the Delay box, type **4**, and then, in the Go to URL box, type **login.asp**. See Figure 9-40.

Figure 9-40   Refresh dialog box

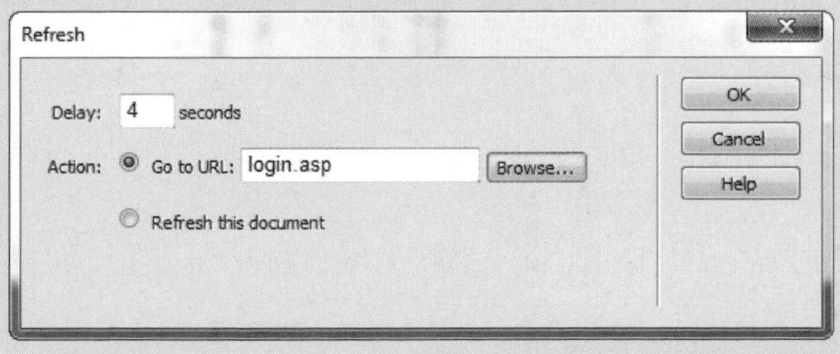

4. Click the **OK** button.

5. Place the insertion point after the heading text and after the closing h1 tag, press the **Right** arrow key or the **Enter** key, if necessary, to move the insertion point to the next line, and then type **Your access was denied. Please enter your login ID and password again.** (including the period).

6. Save the page, and then upload the page to your remote server.

Before you continue, you will test the login.asp page.

To test the login.asp page:

1. Preview the login.asp page in a browser. The login.asp page appears in the browser window. You will enter an invalid username and password.

2. Type **test** in the User name box, type **random** in the Password box, and then click the **Login** button. The login information is invalid, so the access_denied.html page appears in the browser window. After four seconds, the login.asp page is redisplayed. Now, you will enter a valid username and password.

3. Type **nextbest** in the User name box, type **zergrush** in the Password box, and then click the **Login** button. The database.asp page is displayed in the browser window.

4. Close the browser, and then close the pages.

Finally, you will protect the database.asp and database_details.asp pages from unauthorized access by adding the Restrict Access server behavior to the page.

To restrict access to the database.asp and database_details.asp pages:

1. Open the **database.asp** page in Design view.

2. In the **Data** category of the Insert panel, click the **User Authentication button arrow**, and then click **Restrict Access To Page**. The Restrict Access To Page dialog box opens.

3. In the If access denied, go to box, type **access_denied.html**. See Figure 9-41.

Figure 9-41	Restrict Access To Page dialog box

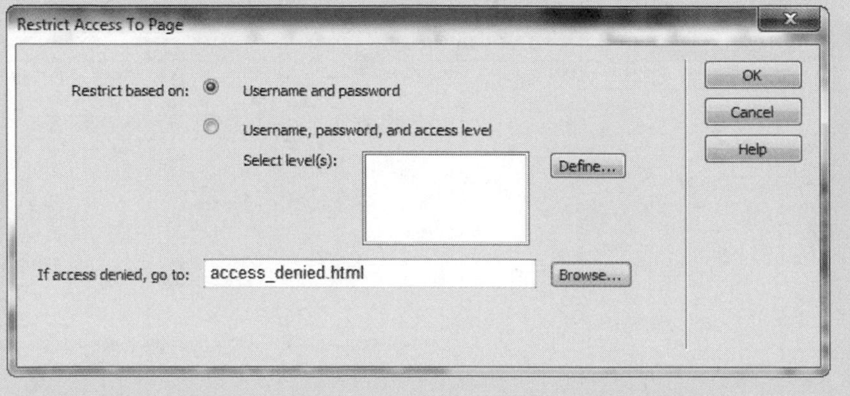

▶ **4.** Click the **OK** button, save the page, and then upload the page to your remote server.

▶ **5.** Open the **database_details.asp** page in Design view, and then repeat Steps 2 through 4 to restrict access to that page. You will test the behavior you added to the pages.

▶ **6.** Preview the database.asp page in a browser. Because you are not logged in, the database.asp page does not display in the browser window. Instead, the access_denied.html page appears for four seconds, and then the login.asp page is displayed.

   Trouble? If the database.asp page does appear, you did not close the browser window after you logged in and you are still logged in. Close any open browser windows and repeat Step 6.

▶ **7.** Close the browser, and then close the pages.

In this session, you created database-driven Web pages for the NextBest Fest site using Access and VBScript for a Windows server. The database functionality will enable Gage to collect data about the preferences of NextBest Fest's customers. Analyzing this data will help shape future marketing plans for NextBest Fest.

REVIEW

Session 9.2 Quick Check

1. In addition to selecting a database, you must also select a(n) _____ that you will use to create server behaviors.
2. What language do you use to create server behaviors when you use an Access database?
3. What is a server behavior?
4. Why do you need the Recordset behavior?
5. Why would you create a login page?
6. What is the purpose of the meta refresh tag?

Practice the skills you learned in the tutorial.

PRACTICE

Review Assignments

Data File needed for the Review Assignments: anti_db.sql or anti_db.mdb

Dan and Cat want to provide users with a way to give feedback and to make requests. You will add a new section to the home page asking users to provide input and you will create a short form so users can provide their name, email address, and comments. The information from the form will be collected in a database. Below the form, you will create an area that displays the comments users have submitted but not their name or email address.

If you are using MySQL and PHP on a Linux server, complete the following steps:

1. Open the **antifest** site you modified in Tutorial 8, and then open the **index.html** page in Design view.

2. Add a new line after the page content, type **feedback**, apply the h2 tag, press the Enter key, type **We would love to hear your thoughts about the fest and any ideas that you have regarding future festivals. If you have anything to contribute, simply fill out and submit the following form. Together we can rock the world.**, and then press the Enter key.

3. Insert a form in the page, enter **comment** as the form name, and then insert a table with 5 rows, 2 columns, 100% table width, 0 border thickness, 0 cell padding, 5 cell spacing, and no header in the form.

4. Align the left column to the Right and Top, and then align the right column to the Left and Top.

5. In the upper-left cell, type **first name:** (including the colon), press the Tab key to move the insertion point to the upper-right cell of the table, insert a Text Field, and then close the Input Tag Accessibility Attributes dialog box. In the Document window, select the TextField. In the Property inspector, enter **first_name** in the TextField box, and then set Max chars to 80.

6. Repeat Step 5 to enter the label **last name:** and the text field **last_name** in the second row of the table, and the label **email address:** and the text field **email_address** in the third row of the table.

7. In the first cell of the fourth row, type **comments:**, and then in the second cell of the fourth row, insert a Textarea field and close the Input Tag Accessibility Attributes dialog box. In the Document window, select the Textarea. In the Property inspector, enter **comments** in the TextField box and set Num lines to 10.

8. In the second cell of the fifth row, insert a Submit button, and then save the page.

9. Connect to an existing database or create the database on your remote server using the **anti_db.sql** file located in the Dreamweaver9\Review folder included with your Data Files. (*Hint*: Obtain the information you need from your instructor or technical support person.)

10. In the Server Behaviors panel, click the document type link in Step 2, select PHP as the document type, and then click the OK button. Click the Update button when prompted to update links.

11. In the index.php page, update the link from the home page navigation text and the logo rollover to index.php, and then save the page.

12. In the Server Behaviors panel, click the testing server link in Step 3, check the Testing check box beside the antifest web server in the server list, and then edit the server. In the Advanced tab, select PHP MySQL as the server model in the Testing Server area, and then click the Save button in each dialog box.

13. In the Server Behaviors panel, add the Recordset behavior, type **anti_record** as the name, click the Define button next to the Connection box, click the New button, type **anti_connect** as the connection name, type **localhost** or the database server

URL as the MySQL server, type your username and password, click the Select button to display a list of databases, select anti_db in the list, click the OK button, click the OK button, click the Done button, select anti_connect as the connection, click contact in the Tables list, click the SELECT button, and then click the OK button. The Recordset behavior is added to the page and appears in the Server Behaviors panel.

14. In the Server Behaviors panel, add the Insert Record behavior, submit values from comment, select anti_connect as the connection, click contact in the Insert table list, click the Browse button, click the index.php page in the local root folder, and then click the OK button in each dialog box. Save the page. The Insert Record behavior is added to the page and appears in the Server Behaviors panel.

15. Upload the page to your remote server (include dependent files), preview the page in a browser, and then close the browser.

16. Double-click the Recordset behavior in the Server Behaviors panel to open the Recordset dialog box, click the Simple button, click the Selected option button in the Columns section, click comments in the Columns box, and then click the OK button.

17. Place the pointer after the form area inside the content div, click the Dynamic Table button in the Dynamic Data list in the Data category of the Insert panel, click the All records option button, set the border to 0, set the cell padding to 3, and then click the OK button. A dynamic table appears below the form in the page.

18. Select the heading text in the top row of the dynamic table and format the text with the h2 tag.

19. Save the page, upload the index.php page to your remote server (include dependent files), preview the page in a browser (updating the page and dependent files on the testing server, if necessary), type a test entry in the form, and then click the Submit button to submit the form. The comment you submitted appears below the form in the page. (*Hint*: If you are sharing a database with classmates, you might see additional comments displayed below the form. If you do not see your comment, refresh the page.)

20. Submit the finished files to your instructor.

If you are using Access and ASP on a Windows server, complete the following steps:

1. Open the **antifest** site you modified in Tutorial 8, and open the **index.html** page in Design view.

2. Add a new line after the page content, type **feedback**, apply the h2 tag, press the Enter key, type **We would love to hear your thoughts about the fest and any ideas that you have regarding future festivals. If you have anything to contribute, simply fill out and submit the following form. Together we can rock the world.**, and then press the Enter key.

3. Insert a form in the page, enter **comment** as the form name, and then insert a table with 5 rows, 2 columns, 100% table width, 0 border thickness, 0 cell padding, 5 cell spacing, and no header in the form.

4. Align the left column to the Right and Top, and then align the right column to the Left and Top.

5. In the upper-left cell, type **first name:** (including the colon), press the Tab key to move the insertion point to the upper-right cell of the table, insert a Text Field, and then close the Input Tag Accessibility Attributes dialog box. In the Document window, select the TextField. In the Property inspector, enter **first_name** in the TextField box, and then set Max chars to 80.

6. Repeat Step 5 to enter the label **last name:** and the text field **last_name** in the second row of the table, and the label **email address:** and the text field **email_address** in the third row of the table.

7. In the first cell of the fourth row, type **comments:**, and then in the second cell of the fourth row, insert a Textarea field and close the Input Tag Accessibility Attributes dialog box. In the Document window, select the Textarea. In the Property inspector, type **comments** in the TextField box and set Num lines to 10.

8. In the second cell of the fifth row, insert a Submit button, and then save the page.

9. Connect to an existing database or upload the database on your remote server using an FTP program and the **anti_db.mdb** file located in the Dreamweaver9\Review folder included with your Data Files. (*Hint*: Obtain the information you need from your instructor or technical support person.)

10. In the Server Behaviors panel, click the document type link in Step 2, click ASP VBScript as the document type, if necessary, and then update the links.

11. In the index.asp page, update the link from the home page navigation text and the link from the logo rollover to index.asp, and then save the page.

12. In the Server Behaviors panel, click the testing server link in Step 3, click the Servers tab in the Site Setup for antifest dialog box, select the antifest web server and check the Testing check box (leave the Remote check box checked as well), and then click the Save button.

13. In the Server Behaviors panel, add the Recordset behavior, type **anti_record** as the name, click the Define button, click the New button, click Custom Connection String, type **anti_connect** as the connection name, type **Provider=Microsoft.Jet.OLEDB.4.0; Data Source=** and the exact file path to your database as the connection string, click the Using Driver on Testing Server option button, if necessary, click the Test button, click the OK button, click the OK button, click the Done button, select anti_connect as the connection, click contact in the Tables list, click the SELECT button, and then click the OK button. The Recordset behavior is added to the page and appears in the Server Behaviors panel. (*Hint*: If you do not know the exact path to your database, ask your instructor or technical support person. If the test is unsuccessful, double-check the connection string and file path for your database or use an outside FTP program to upload the _mmServerScripts folder to the root folder on your remote server and your testing server if you are using a separate testing server.)

14. In the Server Behaviors panel, add the Insert Record behavior, select anti_connect as the connection, click contact in the Insert into table list, click the Browse button, click the index.asp page in the local root folder, click the OK button, click comment in the Get values from list, if necessary, and then click the OK button. Save the page. The Insert Record behavior is added to the page and appears in the Server Behaviors panel.

15. Upload the page to your remote server (include dependent files), preview the page in a browser, and then close the browser. (*Hint*: If the page does not display in the browser, Dreamweaver has not added a piece of code that you need to insert. Open the **index.asp** page in Code view, scroll to approximately Line 130, and locate the following code:

```
<object type="application/x-shockwave-flash"
data="FLVPlayer_Progressive.swf" width="293" height="251">
```

After the opening bracket (and before the word *object*), type **<%%>** and then repeat Step 15.)

16. Double-click the Recordset behavior in the Server Behaviors panel to open the Recordset dialog box, click the Simple button, click the Selected option button in the Columns section, click comments in the Columns box, and then click the OK button.

17. Place the pointer below the form area inside the content div, click the Dynamic Table button in the Dynamic Data list in the Data category of the Insert panel, click the All records option button, set the border to 0, set the cell padding to 3, and then click the OK button. A dynamic table appears below the form in the page.

18. Select the comments text in the top row of the dynamic table and format the text with the h2 tag.

19. Save the page, upload the index.asp page to your remote server (include dependent files), preview the page in a browser (updating the page and dependent files on the testing server, if necessary), type a test entry in the form, and then click the Submit button to submit the form. The comment you submitted appears below the form in the page. (*Hint*: If you are sharing a database with classmates, you might see additional entries in the database. If you do not see your comment, refresh the page.)

20. Submit the finished files to your instructor.

Add database-driven pages to display blog entries in a Web site for a skateboard company.

CHALLENGE

Case Problem 1

Data File needed for this Case Problem: moeb_db.sql or moeb_db.mdb

Moebius Skateboards   Corey wants to create blog entries that appear in the about page of the Moebius Skateboards site. The blog entries will help him communicate with users as well as promote the skateboards he sells and the company's skateboarding team. You will create database-driven pages to create a tool that will enable him to do this. As part of the tool, you will create a form Corey can use to enter blog entries. This form will use the Spry Validation Textarea widget, which is a text area that has extra code around it to ensure that the form will not submit unless text is in the text area. This will ensure that no empty entries will be posted to the site accidentally.

If you are using MySQL and PHP on a Linux server, complete the following steps:

1. Open the **Moebius Skateboards** site you modified in Tutorial 8.

2. In the Files panel, duplicate the contact.html page, rename the copied page as **blog.php**, and then update the links in the file.

3. Open the **blog.php** page in Design view, change the heading text to **Blog Entry**, replace the word *Contact* in the page title with **Blog Entry**, and then delete the content from below the heading to the end of the content div, including the form and form content.

4. Insert a form in the page, enter **blogentry** as the form name, and then insert a table with 2 rows, 2 columns, 100% table width, 0 border thickness, 3 cell padding, 0 cell spacing, and no header in the form.

5. In the upper-left cell, type **blog entry**, align the left column to the Right and Top, and then align the right column to the Left and Top.

⊕ EXPLORE   6. With the insertion point in the upper-right cell of the table, insert a Spry Validation Textarea widget from the Forms tab of the Insert panel, close the Input Tag Accessibility Attributes dialog box, and then click the Spry Textarea tab to select the widget. In the Property inspector, enter **blogentryvalidate** in the Spry Textarea box, and then check the Required check box, if necessary. In the Document window, click the scroll bar of the widget twice to display the text field properties. In the Property inspector, enter **blogentry** in the TextField box, set the Char width to 80, and then set the Num lines to 10.

7. In the lower-right cell of the table, insert a Submit button, and then save the page, clicking the OK button to add Spry scripts to the directory.

8. Connect to an existing database or create the database on your remote server using the **moeb_db.sql** file located in the Dreamweaver9\Case1 folder included with your Data Files. (*Hint*: Obtain the information you need from your instructor or technical support person.)

9. In the Server Behaviors panel, click the document type link in Step 2, select PHP as the document type, and then click the OK button.

10. In the Server Behaviors panel, click the testing server link in Step 3, select the moebius web server from the list in the Servers tab, check the Testing check box, edit the server and check the Use Passive FTP check box in the More Options drop-down menu in the Basic tab, click the Save button, and then click Save again.

11. In the Server Behaviors panel, add the Recordset behavior, type **moeb_record** as the name, click the Define button next to the Connection box, click the New button, type **moeb_connect** as the connection name, type **localhost** or the database server URL as the MySQL server, type your username and password, click the Select button to display a list of databases, click moeb_db in the list, click the OK button, click the OK button, click the Done button, select moeb_connect as the connection, click blog in the Table list, click the SELECT button, select blog from the list, and then click the OK button. The Recordset behavior is added to the page and appears in the Server Behaviors panel.

12. In the Server Behaviors panel, add the Insert Record behavior, submit values from blogentry, select moeb_connect as the connection, click blog in the Insert table list, select 'blog' Does Not Get a Value in the Columns list, select FORM.blogentry in the Value list, click Text in the Submit as list, if necessary, click the Browse button, click the about.html page in the local root folder, and then click the OK button in each dialog box. The Insert Record behavior is added to the page and appears in the Server Behaviors panel.

13. Save the page, upload the page to your remote server (include dependent files), preview the page in a browser, update the page and the dependent files on the testing server, if necessary, and then close the browser.

14. Open the **about.html** page in Design view, click the document type link in the Server Behaviors panel, select PHP in the list, click the OK button, click the Update button to update the links in the pages, click the OK button in the message dialog box, and then update the about link in the navigation text in the about.php page so that the link goes to the about.php page when clicked.

15. Click the blog.php tab, right-click the Recordset behavior in the Server Behaviors panel, click Copy on the context menu, click the about.php tab, right-click in the Server Behaviors panel, and then click Paste on the context menu to paste the Recordset behavior into the page.

✥ EXPLORE
16. Double-click the Recordset behavior in the Server Behaviors panel to open the Recordset dialog box, click the Simple button, if necessary (if the button says Advanced, you are already in Simple), click the Selected option button in the Columns section, click blog in the Columns box, and then click the OK button.

✥ EXPLORE
17. Delete the text below the heading in the content div, click the Dynamic Table button in the Dynamic Data list in the Data category of the Insert panel, click the All records option button, set the border to 0, set the cell padding to 3, and then click the OK button. Delete any extra space between the new table and the heading text.

18. Save the page, upload the about.php and the blog.php page to your remote server (include dependent files), preview the blog.php page in a browser (updating the page and dependent files on the testing server, if necessary), click the Submit button to test that the Spry Validation Textarea widget is working (a message appears, stating that "A value is required."), type a test entry in the form, and then click the Submit button to submit the form. The about.php page with the new entry opens in the browser window. (*Hint*: If you are sharing a database with classmates, you might see additional entries in the database.)

19. Submit the finished files to your instructor.

If you are using Access and ASP on a Windows server, complete the following steps:

1. Open the **Moebius Skateboards** site you modified in Tutorial 8.
2. In the Files panel, duplicate the contact.html page, rename the copied page as **blog.asp**, and then update the links in the file.
3. Open the **blog.asp** page in Design view, change the heading text to **Blog Entry**, replace the word "Contact" in the page title with **Blog Entry**, and then delete the content from below the heading to the end of the content div, including the form and form content.
4. Insert a form in the page, enter **blogentry** as the form name, and then insert a table with 2 rows, 2 columns, 100% table width, 0 border thickness, 3 cell padding, 0 cell spacing, and no header in the form.
5. In the upper-left cell, type **blog entry**, align the left column to the Right and Top, and then align the right column to the Left and Top.

EXPLORE

6. With the insertion point in the upper-right cell of the table, insert a Spry Validation Textarea widget from the Forms tab of the Insert panel, close the Input Tag Accessibility Attributes dialog box, and then click the Spry Textarea tab to select the widget. In the Property inspector, enter **blogentryvalidate** in the Spry Textarea box, and then check the Required check box, if necessary. In the Document window, click the scroll bar of the widget twice to display the text field properties. In the Property inspector, enter **blogentry** in the TextField box, set the Char width to 80, and then set the Num lines to 10.
7. In the lower-right cell of the table, insert a Submit button, and then save the page, clicking the OK button to add Spry scripts to the directory.
8. Connect to an existing database or upload the database on your remote server using an FTP program and the **moeb_db.mdb** file located in the Dreamweaver\Case1 folder included with your Data Files. (*Hint*: Obtain the information you need from your instructor or technical support person.)
9. In the Server Behaviors panel, click the document type link in Step 2, click ASP VBScript in the list, if necessary, and then update the links.
10. In the Server Behaviors panel, click the testing server link in Step 3, in the Servers list, select the moebius web server and check the Testing check box (leave the Remote check box checked as well), and then click the Save button.
11. In the Server Behaviors panel, add the Recordset behavior, type **moeb_record** as the name, click the Define button, click the New button, click Custom Connection String, type **moeb_connect** as the connection name, type **Provider=Microsoft.Jet.OLEDB.4.0; Data Source=** and the exact file path to your database as the connection string, click the Using Driver on Testing Server option button, if necessary, click the Test button, click the OK button, click the OK button, click the Done button, select moeb_connect as the connection, click the Advanced button, if necessary, click blog in the Tables list, click the SELECT button, and then click the OK button. The Recordset behavior is added to the page and appears in the Server Behaviors panel. (*Hint*: If you do not know the exact path to your database, ask your instructor or technical support person. If the test is unsuccessful, double-check the connection string and file path for your database or use an outside FTP program to upload the _mmServerScripts folder to the root folder on your remote server and your testing server if you are using a separate testing server.)
12. In the Server Behaviors panel, add the Insert Record behavior, select moeb_connect as the connection, click blog in the Insert into table list, click the Browse button, click the about.html page in the local root folder, click the OK button, click blogentry in the Get values from list, if necessary, click blog in the Column list, click blogentry inserts into column "blog" (Text) in the Form elements list, and then click the OK button. The Insert Record behavior is added to the page and appears in the Server Behaviors panel.

13. Save the page, upload the page to your remote server (include dependent files), preview the page in a browser, and then close the browser.

14. Open the **about.html** page in Design view, click the document type link in the Server Behaviors panel, select ASP VBScript in the list, click the OK button, click the Update button to update the links in the pages, click the OK button in the message dialog box, and then update the link in the navigation text in the about.asp page so that the link goes to the about.asp page when clicked.

15. Click the blog.asp tab, save the page, right-click the Recordset behavior in the Server Behaviors panel, click Copy on the context menu, click the about.asp tab, right-click in the Server Behaviors panel, and then click Paste on the context menu to paste the Recordset behavior into the page.

⊕ EXPLORE   16. Double-click the Recordset behavior in the Server Behaviors panel to open the Recordset dialog box, click the Simple button, if necessary (if the button says Advanced, you are already in Simple), click the Selected option button in the Columns section, click blog in the Columns box, and then click the OK button.

⊕ EXPLORE   17. Delete the text below the heading in the content div, click the Dynamic Table button in the Dynamic Data list in the Data category of the Insert panel, click the All records button, set the border to 0, set the cell padding to 3, and then click the OK button. Delete any extra space between the new table and the heading text.

18. Save the page, upload the about.asp page and the blog.asp page to your remote server (include dependent files), preview the blog.asp page in a browser (updating the page and dependent files on the testing server, if necessary), click the Submit button to test that the Spry Validation Textarea widget is working (a message appears, stating that "A value is required."), type a test entry in the form, and then click the Submit button to submit the form. The about.asp page with the new entry opens in the browser window. (*Hint:* If you are sharing a database with classmates, you might see additional entries in the database.)

19. Submit the finished files to your instructor.

Add database-driven pages to collect and display a tally of visitors' votes for favorite paintings.

APPLY

Case Problem 2

Data File needed for this Case Problem: cowboy_db.sql or cowboy_db.mdb

Cowboy Art Society   Moni wants visitors to the Cowboy Charlie site to vote for their favorite painting. You will create a form in the home page so that visitors can submit their votes. The form will be connected to a database that stores the votes, and the vote tally will be displayed below the form in the home page.

If you are using MySQL and PHP on a Linux server, complete the following steps:

1. Open the **Cowboy Charlie** site you modified in Tutorial 8, and then open the **index.html** page in Design view.

2. After the existing content in the content div, insert a form into the page, enter **voteform** as the form name, and then, in the form, insert a table with 3 rows, 1 column, 40% table width, 0 border thickness, 2 cell padding, 2 cell spacing, and no header cells.

3. In the top row, type **Select your favorite painting**, and then align the text to the Left and Top.

4. Add a radio group in the second row, name the radio group **vote**, replace "Radio" with **The Bucker** in the first row of both the Label and Value columns, replace "Radio" with **Grubpile** in the second row of both the Label and Value columns, click the Add button to add a new row, replace "Radio" with **A Quiet Day in Utica** in the third row of both the Label and the Value columns, and then click the OK button.

5. Add a Submit button in the third row of the table, typing **Submit** as the button name and the value, if necessary, and then save the page.

6. Connect to an existing database or create the database on your remote server using the **cowboy_db.sql** file located in the Dreamweaver9\Case2 folder included with your Data Files. (*Hint*: Obtain the information you need from your instructor or technical support person.)

7. In the Server Behaviors panel, click the document type link in Step 2, click PHP in the list, click the OK button, update the links, click the OK button to confirm that the index.php page could not be updated, save the index.php page, update the link for the hotspot that covers the entire top banner of the page to the index.php page, and then save the page again.

8. Click the testing server link in Step 3, check the Testing check box for the Cowboy Charlie web server, edit the Server profile, if necessary, adjust the Web URL prefix box, type the URL for your posted site, and then click the Save button in both dialog boxes.

9. In the Server Behaviors panel, add the Recordset behavior, name the recordset **charlie_record**, click the Define button, click the New button, type **charlie_connect** as the connection name, type **localhost** or the database server URL in the MySQL server box, type your username and password, click the Select button to display a list of databases, select the **cowboy_db** database from the list, click the OK button twice, click the Done button, click the Simple button, if necessary, and then click charlie_connect in the Connection list.

⊕ EXPLORE 10. Click the Advanced button, delete all the text in the SQL box, type the following code exactly as it appears, click the Test button, close the test dialog box, and then click the OK button to enter a query that enables the vote tally to be displayed in a dynamic table.

SELECT vote AS Painting, count(vote) AS Votes

FROM vote

GROUP BY vote

ORDER BY vote

11. In the Server Behaviors panel, add the Insert Record behavior, click voteform in the Submit values from list, if necessary, click charlie_connect in the Connection list, click vote in the Insert table list, click 'vote' Gets Value From 'FORM.vote' as 'Text' in the Columns list, click FORM.vote in the Value list, click Text in the Submit as list, if necessary, click the Browse button, click the index.php page in the local root folder (because the totals will be displayed in this page), and click the OK button in each dialog box that appears. The Insert Record behavior is added to the page and appears in the Server Behaviors panel.

12. Save the page, upload the page to your remote server (include dependent files), preview the page in a browser (update the page and dependent files on the testing server), and then close the browser.

⊕ EXPLORE 13. Place the insertion point in a blank line below the form, click Dynamic Table in the Dynamic Data list in the Data category of the Insert panel, click the All records button, set the border to 0, set the cell padding to 3, and then click the OK button.

14. Format the table heading text with the h2 tag.

15. Save the index.php page, upload the page to your remote server (include dependent files), preview the page in a browser (update the page and the dependent files on the testing server, if necessary), click an option button in the form, and then submit the form. The new vote tally appears below the form in the page. (*Hint*: If you are sharing a database with classmates, you might see additional entries in the database.)

16. Submit the finished files to your instructor.

If you are using Access and ASP on a Windows server, complete the following steps:

1. Open the **Cowboy Charlie** site you modified in Tutorial 8, and then open the **index.html** page in Design view.

2. After the existing content in the content div, insert a form into the page, enter **voteform** as the form name, and then, in the form, insert a table with 3 rows, 1 column, 40% table width, 0 border thickness, 2 cell padding, 2 cell spacing, and no header cells.

3. In the top row, type **Select your favorite painting**, and then align the text to the Left and Top.

4. Add a radio group in the second row, name the radio group **vote**, replace "Radio" with **The Bucker** in the first row of both the Label and Value columns, replace "Radio" with **Grubpile** in the second row of both the Label and Value columns, click the Add button to add a new row, replace "Radio" with **A Quiet Day in Utica** in the third row of both the Label and the Value columns, and then click the OK button.

5. Add a Submit button in the third row of the table, typing **Submit** as the button name and the value, if necessary, and then save the page.

6. Connect to an existing database or upload the database to your remote server using an FTP program and the **cowboy_db.mdb** file located in the Dreamweaver9\Case2 folder included with your Data Files. (*Hint*: Obtain the information you need from your instructor or technical support person.)

7. In the Server Behaviors panel, click the document type link in Step 2, click ASP VBScript in the list, click the OK button, update the links in the files, click the OK button to confirm that the index.asp page could not be updated, save the index.asp page, update the link for the hotspot that covers the banner at the top of the page to the index.asp page, and then save the page again.

8. Click the testing server link in Step 3, in the Servers tab, check the Testing check box for the Cowboy Charlie web server, edit the server profile and ensure that the file path information from the Web URL prefix box is the URL for your posted site, and then click the Save button twice. Click OK to re-create the cache.

9. In the Server Behaviors panel, add the Recordset behavior, name the record-set **charlie_record**, click the Define button, click the New button, click Custom Connection String, type **charlie_connect** as the connection name, type **Provider=Microsoft.Jet.OLEDB.4.0; Data Source=** and the exact file path to your database in the Connection String box, click the Using Driver on Testing Server option button, if necessary, click the Test button, click the OK button to close the dialog box stating that the connection was made successfully, click the OK button to close the Custom Connection String dialog box, click the Done button, click the Simple button, if necessary, click charlie_connect in the Connection list, click vote in the Table list, click the Test button, and then click the OK button. (*Hint*: If you do not know the exact path to your database, ask your instructor or technical support person. If the test is unsuccessful, double-check the connection string and file path for your database or use an outside FTP program to upload the _mmServerScripts folder to the root folder on your remote server and your testing server if you are using a separate testing server.)

⊕ **EXPLORE**   10. Click the Advanced button, delete all the text in the SQL box, type the following code exactly as it appears, click the Test button, click the OK button, and then click the OK button to enter a query that will enable the vote tally to be displayed in a dynamic table.

SELECT vote AS Painting, count(vote) AS Votes

FROM vote

GROUP BY vote

ORDER BY vote

11. In the Server Behaviors panel, add the Insert Record behavior, click charlie_connect in the Connection list, click vote in the Insert into table list, click the Browse button, click the index.asp page in the local root folder (because the totals will be displayed in this page), click the OK button, click voteform in the Get values from list, if necessary, click vote in the Column list, click vote inserts into column "vote" (Text) in the Form elements list, and then click the OK button. The Insert Record behavior is added to the page and appears in the Server Behaviors panel.

12. Save the page, upload the page to your remote server (include dependent files), preview the page in a browser, and then close the browser. (*Hint*: If the page will not display, Dreamweaver has not added a piece of code that you need to insert. Open the **index.asp** page in Code view, scroll to approximately Line 100, and locate the following code:

```
<object data="media/cr_art.swf" type="application/x-shockwave-
flash" width="400" height="300" align="top">
```

After the opening bracket, type <%%> (before object) and then repeat Step 12.

⊕ EXPLORE   13. Place the insertion point in a blank line below the form, click Dynamic Table in the Dynamic Data list in the Data category of the Insert panel, click the All records button, set the border to 0, set the cell padding to 3, and then click the OK button.

14. Format the table heading text with the h2 tag.

15. Save the index.asp page, upload the page to your remote server (include dependent files), preview the index.asp page in a browser, click an option button in the form, and then submit the form. The new vote tally appears below the form in the page. (*Hint*: If you are sharing a database with classmates, you might see additional entries in the database.)

16. Submit the finished files to your instructor.

Display coaching topics stored in a database in the home page of a Web site for a life coach.

APPLY

Case Problem 3

Data File needed for this Case Problem: tess_db.sql or tess_db.mdb

Success with Tess   Tess wants to add an online coaching section to the Success with Tess site. In this section, she will provide general information on a wide range of hot coaching topics. You will create a Topics Admin page, and then add a form in the page that enables Tess to enter topic content. To ensure that she does not accidentally submit forms with empty entries, you will use the Spry Validation Textarea, which allows forms to be submitted only when the text area contains content. The form will be connected to a database. Finally, you will add an online coaching section to the coaching.html page and include code to display the content stored in the database.

If you are using MySQL and PHP on a Linux server, complete the following steps:

1. Open the **Success with Tess** site you modified in Tutorial 8.

2. In the Files panel, duplicate the coaching.html page, rename the copied page as **topics.php**, and then open the topics.php page in Design view.

3. Change the heading text to **Topic Input**, replace the word *Coaching* in the page title with **Topics Input**, and then delete the content in the page.

4. Insert a form in the page, enter **topicform** as the form name, and then, in the form, insert a table with 2 rows, 2 columns, 90% table width, 0 border thickness, 3 cell padding, 0 cell spacing, and no header cells.

5. Type **input coaching topic** in the upper-left cell, and then align the text to the Right and Top.

✛ EXPLORE

6. Insert a Spry Validation Textarea widget in the upper-right cell, close the Input Tag Accessibility Attributes dialog box, enter **topicvalidate** as the Spry Textarea name, and then make sure the field is set as Required. Click the scroll bar twice to select the text area, enter **topic** as the field name, set the character width to 80, and then set the number of lines to 10.

7. Add a Submit button in the lower-right cell, and then save the page. Click the OK button in the Copy Dependent Files dialog box to add the SpryAssets folder and files to the site.

8. Connect to an existing database or create the database on your remote server using the **tess_db.sql** file located in the Dreamweaver9\Case3 folder included with your Data Files. (*Hint*: Obtain the information you need from your instructor or technical support person.)

9. In the Server Behaviors panel, select PHP as the document type in Step 2, if necessary.

10. Set up the testing server in Step 3, check the Testing check box for the Tess web server in the Servers tab, and then edit the server profile and enter the URL for your remote site in the Web URL box, if necessary.

11. In the Server Behaviors panel, add the Recordset behavior, click the Simple button, if necessary, name the recordset **tess_record**, click the Define button, click the New button, type **tess_connect** as the connection name, type **localhost** or your database server URL as the MySQL server, type your username and password, click the Select button to display a list of databases, click the tess_db database, click the OK button in each dialog box, click the Done button, click tess_connect in the Connection list, click Simple, if necessary, click topic in the Table list, click the Selected option button, click topic_text in the Columns list, and then click the OK button. The Recordset behavior is added to the page and appears in the Server Behaviors panel.

12. In the Server Behaviors panel, add the Insert Record behavior, click topicform in the Submit values from list, if necessary, click tess_connect in the Connection list, click topic in the Insert into table list, click 'topic_text' does not get a value in the Columns list, click FORM.topic in the Value list, click Text in the Submit as list, if necessary, click the Browse button, click the coaching.html page in the local root folder, and then click the OK button in each dialog box. The Insert Record behavior is added to the page and is visible in the Server Behaviors panel.

13. Save the page, upload the page to your remote server (include dependent files), and then preview the page in a browser (update the page and the dependent files on the testing server, if necessary).

14. Copy the Recordset behavior in the Server Behaviors panel, and then close the page.

15. Open the **coaching.html** page in Design view, select PHP as the document type in Step 2 in the Server Behaviors panel, update the links in the file, paste the Recordset behavior into the Server Behaviors panel in the page, save the coaching.php page, update the Coaching navigation text to link to the coaching.php page, save the page again, and then upload the page to your remote server.

16. Above the Coaching disclaimer heading, enter an **Online Coaching** heading, and then type the following text in the Online Coaching section: **Below I have provided some general information that you may find helpful. Check back frequently for more.**

✛ EXPLORE

17. Place the insertion point in a blank line below the text in the Online Coaching section, click the Dynamic Table button in the Dynamic Data list in the Data category of the Insert panel, click the All records option button, set the border to 0, set the cell padding to 5, click the OK button, and then delete the first row of the dynamic table (the row that shows "topic_text").

18. Save the coaching.php page, upload the page to your remote server (include dependent files), preview the topics.php page in a browser (update the files and dependent files on the testing server, if necessary), type a test entry in the form followed by your name, and then click the Submit button. The coaching.php page with the topic entries appears in the browser. (*Hint*: If you are sharing a database with classmates, you might see additional entries in the database.)

19. Submit the finished files to your instructor.

If you are using Access and ASP on a Windows server, complete the following steps:

1. Open the **Success with Tess** site you modified in Tutorial 8.

2. In the Files panel, duplicate the coaching.html page, rename the copied page as **topics.asp**, and then open the topics.asp page in Design view.

3. Change the heading text to **Topic Input**, replace the word *Coaching* in the page title with **Topic Input**, and then delete the content in the page.

4. Insert a form in the page, enter **topicform** as the form name, and then, in the form, insert a table with 2 rows, 2 columns, 90% table width, 0 border thickness, 3 cell padding, 0 cell spacing, and no header cells.

5. Type **input coaching topic** in the upper-left cell, and then align the text to the Right and Top.

⊕ EXPLORE

6. Insert a Spry Validation Textarea widget in the upper-right cell, close the Input Tag Accessibility Attributes dialog box, enter **topicvalidate** as the Spry Textarea name, and then make sure the field is set as Required. Click the scroll bar twice to select the text area, enter **topic** as the field name, set the character width to 80, and then set the number of lines to 10.

7. Add a Submit button in the lower-right cell, and then save the page. Click the OK button in the Copy Dependent Files dialog box to add the SpryAssets folder and files to the site.

8. Connect to an existing database or upload the database to your remote server using an FTP program and the **tess_db.mdb** file located in the Dreamweaver9\Case3 folder included with your Data Files. (*Hint*: Obtain the information you need from your instructor or technical support person.)

9. In the Server Behaviors panel, select ASP VBScript as the document type in Step 2.

10. Set up the testing server in Step 3, check the Testing check box for the Tess web server in the Servers tab, edit the server profile, and then enter the Web URL for your remote site in the URL box, if necessary.

11. In the Server Behaviors panel, add the Recordset behavior, click the Simple button in the Recordset dialog box, if necessary, name the recordset **tess_record**, click the Define button, click the New button, click Custom Connection String, type **tess_connect** as the connection name, type **Provider=Microsoft.Jet.OLEDB.4.0; Data Source=** followed by the exact file path to your database as the connection string, click the Using Driver on Testing Server option button, click the Test button, click the OK button to confirm the connection was made successfully, click the OK button, click the Done button, click tess_connect in the Connection list, click topic in the Table list in Simple mode, click the Selected option button, click topic_text in the Columns list, and then click the OK button. The Recordset behavior is added to the page and appears in the Server Behaviors panel. (*Hint*: If you do not know the exact path to your database, ask your instructor or technical support person. If the test is unsuccessful, double-check the connection string and file path for your database or use an outside FTP program to upload the _mmServerScripts folder to the root folder on your remote server and your testing server if you are using a separate testing server.)

12. In the Server Behaviors panel, add the Insert Record behavior, click tess_connect in the Connection list, click topic in the Insert into table list, type **coaching.asp** in the After inserting, go to box, click topicform in the Get values from list, if necessary, click topic in the Form elements list, select topic_text in the Column list and Text in the Submit as list, and then click the OK button. The Insert Record behavior is added to the page and appears in the Server Behaviors panel.

13. Save the page, upload the page to your remote server (include dependent files), and then preview the page in a browser.

14. Copy the Recordset behavior in the Server Behaviors panel, and then close the page.

15. Open the **coaching.html** page in Design view, select ASP VBScript as the document type in Step 2 in the Server Behaviors panel, update the links in the pages, click the OK button to confirm that the coaching.asp page could not be updated, paste the Recordset behavior into the Server Behaviors panel, save the coaching.asp page, update the Coaching navigation text to link to the coaching.asp page, save the page again, and then upload the page to your remote server (include dependent files).

16. Above the Coaching disclaimer heading, enter an **Online Coaching** heading, and then type the following text in the Online Coaching section: **Below I have provided some general information that you may find helpful. Check back frequently for more.**

⊕ EXPLORE   17. Place the insertion point in a blank line below the text in the Online Coaching section, click the Dynamic Table button in the Dynamic Data list in the Data category of the Insert panel, click the All records option button, set the border to 0, set the cell padding to 5, click the OK button, and then delete the first row of the dynamic table (the row that shows "topic_text").

18. Save the coaching.asp page, upload the page to your remote server (include dependent files), preview the topics.asp page in a browser (update the files and dependent files on the testing server, if necessary), type a test entry in the form followed by your name, and then click the Submit button. The coaching.asp page with the topic entries appears in the browser. (*Hint*: If you are sharing a database with classmates, you might see additional entries in the database.)

19. Submit the finished files to your instructor.

Create database-driven pages to collect and display customer comments.

CREATE

Case Problem 4

Data File needed for this Case Problem: coffee_db.sql or coffee_db.mdb

Coffee Lounge   Tommy wants you to add a form to the Coffee Lounge site that includes a comments section. After you create the form, you will connect the form to a database and add code to another page to display the customer comments.

1. Open the **Coffee Lounge** site you modified in Tutorial 8, and then open the page in which you will create the form in Design view.

⊕ EXPLORE   2. Create a form in the page that enables customers to enter comments. The form should have a text area for comments and a Submit button for submission. (*Hint*: Use a table to create the form structure and use the Spry Validation Textarea widget to verify that users have entered content into the text area before they submit the form.)

3. If your instructor has not already done so, upload the database on the remote server using the **coffee_db.sql** file (if you are using MySQL and PHP) or create the database on your remote server using the **coffee_db.mdb** file (if you are using Access and ASP) located in the Dreamweaver9\Case4 folder included with your Data Files. (*Hint*: Obtain the information you need from your instructor or technical support person.)

4. Connect the Web site to the database by completing Steps 2 and 3 in the Server Behaviors panel. (*Hint*: Remember to update the link on the .php or .asp page.)

5. Add the Recordset and the Insert Record server behaviors to the page.

6. Copy the Recordset server behavior from the page, open the page in which you want the comments to appear, and then paste the Recordset server behavior in the page.

⊕ EXPLORE

7. Add a customer comments heading in an appropriate location on the page, and then add a dynamic table that displays customer comments in the page. (*Hint*: To add a dynamic table, click the Dynamic Table button in the Dynamic Data list in the Data category of the Insert panel.)

8. Save the pages, upload the pages to your remote server, and then test the pages.

9. Submit the finished files to your instructor.

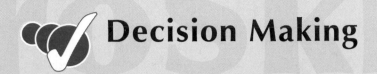

Decision Making

Planning a Personal Web Site

Decision making is the process of choosing between alternative courses of action. To create an effective Web site, you must begin by making a series of decisions about the site's purpose and parameters. Understanding the decision-making process will enable you to make better decisions that will, in turn, lead to the creation of a more effective Web site. This is especially important if you plan to create Web sites professionally.

Obtain Relevant Information

The first step in the decision-making process is to gather all of the information and data that is related, directly or indirectly, to the decisions you will make. When creating a Web site plan, this can include information about the prospective target audience and potential site goals, any site content that you have developed, all collateral materials that you have collected, user data, and research into similar sites. The more complete and relevant the information you gather, the better decisions you can make about the Web site.

Evaluate the Information, Develop Alternatives, and Select the Best Option

The next step in the decision-making process is to use the information that you have collected to develop alternatives and to make predictions regarding the relative value of each alternative. For example, to determine the goals for the site, you can create a list of all the potential goals, and then narrow the list to the top five goals. Prioritize the list with the main site goal as number one; then consider how this will affect the layout, design, and information architecture of the final site. Use this process to develop alternate site goals and to evaluate the effects of each list on the final site, then select the best alternative as the final list of goals for the site.

Prepare an Action Plan

After you have made a decision, you need to create a plan for implementing the decision. Consider all the steps you must take and all the resources that you will need to achieve the desired outcome. For example, once you have made all the decisions about the Web site, you must develop a plan for creating the site. What resources will you need for the project? How will you acquire those resources and how long will it take to get them? What is the timetable for the project? When will you start and how long will each task take? Is there an order in which you must complete the tasks? Can any tasks be performed at the same time? You should select a project manager and then assign milestones to track the progress of the plan's implementation.

Take Action and Monitor Results

After the plan is created and approved, the plan implementation begins. As you make progress, it is important to compare actual activity with the scheduled activity to ensure that you stay on track and on schedule. It is also important to assess how well the implemented plan is achieving the desired results. If elements of your plan have unintended results, it may be necessary to reevaluate your decisions and to adjust your plan. For example, if the Web site is not achieving one of the primary goals, you should reevaluate the importance of that goal or redesign the pages and replace page content to better achieve that goal.

ProSkills

Create a Personal Web Site

Dreamweaver is the industry-standard tool for professional Web design, but it also has a wide user base beyond the professional world. Consider these examples: Individuals use Dreamweaver to create personal Web sites, small businesses use Dreamweaver to create and maintain online catalogs, and educational institutions use Dreamweaver to create promotional information and Web applications. The possibilities are infinite.

In this exercise, you will use Dreamweaver to plan and create a personal Web site with information of your choice, using the Dreamweaver skills and tools presented in Tutorials 1 through 9. Use the following steps as a guide to completing your Web site, keeping in mind the guidelines for decision making provided earlier.

Note: Please be sure *not* to include any personal information of a sensitive nature in the Web site you create to submit to your instructor for this exercise. Later, you can update the Web site with such information for your personal use, but remember that all Web sites you post to a Web server are visible to anyone who has Internet access and a Web browser.

1. Create a list of site goals; review the list for order of importance and wording.
2. Define your target audience, researching the target audience as needed, and create a user profile for the site.
3. Conduct market research to gather information about three similar Web sites, and analyze them.
4. Develop two end-user scenarios for the site.
5. Design the information architecture for the site.
6. Draw a flowchart for the site so that you can visualize the site navigation and page connectivity.
7. Develop a site concept and metaphor.
8. Choose a color palette, fonts, and graphic style for the site. (*Hint*: You might want to create a document that identifies all of your choices, including hexadecimal color codes for each color as well as a breakdown of font attributes by family, font size, color, and style for body text, links, headings, subheadings, and so on.)
9. Create a layout design for the pages of the site.
10. Gather relevant content materials and write the page content for the pages. Consider including a page heading and a summary sentence at the top of each page, and then break page content into smaller sections with subheadings that will guide the target audience through the page.
11. Create a local site definition and a remote site definition.
12. Create a page using divs and CSS styles to lay out the page elements, and then create additional CSS styles to style the page elements and content as appropriate based on your site plan.
13. Export the styles to an external style sheet.
14. Create a main template for the site. Add editable regions to the template and insert placeholder text as appropriate.

ProSkills

15. Design the site navigation system, and then add the navigation to the template, creating appropriate elements. (*Hint*: If you do not have access to a graphics program, you can create a series of text links for the site navigation.)

16. Add an appropriate list of keywords to the head content of the template.

17. Add an appropriate description of the site to the head content of the template.

18. Create at least two library items for elements that you intend to reuse or update frequently, such as footers or information that will appear in more than one page.

19. Use the template to create the pages of your site in the local root folder, and name each page with a descriptive filename.

20. For each page in your site, enter an appropriate page title, add content and graphics, and then apply appropriate CSS styles to format the content. When possible, add graphics as Smart Objects to ensure efficient workflow and updatability.

21. After you have created all the pages for the site, modify the navigation in the template to link each element to the appropriate page, and then save the template and update the pages.

22. Create an image map in at least one Web page.

23. Add a rollover button in at least one Web page.

24. Insert a Flash movie or sound into at least one page.

25. Save the pages, and preview them in a browser. Adjust the pages, as needed.

26. Upload the site to a remote server, and then preview the site over the Internet. Test each page of the site, and adjust the pages in Dreamweaver as needed.

27. Save and close the site, and then submit the completed files to your instructor.

DREAMWEAVER

OBJECTIVES

- Plan and design a Web site
- Create and use a CSS style sheet
- Create Web pages that include text, images, an image map, and a rollover button
- Insert a navigation system
- Create and use library items
- Create an alternate print style sheet
- Insert a video or a sound file using HTML5 or Flash in a Web page
- Preview and test each page in a Web site

Building a Web Site

Case | *Borders*

Borders is a frame shop that specializes in creating contemporary, one-of-a-kind frames for traditional western art. The shop also displays the work of local western artists. Borders caters to young, upwardly mobile city dwellers who want to combine their western roots with urban style. The owners of the shop want to build a Web site that will be used to market their goods and services and to let people know about upcoming events. If the site is successful, the owners plan to add an e-commerce section to the site.

1. Create a list of site goals; review the list for order of importance and the wording.
2. Define a target audience and create a user profile for the site. (*Hint*: Research the target audience as needed.)
3. Conduct market research to gather information about at least four competing Web sites or other Web sites that cater to a similar target audience, and then write a paragraph summarizing your findings. (*Hint*: Look at western themed Web sites, such as *www.cowboycool.com*.)
4. Develop two end-user scenarios for the site.
5. Create an information category outline for the site.
6. Create a flowchart for the site.
7. Develop a site concept and a metaphor for the site. Write a paragraph explaining your choices.
8. Choose a color palette, fonts, and a graphic style for the site. Write a paragraph explaining your choices.
9. Create rough sketches of two layouts for the site. Write a paragraph explaining which layout you prefer and why.
10. Check the layout of the design you prefer for logic, and verify that your design reinforces the site goals and supports the site metaphor.
11. Create a local site definition and a remote site definition.
12. Create a home page for the site using div tags and CSS to lay out the page. Name the Web page with a descriptive filename and save the page. (*Hint*: Remember to use index.html or index.htm as the filename for the home page.)

STARTING DATA FILES

There are no starting Data Files needed for this additional case.

13. Export the existing styles to an external style sheet, and then attach the style sheet to the page.
14. Add CSS styles to the style sheet for background, links, font colors, headings, and other elements, based on what is appropriate for your site.
15. Add an appropriate list of keywords to the head content of the page.
16. Add an appropriate description of the site to the head content of the page.
17. Set an appropriate page title for the Web page you created.
18. Insert navigation into the page. (*Hint*: You can use graphics or text links for site navigation.)
19. Type an appropriate page heading and text content in the Web page, and then apply appropriate CSS styles to format the content.
20. Add at least one image to the Web page and if you have Photoshop CS6, create Smart Objects. (*Hint*: If you don't have an image file to insert, you can use any of the image files included with your Data Files.)
21. Repeat Steps 12 through 20 to create at least three additional first-level pages for the site based on your site plan, but attach the style sheet you created in Step 13 to the subsequent pages.
22. Create at least two library items for elements that you intend to reuse or update frequently, such as footers or upcoming sales information that will be displayed in more than one page. Add the library items to the pages of your site.
23. Save the pages, and then preview the pages in a browser.
24. Create an image map in at least one Web page.
25. Add a rollover button to at least one Web page.
26. Save the pages, and then preview the pages in a browser.
27. Insert a video or sound file using HTML5 or Flash into at least one page. (*Hint*: If you don't have one of these types of files to insert, you can use any of the files included with your Data Files as placeholders.)
28. Preview the site in Live view and in a browser.
29. Upload the site to a remote server and preview the site over the Web, testing each page of the site.
30. Submit the finished files to your instructor.

OBJECTIVES

- Plan and design a fluid grid site
- Create pages using Fluid Grid Layout div tags, media queries, and CSS styles
- Create and use library items
- Create and use a CSS style sheet
- Create Web pages that include text, images, an image map, and a rollover button
- Create and test a form
- Insert a video or a sound file in a Web page using HTML5 or Flash
- Preview and test each page in a Web site

Building a Fluid Grid Web Site with a Form

Case | *Steam Room*

The Steam Room is a late-night tea house and venue for Steam Punk bands. The house features live, steam punk music, a house tribal fusion dance troupe, and outdoor fire poi on the weekends; an improvisational psychedelic jazz jam on Thursday nights; poetry slams on Wednesday nights; experimental film screenings on Tuesday nights; and a book club for cyberpunk titles on Monday nights. In addition, the Steam Room encourages public art by allowing patrons and local artists to arrive with found objects and add them to the collaborative sculptural pieces scattered throughout the venue.

Steam Room owner, Ariella Vale, has decided that the house could benefit from a Web site. She wants to use the site as a marketing tool to promote featured events, the monthly special (a different tea is featured each month), and sales. Ariella also wants to include a page that features a different local nonprofit organization each month. The page should include a blurb about the nonprofit organization, contact information, and, if possible, a link to the nonprofit's Web site. She wants to be able to update this feature page herself. Finally, she wants the layout to be an adaptive design that will adjust layout for desktops, tablets, and mobile devices.

1. Create a list of site goals; review the list for order of importance and the wording.
2. Define a target audience and create a user profile for the site. (*Hint*: Research the target audience as needed.)
3. Conduct market research to gather information about at least four competing Web sites or other Web sites that cater to a similar target audience, and then write a paragraph summarizing your findings.
4. Develop two end-user scenarios for the site.
5. Create an information category outline for the site.

STARTING DATA FILES

steam_formTest.html

6. Create a flowchart for the site.
7. Develop a site concept and a metaphor for the site. Write a paragraph explaining your choices.
8. Choose a color palette, fonts, and a graphic style for the site. Write a paragraph explaining your choices.
9. Create rough sketches of two layouts for the site. Because the site will be adaptive, each layout must include a sketch for the desktop, tablet, and mobile displays. Write a paragraph explaining which layout you prefer and why.
10. Check the layout of the design you prefer for logic, and verify that your design reinforces the site goals and supports the site metaphor.
11. Create a local site definition and a remote site definition.
12. Create the home page for the site using the Fluid Grid Layout and use Fluid Grid Layout div tags, media queries, and CSS styles to lay out the page for desktop, tablet, and mobile display.
13. Add a background and colors to the page, as appropriate, based on your site plan.
14. Add an appropriate list of keywords to the head content of the page.
15. Add an appropriate description of the site to the head content of the page.
16. Create at least three additional CSS styles to format the text in the site; refer to your site plan for the appropriate colors, fonts, and so forth.
17. Insert navigation into the page and create appropriate elements.
18. Create at least two library items for elements that you intend to reuse or update frequently, such as footers or an upcoming events list that will be displayed in more than one page.
19. Duplicate the home page to create the other pages of the site.
20. Rename the Web page with a descriptive filename. (*Hint*: Remember to use index.html or index.htm as the filename for the home page.)
21. Set an appropriate page title for the Web page you created.
22. Open the Web page, type an appropriate page heading and text content, and then apply appropriate CSS styles, if necessary, to format the content.
23. Add at least one image to the Web page and create Smart Objects if you have Adobe Photoshop CS6. (*Hint*: If you don't have an image file to insert, you can use any of the image files included with your Data Files.)
24. Save the page, and then preview the page in a browser.
25. Repeat Steps 19 through 24 to create at least three first-level pages for the site based on your site plan.
26. Create an image map in at least one Web page.
27. Copy the **steam_formTest.html** file located in the AddCases\Case2 folder included with your Data Files to the site's local root folder. This will enable you to test the form.
28. Open the **steam_formTest.html** file in Design view, add the Mark of the Web to the page, and then save the page.
29. Add a rollover button to at least one Web page.
30. Create a form in one Web page to collect appropriate data from visitors.
31. Preview the form in a browser, and then test the form.
32. Insert a video or a sound into at least one page using HTML5 or Flash. (*Hint*: If you don't have one of these types of files to insert, you can use any of the files included with your Data Files as placeholders.)
33. Preview the site in a browser.
34. Upload the site to a remote server and preview the site over the Web, testing each page of the site.
35. Submit the finished files to your instructor.

OBJECTIVES

- Plan and design a Web site
- Create a template
- Create and use a CSS style sheet
- Create and use library items
- Create template-based Web pages that include page headings, text, images, an image map, and a rollover button
- Create and test a form
- Insert a video or sound file using HTML5 or Flash in a Web page
- Preview and test each page in a Web site

Building a Web Site with Database Functionality

Case | *antimag*

Dan and Cat, the promoters of antifest, want to create an online zine to promote the fest and the bands that play at the fest. The monthly online zine will be called *antimag*. Each issue will include band interviews, a calendar of local performances and events, reviews of local performances and new CD releases, and reader reviews and comments. The zine will also include a "Wanted" section for bands looking for new members and a section that features a local venue.

1. Create a list of site goals; review the list for order of importance and the wording.
2. Define a target audience and create a user profile for the site. (*Hint*: Research the target audience as needed.)
3. Conduct market research to gather information about at least four zine Web sites as well as two Web sites that promote local venues and bands, and then write a paragraph summarizing your findings.
4. Develop two end-user scenarios for the site.
5. Create an information category outline for the site.
6. Create a flowchart for the site.
7. Develop a site concept and a metaphor for the site. Write a paragraph explaining your choices.
8. Choose a color palette, fonts, and a graphic style for the site. Write a paragraph explaining your choices.
9. Create rough sketches of two layouts for the site. Write a paragraph explaining which layout you prefer and why.
10. Check the layout of the design you prefer for logic, and verify that your design reinforces the site goals and supports the site metaphor.

STARTING DATA FILES

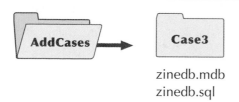

zinedb.mdb
zinedb.sql

11. Create a local site definition and a remote site definition.
12. Create a main template for the site, using div tags and CSS to lay out the page.
13. Add editable regions to the template and insert placeholder text, as appropriate.
14. Add a background and colors to the template, as appropriate, based on your site plan.
15. Add an appropriate list of keywords to the head content of the template.
16. Add an appropriate description of the site to the head content of the template.
17. Create at least three CSS styles to format the text in the site; refer to your site plan for the appropriate colors, fonts, and other elements.
18. Add a navigation system for the site. Create appropriate elements.
19. Create at least two library items for elements that you intend to reuse or update frequently, such as footers or an upcoming events list that will be displayed in more than one page.
20. Use the template to create a Web page.
21. Rename the Web page with a descriptive filename. (*Hint*: Remember to use index.html or index.htm as the filename for the home page.)
22. Set an appropriate page title for the Web page you created.
23. Open the Web page, type an appropriate page heading and text content, and then apply appropriate CSS styles, if necessary, to format the content. (*Hint*: You can use the antifest bands as featured bands.)
24. Add at least one image to the Web page and create Smart Objects if you have Photoshop CS6. (*Hint*: If you don't have an image file to insert, you can use any of the image files included with your Data Files.)
25. Save the page, and then preview the page in a browser.
26. Repeat Steps 20 through 25 to create a home page and at least three first-level pages for the site, based on your site plan.
27. After you have created all the pages for the site, open the template and modify the navigation, selecting each element and adding the link to the appropriate page.
28. Save the template, and then update the pages.
29. Create an image map in at least one Web page.
30. Add a rollover button to at least one Web page.
31. Create a form in one Web page to collect comments from visitors. Use a table to organize the form objects and buttons. Don't forget to include a Submit button. (The zine database located in the AddCases\Case3 folder included with your Data Files includes a full_name field, a comment field, and an email address field.)
32. Upload the **zine** database file located in the AddCases\Case3 folder included with your Data Files to your remote server if you are using ASP, or create the database on your remote server if you are using PHP.
33. Connect the site to the database, and then connect the form page to the database.
34. Add server behaviors to a Web page that will enable users to view the comments that are collected in the database.
35. Upload the site to your remote server, if necessary.
36. Preview the form in a browser, and then test the form by entering appropriate information and submitting the form.
37. Preview the Web page in which comments are displayed.
38. Insert a video or sound file using HTML5 or Flash into at least one page in the site. (*Hint*: If you don't have one of these types of files to insert, you can use any of the files included with your Data Files as placeholders.)
39. Preview the site in Live view and in a browser.
40. Upload the site to a remote server, and then preview the site over the Web, testing each page of the site.
41. Submit the finished files to your instructor.

OBJECTIVES

- Check a site for browser compatibility
- Test links throughout a site
- Conduct Web site usability tests
- Create site reports
- Manage site files when working in a team

Exploring Wrap-Up Tasks and Working in a Team

After you have created a site, several tasks still need to be completed prior to posting the site for the public to view (also called "going live"). You should do a final browser compatibility check to ensure that the site will display the same way across the various browsers you plan to support. You should check the site for broken links and orphaned pages, and then repair broken links and remove pages that are no longer part of the site from the root folder both locally and remotely. You should perform usability tests to ensure that the target audience can navigate through the site easily and to ensure that the goals of the site are reached. A good way to test the site for usability is to watch users interact with the site and then interview the users to get feedback about where the site is successful and areas that might need improvement. You should also take advantage of reporting features in Dreamweaver to check the site for instances of nested and unnecessary tags, accessibility, and so forth.

Many Web sites are created by teams of people. Dreamweaver has several features that help teams work on a site more efficiently. The Check In/Check Out feature enables teams to work together on a site without potentially overwriting each other's work. The workflow reports allow a project manager to find out which member of a team has specific pages and which pages have been recently modified. Another report provides information about HTML attributes.

STARTING DATA FILES

There are no starting Data Files needed for this appendix.

Checking a Site for Browser Compatibility

The **Browser Compatibility Check** feature reviews the code in Web site files and identifies combinations of HTML and CSS that might have rendering problems in certain browsers or are unsupported by the browsers. After you run a Browser Compatibility Check on a page, any potential CSS rendering issues or unsupported CSS code are listed in the Browser Compatibility panel. A confidence rating indicates the likelihood of the bug's occurrence (ranging from a quarter-filled circle for a possible occurrence to a filled circle for a very likely occurrence). For each potential issue, the panel displays a link to documentation about the bug on Adobe CSS Advisor, which is a Web site that details commonly known browser rendering bugs, and offers solutions for fixing them.

By default, the Browser Compatibility Check feature checks against Chrome 7.0, Firefox 1.5, Internet Explorer 6.0, Netscape Navigator 8.0, Opera 8.0, and Safari 2.0. You can choose which of these browsers to check compatibility with and the minimum browser version you plan to support.

Three levels of potential browser-support problems can arise:

- An error indicates CSS code that might cause a serious visible problem in a particular browser, such as causing parts of a page to disappear.
- A warning indicates a piece of CSS code that isn't supported in a particular browser, but that won't cause any serious display problems.
- An informational message indicates code that isn't supported in a particular browser, but that has no visible effect.

Browser compatibility checks do not change the page in any way.

To run a Browser Compatibility Check:

▶ **1.** Open the site you want to check for browser compatibility, and then open the page to check.

▶ **2.** On the Document toolbar, click the **Check browser compatibility** button, and then click **Settings**. The Target Browsers dialog box opens. See Figure A-1.

| Figure A-1 | Target Browsers dialog box |

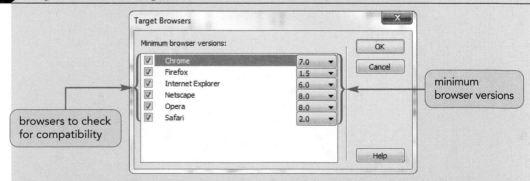

▶ **3.** Click check boxes as needed to select the browsers your target audience might use.

▶ **4.** If necessary, click the version button, and then click the minimum browser version your target audience might use.

▶ **5.** Click the **OK** button. The Browser Compatibility panel opens below the Property inspector. See Figure A-2.

Figure A-2   **Browser Compatibility panel**

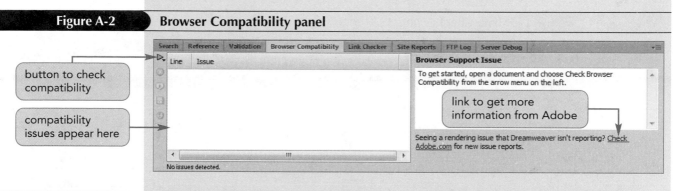

button to check compatibility

compatibility issues appear here

TIP

On the menu bar, you can also click File, point to Check Page, and click Browser Compatibility or click Window, point to Results, and click Browser Compatibility to open the panel.

6. Click the **arrow** button, and then click **Check Browser Compatibility**. Any compatibility issues appear in the left pane of the panel.

7. Double-click an issue in the left pane to select the element affected by that issue, and then make any necessary changes.

Another tool that helps you check a site for browser compatibility is the Adobe BrowserLab. **BrowserLab** is an online service that enables you to test the pages of a site to discover cross-browser compatibility issues and display differences. One unique feature of BrowserLab is that it renders screen shots of your site in different browsers so that you can compare the way the site looks. BrowserLab also integrates with Dreamweaver. You can access it from the Adobe BrowserLab panel if you sign up to use it. Currently, BrowserLab is free with the purchase of Dreamweaver CS6, but the service may become fee-based in the future.

Checking Links Throughout a Site

Before you "go live" with a site, you should check the site for broken links and orphaned files. A **broken link** is a link to a page that no longer exists. An **orphaned file** is a file in the site's root folder that is not linked to by any other file in the site. The **Check Links** feature locates broken links and orphaned files in a site. You can then create a new link to an element that has a broken link and create a link to an orphaned file if you want users to be able to access the file, or you can delete the file from the site's root folder if the file is no longer needed. Be sure to delete the page from both the local root folder and the remote server.

Be aware that checking for broken links does not check links to pages that are located outside of the root folder. Because of this, you should still preview the pages of your site and click the links to test the pages. Also, it is a good idea to periodically check a site for broken links and orphaned files as part of general site maintenance.

To check a site for broken links and orphaned files:

TIP

To check only selected pages, right-click the selected files in the Files panel, point to Check Links, and then click Selected Files.

1. In the Files panel, right-click the root folder, point to **Check Links**, and then click **Entire Local Site**. The Link Checker panel appears below the Property inspector.

2. At the top of the Link Checker panel, click the **Show** button, and then click **Broken Links**, if necessary. The Link Checker panel displays a list of broken links in the site. See Figure A-3. You can fix the links from the panel.

Figure A-3	Link Checker panel

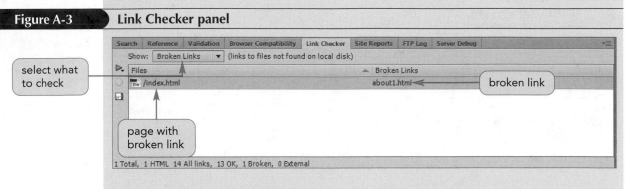

3. In the Link Checker panel, double-click a page with a broken link in the Files list to open that page in the Document window and select the element with the broken link, and then fix the broken link in the Property inspector as usual.

4. At the top of the Link Checker panel, click the **Show** button, and then click **Orphaned Files**. The Link Checker panel displays a list of orphaned files in the site. You can create a link to an orphaned file if needed.

5. Create a link to an orphaned file from an element on another page so users can access that file. You can also delete any unneeded files.

6. In the Link Checker panel, click the orphaned file you want to delete in the Orphaned Files list, and then press the **Delete** key. A dialog box opens, confirming that you want to delete the selected file.

7. Click the **Yes** button to delete the file from the local root folder, and then be sure to delete the file from the remote server, if necessary.

Conducting Web Site Usability Tests

After you finish a site, you should test the site for usability to find potential problems and to ensure that users have a good experience with the site. A good way to test a site for usability is to observe users interacting with the site, and then interview the users about their experiences with the site. When testing large, commercial sites, developers often set up a facility with computers and Internet access and then bring in test groups to observe users navigating through the site. Then, the developers conduct private interviews with the users to find out what they liked, what they did not like, and what confused them. If you are creating a small site, you can conduct more informal tests by asking friends who have not worked on the site but who are part of the target audience to review the site and give you their honest impressions.

In cases in which users have difficulty or confusion during a usability test, the design team often reworks the site to correct the issues, and then conducts a second round of tests to ensure that users will have a good experience before going live with the site.

Creating Site Reports

Site reports provide information about a selected page, a selected group of files, or an entire site. There are two types of reports, workflow and HTML reports, which are described in Figure A-4. **Workflow reports** provide information about changes team members have made to the pages, which you can use to improve collaboration. You must set up a remote connection for the site to run workflow reports. **HTML reports** provide information about HTML attributes, which you can use to clean up the code and ensure consistency within the site.

Figure A-4 **Site reports**

Type	Name	Description
Workflow Reports	Checked Out By	Lists the documents that are checked out by a specified team member
	Design Notes	Lists all the Design Notes (notes with information related to designing the site for yourself or other team members) for selected files or the entire site
	Recently Modified	Lists files that were changed during a specified period of time
HTML Reports	Combinable Nested Font Tags	Lists all the nested font tags that can be combined to clean up the code
	Missing Alt Text	Lists image tags that do not have alternate text
	Redundant Nested Tags	Lists unnecessary nested tags that should be removed from pages to clean up the code
	Removable Empty Tags	Lists all the empty tags that can be removed from pages to clean up the code
	Untitled Documents	Lists all the documents with default titles, duplicate titles, or missing title tags

You can run some or all of these reports for a site.

To run site reports:

1. On the menu bar, click **Site**, and then click **Reports**. The Reports dialog box opens. See Figure A-5.

Figure A-5 **Reports dialog box**

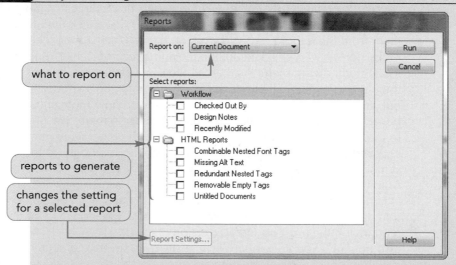

2. Click the **Report on** button, and then click what part of the site you want to create reports for: Current Document, Entire Current Local Site, Selected Files in Site, or Folder. To create a Selected Files in Site report, select the pages you want to report on in the Files panel before opening the Reports dialog box.

3. Click the check boxes next to the reports you want to create.

▶ **4.** For each report you want to create, select the report name in the Select reports box, click the **Report Settings** button, modify the settings as needed, and then click the **OK** button.

▶ **5.** Click the **Run** button. The report results appear in the Site Reports panel that opens below the Property inspector. See Figure A-6.

Figure A-6 ▶ **Site Reports panel**

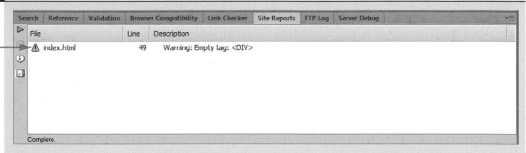

issue from the site report

▶ **6.** In the Site Reports panel, double-click any line to display the corresponding code in the Document window, and then make changes as needed.

Managing Files When Working in a Team

When you work with a team to create a Web site, it is a good idea to establish guidelines to ensure that the workflow moves smoothly. Common guidelines include setting up standard naming conventions that all team members will use and deciding on workflow processes. In addition, Dreamweaver provides several tools to help teams work on a site together.

Check In/Check Out enables a team to coordinate its work as the team members collaborate on pages of a site. This helps prevent one team member from inadvertently overwriting changes that other team members have made to a page. When the Check In/Check Out system is set up, team members must check out files and then download them from the remote server to work on them. When a file is checked out, the name of the person who checked out the file and a red check mark appear in the Files panel to alert other team members that the file is not available. The person who checks out the file sees a green check mark. When team members know who has a file checked out, they can communicate and coordinate workflow more effectively. Team members check in files when they are done working on them. The new version is uploaded to the remote server and is again available to the other team members. After a file is checked in, the local version of the file becomes read-only, as indicated by the lock symbol that appears next to the filename in the Files panel. This prevents any changes from being made to that local version of the file, which may not be the most current version of the file. To modify the page, the file must again be checked out. This ensures that only one team member works on a file at a time and that the team member is working on the most up-to-date version of the file. The Check In/Check Out system is also helpful if you are working with a site from several computer setups.

To set up the Check In/Check Out system:

1. On the menu bar, click **Site**, and then click **Manage Sites**. The Manage Sites dialog box opens.

   Before you can use the Check In/Check Out system, you must associate the local site with a remote server.

2. Select a site, and then click the **Edit** button 🖉. The Site Setup dialog box opens.

3. Click the **Servers** tab, edit your server, and then select the **Advanced** tab.

4. Click the **Enable file check-out** check box to insert a check mark. Additional options appear in the dialog box. See Figure A-7.

Figure A-7	Remote Server in the Site Setup dialog box

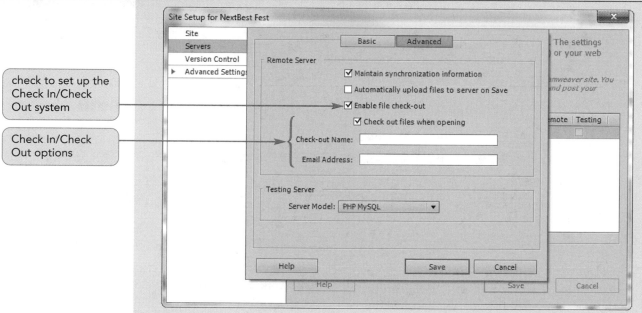

check to set up the Check In/Check Out system

Check In/Check Out options

Trouble? If no additional options appear, your remote access is set to Microsoft Visual SourceSafe.

Trouble? If the Enable file check-out option is not available, you need to set up a remote server for the site.

5. Click the **Check out files when opening** check box, if necessary, to insert a check mark to automatically check out files when you double-click the file in the Files panel.

6. In the Check-out Name box, type the name you want to appear in the Files panel next to files you check out. This lets the team know who to contact about a file that is checked out.

7. In the Email Address box, type your email address. When you check out files, your name will appear as a link in the Files panel that when clicked by a team member opens a message window addressed to you with the file and site name as the subject.

8. Click the **Save** button twice, and then click the **Done** button.

After you set up the Check In/Check Out system, you can check files in and out on a remote server using the Files panel. A green check mark indicates that you have checked out the file. A red check mark indicates that a file is already checked out by another team member. A lock symbol indicates that a file is read-only.

To check out file(s):

1. In the Files panel, select the file(s) you want to check out from the remote server.

2. On the Files panel toolbar, click the **Check Out File(s)** button. The Dependent Files dialog box opens.

3. Click the **Yes** button to download dependent files along with the selected file(s) to be sure you have the most current version available on your local site. The remote version of the file(s) is copied to your local site and, in the Files panel, a green check mark appears next to each file you checked out.

The process to check in a file is similar.

To check in file(s):

1. In the Files panel, select the file(s) you checked out from the remote server.

2. On the Files panel toolbar, click the **Check In** button. The Dependent Files dialog box opens.

3. Click the **Yes** button to upload dependent files along with the selected file(s) to be sure the most current version is available on the remote site. The selected file(s) is copied to the remote site and, in the Files panel, a lock icon appears next to each file you checked in to indicate the file is read-only.

Another way to manage files when working in a team is with **Subversion (SVN)**, a stand-alone versioning control system a team can use to edit and manage files on a remote Web server. Dreamweaver is not a full Subversion client, but team members can get the latest versions of files, modify files, and commit the files. For more information about Subversion, search Adobe Dreamweaver CS6 Help.

GLOSSARY/INDEX

encryption The process of encoding and decoding data so that only the sender and/or receiver can read it, preventing others from being able to understand it. DMR 5

end-user scenario An imagined situation in which the target audience might access a Web site; used to envision actual conditions that an end user will experience while visiting the Web site. DMR 46, DMR 56–57

event The user event and the event handler in a behavior. DMR 386

event handler The code used to refer to the event in a behavior. DMR 386

exiting Dreamweaver, DMR 39

Expanded Tables mode A table mode that temporarily adds cell padding and spacing to all of the tables in the page so that you can more easily select table elements and more precisely position the pointer inside cells. DMR 294

Extensible Hypertext Markup Language. *See* XHTML

Extensible Markup Language. *See* XML

external style sheet A separate file that contains all the CSS styles used in a Web site, which can be used in any page of the Web site to which the style sheet is connected. DMR 136, DMR 148–157
    code, DMR 146–147, DMR 152–154
    creating styles, DMR 151–152
    deleting styles, DMR 150
    moving styles to, DMR 148–150
    style tags, DMR 154–157

F

fair use A doctrine that allows others to reproduce small amounts of an original work specifically for a review, criticism, or illustration of a point without having to obtain the copyright owner's permission. DMR 117

Favorites category, Insert panel, DMR 34

feedback, gathering, DMR 360

.f4v file, DMR 405, DMR 435

file extension A series of characters used by Windows to determine the file type, such as .html or.htm for Web pages. DMR 22

file management by team, DMR A6–A8

File Transfer Protocol (FTP) A common Internet protocol used to copy files from one computer to another over the Internet. DMR 2

filename The name under which a Web page (or other file) is saved. DMR 24

Files panel A panel in Dreamweaver used to manage local and remote site files and folders. DMR 15, DMR 21–23

Find and Replace tool, DMR 119–120

firewall A hardware or software device that restricts access between a computer network and the Internet or between a computer and other computers, protecting the computer behind the firewall. DMR 83

fixed-width layout A page layout that sets pages at a specific size; fixed-width pages display at the specified size in browsers, regardless of the screen resolution. DMR 180–181

.fla file, DMR 405

Flash A widely used animation program that uses vector-based graphics, which can scale and compress to a very small file size without losing quality; used to create and deliver interactive animations for display on the Web. DMR 402, DMR 404, DMR 405–415
    adding video to Web pages, DMR 437–442
    adjusting attributes of Flash movies, DMR 413–415, DMR 429
    deleting video, DMR 442
    embedding movies with sound, DMR 426–429
    embedding sound formats using plug-ins and players, DMR 429
    file types, DMR 405
    files added with video clips, DMR 441–442
    information on Adobe site, DMR 406–408
    inserting Flash movies, DMR 409–413
    pros and cons, DMR 406
    viewing in Apple and mobile devices, DMR 405

Flip Toggle Switch widget, jQuery Mobile, DMR 505

floating positioning Positioning that enables you to create flexible designs that vary in size and position in response to the user agent as well as the screen size and resolution. DMR 179

flowchart A diagram of geometric shapes connected by lines that shows steps in sequence; in Web design, a visual representation of the hierarchical structure of the pages within a site. DMR 58
    creating, DMR 61–62

fluid grid design An approach to Web design that enables designers to create one Web site using a fluid, proportion-based grid and style sheets that rely on the CSS3 media query rule to detect the user's device specifications and to adapt the page layout, text size, image sizes, and other elements based on the viewing environment. DMR 450–481
    adding content, DMR 477–480
    adjusting div width and layout, DMR 466–469
    adjusting margins, padding, and spacing, DMR 472–475
    code, DMR 475–477
    creating a fluid grid page, DMR 453–457
    CSS3 media queries. *See* CSS3 media query
    history of grids in art, DMR 452–453
    styles, DMR 469–471
    viewing pages at different sizes, DMR 455–457
    visually adjusting, DMR 465–475

Fluid Grid div tag, adding, DMR 463–465

.flv file, DMR 405, DMR 435

folder structure, logical, DMR 19

font A set of letters, numbers, and symbols in a unified typeface. DMR 69–73
    advantages and disadvantages, DMR 168
    embedded, DMR 71
    formats, DMR 167
    monospaced, DMR 69–70
    proportional, DMR 70
    sans serif, DMR 69
    selecting, DMR 71
    serif, DMR 69

font color The color that is applied to a font. DMR 71

font kit The fonts, font variations, and description information of a Web font. DMR 167

font size The size of a font. DMR 71

font style The stylistic attributes such as bold, italic, and underline that are applied to a font. DMR 71

font tag An HTML tag that allowed designers to designate in which font and relative font size the Web page should display (as long as the designated font was installed on the user's computer); deprecated in HTML 4.01, its functions were replaced and expanded upon by Cascading Style Sheets. DMR 134

TASK REFERENCE

TASK	PAGE #	RECOMMENDED METHOD
Alternate text, add to graphic or link	DMR 243	Select graphic or link, type text in Alt box in Property inspector or enter in Tag Accessibility Attributes dialog box
AP div, adjust attributes	DMR 215	Select AP div, set attributes in Property inspector
AP div, adjust stacking order	DMR 221	In AP Elements panel, drag AP div to new position
AP div, insert	DMR 204	In Layout category of Insert panel, click Draw AP Div, drag in Document window to draw AP div
AP div, make active	DMR 206	Click in AP div
AP div, move	DMR 206	Select AP div, drag with AP div selection handle to new position
AP div, nest	DMR 224	With Nesting enabled, click in the Parent AP div in the Document window, click Draw AP Div and then draw the new AP Div inside the parent AP Div
AP div, resize	DMR 206	Select AP div, drag resize handle or enter values in Property inspector
AP div, select	DMR 206	In Document window, click edge of AP div or click selection handle of active AP div
AP Elements panel, display	DMR 222	Expand CSS panel group, click AP Elements tab
App, create	DMR 512	*See* Reference box: Creating a Basic App
Behavior, add to object with Behaviors panel	DMR 389	*See* Reference box: Adding a Behavior Using the Behaviors Panel
Behaviors panel, display	DMR 389	Click Window, click Tag Inspector, click Behaviors
Broken links, check site for	DMR A3	In Files panel, right-click root folder, point to Check Links, click Entire Local Site
Broken links, review	DMR A4	In Link Checker panel, click Show button, click Broken Links, double-click page with broken link
Browser compatibility, run check	DMR A2	On Document toolbar, click Check browser compatibility, click Settings, select browsers and versions, click OK
Browser compatibility, see issues	DMR A3	In Browser Compatibility panel, click arrow button, click Check Browser Compatibility, double-click issue
Browser window, close	DMR 11	Click [X] on browser title bar
Cell, select one or more in Standard mode	DMR 295	Ctrl+click one cell or Ctrl+drag across multiple table cells
Check In/Check Out system, set up	DMR A7	On menu bar, click Site, click Manage Sites, select site, click Edit, click Servers tab, edit server, click Advanced tab, check Enable file check-out, enter Check-out Name and Email Address, click Save twice, click Done
Code view, display page in	DMR 25	On Document toolbar, click Code button
Column, select in Standard mode	DMR 296	Click in table, move pointer above column, click column
Comment, add to page	DMR 193	Click in code, on Coding toolbar, click, click [icon], type comment text
Copyright symbol, add to page	DMR 198	In Text category of Insert panel, click Characters button arrow, click Copyright

TASK	PAGE #	RECOMMENDED METHOD
CSS transition, create	DMR 398	Click Window, click CSS Transitions, click ➕, select a Target Rule, select a Transition On option, set transition duration, delay, and timing function, add property, select option in Property list, set the End Value, click Create Transition
Custom script, add to page	DMR 392	Click Script button arrow in Common category of Insert panel, click Script, select type, enter content, click OK
Database, connect Web site to	DMR 545, DMR 571	In Server Behaviors panel, click document type link to select document type, click testing server link to set testing server in site definition
Database, create on remote Linux server	DMR 543	Log into database management interface, run SQL statements to create database
Database, upload to remote Windows server	DMR 569	Click Site, click Manage Sites, click New, click Servers, click, enter server information, click OK, click Done
Database-driven pages, create for Linux server	DMR 539	*See* Reference Window: Creating Database-Driven Pages for a Linux Server
Database-driven pages, create for Windows server	DMR 566	*See* Reference Window: Creating Database-Driven Pages for a Windows Server
Design view, display page in	DMR 25	On Document toolbar, click Design button
Div tag, insert	DMR 191	In Layout category of Insert panel, click Insert Div Tab, click Insert, click location, select or create CSS style, click OK
Div tag content, add	DMR 196	Select placeholder text in div, enter text or image as usual
Document window, make sizable	DMR 28	On title bar, click ⬛
Document window, resize	DMR 29	On status bar, click Window Size button and click option, click ⬛, or click ⬛
Document window, set magnification	DMR 30	On status bar, click Set magnification button, click option
Document window, zoom in	DMR 30	On status bar, click 🔍, click page
Document window, zoom out	DMR 30	On status bar, click 🔍, press Alt, click page
Dreamweaver, exit	DMR 39	Click File, click Exit
Dreamweaver, start	DMR 16	Click Start, click All Programs, click Adobe or Adobe Design Premium CS6, click Adobe Dreamweaver CS6
Editable region, add to template	DMR 346	Click Templates button arrow in Common category of Insert panel, click Editable Region, type name, click OK
Email link, create	DMR 336	Select text in Document window, type mailto: followed by email address in Link box in Property inspector
Expanded Tables mode, switch to	DMR 294	Click Expanded in Layout category of Insert panel
External style sheet, create	DMR 148	*See* Reference box: Moving Styles to a New External Style Sheet
External style sheet, define new style in	DMR 151	*See* Reference box: Defining a Style in an External Style Sheet
File, check in	DMR A8	In Files panel, select file checked out from remote server, click Check In button, click Yes
File, check out	DMR A8	In Files panel, select file, click Check Out File(s) button, click Yes
File, close	DMR 39	On page tab, click ✖

TASK	PAGE #	RECOMMENDED METHOD
File, open in Document window	DMR 23	In Files panel, double-click filename
Files list, view in Files panel	DMR 21	*See* Reference box: Viewing the Files List in the Files Panel
Flash movie, add to Web page	DMR 409	*See* Reference box: Adding a Flash Movie to a Web Page
Flash movie, adjust attributes	DMR 414	Select Flash movie, change attributes in Property inspector
Flash movie with sound, adjust attributes	DMR 429	Select Flash movie, change attributes in Property inspector
Flash movie with sound, embed in Web page	DMR 426	*See* Reference box: Adding a Flash Movie with Sound to a Web Page
Flash video, add to Web page	DMR 438	See Reference box: Adding a Flash Video Clip to a Web Page
Fluid Grid Layout div, add to page	DMR 463	Click Insert Fluid Grid Layout Div Tag button in Layout category of Insert panel
Fluid grid page, create	DMR 453	*See* Reference box: Creating a Web Page Using the Fluid Grid Layout
Fluid grid page, view at different sizes	DMR 455	On status bar, click ▣, ▣, or ▣
Form, add to Web page	DMR 361	Click page location for form, click Form in Forms category of Insert panel
Form, create	DMR 361	*See* Reference box: Creating a Form
Form attributes, add to form	DMR 363	Select form, set attributes in Property inspector
Form data, validate	DMR 390	On status bar, click form tag, in Behaviors panel, click ▼, click Validate Form, set validation options, click OK, in Behaviors panel, click Events arrow, click onSubmit
Form object, add to form	DMR 364	Click in form, click appropriate button in Forms category of Insert panel, type object name and set attributes in Property inspector
Graphic, add to Web page	DMR 242	*See* Reference box: Adding a Graphic to a Web Page
Graphic, adjust brightness and contrast	DMR 255	Select graphic, click ◑ in Property inspector, click OK, drag Brightness and/or Contrast slider, click OK
Graphic, crop	DMR 254	Select graphic, click ◩ in Property inspector, click OK, drag resize handles to set crop area, press Enter
Graphic, format with CSS style	DMR 245	Select graphic, click Class arrow in Property inspector, click style
Graphic, replace	DMR 248	Double-click graphic in Document window, double-click new graphic
Graphic, resample	DMR 253	Select graphic, click ▣ in Property inspector
Graphic, resize	DMR 252	Select graphic, drag resize handles or enter values in W and H boxes in Property inspector
Graphic, sharpen	DMR 256	Select graphic, click △ in Property inspector, click OK, drag Sharpen slider, click OK
Guide, display or hide	DMR 207	Drag to or from horizontal or vertical ruler
Guide, reposition	DMR 207	Drag to new location in Document window
Help, get in Dreamweaver	DMR 35	*See* Reference box: Getting Help in Dreamweaver
Hotspot, create	DMR 264	Click ▢, ◯, or ▽ in Property inspector, drag or click in Document window to create hotspot

TASK	PAGE #	RECOMMENDED METHOD
Hotspot, move, resize, or reposition point	DMR 264	Click ⬉ in Property inspector, drag hotspot or point on hotspot
HTML tag, modify	DMR 137	*See* Reference box: Modifying an Existing HTML Tag
HTML tags, examine in Web pages	DMR 127	*See* Reference box: Examining HTML Tags
Hyperlink, create from graphic	DMR 262	Select graphic, click 🗀 next to Link box in Property inspector, double-click file to link to
Hyperlink, create from text	DMR 125	Select text in Document window, type filename in Link box in Property inspector
Hyperlink, use	DMR 10	Click link in browser window
Image map, create	DMR 263	*See* Reference box: Creating an Image Map
Insert panel, use	DMR 34	Click Insert panel, click category button, click category, click option
Inspect mode, switch to	DMR 371	On Document toolbar, click Inspect button
jQuery Mobile site, create from starter page	DMR 487	Click File, click New, click Page from Sample, click Mobile Starters, click starter page, click OK
Keywords, add to Web page	DMR 326	Click Head button arrow in Common category of Insert panel, click Keywords, type keywords, click OK
Keywords, edit	DMR 327	In Code view, click in keywords list, make changes to keywords as needed in Property inspector or Document window
Library item, add to Web page	DMR 334	Drag library item from library in Assets panel to desired location in page
Library item, create	DMR 332	*See* Reference box: Creating a Library Item
Library item, delete from library	DMR 339	Select library item in library, click 🗑 in Assets panel
Library item, delete from page	DMR 339	Select library item in page, press Delete
Library item, edit	DMR 336	Open library item, make changes as needed, save library item, click Update, click Close
Library item, open	DMR 336	Double-click library item in Assets panel
Live Code view, display page in	DMR 370	Switch to Live view, click Live Code button on Document toolbar
Live view, display page in	DMR 27	On Document toolbar, click Live button
Local site definition, create	DMR 18	*See* Reference box: Setting Up Local Information for a New Site
Mark of the Web, add	DMR 443	*See* Reference box: Adding Mark of the Web to a Web Page
Meta description, add to Web page	DMR 329	Click Head button arrow in Common category of Insert panel, click Description, type description, click OK
Meta description, edit	DMR 330	In Code view, click in description, make changes to description as needed in Property inspector or Document window
MP3 sound file, link to Web page	DMR 432	Select graphic or text, click 🗀 next to Link box in Property inspector, double-click sound file
Multiscreen Preview, view page in	DMR 456	On the Document toolbar, click 📱, click Multiscreen Preview
Nested template, create	DMR 356	Create new page from main template, click Templates button arrow in Common category of Insert panel, click Make Nested Template, type template name, click Save, add or modify template content as needed, save nested template

TASK	PAGE #	RECOMMENDED METHOD
Nonbreaking space, insert	DMR 124	In Text category of Insert panel, click Non-Breaking Space button in Characters list
Orphaned files, check site for	DMR A4	In Files panel, right-click root folder, point to Check Links, click Entire Local Site
Orphaned files, review	DMR A4	In Link Checker panel, click Show button, click Orphaned Files, click link to delete or create link to file
Page, duplicate	DMR 199	In Files panel, right-click page, point to Edit, click Duplicate
Page, rename	DMR 199	In Files panel, select page name, click page name, edit name, press Enter
Page properties, set	DMR 93	Click Modify, click Page Properties, set desired properties, click OK
Page title, add	DMR 89	On Document toolbar, type page title in Title box, press Enter
Password, delete from remote site definition	DMR 101	On menu bar, click Site, click Manage Sites, click site name, click Edit, click Remote Info, uncheck Save check box, click OK, click Done
Photoshop file, insert in Web page	DMR 272	*See* Reference box: Inserting a Photoshop File into a Dreamweaver Web Page
Photoshop file, insert part in Web page	DMR 280	In Photoshop, click ▣ in Tools panel, draw rectangle over area to copy, click Edit, click Copy; in Dreamweaver, click location for partial Photoshop file, click Edit, click Paste, click Format arrow, click format, select optimization settings, click OK, save the file, enter Alt text
Photoshop Smart Object, create	DMR 272	*See* Reference box: Inserting a Photoshop File into a Dreamweaver Web Page
Photoshop Smart Object, edit source file	DMR 276	Select Smart Object in Document window, click Edit in Property inspector, edit and save file in Photoshop
Photoshop Smart Object, update in Dreamweaver	DMR 279	Click Smart Object in Document window, click ⟳ in Property inspector
Prebuilt CSS layout page, create	DMR 182	Click File, click New, click Blank Page, click HTML, click layout, click Create
Preview list, add browser to	DMR 98	Click File, point to Preview in Browser, click Edit Browser List, click ➕, type browser name in Name box, click Browse, click browser program icon, click Open, check Primary browser or Secondary browser check box, click OK, click OK
Remote host, connect	DMR 102	On Files panel toolbar, click 🔌
Remote host, disconnect	DMR 101	On Files panel toolbar, click 🔌
Remote site definition, create	DMR 82	*See* Reference box: Setting Up Remote Servers for FTP Access
Repeating table, add to template	DMR 347	Click Templates button arrow in Common category of Insert panel, click Repeating Table, set table options, type name, click OK
Rollover, create	DMR 282	Click Images button arrow in Common category of Insert panel, click Rollover Image, type name, select original image, select rollover image, select format, click OK

TASK	PAGE #	RECOMMENDED METHOD
Rollover, insert	DMR 266	*See* Reference box: Inserting a Rollover
Row, select in Standard mode	DMR 296	Click in table, move pointer outside left border of row, click row
Rulers, change measurement	DMR 298	Click View, point to Rulers, click measurement
Rulers, show or hide	DMR 298	Click View, point to Rulers, click Show
Select tool, select	DMR 30	On status bar, click ▸
Shockwave movie, add to Web page	DMR 418	*See* Reference box: Adding a Shockwave Movie to a Web Page
Shockwave movie, adjust attributes	DMR 420	Select Shockwave movie, change attributes in Property inspector
Site report, run	DMR A5	Click Site, click Reports, click Report on button, select option, select reports, click Report Settings button, modify settings, click OK, click Run
Spelling, check in page	DMR 118	Click Commands, click Check Spelling
Split view, change orientation	DMR 26	On menu bar, click view, click Split Vertically or Split Horizontally
Split view, display page in	DMR 25	On Document toolbar, click Split button
Standard mode, switch to	DMR 294	Click Standard in Layout category of Insert panel
Style, apply	DMR 142	Select text in Document window, click HTML button in Property inspector, click Class arrow, click style name
Style, create class or ID	DMR 141	*See* Reference box: Creating a Class or ID Style
Style, define in external style sheet	DMR 151	*See* Reference box: Defining a Style in an External Style Sheet
Style, disable or enable	DMR 162	Select style in All Rules pane of CSS Styles panel, right-click property in Properties pane, click Disable or Enable
Style, edit in CSS Styles panel	DMR 158	*See* Reference box: Editing a Style
Style, edit in Properties pane of CSS Styles panel	DMR 160	Select text with style to edit in page, click Current button in CSS Styles panel, click ᴬ𝐳↓ or 🗋, click value for attribute, enter new value, press Enter
Styles, move to external style sheet	DMR 148	*See* Reference box: Moving Styles to a New External Style Sheet
Table, add content to cell	DMR 292	Click in table cell, type text, press Enter to add paragraph within cell
Table, create in Standard mode	DMR 288	*See* Reference box: Inserting a Table
Table, delete structure and content	DMR 299	Select table, press Delete
Table, format with CSS styles	DMR 303	Select table cell, row, or column to format, click Class arrow in Property inspector, click style
Table, import tabular data	DMR 292	Select table, click File, point to Import, click Excel Document (or click Insert, point to Table Objects, click Import Tabular Data), select data file, select formatting, click Open
Table, modify attributes in Standard mode	DMR 297	Select table, change attributes in Property inspector
Table, resize in Standard mode	DMR 298	Select table, drag a resize handle or type value in W box in Property inspector
Table, select in Standard mode	DMR 294	Right-click table, point to Table, click Select Table
Table cells, merge	DMR 300	Select cells to merge, click ⊡ in Property inspector
Table column, adjust span	DMR 301	Right-click cell in column, point to Table, click Increase Column Span or Decrease Column Span

TASK	PAGE #	RECOMMENDED METHOD
Table column, delete	DMR 302	Select column, right-click selected column, point to Table, click Delete Column
Table column, insert	DMR 302	Select column to right of column you want to insert, right-click selected column, point to Table, click Insert Column
Table column, resize	DMR 302	Drag column border left or right
Table header cell, create	DMR 301	Select row, check Header check box in Property inspector
Table row, adjust span	DMR 301	Right-click cell in row, point to Table, click Increase Row Span or Decrease Row Span
Table row, delete	DMR 302	Select row, right-click selected row, point to Table, click Delete Row
Table row, insert	DMR 302	Select cell or row below row you want to insert, right-click selected cell or row, point to Table, click Insert Row
Table row, resize	DMR 302	Drag row border up or down
Template, add region to template	DMR 345	Click Templates button arrow in Common category of Insert panel, click appropriate button
Template, apply to existing Web page	DMR 352	Open page in Document window, select template in Assets panel, click Apply, designate in which regions to place existing content
Template, create	DMR 343	See Reference box: Creating a Template
Template, delete	DMR 355	Select template in Assets panel, click 🗑
Template, edit	DMR 353	Open template in Document window; add, remove, and change elements as needed, save template, click Update, click Close
Template-based page, detach from template	DMR 355	Open template-based page, click Modify, point to Templates, click Detach from Template
Text, copy from another file and paste in Web page	DMR 115	Open file, select text, press Ctrl+C, click in Document window, click Edit, click Paste Special
Text, find and replace in page	DMR 119	Click Edit, click Find and Replace
Text, format using Property inspector	DMR 121	See Reference box: Formatting Text Using the Property Inspector
Text link, create to page with mouse	DRM 211	In HTML pane of Property inspector, click 🌐 and drag to page in Files panel
Theme, apply to jQuery Mobile site	DMR 502	Switch to Split view, turn on Live view, select div tag for page in Code pane, click swatch in jQuery Mobile Swatches panel
Web font, add	DMR 167	See Reference box: Adding a Web Font
Web page, create from template	DMR 349	See Reference box: Creating a Template-Based Page
Web page, create new	DMR 86	See Reference box: Creating an HTML Page in a Site
Web page, open in Document window	DMR 23	In Files panel, double-click filename
Web page, open local page in browser	DMR 8	See Reference box: Opening a Local Web Page in a Browser
Web page, open remote page in browser	DMR 7	Click Address bar in browser window, type URL, press Enter
Web page, preview in browser	DMR 99	Open page to preview, click File, point to Preview in Browser, click browser name
Web page, save existing	DMR 90	Click File, click Save

TASK	PAGE #	RECOMMENDED METHOD
Web page, save new	DMR 88	Click File, click Save As, navigate to save location, type filename in File name box, click Save
Web site, design	DMR 64	*See* Reference box: Designing a Web Site
Web site, preview on Web from remote location	DMR 102	Start browser, type URL of remote site in Address bar, press Enter
Web site, upload to remote server	DMR 100	*See* Reference box: Uploading a Web Site to a Remote Server
Workspace, select configuration	DMR 16	On menu bar, click workspace switcher button, click workspace